Social Stratification

Social Stratification
a multiple hierarchy approach

Vincent Jeffries   *and*   **H. Edward Ransford**

*California State University,
Northridge*

*University of Southern
California*

ALLYN AND BACON, INC.

Boston   London   Sydney   Toronto

To Patty and Lynn

Library of Congress Cataloging in Publication Data

Main entry under title:

Social stratification.

   Bibliography: p.
   Includes index.
   1. Social classes—United States—Addresses, essays,
lectures.   2. Power (Social sciences)—Addresses,
essays, lectures.   3. Social mobility—United States—
Addresses, essays, lectures.   4. Age groups—
Addresses, essays, lectures.   5. Ethnic groups—
Addresses, essays, lectures.   6. Sex role—Addresses,
essays, lectures.   I. Jeffries, Vincent.   II. Rans-
ford, H. Edward.
HN90.S6S58   305.5'0973   79-25382
ISBN 0-205-06858-8

Printed in the United States of America.

Contents

v

Preface

THE TOPIC of stratification, or social inequality, has traditionally been a study of class inequality. Although approaches have ranged from the purely subjective, with emphasis on prestige, to the more objective, stressing power and decision making, the primary focus on class stratification has continued until the present. Other stratification systems, such as ethnicity, sex, and age, have not been as fully considered in stratification texts and readers on the market today.

Social Stratification: A Multiple Hierarchy Approach is different. The class, ethnic, sex, and age hierarchies are given approximately equal attention. It is demonstrated that each of these four strata can be analyzed from a common perspective involving the unequal distribution of power, privilege, and prestige, common experience due to a stratum membership, the existence of an ideology supporting the stratification system, the potential for stratum consciousness and action, and vertical mobility.

Social Stratification is different in a second sense. Although a number of previous works have considered more than class stratification, few, to our knowledge, have made a general attempt to integrate the analysis of the four hierarchies of class, ethnicity, sex, and age. Comparisons across the hierarchies are emphasized, as is the analysis of combinations of particular strata. In this sense, what is termed a *Multiple Hierarchy Approach* is developed and presented.

This is a jointly authored book. There is no junior or senior author. The ideas contained in the multiple hierarchy model of stratification herein presented are the product of a number of years of frequent and close collaboration between the two authors. Though all the chapters, except the first two, are singly authored and were for the most part singly written, the ideas that they contain emerged and were developed from many hours of joint discussions.

V. J. and E. R.

Acknowledgements

VARIOUS REVIEWERS have contributed valuable comments and criticisms during the development and writing of this book. Appreciation is expressed to Joan Acker, Kenneth Berry, Lucile Duberman, Bruce K. Eckland, D. Stanley Eitzen, Martha E. Gimenez, Norval D. Glenn, Patricia Ann Jeffries, Barbara Lasslett, James R. Lincoln, Richard T. Morris, Charles Mueller, Edward Nelson, Robert Perrucci, Lynn Ransford, George Ritzer, and David R. Simon.

A major debt of gratitude is due to Gary Folven, Social Science Editor for Allyn and Bacon. His constant encouragement, good judgement, and sound advice played a very important role in this project from inception to finish. The assistance of Al Levitt of Allyn and Bacon in the final stages of this project is also appreciated.

We are grateful to Cynthia Hartnett for her careful editing of the entire manuscript. Patricia Ann Jeffries and Lynn Ransford made valuable contributions to the conceptual clarity and readability of the entire manuscript. Thanks also are due to Grace Sheldrick of Wordsworth Associates for her thoughtful final editing.

Thanks are also due to Emmi Stein, Jackie Sanchez, and Kathi Speck for typing the manuscript.

Any errors or misinterpretations are solely our responsibility.

V. J. and E. R.

PART I

The Multiple Hierarchy Model

1

From a Single to a Multiple Hierarchy Approach

ANY SOCIETY is divided in varying gradations, between the powerful and the powerless, the rulers and the ruled, the rich and the poor, the honored and the despised. The study of social stratification identifies and investigates the characteristics of such social inequalities; the means by which systems of inequality emerge and are maintained; the influence of social hierarchies upon groups and individuals; and the way in which social hierarchies change through time.

Social stratification always connotes a hierarchial arrangement of groups. Any aggregate of individuals occupying the same position in a social hierarchy is referred to as a *stratum*. The very rich, for example, occupy an upper stratum. The very poor occupy the lowest stratum. For sociologists, the terms *upper* and *lower* do not signify judgements of personal worthiness or favorable or unfavorable characteristics of different people. Lower simply means low access to society's rewards—of money, power or prestige.

The study of social stratification has focused primarily upon the hierarchy of social class, and social classes are always tied to the distribution of economic wealth. Karl Marx laid the foundation for the modern study of social classes. For Marx, class position was determined by the degree to which a person or group controlled the means of production in society. In Marxian terms, there are two principle classes. Those people who own the raw materials, tools, technology, and the other ingredients that go into the production process are the privileged and the societal decision makers. By contrast, a second group, a working class who owns no components of the economic production system, is, as a result, both powerless and lacking in privilege. According to Marx, these two economic classes have been in conflict with one another throughout history—lord and serf in the age of feudalism, capitalist and wage-earner in the age of industrial capitalism.

Influenced by Marxian concepts, sociologists in the United States have emphasized the economic dimension mainly in terms of wealth, property holdings, and control over the production system. Sociologists have an equally important tradition of viewing

An asterisk (*) accompanying a citation indicates a selection that is included in this volume.

3

stratification systems in terms of prestige. Max Weber introduced the dimension of status, or prestige, which refers to the distribution of social honor. Certain activities, life styles and occupations have greater prestige or honor attached to them than others. Upper white-collar jobs are usually accorded greater prestige than blue-collar jobs, for example. Drawing from Marx's and Weber's contributions, the measurement of social class in the United States has focused on such factors as a person's authority over others in work, occupational prestige, education, and wealth. An individual's position in the class stratification system may be determined by a combination of these factors.

The frame of reference presented here departs from the usual emphasis on the class order. An exclusive emphasis on social class limits one's understanding of the complexities of social inequality in modern societies. Therefore, we emphasize multiple hierarchies—class is one of them, but ethnicity, sex, and age are also important. The chapters and readings in this book present a *multiple hierarchy* model of stratification in which class, ethnicity, sex and age are viewed as separate but interrelated hierarchies of social inequality.

Sex, ethnic, and age stratification, which have usually been analyzed separately, are tied together in this book in an overall scheme of social stratification. A unified model incorporating these four hierarchies enables us to study combinations of stratification positions such as young-white-female or black-aged-lower-class combinations.

ETHNICITY, SEX, AND AGE
AS SEPARATE HIERARCHIES

Recent years have seen an increasingly large body of research on the disadvantaged status of women, ethnic minorities, and age groups such as youth and the aged. The protest movements of the 1960s and early 1970s drew special attention to ethnic and sex inequalities in the United States.

Although ethnicity, sex, and age are among the most obvious criteria of social stratification, sociologists have not commonly discussed them as distinctive stratification hierarchies. Only in the case of ethnicity do we find a school of thought that defines blacks as a "quasi-caste" group, a racial order into which one is born, which restricts equalitarian contact with whites and limits access to social rewards (Blau, 1974; Duberman, 1976). In the case of age and sex, one finds stratification perspectives just recently emerging. Many in the field are not used to thinking of age and sex in hierarchical terms. But "if, following Sorokin(1959:11), stratification is defined as the differentiation of a population into a hierarchy of layers, and if this means an unequal distribution of rights and privileges, power and influence, . . ." then it seems quite certain that ethnicity, sex, and age can be considered bases of stratification systems (Lieberson, 1970:172). Even casual observation reveals that typically whites have more privilege, power, and prestige than blacks in American society; that men have more privileges and influence than women; and that children and the aged have less social honor, influence, and privileges than do young and middle-aged adults.

When ethnicity, sex, and age have been considered by sociologists, they usually have been seen only as variables that affect the socioeconomic distribution—not as distinctive hierarchies in their own right. For example, the common explanation of why blacks, women, and the aged have less power in society is that they are over-represented in low occupation and income categories. Certainly, the socioeconomic or class standing of a group is a crucial part of its stratification standing. But, in addition, the distribution of social rewards—power, privilege, and prestige—is determined by ethnic, sex, and age-group membership *per se*. That is, we perceive four somewhat distinct stratification systems (class, ethnicity, sex, and age), each with strata that are independently linked to the rewards of power, privilege, and prestige.

The few accounts that have introduced this more multidimensional view of stratification (Lenski, 1966; Acker, 1973; Lieberson, 1970, Duberman, 1976) have not always been well received (Parkin, 1971; Mayer and Buckley, 1970). Among many in the field there appears to be some resistance to "breaking open" stratification logic to a multi-hierarchy approach.

One major purpose of this chapter is to disengage ethnicity, sex, and age from a strictly socioeconomic framework and to establish each as an independent stratification heirarchy. Some long-held assumptions justifying the class approach need to be unearthed and challenged. In the following pages, we will review these assumptions, explain why a single stratification scheme may no longer be valid for describing the contemporary United States, and why a multiple hierarchy model is more accurate.

TRADITIONAL ASSUMPTION I OF SINGLE HIERARCHY MODEL:

The family is the proper unit of analysis in studying stratification systems.

> A young woman in an upper middle-class family, in which the father is a lawyer, shares the same status as her brother. She and her brother (and their mother, too) are considered to be upper middle-class because of the father's (husband's) occupation.
>
> Are the young woman's chances to become a lawyer the same as her brother's? Probably not. Therefore, the woman's position in the sexual stratification hierarchy must be considered apart from her status as an upper middle-class family member.

Many sociologists have viewed the family as the basic unit of stratification. That is, families, rather than individuals, are upper, middle, or lower in class standing. In industrial societies, the occupational achievement and income of the family breadwinner define the stratification positions of all family members. Traditionally, the male head of the household determines the class of the family unit. Although women have entered the labor force in ever increasing numbers, the man's occupation usually contributes most to the prestige and income of the household. Further, it is argued that the family is the unit that places the newborn child in the reward structure at birth. "This placement function could not take place if the family did not form a unit with respect to rank order, its members sharing the same rank and being treated as social equals'' (Mayer and Buckley, 1970:10). This point of view does not completely rule out sex and age inequalities but the latter are not considered legitimate stratification hierarchies because they occur under the more significant and broad umbrella of family class position. In any family, the man may have more power and privileges than the woman and the adults far more power and privileges than the children, but, in traditional studies, *all members of a household are viewed as members of the same social class*.

As will become increasingly evident, our position is quite different. We view ethnicity, sex, and age as separate stratification hierarchies that cut across class lines. Of course, a person's life chances of finishing college, travelling to Europe, avoiding a police record, and obtaining an interesting and challenging job are highly related to family class position. But a person's age, sex, and race also have a powerful impact on his or her life chances. Males, for example, traditionally have had a much greater choice of occupation than females. And whatever their family class background, blacks and Chicanos often experience separate and unequal education in segregated inner-city schools. Race, sex, and age positions therefore signify different access lines to the rewards of power, privilege, and prestige. If one is old, black, or female, there are barriers to acquiring social rewards that cannot be fully explained by family class position alone. Accordingly, we stress the *individual* rather than the family group as the unit of analysis. Individuals occupy different positions on four separate hierarchies (Acker, 1973).

The Family and Inheritance

Stratification systems are *institutionalized inequalities*—inequalities that are persistent and that are passed on through time. Traditionally, the family is viewed as the unit through which social inequalities are maintained through inheritance. From this view, social class is presumed to be the only legitimate hierarchy because only in the case of class is there a regular network of people (the family) to pass on wealth and resources through generations. Children inherit property and wealth from their parents and other members of their kinship group. In addition, the family is a powerful socializing force, inculcating basic attitudes and skills that tend to perpetuate social classes.

On the other hand, so the argument goes, sex and age cannot provide clear bases for enduring systems of inequality because they involve individual traits that cannot be transferred. We reject this view. Discriminatory behavior toward race, sex, and age groups is powerful enough to institutionalize and so to perpetuate disadvantaged strata through time. Established laws, customs, and practices have prevented racial minorities, women, youth, and the aged from occupying favorable positions in society. These basic laws, customs, and practices have existed for a very long time and will continue to produce inequalities for some time to come. Therefore, there are other means by which society passes on inequalities, generation after generation. Although institutionalized racism, sexism, and ageism may not involve tangible exchanges such as money and property, they do create enduring systems of rank.

The Family Remains Important
in the Multiple Hierarchy Approach

The viewpoint presented in this book is that the *individual* rather than the *family* is the basic unit of stratification. This is not to say that the family is inconsequential in determining stratification rewards. We are not relegating the family unit to some remote position in the stratification arena. Indeed, some of the most important determining factors of an individual's access to power, privilege, and prestige are played out or determined within the family context.

If it were not for the family, it would be more difficult to conceptualize sex and age inequalities as separate hierarchies. For example, the same family institution that passes on inherited wealth (a class function) also passes on barriers to female achievement by socializing young women into traditional gender-role models. Further, as parents exert a great deal of power and discipline over children, they set the stage for age stratification in which the legitimate authority of parents over children is echoed in a great many institutions (for example, the subordinate position of children in most schools and the limited rights of children in the legal system). Thus, the multiple hierarchy model presented here does not preclude a focus on the family as a factor in social stratification, but rather depends to a certain degree on the family institution as one basis for viewing sex, age, and ethnicity as hierarchies independent of class.

TRADITIONAL ASSUMPTION II OF THE SINGLE
HIERARCHY APPROACH:

All inequality in our society comes back to class (especially economic) inequality. If class position is held constant, there is very little remaining for race, sex, or age inequality to explain.

This second assumption of the single hierarchy approach views race, sex, or age as "quasi-variables" in stratification which are far less important than social class. Being old, female, or black may add a small increment of disadvantage to a low class position, but in a relative comparison of inequalities, the fact of being poor is by far most important. From this point of view, disadvantages due to one's ethnicity, sex, or age can be explained by looking at class position alone. Parkin makes this point most explicitly in his discussion of sex inequality compared to class inequality: ". . . and if the wives and daughters of unskilled laborers have things in common with the wives and daughters of wealthy land-owners, there can be no doubt that the *differences* in their overall situation are far more striking and significant. *Only if the disabilities attaching to female status were felt to be so great as to override differences of a class kind would it be realistic to regard sex as an important dimension of stratification*" (Parkin, 1971:15, emphasis added). In other words, inequality by sex pales beside class inequality. There is much to debate over this assertion.

First, it can be argued that the disabilities of one dimension (sex, in this example) do not have to be greater or even as great as those of social class to be considered a separate stratification hierarchy. What is important is that the social inequalities attached to sex are *significant* and *patterned,* and that this is true for women at lower as well as higher levels of social class. For example, one disability that women of all class levels have faced is socialization into the belief that a woman can only occupy certain roles in our society, such as homemaker, secretary, or nurse.

> . . . the well-socialized American girl learns three clear lessons. . . . With regard to her personality, she 'knows' that to be truly feminine she will be sweet, expressive, not too intelligent, nurturing, cooperative, pretty and fairly passive. With regard to her capability, she 'knows' she will always be less capable and less important than most men. With regard to her future, she 'knows' she will be a wife and mother (Weitzman, 1975:127).

If family class position is the prime determiner of one's social status, then a woman raised in a wealthy family should experience few disabilities indeed. But until recently the major choice for a young woman from a wealthy family was whether or not she was going to marry a wealthy man. Her choices rarely involved her own achievement, career, or individual self-actualization.

Regardless of social class background, women, the aged, and minorities face high degrees of discrimination in all institutions. In the economic sector, women are largely confined to the most monotonous work under the supervision of men. They are treated unequally with regard to pay, promotion, and responsibility (Freeman, 1975). The few women who do reach positions of authority and prestige may yet face high degrees of work strain, isolation from co-workers and are not recognized for their authority and talents (Miller*et al.,* 1975). Similarly, a number of studies have shown that even among blacks who have achieved high levels of education or occupational status or who score high in ability tests, significant discrepancies in social rewards remain when blacks are compared with whites with similar achievement levels (Butler, 1976; Blau and Duncan, 1967).

Recent consciousness-raising and political efforts among women, youth, and ethnic minorities exemplify further the distinctions made on these bases, apart from class. For example, women from a variety of class, ethnic and marital situations have joined together in common consciousness to protest a separate set of inequities faced by women.

SUMMARY

The preceding discussion leads to a basic orientation of this book:

1. Although the social class position of a male breadwinner often determines certain rewards, privileges, or disabilities for an entire family, the ethnicity, sex, and age positions of individuals (in families or as single persons) are important stratification dimensions.
2. Because individuals of the same sex, age, or race face common disabilities and have the potential to mobilize for common action (regardless of family class position) we prefer to emphasize stratification among individuals rather than families.

3. A person can be regarded as occupying different ranks on each of the four hierarchies (class, ethnicity, sex, and age) rather than occupying a single position on one stratification structure.

Throughout this discussion on stratification, we have distinguished between a single hierarchy (class) model and a multiple hierarchy model. Figure 1–1 compares the two approaches.

The traditional class model shows that visible ethnic minorities, women, and the aged face barriers in reaching positions in the class hierarchy and as a result of this lower income, occupational, and educational standing, they have lesser degrees of power, privilege, and prestige in society. In the multiple hierarchy model, the distribution of rewards does not depend on social class as an intervening link. Ethnicity, sex, age, and class, as separate stratification systems, directly determine access to power, privilege, and prestige.

It is not that one model is correct and the other is incorrect—rather that the literature has stressed one (class model) almost to the exclusion of the other (multiple hierarchy model). In this book, both models are seen as valid and both will be discussed. However, the multiple hierarchy model is emphasized as a new frontier of stratification research, one that is more comprehensive and valid for studying social inequality in contemporary times.

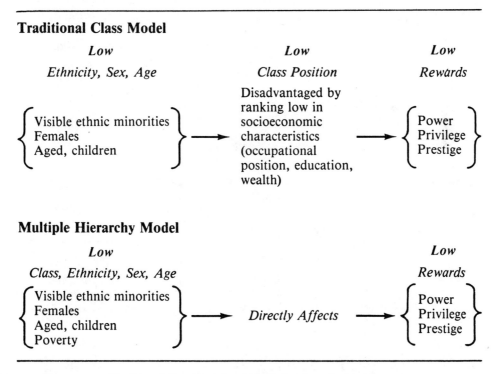

Figure 1–1. *Traditional Class Model and Multiple Hierarchy Model*

THE MULTIPLE HIERARCHY MODEL

This stratification model is illustrated in Figure 1–2. Note that the arrows connect each hierarchy with power, privilege, and prestige. A stratum or position in each hierarchy (such as upper class, white ethnic, or female) represents an aggregate of people who share the same access to these social rewards. The higher the position in each hierarchy, the greater the access to power, privilege and prestige. The lower the position, the greater the degree of powerlessness, the fewer the opportunities to acquire valued objects and experiences, and the more reduced the prestige.

Each of the four hierarchies shown in Figure 1–2 can be defined as follows. *Class* stratification is a composite of economic assets, occupational position, and educational attainment.

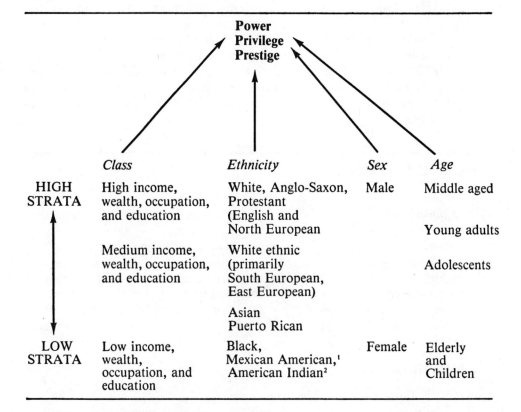

Figure 1-2. *Multiple Hierarchies of Stratification*

1. Although *Hispanic* is the term used most widely to include Mexican Americans or Chicanos, Cubans, Puerto Ricans, South Americans, and other Spanish-speaking people, lumping together all Spanish-speaking people under the term *Hispanic* would blur sociological analysis. Language often is all that Hispanic people share.

Chicanos or Mexican Americans are discussed most in this book because 1) they represent 60 to 70 percent of the Hispanic population of the United States, depending on the inclusion of illegal aliens, and 2) their historical experiences fit a model of conquest and colonization—important factors when power inequality determines positions in the ethnic hierarchy.

2. The terms *American Indian* and *Native American* are used interchangeably in this text.

The term *ethnic group* or *ethnicity* is used in a broad way to include 1) people distinguishable primarily by visible physical criteria, that is, racial groups such as blacks; 2) cultural populations distinguishable by language, heritage, nationality, or special traditions (such as Poles, the Irish, Jews, or Italians); and 3) groups such as American Indians who are differentiated by both cultural and physical differences. Throughout this book, there is a greater focus on the visible ethnic minorities (1 and 3 above) and especially those minorities conquered by force—blacks, Mexican Americans, and American Indians.

The *sex* hierarchy includes two strata: male and female. In the case of the *age* hierarchy, there are points in the life cycle that are related to the distribution of power, privilege and prestige—childhood, adolesence, young adulthood, middle age, and old age. Age is related to power, privilege, and prestige and also to what society expects people to do at these points in life. Norms, conventions, and constraints are applied to all age groups.

For the individual, the end result of his or her position in all the hierarchies taken together ultimately determine one's access to power, privilege, and prestige (refer again to Figure 1–2).

Power

Power is defined here as the likelihood of individuals or groups exerting their will over others, even when there is opposition or resistance from others. If you can enforce your will on people who do not want to be controlled by you, then you have power. The use of force is the ultimate manifestation of the possession of power. The protests of blacks and anti-war demonstrators in the 1960s in many instances were finally contained by the use of force. There are other far less obvious ways in which power is exerted. The chief of these is through the exercise of authority. When power relations are viewed as legitimate or natural, we use the term *authority*. *Authority* means that force has been institutionalized such that people accept orders or direction without question. Serfs in the Middle Ages, for example, did not question the exercise of power by the nobility and the clergy. In a similar way, until very recently, most wives accepted the dictates of their husbands. Whether power is exercised through force or through authority, some groups in society are able to realize their will far more often than other groups.

Privilege

Privilege refers to the rights, advantages, and immunities associated with a position in a hierarchy. The distribution of privilege divides society into the "haves" and the "have-nots." Those in higher strata have immunities, benefits, prerogatives, liberties, and options that are less available to those of lower strata. Privilege has two major aspects: economic and cultural. 1) Some privileges are directly related to the economic position of individuals. People with great wealth can purchase many advantages, such as the best medical care, and can avoid disadvantages, such as spending time in jail. 2) Other privileges, which are not related directly to economic factors are *cultural privi-*

leges. Cultural norms and constraints give advantages and disadvantages selectively. For example, until recently, women have been locked into fairly rigid role prescriptions for femininity and child rearing.

Prestige

Prestige refers to the distribution of social honor or status. In any society, groups are evaluated differently. Some have high prestige, while others have low prestige and are looked down on. This ranking of individuals and groups involves a consensus of opinion on the criteria for conferring prestige. Such judgements are in part a reflection of the dominant values of a society. Thus, in the United States, where material success is highly valued, the possession of wealth is an attribute that tends to confer prestige.

A more detailed analysis of power, privilege and prestige and their interrelationships is presented in chapter 3. Gerhard Lenski*(1966), whose article is included in the selected readings for this chapter, presents an interesting theory that draws connections between power, privilege, and prestige. Lenski sees power as the central variable in stratification. People with greater resources of power can seize a larger share of the economic surplus. Privilege is thus determined by power. Lenski describes prestige as a function of power and privilege in that those in powerful positions with a greater amount of the economic surplus have, as a result, greater prestige.

SUMMARY

This book presents an approach to the study of social stratification that differs from the dominant tradition in the field. We have attempted to show that stratification can be expanded from a primary focus on class to a model that includes four hierarchies—class, ethnicity, sex, and age. A model with four hierarchies increases our understanding of inequality in American society.

Chapter 2 continues the introduction to the multiple hierarchy model. In particular, it is shown that important gains in understanding are made when two or more hierarchies are jointly considered.

REFERENCES

Acker, Joan. 1973. "Women and Social Stratification: A Case of Intellectual Sexism." *American Journal of Sociology* 78 (January): 936–945.

Blau, Peter M. 1974. "Presidential Address: Parameters of Social Structure." *American Sociological Review* 39 (October): 615–635.

Blau, Peter M. & Otis Dudley Duncan. 1967. *The American Occupational Structure*. New York: John Wiley & Sons.

Butler, John S. 1976. "Inequality in the Military: An Examination of Promotion Time for Black and White Enlisted Men." *American Sociological Review* 41 (October): 807–818.

Duberman, Lucile. 1976. *Social Inequality*, Philadelphia: J. B. Lippincott.

Freeman, Jo., ed. 1975. *Women: A Feminist Perspective*. Palo Alto, Calif.: Mayfield Publishing Co.

Lenski, Gerhard E. 1966. *Power and Privilege*. New York: McGraw-Hill.

_____1966. "The Dynamics of Distributive Systems." In Gerhard E. Lenski (ed.), *Power and Privilege*. New York: McGraw-Hill.

Lieberson, Stanley. 1970. "Stratification and Ethnic Groups." In Edward O. Laumann (ed.), *Social Stratification: Research and Theory for the 1970's*. Indianapolis: The Bobbs-Merrill Company.

Mayer, Kurt B. & Walter Buckley. 1970. *Class and Society*. New York: Random House.

McTavish, Donald G. 1971. "Perceptions of Old People: A Review of Research Methodologies and Findings." *The Gerontologist* (Winter): 90–108.

Miller, Jon, Sanford Labovitz, & Lincoln Fry. 1975. "Differences in the Organizational Experiences of Men and Women: Resources, Vested Interests and Discrimination." *Social Forces* (December): 365–381.

Parkin, Frank. 1971. *Class Inequality and Political Order*. New York: Frederick A. Praeger.

Sorokin, Pitirim A. 1959. *Social and Cultural Mobility*. Glencoe, IL: Free Press.

Weitzman, LeMore J. 1975. "Sex Role Socialization." In Jo Freeman (ed.), *Women: A Feminist Perspective*. Palo Alto, Calif.: Mayfield Publishing Co.

Not being able to make that which is just strong, man has made that which is strong just. Pascal

The Dynamics of Distributive Systems

Gerhard Lenski

IN ANALYSES of social stratification, it is a temptation to turn immediately to the interesting and much debated structural problems, such as those concerning the nature, number, and composition of classes. While such questions must inevitably be a part of any adequate treatment of the subject, they are secondary in importance to questions about the processes which give rise to the structures. Moreover, to attempt to deal with the structural problems without prior attention to these processes, as is sometimes done, is to put the cart before the horse and create confusion. For these reasons, the present chapter will be concerned chiefly with problems of dynamics, reserving most structural problems for the next chapter.

TWO LAWS OF DISTRIBUTION

When one seeks to build a theory of distribution on the postulates about the nature of man and society set forth in the last chapter, one soon discovers that these lead to a curious, but important, *dualism*. If those postulates are sound, one would predict that almost all the products of men's labors will be distributed on the basis of two seemingly contradictory principles, *need* and *power*.

In our discussion of the nature of man, it was postulated that where important decisions are

involved, most human action is motivated either by self-interest or by partisan group interests. This suggests that power alone governs the distribution of rewards. This cannot be the case, however, since we also postulated that most of these essentially selfish interests can be satisfied only by the establishment of cooperative relations with others. Cooperation is absolutely essential both for survival and for the efficient attainment of most other goals. In other words, men's selfish interests compel them to remain members of society and to share in the division of labor.

If these two postulates are correct, then it follows that *men will share the product of their labors to the extent required to insure the survival and continued productivity of those others whose actions are necessary or beneficial to themselves.* This might well be called the first law of distribution, since the survival of mankind as a species depends on compliance with it.

This first law, however, does not cover the entire problem. It says nothing about how any *surplus*, i.e., goods and services over and above the minimum required to keep producers alive and productive, which men may be able to produce will be distributed. This leads to what may be called the second law of distribution. If we assume that in important decisions human action is motivated almost entirely by self-interest or partisan group interests, and if we assume that many of the things men most desire are in short supply, then, as noted before, this surplus will inevitably give rise to conflicts and struggles aimed at its control. If, following Weber, we define power as the probability of persons or groups carrying out their will even when opposed by others,[1] then it follows that *power will determine the distribution of nearly all of the surplus possessed by a society*. The qualification "nearly all" takes account of the very limited influence of altruistic action which our earlier analysis of the nature of man leads us to expect.

This second law points the way to another very important relationship, that between our two chief variables, power and privilege. If privilege is defined as possession or control of a portion of the surplus produced by a society, then it follows that *privilege is largely a function of power, and to a very limited degree, a function of altruism*. This means that to explain most of the distribution of privilege in a society, we have but to determine the distribution of power.

To state the matter this way suggests that the task of explaining the distribution of privilege is simple. Unfortunately, this is not the case since there are many forms of power and they spring from many sources. Nevertheless, the establishment of this key relationship reduces the problem to more manageable proportions, since it concentrates attention on one key variable, power. Thus if we can establish the pattern of its distribution in a given society, we have largely established the pattern for the distribution of privilege, and if we can discover the causes of a given distribution of power we have also discovered the causes of the distribution of privilege linked with it.

To put the matter this way is to invite the question of how the third basic element in every distributive system, *prestige*, is related to power

and privilege. It would be nice if one could say that prestige is a simple function of privilege, but unfortunately this does not seem to be the case. Without going into a complex analysis of the matter at this point, the best that can be said is that empirical evidence strongly suggests that *prestige is largely, though not solely, a function of power and privilege, at least in those societies where there is a substantial surplus.*[2] If this is true, it follows that even though the subject of prestige is not often mentioned in this volume, its pattern of distribution and its causes can largely be deduced from discussion of the distribution of power and privilege and their causes in those societies where there is an appreciable surplus.

Graphically, the relationship between these three variables, as set forth in the propositions above, can be depicted in this way:

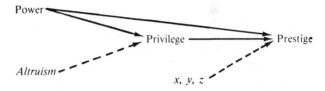

The solid lines indicate major sources of influence, the dashed lines secondary sources.

To make this diagram complete, one other dashed line should probably be added, indicating some feedback from prestige to power. Thus a more accurate representation of the relationships would look like this:

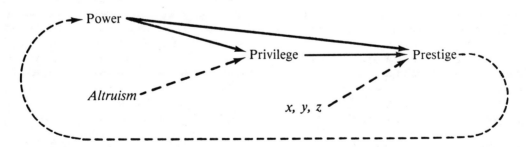

1. See Max Weber, *The Theory of Social and Economic Organization*, translated by A. M. Henderson and Talcott Parsons (New York: Free Press, 1947), p. 152, or Max Weber, *From Max Weber: Essays in Sociology*, translated by H. H. Gerth and C. Wright Mills (Fair Lawn, N.J.: Oxford University Press, 1946), p. 180.

2. For evidence supporting this generalization, see p. 430. I have not attempted to establish this generalization by deductive logic since this would be a major undertaking requiring the introduction of new postulates and would divert the analysis from its primary task. For the same reason I have not attempted to deal with prestige in other parts of this volume except incidentally.

Power is the key variable in the triad from the causal and explanatory standpoint. Hence, it is with this variable that we shall be primarily concerned in the analysis which follows.

THE VARIABLE ASPECTS
OF DISTRIBUTIVE
SYSTEMS

As the statement of the two laws indicates, the second law does not have any effect on the distributive process until the conditions specified in the first have been satisfied. Until the necessities of life have been made available to enough productive, mutually interdependent members of the group, there is no surplus to be fought over and distributed on the basis of power. Thus, as a first hypothesis we would be led to predict that *in the simplest societies, or those which are technologically most primitive, the goods and services available will be distributed wholly, or largely, on the basis of need.*

As the productivity of societies increases, the possibility of producing a surplus steadily increases, though it should be noted that the existence of a surplus is not a function of technological advance alone. Even though we cannot say that the surplus available to a society increases proportionately with advances in the level of technology, such advances increase the probability that there will be a surplus and also that there will be a sizable surplus. Hence, as a second hypothesis we are led to predict that *with technological advance, an increasing proportion of the goods and services available to a society will be distributed on the basis of power.*

In view of the dualistic basis of the distributive process, and the variations to which this must necessarily give rise, it would be unwise to attempt to develop a single general theory of distribution or stratification to cover all societies. Rather, we will gain far more if we follow the example of the economists in their analyses of the behavior of markets. As they discovered years ago, it is impossible to create a single general theory of market behavior except of the most limited nature. In order to deal effectively with most of the more complex aspects of market behavior, it is necessary to take account of the existence of different kinds of markets. This has led to the distinction between theories of perfect and imperfect competition. The latter can be further subdivided into theories of oligopoly, monopoly, monopsony, and so forth. In other words, on closer inspection the theory of market behavior turns out to consist of a small number of general principles which constitute the general theory of markets, and a whole series of more limited principles applicable only under specific conditions.

The same approach is required in stratification theory, if our analysis up to this point is sound. If the first two laws of distribution and the two hypotheses based on them are valid, then *the nature of distributive systems will vary greatly, depending on the degree of technological advance in the societies involved.* The variations should be every bit as great as those which differentiate markets where perfect competition prevails from those where imperfect competition holds sway.

For this reason, the major part of this volume will be devoted to a series of analyses of distributive systems in specific types of societies, with the types defined in technological terms. The handful of universally applicable principles of distribution can be dealt with quite briefly and with reasonable adequacy in this chapter and the next.

While the foregoing is reason enough to base our special theories on societal types defined in technological terms, there is one other great advantage derived from this approach. Past research has made it clear that technology is never an isolated variable in sociocultural systems. On the contrary, it tends to be linked fairly closely with a whole series of other variables which evidently stand in a dependent relationship to it.[3] This is especially true of many social organizational variables which are linked with distributive systems and tend to define their limits of possible

3.   See, for example, L. T. Hobhouse, G. C. Wheeler, and M. Ginsberg, *The Material Culture and Social Institutions of the Simpler Peoples* (London: Chapman & Hall, 1930) and Alvin W. Gouldner and Richard A. Petersen, *Notes on Technology and the Moral Order* (Indianapolis: Bobbs-Merrill, 1962) for broadly comparative studies, or Ralph Linton, *The Tanala: A Hill Tribe of Madagascar* (Chicago: Field Museum of Natural History, 1933) for an excellent case study.

variation, e.g., nature and extent of division of labor, maximum community size, etc. Hence, *by classifying societies on the basis of technology, we are, in effect, simultaneously controlling, wholly or in part, many other relevant variables.* The value of this will become evident beginning in Chapter 5.

To say that many other characteristics of human societies vary with technology is not to say that all do. Clearly some do not, and others do so only to a limited degree. Wilbert Moore has suggested that supernatural beliefs and aesthetic forms are not so closely correlated with technology as most forms of social organization.[4] The same may also be true of certain basic aspects of family life. However, while these exceptions deserve recognition and careful consideration, they do not vitiate the basic principle involved.

It should also be noted that classifying societies on the basis of the nature of their technology does not imply that all those in a single category have *identical* distributive systems any more than that all oligopolistic markets function the same way. Obviously there are variations within each societal type just as within each type of market, and an effort will be made to identify and account for the more important of them. However, these may be thought of as *second-order variations,* which are best dealt with after the first-order variations have been established and the internal uniformities associated with them clearly delineated.

In dealing with these second-order variations we shall sometimes have to rely on inductive logic to establish both causal and descriptive generalizations. However, this will not always be the case. Sometimes deductive logic can be employed. For example, if the size of a society's surplus affects the nature of its distributive system, and if the size of the surplus depends to some degree on the nature of the physical environment, then we should predict that *differences in the physical environment will lead to secondary differences in distributive systems.* More specifically, the richer the environment, the larger the surplus and the greater the importance of power in the distributive process.

There are also reasons for predicting that the influence of environmental differences will be greater in primitive societies than in those which are technologically more advanced. To begin with, technological advance makes possible the geographical expansion of societies, and the larger the territory occupied by a society, the less the probability that the total environment will be extremely favorable or unfavorable and the greater the probability that it will include a mixture of favorable and unfavorable land. Hence, environmental variation should be less among the larger, technologically advanced societies than among the smaller, more primitive. In addition, technological advance frequently means the development of alternative solutions to the various problems of production. Technologically advanced societies, therefore, should be less hampered by environmental limitations than primitive societies are, and thus *environmental variation should have less effect on the level of productivity in advanced societies than in primitive.*

Another important source of secondary variation has been identified by Stanislaw Andrzejewski in his important but neglected book, *Military Organization and Society.*[5] As he has shown, both deductive logic and empirical data indicate that *the degree of inequality in societies of a given level of technological development tends to vary inversely with what he calls "the military participation ratio,"* that is *the proportion of the adult male population utilized in military operations.* Where most adult males are utilized for such purposes, the degree of inequality tends to be less than in those in which military needs are supplied by a small force of military specialists. Thus, this factor can also be used to explain some of the secondary variations which are found among societies of the same technological type.

A third source of secondary variations which can be anticipated is the technological variation which exists even among societies classified in the same category. No two societies are identical from the technological standpoint, and their classification into technological types is based on similarities (or identity) with respect to certain fundamental characteristics and ignores secondary

4. Wilbert E. Moore, *Social Change* (Englewood Cliffs, N.J.: Prentice-Hall, 1963), pp. 72–76.

5. (London: Routledge, 1954), especially chap. 2.

differences. If primary differences in technology cause major differences in distributive systems, *one would expect these secondary differences in technology to generate lesser differences in distributive systems.* Thus, one would expect considerable differences between a society in the first stages of industrialization and one which is highly industrialized, just as one would expect differences between a hunting and gathering society with no alternative mode of food production and one which has some rudimentary forms of horticulture to supplement its diet.

Finally, as will become evident later in this chapter, *one can expect secondary variations associated with the stage a society occupies in what I shall call "the political cycle"* (see page 59 of this chapter). In effect, this is a measure of the degree to which the prevailing distributive system is accepted as legitimate. While this is linked somewhat with the level of technological development of societies, it is no simple function of this variable and hence exercises a substantially independent influence.

FORCE AND ITS TRANSFORMATION

Of the two principles which govern the distributive process, need and power, the first is relatively simple and poses few problems of great importance or difficulty. Unhappily, the same cannot be said of the second. Of all the concepts used by sociologists, few are the source of more confusion and misunderstanding than power. Hence it is necessary to spell out in some detail the nature of this concept and how it functions in the distributive process.

As a starting point, it may be well to return briefly to one of the postulates introduced in the last chapter. There it was assumed that survival is the chief goal of the great majority of men. If this is so, then it follows that *the ability to take life is the most effective form of power.* In other words, more men will respond more readily to the threat of the use of *force* than to any other. In effect, it constitutes the final court of appeals in human affairs; there is no appeal from force in a given situation except the exercise of superior force.

Hence force stands in the same relationship to other forms of power as trumps to the other suits in the game of bridge, and those who can exercise the greatest force are like those who control trumps.

This fact has been recognized by countless observers of the human scene in every age. As Pascal put it, "Not being able to make that which is just strong, man has made that which is strong just." Cicero made the same point when he said, "Laws are dumb in the midst of arms," and Hobbes asserted that "Covenants without the sword are but words, and of no strength to secure a man at all."

This principle is also recognized by the leaders of nations, the practical men of affairs. Every sovereign state restricts, and where possible prohibits, the independent exercise of force by its subjects. States may be tolerant of many things, but never of the growth of independent military organizations within their territories. The reason is obvious: any government which cannot suppress each and every forceful challenge to its authority is overthrown. Force is the foundation of sovereignty.

On this point there is no dispute between conservatives and radicals. Their arguments are concerned only with the ends served by the state's use of force. Conservatives insist that might is employed only as the handmaiden of right, to restrain and rebuke those who put self-interest above the common good, while radicals maintain that the state employs might to suppress right, in defense of selfish interests.

If force is the foundation of political sovereignty, it is also the foundation of the distributive system in every society where there is a surplus to be divided. Where coercive power is weak, challenges inevitably occur and the system is eventually destroyed and replaced by another based more firmly on force. Men struggling over control of the surplus of a society will not accept defeat so long as there is a higher court of appeals to which they may take their case with some likelihood of success and profit to themselves.

The principle involved here is essentially the same as the principle of escalation with which modern military men are so concerned. Small wars based on small weapons inevitably grow into more deadly wars utilizing more deadly weapons if, by advancing the level of conflict, one of the parties anticipates turning defeat into victory. Similarly, in the case of conflicts within societies, the parties involved are always motivated to take the issue to the final court of appeals so long as there is the likelihood of benefiting by it. While men will not resort to armed revolution for trivial gains, when control over the entire surplus of a society is involved, the prospect is more enticing. The attractiveness varies directly with the weakness of the current regime.

Nevertheless, as Edmund Burke, the famed English conservative, recognized, "The use of force alone is but temporary. It may subdue for a moment; but it does not remove the necessity of subduing again: and a nation is not governed, which is perpetually to be conquered." Though force is the most effective instrument for seizing power in a society, and though it always remains the foundation of any system of inequality, it is not the most effective instrument for retaining and exploiting a position of power and deriving the maximum benefits from it. Therefore, regardless of the objectives of a new regime, once organized opposition has been destroyed it is to its advantage to make increasing use of other techniques and instruments of control, and to allow force to recede into the background to be used only when other techniques fail.

If the new elite has materialistic goals and is concerned solely with self-aggrandizement, it soon discovers that the rule of might is both inefficient and costly. So long as it relies on force, much of the profit is consumed by the costs of coercion. If the population obeys only out of fear of physical violence, a large portion of the time, energy, and wealth of the elite are invariably consumed in the effort to keep it under control and separate the producers from the product of their labors. Even worse, honor, which normally ranks high in the scale of human values, is denied to those who rule by force alone.[6]

6. For a good discussion of the limitations of rule by force, see Robert Dahl and Charles Lindblom, *Politics, Economics, and Welfare* (New York: Harper & Row, 1953), pp. 107–109. See also Karl A. Wittfogel, *Oriental Despotism: A Comparative Study of Total Power* (New Haven, Conn.: Yale University Press, 1957), chap. 4.

If materialistic elites have strong motives for shifting from the rule of might to the rule of right, ideologically motivated elites have even stronger. If the visions and ideals which led them to undertake the terrible risks and hardships of revolution are ever to be fulfilled, the voluntary cooperation of the population is essential, and this cannot be obtained by force. Force is, at best, the means to an end. That end, the establishment of a new social order, can never be fully attained until most members of society freely accept it as their own. The purpose of the revolution is to destroy the old elite and their institutions, which prevent the fulfillment of this dream. Once they are destroyed, an ideological elite strives to rule by persuasion. Thus *those who seize power by force find it advantageous to legitimize their rule once effective organized opposition is eliminated.* Force can no longer continue to play the role it did. It can no longer function as the private resource of a special segment of the population. Rather it must be transformed into a public resource used in the defense of law and order.

This may seem to be the equivalent of saying that those who have at great risk to themselves displaced the old elite must now give up all they have won. Actually, however, this is not at all necessary since, with a limited exercise of intelligence, force can be transformed into authority, and might into right.

There are various means by which this transformation can be effected. To begin with, by virtue of its coercive power, a new elite is in a good position to rewrite the law of the land as it sees fit. This affords them a unique opportunity, since by its very nature law is identified with justice and the rule of right. Since legal statutes are stated in general and impersonal terms, they appear to support abstract principles of justice rather than the special interests of particular men or classes of men. The fact that laws exist prior to the events to which they are applied suggests an objective impartiality which also contributes to their acceptance. Yet laws can always be written in such a way that they favor some particular segment of society. Anatole France saw this clearly when he wrote, "The law in its majestic equality forbids the rich as well as the poor to sleep under bridges, to beg in the street, and to steal bread." Edwin

Sutherland provided detailed documentation of the presence of such bias, as have a host of others.[7] In short, laws may be written in such a way that they protect the interests of the elite while being couched in very general, universalistic terms.

Often a new elite finds that it does not even need to change the laws to accomplish its ends. Typically the old laws were written to serve the interests of the holders of certain key offices, and once these offices have been seized, the new elite can use them as resources to build their fortunes or attain other goals.

Institutions which shape public opinion serve as a second instrument for legitimizing the position of new elites. Through the use of a combination of inducements and threats, educational and religious institutions, together with the mass media and other molders of public opinion, can usually be transformed into instruments of propaganda for the new regime. A determined and intelligent elite working through them can usually surround itself with an aura of legitimacy within a few months or years.

The concept of "propaganda," or the manipulation of consensus, is an integral element in the synthetic theory of stratification. A recognition of this phenomenon and the special role it plays in the distributive process enables us to avoid the impasse which has driven Dahrendorf and others to despair of ever reconciling the conservative and radical traditions. Consensus and coercion are more closely related than those who preach the Janus-headed character of society would have us believe. *Coercive power can often be used to create a new consensus.*

There is probably no better example of this than the Soviet Union. Here a small minority seized control of the machinery of state in 1917 and used the coercive powers of the state to transform the educational system of the nation and the mass media into one gigantic instrument of propaganda. Within a single generation the vast majority of Russians were converted to a sincere and genuine support of most of the basic elements of the Communist Party's program.[8]

In the short run, propaganda may be used to support a great variety of programs and policies adopted by an elite. In the long run, however, its basic aim is the dissemination of an ideology which provides a moral justification for the regime's exercise of power. Gaetano Mosca put it this way:

> Ruling classes do not justify their power exclusively by *de facto* possession of it, but try to find a moral and legal basis for it, representing it as the logical and necessary consequence of doctrines and beliefs that are generally recognized and accepted.[9]

Most of the theories of political sovereignty debated by philosophers have been intellectualized versions of some popular ideology. This can be seen in the now discredited belief in the divine right of kings. In our own day, the belief in popular sovereignty serves the same justifying function. A basic element in our current American ideology is the thesis expressed by Lincoln that ours is a "government of the people, by the people, for the people." Another basic element is incorporated in Francis Scott Key's oftsung phrase, "the land of the free." It is difficult to exaggerate the contribution of these beliefs to the political stability of our present political system and of the distributive system based on it.

Finally, the transformation of the rule of might into the rule of right is greatly facilitated by the pressures of daily life, which severely limit the political activities of the vast majority of mankind. Though the majority may become politically active in a significant way for a brief time in

---

7. Edwin Sutherland, *White Collar Crime* (New York: Holt, 1949). For a very different kind of documentation of the partiality of laws, see Philip Stern, *The Great Treasury Raid* (New York: Random House, 1964) or any of the many excellent books on political lobbying by vested interests and the benefits derived therefrom.

8. For documentation of this sweeping generalization, see Alex Inkeles and Raymond Bauer, *The Soviet Citizen* (Cambridge, Mass.: Harvard University Press, 1959). On the basis of interviews with hundreds of displaced persons from the Soviet Union immediately after World War II, these writers concluded that there was only limited questioning of the wisdom of state socialism, centralized planning, and the other major elements of Soviet domestic policy. The chief criticisms were directed at the means employed by the Party in achieving its ends—especially the use of terror. This same conclusion has been reached by most other experts on the Soviet Union.

9. Gaetano Mosca, *The Ruling Class,* translated by Hannah Kahn (New York: McGraw-Hill, 1939), p. 70.

a revolutionary era, the necessity of securing a livelihood quickly drives most from the political arena. For better or worse, few men have the financial resources which enable them to set aside their usual economic activities for long. As a result, the affairs of state in any civilized society, and in many that are not, are directed by a small minority. The majority are largely apolitical. Even in popular democracies the vast majority do no more than cast a ballot at infrequent intervals. The formulation of public policy and the various other tasks required by the system are left in the hands of a tiny minority. This greatly facilitates the task of a new regime as it seeks to make the transition from the rule of might to the rule of right.

THE RULE OF RIGHT

On first consideration it may seem that the rule of right is merely the rule of might in a new guise, and therefore no real change can be expected in the distributive process. Such a view is as unwarranted as that which denies the role might continues to play in support of vested interests, even under the rule of right. The fact is that, as the basis of power is shifted from might to right, certain subtle but important changes occur which have far-reaching consequences.

To begin with, if the powers of the regime are to be accepted as rightful and legitimate they must be exercised in some degree, at least, in accord with the conceptions of justice and morality held by the majority—conceptions which spring from their self-interest and partisan group interests. Thus, even though the laws promulgated by a new elite may be heavily slanted to favor themselves, there are limits beyond which this cannot be carried if they wish to gain the benefits of the rule of right.

Second, after the shift to the rule of law, the interests of any single member of the elite can no longer safely be equated with the interests of the elite as a whole. For example, if a member of the new elite enters into a contractual arrangement with some member of the nonelite, and this turns out badly for him, it is to his interest to ignore the law and break the contract. However, this is not to the interest of the other members of the elite

since most contractual arrangements work to their benefit. Therefore, it is to their interest to enforce the law in support of the claims of the nonelite to preserve respect for the law with all the benefits this provides them.

Vilfredo Pareto, the great Italian scholar who has contributed so much to our understanding of these problems, has pointed out a third change associated with the shift from the rule of might to the rule of right. As he observed, those who have won power by force will, under the rule of right, gradually be replaced by a new kind of person and in time these persons will form a new kind of elite. To describe the nature of this change, Pareto wrote of the passing of governmental power from "the lions" to "the foxes."[10] The lions are skilled in the use of force, the foxes in the use of cunning. In other words, the shift from the rule of might means that new skills become essential, and therefore there is a high probability that many of the elite will be displaced because they lack these skills. This displacement is greatly facilitated by the fact that the interests of the elite as a class are no longer identical with the interests of each individual member, which means that individually they become vulnerable. Even those who hang on are forced to change, so that in time the nature of the elite as a class is substantially altered, provided it is not destroyed first by a new leonine revolution or coup. Though this change means increased reliance on intelligence and less on force, as Pareto's choice of the term "fox" and his emphasis on "cunning" indicate, the shift to the rule of right is not the beginning of the millennium when lambs can lie down safely with lions—or foxes. Nor is it the end of the era in which self-interest and partisan group interests dominate human action.

As Pareto's analysis suggests, the rule of the foxes means not merely the rise and fall of individuals, but also changes in the power position of whole classes. Specifically, it means some decline in the position of the military and a corresponding rise by the commercial class and the class of

10. See Vilfredo Pareto, *The Mind and Society*, translated by A. Bongiorno and Arthur Livingstone and edited by Livingstone (New York: Harcourt, Brace & World, 1935), vol. III, especially paragraphs 2170–2278.

professional politicians, both of which are traditionally skilled in the use of cunning. To a lesser degree, it means some improvement in the status of most of the nonmanual classes engaged in peaceful, civilian pursuits.

Fourth, and finally, the transition from the rule of might to the rule of right usually means greater decentralization of power. Under the rule of might, all power tends to be concentrated in the hands of an inner circle of the dominant elite and their agents. Independent centers of power are viewed as a threat and hence are destroyed or taken over. Under the rule of right, however, this is not the case. So long as they remain subject to the law, diverse centers of power can develop and compete side by side. This development is not inevitable, but it can, and probably will, happen once the elite no longer has to fear for the survival of the new regime. As many observers have noted, the degree of unity within a group tends to be a function of the degree to which the members perceive their existence as threatened by others.

In view of these changes, it becomes clear that shifts from the rule of might to the rule of right and vice versa constitute one of the more important sources of variation within societal types defined in technological terms. In other words, even among societies at the same level of technological development, we must expect differences along the lines indicated above, reflecting differences in their position on the might-right continuum.

THE VARIETIES OF INSTITUTIONALIZED POWER

As the foregoing makes clear, *with the shift from the rule of might to the rule of right, power continues to be the determinant of privilege, but the forms of power change.* Force is replaced by institutionalized forms of power as the most useful resource in the struggle between individuals and groups for prestige and privilege, though force still remains in the picture as the ultimate guarantee of these more genteel forms.

Institutionalized power differs from force in a number of ways which deserve note. To begin with, it is a socially acceptable form of power, which means that those who exercise it are less likely to be challenged and more likely to obtain popular support than are those who use force. Second, institutionalized power tends to be much more impersonal. Individuals claim the benefits of institutionalized power not because of their personal qualities or accomplishments, which might easily be challenged, but simply because they occupy a certain role or office or own a certain piece of property. To be sure, it is often assumed that those who enjoy the benefits of institutionalized power are entitled to them by virtue of superior accomplishments or personal qualities, but this is not the crucial issue and the beneficiary does not have to demonstrate these things. It is enough just to be the occupant of the role or office or the owner of the property. Institutionalized power insures that the benefits flow automatically to such persons without regard to their personal qualities or accomplishments. This is, of course, the chief reason why those who gain power by force strive to convert force into institutionalized power.

Institutionalized power takes many forms, but it always involves the possession of certain enforceable rights which increase one's capacity to carry out one's own will even in the face of opposition. It would be impossible to identify and discuss all these many forms here, but it is important to identify some of the more basic and show their varied nature.[11]

One of the basic distinctions within the category of institutionalized power is that between *authority* and *influence.* Authority is the enforceable right to command others. Influence, by contrast, is much more subtle. It is the ability to manipulate the social situation of others, or their perception of it, by the exercise of one's resources and rights, thereby increasing the pressures on others to act in accordance with one's

---

11. There have been numerous attempts to classify the various forms of power, but none have been completely successful. For three of the better efforts, see Herbert Goldhamer and Edward Shils, "Types of Power and Status," *American Journal of Sociology,* 45 (1939), pp. 171–182; Harold Lasswell and Abraham Kaplan, *Power and Society: A Framework for Political Inquiry* (New Haven, Conn.: Yale University Press, 1950), chap. 5; and Robert Bierstedt, "An Analysis of Social Power," *American Sociological Review,* 15 (1950), pp. 730–738.

own wishes.[12] Though these two forms of institutionalized power are quite distinct on the analytical level, they are often hopelessly intertwined on the empirical.

Institutionalized power varies not only in the mode of its action but also in terms of the foundations on which it rests. Here one can speak of a distinction between *the power of position* and *the power of property*. The power of position means *the power which rightfully belongs to the incumbent of any social role or organizational office possessing authority or influence*. This can be seen in the case of officers of state who enjoy great authority and influence so long as they continue to occupy their post, but who lose it when they are replaced. While this is one of the more impressive examples of the power of position, the same basic phenomenon can be seen in the case of the incumbents of a host of lesser roles. One must include under this heading not merely positions in political organizations, but also those in economic, religious, educational, and military organizations, together with age and sex roles, roles in kin groups, roles in racial and ethnic groups, and every other kind of role or office with authority or influence.

A second foundation on which institutionalized power commonly rests is the *private ownership of property*. Though property and position have often been closely linked, the connection is neither necessary nor inevitable. The ownership of property is frequently dissociated from occupancy of a particular office or role. Since property is, by definition, something in short supply and hence of value, the owner of property controls a resource which can be used to influence the actions of others. The more he owns, the greater is his capacity to influence, and thus the greater his power. In some instances, as in the ownership of slaves or of a political office which has been purchased,[13] the power of property can take the form of authority. It also takes the form of authority to the extent that the owner is entitled to proscribe certain actions by others—that is, order them *not* to do certain things, such as trespass on his land.

Before concluding this brief introduction to institutionalized power, it may be well to take note of Simmel's observation that where the rule of law or right prevails, there is always a two-way flow of influence (and sometimes, one might add, of authority as well) between the more powerful and the less powerful.[14] This point is easily forgotten, since the very concept "power" suggests a one-directional flow. To say that there is a two-way flow does not mean that the flow is equally strong in both directions, but it does mean that one should not ignore the secondary flow or the factors responsible for it and the consequences of it.[15]

---

12. In many sociological writings the relationship between power and influence is extremely confusing. Sometimes they are treated as synonymous, other times as two distinct phenomena with no area of overlap. Influence should be treated as one special type of power. This approach is consistent both with good English usage and with the insights of some of the abler social theorists. For example, *Webster's Collegiate Dictionary* (5th ed.) defines influence as "the act or the power of producing an effect *without apparent force or direct authority*" (emphasis added).

13. On the purchase of offices, see pp. 224–225.

14. Georg Simmel, *The Sociology of Georg Simmel,* edited and translated by Kurt Wolff (New York: Free Press, 1950), part 3.

15. More recently the same point was made by Robert Dahl and Charles Lindblom in their book *Politics, Economics and Welfare,* part 4, where they point to the existence of four sociopolitical systems, two of which, price systems and polyarchical systems, involve some measure of influence by the less powerful over the more powerful.

2

Applications of a Multiple Hierarchy Approach

THE STUDY of stratification furnishes a perspective on human behavior, how societies are organized, and how they change. It can be applied as a prism that captures and focuses certain pieces of reality.

Karl Marx established several points of reference that still constitute major areas of theory and research in social stratification in various types of societies: (1) the idea of the primacy of the economic production system in determining which groups have power and privilege in a society; (2) the idea that stratification systems involve tension, conflict, and competition because a ruling class always attempts to increase its profits and rewards at the expense of a subordinate laboring class; (3) the idea that the controlling economic group justifies its exploitation by developing ideologies to support the status quo; (4) the idea of group consciousness among members of a similar stratum and the recognition that such consciousness can take the form of political action resulting in social change; and (5) the idea that an individual's position in the social structure shapes his or her beliefs, behavior, and life experience.

Drawing from Marx and others, we have based this book on five basic concepts pertaining to social stratification. Each concept is explained briefly in this chapter and concentrated on exclusively in later chapters. Each concept represents a traditional area of study containing a substantial body of theory and research.

1. Unequal distributions
2. Common experiences
3. Supporting ideology
4. Stratum consciousness and action
5. Vertical mobility

These five stratification concepts form the organizational framework of this book. These basic concepts will be applied to each of the four hierarchies, going beyond the

An asterisk (*) accompanying a citation indicates a selection that is included in this volume.

usual single focus on social class. Each concept will be applied to ethnic, sex, and age stratification as well as to class. For example, in the case of stratum consciousness, it is not only class groups that have the potential for feelings of solidarity and shared fate, but ethnic, sex, and age groups as well. Major emphasis will be placed on *comparisons* across the four hierarchies. There may be greater potential for stratum consciousness among blacks than among women, for example, since blacks often live in highly unequal ghetto communities where grievances and a sense of shared fate can easily develop, whereas women live in separate families and, in most instances, live in close relationship with men, who are members of the superordinate strata.

A second major emphasis is on the effects of *combinations* of stratification positions, such as old and black, or poor and white, or young and middle class. With a multiple hierarchy model, the complex social worlds created by the juxtaposition of two or more such positions can be brought into sharp focus, as can their effects on social processes and individual attitudes and behavior.

These basic concepts can also be stated as propositions, providing a more elaborated statement of their place in the context of the study of social stratification.

Concept 1. The Most Basic Characteristic Of Stratification Is An Unequal Distribution Of Power, Privilege, And Prestige.

Concept 2. Those Who Occupy The Same Position In A Given Hierarchy Will Hold Certain Experiences, Situations, And Social Expectations In Common.

Concept 3. All Stratification Hierarchies Are Supported By An Ideology—A Network Of Interrelated Beliefs, Norms And Values—That Gives Legitimacy And Acceptance To The Unequal Distribution Of Power, Privilege, And Prestige.

Concept 4. All Stratification Systems Have The Potential For The Development Of Stratum Consciousness And Action Directed Toward Changing The Distribution Of Power, Privilege, And Prestige.

Concept 5. All Stratification Systems Are Characterized By Vertical Mobility—Movement Up Or Down, To Greater Or Lesser Power, Privilege, And Prestige—Of Both Individuals And Groups.

Each of these five propositions refers to a fundamental property of stratification systems. Social stratification exists only when groupings exhibit to some degree the characteristics stated in these propositions. When one or more of these features of social organization are absent, a developed hierarchy of social strata cannot be said to exist. By demonstrating that these five basic propositions, which have been central to the study of class stratification, are also applicable to ethnic, sex, and age groupings in the United States, the multiple hierarchy perspective provides a synthesis which systematically extends the scope of existing theories and frames of reference in the study of stratification.

The basic organization of this book entails an analysis of class, ethnic, sex, and age stratification from the perspectives provided by the five basic concepts and their attendant propositions. Within this context, emphasis is placed on comparisons and combinations relative to these four hierarchies. Figure 2–1 illustrates the basic plan of organization.

Unequal distribution, supporting ideology, common experience, stratum consciousness and action, vertical mobility

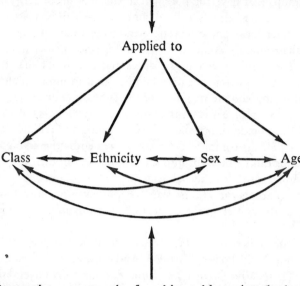

I   *Comparisons* among the four hierarchies using the basic five concepts. For example, differences in the distribution of power by ethnicity and sex.

II *Combinations* or joint effects among the hierarchies. For example, old, female, and poor; young adult, white, and male.

Figure 2-1.   *Five Basic Concepts of Social Stratification Used in This Book*

The following pages present a brief discussion of the five organizing concepts and examples of comparisons and combinations pertaining to each.

CONCEPT 1: UNEQUAL DISTRIBUTION OF POWER, PRIVILEGE, AND PRESTIGE

Power, privilege, and prestige were defined in chapter 1. Social classes, as groups based on wealth, occupation and education, have already been extensively linked to the rewards of power, privilege, and prestige. What is new and interesting is the recent application of these concepts to sex, ethnicity, and age. The need for this type of analysis is evidenced by the newly emerging consciousness among these groups in the world today.

The study of differential gender roles has a long history, but only recently have the relations between males and females been clearly conceptualized as unequal in power and privilege (Collins, 1971; Polatnick,* 1973–74).

There has been a shift from the fairly neutral idea that men and women play very different roles in our society (nurturant homemaker vs. instrumental breadwinner) to the view that men are in positions from which they are able to control the lives of women and limit their access to privilege and prestige. Women are not likely to acquire power, income, and social honor in the larger society from their roles as housewives. Unequal distribution of power between the sexes is also apparent in the occupational structure. Women are often employed in occupations that require them to take orders from men. When women do have authority over others, they usually give orders to other women or children, seldom to men.

Similarly, even though differential prestige among ethnic groups has been studied since the early part of this century (Bogardus; 1928; Simpson and Yinger, 1972: 139–164), it is only in the 1960s and 1970s that one finds a clear emphasis on unequal power as the foundation of ethnic-racial stratification, as seen in works such as those of Blauner (1972) and Olsen* (1970). Recent scholarly articles focus on: (a) the fact that blacks, American Indians, and Mexican-Americans are *conquered* minorities who have faced a very different set of experiences from those of white ethnic groups who voluntarily came to the United States; (b) the institutions, housing, and economics of Indian reservations and black ghettos have been largely controlled by white outsiders; and (c) racism is increasingly viewed as an institutional problem rather than a problem of prejudiced personalities.

The study of age from a stratification perspective is just emerging at the time of this writing and can probably be said to have received its major impetus from the pioneer work of Riley, Johnson, and Foner (1972). Increasingly, age groups such as children and the elderly are being viewed as groups with low degrees of power, privilege, and prestige. At retirement, older people are stripped of income and positions that grant power and prestige in the larger society—they are defined as nonproductive members of society. The powerless position of children is increasingly questioned. For example, Farson* has presented a Bill of Rights for children (Farson, 1974). Child abuse centers for battered children exist for the first time, and many child-rearing practices now put emphasis on a democratic solution to problems rather than on unquestioned obedience and submission to parental authority.

Power, Privilege, and Prestige: Comparisons and Combinations

The multiple hierarchy approach centers on comparisons and combinations of hierarchical positions. A comparative framework would note that visible ethnic minorities, women, and the aged have all interacted with more powerful strata that have limited their options and defined the kinds of occupations and roles open to them. However, striking differences exist in the way power has been exerted. In the United States, blacks and American Indians were conquered by force and placed in institutional systems of dependency and total control (slavery and Bureau of Indian Affairs control of reservations). Women and the aged have not faced as striking and overt forms of force and coercion as the conquered minorities, nor have they lived in subjugated communities, such as ghettos and reservations. Rather, unequal power and privilege by sex and age have taken place in the form of laws (mandatory retirement) and unwritten customs and roles that have excluded these groups from full participation in positions that command honor and power.

A combinations perspective on power, privilege, and prestige explores the joint effects of two or more hierarchies upon the distribution of these rewards. Those who are black, old, and poor face greater barriers to power, privilege, and prestige than those with one of these characteristics.

CONCEPT 2: CORRELATES, OR
COMMON EXPERIENCES

How an individual behaves, thinks, or generally views the world stems in some degree from his or her location in the social structure. When individuals occupy similar statuses in the social structure, their construction of reality is likely to be similar, since the life circumstances influencing their social perception are somewhat alike. Conversely, when individuals occupy different statuses in the social structure, their views on a variety of topics and issues are likely to be different. These facts allow us to use each of the four hierarchies as a predictive variable. That is, they allow us to correlate many life styles, behaviors, and attitudes with a stratification position. To illustrate, numerous studies have shown that there are striking differences in rates of mental illness and in political voting behavior according to one's social class. Severe mental illness (psychoses) is much more likely to be found in the poverty stratum than in the working, middle, or upper class strata (Hollingshead and Redlich, 1958).

Ethnic, sex, and age strata also constrain and shape human behavior. For example, sex roles shape a woman's behavior toward feminine ideals; old age limits options in terms of travel, mobility, and all the services and comforts that money can buy. Thus, each hierarchy can be viewed as the predictive cause of certain outcomes.

Correlates: Combinations and Comparisons

The correlates (or common experiences) tradition focuses on the ways in which class, age, sex, and ethnicity combine or compete to influence a variety of predicted outcomes.

One of the most interesting and unexplored areas of research is how hierarchies combine to form cumulative effects. If each of the four hierarchies can be independently related to disadvantages in power, privilege, and prestige, then the combined effect of two or more low positions can lead to severe disadvantages. Instead of a single (class) stratification order, one can visualize a society in which some face multiple, stacked layers of inequality.

Aged blacks are one such group in which racism, ageism, and poverty operate to create extreme deprivation. Recognizing their special status at the White House Conference on Aging in 1971, they came represented by their own National Caucus for the Black Aged. Aged blacks felt subject to a combination of disadvantages requiring a special organization that was sensitive to their unique needs and that would create policies and actions most beneficial to them (Jackson, 1974). Other recently published studies have similarly examined the double jeopardy caused by the combination of low statuses. Clark* (1971) has documented the difficulties of the aged poor in the inner city, and Murray (1970) has noted the particular disadvantages encountered by the black female. Shortridge (1975) has analyzed the disadvantaged situation of the working poor woman.

Correlates, or common experiences, can be studied at a comparative level by asking which of two or more stratification positions has the greater impact upon a given outcome. Scholars frequently debate whether race or sex has more influence on earnings, for example. In comparing males and females and blacks and whites, Almquist (1975) found that being female was a greater liability than being black, with respect to income.

CONCEPT 3: SUPPORTING IDEOLOGIES

All systems of social stratification develop a rationale and justification for the unequal distribution of power, privilege, and prestige. The analysis of ideologies places systems of social inequality in a cultural context and examines how culture influences the maintenance of stratification.

To the degree that stratification hierarchies are not maintained by force, they must be accepted to some extent by the members of subordinate strata. Supporting ideologies perform this function. Without this acceptance, constant strife and conflict or the continued use of physical force to repress such dissent is inevitable. Members of subordinate strata will accept their position, even if it entails considerable hardship and manifest inequalities, if the prevailing culture gives a satisfactory explanation for their deprivations. Conversely, those in superordinate positions can live comfortably and in good conscience with their favored position if culturally sanctioned justifications are readily available. Thus, depending on their position in a hierarchy, supporting ideologies fulfill somewhat different functions for individuals. In general, they provide a rationale for existing social inequalities, and in so doing give stability and a degree of tranquility to society.

When supporting ideologies are a generally accepted part of the culture and prevailing social expectations, they become enhanced with the tremendous force of public opinion and established tradition. Unquestioned assumptions regarding human nature and the social order come to be taken for granted. Thus, Bem and Bem * (1972) have referred to the "Unconscious Ideology" of sex role socialization that places, and helps to maintain, women in a subordinate position to men.

Ideologies are regarded as loosely interrelated systems of beliefs, norms, and values. *Beliefs* refer to opinions or judgements about some aspects of reality. For example, various studies (McTavish, 1971; National Council of Aging, 1975) have indicated a prevalence of negative beliefs about the aged in the United States. *Norms* refer to standards of correct and incorrect behavior. Thus, there are various norms pertaining to the age at which people should do things such as marry, decide on a career, become grandparents, and retire (Neugarten, Moore, and Lowe, 1965). *Values* refer to conceptions of desirable ends. For example, youth and youthfulness are idealized and highly regarded in the United States. The aforementioned beliefs, norms, and values are parts of a much larger and to some degree uncharted ideology supporting that aspect of the age stratification system in the United States which places the elderly in a subordinate position.

Supporting Ideologies: Comparisons and Combinations

The multiple hierarchy approach provides a perspective for comparing similarities and differences in ideologies that support stratification in different hierarchies. For example, the ideologies supporting the systems of class, ethnic, sex, and age stratification in the United States all entail a set of generally accepted negative beliefs regarding those in the lowest positions of these hierarchies. According to one set of cultural beliefs, women are said to be unsuited for high occupational positions because their "natural" temperament is more passive, dependent, nurturant, and emotional. They thus lack the objective, logical, aggressive characteristics necessary to lead and organize others. The aged are also believed to be unfit for many occupational positions, but for different reasons. They are seen as unfit because of a presumed loss in physical health and vigor, outmoded skills, and less flexibility in thought. Mandatory retirement is based, in part, on these beliefs. Racial minorities and the poor are also the object of prevalent negative beliefs that serve to justify a denial of full opportunities.

The comparative approach also provides for the analysis of the manner in which particular beliefs, norms, or values may support and maintain inequality in more than one hierarchy. For example, one set of ideas that serves to explain the low position of both the poor and racial minorities stresses free will and individual effort. The white poor and lower class blacks are both regarded as being in low positions because they have not exerted the necessary effort. According to this ideology, the system is open and just and those who fail to work hard and plan ahead deserve to be poor. Their low position is seen as a result of a lack of individual effort. From this viewpoint, advantages of birth, or barriers of discrimination, are given only slight consideration (Feagin* 1972; Schuman*, 1975).

Combinations of ideologies can emerge when the beliefs, norms, and values of two or more hierarchies overlap or reinforce each other. Certain beliefs and values are associated with growing old in the youth-oriented society of the United States. Both men and women must cope with the social negativism associated with old age. But various studies (Bell, 1970; Sontag*, 1972) show that aging is socially evaluated more negatively for women than for men. Middle-aged and older women face double standards and double jeopardies that men of the same age do not face. Since the cultural ideals surrounding women stress physical beauty and childbearing, when a woman loses these qualities in her middle or later years she especially faces a loss of prestige and reduced options for the future. Men, in contrast, often reach the heights of their careers in the middle years and have many occupational sources of power and prestige to offset the negative ideologies surrounding aging. Thus, various ideas pertaining to age and sex stratification combine to produce a double standard of aging that seriously disadvantages women but not men.

CONCEPT 4: STRATUM CONSCIOUSNESS
AND ACTION

The study of stratum consciousness concentrates on the role of social strata in generating social movements and other activities aimed at bringing about social and cultural change. It analyzes the conditions under which members of the subordinate strata will: (1) develop a shared perception of injustice regarding the distribution of power, privilege, and prestige, and (2) engage in collective action to change their disadvantaged position.

Class consciousness has long been a central concern in the analysis of the structure and dynamics of class stratification. But a strictly class model of consciousness is not adequate to explain the consciousness raising and protest of groups such as blacks and women in recent years. The multiple hierarchy model provides a frame of reference for the study of consciousness and action beyond the limited range of class stratification.

Stratum Consciousness and Action: Comparisons and Combinations

The comparative approach focuses attention on the uniformities of consciousness and action across different hierarchies. Regardless of the hierarchy involved, consciousness entails such elements as a developing sense of group identification, a perspective of shared fate, solidarity, and a growing sense of injustice over the distribution of rewards. Statum consciousness involves a redefinition of the situation. For example, with the development of consciousness, the definition of problems shifts from an individual to a social level. What were previously regarded as individual failings or pathologies become regarded as social problems. Thus, comparing across strata, the ''Black is Beautiful'' facet of the black movement and the consciousness-raising groups in the women's movement both involve a deliberate and explicit rejection of negative definitions of the self that are contained in the dominant culture.

The multiple hierarchy model also provides for the comparative study of the pattern of development of consciousness and action in different hierarchies. The multiple hierarchy approach provides a comparative frame of reference for asking why consciousness and action have developed in some hierarchies and not in others. This focus of the multiple hierarchy model necessitates a more thorough study of the relationship between social stratification and social change. For example, the aged in the United States have not developed stratum consciousness nor engaged in social protest to near the extent that ethnic minorities and women have. Kasschau (1977) reasons that because many older persons try to deny their ages and to appear younger, they are not likely to identify with the interests of the aged stratum or to engage in action on their behalf. Kasschau also notes that the legal system has less clearly and consistently defended the civil rights of the aged compared with those of women and ethnic minorities. And the mass media has paid far less attention to age discrimination compared with discrimination based on ethnicity and sex. In short, there appears to be a special set of cultural and social forces that have weakened the potential for age consciousness, compared with sex and ethnic consciousness.

The impact of particular combinations of hierarchical positions on the development of consciousness and action can be explored. For example, two kinds of consciousness may sometimes reinforce one another. Leggett (1968) found that black union workers who identified strongly with their class, that is, with the grievances and interests of the working man, also expressed high degrees of black pride and consciousness. Black consciousness seemed to go with class consciousness, and when both were present, there was greater expressed militance or willingness to engage in strikes and other class actions. A parallel result was observed by Ransford* (1977) in a study of black respondents interviewed shortly after the Watts (Los Angeles) riot of 1965. Blacks who expressed both working class consciousness and black consciousness interpreted the Watts riot in positive terms and were more willing to take radical action, including violence, to correct racial injustices.

In contrast to these studies in which positions in two hierarchies enhance the development of stratum consciousness, other studies have indicated that the cross pressures engendered by two statuses can reduce, limit, or prevent the development of consciousness and action. For example, Nieto* (1974) has described how stress on traditional sex roles and the established family pattern influence Mexican American women to limit their expectations relative to the women's liberation movement. Many support such issues as equal pay and job opportunities, but are resistant to pushing for a more equalitarian situation with respect to various aspects of the husband-wife relationship.

CONCEPT 5: VERTICAL MOBILITY

Vertical mobility is an important aspect of change within systems of social stratification. The study of vertical mobility focuses on movement up or down a hierarchy. Such movement may be simply from one stratum to another or may involve a more dramatic shift from the top to the bottom of the structure, or vice-versa. Mobility of this degree usually occurs when major social movements produce revolutionary social or cultural change. Vertical mobility may be experienced by individuals or by groups. In the case of individual mobility, the relative distance between strata remains the same and emphasis is placed on how far given individuals have moved from some baseline starting point. Sons, for example, who achieve higher occupational positions than their fathers are said to be upwardly mobile in the class hierarchy. Group mobility in contrast refers to the ascendance or descendance of an entire stratum (or at least a major portion of that stratum). If women or blacks have made significant gains in power, privilege, and prestige over a twenty year time period, we can conclude that group mobility has taken place.

In this book, sex and ethnic mobility are considered only at the group level. Obviously, it is difficult for individuals to change their gender or their skin color, and this rarely occurs. However, aggregate or group mobility for women or blacks may be the object of meaningful and important inquiries.

Social class and age can be considered at both the individual level and the group level. One can study the mobility of individuals through occupational positions (class hierarchy) as well as the mobility of an entire occupational stratum, such as blue collar workers. Similarly, age can be studied individually as the movement of individuals through life stages (such as childhood, adolescence, young adulthood, maturity, and old age) as well as at the group level (e.g., the relative social status of the aged through time). Both individual and group mobility continually occur in any system of stratification, although their degree and form may differ considerably.

Mobility: Comparisons and Combinations

To illustrate group mobility with comparative data, Szymanski (1974) found that although blacks had been upwardly mobile in occupational position in the period from 1940 to 1970, there had been little change in the occupational position of women. This study is an example of how the relative upward and downward mobility of sex and ethnic groups can be gauged with comparative data.

A combinations approach to social stratification considers what results when individuals or groups ascend or descend more than one hierarchy. For example, at the individual level, there is a pattern for persons simultaneously to ascend the class and age hierarchies. For many individuals, increases in age are accompanied by increases in occupational rank, authority, and salary. This dual track mobility often continues until retirement. However, dual hierarchy mobility may not be this neat and synchronized.

Sometimes a high position may be achieved in one hierarcy but the full prerogatives of that position be denied because of low position in another hierarchy. For example, minority persons or women who have moved into high occupational positions (such as a black doctor or a woman manager) may find access to information, full respect of co-workers, decision-making opportunities, and open channels of communication all limited by a residue of racial or sexual barriers. Miller, Labovitz, and Fry (1975) have illustrated that some of these deprivations were suffered by women in high-level positions in large formal organizations. This type of "incomplete mobility" has been relatively ignored in studies of vertical mobility. The progress of ethnic minorities and women has been viewed almost exclusively in class terms, with the unstated assumption that the achievement of class equality represents full equality.

CONCLUSIONS

This book presents an approach to the study of social stratification that is different from the dominant tradition in the field and in its current emphasis. In expanding the basic frame of reference for studying stratification from a single (class) hierarchy model to a four hierarchy model—class, ethnicity, sex and age—this work is consistent with what appears to be a growing trend in recent years. This trend, however, is in a very early stage of development, and a great deal of conceptual and empirical work still needs to be done. This book breaks new ground by: 1) systematically connecting each of the five stratification concepts—unequal power, privilege, and prestige; supporting ideology; common experiences; stratum consciousness and action; vertical mobility—to each of the four hierarchies of class, ethnicity, sex and age; 2) developing a comparative perspective across the four hierarchies, thus noting similarities and differences across class, ethnicity, sex and age stratification; and 3) calling attention to the combination or joint effects that occur when examining two or more hierarchies in interaction.

These five basic concepts of stratification, which are reflected in subsequent chapter titles, serve as the organizational framework of this book.

The writings of Pitirim A. Sorokin (1964, 1969*) influenced our development and expansion of the multiple hierarchy approach. Sorokin was one of the first to conceptualize the joint effect of two or more hierarchies, which he referred to as "multi-bonded" stratification. He was far ahead of his time in breaking out of the class mold and considering a number of other hierarchies: sex, age, race, kinship, locality, religion, and political parties, to mention a few. Sorokin's approach to stratification is illustrated by the selection from his writings, which is included at the end of this chapter.

REFERENCES

Almquist, Elizabeth M. 1975. "Untangling the Effects of Race and Sex: The Disadvantaged Status of Black Women." *Social Science Quarterly* 56 (June): 129–142.

Bell, Inge Powell. 1970. "The Double Standard of Aging." *Trans-Action* (November–December): 75–80.

Bem, Sandra L. and Daryl J. Bem. 1972. "Homogenizing the American Woman: The Power of an Unconscious Ideology." Unpublished Paper. (Included in this volume.)

Blauner, Robert. 1972. "Colonized and Immigrant Minorities." In Robert Blauner, *Racial Oppression in America*. New York: Harper and Row.

Bogardus, Emory. 1928. *Immigration and Race Attitudes*. Indianapolis: D.C. Heath.

Clark, Margaret. 1971. "Patterns of Aging Among the Elderly Poor of the Inner City." *The Gerontologist* (Spring): 58–65.

Collins, Randall. 1971. "A Conflict Theory of Sexual Stratification." *Social Problems* 19 (Summer): 3–21.

_____1975. *Conflict Sociology*. New York: Academic Press.

Farson, Richard. 1974. "Birthrights: A Children's Bill of Rights." *Ms* 2 (March): 67–69, 71, 94, 95.

Feagin, Joe R. 1972. "God Helps Those Who Help Themselves." *Psychology Today* 6 (November): 101.

Hollingshead, August B. and Frederick C. Redlich. 1958. *Social Class and Mental Illness*. New York: John Wiley and Sons.

Jackson, Jacquelyne Johnson. 1974. "NCBA, Black Aged and Politics." *The Annals of the American Academy of Political and Social Science* 415 (September): 138–159.

Kasschau, Patricia L. 1977. "Age and Race Discrimination Reported by Middle-Aged and Older Persons." *Social Forces* 55 (March): 728–742.

Leggett, John C. 1968. Class, Race and Labor. New York: Oxford University Press.

McTavish, Donald G. 1971. "Perceptions of Old People: A Review of Research Methodologies and Findings." *The Gerontologist* (Winter): 90–108.

Miller, Jon, Sanford Labovitz, and Lincoln Fry. 1975. "Differences in the Organizational Experiences of Men and Women: Resources, Vested Interests and Discrimination." *Social Forces* (December): 365–381.

Murray, Pauli. 1970. "The Liberation of Black Women." In Mary Thompson (ed.), *Voices of the New Feminism*. Boston: Beacon.

National Council on Aging. 1975. *Perspective on Aging* 4 (March/April): 3–6, 13–15, 16, 18.

Neugarten, Bernice L., Joan W. Moore, and John C. Lowe. 1965. "Age Norms, Age Constraints and Adult Socialization." *American Journal of Sociology* 70 (May): 710–717.

Nieto, Consuelo. 1974. "The Chicano and the Women's Rights Movement." *Civil Rights Digest* 6 (Spring): 36–42.

Olsen, Marvin E. 1970. "Power Perspectives on Stratification and Race Relations." In Marvin E. Olsen (ed.), *Power in Societies* New York: Maxmillan: pp. 296–304.

Palmore, Erdman and Frank Whittington. 1971. "Trends in the Relative Status of the Aged." *Social Forces* 50 (September): 84–90.

Polatnick, Margaret. 1973–1974. "Why Men Don't Rear Children: A Power Analysis" *Berkeley Journal of Sociology* 18: 46–86

Ransford, H. Edward. 1977. "Stratum Solidarity in a Period After the Watts Riot." In H. Edward Ransford, *Race and Class in American Society: Black, Chicano and Anglo.* Cambridge, Mass.: Schenkman 136–144.

Riley, Matilda White, Marilyn Johnson, and Anne Foner. 1972. *Aging and Society: A Sociology of Age Stratification* New York: Russell Sage Foundation.

Schuman, Howard. 1975 "Free Will and Determinism in Public Beliefs about Race." In Norman R. Yetman and C. Hoy Steele (eds.), *Majority and Minority.* Boston: Allyn and Bacon: pp. 375–380.

Shortridge, Kathleen. 1975. "Working Poor Women." In Jo Freeman (ed.), *"Women" A Feminist Perspective* Palo Alto, Calif.: Mayfield.

Simpson, George Eaton and J. Milton Yinger. 1972. *Racial and Cultural Minorities.* New York: Harper and Row.

Sontag, Susan. 1972. "The Double Standard of Aging." *Saturday Review* (September): 119–126.

Sorokin, Pitirim A. 1964. *Social and Cultural Mobility.* Glencoe, Ill.: Free Press.

——————————1969. *Society, Culture and Personality.* New York: Cooper Square Publishers, Inc.

Szymanski, Albert. 1974. "Race, Sex, and the U.S. Working Class." *Social Problems* 21 (June): 706–725.

Social Stratification

Pitirim A. Sorokin

I. THE STRATIFICATION OF SOCIAL GROUPS

THE SOCIAL structure of the human population does not consist merely in the differentiation of the population into unibonded and multibonded groups. It consists also in the fact of the stratification of organized groups—stratification within any single group and stratification of several groups with respect to one another. Thus to be more or less complete, a knowledge of social structure requires recognition not only of social differentiation but of social stratification as well. The first concerns the division of the population along the vertical lines of the groups; the second refers to the division of the population along the horizontal lines. The real social strata of a group, as well as groups with respect to one another, are ranked as superior and inferior, higher and lower, controlling and controlled, dominating and subordinated, privileged and disfranchised. If the sociocultural world of human groups were only a "one-story structure," the essentials of that structure would be learned through a study of its social differentiation. If it is, as indeed it happens to be, a "many-storied structure" then one must know also its stratificational aspect. This explains why a study of social stratification is now in order.

II. CLASSIFICATION OF THE FORMS OF STRATIFICATION OR INEQUALITIES

Like social differentiation, social stratification has many forms and can be classified in many different ways. For sociological purposes, the following appear to be the most important: (1) official and unofficial organized real strata, "as if" organized strata, and nominal, statistical pseudo strata (plurels); (2) intragroup and intergroup stratification; (3) unibonded and multibonded stratification. Then each of the unibonded and multibonded strata can be subclassified into open (nonhereditary), closed (hereditary), and intermediary. There are among the intermediary forms those that are *legally sanctioned* by the official law of the state or some other group, and those that are *factual*, that is, without specific legal sanctioning.

The multibonded strata can be classified, according to the number of the stratifying bonds, into double, triple, quadruple, and so on. They can be further classified as a) innerly solidary, or affine; b) antagonistic, or disaffine; and c) neutral. Let us now make an analysis of the nature of each of these forms, one by one, of their combinations, in order to gain a more adequate knowledge of social stratification.

1. The Organized Real Strata, the "As If" Organized Strata, and the Nominal, Pseudo Strata

An *organized real social stratum of a group*, or of a constellation of groups, is composed of the totality of the members interacting with one another and having all the characteristics of a real social group: causal and meaningful unity, reality, individuality, interdependence of its members, government, and so on (see Chapter 8). Whether composed of many or a few or even of one member, the real social stratum lives and functions amidst other strata as a real organized social group with all its essential characteristics (Chapter 4). The real social strata ordinarily are defined legally by the official law of the group, like the ranks of the pope-cardinal-archbishop-bishop hierarchy in the church group, like the full-associate-assistant professor-instructor grading in the university, and so on for other groups. The ranking of the official law may or may not coincide with the ranking of the unofficial convictions of the members of the group. Officially, the rank of the French or the Russian nobility on the eve of the French and Russian Revolutions was the highest among all the estates of the respective countries; but according to the unofficial-law convictions of a considerable part of the French and Russian populations, the "superiority and prestige" of the nobilities was not respected and their official high position was in fact resented and considered unjustified. There are many cases where the rankings of the official and unofficial laws coincide. Now and then the real strata exist factually, that is, without specific legal sanctioning, official or unofficial. Thus in many populations the strata of the rich and of the poor exist as real strata, but they are not defined or sanctioned legally. Whether legally sanctioned or merely existing factually, the real unibonded or multibonded social stratum is always an objectively given real collectivity, easily observable and existing independently of the subjective ranking of observers and investigators.[1]

An "as if" real and organized stratum of a group, or of a constellation of groups, is composed of the totality of the individuals who have the same position—rights, duties, functions, etc.—in the hierarchy of strata, and who therefore think, feel, and act similarly so far as such a similarity is imposed on them by the similarity of their stratum-positions. However, they are not expressly organized into one body, with its own government, regulations, planned and consciously pursued policy, and so on. Many of such members may not even be aware of their co-belonging to the same stratum. The strata of slaves, serfs, and criminals, are examples of such "as if" organized strata. Their social status was precisely defined by law, but did not have any committee, they were often scattered over a wide territory, and they did not react directly with one another. Nevertheless, they acted and felt similarly, like the partisans and guerillas of the same army.

A purely nominal or statistical stratum (a plurel) does not have the essential traits of a real group and does not exist as such in reality. When, for instance, statisticians divide the population into income-groups: below $100, $101 to $150, $151 to $200, $201 to $251, and so on, such economic strata are nominal groups. The persons receiving from all sources an income between $101 and $150 are not necessarily more closely connected with one another than with persons receiving, especially all from the same source, $76 to $100, or $151 to $175. When W. L. Warner and P. S. Lunt divide the Population of Yankee City into six strata: upper-upper, lower-upper, upper-middle, lower-middle, upper-lower, and lower-lower they are constructing wholly nominal strata. Their own material shows that neither economically, or by the volume of rights and duties, nor in behavioral, occupational, or any other way,

---

1. For this reason all the studies of social stratification in which the strata are obtained through a ranking of the observers themselves, or through a vague reference to "the status" or "social class" or "prestige" ranked subjectively by one or a group of evaluators—all these studies actually deal not with the real social strata but with either "as if organized strata" or, in most cases, with purely "nominal plurels" taken incorrectly for a real stratum. Such studies remain largely fruitless. See the examples of such mistakes as well as attempts to avoid them in the works of Warner and Lunt, cited; in W. H.

Form, "Status Stratification in a Planned Community," *ASR*, X, pp. 605-13; E. H. Bell, "Social Stratification in a Small Community," *Scientific Monthly*, 1934, pp. 157-164; H. Speier, "Honor and the Social Stratification," *SR*, II, pp. 74-97; M. Smith, "An Empirical Scale of Prestige Status of Occupations," *ASR*, 1943, pp. 185-192; D. Anderson and P. E. Davidson, *Ballots and the American Class Struggle* (Stanford University Press, 1939). See the vast literature on stratification in my *Mobility*.

do these strata live and function as real organized or even "as if" organized unities.[2] Still more nominal are most of their 89 stratified positions in Yankee City. These positions are the cuts of a social "mince pie" rather than organs and cells of a living body. Subsequently we shall deal mainly with the organized real and with the "as if" organized strata, paying little attention to the nominal plurels.

2. The Intragroup and Intergroup Strata (Inequality)

We have distinguished further intragroup and intergroup stratification. In our analysis of the organized groups (see Chapter 4), it has been indicated that the distributive and organizational functions of law create a stratification in any organized group. In order to prevent clashes among its members and enforce the official law, any organized group establishes a long or short hierarchy of superior and inferior authorities, and ranks its members into a very definite, clear-cut order in which the decision of each superior authority or stratum is mandatory upon the respective inferior rank or authority. Such an hierarchization of the authority or of the rights and duties leads to a clear-cut stratification of all members of any organized group. This explains why *the organization and stratification are inseparable and why stratification is an inalienable trait of any organized group*. In other words, unequal distribution of

2. See their *The Social Life of a Modern Community and The Status System* (quoted). Somewhat humorous evidence of the nominality of their strata is given in the fact that, having artificially divided the population into these six strata, they subsequently find that members of the same stratum behave differently and that in the associations, cliques, and in many other ways, these strata are intermixed to such an extent that they are forced to make another "discovery," namely, that associations, cliques, occupations, and many other devices serve as the "integrating links" between the strata, uniting them into one community. The real situation is much simpler. Most of their strata not being real ones, they do not exist. Therefore their members are naturally intermingled. Their second "discovery" cancels their first, and both together show the nominal nature of their six stratified classes. Another conspicuous example of purely nominal plurels substituted for real groups is given in most of the complex and fruitless classifications of S. C. Dodd's *Dimensions of Society* (New York, 1942).

rights-duties-roles-functions is an inherent trait of an organization. Whatever organized empirical group we take, from the family, clan, tribe, to age, sex, racial, language, state, religious, occupational, economic and other groups, they are all stratified into a number of either legal and clearly-cut strata or into a factual and somewhat muddled set of strata, superior and inferior, dominant and subordinate. In both cases these strata exist objectively, making unnecessary the subjective ranking of observers. We shall see this in the next section of this chapter.

Side by side with the intragroup stratification (inequality), there is intergroup stratification, or inequality among groups, whether these groups are of the same or different nature with respect to their unibonded or multibonded characteristics. Different states, different occupational, religious, or other groups, are not situated on the same level, but on different levels so far as their prestige, controlling influence, domination, and other powers are concerned. In other words, groups are stratified one with respect to another. There are big and small state powers; there are skilled and the unskilled; there are the professional and the big business occupations; there are the monopolistic, privileged religions, and the suppressed, persecuted, and disfranchised ones. These are all examples of such intergroup stratification of groups in the same class. There is also, in somewhat more confused condition, stratification among groups which are of a different nature. There is ranking of the state and religious groups (witness the struggle for supremacy between the state and the church in the Middle Ages); there is ranking of occupational and nationality groups, and so on. In more detailed form, these stratifications will be outlined in the next section. For the present, the above definitions will suffice for the subsequent discussion.

3. Unibonded and Multibonded Stratification

Our concept of unibonded and multibonded groups is also applicable to social strata. *Stratification within any unibonded group is a unibonded stratification; stratification within a multibonded group is a multibonded stratifica-*

tion. It should be remembered that the uni-bonded groups are those in which the grouping of members is centered around one main class of values-meanings-norms. The multibonded groups are those in which the *raison d'être* of the group is a coalescence of two or a greater number of the sets of the unibonded values-meanings-norms. In accordance with this conception, the stratification in the unibonded groups is based on the same main value on which is based the existence of the group itself. The *raison d'être* of the stratification in such a group is a bigger and better realization of this value: in economic groups of the economic value; in kinship groups, the kinship value; in religious groups, the religious value, and so on. This does not exclude the other values as secondary ones or as a by-product. But, as a rule, an economic group does not exist because of and for the sake of better propagation of religion, nor the religious group for making money. The stratification within an economic or religious group exists for the bigger and better realization of the economic and religious values respectively. For these reasons they are unibonded, the economic with the richer and poorer strata, the religious with the strata of pope, cardinal, bishop, priest, and plain parishioner. Each is based on its own main value, each representing a gradation of this unibonded value in its upper and lower ranks.

Since a multibonded group realizes the main values of two or a greater number of the unibonded groups, its stratification will also be a multibonded stratification whose *raison d'être* is a realization of these compounded values. Hence the unibonded and multibonded stratification and the strata. A unibonded real or "as if" real stratum is made up of the totality of the members of a unibonded group united into a real stratum by similar rights, duties, and apportionment of the main value of the group, by similar status and role in its realization and enjoyment. The status, role, and apportionment will always tangibly, and sometimes formally, be different from those of the other strata of the same group. A multibonded real stratum in a multibonded group is composed of the totality of the members united into one rank by a similarity of their rights-duties in regard to a similar apportionment, status and role in the realization of the compounded values of the group. This apportionment, role, and

status is clearly different from those of other strata in the same group. Hence, *qualitatively there are as many unibonded and multibonded forms of stratification (inequality) as there are unibonded and multibonded groups.* Let us briefly consider these forms of stratification and inequality.[3]

III. FORMS OF UNIBONDED STRATIFICATION (INEQUALITY)

1. Intra- and Interracial Stratification (Inequality)

If racial groups are organized, we have a racial stratification within each of the racial groups into leaders, influential layers, and plain members. There is also a stratification of the racial groups one with respect to the others, for instance, the white race legally or factually being superior to and dominant over the black race, the ranking involving a series of privileges for the white and disfranchisement for the other race. In some populations and periods, this stratification of different racial groups assumed the sharpest, most rigidly organized legal and factual forms, with the "inferior" race turned into slaves and serfs and with the "superior" race becoming an autocratic master; with the "inferior" race dispossessed of practically all political, civil, economic, or other rights, pitilessly exploited by the "superior" racial group, and treated worse than cattle. Human history is full of such racial stratifications. In a population where different racial groups exist side by side, racial inequalities lead often to a clear-cut, legal ranking of different races into several strata from the highest to the lowest, with decreasing privileges and increasing disfranchisement of all kinds as we move from the

---

3. Here I am following the classification of my *Sistema Soziologii* (Petrograd, 1921) Vol. II, pp. 173–178, 249–258. In my monographic *Mobility* I gave a more detailed study of the economic, occupational, and sociopolitical forms of stratification, stressing at the same time that "the concrete forms of stratification are numerous." *Ibid.,* p. 12. The classification of the forms of stratification with the subsequent outline of the main unibonded and multibonded stratifications clarifies, to a considerable degree, the prevalent vagueness of the concept of stratification as well as of its forms.

"superior" to the "inferior" race groups. Thus, even now in the United States, the order of the white, the yellow, and the black "races" is one such form of stratification. Another, and more detailed form, in which the population and law-givers mix racial and biosocial stocks or nationality groups is illustrated by such stratifications as the Mayflower descendants, the Daughters and Sons of the American Revolution, the native-born Yankees, the Anglo-Saxons, the Dutch-German-Scandinavian-Irish-French, the Italian-Jewish-Russian-Polish-Finnish-Greek-Armenian, the Chinese-Japanese-Oriental, the Negro and other "African" blacks. This order varies, depending upon the state and the stratifiers, but in this or that form it is widely spread, daily used, functions in hundreds of social relationships, and manifests itself even in legal forms, whether in the size of the quota of immigrants permitted for each "stock," in the total exclusion of Orientals, or in many other forms, not to mention many legal and factual disfranchisements of the Negro and other "Africans."[4]

Regardless of the magnitude of the privileges and disfranchisements of different racial, or what is thought to be racial, strata, the stratification is unibonded, based upon the assumption of racial heterogeneity, and it is different from all other forms of unibonded and multibonded stratifications. It groups in one stratum, by the bond of racial similarity, and ignores economic, religious, or any nonracial bond. Such interracial

4.   The Immigration Acts of 1921, 1924, 1929, and 1934 clearly reflect the United States "official" stratification, ranking, favoring, and discrimination against various European "stocks" and "races." Of the total 100% of immigration, it alloted 55.5% to Great Britain and Ireland, 17.2% to Germany, and only 1.8% to Russia, and from .2% to 4% to all the countries of eastern, southern and central Europe. It excluded entirely the Japanese and most of the other "yellow" races and also the "African" races. It favored decidedly the "races" of northwestern Europe, assigning to them 83% of the total European immigration, instead of the 21% supplied by this area before 1921. It apportioned only 16% of the European total to the eastern, southern and central European groups, instead of the 80% of the total supplied by these areas before the Acts. The Acts remain the striking evidence of both legal and factual discrimination against and the favoring of specified "racial stocks," and this evidence invalidates all the pious speech-reactions denouncing racial discrimination, all the official and unofficial verbosity that has daily flooded the nation not only during the war, but after it.

stratification is usually followed by the creation of many ideologies[5] rationalizing racial inequality in terms of the notion of a "chosen people," the idea of "blue blood," or some complicated ideology like those theories of A. Gobineau, H. S. Chamberlain, O. Ammon, V. de Lapouge, K. Pearson, and F. Galton, of many eugenists and geneticists, plus the popular beliefs about the inequality of races and the superiority of the ideologists' own race.

2.   Intra- and Intersex Stratification (Inequality)

This is another form of unibonded stratification. Biological sex-differences are seized upon for building a superstructure of sociocultural inequalities between male and female groups. It elevates the groups and members of one sex, usually the male, into the superior, privileged, and dominant stratum, and it degrades the other sex group, usually female, to inferior, disfranchised, and subordinate status. In some populations the contrast between the status of men and women is enormous. Women are often deprived of all rights and men, as *paterfamilias,* are given the right of life and death over their women. In other societies the factual and legal difference in the status of the sex groups is not so great. Nevertheless, in whatever form, it exists in practically all populations at all times. Even in the most democratic countries, at the present time, the full factual and legal equality of the sexes has not been attained. The economic, political, and other legal rights of women are still not equal to those of men, in several respects. Factual discrimination against women, beginning with the well-known "double standard of sexual morality" and ending with hundreds of other disfranchisements, still exists. The stratification is unibonded in sexual

5.   See an analysis and criticism of all these theories in my *Theories*, Ch. 5. Characteristic detail: even ranking done by scholars supposedly free from racial prejudice shows its contagious effect. For instance, the ranking of the population of Yankee City by Warner and Lunt is based upon the hidden assumption that the Yankee native population is socially superior and belongs only to the upper-upper and lower-upper. This implicit assumption is the real basis of their stratification into six strata.

terms. It is based on the sex-difference and is not reducible to any other basis or form.

There is also intrasex stratification in organized groups of both men and women. Organizations of women are stratified into leaders and led, ruling committee members and ordinary members, influential and less influential. Such layers of "women-aristocrats" and "women-plebs" exist in all local, provincial, state, and national women's organizations. The same is true of all groups of men. In comparison with the intersex stratification, this intrasex hierarchy of men or women assumes other forms of stratification as well, e.g., occupational, political, and so on.

3. Intra- and Interage Group Stratification (Inequality)

All that has been said of sex-stratification is equally applicable to the inequalities of various age-groups. Legally and factually in all societies the age groups have been stratified, with different rights, duties, status, roles, privileges, disfranchisements. In some populations the contrast between age-groups is quite striking, with the younger groups deprived of all rights and subordinated entirely to the older people. In others the differences have been fewer, milder, and more limited. But in none of the populations has there been realized the real legal and factual equality of the status of different age-groups. Even in the most advanced democracies, the younger age-groups are deprived of many rights and privileges—economic, occupational, political, and civic.

There is also an undeveloped stratification within each of the organized age-groups, especially in the disfranchised ones. There are leaders and led, influential and non-influential strata within the same age group. The stratification of various "youth organizations" and movements into leaders, committee members, and ordinary members exists in local, state, and national youth groups. Within the organized groups of the same age, say of youth, there are the "youth aristocracy" and the "youth plebs." In such movements and groups as the Townsend movement, an organized elderly age group trying to get privileges at the cost of the younger age groups, there are the national leaders, the state leaders, the county and city leaders of various ranks and degrees of influence, a series of intermediary strata, and finally the ordinary members of the organization—mere voters, payers, and supporters. The concrete forms of the intra-age group stratification or inequality are many. Often they merge with the stratification and inequality in other organized groups.

4. Intra- and Intergroup Kinship Stratification (Inequality)

Each kinship group is stratified into a series of ranks based on blood-kinship, "classificatory" kinship, and artificial-kinship. There are the chiefs of the kins; the high, usually elderly, ranks of the most influential, most honored, most dominating kinship aristocracy; the several intermediary ranks; and the least influential, dominated, and lowest ranks of the kins. The concrete forms of this ranking vary from kinship group to kinship group.[6] Superiority and higher prestige of kinship aristocracy may be due now to age, now wealth, now sacrifice and heroic deeds, now to the number of scalps obtained, now to the endurance of torture, and now to services rendered the group. But, whatever the concrete form, the status of kinsmen in a group is not equal and there is always a clear-cut or somewhat muddled set of ranks of superior and inferior strata.

Interkinship stratification manifests itself in a hierarchy of ranks of different interacting kinship groups. In a conglomerate population consisting of several kinship groups, whether among the preliterate or historical populations, the kindreds, gentes, and families (in which the kinship tie is one of the bonds) have hardly ever been equal in their status, influence, prestige, honor, and functions. Legally or factually there have always been the leading, the aristocratic, the superior kinship groups, gentes and families and the subordinated, led, uninfluential, and submerged ones. When the kinship tie coalesced

6. For examples of concrete forms among preliterate kinship groups, see the cited works of Thomas, Kroeber, Hobhouse, Wheeler, Ginsberg, Lowie, Thurnwald, Radcliffe-Brown, and others.

with other bonds and there arose multibonded social estates, kinship stratification assumed the legal and clear-cut forms of the hereditary kindreds of the Spartiates and the non-Spartiates and slaves in Sparta; of the Eupatridai, the common Orgeones, and slaves in Athens; the patricians and the plebeians in Rome, with other intermediary and unfree strata; of several orders ranging from nobility to slaves in other populations. Even in contemporary England, the families are still ranked in sixty-five orders of hereditary and nonhereditary dignities—all above the common families. The royal family is at the top, then come the basic ranks of the dukes, marquises, earls, viscounts, barons, knights, baronets, companions, esquires, and gentlemen. In some form, such a ranking of various kindreds and families exists in practically every population. Even in the democratic United States, one can hardly find a village or city, not to mention the nation, in which there is not some stratification of its families into the leading, the higher, the blue blood, the aristocratic, the influential, and into the submerged, the good-for-nothing, with several grades in between. On a nation-wide scale, the kinship groups of the descendants of the Mayflower, of the Daughters and Sons of the American Revolution, of the Sixty Families,[7] to mention but a few, are examples of this kind of stratification. Finally, the role of kinship groups in the appraisal, appointment, and promotion of a person of "good family" in business, the professions, politics, is known to everybody. There is a tendency of kins occupying a high position to open or hidden nepotism. Although denounced incessantly, especially in the so-called equalitarian societies, stratification on the basis of kinship continues to exist everywhere. Its concrete forms change, but its essence remains immortal.

5. Intra- and Intergroup Locality Stratification (Inequality)

Any territorial group, be it a village, a city, or a precinct, not to mention larger territorial units, has its local aristocracy, its intermediate strata, and its under-dogs. Since any territorial group represents a conglomeration of various unibonded and multibonded groups, the concrete forms of the stratification of local groups are also manifold, overlapping and sometimes "muddled." Nevertheless they all assume a territorially bounded character and manifest themselves in various "locality forms." First, there are the locally elected or appointed authorities in charge of the local needs: economic, sanitary, educational, etc. The local chief, mayor, alderman, selectmen, and so on, make up the upper governing stratum of the population, as a form of local aristocracy. Second, in many cities and even villages the territorial stratification appears in the division of residential areas into exclusive, restricted, plebeian, unrestricted, and slums; into streets and areas occupied by the royal, financial, intellectual, and other aristocracies, as, for example, the Boston Brahmins on Beacon Hill. There are areas for the middle strata and for the lowest, the outcasts and dregs of society. Another form of locality stratification is the division of the local population into "society" and common mortals; into the "exclusive" cliques, the country club sets, and other associations of the upper class; and into the lower plebs not admitted to these aristocratic strata. Even in a village there are several layers of superior and inferior gradations, with the members of the same stratum treating each other as equals and those of different strata discriminating as between superiors and inferiors.[8] Concrete variations on the pattern are numerous, but the general pattern of stratification is essentially constant. The local character is manifest in the fact that most of the "highest local aristocracy" cease to be an aristocracy outside of the limits of the given locality. The "great man" of a given village or precinct turns into an unknown, insignificant common mortal beyond the boundaries of his local group.

Besides the intralocality stratification, there is interlocality stratification. Many national or even international groups like the state, religious groups, occupational unions, political parties, business corporations, are divided into the state, the county, the city, the village, and other local

---

7. See F. Lundberg, *America's Sixty Families* (New York, 1937).

8. See concrete examples in Sinclair Lewis's *Cass Timberlane* (New York, 1945). In the city of Grand Republic, Cass Timberlane, Dr. Drover, Bradd Criley, and others are the local aristocracy.

subgroups. In this territorial subdivision of social systems, the leaders or aristocracy of the larger territorial units are factually and often legally superior to those of the smaller territorial units. The president of the state is superior to the governors of the province, and so on. The president of the United States Steel Corporation or of the American Federation of Labor is superior to the presidents or chiefs or managers of smaller territorial units of the Corporation or of the local labor union. As a result, the territorial "aristocracies" of various kinds range into a hierarchy of the superior and inferior strata. There is another variation. In many countries the whole population of a certain territory is deprived of a series of rights and privileges. For instance in pre-revolutionary Russia the population of certain territories did not have the right of self-government (municipal and semstvo) and other privileges. Likewise, in England before the reforms of 1830–1834, the representation in Parliament was grossly favorable to some localities. The variety of interterritorial stratification exists in some form in all countries. In a city not all the "exclusive" areas are equal. At one time the Back Bay in Boston was equal to Beacon Hill, but later it became less aristocratic.[9] There were several "aristocratic" areas of Paris, but not all of these were equal. The same is true of various exclusive localized societies, cliques, Junior Leagues, clubs, and associations. Whatever their concrete and ever-changing patterns, the fact of interlocality group stratification is perennial and general.

6. Intra- and Internationality Stratification (Inequality)

Intranationality stratification exists everywhere. There is the highest stratum, composed of national heroes, of the great political, scientific, artistic, religious, and cultural men and women, who are the pride and glory of the group; then there is the stratum of the members of commit-

tees of the various nationality organizations and associations, in the form of the historical aristocracy of a given nationality; there are the middle groups; and lastly, the common people. These strata are relatively clear-cut, especially in the language groups that are suppressed and disfranchised by the state government or other powers. As most of the members of the language groups are hardly organized, their inner stratification is generally somewhat "anarchical," not brought into one clear-cut hierarchy. When a language group creates an almost coterminous state organization, as it often does, purely language group stratification merges with the state hierarchy, assumes its clearness and definiteness, and becomes the same thing as the intrastate stratification.

Internationality stratification is a perennial and practically universal phenomenon. Now and then it assumes clear-cut and objective forms, when certain nationalities are legally ranked in the order of their superiority and inferiority with a respective distribution of privileges and disfranchisements. Thus in ancient Rome the population was stratified into several classes: the full-fledged citizens of Rome, that is, *cives;* the less privileged, like the *latini;* the members of the *civitates cum suffragio* and *sine suffragio, civitates foederatae* and *liberae,* subdivided into *aequum* and *iniquum;* the provincial strata of the *peregrini, peregrini dediticii,* and so on; each stratum having different status, rights, duties, privileges, and disfranchisements. At the source of many of these divisions lay the fact of conquest, but up to the extension of Roman citizenship upon all the free population except the *peregrini dediticii,* in 212 A.D., the lines of stratification went, to a great extent, along the lines of the nationality or language groups.[10] In Russia before the revolution certain language groups, from the Poles to the many aboriginal groups of Asia, were legally deprived of certain rights and privileges possessed by other language-groups in Russia. Some of the non-Russian groups like the Finns had more political and other rights than the Russian-language groups. In the contemporary French, British, and Dutch empires, not to mention many other

9. See the facts in an excellent analysis in W. Firey's work, quoted. Also, P. Hatt, "The Relation of Ecological Location to Status Position," *ASR*, 1941, pp. 481–85; also M. A. Gibbard, "The Status Factor in Residential Succession," *AJS*, May, 1941. Cf. C. Shaw and M. McKay, *Juvenile Delinquency and Urban Areas* (Chicago, 1940).

10. See T. Mommsen, *Abriss des Römische Staatsrecht* (Berlin, 1893); I. Pokrovsky, *Istoria Rimskago Prava* (Petrograd, 1924).

states, the subjects in the colonies and posses-sions, belonging to nationalities different from the French, British, or Dutch, are ranged into sev-eral classes according to their comparative disfran-chisements. In whatever form, nearly everywhere that state populations are made up of different language groups, there exists either legal or fac-tual form of internationality stratification. Even in the United States there are many forms of it manifest in the ranking of Americans of various nationalities into a series of superiors and inferiors by the native-born of native parents, and by other language groups. The Yankees and Old Ameri-cans regard themselves as the highest group.[11] Then come in various orders British-Americans, Scandinavian- or German-Americans, French- or Irish-Americans; all the rest of the other Ameri-can nationalities are ordinarily ranked below these ''aristocratic'' groups. The rank order of Ameri-can nationalities made by the Jewish- or Italian- or Russian-Americans naturally differs in that it puts their own nationality at the top and others in a descending order. But a hierarchical ranking is made by practically all American language groups. It manifests itself in various ''exclusive'' associations, societies, clubs, resorts, residential districts, and so on, which admit the ''superior'' nationalities to membership, and exclude the ''inferior'' ones. It externalizes itself in other forms of ''social distance'' which these groups and individuals believe to exist between their rank and that of the other nationalities.[12] It ex-presses itself in our immigration laws, excluding

from immigration and thus from citizenship a large number of racial and language groups of the East, Africa, and other continents.[13] It manifests itself in the terms of *jus connubium* and *jus con-vivium,* which legally or factually favor or disfavor certain internationality marriages and result in different amounts of intermarriages of different nationalities, even in a democratic country like the United States.[14] To sum up: Intra- and inter-group nationality stratification is almost universal and perennial; its concrete manifestations change, its essence remains.

7. Intra- and Interstate Stratification (Inequality)

The state is the group with possibly the clearest legal and factual stratification. Being a clearing-house for many other groups, its stratifi-cation, as we have seen, serves also to express the stratification of other groups. The state constitu-tion and official law give a detailed map of the structure of the hierarchy of its authorities. At the top there is a monarch or president or dictator or Führer. Then comes the cabinet with its secre-taries or their equivalent; then undersecretaries, assistant secretaries of various ranks (first, second, etc.); then the chiefs of divisions, assistant chiefs of the divisions, and so on, down to the pettiest official, policeman, and plain citizen. A similarly clear-cut hierarchy of ranks may be seen in the judicial order of the state, beginning with the supreme court or judge and ending with the low-est local justices and court agents. There is also a pyramid among the legislative authorities, with the supreme organ at the top—the parliament, congress, the monarch's legislative group; and then a series of subordinated provincial and local legislative organs. The state army and navy have

11.   See Warner and Lunt, *op. cit.* A study shows that sixth grade children found 26 favorable traits in Americans, 6 neutral, and none unfavorable. See R. Zeligs, ''Racial Atti-tudes of Children,'' *Sociology and Social Research,* XXI (1937), p. 364. See various rankings of nationalities by 1725 adults, 200, and then 12 children, in R. Zeligs, ''Tracing Racial Attitudes,'' *Ibid.,* XXIII (1938), p. 50.

12.   For instance, 269 native American whites, mainly middle class persons, gave the following ranks of social near-ness in terms of their neighbor-preferences: Irish, German, Swedish, Jewish, Italian, Armenian, Japanese, Mexican, Filipino, Negro. E. Monjar, ''Racial Distance Reactions,'' *Sociology and Social Research,* XXI (1937), p. 559. In a series of other studies published in this journal, the rank order of language groups varies. On the other hand, the rank of the whites, evaluated by Negroes, is very low. See, for instance, M. C. Hill, ''Basic Racial Attitudes towards Whites in an Oklahoma All-Negro Community,'' *AJS* (1944), pp. 519–523.

13.   See *U.S. Immigration Laws and Rules* (Washington, 1930). E. Bogardus, ''From Immigration to Exclusion,'' *Sociology and Social Research,* XXXIV (1940), pp. 272–278.

14.   See R. Kennedy, ''Single or Triple Melting Pot,'' quoted; J. Drachsler, *Intermarriage in New York City* (New York, 1921); W. Weatherly, ''Race and Marriage,'' *AJS,* XV; A. E. Jenks, ''Ethnic Census in Minneapolis,'' *Ibid.,* XVII; U. Z. Engelman, ''Intermarriage Among Jews in Germany,'' *Sociology and Social Research* (1935), pp. 34–40.

ranks from supreme commander, marshals, down to privates and seamen, with many intervening ranks. Depending on the type of state, these hierarchies vary in their concrete forms, but in all states they are clearly defined and furnish us with a long series of ranks of authorities.

Interstate stratification is clear in federations and confederations, with the federal authorities being superior to the several state authorities. In some cases there is a legal ranking within these federated states. Less clear-cut, but unquestionable factual stratification exists among the interacting "sovereign" states, where there are "big" and "small" powers. Many interstate relationships are defined by international law. There is an order of precedence of diplomatic representatives of the various states at different seats of government, and there is the comparative prestige and authority of the military, financial, and other agents of a state. The interstate ranking of the "sovereign" states and of their representatives is full of gradations and precedences.

This influential role of the state and its clear-cut stratification explains why an individual's social position is largely determined by his state membership and by the specific stratum in the state hierarchy to which he belongs. Regardless of the individual's positions in other groups, his high state position, e.g., monarch, president, cabinet minister, marshal, or supreme commander, in a powerful state is sufficient to make him a "conspicuous somebody" in the human world and to rank him among "the highest" on earth.[15]

8. Intra- and Interpolitical Party Stratification (Inequality)

Any political party has a long or short hierarchy of its bosses and bossed, ranging from the leader, chief, president, to members of the central committee or caucus, to big and small financial supporters, to influential members of the provincial committees, and ending with the precinct leader and plain voting member. Since it is a fighting organization, no political party can be

free of such stratification. The Equalitarian, the Socialist, the Communist, the Syndicalist, and the Anarchist (so far as they are organized) parties are not exceptions to this rule. If anything, the rigidity of stratification, the dictatorial autocracy of the higher bosses, is much more severe and autocratic in such parties than in the conservative bourgeois parties. Some of these radical parties, like the Syndicalist, Communist, and the like, explicitly profess the principle of the selected party elite, which is entitled to rule the majority as it pleases, in accordance only with its own decisions. The power of the heads of such Equalitarian, Socialist, Communist, Syndicalist, National Socialist, and Jacobin parties, whether the head be Lenin or Stalin, Robespierre or L. A. Blanqui, Hitler or Mussolini, is autocratic. As to the role of the plain party members in such parties, it is, in the words of a Syndicalist theorizer, E. Fournière, the role of the zeros, whose only function is to increase the weight of the figure on the left, that is, the party leader or boss.[16]

The interparty stratification manifests itself quite clearly in countries with one dictatorial party, as in Cromwellian England, Jacobin France, Communist Russia, Nazi Germany, or Fascist Italy. All other parties are suppressed. The dictatorial party has a monopoly of privileges, and for other parties the concentration camp, confiscation of property, and even execution prevail. In a milder form, this inequality exists also in democratic countries. There is a system of spoils and booty for the victorious party and disfranchisement for the defeated parties. Almost all the coveted state positions, innumerable sinecures, explicit and implicit, direct and indirect economic and other advantages go to the victorious party. There may even be punishing measures against the defeated parties. If the fight for spoils and power flares into civil war between the parties, then their stratification becomes almost limitless; one party tends to exterminate the other with the utmost ferocity.

---

15. See the details on state stratification in my *Social Mobility*, Chps. II, V.

16. E. Fournière, *La sociocratie* (Paris, 1910), p. 117. See, on these autocratic, oligarchic features of such parties, V. Pareto, *Systèmes socialistes* (2nd. ed., Paris, 1926); also the quoted works of R. Michels, M. Ostrogorsky, H. Lagardelle, G. Sorel, and others; P. Kropotkin, *The Speeches of a Rebel* (in Russian, Moscow, 1919); M. Bakunin, *The State and Anarchy* (in Russian, Moscow, 1919).

9. Intra- and Interoccupational Stratification (Inequality)

The members of any given occupation are stratified into many ranks. In the automobile or steel industry we have a long hierarchy beginning with the Henry Fords, the presidents of U.S. Steel and General Motors, and ranging to the lowest unskilled workers and office boy in these occupations, with a large number of intermediary strata. The professions are not excluded from this stratification. In teaching there is a hierarchy topped by the state secretaries of education, presidents of universities and of academies of science and the like, with intermediate strata of university deans, full-, associate- and assistant-professors; then come principals and teachers in high schools; and last there are the elementary school teachers.

The intraoccupational stratification manifests itself in another general form; in almost all occupations there are three main strata. First, the masters or entrepreneurs, those who are their own "bosses" and organize, direct; and control the activities of all the employees; second, the higher employees—directors, managers, high engineers, who, although subordinated to the masters, control and manage those below them; third, the clerical and subordinate employees and wage earners, who do largely routine or manual work, controlled and organized by the higher strata. Each of these basic strata is often stratified within itself. Under different names these basic intraoccupational strata are found in the past as well as in the present, in private as well as in governmental occupations. In the occupational group of the same caste there is a variation of these divisions. In the Roman or Chinese, medieval or Egyptian guild systems, the ranks of the apprentices, of the ordinary members (*populus, plebs, valets*), and of the *magistri* is an illustration.[17]

The intraoccupational stratification exists in many other forms. The upper strata of an occupational group control the lower ones; they have greater prestige, better economic remuneration, and other advantages. Often the distance between the head of a big occupational enterprise, like Henry Ford, and the lowest wage-earner in the same occupation is as great as between the autocratic monarch of an empire and his humblest subject.

The interoccupational stratification is also a universal and perennial phenomenon. From the standpoint of attractiveness, prestige, remuneration, power, domination and subordination, the unskilled manual occupations have usually occupied the lowest position. Then come the semiskilled, the skilled; the semiprofessional, including the clerical, small business, and petty officials; the highly qualified professionals, including big business and government, being at the top. This basic pyramid of occupations, with minor and temporary variations, is a general uniformity of the interoccupational stratification. The occupations that require a high degree of intelligence, are highly important for the population, and that consist of intellectual creative work of sociocultural organization and control, have regularly been the superior occupations. The occupations consisting of manual, uncreative work, requiring only intelligence for their performance, have regularly been the most inferior.[18]

Within the basic occupational strata there are many subdivisions. These strata have existed partly in an organized, partly in an "as if" orga-

---

17. Cf. Saint Leon, E. Martin, *Histoire de Corporation de Mètiers* (Paris, 1922); J. P. Waltzing, *Etude historique sur les corporations professionelles chez les Romains* (Louvain, 1895), 2 Vols.; J. M. Lambert, *Two Thousand Years of Guild Life* (Hull, 1891); F. Poland, *Geschichte des griechischen Vereinswesen* (Berlin, 1935).

18. See the facts, details, and literature in my *Mobility*, Ch. 6. The general order of occupations is similar to F. W. Taussig's, F. E. Barr's, and other generally accepted scales of occupations. As one goes from the top to the bottom occupations, the indices of the required intelligence decrease, economic remuneration decreases; functions of social control and organization (cultural, economic, military, governmental, etc.) decrease; creativeness decreases; subordination increases. The top occupations have always been those of the aristocracy and upper social strata, while unskilled manual work was the occupation of the strata of slaves and serfs in unfree society and of the least paid, most subordinate unskilled labor in the free societies. See also M. Smith, "Measuring Occupations," *Sociology and Social Research* (1935), pp. 40–50; O. Machotka, "Social Stratification." *Ibid.* (1937), pp. 3–13. Also referred studies of D. Anderson, P. E. Davidson, W. H. Form, H. Speier; A. Obrdlik, *Povolani*, quoted. In this last study the prestige order of various occupations is different, but because they are rated by the members of the respective occupations from the standpoint of social utility. It is to be understood that I state the situation as it has been, regardless of what it ought to be.

nized, and in an unorganized form, from earliest time.

10. Intra- and Intereconomic Group Stratification (Inequality)

All groups, except, perhaps, the familistic family and a small group of the most intimate friends with a real community of economic values, are stratified economically into richer and poorer members. Measured by amount of property, income, economic rights and duties, economic plane of living, or in any other way, the members of the racial-sex-age-kinship-territorial-language-state-occupational-religious or any other group have always been economically unequal. The height and profile of the economic pyramid fluctuate from group to group, period to period, but the stratification remains. Even religious groups with common property, even Communist and Socialist and other groups, could not eliminate the economic inequality, in spite of their intention to do so. Communism in Soviet Russia is typical in this respect. As early as 1918 the Soviet Government had to introduce wage differentials, with a ratio of 175 to 100 as maximum and minimum, and with more than thirty intervening levels. Since then the inequality has kept on growing. In ancient Greece and Rome all the free population was divided formally, e.g., as in the reforms of Solon and Servius Tullius, into several clear-cut economic strata, with respective rights and duties. In other groups the formal stratification may be absent, but the factual stratification stands solid and sometimes strikingly high.

Economic stratification exists not only within a group but also among different groups, either of the same or different natures. Among states, there are the richer and the poorer and less prosperous. This is also true of different religious, political, occupational, and other groups. And it is true in regard to groups of a different nature. Intra- and intergroup equality remains merely an ideal hoped for by many; thus far it has hardly ever been realized in human history. The total social position of every individual depends greatly upon the economic stratum in which he belongs; the rich always occupy a higher position than the poor in the total or integral sociocultural pyramid.

11. Intra- and Interreligious Group Stratification (Inequality)

As soon as a religious group is organized, its stratification emerges. Ordinarily, as in state groups, it is clear-cut. The pope, patriarch, dalai-lama, *pontifex maximus, rex sacrificulus,* the primate, or supreme priest is at the top of the hierarchy; then there is the stratum of cardinals, metropolitans, archbishops, and bishops; then the priests of different ranks and dignities; the various deacons; and finally the plain believers, below whom there may be a stratum of pagans, disbelievers, heretics, and generally the "damned souls." The actual number of the ranks varies in different religions, but in all religions the stratification exists.[19] In almost all religions each superior stratum is believed to be endowed with a greater proportion of divine grace and holiness, has the dominant legal authority, binding the lower ranks, greater prestige, and usually better economic conditions. The contrast between the highest stratum and a disbeliever or heretic is often as great, sometimes greater, than that between an autocratic monarch and a criminal or slave. Many attempts to organize a religious group without stratification have failed as soon as the group reached some modest size. Even such attempts—probably the most earnest—as that of St. Francis of Assisi failed during St. Francis' own lifetime.

There is also interreligious stratification. In populations without religious freedom it manifests itself in the monopolistic position of the obligatory religion and in the suppression of all the other religious groups, including the persecution and disfranchisement of their members. The situation is identical to that in which a monopolistic political party suppresses all other parties. In populations like pre-Revolutionary Russia and in England, the stratification takes a milder form in which one religion is favored as the national religion, the Russian Orthodox and Anglican for example, with the other religions suffering various degrees of comparative disfranchisement. In many populations there are the religions of the

19. See J. Wach, *op. cit.,* Chps. 5, 7, and Appendix, for concrete forms of ranks of the religious hierarchies in various preliterate and historical religions.

aristocracy, of the middle classes, and of the slaves; religions of different occupations and economic strata; of different kinship groups, and so on.[20]

Subjectively, from the standpoint of a believer, interreligious stratification consists in a belief and in accompanying practices that the believer's religion is the only true one, all the others being untrue, inferior, and "damned." The concrete objective and subjective forms of interreligious stratification are many.

12. Stratification of Other Unibonded Groups

Stratification exists among other unibonded groups. All educational institutions, from elementary school to university, are stratified, each within itself and any one with respect to all the others. The same is true of scientific, philosophical, artistic, philanthropic, and other organized "ideological" groups, e.g., hospitals, symphony orchestras, theaters, the Red Cross, etc. Criminal gangs are stratified into boss, main henchmen, and plain members. The height of the pyramid, the number of ranks, the size of each stratum fluctuate widely from group to group, but intra- and intergroup stratification is present in all of them.

As any stratification means "superiority and inferiority," "domination and subordination," it generates an incessant struggle of the members of the various strata, all seeking to climb up the ladder to a higher place in the hierarchy. There are inflated and deflated ambitions, rivalries, jealousies, envy, hatred, and their consequences: mutual conflict of the members of the different strata for promotion, for differential shares in advantages and disadvantages. The Darwinian struggle for existence is too vague and too general a formula. Intra- and intergroup struggle for higher places in the hierarchy of stratification are more intense forms of the struggle for existence.[21] However, all this will be discussed more fully later.

20. See especially J. Wach, *op. cit.*, Ch. 6.

21. See N. K. Mikhailovsky, "Struggle for Individuality," in his *Works* (in Russian).

IV. MULTIBONDED STRATIFICATION

1. Double, Triple, and More Complex Strata

Since by definition the multibonded stratification is the multibonded group viewed in its stratified aspect, the multibonded forms of stratification fall in the same classes as those of the multibonded groups. By the number and nature of the unifying bonds we can distinguish the double, the triple, quadruple, and more complex "superior and inferior" strata in the respective double, triple, quadruple multibonded groups. If a person or a set of persons in a given population occupies a high position in both its state and economic stratifications, such a person gives us a double—the state plus economic—aristocracy. If a group occupies a high position in a religious order, say that of bishops, and a high position in a political party and the state as well, such a group gives us a triple upper stratum—the religious, plus political party, plus state. If a set of persons belongs to the chiefs of the noblest kinship groups, are the richest, perform the creative and most aristocratic occupational functions, and at the same time are the highest state officials, such a group gives us a quadruple aristocracy—kinship, economic, occupational, state. On the other hand, a group of persons who are economically poorest, unskilled occupationally, of inferior race, illiterate, belongs to a quadruple stratum of underdogs, and so on.

Combining the number of the unibonded stratifying ties with their nature we can have as great a number of different multibonded strata in a given population as the binomial formula of Newton defines. Factually, most of such combined strata do exist within any large population.

The stratified system of castes, orders, and classes analyzed in Chapter 14 gives additional concrete examples of multibonded strata. The upper and lower castes are superior or inferior not on a single basis but on a multiple basis. The Brahmins are superior to the Sudras in race, religion, occupation, kinship, language, education, and so on. Likewise, the social estate of the nobles in comparison with that of the free population and slaves is superior not for one reason but for three: occupational, economic, and state. The less strict stratification of social classes is due not to one stratifying factor but at least two factors; the upper classes are richer and discharge higher occupational functions, the state legal stratification playing a much more modest role than in the case of the triple stratum of the social order. In the class population, all citizens are declared to be legally equal in regard to state law.

There are in any population many different double, triple, and quadruple strata. The caste, class, order, family, and tribe, which have been analyzed, with their intra- and interstrata, are only a few, though the most important, of these different multibonded stratified groups.

Here again we see the crude state of the social sciences in respect to their knowledge and classification of the forms of social stratification and of the number and variety of the strata. We have seen that the social sciences do not have any systematic taxonomy of social groups. Now we can note that they do not have any taxonomy of the forms of social stratification and of the social strata. Out of the several dozens, the hundreds even, of various multibonded and unibonded social strata which exist in any large population, especially in urbanized and industrialized aggregations, the current texts in sociology and the social sciences mention only a few, like social class, social order, caste, and even these few are poorly defined in their structural composition.

There is another error: that is the tendency to treat groups and strata nominalistically, to cut them into nice statistical slices of mince pie, to create in this way hundreds of cubes of the social body, and to process them through routine quantitative operations, thus giving "scientific" looking diagrams and formulas and figures which, however, do not give any idea of the real anatomy, cytology, and morphology of the social organism. The works of Warner and Lunt and S. C. Dodd, which have been mentioned, are examples of this error.

The classification of the present work points out a new field of real social taxonomy and stratigraphy in sociology and the social sciences. It enables an investigator to analyze precisely the social differentiation and stratification of any given population into the real and "as if" real groups and strata. As we shall see further, it en-

ables us to define precisely the position of every individual in the complex sociocultural world.

An actual detailed enumeration of all the double, triple, and more complex strata is outside the scope of this work. The definitions being given, any intelligent researcher can apply them to any concrete population under his investigation. Instead of such an actual enumeration, we shall pay attention to other important classes of social strata viewed from additional standpoints.

2. Innerly Antagonistic (Disaffine), Solidary (Affine), and Neutral Multibonded Groups

We must further distinguish the innerly antagonistic or disaffine, the innerly solidary or affine, and the innerly neutral multibonded strata. By the *innerly antagonistic,* and closely connected with it, the *disaffine,* multibonded stratum is meant that made up of the mutually contradictory, uncongenial bonds-values that make the social position of its members innerly contradictory. The members of such an innerly contradictory stratum are urged by the mutually uncongenial or contradictory bonds to the self-contradictory behavior and mentality. Likewise, such a disaffine stratum appears as a self-contradictory stratum to the outsiders who are in contact with it.

The innerly solidary or affine multibonded stratum is that in which the compounded stratifying bonds are mutually congenial, and urge its members to the same behavior and mentality. Finally, the *innerly neutral multibonded stratum* is that in which there is no mutual antagonism among the compounded bonds and no mutual solidarity as well. If one imagines a person who is a monarch, a pauper, and a member of a suppressed political party, one has a picture of an innerly antagonistic stratum of the person: highest in his state group, lowest economically, and low in the political party. These three variables are obviously irreconcilable and mutually antagonistic; together they force the person to an impossible and self-contradictory behavior and mentality. As a monarch he has to behave and has to be treated with the dignity, honor, respect, and authority due a monarch. As a pauper he has to behave and be treated as paupers behave and are treated. Two lines of conduct of the person and of the others are obviously irreconcilable, neither objectively nor subjectively possible. "While it is not difficult to preserve one's social prestige by doing nothing, it is difficult to keep it when one possesses nothing," rightly says C. Bouglé.[22] As a result such a coalescence of the stratifying bonds cannot last long and is bound to lead to a decomposition; either the monarch becomes rich and a high member of the dominant party, or he has to cease being a monarch.

There are further examples of anomalous double strata: high occupationally, but low in race and religion; high in nationality or kinship, but low in economic status; rich slaves; poor aristocrats. A member of one of these disaffine strata finds himself "exalted" in one respect and an "underdog" in another. In this way the dilemmas, contradictions, and muddleness of the status of a person appear.[23]

One must not think that such groups are something exotic, infrequent, and without general significance. It is true that the "unnatural" or disaffine strata do not happen as frequently as the "natural" or affine, and when they happen they tend to decompose rapidly and be replaced by the affine coalescence of the stratifying bonds. Both forms are general forms and have a deep significance for an understanding of many social phenomena and processes. This can be seen from the following typical and factual cases.

The high strata of most of the unibonded groups comparatively easily coalesce together and make an innerly solidary multibonded stratum of the privileged multibonded aristocracy. For instance, the high governmental stratum in the state easily compounds with the rich.[24] These two bonds are mutually affine and solidary; therefore

give frequent, durable, and stable coalescence in the form of this double stratum. Once in a while, however, we have in a population two double disaffine groups; one is economically richer but occupies a lower stratum in the state stratification than the other. Such an example is found in the position of the nobility and bourgeoisie on the eve of the French Revolution. The "third estate" was richer, but politically it was, to speak in the terms of its mouthpiece, l'Abbé Sieyès, "nothing" in comparison with the nobility. Two such "unnatural" double strata evidently could not last long; they were bound to decompose and be replaced by two innerly "affine" double strata. Either the rich had to get the high state position or the nobility had to become rich. The French Revolution consisted in the decomposition of these two disaffine strata and in the creation of two new affine strata. The rich third estate "became everything," in the terms of the same Sieyès. The Revolution, in chemical terms, performed a double reaction of transposition of the elements of the two disaffine molecules. Similar was one of the central processes of the Russian Revolution of 1905 and then of the Communist Revolution. At the beginning of the twentieth century, the Russian nobility became impoverished and poorer than the growing industrial, financial, and commercial bourgeoisie, which belonged to a notably lower stratum in the state hierarchy. The Revolution of 1905 and subsequent years dissolved both disaffine double groups; the nobility lost its privileges and controlling power in the state while the bourgeoisie elevated itself and became, through the Constitution of 1906, the most important double stratum. In ancient Greece, when the nobles became richer than the king, the monarchy was liquidated and replaced by the aristocracy of the nobility. When the Athenian nobility of the *eupatridae* was economically outstripped by the new rich class, struggle followed and there emerged the Solonian stratification of the free population into four classes on the basis of wealth, the highest with an income of 500 medimni of corn and the lowest with below 200 medimni. At the end of the Republican period in Rome, a new stratum of the Equestrians became richer than the noble Senatorial class. After a series of civil wars and revolutions there was a rearrangement of classes in which wealth and privileged position in the state

22. C. Bouglé, *La démocratie devant la science* (Paris, 1906), p. 92.

23. See some facts and considerations in E. C. Hughes, "Dilemmas and Contradictions of Status," AJS (1945), pp. 353–60.

24. This is true of the rich and the state ruling class among preliterate as well as historical populations. See facts for the preliterate and historical populations in W. I. Thomas, *Primitive Behavior*, pp. 361–420; G. Landtman, *The Origin*, quoted; M. Kovalevsky, *Sociology* (in Russian, St. Petersburg, 1912), Vol. II, pp. 188 ff.; M. Diakonoff, *Studies of Social and Political Organization of Russia* (in Russian, St. Petersburg, 1910), pp. 82 ff.

hierarchy were compounded as stratifying bonds. The same process has gone on for the European nobility and the bourgeoisie since the beginning of the industrial revolution.

In other cases the wealthy may not gain the high state position. The impoverished aristocracy may, by use of force, seize enough wealth to maintain its position. The Spartan aristocracy maintained its position in this way for many decades. Such was also the way of many other aristocracies. Many revolutionary groups obtain wealth after their revolution and thus establish a new "affine" aristocratic stratum. Recent examples are the Nazis and Communists. Poor conquerors who subjugate another country, like William the Conqueror, take for their own group, e.g., the Normans, the riches of the subjugated people, the Anglo-Saxons. The Spanish Conquistadors behaved in the same way and so did practically all the conquerors. These facts—and they occur daily in human history—show that affine and disaffine strata are fairly frequent in populations of all times and all countries. Generally when innerly disaffine strata appear one can expect an orderly or violent liquidation of such strata and the substitution of new affine strata for them. The chemical reaction of transposition is to be expected in such a situation. It may happen in either of two ways: the rich may get power, or the powerful may seize wealth. Both ways have happened many times in history.

Another general variation of such processes of "transposition" is furnished by the perennial tragi-comedy of history staged by the equalitarian-Communist, Socialist, and Equalitarian-revolutionary groups. The first act of the play consists in the fiery speeches and actions of the equalitarians—mostly poor and disfranchised—who denounce the economic and other inequalities and organize to overthrow the rich strata. The equalitarians make up a triple stratum: economically poor, low position in the state, and members of equalitarian political parties. Its equalitarian, communist, socialist ideology is affine to such a stratum. During the revolution, if the group overthrows the upper economic and state strata and occupies their place, it transforms itself into a conspicuously disaffine stratum: it is in the embarrassing position of finding that its equalitarian ideology does not square with its economic position. Its mottoes—"redistribution of wealth,"

"expropriation of the exploiters," "take what has been stolen by the rich classes," "down with private property," "down with the government and aristocracy," "*aequatio bonorum*," "*pecunias a equare*," and so on—these slogans can now only be directed against the revolutionary aristocracy itself. Evidently such a position is impossible. The new ruling and economic aristocracy must give up its place or the old party standard must be replaced by a new one, fitting to the new position of the party. This second way usually takes place in the form of a gradual transformation of the party's ideology and the party itself from the previous equalitarian, Communist, Socialist, and poor party into a new party rejecting its previous principles and becoming aristocratic. R. Pöhlmann, in his study of Equalitarian, Communist, Socialist, and revolutionary movements of Greece, a study which is still pre-eminent, very well sums up the situation by saying that after an elevation to the top such revolutionary strata "now had every reason to fear the outburst of new revolutions, for in a new revolution with its re-distribution of wealth and privileges they could only lose without any gain; therefore they needed not to go about any more masquerading as proletarian revolutionaries. Usually, in these conditions, they rapidly acquired the most reactionary ideology in economics as well as in politics; they turned into partisans of the *Beati possidentes* (Blessed are those who possess). Now they worried little over the growth of a new inequality. They would not listen to the idea of a new division of property (and of all the other privileges) now that they themselves were the rich and privileged. Consequently their equalitarian-socialist fraternity lasted only till the rich and privileged were conquered and the process of spoliation was accomplished."[25] Such a story has invariably happened with all successful revolutions so far as the economic and social redistribution of wealth is concerned.[26] The latest corroboration of it is given in the facts of the Russian Revolution. Already the ideology, policy, and structure of the Communist Party and the so-

25. R. Pöhlmann, *Geschichte der sozialen Frage und der Sozialismus in der antiken Welt* (München, 1912), pp. 469 ff.

26. See my *Sociology of Revolution, passim;* my *Calamity*, Chps. 8 and 15. See facts and literature in these works.

called Communist Government are about opposite to what they were before and at the beginning of the Revolution. The party and government are transformed into a new "affine" stratum of triple aristocracy, which has the highest economic, state, and managerial positions. Naturally it has already manufactured a new ideology having little similarity to the previous one.[27]

To give another example, if in the United States the Negro race continues to be considered inferior, and if the Negroes become richer than the whites, two double disaffine strata will be created. Such a situation is bound to provoke, in either way, the "chemical reaction of transposition"; either the whites become richer or the Negroes become an equal race. As a matter of fact, in some of the southern states, where there are prosperous Negroes and "poor whites," such a situation already exists. Now and then it causes one of the reactions of transposition, in the form of lynching and pillaging the Negroes or in the steady elevation of the rank of the Negro group.

Generally the consolidation of the upper strata of two or a greater number of the unibonded group produces an affine multibonded stratum (*similia similibus curantur*) while a coalescence of the high stratum in one or some of the unibonded groups with the low stratum in others builds an innerly antagonistic, disaffine multibonded stratum, a house divided against itself.

As a rule the multibonded strata of various populations are affine innerly and represent a coalescence of the upper ranks of two or more unibonded groups with one another, and of their lower ranks with the lower ranks of the other. But such an affine coalescence is never perfect. Not one hundred per cent of the upper strata of two or more unibonded groups merge in the multibonded upper stratum, but only a part. The same is true of the lower or middle strata of each of the coalescing unibonded groups. There are always some discrepancies in the secondary rankings and

sometimes a sharp disaffinity. Not all the richest persons are highest in the state government, in the religious group, in the blood kinship groups, in the political parties, in the language groups or scientific societies, and so on. Not all the bosses of a political party are the popes or cardinals in the church group, or the presidents or monarchs in the state groups. In short, *the correlation of the affine strata is never perfect.* The stratified pyramids of the unibonded groups never consolidate in such a way that all their strata coincide and create one integral consolidated social pyramid, in which all the tops of the unibonded pyramids make one integral top and all the middle and lowest strata consolidate into one integral middle or lowest stratum. The actual "sky line" of the total stratification rather takes the shape of the skyline of a mountain range with several peaks of different pyramids not entirely merged.

There are several forms of social aristocracy and of social underdogs, not to mention of the middle strata. We have several unibonded aristocratic strata: the aristocracy of the state government, of the religious, economic, occupational, racial, language, age, sex, kinship groups; the aristocracy of science, arts, education, and of other unibonded groups. There are several forms of the multibonded aristocracies: upper castes, upper social orders and classes, and many other forms.[28] The same is true of the middle strata and of the lowest ranks in each of the unibonded and multibonded groups. The upper ranks of many unibonded groups in a given population tend to consolidate into several multibonded aristocracies. But the merger is never total and perfect. For instance in the United States, top ranks of the state, of finance, occupational unions, the professions, of the religious groups, of the "blue blood registerites," of the stars of science and the arts, are in fairly close contact with one another. They are interlocked through several groups, institutions, activities, and enterprises. They compose an informal but real multibonded upper stratum that exerts a very strong influence upon the whole

27.   See my *Russia and the United States* (New York, 1944), Ch. 9; B. Moore, Jr., "The Communist Party of the Soviet Union: 1928–1944," *ASR* (1944), pp. 266–78; N. S. Timasheff, "Vertical Social Mobility in Communist Society," *AJS* (1944), pp. 9–21; N. S. Timasheff, *The Great Retreat* (New York, 1946).

28.   This means that T. H. Marshall's interpretation of my position as denying the existence of social classes is grossly inaccurate. I contend only that social class is one of the multibonded groups and stratifications.

course of the sociocultural process. The names of such stars, celebrities, statesmen, captains of finance and industry may be found together in almost every copy of a newspaper. They compose the "cream" of various "Who's Who." They think and act in a fairly concerted way. They make the upper "few hundred families" into an American "consolidated aristocracy."

But since the consolidation is not perfect, another part of the same ranks make up another "consolidated aristocracy," with fairly different policies and activities. Some rich people belong to the Protestant and Catholic and even atheistic religions; some to the Republican, Democratic, and, as a rare exception, even to the Communist Party. Some occupy high governmental positions in Washington, but others are in opposition. Some belong to the "registerites" but others don't. Some prefer Harvard bosses, others Yale or Chicago bosses. Some finance liberal papers, the others conservative ones. On many political and social issues they differ. And so it goes. The same is true of governmental, occupational, scientific, nationality, and other "aristocracies." The real leaders of even science and religion are often found in different factions and cliques. This is what is meant by saying that the consolidation is not complete or perfect.

The same is still more true of the less organized middle and lower strata in unibonded groups.

Even the highest leaders of some of the unibonded groups find themselves excluded from various consolidated aristocracies. For instance the most prominent leaders of the Negroes are tolerated, but not admitted to the several consolidated aristocracies. Some of these do not admit Jewish or other leaders of the upper ranks. The *nouveaux riches* are often disdained. The leaders of Communist and similar parties cannot become members of the high strata of the Catholic and other religious groups. On the other hand, the Communist leaders or the new millionaires not infrequently scorn the blue blood aristocracy or the upper hierarchy of the Catholic and other churches. The leaders of a given nationality group may humiliate, abuse, and destroy the leaders of another nationality group to which they were inimical. Add to this the incessant change of

sociocultural conditions which inexorably leads to the elevation of a new multibonded stratum and undermines the established aristocracy, creating incessantly new innerly disaffine groups.

As a result there are always several discrepancies and contradictions in the consolidation of the multibonded strata, several disaffine strata, small or large, with self-contradictory positions for their members. There are the respective jealousies, disappointments and the ensuing struggle, because in such conditions "those who aim at equality will be ever ready for sedition, if they see those whom they esteem their equals possess more than they do; and those who are not content with equality but aim at superiority, if they think that while they deserve more than they have only are equal with or less than their inferiors."[29]

Concrete forms of the innerly disaffine multibonded strata have been very diverse in human history. When such strata are small, the decomposition passes without notice. But when they are large, the process of their decomposition and replacement by the new affine multibonded strata becomes quite "noisy" and ordinarily assumes the form of riots, revolts, conquests, revolutions, wars, or radical social reform movements. As a matter of fact there has hardly been any important historical internal revolution or reform which has not been due, to a large extent, to the existence of such "abnormal" strata and has not consisted, to a large extent also, in the "reaction of transposition." Before any revolution or reform in a society there are always some such strata and when the smoke-screen of revolutionary movement has passed, one ordinarily finds new affine strata.

A study of the social processes from this standpoint opens a new and promising field of "sociological chemistry" of social groups, processes, and strata. Herein lies additional evidence of the importance of our classification of groups and strata for scientific purposes.

---

29. Aristotle, *Politics*, 130–132. In the next chapter it will be shown that there are two different types of the sky-lines of aristocracies of various populations: one where various peaks are dominated by one tallest peak; another where there is no dominant peak among several tops of various unibonded and multibonded pyramids.

V. ADDITIONAL SUB-FORMS OF THE UNIBONDED AND MULTIBONDED STRATA

Some of the unibonded and multibonded strata are *legally defined and maintained by the official law of the respective groups*. The legal provisions indicate precisely who can and cannot be their members; what is the position of each rank in the hierarchy of the strata; to what strata it is superior and inferior; what exactly are its rights and duties, its functions and role. Examples of legally defined hierarchies are the official and legal hierarchies of the state, the hierarchy of the church, and the hierarchy of some occupational unions. Among the multibonded strata, the hierarchy of social orders and castes provide an example of the legally defined multibonded pyramid of strata. The official law of the state, together with the official code of the nobility as the upper social order, defines who may become a member, when, and under what conditions, of the nobility, the bourgeoisie, or even of the stratum of the serfs and slaves. The official law of religion plus the official law of the castes themselves determine who may become a member of a caste, when, and under what conditions.

Other unibonded and multibonded strata exist only factually, in the form of less precisely defined layers. There are no legal obstacles, only factual ones, to becoming a member. If one overcomes these, he can enter the stratum. The hierarchy of social classes is an example of a multibonded stratum of the factual character. Also factual in their nature is the intragroup hierarchy of the organized portions of nationality, occupational, and political party groups. So also are some of the "as if" organized strata.

This distinction is important per se, but has a particular significance for the phenomena of vertical mobility which are described further on.

Unibonded and multibonded groups are either legally or factually or in both ways *closed and hereditary* or *open and non-hereditary*. Some are intermediate between these. The caste is a closed and hereditary stratum. The social estate is less closed and less hereditary than a caste, but more so than social class. The upper social classes are more closed than the lower ones. Generally, the upper strata of almost all unibonded and multibonded groups tend to be more closed than the lower strata, so far as an infiltration of outsiders into membership is concerned. Since the upper strata give more privileges and advantages of both economic and noneconomic character, the number of vacancies is far fewer than the number of persons who would like to occupy them. Hence the barriers and obstacles of either legal or factual nature. The lower strata have fewer advantages and more burdens; they do not need to bar their gates to newcomers.

Finally, *some of the organized strata are centralized in their government, others decentralized*. The states and some religious organizations like the Catholic, the Mohammedan, and parties like the Communist and Nazi, are centralized; there is a central supreme government, a central führer, chief, pope, and the like. Castes, classes, and some other groups, such as Protestant denominations, are decentralized. They do not have any centralized government, head, or committee.

VI. CONCLUSIONS

The preceding discussion has given the main types of the unibonded and multibonded stratification of the population. It shows a much more complex picture, containing more varied forms of stratification, than is usually depicted. It lays down the solid foundation for a social taxonomy and stratigraphy. It puts an end to the anarchic and crude state of the current structural analysis and classification of social groups and strata.

A series of important conclusions in regard to the general traits of social differentiation and stratification and in regard to the individual follow from the development of this systematic theory. It is better, however, to postpone the discussion of these results until after the analysis of the population generally. We turn now to this analysis as the last step in the study of the structural aspect of social phenomena.

PART II

The Traditional Class Approach to Stratification

3

Basic Concepts and Theories of Class Stratification

Vincent Jeffries

THE STUDY of class stratification has been characterized by considerable divergence and disagreement. Some scholars have viewed stratification primarily in terms of differences in power, while others have emphasized subjective opinions as its most important basis. Some have conceived of stratification as a coercive system of institutionalized injustice; others have seen it as a division of labor reflective of individual effort and ability. Stratification also has been viewed as an expression of commonly held values, and, by others, as a balance of conflicting interests in society.

This chapter presents basis theoretical models that reflect this variety of approaches to the study of social stratification. The relationships between social class and power, privilege, and prestige will be examined and the views of scholars who have had a major influence upon the study of class stratification will be presented. The contributions of Karl Marx* (1956; 1959; Mills* 1962), Max Weber* (1947; 1958*; Gerth and Mills 1958), and Kingsley Davis and Wilbert E. Moore* (1945) are further illustrated by selections from their writings.

THEORETICAL PERSPECTIVES

Functional and Conflict Theories

Functional and conflict theories are among the major schools of sociological thought; both have a long history commonly dated back to the nineteenth century (Ritzer, 1975; Turner, 1978). Although they are often contrasted, these two schools of thought also share many common assumptions (Ritzer, 1975; Lenski, 1966). Function-

An asterisk (*) accompanying a citation indicates a selection included in this volume.

alism is frequently regarded as growing out of the works of late nineteenth and early twentieth century theorists such as Emile Durkheim (1960), and Herbert Spencer (1972), whereas the beginnings of conflict theory are particularly associated with the writings of Karl Marx (Mills*, 1962). Recent theorists identified with functionalist theory, who have also contributed to the study of social stratification, are Talcott Parsons (1953) and Kingsley Davis and Wilbert E. Moore*(1945). Ralf Dahrendorf (1957), Randall Collins (1975) and C. Wright Mills*(1956, 1959, 1963*) are writers who emphasize conflict theory in the study of stratification.

These two schools of thought have a long past in the history of ideas relating to social inequality. They have been variously designated as the conservative and radical (Lenski, 1966:3–23), conflict and order (Horton, 1966), integration and coercion (Dahrendorf, 1959), and conflict and functional (Roach, Gross and Gursslin, 1969:54–55) perspectives. The terms conflict and functional will be used here, although the presentation of these models draws heavily from all of the authors cited above. The conflict and functional models provide basic perspectives that can be applied to class stratification, as well as ethnic, sex, and age stratification.

Conflict and functional theories both imply a basic conception of the nature of society from which views of stratification systems derive. Functional theories of society say that there is a predominant tendency toward order and stability in societies. Commonly held values and traditions form the basis for the integration of society. The various segments or institutions of society are closely interrelated and contribute to the cohesion of that society. For example, the political, economic, and family institutions all make vital contributions to the social order. The family provides for the care of the helpless child, the political institution regulates the distribution of power, the economic institution controls the distribution of scarce resources. Each institution or segment of society makes a contribution to the larger whole. In addition, societies achieve some degree of integration because of commonly held values. These values are beliefs held in high regard, or cultural ideals. The most salient values in a society unite diverse segments of that society toward common purposes and actions. Social control exerted through existing institutions is regarded as necessary and beneficial both to the individual and to society. From the functionalist perspective, individual development and fulfillment are best achieved by conformity to existing norms and values, and deviant behavior is usually viewed as undesirable. Social change is regarded as basically orderly and evolutionary, representing a gradual unfolding of potentials inherent in society.

The above discussion outlines the most general image of society that is derived from a functional perspective. Out of this general tradition there comes a very specific view of stratification. Stratification, or the unequal distribution of rewards, is seen as making a contribution to the social order. That is, stratification actually contributes to the social cohesion and integration of society. But how is it possible that the unequal distribution of rewards can make a positive contribution to society? Davis and Moore* (1945) present the clearest statement of functionalism applied to stratification. These authors consider that the unequal distribution of rewards to different social positions is necessary to ensure that vital positions in the social structure are filled by competent individuals. Some positions or occupations in a society are more vital to the integration of that society than are others. In the political institution, for example, most people would regard the position of Supreme Court Justice as more vital to the integration of society than the position of court clerk. But those positions that make the biggest contribution to societal cohesion involve long and difficult training periods and considerable investments in time and energy. To be sure that these important positions are filled by competent people on a regular basis, society must attach greater rewards to these positions, such as money, status, work challenge and ego enhancement. In effect, the unequal distribution of rewards is a large scale motivation device to insure that competent individuals will try to reach important positions and will carry out the duties of those positions. Rewarding some positions more than others results in social hierarchies of wealth, status, and power. The functionalist does not view this unequal distribution as illegitimate or unjust but, rather, as essential to the social order.

For years after its publication, comment and debate regarding the contents of the Davis and Moore*(1945) article have appeared in the scholarly literature, as for example, in statements by Tumin (1953), Buckley (1958), Wrong (1959), and Stinchecombe (1963). Some have criticized the theory as being static or excessively conservative in that it takes the *existing* distribution of rewards as inherently "natural" or functionally the best distribution. Functional theory ignores the dynamics of social change and the fact that there may be serious inequities in the distribution of rewards in a given society.

Others criticize the Davis-Moore functional theory on the grounds that it ignores power. The theory assumes an open system and the smooth recruitment of motivated, talented individuals to functionally important positions. But those in power often attempt to hold on to their power and to restrict others from reaching these positions.

The Davis-Moore theory has also been criticized for its methodology. There are no objective standards to determine functional importance. How are we to determine the exact functional importance of a given position? The problem becomes especially acute when considering middle level occupations. How does one determine the relative functional importance among occupations like social worker, teacher, and musician? Despite these criticisms, the functional theory has survived and provides one major view on stratification in society. Figure 3–1 presents the basic premises of a functional theory of stratification.

---

1. Stratification is a social structure which expresses common values and traditions. As such it provides a basis for the integration and stability of society.
2. The distribution of power, privilege, and prestige is basically just, necessary, and beneficial to both individual and societal welfare.
3. The exercise of power to maintain an existing system of privileges in society is minimal.
4. The institutions of society embody consensual values and carry out policies that serve the common good.
5. Society must attach unequal rewards to social positions in order to ensure that they are filled by capable individuals.
6. The positions individuals occupy in society are primarily a function of their talents and their efforts in developing those talents.

Figure 3–1. *Functional Theory Applied to Social Stratification*

The conflict model presents a very different view of the basic nature of society. From the conflict perspective, society's predominant bent is toward instability and change. Society is composed of groups with conflicting interests in continual but varying degrees of opposition. According to conflict theory, social control is exerted through existing institutions by the use of force, coercion, and manipulation. Social control retards or prevents the development of the full potential of individuals and society. What society defines as deviant behavior is often regarded by conflict theorists as promoting personal growth and beneficial changes in social organization. Social change is regarded as involving fundamental alterations in existing institutions and is therefore revolutionary by nature.

The general image of society as seen from a conflict perspective gives rise to a specific view of stratification. The division of society into upper and lower strata represents coercion and antagonism between classes. Often the advantages and profits that accrue to one class represent losses for another class. Karl Marx's theory is a prime example of the conflict stratification approach. The stratification system is regarded as a source of social conflict because the owners of the means of production (higher stratum) seek to use their position for their own narrow interests to the detriment of the exploited working class. The unequal power and conflict of interests between strata frequently lead to protest, disruption and change in society. Figure 3–2 presents the basic premises of the conflict theory of stratification.

Synthesis of Functional and Conflict Perspectives

Gerhard Lenski (1966:17–23) has noted the development and increasing emergence of a synthesis of the conflict and functional models of stratification. The valid insights of both are being incorporated into a more empirically based theory of social stratification. This gradually developing synthesis is the result of the relatively recent application of the scientific method to the study and analysis of social stratification. The disciplined merging of ideas and data that this involves is in contrast to the previous em-

---

1. Stratification is an expression of divergent group interests. As such it is a source of conflict in society.
2. The distribution of power, privilege, and prestige is basically unjust, unnecessary, and detrimental to individual and social welfare.
3. The exercise of power through both manipulation and coercion plays a major role in maintaining the system of privileges in society.
4. The institutions of society serve to enhance the advantages of the upper stratum at the expense of the rest of society.
5. Unequal rewards for social positions serve to maintain and enhance the interests of the upper stratum.
6. The positions individuals occupy in society are primarily a function of unequal access to motivation, training, and channels of advancement.

Figure 3–2. *Conflict Theory Applied to Social Stratification*

phasis on moral evaluation with respect to the existence of social inequality. Early examples of this more systematic and empirical approach are seen in the works of Max Weber*(1958) and Pitrim A. Sorokin*(1969*, 1959); Lenski's (1966) work and that of Stanislaw Ossowski (1963) and Pierre van den Berghe (1963) represent more recent advances in the search for a viable synthesis. ·

The synthesis of these two perspectives is based in part on the assumption that the conflict and functional models emphasize aspects of society that are both complementary and inseparable. Pierre van den Berghe (1963) cites four areas of convergence and overlap between these two apparently contrasting models. Both are holistic; that is, both view society as a system of interrelated parts. Second, both models are concerned with the dual role of conflict as well as consensus. Consensus, emphasized by functionalists, and conflict, emphasized by conflict theorists, can have the opposite effect. For example, conflict can ultimately contribute to integration, such as when conflict over diverse issues keeps a major cleavage from developing, thus helping to maintain a certain level of societal integration. In other instances, consensus can lead to disintegration and change. This can be observed in instances of rigid stress on impractical and unworkable norms. Another example is the emphasis on values, such as those of competition and individualism, which, if strongly subscribed to by a sufficiently large number of individuals, are likely to be socially disruptive. A third similarity between the conflict and functional models is that both emphasize an evolutionary view of social change. Despite differences within this context, both models hold that a given state of a social system presupposes certain previous states out of which the existent structure developed. The fourth major area of overlap is the long-range tendency toward social integration that both models describe. In the conflict view, this comes about through a progression to ever higher stages of development brought about through the resolving of conflicts, whereas in the functional view it is achieved primarily through value consensus.

Symbolic Interactionist Theory

Another theory for understanding the structure and dynamics of stratification systems is symbolic interactionism (See especially Blumer, 1969; Rose, 1962; Shibutani, 1961; Thomas, 1958; Turner, 1962, 1976.) Although symbolic interactionism is a major theoretical school in sociology, it has seldom been applied to the study of social stratification. An exception to this is the work of Shibutani and Kwan (1965).

Symbolic interactionist theory entails a more detailed and explicit frame of reference for examining the relationship between society, culture, and the individual than is provided by either the conflict or the functional models. It gives particular insight into the ways in which stratification systems affect the psyches and life histories of individuals. It examines the manner in which the action of individuals has import for both the maintenance and the change of systems of social stratification.

Symbolic interactionist theory assumes that society and culture constitute the effective environment of individuals. Society in the broadest sense refers to social interaction between individuals and the interrelationships that exist between groups. Society encompasses situations of interaction ranging from one-to-one encounters to large scale relations between groups. Such interactions can also range from spontaneous ones to those that are highly structured. Culture refers to relatively organized systems of mean-ings. Such meanings include beliefs, or conceptions of the nature of reality; norms, or standards of correctness; values, or ends that are considered to be desirable; and roles, or conventional patterns of claims and obligations in social relationships. Cultural mean-ings can be general, in the sense that they are widely shared in a given society, or they may be subcultural—that is, characteristic of particular groupings. Although societies and cultures tend to be systematic and organized, they are also dynamic, in the sense that they are constantly changing.

From the interactionist perspective, human personality is viewed as a relatively organized system of meanings. Hence, there is a certain order and predictability to the behavior of individuals. Individuals tend to select and emphasize key meanings from among those available in their environment. These key meanings comprise what may be termed the "life organization" of the individual (Thomas, 1958). Life organization constitutes schemes of conduct that provide stability and direction in day-to-day interac-tion. Also central to the organization of personality is the conception of self. Self refers to the overall meaning that the individual ascribes to himself or herself. The concept of self held by the individual affects the way he or she relates to others. Personality and its elements continually evolve throughout the lifetime of an individual. Each individual personality develops in its own unique way, choosing and selecting within the limits of available cultural alternatives.

Interactionist theory holds that the study of human behavior must deal with two basic kinds of data, that pertaining to individuals and that pertaining to society and cul-ture. In order to analyze and explain structure or process on either level, both individ-uals and cultural data must be taken into account. Personality, on the one hand, and social structures and cultures on the other, develop out of and are reaffirmed in the con-tinual process of social interaction. The mutual interdependence between the individual and the sociocultural necessitates consideration of both to explain phenomena at either level.

The dimension of meaning, or the definition of the situation, is considered by symbolic interactionists to be of major importance at both the individual and the socio-cultural levels of analysis. Individuals ascribe meanings to situations, events, and ideas, and their definition of the situation is a key element in their relations to them. In a sim-ilar vein, there are consensual meanings that are characteristic of particular subcultures and cultures and that represent generally agreed on and socially supported definitions of the situations.

A significant proportion of human thought and behavior is directly affected by socialization into subcultures and the general culture. Socialization, the process by which individuals are taught the ways of their society, entails the internalization of cul-turally shared meanings. Much of the uniformity and predictability of human behavior is due to the pervasive influence of such culturally accepted definitions of the situations. While socialization accounts for similarities among human beings, it also accounts for diversity. Through socialization into different cultures and subcultures, individuals develop different systems of life organization and behavior patterns. Symbolic inter-actionists say that individual diversity also results from individual differences in natural endowment and temperament and the effect of choices made between available altern-atives, both of which to some degree transcend the socialization process.

Used to explain social stratification, symbolic interactionist theory yields the propositions which are presented in Fig.3-3.

Symbolic interactionist theory is applied to social stratification in later sections of this book. This theoretical perspective is especially useful for bringing into focus the dynamic interplay between systems of stratification, an individual's life within them, and his or her interpretation of them. This interplay determines how prevailing social practices and structures are maintained or changed. It also provides a perspective that emphasizes some of the processes through which stratification systems shape and mold the psyche and life history of the individual.

Application of the Theories

The functional, conflict, and symbolic interactionist perspectives contain different insights regarding the nature of social organization and change. When all three are applied to a given topic, a more comprehensive view can be obtained than with any single one of these approaches because they ask different questions and focus attention upon contrasting aspects of the same thing. The ghetto protests of the 1960s and the circumstances surrounding them serve as an example of how each of these theories contributes to the understanding of social phenomena.

The emphasis on a common core of values, which is central to functional theory, raises questions regarding various aspects of the protests. One area of inquiry involves the relationship between values such as equality of opportunity and the dignity of all people and the protests of blacks in the United States. Failure to have full access to these values may be regarded as a primary reason for the protests in Watts, Detroit, and other cities in the United States. Various attempts to better the condition of blacks, which

---

1. Any stratification system is invested by the members of society with meanings pertaining to its characteristics and the reasons for its existence.
2. The structure and dynamics of stratification must be understood within the context of the meanings individuals ascribe to it, to themselves, and to their position in the stratification system.
3. The socialization process, in terms of both experiential and ideological content, reflects the position of the individual in the stratification system. Thus, characteristic patterns of life organization and characteristic views of stratification are likely to be associated with positions in particular social strata. Such meanings are likely to be different in different social strata.
4. Stratification systems are maintained through socialization into the meanings that support and justify them. Such socialization will differ from one strata to another.
5. Change within stratification systems rests in part upon how readily individuals accept new meanings about the nature of stratification and their place within it. Such susceptibility differs from one stratum to another.

Figure 3-3. *Symbolic Interactionist Theory Applied to Social Stratification*

were generated by these protests, can also be seen as growing out of these consensual values, and reaffirming them. The protests may be seen from the perspective of functionalism as ultimately generating a trend toward greater value consistency and equilibrium through their stimulation to remove inconsistencies between dominant values and the treatment of blacks. Functional theory also directs attention to the question of what elements in the culture have contributed to the prejudice and discrimination against blacks that were causes of the protests.

The conflict approach focuses attention on the disparate group interests that were expressed in the ghetto uprisings. What these interests are and how they are rooted in social structure are of central concern. The unequal distribution of power, privilege, and prestige and its role in the protests is a basic question from the perspective of conflict theory. The place of force and manipulation in keeping blacks in a disadvantaged position, and in quelling the protests, is another area of investigation deriving from a conflict perspective. Conflict theory also directs attention to the manner in which uprisings, such as those in the ghettos during the 1960s, serve to bring about social change. Under what conditions will those in control of the power structure be responsive to this type of activity, and, what is the role of such protests in ultimately changing the distribution of power, privilege, and prestige?

The symbolic interactionist perspective focuses attention on the riots as a form of social interaction. Shared meanings regarding the protests should emerge from this process of interaction, particularly among those in the black community, but also throughout the general population. Different meanings regarding the riot should develop in different locations of the social structure that possess different subcultures, the tenants of which provide a perspective through which the riots are interpreted. The interactionist approach also highlights the role of individual personality in determining the meanings ascribed to the protests. Each individual brings a constellation of meanings to the situation that influence his or her definition and ultimate reaction to it. The interactionist approach focuses attention on the particular meanings that may influence participation in the protests, and reactions to them.

POWER, PRIVILEGE, AND PRESTIGE

The basic concerns of the study of social stratification are expressed in the concepts of power, privilege, and prestige. Despite differences and divergences within the field, scholars have consistently emphasized one or more of these three attributes of stratification systems. Functional theorists have generally tended to give greatest primacy to prestige, usually conceptualizing stratification as subjective ranking on the basis of some criteria. Privilege is most often the secondary emphasis in functional theories, whereas power is usually given minor notice or ignored. Conflict theorists tend to place greatest stress on power. They give privilege secondary emphasis, and prestige is commonly viewed as of least significance. The three concepts of power, privilege, and prestige thus serve as a basis from which the field of stratification can be organized and from which differing theoretical approaches can be integrated around a common core of basic concepts.

Stratification by definition entails an unequal distribution of power, privilege, and prestige. If there are no such inequalities, then social stratification does not exist. This orientation toward power, privilege, and prestige in the analysis of stratification systems builds most directly on the traditions established by Marx (1956; Mills*, 1962:81–95), Weber* (1958:180–195), and such later theorists as Mills* (1963: 305–323), Sorokin* (1969*:256–295; 1959), and Lenski* (1966:43–72).

Power

Max Weber* (1958:180) defines power as "the chance of a man or number of men to realize their own will in a communal action, even against the resistance of others who are participating in the action." A later theorist, Robert Bierstedt, observes that power, when made manifest through force, "compels a change in the course of action of an individual or a group against the wishes of the individual or the group" (1974:358). In terms of social stratification, the unequal distribution of power allows members of a higher stratum to exert their will on members of a lower stratum. This ability to achieve aims in communal action may in some instances be due to the application of force, or to the threat of force. In other instances, this ability to realize aims may be due to voluntary compliance based on the acceptance of the right of one party to issue commands.

Various scholars such as Bierstedt (1974:350–366) and Gerhard Lenski* (1966: 43–72), have viewed power as the element leading to the creation and maintenance of any stratification system. This emphasis on the distribution of power as the fundamental criterion of stratification systems finds its earlier beginnings in the writings of Karl Marx and Max Weber. Marx (Mills*, 1962:81–95; see also Marx, 1956) conceptualized the stratification system as a hierarchy of power based on control of the productive processes of society. Social classes, which are a reflection of the economic base of production, are the social groupings through which power is held and exercised.

Weber* (1946:180–195) expanded Marx's formulation of the basis of power. In so doing, Weber broadened and extended Marx's singular emphasis on class stratification to a multidimensional theory of social stratification. Class, which to Weber involves position in the market place relative to the use of property and exchange of goods and services for economic advantage, was but one basis of access to power. Status, the social honor and prestige accorded to groups within a society, was emphasized by Weber as another major source of power. A third basis of power was party. To Weber, parties are basic to the political order and constituted of groups specifically organized to maintain or to alter the distribution of power in society.

Bierstedt identifies three major sources of power (1974:363–366; see also Bierstedt, 1950). The first of these is the number of individuals, especially if that constitutes a majority. Numbers give power, and other things being equal, the larger group can control the smaller. That such is not always the case is due in part to what Bierstedt identifies as a second source of power, which is organization. Well-organized and disciplined groups with a clearly defined purpose can control larger unorganized groups. When these two factors are combined, an organized majority then exists, and such a group can be extremely powerful. A third source of power is resources, which can vary from knowledge, to military armaments, to natural resources.

The most fundamental manifestation of power is physical force. Those people who can activate and control physical force, which in modern industrial societies are law enforcement agents and the military, have the ability to realize their will against the opposition of others. Control over the means of force was a major factor in the conquest and subjugation of blacks, Mexicans and American Indians in the earlier history of the United States. Superior force was also used by large corporations against labor unions in the nineteenth and early twentieth centuries. Corporations were often able to successfully call on the federal courts to issue injunctions against labor strikes. If this tactic failed, corporations were frequently able to prevail on state and federal authorities to bring in troops to quell labor related disturbances. In more recent times, the protests of blacks in the ghetto riots of the 1960s were put down by the use of superior force.

Power is often most effectively exercised through the occupancy of key positions in major institutional spheres, such as the political, religious, and economic. In his classic work on power in the United States, C. Wright Mills (1959) has analyzed how the corporate, political, and military elite are able to realize their will by occupying key decision-making positions. Mills believes there is an "interlocking directorate" of the elite from these three sectors of society. Members of this elite move from positions of power in one institutional sphere to positions of power in another. This movement enables them to make basic policy decisions that serve their interests in the allocation of economic and other resources. Decision-making power finds its focus in key positions in these three sectors, while other areas of society are subordinated to them. In Mills's view, the corporate rich are the apex of this national power structure and from this position are able to initiate action within the political and military spheres. In a related study (which is discussed in some detail in the next chapter), Domhoff (1967) elaborates and further documents many of Mills's ideas, although contending that Mills overestimates the place of the military in the national structure of power.

Power also can be exercised by influencing the minds of other people so that they think in a manner consistent with the realization of goals desired by those with power. In modern industrialized societies, the control of the mass media gives unparalleled opportunity to mold and influence public opinion. The history of modern totalitarian regimes reveals a hostility to the free press and concerted efforts to maintain exclusive control of the means of mass communication by the ruling strata. William Shirer (1964), for example, has described how the Nazi party was able to mold the opinions of the German people to such an extent that their perceptions of events leading up to World War II differed radically from those prevalent in other countries of Europe. By controlling the flow of information, the party was able to create and maintain among the German populace totally false perceptions of Germany's actions in international affairs.

Although force is the ultimate manifestation of power, to maintain a stratification system solely by force is extremely costly and deprives those in control of the system of many of its benefits (Lenski, 1966:50–58). In order to avoid the constant use of force, ruling strata attempt to institutionalize and make legitimate their position once control is gained. Compliance by a populace through fear of physical force is gradually replaced by the exercise of power through authority. When power is exerted through authority, commands are willingly obeyed because the population considers them to be legitimate.

Max Weber laid the foundations for the systematic study of authority by developing a typology of types of legitimate authority (Weber, 1947:324–386). Weber believed that power is legitimized through three types of authority: traditional, legal, and charismatic. Although he described these types of authority separately, Weber recognized that legitimated power usually rests on some combination of the three.

Traditional authority rests on the acceptance of established traditions and on the acceptance of those who occupy positions of high status in accordance with these traditions. Obedience is owed to those in positions of authority because tradition says so, not because written and enacted laws specify so. The extent of authority is also defined by tradition. For centuries the authority structure of China rested primarily on such a basis of tradition.

Legal authority is based on the acceptance of normative rules, or laws, and accordingly, on a belief in the rights of those who exercise authority under these rules. This type of authority involves a set of abstract norms, which are usually established through rational means directed at attaining group interests. Legal authority is located in positions, rather than in individuals. In a society regulated by legal authority, many social activities are organized by rules, specific spheres of competence, and a hierarchy of positions. The administrative staff of organizations is separated from ownership of the means of production. This type of authority is exemplified in the bureaucratic organization of corporations and the military.

In charismatic authority, commands are obeyed because of the personal qualities of individuals who issue them. Charismatic authority, at least in its early stages, often develops outside of, and is frequently contrary to, already established systems of authority. Hence Weber also referred to the routinization of charisma, the process by which a charismatic leader and his or her followers seek to maintain authority based upon some combination of legal or traditional grounds.

The relationship between power and authority is discussed by Robert Bierstedt (1974:337–366). Authority is defined as institutionalized power. That is, authority incorporates power within the recognized and stabilized procedures of society. Authority thus places the mantle of the normative system around the use of power. Further, it links power to specific social positions and specifies when and in what manner power may be exercised.

Authority is closely related to the prevailing culture. Authority is linked to positions in a group or society, and not to individuals (Bierstedt, 1974:337–349). It is exercised on the basis of the norms attached to such positions. A person occupying a position of authority is obligated to make decisions and to enforce them, according to the normative system of society. Norms therefore define the rights and duties, and privileges and obligations, which are associated with a given position and its sphere of authority.

Systems of authority, like customs, norms, and other consensual aspects of culture, exert strong pressures toward conformity (Bierstedt, 1974). Conformity is usually rewarded in some manner, such as by social approval, whereas violation of the norms of authority carries various negative sanctions. Bierstedt notes that people obey authority for the same reasons that they conform to cultural expectations in general. A major reason individuals submit to authority can be found in the powerful indoctrination inherent in the socialization process. Another factor is that habituation to custom can become so deeply rooted that obedience to authority takes place without conscious reflection or effort. Recognition of the utility of some traditional practices is another reason that authority is such a compelling force in social life. And submission to authority can be a way of expressing group identification, whether to a group the individual belongs to or, in the case of some reference groups, to one which is simply a point of identification. For example, first-year university students who join fraternities or sororities commonly accept a subordinate position during their first year of membership. This is partly an expression of their desire for full acceptance and a way of demonstrating a willingness to follow the traditions of the group.

The links between culture, authority, and the exercise of power are both complex and numerous. Power can be exercised because individuals have been socialized to accept cultural beliefs that support existing distributions of power, privilege, and prestige. Stratification systems, for example, are always characterized by ideologies that legitimize the superordinate groups' "natural right" to rule. Both Feagin*(1972) and Huber and Form (1973) have noted how beliefs regarding individual responsibility and an open system have served to maintain the existing system of class stratification in the United States. This same complex of widely held cultural beliefs is used to justify the subordinate position of blacks in this country (Schuman*, 1975). In like manner the traditional beliefs about the nature of men and women serve to maintain the system of sexual stratification (Bem and Bem*, 1970; Polatnick*, 1973–74). The potency of such widely accepted ideas in maintaining existing systems of stratification is enhanced by their incorporation within traditional roles involving dominance and submission. The lifetime socialization into such roles is extremely influential, partly because it is frequently unquestioned and taken for granted. Thus, Bem and Bem* (1972) refer to the "unconscious ideology" involved in traditional sex roles which, in a variety of ways, serves to maintain and enhance the subordinate position of women relative to that of men. The influence of such ideas in supporting systems of stratification and the differential exercise of power they entail is the topic of a later chapter in this volume.

Privilege

Power pertains to the ability of individuals or groups to realize their will in communal actions; privilege refers to the social distribution of goods, services, situations, and experiences that are highly valued and beneficial. Privilege also refers to the rights and duties, claims and obligations, deprivations and advantages associated with position in a stratum in a given social hierarchy. Those in higher strata have immunities, advantages, prerogatives, liberties, and options that are relatively less available to those of lower strata. In this sense, in almost all societies certain strata clearly have more privileges than others.

Gerhard Lenski* has defined privilege as the "possession or control of a portion of the surplus produced by a society" (1966:45). This definition and the examples given by Lenski throughout his analysis of stratification systems indicate that privilege is closely linked to economic position, and that economically related resources—those that money can buy—are the major dimension of privilege. We feel that this position is too narrow a view of the innumerable socially patterned and regularized advantages and disadvantages that are so central to the essence of social stratification. Hence two major types of privilege are distinguished: those that are closely related to the possession of economic resources, and those that are closely related to social expectations and norms. In this sense, privilege has two major aspects: what money can buy, or enable one to avoid, and what the culture of society confers or withholds.

Economically related privileges are those that can usually be obtained if one has sufficient economic assets. These include a wide range of goods and services. Legal services and medical care, for example, are closely linked with the ability to pay for such services. If one has enough money, an almost infinite variety of material goods, comforts, and advantages can be purchased and many unpleasant situations avoided.

Economically related privileges are largely determined by social class position, but they are not identical to it. The class system is viewed in this work as a social hierarchy based on wealth, or total economic assets, occupation, and education. Class position is thus based primarily on economic position. In contrast, economically related privileges pertain to the advantageous situations and circumstances that can be obtained through the use of economic assets, not to the assets themselves. For example, the possession of economic assets totaling over $250,000 would place the individual in the upper class. The ability to use these assets to send one's children to private schools, to hire live-in help, or to fly to Europe periodically for rest and relaxation is a manifestation of a high level of economically related privileges. In a similar vein, the possession of economic assets of less than $2,500 would place the individual in the lower class. The fact that such an individual would be unable to send his or her children to any school other than the local public school, could not hire help for home maintenance, and would not be able to travel on vacations is a reflection of a low level of economically related privileges. High class position gives access to many privileges that money can purchase, whereas low class position makes such access difficult or impossible.

This relationship between economically related privilege and the class system is illustrated by the vastly different treatment of the rich and the poor in institutional spheres in the United States (Duberman, 1976:162–227). The criminal justice system, for example, has essentially two kinds of justice, one for the rich and one for the poor. The poor are likely to be represented by inadequate legal counsel, to be assumed to be guilty, and to be labeled as criminal. The poor also are less likely to receive short or suspended sentences. These patterned inequalities are similarly manifested in the area of health care. In physical, mental, and dental health, the poor do not have the same advantages as do those in higher social classes.

The second major category of privileges derives from cultural norms and traditions. These cultural privileges pertain to the advantages, freedoms, and opportunities awarded to some individuals on the basis of position in a social hierarchy. These same privileges are withheld from others by virtue of their lower stratum membership. For example, women have been far more restricted in choice of occupation, career training, and socially accepted behavior patterns than have men. And until recent years, blacks were almost completely confined to the more undesirable and low paying occupations in society. In some areas of the country, blacks were subjected to a rigid code of racial etiquette that expressed and maintained a system of superordination and subordination between blacks and whites. Mandatory retirement is another example of the differential distribution of cultural privileges. Millions of persons in the United States are denied gainful employment in their lifetime occupations simply because they have reached a certain age, most usually age sixty-five.

These examples illustrate that prevailing and traditional beliefs, values, and norms—that is, the dominant culture— confer and deny many privileges on a basis that has little to do with economic position. Further, in many instances the denial of such privileges cannot be changed by bargaining with economic resources. Although the situation has changed considerably in the past two decades, in times previous to this being a black person meant being denied many privileges routinely accorded to whites in the United States. Even though wealthy blacks were able to avoid some discrimination, possession of wealth did not entirely eliminate deprivations such as separate and inferior public facilities, the denial of access to many circumstances and situations available to whites, and the respect and courtesy of strangers. In a similar vein, high status women still suffer the denial of privileges accorded to men of similar position (Miller, Labovitz, and Fry*, 1975).

Prestige

Prestige refers to the distribution of social honor, or status. In any society, some groups are evaluated differently from others. Some are regarded highly and are given respect and deference, while others are looked down on. In relation to social stratification, prestige is the differential ranking of individuals or groups according to some criteria determined by society. Prestige must be conferred or withheld. It cannot be simply taken by its recipient. In this sense, it requires some degree of community consensus about what qualities are desirable and undesirable. Prestige rankings thus reflect the values emphasized in a given society. Prestige is often accorded to individuals on the basis of factors such as religious association, family background, wealth, power, occupation, and ethnicity.

Max Weber* (1958:180–195) first systematically analyzed the role of prestige or "status" in social stratification. Weber regarded the status hierarchy as a distinct dimension of stratification systems, based on the positive or negative evaluation of social honor. Emphasis is placed on status groups, that is, on individuals who have similar claims to social honor or prestige, by virtue of such criteria as family background, ethnicity, or occupation. These groups tend to form communities, and to express their status position through a distinctive "style of life," which also is a necessity for group membership. Status group members erect barriers of social exclusion to enhance and maintain their position and to limit the entrance of outsiders. Debutante parties, country clubs, and marriage restricted to a status circle are contemporary examples of these exclusionist practices.

The works of W. Lloyd Warner and his associates (Warner and Lunt, 1941; Warner, Meeker, and Eells, 1960; Warner, et al., 1963) treat prestige as the basis of stratification. They define social classes as aggregates of individuals who are ranked by members of a given community on a continuum from superior to inferior positions. The number of classes in a community and the criteria for ranking are also regarded as determined by the subjective evaluation of community members.

In addition to describing the characteristics of classes in a community, another focus of the work of Warner and his associates was to examine the impact of class position upon other areas of social participation and behavior. The relationships between social classes and the family, participation in voluntary associations and cliques, the church, and the school are examined in detail. The investigation indicated that the prestige stratification system has definite effects in these other spheres of social structure.

Before the publication of the works of Warner, *et al.*, sociologists in the United States had devoted relatively little attention to the systematic study of stratification. The work of Warner and his associates produced considerable controversy and criticism surrounding such issues as the methodology of the study, the failure to make precise analytical distinctions regarding separable elements of stratification (such as power, economic, and prestige aspects), the primacy given to the prestige dimension of stratification, and the presumed inability to extend the results to larger cities or the nation as a whole (see for example, Kornhauser, 1953; Mills, 1942). Criticisms notwithstanding, Warner's work had numerous worthwhile features and gave much needed impetus to the study of patterns of social stratification in the United States. It is discussed in further detail in chapter 4.

Prestige rankings have been studied most often in relation to occupational prestige. Because of the relative anonymity of individual life in urbanized society, occupation has become a principal criterion by which individuals are evaluated. Many studies conducted in the United States and in other countries have examined how samples of respondents rank occupation and, in some instances, the reasons for such ranking.

One of the most comprehensive of these studies in the United States is by North and Hatt (1947). Data for the study consists of a nationwide study of approximately 3,000 adults who were asked questions designed to explore basic attitudes about occupations. Respondents were asked whether "excellent," "good," "average," or "poor" best described their "own personal opinion of the general standing" of ninety different occupations. The most frequent reasons given for designating a job as excellent were high pay (18 percent); an essential job that serves humanity (16 percent); preparation requiring considerable education, hard work, and money (14 percent); and the social prestige associated with a job (14 percent). United States Supreme Court Justice, physician, and state governor were the three most highly rated occupations. When the ninety occupations were classified by groups, government officials had the highest average score, followed by professional and semi-professional workers. At the other end of the scale unskilled, low paying, "dirty" jobs with little public responsibility tended to rank at or near the bottom. The lowest groups of occupations were service workers and laborers, with the lowest three specific occupations being garbage collector, street sweeper, and shoe shiner.

The North and Hatt (1947) study was replicated in 1963 (Hodge, Siegel, and Rossi, 1966). The follow-up study showed that occupational prestige rankings were extremely stable over time, with few differences between 1947 and the 1963 studies. Small changes were observed, however. One notable change was a small shift upward in prestige of the aggregate score of blue collar occupations.

THE INTERRELATIONSHIPS BETWEEN POWER, PRIVILEGE, AND PRESTIGE

The position is taken in this volume that power establishes and maintains systems of social stratification. This view is similar to that of Lenski* (1966:43–72), who argues that while there is a mutual influence between power, privilege, and prestige, the primary direction is from power to privilege to prestige.

Power is considered predominant in stratification systems for a variety of reasons. As the ultimate use of power, force has a profound effect on determining privileges. Once power is legitimized in the form of authority, the potential for determining both privilege and prestige is further enhanced. In the 1950s the leaders of the movement for black liberation perceived this central role of power in changing the position of disadvantaged groups in the stratification system (Olsen,* 1970). Instead of trying to change white attitudes of social prejudice, blacks turned to more direct attempts to gain power. To attack inequities in social structure effectively, power was clearly necessary.

Of central importance in the relationship between power, privilege, and prestige is the fact that to the degree that a group holds power, it can control the vital processes of society and manipulate parts of the social structure to its advantage. By placing individuals in high ranking positions from which they can make far-reaching decisions, the balance of privilege can be drastically altered.

Power gives control over major institutional spheres. The holders of power are able to influence the allocation of the economic surplus of society, the wage and price levels of the economy, the society's legal structure, educational institutions, and the mass media. If the exercise of power is not limited in some way, such as by constitutional government or a system of checks and balances among power holders, control over these institutional spheres can radically change the distribution of privilege and prestige in society in a relatively short period of time.

Our position, similar to that of Lenski* (1966), is that prestige derives principally from power and privilege. Power and privilege are likely to lead to authority, material advantages, the opportunity to develop talents and skills, the ability to engage in socially valued experiences, and the occupancy of key decision-making positions. Since all of these attributes are generally socially valued ones, they are likely to lead to increased prestige.

The aforementioned perspective does not assume a universal causal direction between these basic stratification criteria, but rather a predominant direction of influence. However, there is certainly some degree of feedback in which increased privileges may lead to increased power and in which increased prestige may lead to advantages of privilege and power. For example, privilege in the form of increased educational opportunities can qualify individuals for high level decision-making positions; this in turn would give increased power. Such has been the case with respect to some ethnic minorities and women in recent years in the United States. Prestige also can react directly on power and privilege. For example, the prestige accorded to the wealthy in the United States is undoubtedly a factor in the differential treatment by the courts of white collar crime as compared to other types of criminal behavior. In these cases, the usual pattern is one of very light sentences, or more often fines, even though such white collar crimes often entail extensive monetary losses.

Individuals or groups that have prestige are given deference, favors, and advantages in a variety of instances and situations. Prestige provides access to privileges that would otherwise not be given and can contribute to the realization of aims in communal action. Although functional theories tend to place little emphasis on the role of power in stratification systems, their perspective provides a holistic view which illuminates the manner in which prestige can so influence the distribution of power and privilege. The allocation of prestige and rewards to various social positions, as well as the general profile of stratification systems, are seen from the functionalist orientation as a reflection of the hierarchy of values in the dominant culture. For example, Parsons (1953) notes that the high accord given to the values of achievement according to universalistic criteria and performance, which are stressed in the culture of the United States, emphasize productive activity in the economy, or occupation, as the primary source of evaluation and ranking. In a similar vein, Davis and Moore* (1945) emphasize the relationship between dominant values and the differential evaluation of activities. Functional theories thus focus attention on the fact that prestige can be deeply imbedded in traditional customs and values. Prestige does not exist in a vacuum but rather is linked to a variety of symbols that can activate the bestowal of deference. The effect of culturally prescribed prestige upon human behavior can be considerable under these conditions.

SOCIAL CLASSES

The term *social class* has been given a variety of meanings in scholarly usage (Duberman, 1976:56–64). The conception of social classes discussed here derives principally from Karl Marx (1956; Mills*, 1962), Max Weber* (1958), Pitirim A. Sorokin (1969: 271–275), and C. Wright Mills* (1963).

In many respects, Karl Marx established the foundation for the systematic study of social classes. To Marx, classes are first and foremost aggregates of individuals who occupy a common position in relation to the means of production. Although recognizing a variety of classes, Marx emphasized the role of two classes composed of those who control the productive structure and processes and those who must sell their labors. In the European society of the nineteenth century, these two basic classes were the capitalists, or bourgeoisie, and the wage workers, or the proletariat.

Marx viewed classes as objective features of social structure that represent the societal expression of the division of labor characteristic of the economic base of a given society. According to Marx, class stratification is the focal point of both social organization and social change. Class position constitutes a set of real life experiences and conditions which confront individuals and to a large extent determine what both their life experiences and their perceptions of the social world will be.

More than any other theorist, Karl Marx focused attention on the importance of social classes as a major factor in understanding social change and broad historical trends. The central fact of such changes is the struggle between social classes. The class struggle is the expression of the irreconcilable interests of those who control the economic processes of society, and thus hold power, and those who do not.

The development of class consciousness is to Marx the basic mechanism through which fundamental structural changes occur in society (Mills*, 1962). Consciousness grows out of continued and progressively intense conflict between those who own and control the means of production and those who own nothing and have only their labor to sell. Class consciousness includes an awareness of one's own class and of other classes, a feeling of group identity based on a common class position, a sense of injustice, and an awareness of the need for collective political action to change the existing social structure. Marx believed that with the continued development of class consciousness and the intensification of class conflict, society would become polarized between the owners of the means of production and the rest of society. Since the holders of power would never voluntarily give it up, revolution would be necessary.

Max Weber* (1958*; see also Weber, 1947: 424–429) regarded classes as aggregates of individuals who have common life chances with respect to the market place. Life chances entail the opportunities for attaining advantages through the possession and control of property and the exchange of goods and services. Classes to Weber, as to Marx, are a phenomenon of the economic sector of society, and power is derived from the relationship of individuals and groups to the economic processes and structure of society. Weber, however, says that status, or social honor, and parties, which are groups devoted to the acquisition and maintenance of power, are also major factors related to access to power. Status and party are often closely related to class. For example, the criteria of status in a given society may be based partly on class position, as is the case in the United States, where wealth usually gives status. Parties often represent class interests, and are thereby also often closely linked to the class structure.

Following in very much the same tradition as Marx and Weber, Sorokin (1969:271–275) sees social classes as based on occupational and economic bonds, with the additional bond of being members of the same stratum. This latter component entails a similarity of rights and duties, and advantages and disadvantages, relative to other strata. Elaborating on this basic conception, Sorokin lists a number of the characteristics of social classes. Classes are legally open groups, but in reality are semiclosed. Members of a given social class possess common interests by virtue of their class situation. The interests of one class are in opposition to those of other classes. Social classes are partly organized and partly possess a consciousness of common membership in the same class. Classes are characteristic of western societies in the eighteenth, nineteenth, and twentieth centuries. The major classes during this period have been the industrial-labor or proletarian class; the peasant-farmer class; the class of large landowners, which is considerably reduced in size from what it once was; and the capitalist class, which is gradually being transformed into the managerial class. Each of these major classes is divided into subclasses.

C. Wright Mills* (1963) defines class membership according to an individual's amount and source of income. On this basis, a class is composed of individuals with similar life chances because of a similar class situation. Favorable life chances involve a wide variety of advantages, such as good medical care, educational opportunities, and exposure to the fine arts. Life chances are primarily related to the opportunity for selling services on the labor market; hence, they are directly related to occupational skills and qualifications.

The perspective adopted here regarding social classes builds on and is basically consistent with that contained in the writings of the previously discussed theorists. Social classes are viewed as social and economic groups constituted by a coalescence of economic, occupational, and educational bonds. In a sense, each of these components of class have their own separate hierarchies. They are interrelated yet distinct phenomena that can, and in some instances do, exhibit disparities in positions among individuals or groups when they are compared across the three hierarchies. For example, many university professors who have Doctor of Philosophy degrees have low- to middle-level incomes. On the other hand, some individuals who have made considerable wealth do not have a college education. However, economic position in terms of total wealth, occupation, and education are far more often than not closely related. It is the strata formed by the coalescence of these factors that are here referred to as social classes. Greater wealth, a relative degree of autonomy and initiative in one's occupation, some authority in one's occupation, and a high degree of education tend to go together. At the other end of the social scale, poverty, little autonomy, individuality, or authority in one's occupation, and a low level of education tend to occur together.

The economic aspect of class is considered to be of greatest importance. Social classes are primarily economic groups. Income, property, stocks and bonds, or other forms of wealth are major elements of the economic attributes of social class. The total economic assets, or wealth, possessed by an individual or group constitutes position in the economic aspect of the social class hierarchy. From the economic viewpoint, "upper" class refers to those who have great wealth. Such wealth usually involves high income, and chances for future income from property ownership, inheritance, or investment. In addition, many at the top of the economic order have a high degree of control over the production process as stockholders, owners, or directors of business enterprises, which further enhances opportunities for acquiring more economic advantages.

Social classes, however, are more than economic groups; they are also occupational groups. Certain kinds of occupational environments and experiences are an important dimension of social class. Working class for example, refers not only to a middle or lower position in terms of economic assets, but also to a specific occupational environment. The following summary describes many working-class occupations. The working-class occupational groups make their living by selling their services or labor (rather than capital) in the marketplace. The working class does not own or control the instruments of production. Its members are often in subordinate positions in occupational hierarchies and accordingly have little opportunity to exercise independent thought, initiative, and creativity in their work. The nature of their work often is boring and repetitious and the pace of work is outside of their control. The working class is usually paid hourly wages, rather than monthly salaries for some designated work assignment.

Many scholars have studied occupations almost solely as a hierarchy of prestige. In contrast, the perspective taken in this volume toward occupation as a component of social class emphasizes structural factors, such as the amount of income associated with a given occupation, position in the productive process, and the amount of initiative and independence, authority and power, associated with the occupation. The prestige associated with occupations is considered to be derived primarily from these structural factors, but is not inherent to the definition of social class.

Education is the third component of social class, providing an important avenue of access to higher occupational and economic positions. Failure to achieve certain levels of education will in most instances bar an individual from middle and higher level occupational positions and their attendant advantages in accumulating wealth. Lack of a high school diploma virtually closes access to the vast majority of middle level occupations. Completion of a Bachelor of Arts degree is in many instances a prerequisite for the more desirable white collar jobs. Professional degrees, such as the M.D. and law degrees give access to high occupational positions and very favorable wealth making opportunities.

Social classes as the coalescence of economic, occupational, and educational bonds are considered to be objective features of social structure. The views people have of the stratification system are separate and distinct from its existence as part of social structure and organization. This emphasis on the objective nature of stratification is also applicable to the existence of class consciousness. Some argue that the term "social class" should only be used to refer to members of a stratum who feel a sense of belonging together and have a defined set of common interests. The idea advanced here is that groups sharing generally similar levels of wealth, occupation, and education—that is, classes—have a potential for class consciousness that may or may not be realized. The conditions under which class consciousness develops and those which make its emergence difficult are major areas of theory and investigation in the study of social stratification, but are not considered as being intrinsic to the definition of social class.

THE RELATIONSHIPS BETWEEN SOCIAL CLASSES
AND THE UNEQUAL DISTRIBUTION OF POWER,
PRIVILEGE, AND PRESTIGE

Class position as the coalescence of economic and occupational and educational bonds is directly related to the unequal distribution of power, privilege, and prestige. In general, the higher the class position, the greater the degree of power, privilege, and prestige. Higher classes also have greater access to these attributes than do lower classes.

As a component of social class, wealth is directly related to both the possession of and access to power. In sufficient quantity, monetary assets can greatly increase the ability of an individual or group to realize its will in communal action. In innumerable ways, money can be used to influence and, if necessary, to coerce. In contrast, a scarcity of economic assets makes influencing social forces to one's advantage difficult. In most instances, the only way that groups without an economic surplus can make their cause known and further their interests is to resort to public demonstrations and disruptive tactics.

Besides its bearing on power, wealth can provide increased privileges. For example, if one has enough money, one usually also has time to devote to self-actualizing and enjoyable pursuits and experiences. One is assured of superior legal and medical services and educational and cultural opportunities. A low-income, unskilled worker, on the other hand, may spend sixty hours or more in physically exhausting or psychically stultifying work in order to have minimal food and shelter for the family. Under these conditions, the need for medical and legal services can present an insurmountable barrier, and neither time nor resources are available for educational or cultural experiences.

Since social honor is usually conferred on the wealthy, the economic aspects of class are also related to prestige. This is perhaps particularly true in the United States, which has had a long tradition of conferring prestige on the holders of wealth (Huber, 1971).

Occupation is, of course, closely related to income and wealth, but can be considered separately with respect to its particular effects upon power, privilege, and prestige. Power can be exercised through decision-making positions in occupations that promulgate policies affecting group interests. If a group has no individuals in higher level decision-making positions in various institutional spheres (such as education, law enforcement, or the judiciary), then its members can suffer various disadvantages because of a lack of knowledge or understanding regarding their particular problems, grievances, and subcultural patterns. Women, blacks, and other minorities, for example, have often been unfairly treated in educational and legal processes because they have lacked a voice in the policy and decision-making positions of these spheres of activity.

Different occupations entail different types of work-related privileges. Some occupations involve interesting work and a variety of self-actualizing experiences. Others involve the extreme of alienated labor, in which work is simply a means to an end and has no intrinsic satisfaction, as in the case of many automobile workers (Chinoy, 1965). The occupations of higher level white-collar workers are usually more desirable than those of most blue-collar workers. This is particularly true when unskilled segments of the labor force are compared with upper level white-collar positions.

The distribution of prestige in society is also related to occupation. Prestige is often conferred on the basis of occupational position. Generally, people in white-collar occupations and in occupations requiring extensive training have more prestige than people in blue-collar occupations and those requiring little training. Thus, the occupational characteristics of a given stratum affect the amount of prestige that will be bestowed on its members.

Education, the third component of social class, is also related to the ability to acquire power, privilege, and prestige. It is often a prerequisite to positions of power, especially to those in bureaucratic structures and in professional organizations. These positions, such as university president or director of a research laboratory, are invested with power and can also serve as a springboard to higher level positions, such as advisor to government officials or a place on corporate boards of directors. Education is also a prerequisite to many highly lucrative occupations. The income from such occupations allows an individual to purchase various privileges, such as the best medical care, a comfortable home, and a university education at elite schools for one's children. Education also confers basic knowledge and skills, such as those in writing and communication, which can be used in acquiring and maintaining privileges. The value of these skills is illustrated in a study by Fellman, Brandt, and Rosenblatt (1970). These authors document the inability of working-class persons to adequately deal with government officials planning to radically alter their neighborhood by highway construction. Education also confers prestige on individuals, particularly if one has advanced professional degrees. The prestige can then be converted, in some instances, into increased privilege and power.

CONCLUSIONS

This chapter has considered some of the major concepts and theories that form the basis for the systematic study of class stratification. The study of social stratification has been characterized by the differing perspectives of conflict and functional theories. The position taken in this volume is that both the conflict and functional approaches have value in the study of stratification. Although either theory in its extreme form tends to be one-sided and incomplete, both contain valid insights about social stratification. Both theoretical models provide guideposts to which actual societies or theories of stratification can be compared.

To the traditional conflict and functional approaches to the study of stratification was added the frame of reference provided by symbolic interactionist theory. This perspective is particularly applicable to certain problems in the field of stratification having to do with the relationships between individual psyche and behavior and social structure. Each of these three theories—conflict, functional, and symbolic interactionist—will be used as a frame of reference at different points throughout this book to interpret and deepen understanding of various topics. Each is regarded as making a unique contribution to the analysis of particular phenomena in social stratification.

The concepts of power, privilege, and prestige were identified as fundamental to the study of social stratification because they encompass the central concerns of this field of investigation. These three basic concepts also provide a fundamental orientation that encompasses the sometimes extreme divergences found in various approaches to the study of stratification. The concept of social class and the relationship between classes and power, privilege, and prestige was also considered.

In chapter 4, more specific topics of class stratification will be discussed. Methods used to measure social class will be considered, and data pertaining to the distribution of wealth, levels of education, and occupational characteristics of the population of the United States will be presented. To illustrate the characteristics of the major social classes and their impact on the life histories of individuals, some studies of class stratification will be briefly summarized.

REFERENCES

Bem, Sandra L. and Daryl J. Bem. 1972. "Homogenizing the American Woman: The Power of an Unconscious Ideology." Unpublished paper.

Bierstedt, Robert. 1950. "An Analysis of Social Power." *American Sociological Review* 15 (December): 730–738.

_____. (1974) *The Social Order*. New York: McGraw–Hill.

Blumer, Herbert. 1969. *Symbolic Interactionism*. Englewood Cliffs, N.J.: Prentice-Hall.

Buckley, Walter. 1958. "Social Stratification and the Functional Theory of Social Differentiation." *American Sociological Review* 23 (August): 369–375.

Chinoy, Ely. 1965. *Automobile Workers and the American Dream*. Boston: Beacon Press.

Collins, Randall. 1975. *Conflict Sociology*. New York: Academic Press.

Dahrendorf, Ralf. 1959. *Class and Class Conflict in Industrial Society*. Stanford, Calif.: Stanford University Press.

Davis, Kingsley and Wilbert E. Moore. 1945. "Some Principles of Stratification." *American Sociological Review* 10 (April): 242–249.

Domhoff, G. William. 1967. *Who Rules America*. Englewood Cliffs, N.J.: Prentice-Hall.

Duberman, Lucile. 1976. *Social Inequality*. Philadelphia: J. B. Lippincott.

Durkheim, Emile. 1960. *The Division of Labor in Society*. Glencoe, Ill.: The Free Press.

Feagin, Joe R. 1972. "God Helps Those Who Help Themselves." *Psychology Today* 6 (November): p. 101.

Fellman, Gordon, Barbara Brandt, and Roger Rosenblatt. 1970. "Dagger in the Heart of Town." *Trans-Action* 7 (September): 38–47.

Gerth, H. H. and C. Wright Mills. 1958. *From Max Weber*. New York: Oxford University Press.

Haer, John L. 1957. "Predictive Utility of Five Indices of Social Stratification." *American Sociological Review* 22 (October): 541–546.

Hatt, Paul K. and C. C. North. National Opinion Research Center. 1947. "Jobs and Occupations: A Popular Evaluation." *Opinion News* 9 (September): 3–13.

Hodge, Robert W., Paul M. Siegel and Peter H. Rossi. 1966. "Occupational Prestige in the United States: 1925-1963." In Reinhard Bendix and Seymour Martin Lipset (eds.) *Class, Status and Power*. New York: Free Press. Pp. 322–334.

Horton, John. 1966. "Order and Conflict Theories of Social Problems as Competing Ideologies." *American Journal of Sociology* 71 (May): 701–713.

Huber, Joan and William H. Form. 1973. *Income and Ideology*. New York: Free Press.

Huber, Richard M. 1971. *The American Idea of Success*. New York: McGraw-Hill.

Kornhauser, Ruth Rosner. 1953. "The Warner Approach to Social Stratification." In Reinhard Bendix and Seymour Martin Lipset (eds.) *Class, Status and Power*. Glencoe, Ill.: Free Press.

Lenski, Gerhard E. 1966. *Power and Privilege*. New York: McGraw-Hill.

——————. 1966. "The Dynamics of Distributive Systems." In Gerhard E. Lenski *Power and Privilege*. New York: McGraw-Hill.

Marx, Karl. 1956. *Selected Writings in Sociology and Social Philosophy*. J. B. Bottomore and Maximilien Rubel (eds.) New York: McGraw-Hill.

Marx, Karl and Friedrich Engels. 1959. *Basic Writings on Politics and Philosophy*. Lewis S. Feuer (ed.) New York: Doubleday.

Miller, Jon, Sanford Labovitz, and Lincoln Fry. 1975. "Differences in the Organizational Experiences of Men and Women: Resources, Vested Interests and Discrimination." *Social Forces* 54 (December): 365–381.

Mills, C. Wright. 1942. "The Social Life of a Modern Community." *American Sociological Review* 8 (April): 263–271.

——————. 1956. *White Collar*. New York: Oxford University Press.

——————. 1959. *The Power Elite*. New York: Oxford University Press.

——————. 1962. "Inventory of Ideas." In *The Marxists*. New York: Dell Publishing Company, pp. 81–95.

——————. 1963. "The Sociology of Stratification." In Irving Louis Horowitz (ed.) *Power, Politics and People*. New York: Ballantine Books. pp. 305–323.

Olsen, Marvin E. 1970. "Power Perspectives on Stratification and Race Relations." In Marvin E. Olsen (ed.) *Power in Societies*. New York: MacMillan. Pp. 296–304.

Ossowski, Stanislaw. 1963. *Class Structure in the Social Consciousness*. New York: Free Press.

Parsons, Talcott. 1953. "A Revised Analytical Approach to the Theory of Social Stratification." In Reinhard Bendix and Seymour Martin Lipset (eds.) *Class, Status and Power*. Glencoe, Ill.: The Free Press. Pp. 92–128.

Polatnick, Margaret. 1973–1974. "Why Men Don't Rear Children: A Power Analysis." *Berkeley Journal of Sociology* 18: 45–86.

Ritzer, George. 1975. *Sociology A Multiple Paradigm Science*. Boston: Allyn and Bacon.

Roach, Jack L., Llewellyn Gross, Orville Gursslin. 1969. *Social Stratification in the United States*. Englewood Cliffs, N.J.: Prentice-Hall.

Rose, Arnold M. 1962. "A Systematic Summary of Symbolic Interactionist Theory." In Arnold Rose (ed.) *Human Behavior and Social Processes*. Boston: Houghton Mifflin. Pp. 3–19.

Schuman, Howard. 1975. "Free Will and Determinism in Public Beliefs about Race." In Norman R. Yetman and C. Hoy Steele (eds.) *Majority and Minority*. Boston: Allyn and Bacon. Pp. 375–380.

Shibutani, Tamotsu. 1961. *Society and Personality*. Englewood Cliffs, N.J.: Prentice-Hall.

Shirer, William L. 1964. *The Rise and Fall of the Third Reich*. Greenwich, Conn.: Fawcett.

Sontag, Susan. 1972. "The Double Standard of Aging." *Saturday Review* (September): 119–126.

Sorokin, Pitirim A. 1959. *Social and Cultural Mobility*. Glencoe, Ill.: The Free Press.

––––––––––––. 1969. *Society Culture and Personality*. New York: Cooper Square.

––––––––––––. 1969. "Social Stratification." In Pitirim A. Sorokin *Society, Culture and Personality*. New York: Cooper Square Publishers. Pp. 256–295.

Spencer, Herbert. *On Social Evolution*. 1972. J. D. Y. Peel (ed.) Chicago: University of Chicago Press.

Stinchcombe, Arthur L. 1963. "Some Empirical Consequences of the Davis-Moore Theory of Stratification." *American Sociological Review* 28 (October): 805–808.

Thomas, William I. and Florian Znaniecki. 1958. *The Polish Peasant in Europe and America*. New York: Dover Publications.

Tumin, Melvin M. 1953. "Some Principles of Stratification: A Critical Analysis." *American Sociological Review* 18 (August): 387–397.

Turner, Jonathan H. 1978. *The Structure of Sociological Theory*. Homenwood, Ill.: Dorsey Press.

Turner, Ralph H. 1962. "Role-Taking: Process Versus Conformity." In Arnold Rose (ed.) *Human Behavior and Social Processes*. Boston: Houghton Mifflin. Pp. 20–40.

––––––––––––. 1976. "The Real Self: From Institution to Impulse." *American Journal of Sociology*. 81 (March): 989–1016.

Van den Berghe, Pierre. 1963. "Dialectic and Functionalism: Toward a Theoretical Synthesis." *American Sociological Review* 28 (October): 695–705.

Warner, W. Lloyd and Paul S. Lunt. 1941. *The Social Life of a Modern Community*. New Haven: Yale University Press.

Warner, W. Lloyd, Marchia Meeker, and Kenneth Eells. 1960. *Social Class in America*. New York: Harper and Brothers.

Warner, W. Lloyd, J. O. Low, Paul S. Lunt, Leo Srole. 1963. *Yankee City*. New Haven: Yale University Press.

Weber, Max. 1947. *The Theory of Social and Economic Organization*. Glencoe, Ill.: Free Press.

––––––––––––. 1958. "Class, Status and Party." In H. H. Gerth and C. Wright Mills *From Max Weber*. New York: Oxford University Press.

Wrong, Dennis H. 1959. "The Functional Theory of Stratification." *American Sociological Review* 24 (December): 772–782.

Inventory of Ideas

C. Wright Mills

THE DISTINCTIVE character of Marx's "scientific socialism," I think, lies in this: his images of the ideal society are connected with the actual workings of the society in which he lived. Out of his projections of the tendencies he discerns in society as it is actually developing he makes up his image of the future society (the post-capitalist society that he wants to come about). That is why he refuses, at least in his maturity, to *proclaim* ideals. Morally, of course, he condemns. Sociologically, he points to the results of that which he condemns. Politically, he directs attention to the agency of historical change—the proletariat—and he argues, with facts and figures, theories and slogans, that this developing connection between human agency and implicit goal is the most important trend in capitalist society. For by the development of this agency within it, capitalist society itself will be overthrown and socialism installed. The historical creation of the proletariat is the central thrust within the capitalist realm of necessity. That thrust is driving capitalism toward the revolutionary leap into the socialist epoch, into the realm of freedom.

This connection of ideal or goal with agency is at once a moral and an intellectual strategy. It sets Marx off from those he characterized as utopian socialists. This connection between built-in agency and socialist ideal is the political pivot around which turn the decisive features of his model of society and many specific theories of historical trend going on within it. It also provides a focus in social theory for the moral discontent registered in socialist aspirations; and on occasion, a new focus for liberal ideals as well. And it leads—as we shall presently see—to the direst ambiguities of marxian doctrine: this connection between ideal and agency has been at the bottom of the continual second thoughts, metaphysical squabbles, and major revisions by marxists who have come after Marx.

To explain the economic and psychological mechanics by which this built-in historical agency is developed, and how this development inevitably leads to the overthrow of capitalism—these are the organizing points of classic marxism. To explain delays in this development and find ways to facilitate and speed it up, or patiently to wait for it—these are the points from which subsequent varieties of marxism depart.

The remarkable coherence of Marx's system, the close correlation of its elements is in large measure a reflection of the consistency with which he holds in view the central thrust toward the development of the proletariat and its act of revolution. If we keep this in mind, we will not violate marxism as a whole. We must now attempt to set forth, for the moment without criticism, a brief inventory of the most important conceptions and propositions of classic marxism.[1]

1. The Economic Basis of a Society Determines Its Social Structure As a Whole, As Well As the Psychology of the People within It.

Political, religious, and legal institutions as well as the ideas, the images, the ideologies by

1. In this chapter, I do not quote Marx's phrases; the readings, I am hopeful, will have made these clear.

means of which men understand the world in which they live, their place within it, and themselves—all these are reflections of the economic basis of society.

This proposition rests upon the master distinction within Marx's materialist model of society: the economic base (variously referred to as the mode of economic production, the substructure, the economic foundation) is distinguished from the rest of the society (called the superstructure or institutional and ideological forms). In the economic base, Marx includes the forces and the relations of production. In capitalism the latter means essentially the institution of private property and the consequent class relations between those who do and those who do not own it. The forces of production, a more complex conception, include both material and social elements: (a) natural resources, such as land and minerals, so far as they are used as objects of labor; (b) physical equipment such as tools, machines, technology; (c) science and engineering, the skills of men who invent or improve this equipment; (d) those who do work with these skills and tools; (e) their division of labor, insofar as this social organization increases their productivity.

2.   The Dynamic of Historical Change Is the Conflict between the Forces of Production and the Relations of Production.

In earlier phases of capitalism, the relations of production facilitate the development of the forces of production. One cannot find a more handsome celebration of the work of capitalists in industrialization than in the pages of Marx's *Capital*. But in due course the capitalist organization of industry—the relations of production—come to fetter the forces of production; they come into objective contradiction with them. "Contradiction" I take to mean a problem that is inherent in and cannot be solved without modifying, or "moving beyond," the basic structure of the society in which it occurs. For Marx, "the basic structure" means the capitalist economy.

Continuous technological development and its full use for production conflicts with the interest of the property owners. The capitalists pro-

hibit the utilization of new inventions, buying them up to avoid the loss of their investment in existing facilities. They are interested in increased productivity and in technical progress only as profits can thereby be maintained or increased. Thus capital itself is "the real historical barrier of capital production."

3.   The Class Struggle between Owners and Workers Is a Social, Political and Psychological Reflection of Objective Economic Conflicts.

These conflicts lead to different reactions among the members of the different classes of bourgeois society. The "objective" contradiction within the capitalist economy, in brief, has its "subjective" counterpart in the class struggle within capitalist society. In this struggle the wage-workers represent the expanding forces of production and the owners represent the maintenance of the established relations of production (property relations mainly) and with them, the exploitation of the unpropertied class.

History is thus an objective sequence, a dialectic, a series of contradictions and of their resolutions. History is also a struggle between classes. These two ways of thinking are, within marxism, quite consistent. For Marx held that the revolution will result from the developing material forces of production as they come into conflict with the relations of production; this revolution will be realized by the struggle of the classes, a struggle caused by the objective, economic contradiction.

The point may be put more abstractly, in line with the "dialectical" method. In Marx's view, continual change—and change into its opposite—is inherent in all reality, and so in capitalist society. The dialectical method is a way of understanding the history of a social structure by examining its conflicts rather than its harmonies. In brief, and in ordinary language, the "laws of dialectics" are as follows: (a) if things change enough, they become different, qualitatively, from what they were to begin with; (b) one thing grows out of another and then comes into conflict with it; (c) history thus proceeds by a series of conflicts and resolutions rather than merely by minute and gradual changes.

4. Property As a Source of Income Is the Objective Criterion of Class; within Capitalism the Two Basic Classes Are the Owners and the Workers.

Marx left unfinished his categories of social stratification. A few definitions and remarks are available in *Capital* along with his class analysis of historical events and remarks made in his more abstracted model of capitalist society. From all these, his conceptions and theories appear to be as follows:

The basic criterion of class is the relation of men to the means of production, an objective criterion having primarily to do with economic and legal fact. Those who own the means of production are bourgeoisie, those whom they hire for wages are proletariat. So defined, these terms point to aggregates of people, not to social organizations or psychological matters.

In this objective sense, Marx writes in *The German Ideology,* "the class . . . achieves an independent existence over and against individuals, so that the latter find their condition of existence predestined and hence have their position in life and their personal development assigned to them by their class, become subsumed under it."

This statement can be made empirically, as Max Weber later did, in a way that does not violate Marx's meaning. The chances for an individual to achieve that which he values, and even the values themselves, are dependent upon the objective, economic class-position he occupies. At least for statistical aggregates, this is so, irrespective of any psychological opinions or attitudes.

5. Class Struggle Rather Than Harmony—"Natural" or Otherwise—Is the Normal and Inevitable Condition in Capitalist Society.

Marx's denial of any theory of natural harmony is an affirmation that in capitalist society

conflicts of interest are basic. By "basic" we are to understand: irremediable within the system: if one interest is fulfilled, the other cannot be. For Marx and for most marxists, the general and basic conflict of interest comes from the division between propertied and nonpropertied classes. Whether these classes are aware of it or not, there is an inevitable conflict of interest between them, defined by the relation of each to the means of production. A contradiction of their basic interests prevails.

6. Within Capitalist Society, the Workers Cannot Escape Their Exploited Conditions and Their Revolutionary Destiny by Winning Legal or Political Rights and Privileges; Unions and Mass Labor Parties Are Useful As Training Grounds for Revolution, but Are Not a Guarantee of Socialism.

Middle-class democracy is always and necessarily based upon economic inequalities and exploitation. Hence Marx continually warns against reformist illusions, and exposes them by reference to the objective contradiction between productive forces and productive relations. There is only one way out: the wageworkers must themselves, by their successful struggle as a propertyless class against the property-owning class, resolve the objective contradiction. They themselves must liberate the constructive forces of production by overturning the entire superstructure that is rooted in the capitalist relations of production. The productive forces, now fettered by capitalist rigidity, will then go forward at an enormously accelerated rate of progress.

7. Exploitation Is Built into Capitalism As an Economic System, Thus Increasing the Chances for Revolution.

Whatever his wages may be, under capitalism the worker is economically exploited. That is the practical meaning of Marx's doctrine of "surplus value." Only human labor, for Marx, can create value. But by the application of his labor power, the worker produces a greater value than he is paid for by the capitalist for whom he works. The "surplus value" thus created is appropriated by the capitalist class, and so the worker under capitalism is exploited.

8. The Class Structure Becomes More and More Polarized, Thus Increasing the Chance for Revolution.

The composition of capitalist society will undergo these changes: (a) the bourgeoisie or middle class will decrease in numbers; (b) the wageworkers will increase in numbers; (c) all other "intermediary classes" will fade out of the political picture, as the society is polarized between bourgeoisie and proletariat. In general, by "intermediary" classes Marx means the petty bourgeoisie, those of small property; and not white collar employees.

9. The Material Misery of the Workers Will Increase, As Will Their Alienation.

The increasing misery of the wageworkers refers not only to the physical misery of their life conditions but also to the psychological deprivation arising from their alienation. It is essential to keep these separate, and to remember that for Marx the latter seemed the more important, that alienation could exist and deepen even if material standards of living were improved. However, he expected that the workers will increasingly suffer in both respects, although many latter-day marxists stress the psychological deprivation, the alienation of men at work.

It is to misunderstand Marx, I believe, to equate alienation with whatever is measured as "work dissatisfaction" by industrial psychologists in the USA today. Behind Marx's difficult conception of alienation there is the ideal of the human meaning he believes work ought to have and which he believes it will come to have in a socialist society.

According to Marx, wage work under capitalism is an activity by which men acquire the things they need. It is an activity undertaken for ulterior ends and not in itself a satisfying activity. Men are alienated from the process of their work itself, it is external to them, imposed by social conditions. It is not a source of self-fulfillment but rather a miserable denial of self. They do not "develop freely" their physical and mental energies by their work, but exhaust themselves physically and debase themselves mentally.

Moreover, in work the laborer gives over to the owner the control of his activity: "It is not his work, but work for someone else . . . in work he does not belong to himself but to another person." At work, men are homeless; only during leisure do they feel at home.

Finally, work results in the creation of private property; the product of the work belongs to another. The worker empties himself into this product; the more he works the greater his product, but it is not his. Private property, accordingly, causes him to be alienated. Thus the alienation of labor and the system of private property are reciprocal.

Alienation, working together with economic exploitation, leads to increasing misery—and so in due course, to the formation of the proletariat as a class-for-itself.

10. The Wageworkers—a Class-in-itself—Will Be Transformed into the Proletariat, a Class-for-itself.

The first phase—a class-in-itself—refers to the objective fact of the class as an aggregate, defined by its position in the economy.

The second—a class-for-itself—refers to the members of this class when they have become aware of their identity as a class, aware of their common situation, and of their role in changing or in preserving capitalist society. Such class consciousness is not included in the objective definition of the term "class"; it is an expectation, not a definition. It is something that, according to Marx, is going to develop among the members of the classes. How it will develop he does not make as clear as why it will, for according to his analysis of their condition, as the interests of the two classes are in objective and irremediable conflict, their members will eventually become aware of their special interests and will pursue them.

Ideas and ideology are determined (as stated in proposition 1) by the economic bases of a society. The class consciousness of the proletariat will follow this rule. The ideas men come to have are generally determined by the stage of history in which they live, and by the class position they occupy within it. There is not, however, a universal and certainly not an immediate one-to-one correlation. The ideas of the ruling class in a given society are generally the ruling ideas of that epoch. Men who are not in this ruling class but who accept its definitions of reality and of their own interests are "falsely conscious." But in due course, true class consciousness will be realized among the proletariat.

The workers will become increasingly class conscious and increasingly international in their outlook. These economic and psychological developments occur as a result of the institutional and technical development of capitalism itself. In this process, the proletariat will abandon nationalist allegiances and take up loyalties to their own class, regardless of nationality. Like the relations of production, nationalism fetters their true interest which is to release the forces of production.

11. The Opportunity for Revolution Exists Only When Objective Conditions and Subjective Readiness Coincide.

Neither the objective conditions for successful revolution nor revolutionary urges within the proletariat, in Marx's view, continuously increase. Both ebb and flow with the developing of objective conditions and the resulting political and psychological ones. Sometimes Marx emphasizes the subjective factor of revolutionary class war, sometimes the underlying objective developments. Thus in 1850:

"Under the conditions of this general prosperity, when the productive forces of bourgeois society develop as abundantly as is at all possible within the existing bourgeois conditions, there can be no question of a real revolution. Such a revolution is only possible in those periods when the two factors, the modern productive forces and the bourgeois forms of production, come to contradict one another."

The proletariat must do the job by its own revolutionary action as a proletariat, but can succeed only under the correct objective conditions. Sooner or later, the will and the conditions will coincide. Many trends, already indicated, facilitate this. In addition, another rule points toward the proletarian revolution:

12. The Functional Indispensability of a Class in the Economic System Leads to Its Political Supremacy in the Society As a Whole.

This unstated premise of Marx is the underlying assumption, I believe, of the marxist theory of power. On this premise the capitalists have replaced the nobles, and capitalism has succeeded feudalism. In a similar manner, reasoned Marx, the proletariat will replace the bourgeoisie, and socialism replace capitalism. Old rulers who were once functionally indispensable are so no longer. In the course of capitalist development the bourgeoisie, like the feudal nobles before them, have become parasitical. They cannot help this. It is their destiny. And so they are doomed.

13. In All Class Societies the State Is the Coercive Instrument of the Owning Classes.

This of course follows from the theory of power, just stated; and from the conception of the superstructure as economically determined. The state is seen as an instrument of one class and, in advanced capitalism, of a class that is in economic decline. The class of which the state is the coercive instrument is no longer economically progressive, no longer functionally indispensable, and yet it still holds power. It must, therefore, act increasingly by coercion.

14. Capitalism Is Involved in One Economic Crisis After Another. These Crises Are Getting Worse. So Capitalism Moves into Its Final Crisis—and the Revolution of the Proletariat.

As the proletariat are subjectively readied, the objective mechanics of capitalism moves the system into increasingly severe crises. The economic contradictions that beset it insure increasing crisis. This cannot be halted until the base of capitalism is abolished, for crisis is inherent in the nature of this system.

15. The Post-Capitalist Society Will First Pass Through a Transitional Stage—That of the Dictatorship of the Proletariat; Then It Will Move into a Higher Phase in Which True Communism Will Prevail.

No one, Marx held, can say exactly what the nature of post-capitalist society will be. Only utopians and dreamers draw up detailed blueprints of the future. Just as he does not like to proclaim ideals, so Marx dislikes to go into explicit detail about the future. Either kind of discussion seems to him "idealistic" in the sense of "irrelevant" or "unrealistic." Nonetheless it is possible to find in the relevant texts, mainly his *Critique of the Gotha Program*, Marx's image of the future society:

The transitional stage may be equated with the revolution. The appropriating class will itself be expropriated, the owners' state will be broken up, the productive facilities transferred to society in order to permit a rational planning of the economy. In this first stage, society will be administered and defended against its enemies by a dictatorship of the revolutionary proletariat. This will probably be something like what he supposed the Paris Commune of 1871 to have been. Still "stamped with the birth-marks of the old society, the newborn society will be limited in many ways by inheritances from the old, capitalist society."

But history will not end there. A higher phase—that of communism—will develop; it will be characterized, first, by the fact that the proletariat as a revolutionary class (not just an aggregate of wageworkers) will form "the immense majority" of the population. The proletariat will be the nation; and so in the nation there will be no class distinctions and no class struggle. More than that, specialization of labor itself, as known under capitalism, with all its deformation of men, will not exist. The inherited opposition of manual and mental labor, the conflict between town and country, will disappear.

Second, the state will wither away, for the only function of the state is to hold down the exploited class. Since the proletariat will be virtually the total population, and thus cease to be a proletariat, they will need no state. Anarchy of production will be replaced by rational and systematic planning of the whole. Only in its second phase, when it has eliminated the remaining vestiges of capitalism and developed its own economic base, will society proceed on principles quite distinct from those of capitalism. Only then will men cease to govern men. Man will administer things. Public authority will replace state power. Only then will the ruling principle of communist society be: "From each according to his abilities, to each according to his needs."

16. Although Men Make Their Own History, Given the Circumstances of the Economic Foundation, the Way They Make It and the Direction It Takes Are Determined. The Course of History Is Structurally Limited to the Point of Being Inevitable.

I have noted that in Marx's historical model of society the agency of change is intrinsically connected with socialist ideals. His major propositions and expectations have to do with the development of its historic agency, and with the revolutionary results of that development. Two general questions of interpretation arise when we confront this central view: (a) In general, does Marx believe in historical inevitability? (b) In connection with the mechanics of the central thrust, does he hold that the economic factor is the determining factor in capital society? These questions have been much argued over, as well they might be; for later marxists, notably Lenin, they have been of leading political urgency. Major party strategy has been debated in terms of different answers to them.

My answer to both questions is Yes. Classic marxism contains only one general theory of how men make history. Only in such terms as it provides do all the specific conceptions and theories of Marx make sense. That theory of history-making, very briefly, is as follows:

". . . each person follows his own consciously desired end, and it is precisely the resultant of these many wills operating in different directions and of their manifold effects upon the outer world that constitute history . . . the many individual wills active in history for the most part produce results quite other than those they intended—often quite the opposite: their motives [of individuals] therefore in relation to the total result are likewise only of secondary significance. On the other hand, the further question arises: what driving forces in turn stand behind these motives? What are the historical causes which translate themselves into these motives in the brains of these actors?"[2]

In the historical development of marxism, as we shall later see, there is always the tension between history as inevitable and history as made by the wills of men. It will not do, I think, to lessen that tension by "re-interpreting" or "explaining" what Marx plainly wrote on the theme. Politicians who must justify decisions by reference to founding doctrine may need to do that. We do not. It is better to try to keep the record straight, and to designate departures from classic marxism as departures.

Aside from the documentary evidence, I believe that Marx is a determinist for the following reasons:

(a) The question of the historical agency is clearly bound up with the problem of historical inevitability and with the ideal of socialism. However ambiguous assorted quotations may make the point seem, classic marxism does differ from utopian socialism and from liberalism precisely on this point. It may be that in arguing against utopian socialism and against liberalism Marx stresses the idea of inevitability. Be that as it may,

I am less concerned with *why* he held this view than with the fact that he did.

(b) Marx's refusal to preach ideals and his reluctance to discuss the society of the future makes no sense otherwise. Because he did believe in the historical inevitability, as he saw it, he can treat socialism not as an ideal, a program, a choice of means, or as a matter of or for political decision. He can treat it as a matter for scientific investigation.

(c) He did not try to persuade men of any new moral goals, because he believed that the proletariat would inevitably come to them. "In the last analysis," social existence determines consciousness. Historical developments will implant these goals into the consciousness of men, and men will then act upon them. The individual has little choice. If his consciousness is not altogether determined, his choice is severely limited and pressed upon him by virtue of his class position and all the influences and limitations to which this leads.

(d) Historically, the idea of Progress has been fully incorporated into the very ethos of marxism. Marx re-seats this idea—in the development of the proletariat. This becomes the gauge for moral judgments of progress and retrogression. Generally in his temper and in his theories of the master trends of capitalism in decline Marx is quite optimistic.[3]

17. The Social Structure, As Noted in Proposition Number 1, Is Determined by Its Economic Foundations; Accordingly, the Course of Its History Is Determined by Changes in These Economic Foundations.

I have held this point until the end, because it is a point of great controversy. There is a tendency among some marxists to attempt to "defend" Marx's economic determinism by

---

2. F. Engels, *Ludwig Feuerbach* (New York, 1935), pp. 58–59.

3. Despite its earlier notions of progress, liberalism is no longer congenial to ideas of historical inevitability. Such notions collide too obviously with its basic principle of liberty for the individual and the celebration of voluntary associations. Later liberals—at least its more knowledgeable spokesmen—tend to be rather pessimistic about the idea of progress itself; later marxists do not.

qualifying it. They do this in the manner of Engels' later remarks (made in letters) about the interplay of various factors, or by opposing to it a vague sociological pluralism, by which everything interacts with everything and no causal sequence is ever quite determinable. Neither line of argument, even when put in the abstruse terms of "dialectical materialism," seems very convincing or helpful. Moreover, to dilute the theory in these ways is to transform it from a definite theory, which may or may not be adequate, into equivocation, a mere indication of a problem.

Marx stated clearly the doctrine of economic determinism. It is reflected in his choice of vocabulary; it is assumed by, and fits into, his work as a whole—in particular his theory of power, his conception of the state, his rather simple notions of class and his use of these notions (including the proletariat as the agency of history-making). We may of course assume with Engels that he allows a degree of free-play among the several factors that interact, and also that he provides a flexible time-schedule in which economic causes do their work. But in the end—and usually the end is not so very far off—economic causes are "the basic," the ultimate, the general, the innovative causes of historical change.

To Marx "economic determinism" does *not* mean that the desire for money or the pursuit of wealth, or calculation of economic gain is the master force of biography or of history. In fact, it does not pertain directly to *motives* of any sort. It has to do with the social—the class—context under which motives themselves arise and function in biography and in history. The *causes* of which Marx writes are causes that lie behind the motives which propel men to act. We must understand this in the terms of his model of history-making: "Marx examines the causal nature of the resultants of individual wills, without examining the latter in themselves; he investigates the laws underlying *social* phenomena, paying no attention to their relation with the phenomena of the individual consciousness."[4]

Such are the bare outlines of classic marxism. In summary, it consists of a model of

maturing capitalist society and of theories about the way this society and the men within it are changing. In this society, the productive facilities are owned privately and used to make private profit; the rest of the population works for wages given by those who own. It is a society that is changing because its forces of production come into increasing conflict with the organization of its economy by the owners and by their state.

At bottom, developments of its economic basis—in particular its economic contradictions—are making for changes in all its institutions and ideologies. Increasingly resulting in crisis, increasingly deepening the exploitation of men by men, these contradictions are causing the development of the historical agency which upon maturity is destined to overturn capitalism itself. That agency is the proletariat, a class which within capitalism is being transformed from a mere aggregate of wageworkers into a unified and conscious class-for-itself, aware of its common interests, and alert to the revolutionary way of realizing them.

The objective or institutional conflicts are a fact of capitalist life, but may not yet be reflected fully as the class struggle of owners and workers. Now a minority, concerned only with their immediate interests, the workers are growing more and more exploited, more alienated, more miserable, and more organized; in their ranks what men are interested in is coming to coincide with what is to men's interest; and the workers are becoming more numerous. They are coming to be "the self-conscious independent movement of the immense majority" in pursuit of their real and long-run interests. They are coming to true self-consciousness because self-consciousness itself is being changed by the relations of production men enter into independent of their will. And having become self-conscious, they cannot pursue their interests, they cannot raise themselves up, "without the whole super-incumbent strata of official society being sprung into the air."[5]

That is why when the time is ripe, when capitalism is mature and the proletariat ready, the revolution of the proletariat by the most politically alert sector of the proletariat is going to occur. Then bourgeois institutions and all their

4. Nikolai Bukharin, *Economic Theory of the Leisure Class* (New York, 1927), p. 40.

5. Löwith, *op. cit.*, p. 41.

works will be smashed. In turn, the post-capitalist society of socialism will evolve into the communist realm of freedom.

Comprehending every feature of man's activities, human and inhuman, Marx's conception is bitterly filled with sheer intellect and with brilliant leaps of the mind; it is at once analysis, prophecy, orientation, history, program. It is "the most formidable, sustained and elaborate indictment ever delivered against an entire social order, against its rulers, its supporters, its ideologists, its willing slaves, against all whose lives are bound up with its survival."[6]

No sooner were its outlines stated than it began to be revised by other men who were caught up in the torment of history-making. Then the intellectual beauty of its structure, the political passion of its central thrust began to be blunted by the will of political actors and the recalcitrance of historical events.

6. Isaiah Berlin, *Karl Marx* (New York, 1959), p. 21.

Class, Status, Party

Max Weber

ECONOMICALLY DETERMINED *Power and the Social Order.* Law exists when there is a probability that an order will be upheld by a specific staff of men who will use physical or psychical compulsion with the intention of obtaining conformity with the order, or of inflicting sanctions for infringement of it. The structure of every legal order directly influences the distribution of power, economic or otherwise, within its respective community. This is true of all legal orders and not only that of the state. In general, we understand by "power" the chance of a man or of a number of men to realize their own will in a communal action even against the resistance of others who are participating in the action.

"Economically conditioned" power is not, of course, identical with "power" as such. On the contrary, the emergence of economic power may be the consequence of power existing on other grounds. Man does not strive for power only in order to enrich himself economically. Power, including economic power, may be valued "for its own sake." Very frequently the striving for power is also conditioned by the social "honor" it entails. Not all power, however, entails social honor: The typical American Boss, as well as the typical big speculator, deliberately relinquishes social honor. Quite generally, "mere economic" power, and especially "naked" money power, is by no means a recognized basis of social honor. Nor is power the only basis of social honor. Indeed, social honor, or prestige, may even be the basis of political or economic power, and very frequently has been. Power, as well as honor, may be guaranteed by the legal order, but, at least normally, it is not their primary source. The legal order is rather an additional factor that enhances the chance to hold power or honor; but it cannot always secure them.

The way in which social honor is distributed in a community between typical groups participating in this distribution we may call the "social order." The social order and the economic order are, of course, similarly related to the "legal order." However, the social and the economic order are not identical. The economic order is for us merely the way in which economic goods and services are distributed and used. The social order is of course conditioned by the economic order to a high degree, and in its turn reacts upon it.

Now: "classes," "status groups," and "parties" are phenomena of the distribution of power within a community.

Determination of Class-Situation by Market-Situation. In our terminology, "classes" are not communities; they merely represent possible, and frequent, bases for communal action. We may speak of a "class" when (1) a number of people have in common a specific causal component of their life chances, in so far as (2) this component is represented exclusively by economic interests in the possession of goods and opportunities for income, and (3) is represented under the conditions of the commodity or labor markets. [These points refer to "class situation," which we may express more briefly as the typical chance for a supply of goods, external living conditions, and personal life experiences, in so far as this chance is determined by the amount and kind of power, or lack of such, to dispose of goods or skills for the sake of income in a given economic order. The term "class" refers to any group of people that is found in the same class situation.]

It is the most elemental economic fact that the way in which the disposition over material property is distributed among a plurality of people, meeting competitively in the market for the purpose of exchange, in itself creates specific life chances. According to the law of marginal utility this mode of distribution excludes the non-owners from competing for highly valued goods; it favors the owners and, in fact, gives to them a monopoly to acquire such goods. Other things being equal, this mode of distribution monopolizes the opportunities for profitable deals for all those who, provided with goods, do not necessarily have to exchange them. It increases, at least generally, their power in price wars with those who, being propertyless, have nothing to offer but their services in native form or goods in a form constituted through their own labor, and who above all are compelled to get rid of these products in order barely to subsist. This mode of distribution gives to the propertied a monopoly on the possibility of transferring property from the sphere of use as a "fortune," to the sphere of "capital goods"; that is, it gives them the entrepreneurial function and all chances to share directly or indirectly in returns on capital. All this holds true within the area in which pure market conditions prevail. "Property" and "lack of property" are, therefore, the basic categories of all class situations. It does not matter whether these two categories become effective in price wars or in competitive struggles.

Within these categories, however, class situations are further differentiated: on the one hand, according to the kind of property that is usable for returns; and, on the other hand, according to the kind of services that can be offered in the market. Ownership of domestic buildings; productive establishments; warehouses; stores; agriculturally usable land, large and small holdings—quantitative differences with possibly qualitative consequences—; ownership of mines; cattle; men (slaves); disposition over mobile instruments of production, or capital goods of all sorts, especially money or objects that can be exchanged for money easily and at any time; disposition over products of one's own labor or of others' labor differing according to their various distances from consumability; disposition over transferable monopolies of any kind—all these distinctions differentiate the class situations of the propertied just as does the "meaning" which they can and do give to the utilization of property, especially to property which has money equivalence. Accordingly, the propertied, for instance, may belong to the class of rentiers or to the class of entrepreneurs.

Those who have no property but who offer services are differentiated just as much according to their kinds of services as according to the way in which they make use of these services, in a continuous or discontinuous relation to a recipient. But always this is the generic connotation of the concept of class: that the kind of chance in the *market* is the decisive moment which presents a common condition for the individual's fate. "Class situation" is, in this sense, ultimately "market situation." The effect of naked possession *per se,* which among cattle breeders gives the nonowning slave or serf into the power of the cattle owner, is only a forerunner of real "class" formation. However, in the cattle loan and in the naked severity of the law of debts in such communities, for the first time mere "possession" as such emerges as decisive for the fate of the individual. This is very much in contrast to the agricultural communities based on labor. The creditor-debtor relation becomes the basis of "class situations" only in those cities where a "credit market," however primitive, with rates of interest increasing according to the extent of dearth and a factual monopolization of credits, is developed by a plutocracy. Therewith "class struggles" begin.

Those men whose fate is not determined by the chance of using goods or services for themselves on the market, e.g. slaves, are not, however, a "class" in the technical sense of the term. They are, rather, a "status group."

Communal Action Flowing from Class Interest. According to our terminology, the factor that creates "class" is unambiguously economic interest, and indeed, only those interests involved in the existence of the "market." Nevertheless, the concept of "class-interest" is an ambiguous one: even as an empirical concept it is ambiguous as soon as one understands by it something other than the factual direction of interests following with a certain probability from the class situation for a certain "average" of those people subjected to the class situation. The class situation and other circumstances remaining the same, the direction in which the individual worker, for instance, is likely to pursue his interests may vary widely, according to whether he is constitutionally qualified for the task at hand to a high, to an average, or to a low degree. In the same way, the direction of interests may vary according to whether or not a *communal* action of a larger or smaller portion of those commonly affected by the "class situation," or even an association among them, e.g. a "trade union," has grown out of the class situation from which the individual may or may not expect promising results. [Communal action refers to that action which is oriented to the feeling of the actors that they belong together. Societal action, on the other hand, is oriented to a rationally motivated adjustment of interests.] The rise of societal or even of communal action from a common class situation is by no means a universal phenomenon.

The class situation may be restricted in its effects to the generation of essentially *similar* reactions, that is to say, within our terminology, of "mass actions." However, it may not have even this result. Furthermore, often merely an amorphous communal action emerges. For example, the "murmuring" of the workers known in ancient oriental ethics: the moral disapproval of the work-master's conduct, which in its practical significance was probably equivalent to an increasingly typical phenomenon of precisely the latest industrial development, namely, the "slow down" (the deliberate limiting of work effort) of laborers by virtue of tacit agreement. The degree in which "communal action," and possibly "societal action," emerges from the "mass actions" of the members of a class is linked to general cultural conditions, especially to those of an intellectual sort. It is also linked to the extent of the contrasts that have already evolved, and is especially linked to the *transparency* of the connections between the causes and the consequences of the "class situation." For however different life chances may be, this fact in itself, according to all experience, by no means gives birth to "class action" (communal action by the members of a class). The fact of being conditioned and the results of the class situation must be distinctly recognizable. For only then the contrast of life chances can be felt not as an absolutely given fact to be accepted, but as a resultant from either (1) the given distribution of property, or (2) the structure of the concrete economic order. It is only then that people may react against the class structure not only through acts of an intermittent and irrational protest, but in the form of rational association. There have been "class situations" of the first category (1), of a specifically naked and transparent sort, in the urban centers of Antiquity and during the Middle Ages; especially then, when great fortunes were accumulated by factually monopolized trading in industrial products of these localities or in foodstuffs. Furthermore, under certain circumstances, in the rural economy of the most diverse periods, when agriculture was increasingly exploited in a profit-making manner. The most important historical example of the second category (2) is the class situation of the modern "proletariat."

Types of "Class Struggle." Thus every class may be the carrier of any one of the possibly innumerable forms of "class action," but this is not necessarily so. In any case, a class does not in itself constitute a community. To treat "class" conceptually as having the same value as "community" leads to distortion. That men in the same class situation regularly react in mass actions to such tangible situations as economic ones in the direction of those interests that are most adequate to their average number is an important and after all simple fact for the understanding of historical events. Above all, this fact must not lead to that kind of pseudo-scientific operation with the concepts of "class" and "class interests" so frequently found these days, and which has found its most classic expression in the statement of a talented author, that the individual may be in error concerning his interests but that the "class" is "infallible" about its interests. Yet, if classes as such are not communities, nevertheless class situations emerge only on the basis of communalization. The communal action that brings forth class situations, however, is not basically action between members of the identical class; it is an action between members of different classes. Communal actions that directly determine the class situation of the worker and the entrepreneur are: the labor market, the commodities market, and the capitalistic enterprise. But, in its turn, the existence of a capitalistic enterprise presupposes that a very specific communal action exists and that it is specifically structured to protect the possession of goods *per se,* and especially the power of individuals to dispose, in principle freely, over the means of production. The existence of a capitalistic enterprise is preconditioned by a specific kind of "legal order." Each kind of class situation, and above all when it rests upon the power of property *per se,* will become most clearly efficacious when all other determinants of reciprocal relations are, as far as possible, eliminated in their significance. It is in this way that the utilization of the power of property in the market obtains its most sovereign importance.

Now "status groups" hinder the strict carrying through of the sheer market principle. In the present context they are of interest to us only from this one point of view. Before we briefly consider them, note that not much of a general nature can be said about the more specific kinds of antagonism between "classes" (in our meaning of the term). The great shift, which has been going on continuously in the past, and up to our times, may be summarized, although at the cost of some precision: the struggle in which class situations are effective has progressively shifted from consumption credit toward, first, competitive struggles in the commodity market and, then, toward price wars on the labor market. The "class struggles" of antiquity—to the extent that they were genuine class struggles and not struggles between status groups—were initially carried on by indebted peasants, and perhaps also by artisans threatened by debt bondage and struggling against urban creditors. For debt bondage is the normal result of the differentiation of wealth in commercial cities, especially in seaport cities. A similar situation has existed among cattle breeders. Debt relationships as such produced class action up to the time of Cataline. Along with this, and with an increase in provision of grain for the city by transporting it from the outside, the struggle over the means of sustenance emerged. It centered in the first place around the provision of bread and the determination of the price of bread. It lasted throughout antiquity and the entire Middle Ages. The propertyless as such flocked together against those who actually and supposedly were interested in the dearth of bread. This fight spread until it involved all those commodities essential to the way of life and to handicraft production. There were only incipient discussions of wage disputes in antiquity and in the Middle Ages. But they have been slowly increasing up into modern times. In the earlier periods they were completely secondary to slave rebellions as well as to fights in the commodity market.

The propertyless of antiquity and of the Middle Ages protested against monopolies, preemption, forestalling, and the withholding of goods from the market in order to raise prices. Today the central issue is the determination of the price of labor.

This transition is represented by the fight for access to the market and for the determination of the price of products. Such fights went on between merchants and workers in the putting-out system of domestic handicraft during the transition to modern times. Since it is quite a general phenomenon we must mention here that the class antagonisms that are conditioned through the market situation are usually most bitter between those who actually and directly participate as opponents in price wars. It is not the rentier, the share-holder, and the banker who suffer the ill will of the worker, but almost exclusively the manufacturer and the business executives who are the direct opponents of workers in price wars. This is so in spite of the fact that it is precisely the cash boxes of the rentier, the share-holder, and the banker into which the more or less "unearned" gains flow, rather than into the pockets of the manufacturers or of the business executives. This simple state of affairs has very frequently been decisive for the role the class situation has played in the formation of political parties. For example, it has made possible the varieties of patriarchal socialism and the frequent attempts—formerly, at least—of threatened status groups to form alliances with the proletariat against the "bourgeoisie."

Status Honor.   In contrast to classes, *status groups* are normally communities. They are, however, often of an amorphous kind. In contrast to the purely economically determined "class situation" we wish to designate as "status situation" every typical component of the life fate of men that is determined by a specific, positive or negative, social estimation of *honor.* This honor may be connected with any quality shared by a plurality, and of course, it can be knit to a class situation: class distinctions are linked in the most varied ways with status distinctions. Property as such is not always recognized as a status qualification, but in the long run it is, and with extraordinary regularity. In the subsistence economy of the organized neighborhood, very often the richest man is simply the chieftain. However, this often means only an honorific preference. For example, in the so-called pure modern " democracy," that is, one devoid of any expressly ordered status privileges for individuals, it may be that only the families coming under approximately the same tax class dance with one another. This example is reported of certain smaller Swiss cities. But status honor need not necessarily be linked with "class situation." On the contrary, it normally stands in sharp opposition to the pretensions of sheer property.

Both propertied and propertyless people can belong to the same status group, and frequently they do with very tangible consequences. This "equality" of social esteem may, however, in the long run become quite precarious. The "equality" of status among the American "gentlemen," for instance, is expressed by the fact that outside the subordination determined by the different functions of "business," it would be considered strictly repugnant—wherever the old tradition still prevails—if even the richest "chief," while playing billiards or cards in his club in the evening, would not treat his "clerk" as in every sense fully his equal in birthright. It would be repugnant if the American "chief" would bestow upon his "clerk" the condescending "benevolence" marking a distinction of "position," which the German chief can never dissever from his attitude. This is one of the most important reasons why in America the German "clubbyness" has never been able to attain the attraction that the American clubs have.

Guarantees of Status Stratification.   In content, status honor is normally expressed by the fact that above all else a specific *style of life* can be expected from all those who wish to belong to the circle. Linked with this expectation are restrictions on "social" intercourse (that is, intercourse which is not subservient to economic or any other of business's "functional" purposes). These restrictions may confine normal marriages to within the status circle and may lead to complete endogamous closure. As soon as there is not a mere individual and socially irrelevant imitation of another style of life, but an agreed-upon communal action of this closing character, the "status" development is under way.

In its characteristic form, stratification by "status groups" on the basis of conventional styles of life evolves at the present time in the United States out of the traditional democracy. For example, only the resident of a certain street ("the street") is considered as belonging to "society," is qualified for social intercourse, and is visited and invited. Above all, this differentiation evolves in such a way as to make for strict submission to the fashion that is dominant at a given time in society. This submission to fashion also exists among men in America to a degree unknown in Germany. Such submission is considered to be an indication of the fact that a given man *pretends* to qualify as a gentleman. This submission decides, at least *prima facie,* that he will be treated as such. And this recognition becomes just as important for his employment chances in "swank" establishments, and above all, for social intercourse and marriage with "esteemed" families, as the qualification for dueling among Germans in the Kaiser's day. As for the rest: certain families resident for a long time, and, or course, correspondingly wealthy, e.g. "F.F.V., i.e. First Families of Virginia," or the actual or alleged descendants of the "Indian Princess" Pocahontas, of the Pilgrim fathers, or of the Knickerbockers, the members of almost inaccessible sects and all sorts of circles setting themselves apart by means of any other characteristics and badges . . . all these elements usurp "status" honor. The development of status is essentially a question of stratification resting upon usurpation. Such usurpation is the normal origin of almost all status honor. But the road from this purely conventional situation to legal privilege, positive or negative, is easily traveled as soon as a certain stratification of the social order has in fact been "lived in" and has achieved stability by virtue of a stable distribution of economic power.

"Ethnic" Segregation and "Caste."
Where the consequences have been realized to their full extent, the status group evolves into a closed "caste." Status distinctions are then guaranteed not merely by conventions and laws, but also by *rituals*. This occurs in such a way that every physical contact with a member of any caste that is considered to be "lower" by the members of a "higher" caste is considered as making for a ritualistic impurity and to be a stigma which must be expiated by a religious act. Individual castes develop quite distinct cults and gods.

In general however, the status structure reaches such extreme consequences only where there are underlying differences which are held to be "ethnic." The "caste" is, indeed, the normal form in which ethnic communities usually live side by side in a "societalized" manner. These ethnic communities believe in blood relationship and exclude exogamous marriage and social intercourse. Such a caste situation is part of the phenomenon of "pariah" peoples and is found all over the world. These people form communities, acquire specific occupational traditions of handicrafts or of other arts, and cultivate a belief in their ethnic community. They live in a "diaspora" strictly segregated from all personal intercourse, except that of an unavoidable sort, and their situation is legally precarious. Yet, by virtue of their economic indispensability, they are tolerated, indeed, frequently privileged, and they live in interspersed political communities. The Jews are the most impressive historical example.

A "status" segregation grown into a "caste" differs in its structure from a mere "ethnic" segregation: the caste structure transforms the horizontal and unconnected coexistences of ethnically segregated groups into a vertical social system of super- and subordination. Correctly formulated: a comprehensive societalization integrates the ethnically divided communities into specific political and communal action. In their consequences they differ precisely in this way: ethnic coexistences condition a mutual repulsion and disdain but allow each ethnic community to consider its own honor as the highest one; the caste structure brings about a social subordination and an acknowledgment of "more honor" in favor of the privileged caste and status groups. This is due to the fact that in the caste structure ethnic distinctions as such have become "functional" distinctions within the political societalization (warriors, priests, artisans that are politically important for war and for building, and so on). But even pariah people who are most despised are usually apt to continue cultivating in some manner that which is equally peculiar to ethnic and to status communities: the belief in their own specific "honor." This is the case with the Jews.

Only with the negatively privileged status groups does the "sense of dignity" take a specific deviation. A sense of dignity is the precipitation in individuals of social honor and of conventional demands which a positively privileged status group raises for the deportment of its members. The sense of dignity that characterizes positively privileged status groups is naturally related to their "being" which does not transcend itself, that is, it is to their "beauty and excellence." Their kingdom is "of this world." They live for the present and by exploiting their great past. The sense of dignity of the negatively privileged strata naturally refers to a future lying beyond the present, whether it is of this life or of another. In other words, it must be nurtured by the belief in a providential "mission" and by a belief in a specific honor before God. The "chosen people's" dignity is nurtured by a belief either that in the beyond "the last will be the first," or that in this life a Messiah will appear to bring forth into the light of the world which has cast them out the hidden honor of the pariah people. This simple state of affairs, and not the "resentment" which is so strongly emphasized in Nietzsche's much admired construction in the *Genealogy of Morals,* is the source of the religiosity cultivated by pariah status groups. In passing, we may note that resentment may be accurately applied only to a limited extent; for one of Nietzsche's main examples, Buddhism, it is not at all applicable.

Incidentally, the development of status groups from ethnic segregations is by no means the normal phenomenon. On the contrary, since objective "racial differences" are by no means basic to every subjective sentiment of an ethnic community, the ultimately racial foundation of status structure is rightly and absolutely a question of the concrete individual case. Very frequently a status group is instrumental in the production of a thoroughbred anthropological type. Certainly a status group is to a high degree effective in producing extreme types, for they select personally qualified individuals (e.g. the Knighthood selects those who are fit for warfare, physically and psychically). But selection is far from being the only, or the predominant, way in which status groups are formed: Political membership or class situation has at all times been at least as frequently decisive. And today the class situation is by far the predominant factor, for of course the possibility of a style of life expected for members of a status group is usually conditioned economically.

Status Privileges. For all practical purposes, stratification by status goes hand in hand with a monopolization of ideal and material goods or opportunities, in a manner we have come to know as typical. Besides the specific status honor, which always rests upon distance and exclusiveness, we find all sorts of material monopolies. Such honorific preferences may consist of the privilege of wearing special costumes, of eating special dishes taboo to others, of carrying arms—which is most obvious in its consequences—the right to pursue certain non-professional dilettante artistic practices, e.g. to play certain musical instruments. Of course, material monopolies provide the most effective motives for the exclusiveness of a status group; although, in themselves, they are rarely sufficient, almost always they come into play to some extent. Within a status circle there is the question of intermarriage: the interest of the families in the monopolization of potential bridegrooms is at least of equal importance and is parallel to the interest in the monopolization of daughters. The daughters of the circle must be provided for. With an increased inclosure of the status group, the conventional preferential opportunities for special employment grow into a legal monopoly of special offices for the members. Certain goods become objects for monopolization by status groups. In the typical fashion these include "entailed estates" and frequently also the possessions of serfs or bondsmen and, finally, special trades. This monopolization occurs positively when the status group is exclusively entitled to own and to manage them; and negatively when, in order to maintain its specific way of life, the status group must *not* own and manage them.

The decisive role of a "style of life" in status "honor" means that status groups are the specific bearers of all "conventions." In whatever way it may be manifest, all "stylization" of life either originates in status groups or is at least conserved by them. Even if the principles of status conventions differ greatly, they reveal certain typical traits, especially among those strata which are most privileged. Quite generally, among privileged status groups there is a status disqualification that operates against the performance of common physical labor. This disqualification is now "setting in" in America against the old tradition of esteem for labor. Very frequently every rational economic pursuit, and especially "entrepreneurial activity," is looked upon as a disqualification of status. Artistic and literary activity is also considered as degrading work as soon as it is exploited for income, or at least when it is connected with hard physical exertion. An example is the sculptor working like a mason in his dusty smock as over against the painter in his salon-like "studio" and those forms of musical practice that are acceptable to the status group.

Economic Conditions and Effects of Status Stratification. The frequent disqualification of the gainfully employed as such is a direct result of the principle of status stratification peculiar to the social order, and of course, of this principle's opposition to a distribution of power which is regulated exclusively through the market. These two factors operate along with various individual ones, which will be touched upon below.

We have seen above that the market and its processes "knows no personal distinctions": "functional" interests dominate it. It knows nothing of "honor." The status order means precisely the reverse, viz.: stratification in terms of "honor" and of styles of life peculiar to status groups as such. If mere economic acquisition and naked economic power still bearing the stigma of its extra-status origin could bestow upon anyone who has won it the same honor as those who are interested in status by virtue of style of life claim for themselves, the status order would be threatened at its very root. This is the more so as, given equality of status honor, property *per se* represents an addition even if it is not overtly acknowledged to be such. Yet if such economic acquisition and power gave the agent any honor at all, his wealth would result in his attaining more honor than those who successfully claim honor by virtue of style of life. Therefore all groups having interests in the status order react with special sharpness precisely against the pretensions of purely economic acquisition. In most cases they react the more vigorously the more they feel themselves threatened. Calderon's respectful treatment of the peasant, for instance, as opposed to Shakespeare's simultaneous and ostensible disdain of the *canaille* illustrates the different way in which a firmly structured status order reacts as compared with a status order that has become economically precarious. This is an example of a state of affairs that recurs everywhere. Precisely because of the rigorous reactions against the claims of property *per se,* the "parvenu" is never accepted, personally and without reservation, by the privileged status groups, no matter how completely his style of life has been adjusted to theirs. They will only accept his descendants who have been educated in the conventions of their status group and who have never besmirched its honor by their own economic labor.

As to the general *effect* of the status order, only one consequence can be stated, but it is a very important one: the hindrance of the free development of the market occurs first for those goods which status groups directly withheld from free exchange by monopolization. This monopolization may be effected either legally or conventionally. For example, in many Hellenic cities during the epoch of status groups, and also originally in Rome, the inherited estate (as is shown by the old formula for indiction against spendthrifts)

was monopolized just as were the estates of knights, peasants, priests, and especially the clientele of the craft and merchant guilds. The market is restricted, and the power of naked property *per se,* which gives its stamp to "class formation," is pushed into the background. The results of this process can be most varied. Of course, they do not necessarily weaken the contrasts in the economic situation. Frequently they strengthen these contrasts, and in any case, where stratification by status permeates a community as strongly as was the case in all political communities of antiquity and of the Middle Ages, one can never speak of a genuinely free market competition as we understand it today. There are wider effects than this direct exclusion of special goods from the market. From the contrariety between the status order and the purely economic order mentioned above, it follows that in most instances the notion of honor peculiar to status absolutely abhors that which is essential to the market: higgling. Honor abhors higgling among peers and occasionally it taboos higgling for the members of a status group in general. Therefore, everywhere some status groups, and usually the most influential, consider almost any kind of overt participation in economic acquisition as absolutely stigmatizing.

With some over-simplification, one might thus say that "classes" are stratified according to their relations to the production and acquisition of goods; whereas "status groups" are stratified according to the principles of their *consumption* of goods as represented by special "styles of life."

An "occupational group" is also a status group. For normally, it successfully claims social honor only by virtue of the special style of life which may be determined by it. The differences between classes and status groups frequently overlap. It is precisely those status communities most strictly segregated in terms of honor (viz. the Indian castes) who today show, although within very rigid limits, a relatively high degree of indifference to pecuniary income. However, the Brahmins seek such income in many different ways.

As to the general economic conditions making for the predominance of stratification by "status," only very little can be said. When the bases of the acquisition and distribution of goods are relatively stable, stratification by status is favored. Every technological repercussion and economic transformation threatens stratification by status and pushes the class situation into the foreground. Epochs and countries in which the naked class situation is of predominant significance are regularly the periods of technical and economic transformations. And every slowing down of the shifting of economic stratifications leads, in due course, to the growth of status structures and makes for a resuscitation of the important role of social honor.

Parties. Whereas the genuine place of "classes" is within the economic order, the place of "status groups" is within the social order, that is, within the sphere of the distribution of "honor." From within these spheres, classes and status groups influence one another and they influence the legal order and are in turn influenced by it. But "parties" live in a house of "power."

Their action is oriented toward the acquisition of social "power," that is to say, toward influencing a communal action no matter what its content may be. In principle, parties may exist in a social "club" as well as in a "state." As over against the actions of classes and status groups, for which this is not necessarily the case, the communal actions of "parties" always mean a societalization. For party actions are always directed toward a goal which is striven for in planned manner. This goal may be a "cause" (the party may aim at realizing a program for ideal or material purposes), or the goal may be "personal" (sinecures, power, and from these, honor for the leader and the followers of the party). Usually the party action aims at all these simultaneously. Parties are, therefore, only possible within communities that are societalized, that is, which have some rational order and a staff of persons available who are ready to enforce it. For parties aim precisely at influencing this staff, and if possible, to recruit it from party followers.

In any individual case, parties may represent interests determined through "class situation" or "status situation," and they may recruit their following respectively from one or the other. But they need be neither purely "class" nor purely "status" parties. In most cases they are partly class parties and partly status parties, but sometimes they are neither. They may represent ephemeral or enduring structures. Their means of attaining power may be quite varied, ranging from naked violence of any sort to canvas-sing for votes with coarse or subtle means: money, social influence, the force of speech, suggestion, clumsy hoax, and so on to the rougher or more artful tactics of obstruction in parliamentary bodies.

The sociological structure of parties differs in a basic way according to the kind of communal action which they struggle to influence. Parties also differ according to whether or not the community is stratified by status or by classes. Above all else, they vary according to the structure of domination within the community. For their leaders normally deal with the conquest of a community. They are, in the general concept which is maintained here, not only products of specially modern forms of domination. We shall also designate as parties the ancient and medieval "parties," despite the fact that their structure differs basically from the structure of modern parties. By virtue of these structural differences of domination it is impossible to say anything about the structure of parties without discussing the structural forms of social domination *per se*. Parties, which are always structures struggling for domination, are very frequently organized in a very strict "authoritarian" fashion. . . .

Concerning "classes," "status groups," and "parties," it must be said in general that they necessarily presuppose a comprehensive societalization, and especially a political framework of communal action, within which they operate. This does not mean that parties would be confined by the frontiers of any individual political community. On the contrary, at all times it has been the order of the day that the societalization (even when it aims at the use of military force in common) reaches beyond the frontiers of politics. This has been the case in the solidarity of interests among the Oligarchs and among the democrats in Hellas, among the Guelfs and among Ghibellines in the Middle Ages, and within the Calvinist party during the period of religious struggles. It has been the case up to the solidarity of the landlords (international congress of agrarian landlords), and has continued among princes (holy alliance, Karlsbad decrees), socialist workers, conservatives (the longing of Prussian conservatives for Russian intervention in 1850). But their aim is not necessarily the establishment of new international political, i.e. *territorial*, dominion. In the main they aim to influence the existing dominion.

Some Principles of Stratification

Kingsley Davis and Wilbert E. Moore

IN A previous paper some concepts for handling the phenomena of social inequality were presented.[1] In the present paper a further step in stratification theory is undertaken—an attempt to show the relationship between stratification and the rest of the social order.[2] Starting from the proposition that no society is "classless," or unstratified, an effort is made to explain, in functional terms, the universal necessity which calls forth stratification in any social system. Next, an attempt is made to explain the roughly uniform distribution of prestige as between the major types of positions in every society. Since, however, there occur between one society and another great differences in the degree and kind of stratification, some attention is also given to the varieties of social inequality and the variable factors that give rise to them.

Clearly, the present task requires two different lines of analysis—one to understand the universal, the other to understand the variable features of stratification. Naturally each line of inquiry aids the other and is indispensable, and in the treatment that follows the two will be interwoven, although, because of space limitations, the emphasis will be on the universals.

Throughout, it will be necessary to keep in mind one thing—namely, that the discussion relates to the system of positions, not to the individuals occupying those positions. It is one thing to ask why different positions carry different degrees of prestige, and quite another to ask how certain individuals get into those positions. Although, as the argument will try to show, both questions are related, it is essential to keep them separate in our thinking. Most of the literature on stratification has tried to answer the second question (particularly with regard to the ease or difficulty of mobility between strata) without tackling the first. The first question, however, is logically prior and, in the case of any particular individual or group, factually prior.

THE FUNCTIONAL NECESSITY OF STRATIFICATION

Curiously, however, the main functional necessity explaining the universal presence of stratification is precisely the requirement faced by any society of placing and motivating individuals in the social structure. As a functioning mechanism a society must somehow distribute its members in social positions and induce them to perform the duties of these positions. It must thus concern itself with motivation at two different levels: to instill in the proper individuals the desire to fill certain positions, and, once in these positions, the desire to perform the duties attached to them. Even though the social order may be relatively static in

From Kingsley Davis and Wilbert E. Moore, "Some Principles of Stratification," *American Sociological Review*, Vol 10, April 1945, pp. 242–249. By permission of the American Sociological Association and the authors.

1. Kingsley Davis, "A Conceptual Analysis of Stratification," *American Sociological Review*, 7: 309–321, June, 1942.

2. The writers regret (and beg indulgence) that the present essay, a condensation of a longer study, covers so much in such short space that adequate evidence and qualification cannot be given and that as a result what is actually very tentative is presented in an unfortunately dogmatic manner.

form, there is a continuous process of metabolism as new individuals are born into it, shift with age, and die off. Their absorption into the positional system must somehow be arranged and motivated. This is true whether the system is competitive or non-competitive. A competitive system gives greater importance to the motivation to achieve positions, whereas a non-competitive system gives perhaps greater importance to the motivation to perform the duties of the positions; but in any system both types of motivation are required.

If the duties associated with the various positions were all equally pleasant to the human organism, all equally important to societal survival, and all equally in need of the same ability or talent, it would make no difference who got into which positions, and the problem of social placement would be greatly reduced. But actually it does make a great deal of difference who gets into which positions, not only because some positions are inherently more agreeable than others, but also because some require special talents or training and some are functionally more important than others. Also, it is essential that the duties of the positions be performed with the diligence that their importance requires. Inevitably, then, a society must have, first, some kind of rewards that it can use as inducements, and, second, some way of distributing these rewards differentially according to positions. The rewards and their distribution become a part of the social order, and thus give rise to stratification.

One may ask what kind of rewards a society has at its disposal in distributing its personnel and securing essential services. It has, first of all, the things that contribute to sustenance and comfort. It has, second, the things that contribute to humor and diversion. And it has, finally, the things that contribute to self respect and ego expansion. The last, because of the peculiarly social character of the self, is largely a function of the opinion of others, but it nonetheless ranks in importance with the first two. In any social system all three kinds of rewards must be dispensed differentially according to positions.

In a sense the rewards are "built into" the position. They consist in the "rights" associated with the position, plus what may be called its accompaniments or perquisites. Often the rights, and sometimes the accompaniments, are func-

tionally related to the duties of the position. (Rights as viewed by the incumbent are usually duties as viewed by other members of the community.) However, there may be a host of subsidiary rights and perquisites that are not essential to the function of the position and have only an indirect and symbolic connection with its duties, but which still may be of considerable importance in inducing people to seek the positions and fulfil the essential duties.

If the rights and perquisites of different positions in a society must be unequal, then the society must be stratified, because that is precisely what stratification means. Social inequality is thus an unconsciously evolved device by which societies insure that the most important positions are conscientiously filled by the most qualified persons. Hence every society, no matter how simple or complex, must differentiate persons in terms of both prestige and esteem, and must therefore possess a certain amount of institutionalized inequality.

It does not follow that the amount or type of inequality need be the same in all societies. This is largely a function of factors that will be discussed presently.

THE TWO DETERMINANTS OF POSITIONAL RANK

Granting the general function that inequality subserves, one can specify the two factors that determine the relative rank of different positions. In general those positions convey the best reward, and hence have the highest rank, which a) have the greatest importance for the society and b) require the greatest training or talent. The first factor concerns function and is a matter of relative significance; the second concerns means and is a matter of scarcity.

Differential Functional Importance

Actually a society does not need to reward positions in proportion to their functional importance. It merely needs to give sufficient reward to them to insure that they will be filled competently. In other words, it must see that less essential positions do not compete successfully with more essential ones. If a position is easily filled, it need not be heavily rewarded, even though important. On the other hand, if it is important but hard to fill, the reward must be high enough to get it filled anyway. Functional importance is therefore a necessary but not a sufficient cause of high rank being assigned to a position.[3]

Differential Scarcity of Personnel

Practically all positions, no matter how acquired, require some form of skill or capacity for performance. This is implicit in the very notion of position, which implies that the incumbent must, by virtue of this incumbency, accomplish certain things.

There are, ultimately, only two ways in which a person's qualifications come about: through inherent capacity or through training. Obviously, in concrete activities both are always necessary, but from a practical standpoint the scarcity may lie primarily in one or the other, as well as in both. Some positions require innate talents of such high degree that the persons who fill them are bound to be rare. In many cases, however, talent is fairly abundant in the population but the training process is so long, costly, and elaborate that relatively few can qualify. Modern medicine, for example, is within the mental

capacity of most individuals, but a medical education is so burdensome and expensive that virtually none would undertake it if the position of the M.D. did not carry a reward commensurate with the sacrifice.

If the talents required for a position are abundant and the training easy, the method of acquiring the position may have little to do with its duties. There may be, in fact, a virtually accidental relationship. But if the skills required are scarce by reason of the rarity of talent or the costliness of training, the position, if functionally important, must have an attractive power that will draw the necessary skills in competition with other positions. This means, in effect, that the position must be high in the social scale—must command great prestige, high salary, ample leisure, and the like.

How Variations Are to Be Understood

In so far as there is a difference between one system of stratification and another, it is attributable to whatever factors affect the two determinants of differential reward—namely, functional importance and scarcity of personnel. Positions important in one society may not be important in another, because the conditions faced by the societies, or their degree of internal development, may be different. The same conditions, in turn, may affect the question of scarcity; for in some societies the stage of development, or the external situation, may wholly obviate the necessity of certain kinds of skill or talent. Any particular system of stratification, then, can be understood as a product of the special conditions affecting the two aforementioned grounds of differential reward.

MAJOR SOCIETAL FUNCTIONS AND STRATIFICATION

Religion

The reason why religion is necessary is apparently to be found in the fact that human society achieves its unity primarily through the

---

3. Unfortunately, functional importance is difficult to establish. To use the position's prestige to establish it, as is often unconsciously done, constitutes circular reasoning from our point of view. There are, however, two independent clues: *a)* the degree to which a position is functionally unique, there being no other positions that can perform the same function satisfactorily; *b)* the degree to which other positions are dependent on the one in question. Both clues are best exemplified in organized systems of positions built around one major function. Thus, in most complex societies the religious, political, economic, and educational functions are handled by distinct structures not easily interchangeable. In addition, each structure possesses many different positions, some clearly dependent on, if not subordinate to, others. In sum, when an institutional nucleus becomes differentiated around one main function, and at the same time organizes a large portion of the population into its relationships, the *key* positions in it are of the highest functional importance. The absence of such specialization does not prove functional unimportance, for the whole society may be relatively unspecialized; but it is safe to assume that the more important functions receive the first and clearest structural differentiation.

possession by its members of certain ultimate values and ends in common. Although these values and ends are subjective, they influence behavior, and their integration enables the society to operate as a system. Derived neither from inherited nor from external nature, they have evolved as a part of culture by communication and moral pressure. They must, however, appear to the members of the society to have some reality, and it is the role of religious belief and ritual to supply and reinforce this appearance of reality. Through belief and ritual the common ends and values are connected with an imaginary world symbolized by concrete sacred objects, which world in turn is related in a meaningful way to the facts and trials of the individual's life. Through the worship of the sacred objects and the beings they symbolize, and the acceptance of supernatural prescriptions that are at the same time codes of behavior, a powerful control over human conduct is exercised, guiding it along lines sustaining the institutional structure and conforming to the ultimate ends and values.

If this conception of the role of religion is true, one can understand why in every known society the religious activities tend to be under the charge of particular persons, who tend thereby to enjoy greater rewards than the ordinary societal member. Certain of the rewards and special privileges may attach to only the highest religious functionaries, but others usually apply, if such exists, to the entire sacerdotal class.

Moreover, there is a peculiar relation between the duties of the religious official and the special privileges he enjoys. If the supernatural world governs the destinies of men more ultimately than does the real world, its earthly representative, the person through whom one may communicate with the supernatural, must be a powerful individual. He is a keeper of sacred tradition, a skilled performer of the ritual, and an interpreter of lore and myth. He is in such close contact with the gods that he is viewed as possessing some of their characteristics. He is, in short, a bit sacred, and hence free from some of the more vulgar necessities and controls.

It is no accident, therefore, that religious functionaries have been associated with the very highest positions of power, as in theocratic regimes. Indeed, looking at it from this point of view, one may wonder why it is that they do not get *entire* control over their societies. The factors that prevent this are worthy of note.

In the first place, the amount of technical competence necessary for the performance of religious duties is small. Scientific or artistic capacity is not required. Anyone can set himself up as enjoying an intimate relation with deities, and nobody can successfully dispute him. Therefore, the factor of scarcity of personnel does not operate in the technical sense.

One may assert, on the other hand, that religious ritual is often elaborate and religious lore abstruse, and that priestly ministrations require tact, if not intelligence. This is true, but the technical requirements of the profession are for the most part adventitious, not related to the end in the same way that science is related to air travel. The priest can never be free from competition, since the criteria of whether or not one has genuine contact with the supernatural are never strictly clear. It is this competition that debases the priestly position below what might be expected at first glance. That is why priestly prestige is highest in those societies where membership in the profession is rigidly controlled by the priestly guild itself. That is why, in part at least, elaborate devices are utilized to stress the identification of the person with his office—spectacular costume, abnormal conduct, special diet, segregated residence, celibacy, conspicuous leisure, and the like. In fact, the priest is always in danger of becoming somewhat discredited—as happens in a secularized society—because in a world of stubborn fact, ritual and sacred knowledge alone will not grow crops or build houses. Furthermore, unless he is protected by a professional guild, the priest's identification with the supernatural tends to preclude his acquisition of abundant worldly goods.

As between one society and another it seems that the highest general position awarded the priest occurs in the medieval type of social order. Here there is enough economic production to afford a surplus, which can be used to support a numerous and highly organized priesthood; and yet the populace is unlettered and therefore credulous to a high degree. Perhaps the most extreme example is to be found in the Buddhism of Tibet, but others are encountered in the Catholicism of feudal Europe, the Inca regime of

Peru, the Brahminism of India, and the Mayan priesthood of Yucatan. On the other hand, if the society is so crude as to have no surplus and little differentiation, so that every priest must be also a cultivator or hunter, the separation of the priestly status from the others has hardly gone far enough for priestly prestige to mean much. When the priest actually has high prestige under these circumstances, it is because he also performs other important functions (usually political and medical).

In an extremely advanced society built on scientific technology, the priesthood tends to lose status, because sacred tradition and supernaturalism drop into the background. The ultimate values and common ends of the society tend to be expressed in less anthropomorphic ways, by officials who occupy fundamentally political, economic, or educational rather than religious positions. Nevertheless, it is easily possible for intellectuals to exaggerate the degree to which the priesthood in a presumably secular milieu has lost prestige. When the matter is closely examined the urban proletariat, as well as the rural citizenry, proves to be surprisingly god-fearing and priest-ridden. No society has become so completely secularized as to liquidate entirely the belief in transcendental ends and supernatural entities. Even in a secularized society some system must exist for the integration of ultimate values, for their ritualistic expression, and for the emotional adjustments required by disappointment, death, and disaster.

Government

Like religion, government plays a unique and indispensable part in society. But in contrast to religion, which provides integration in terms of sentiments, beliefs, and rituals, it organizes the society in terms of law and authority. Furthermore, it orients the society to the actual rather than the unseen world.

The main functions of government are, internally, the ultimate enforcement of norms, the final arbitration of conflicting interests, and the overall planning and direction of society; and externally, the handling of war and diplomacy. To carry out these functions it acts as the agent of the entire people, enjoys a monopoly of force, and controls all individuals within its territory.

Political action, by definition, implies authority. An official can command because he has authority, and the citizen must obey because he is subject to that authority. For this reason stratification is inherent in the nature of political relationships.

So clear is the power embodied in political position that political inequality is sometimes thought to comprise all inequality. But it can be shown that there are other bases of stratification, that the following controls operate in practice to keep political power from becoming complete: *a)* The fact that the actual holders of political office, and especially those determining top policy must necessarily be few in number compared to the total population. *b)* The fact that rulers represent the interest of the group rather than of themselves, and are therefore restricted in their behavior by rules and mores designed to enforce this limitation of interest. *c)* The fact that the holder of political office has his authority by virtue of his office and nothing else, and therefore any special knowledge, talent, or capacity he may claim is purely incidental, so that he often has to depend upon others for technical assistance.

In view of these limiting factors, it is not strange that the rulers often have less power and prestige than a literal enumeration of their formal rights would lead one to expect.

Wealth, Property, and Labor

Every position that secures for its incumbent a livelihood is, by definition, economically rewarded. For this reason there is an economic aspect to those positions (e.g. political and religious) the main function of which is not economic. It therefore becomes convenient for the society to use unequal economic returns as a principal means of controlling the entrance of persons into positions and stimulating the performance of their duties. The amount of the economic return therefore becomes one of the main indices of social status.

It should be stressed, however, that a position does not bring power and prestige *because* it draws a high income. Rather, it draws a high income because it is functionally important and the available personnel is for one reason or another scarce. It is therefore superficial and erroneous to regard high income as the cause of a man's power and prestige, just as it is erroneous to think that a man's fever is the cause of his disease.[4]

The economic source of power and prestige is not income primarily, but the ownership of capital goods (including patents, good will, and professional reputation). Such ownership should be distinguished from the possession of consumers' goods, which is an index rather than a cause of social standing. In other words, the ownership of producers' goods is properly speaking, a source of income like other positions, the income itself remaining an index. Even in situations where social values are widely commercialized and earnings are the readiest method of judging social position, income does not confer prestige on a position so much as it induces people to compete for the position. It is true that a man who has a high income as a result of one position may find this money helpful in climbing into another position as well, but this again reflects the effect of his initial, economically advantageous status, which exercises its influence through the medium of money.

In a system of private property in productive enterprise, an income above what an individual spends can give rise to possession of capital wealth. Presumably such possession is a reward for the proper management of one's finances originally and of the productive enterprise later. But as social differentiation becomes highly advanced and yet the institution of inheritance persists, the phenomenon of pure ownership, and reward for pure ownership, emerges. In such a case it is difficult to prove that the position is functionally important or that the scarcity involved is anything other than extrinsic and accidental. It is for this reason, doubtless, that the institution of private property in productive goods becomes more subject to criticism as social development proceeds toward industrialization. It is only this pure, that is, strictly legal and functionless ownership, however, that is open to attack; for some form of active ownership, whether private or public, is indispensable.

One kind of ownership of production goods consists in rights over the labor of others. The most extremely concentrated and exclusive of

such rights are found in slavery, but the essential principle remains in serfdom, peonage, encomienda, and indenture. Naturally this kind of ownership has the greatest significance for stratification, because it necessarily entails an unequal relationship.

But property in capital goods inevitably introduces a compulsive element even into the nominally free contractual relationship. Indeed, in some respects the authority of the contractual employer is greater than that of the feudal landlord, inasmuch as the latter is more limited by traditional reciprocities. Even the classical economics recognized that competitors would fare unequally, but it did not pursue this fact to its necessary conclusion that, however it might be acquired, unequal control of goods and services must give unequal advantage to the parties to a contract.

Technical Knowledge

The function of finding means to single goals, without any concern with the choice between goals, is the exclusively technical sphere. The explanation of why positions requiring great technical skill receive fairly high rewards is easy to see, for it is the simplest case of the rewards being so distributed as to draw talent and motivate training. Why they seldom if ever receive the highest rewards is also clear: the importance of technical knowledge from a societal point of view is never so great as the integration of goals, which takes place on the religious, political, and economic levels. Since the technological level is concerned solely with means, a purely technical position must ultimately be subordinate to other positions that are religious, political, or economic in character.

Nevertheless, the distinction between expert and layman in any social order is fundamental, and cannot be entirely reduced to other terms. Methods of recruitment, as well as of reward, sometimes lead to the erroneous interpretation that technical positions are economically determined. Actually, however, the acquisition of knowledge and skill cannot be accomplished by purchase, although the opportunity to learn may be. The control of the avenues of training may inhere as a sort of property right in certain families or classes, giving them power and prestige in

---

4. The symbolic rather than intrinsic role of income in social stratification has been succinctly summarized by Talcott Parsons, "An Analytical Approach to the Theory of Social Stratification," *American Journal of Sociology*, 45: 841–862, May, 1940.

consequence. Such a situation adds an artificial scarcity to the natural scarcity of skills and talents. On the other hand, it is possible for an opposite situation to arise. The rewards of technical position may be so great that a condition of excess supply is created, leading to at least temporary devaluation of the rewards. Thus "unemployment in the learned professions" may result in a debasement of the prestige of those positions. Such adjustments and readjustments are constantly occurring in changing societies; and it is always well to bear in mind that the efficiency of a stratified structure may be affected by the modes of recruitment for positions. The social order itself, however, sets limits to the inflation or deflation of the prestige of experts: an oversupply tends to debase the rewards and discourage recruitment or produce revolution, whereas an under-supply tends to increase the rewards or weaken the society in competition with other societies.

Particular systems of stratification show a wide range with respect to the exact position of technically competent persons. This range is perhaps most evident in the degree of specialization. Extreme division of labor tends to create many specialists without high prestige since the training is short and the required native capacity relatively small. On the other hand it also tends to accentuate the high position of the true experts—scientists, engineers, and administrators—by increasing their authority relative to other functionally important positions. But the idea of a technocratic social order or a government or priesthood of engineers or social scientists neglects the limitations of knowledge and skills as a basic for performing social functions. To the extent that the social structure is truly specialized the prestige of the technical person must also be circumscribed.

VARIATION IN STRATIFIED SYSTEMS

The generalized principles of stratification here suggested form a necessary preliminary to a consideration of types of stratified systems, because it is in terms of these principles that the types must be described. This can be seen by trying to delineate types according to certain modes of variation.

For instance, some of the most important modes (together with the polar types in terms of them) seem to be as follows:

A) The Degree of Specialization

The degree of specialization affects the fineness and multiplicity of the gradations in power and prestige. It also influences the extent to which particular functions may be emphasized in the invidious system, since a given function cannot receive much emphasis in the hierarchy until it has achieved structural separation from the other functions. Finally, the amount of specialization influences, the bases of selection. Polar types: *Specialized, Unspecialized.*

B) The Nature of the Functional Emphasis

In general when emphasis is put on sacred matters, a rigidity is introduced that tends to limit specialization and hence the development of technology. In addition, a brake is placed on social mobility, and on the development of bureaucracy. When the preoccupation with the sacred is withdrawn, leaving greater scope for purely secular preoccupations, a great development, and rise in status, of economic and technological positions seemingly takes place. Curiously, a concomitant rise in political position is not likely, because it has usually been allied with the religious and stands to gain little by the decline of the latter. It is also possible for a society to emphasize family functions—as in relatively undifferentiated societies where high mortality requires high fertility and kinship forms the main basis of social organization. Main types: *Familistic, Authoritarian (Theocratic* or sacred, and *Totalitarian* or secular), *Capitalistic.*

C) The Magnitude of Invidious Differences

What may be called the amount of social distance between positions, taking into account the entire scale, is something that should lend itself to quantitative measurement. Considerable differences apparently exist between different societies in this regard, and also between parts of the same society. Polar types: *Equalitarian, Inequalitarian.*

D) The Degree of Opportunity

The familiar question of the amount of mobility is different from the question of the comparative equality or inequality of rewards posed above, because the two criteria may vary independently up to a point. For instance, the tremendous divergences in monetary income in the United States are far greater than those found in primitive societies, yet the equality of opportunity to move from one rung to the other in the social scale may also be greater in the United States than in a hereditary tribal kingdom. Polar types: *Mobile* (open), *Immobile* (closed).

E) The Degree of Stratum Solidarity

Again, the degree of "class solidarity" (or the presence of specific organizations to promote class interests) may vary to some extent independently of the other criteria, and hence is an important principle in classifying systems of stratification. Polar types: *Class organized, Class unorganized.*

EXTERNAL CONDITIONS

What state any particular system of stratification is in with reference to each of these modes of variation depends on two things: 1) its state with reference to the other ranges of variation, and 2) the conditions outside the system of stratification which nevertheless influence that system. Among the latter are the following:

A) The Stage of Cultural Development

As the cultural heritage grows, increased specialization becomes necessary, which in turn

contributes to the enhancement of mobility, a decline of stratum solidarity, and a change of functional emphasis.

B) Situation with Respect to Other Societies

The presence or absence of open conflict with other societies, of free trade relations or cultural diffusion, all influence the class structure to some extent. A chronic state of warfare tends to place emphasis upon the military functions, especially when the opponents are more or less equal. Free trade, on the other hand, strengthens the hand of the trader at the expense of the warrior and priest. Free movement of ideas generally has an equalitarian effect. Migration and conquest create special circumstances.

C) Size of the Society

A small society limits the degree to which functional specialization can go, the degree of segregation of different stata, and the magnitude of inequality.

COMPOSITE TYPES

Much of the literature on stratification has attempted to classify concrete systems into a certain number of types. This task is deceptively simple, however, and should come at the end of an analysis of elements and principles, rather than at the beginning. If the preceding discussion has any validity, it indicates that there are a number of modes of variation between different systems, and that any one system is a composite of the society's status with reference to all these modes of variation. The danger of trying to classify whole societies under such rubrics as *caste, feudal,* or *open class* is that one or two criteria are selected and others ignored, the result being an usatisfactory solution to the problem posed. The present discussion has been offered as a possible approach to the more systematic classification of composite types.

4

Class Stratification in the United States: Methods and Empirical Studies

Vincent Jeffries

THE DEVELOPMENT of a generally accepted theory of class stratification must depend on valid knowledge of social classes and their functions in the social structure. In order to obtain such knowledge, an adequate methodology to systematically study social classes is necessary. At the present time, however, there is no generally accepted measure of social class whose validity is clearly established.

Several problems contribute to a lack of greater methodological advancement and sophistication in the field of stratification. The diversity of theoretical approaches to the study of class is reflected in a diversity of methodological techniques designed to gather and to measure empirical data about the class structure. This lack of uniformity and direction is compounded by considerable disagreement about the generic definition of social class. Another major problem is the lack of systematic linkage between theories, basic concepts, and methodological techniques. Empirical studies of stratification often lack a theory to guide them, and often use a very poorly defined concept of social class.

Determining the place of individuals within a system of social classes is most often done by one of three general methods: the objective, the self-placement, and the reputational (Roach, Gross, Gursslin, 1969:103–104). In the objective method, individuals are placed in a social class according to some criteria determined by the investigator. The most frequently used single measure is occupation. This is often combined into an index with factors such as education, income, or residence. In the self-placement method, an individual places himself or herself in a class position, such as ''upper'', ''middle'', or ''lower''. Either fixed responses or open-ended questions may be used. In

An asterisk (*) accompanying a citation indicates a selection included in this volume.

the reputational approach, a panel of "judges," who are usually long-time residents of the community under study, is used. Their opinions typically determine both the criteria of stratification and the placement of individuals within the class system.

Both the reputational and the self-placement methods depend in the final analysis on the subjective perceptions and judgements of those interviewed about the stratification system (Roach, Gross, Gursslin, 1969:103). The views of members of a community under study or opinions of respondents being interviewed are the primary basis for determining the nature and number of social classes and for placing individuals within them. In the objective method, both the criteria of class and the placement of individuals are ultimately determined by the investigator. The criteria, however, may involve the investigator's assessment of the subjective judgements of others. Thus, the construction of occupational prestige scales, and of various indices of class position, often involve the investigator's judgment of what a society perceives as prestigious and the basis for such evaluation. Other examples of the objective approach are when factors such as power or wealth are paramount in determining the components of a measure of social class position, and the placement of individuals.

Various authors have noted the lack of an adequate relationship between theory and methods in the study of social classes (Reissman, 1959:160–166; Roach, Gross, Gursslin, 1969:74–80, 106). There is often little, if any, correspondence between a theory of stratification and the procedures used for measuring social classes. Many studies briefly comment on the nature of social classes, choose some established measure and then proceed to investigate the relationship between "social class" and some phenomenon such as political attitudes or child-rearing practices. Such procedures provide little in the way of guidelines toward developing either more adequate theory or better research techniques to measure social class.

Another reason for the lack of a generally agreed on measure of class stratification is that there is no consensus regarding the meaning of the concept of social class (Duberman, 1976:56–64; Roach, Gross, Gursslin, 1969:74–83). This is, of course, partly due to more fundamental disagreements with respect to basic theory. Some theorists, such as those considered in detail in the previous chapter, view classes as primarily objective conditions and as attributes of social structure. Others, such as W. Lloyd Warner and his associates and Richard Centers (1949), conceptualize classes as primarily subjective in nature. To Warner, a class is "two or more orders of people who are believed to be, and are accordingly ranked by the members of the community, in socially superior and inferior positions" (Warner, Low, Lunt, Srole, 1963:36). To Centers, class is a "psychological phenomenon" in that "a man's class is part of his ego, a feeling on his part of belongingness to something; and identification with something larger than himself" (1949:27).

In contrast to the objective views of class presented in the previous chapter, Warner and Centers both, in their own ways, view classes as finding their fundamental basis in subjective meanings. To Warner, community consensus in both prestige rankings and the criteria for conferring status is paramount, whereas to Centers, it is the individual's own sense of self-identification.

In line with this conception of social class, the methodology of Warners's earlier work was devised explicitly to ascertain the evaluation of individuals by others in the community. His methodology, which he calls Evaluated Participation (E.P.), is an example of the reputational approach and involves six techniques. One technique is Matched Agreements, in which social class position can be indicated by two or more informants who place the same individual in the same social class. Rating by Status Reputation is another technique. In this, an individual is placed in a given class because informants report that the individual engages in certain activities and possesses certain traits which are considered to be superior or inferior. In the technique of Rating by Institutional Membership, the individual is placed in a given class because he or she is said to belong to a certain group, such as a clique or association, which is ranked by the consensus of informants as superior or inferior.

Centers's (1949) conception of social class is also reflected in his methodology, which involves subjective self-placement in a given class as determined by response to the following question: "If you were asked to use one of these four names for your social class, which would you say you belonged in: the middle class, lower class, working class, or upper class" (1949:76)?

An early and often used objective measure of class, or socioeconomic status, was developed by Alba Edwards for the Bureau of the Census. The United States Census has used Edwards's grouping of occupations, with appropriate modifications, as the major basis for categorizing workers since the 1930 census (Miller, 1977:243–245). The Edwards's classification also has been the basis for many later scales used widely in social research. Leonard Reissman (1959:145–146) notes that Edwards tried to develop a classification that would combine all occupations into a few basic categories. These basic categories also were to represent similar lifestyles and similar social and economic characteristics. The six major occupational groups in Edward's classification are: professionals; proprietors, managers, and officials; clerks and kindred workers; skilled workers and foremen; semi-skilled workers; and unskilled workers. Each of these groups were regarded by Edwards as representing real distinct social and economic groups.

A frequently used objective measure of social class is the Index of Status Characteristics (I.S.C.), developed by W. Lloyd Warner and his associates (Warner, Meeker, and Eells, 1960:121–159); see also Robinson, Athanasiau, and Head, 1969:362–366). The components of the Index are regarded as symbols that are evaluated with respect to their social status in accordance with the investigator's assessment of appropriate cultural traditions. Thus, although the Index is objective in terms of assignment of class position, it is based on the investigator's evaluation of the subjective consensus regarding symbols of status. The Index is composed of four factors: occupation, source of income, house type, and dwelling area. Individuals are ranked on each of these factors on a scale ranging from a low score of 1 to a high score of 7. These scores are then weighted and summed for a total score which indicates the individual's place in the class hierarchy.

The Index of Social Position (The I.S.P.) is another widely used objective measure of social class. (Hollingshead and Redlich, 1964:387–397; Hollingshead, 1971; see also Miller, 1977:230–238). A brief consideration of this Index illustrates how such measures are constructed. There are both two- and three-factor forms of the I.S.P. The three-factor Index is composed of occupation, education, and residence. The two-factor Index includes only occupation and education.

In the I.S.P. the occupation of the head of household is coded on a seven-point scale, which includes the following categories: executives, proprietors of large concerns, and major professionals; managers, proprietors of medium-sized businesses, lesser professionals; administrative personnel of large concerns, owners of small independent businesses, semi-professionals; owners of little businesses, clerical and sales workers; technicians; skilled workers; semi-skilled workers and unskilled workers.

The occupation scale is a modification of the Edwards's system used by the Census Bureau. The Index of Social Position scale of occupations, however, ranks professions into different groups and ranks businesses by their size and monetary value. This occupational hierarchy is intended to represent the differential values placed upon various occupations according to the skill they involve. It is also intended to reflect the amount of power and control over others that is characteristically associated with an occupation.

Education of the head of household is also divided into seven categories, as follows: graduate professional training; college or university graduate; partial college training; high school graduate; partial high school training; junior high school; less than seven years of school. Education is intended to reflect tastes, attitudes, and behavior patterns. These characteristics are assumed to have a tendency to be similar at a similar level of education.

Residences are ranked on a six point scale, from the richest to the poorest areas. Residence is viewed as reflective of a family's mode of living.

In constructing the Index of Social Position, scores on occupation, education, and residence were correlated with that of judged class position. This latter measure was constructed on the basis of data gathered in extensive interviews, and represented the judgement of Hollingshead and Redlich (1964) pertaining to the appropriate position of households in one of five class levels. On the basis of a statistical analysis of the relationship between judged class position and occupation, education, and residence, each of these factors was weighted. A weight of 9 was assigned for occupation, 5 for education, and 6 for residence. With a possible range from 1 thru 7 for occupation and education and a possible range from 1 thru 6 for residence, the distribution for scores on the three-factor Index of Social Position range from a possible low of 20 to a possible high of 134, with lower scores indicating higher class position. The continuum of scores on the I.S.P. gathered from a sample of the community of New Haven was then cut according to what seemed natural divisions in the distribution to yield five class divisions. Individuals and families could then be placed in one of the five classes on the basis of their scores on the I.S.P. For example, a family whose head holds a clerical job ($4 \times 9 = 36$), is a high school graduate ($4 \times 5 = 20$), and lives in a middle rank residential area ($3 \times 6 = 18$) would have a total I.S.P. score of 74, placing the family in class III.

Since the use of residence required a slow and costly procedure of ranking areas within a community, a two-factor Index of Social Position was developed, utilizing only occupation and education. For this Index, occupation was given a weight of 7 and education a weight of 4.

A study by Joseph A. Kahl and James A. David (1955) provides information pertaining to the interrelationships between various measures of social class. Nineteen measures of class, or "socioeconomic status" were administered to a sample of 219 males. These measures included W. Lloyd Warner's occupational categories, subject's education, census occupational categories, a self-identification measure from Richard

Centers's study, source of income, annual family income, and measures of the subject's house and residential area. Each of these measures was dichotomized as closely as possible to the median and then subjected to correlational and factor analysis.

Results showed relatively high positive correlations among the various measures of social class, indicating that they were all reflective in varying degrees of the same underlying factor. Even though it could be generally said that the indices were measuring a single dimension of social and economic attributes, a more precise evaluation of the results showed two separable factors. The first of these was composed of the various measures of occupation, and other variables such as education, which are closely related to occupation. The second factor clustered around various measures of residential area and dwelling, and socioeconomic data pertaining to the subject's parents. The best single index of the general socioeconomic cluster was occupation. Source of income or education appeared to be the most suitable variables to be combined with occupation, if a multiple factor measure was desired.

A study by John L. Haer (1957) provides further information regarding the various indices of stratification. The aim of this investigation was to ascertain the relative scientific utility of different indices. This property was determined by the criterion of their effectiveness in predicting variables which studies have shown to be related to social stratification.

Data was gathered from a representative sample of 320 individuals. Each individual was placed according to five indices of social stratification. Two subjective measures were used, in which respondents were asked to place themselves in a social class. One measure was a question asking respondents to place themselves in a stated list of classes, such as "working" or "middle." This index is similar to that used by Richard Centers (1949) in his study. Respondents were also asked an open-ended question, in which they placed themselves in a class position. Three objective measures were employed, in which respondents were placed in strata according to some criteria. Occupation and education were used as separate indices. The Index of Status Characteristics from Warner's studies (Warner, Meeker, and Eells, 1960) was also included as an objective measure of stratifiation, involving in this instance the total score based upon occupation, source of income, house type, and dwelling area. All five indices were found to be closely associated statistically, indicating that each measure in some way reflects the same phenomenon of social stratification.

Twenty-two attitudinal and behavioral variables found in previous studies to be associated with stratification were related to the aforementioned five indices of stratification. These variables represent eight areas of life experience, including voluntary organization membership, political behavior, religious experiences, and reading habits. The results showed that overall the Index of Status Characteristics was the best predictor of the various attitudinal and behavioral correlates of stratification. This superiority of the I.S.C. was shown to be due to the fact that it is a composite measure, rather than to the separate predictability of any of its components.

Several conclusions regarding the relative worth of different measures of stratification emerged from the study. Haer (1957) observes that the findings indicate a more useful concept of class stratification is one which emphasizes several factors, rather than relying on any single one. The study also indicated that objective indices have generally higher predictability than subjective indices. Measures with a continuous series of gradations, such as the I.S.C., also appeared to be more predictive than measures with broad discrete categories, such as those in which wide ranges of occupations are grouped together into a relatively small number of ranked levels.

The studies by Kahl and Davis (1955) and Haer (1957) provide a perspective for assessing the various measures of social class. Both studies indicate that, despite the variability in methods, most measures seem to be tapping the same basic phenomenon. This is not to say that the measures are equally adequate. The finding of Haer that composite measures are more adequate for prediction is consistent with the multidimensional view of class advanced by many theorists, and presented in the previous chapter of this book.

Despite differences in method and theory, there seems to be general, although by no means complete, agreement that class involves the three components of occupation, education, and economic assets in some way. As Lucille Duberman says in suggesting the use of the term "social classes" to refer to certain distinct groups in the United States:

> The fact remains that there are discernible social entities, admittedly with blurred boundaries, in American society and in almost all societies in the world. These groups are based primarily on educational, occupational, and income levels, and have different life styles, value different things, have different beliefs, seek different goals, and are treated differently by societal institutions (Duberman, 1976:162–163.

This general perspective is similar to that presented in this book and also is an orientation toward social classes and stratification similar to that expressed by C. Wright Mills* (1963) in the selection at the end of this chapter. With this general view of the nature of class stratification as a frame of reference, the following section explores the distribution of wealth, occupation, and education in the United States, and their interrelationships.

WEALTH, OCCUPATION, AND EDUCATION: DISTRIBUTIONS AND RELATIONSHIPS IN THE UNITED STATES

Although information on wealth in the United States is incomplete and difficult to obtain, a clear picture of its basic distribution can be constructed. Data show a high degree of concentration of wealth in the hands of a relatively small number of individuals and families. This trend has existed from the earliest colonial times to the present.

A recent study by Jonathan H. Turner and Charles E. Starnes (1976) presents a comprehensive description and analysis of the distribution of wealth in the United States. These authors define wealth as "total economic assets." Wealth thus encompasses income, other monetary assets, and also various economic holdings which can be converted into money such as stocks, bonds, real estate, equity in homes, automobiles, and trusts.

Since 1810, the richest 1 percent of the population has consistently held about 25 percent of the total wealth of the country (Turner and Starnes, 1976). The data in Table 4-1 show that in selected years from 1922 to 1972, 1 percent of the population has held somewhere between 20 to 36 percent of the total personal wealth in the United States.

Income is the money received for labor, services, or from property ownership and other investments. Although it is only a part of total wealth, its distribution provides a way of examining the concentration of wealth, since one of the principal sources of wealth is income. Table 4-2 shows the distribution of family income in the United States in 1975. The data show that only 1.4 percent of all families have incomes of $50,000 or more. In numerical terms, this is 783,000 families out of a total of 56,244,000. Over half of all families received less than $15,000 in yearly income in 1975, with a median income for all families of $13,719.

Table 4-3 focuses more directly on the wealthy by presenting the distribution of wealth among those with estate tax returns of $60,000 or more in 1962 and 1972. In both years almost 80 percent of the wealthy had less than $200,000 in assets. At the other end of the hierarchy, approximately 5 percent of the wealthy had holdings of one million dollars or more. Great wealth is thus concentrated in the hands of a very small number of individuals and families.

Table 4-1. *Percent Share of Personal Wealth Held by Top 1 Percent of the Population: 1922-1972 (selected years)*

Year	Percent Share of Top 1 Percent* %
1922	31.6
1929	36.3
1933	28.3
1939	30.6
1945	23.3
1949	20.8
1953	24.3
1954	24.0
1956	26.0
1958	23.8
1962	22.0
1965	23.4
1969	20.1
1972	20.7

*Covers persons 21 years old and over.

Source: Adapted from U.S. Department of Commerce, Bureau of the Census, *Pocket Data Book, U.S.A. 1976:* November, 1976, p. 229.

Table 4-2. *Total Money Income of Families in 1975*

Total Money Income	Families	
	Percent %	Number (thousands)
Under $ 5,000	12.0	6,766
$ 5,000–9,999	21.1	11,920
$10,000–14,999	22.3	12,561
$15,000–19,999	18.7	10,548
$20,000–24,999	11.6	6,518
$25,000–49,999	12.7	7,148
$50,000 and over	1.4	783
Total families	100.00	56,244

Source: Adapted and abridged from U.S. Department of Commerce. Bureau of the Census. *Current Population Reports.* "Consumer Income" Series P-60, No. 105, June, 1977, p. 2.

Table 4-3. *Personal Wealth of Top Wealth-Holders** : 1962–1972*

Top wealth-holders with gross estate of:	Year			
	1962		1972	
	Number (thousands)	Percent %	Number (thousands)	Percent %
$ 60,000–$ 99,999	1,593	38.6	4,938	38.5
$100,000–$199,999	1,627	39.4	5,175	40.4
$200,000–$499,999	692	16.7	2,059	16.1
$500,000–$999,999	149	3.6	425	3.3
$1 million–$10 million	69	1.7		
$10 million or more	2	*	222	1.7
Total	4,132	100.00	12,819	100.00

*Less than .5 percent

**Based on estate tax returns with gross assets of $60,000 or more.

Source: Adapted and abridged from U.S. Department of Commerce, Bureau of the Census, *Pocket Data Book, U.S.A. 1976,* November 1976, p. 229.

Table 4-4 illustrates the concentration of wealth in terms of billion of dollars, again in the years 1962 and 1972. In 1962, the wealthiest 1 percent of the population together held 548 billion dollars in gross personal assets, out of a total for all persons of 2,094 billion dollars. In 1972 the top 1 percent held 1,047 out of 4,256 billion dollars. Most of this wealth held by the top 1 percent is actually held by those within the top .5 percent. Thus, 384 out of 487 billion dollars in 1962, and 721 out of 916 billion dollars in 1972, was held by this smaller segment of the wealthy. The wealth held by the top .5 percent is 79 percent of the total wealth of the top 1 percent of the population in 1962 and 1972.

Table 4-4. *Personal Assets in Billions of Dollars for All Persons, Top One-Half Percent, and Top One Percent of the Population: 1962 and 1972*

| | | Gross Personal Assets (In Billions of Dollars) | |
	All Persons	Top One-Half Percent	Top One Percent
1962			
Total assets	2,094	432	548
Liabilities	314	48	61
Net worth	1,780	384	487
1972			
Total assets	4,256	822	1,047
Liabilities	809	101	131
Net worth	3,447	721	916

Source: Adapted from U.S. Department of Commerce, Bureau of the Census, *Pocket Data Book U.S.A. 1976*, November 1976, p. 229.

Turner and Starnes (1976) frequently present data from a study of wealth distribution in the United States conducted by Projector and Weiss (1966) and released by the Board of Governors of the Federal Reserve System. This investigation gathered data pertaining to both the size and composition of wealth held by the population of the United States in 1962. The sample was drawn according to "consumer units," which may be either individuals living alone or families. A distinctive feature of this study is that those people with considerable wealth were sampled at much higher rates than were other segments of the population. As a result, data was gathered regarding the wealthy that had not previously been available and that has not since been updated. The study is thus unique and provides data worthy of careful consideration, despite the fact that it would otherwise be viewed as outdated.

Table 4-5, which is constructed from the data gathered in the Projector and Weiss (1966) study, shows that in 1962 less than 3 percent of the "consumer units" studied had $100,000 or more, and less than 7 percent held wealth of $50,000 or more. Turner and Starnes (1976) cite further data supporting the idea that most personal wealth is concentrated in the hands of a relatively small segment of the population. Data show that 76 percent of the wealth and 57 percent of the income in the United States is held by 20 percent of the consumer units.

The holding of wealth can also be analyzed in terms of the types of assets possessed by those with varying levels of wealth. Table 4-6 presents data of this nature. It can be seen that most consumer units have some liquid assets, such as cash or a checking account, and an automobile, whereas considerable numbers among those at the lower and middle levels of wealth also have some assets in a home. Note the higher percentages, at the higher levels of wealth, who hold assets in business, professions and in investments and trusts. For example, even though only 4 percent of those with total assets less than $1,000 have investment assets, 93 to 99 percent of those in the three

Table 4-5. *Size of Net Worth, 1962*

Net Worth**	Percent Distribution of Consumer Units
Negative	11
Zero	5
$1–999	12
$1,000–4,999	17
$5,000–9,999	15
$10,000–24,999	23
$25,000–49,000	10
$50,000–99,999	4
$100,000–199,999	1
$200,000–499,999	1
$500,000–999,999	*
$1,000,000 and over	*

*Indicates amounts insignificant in terms of the particular unit (for example, less than ½ of 1 percent).

**Net worth is defined as wealth minus unsecured debts.

Source: Abridged and adopted from Dorothy S. Projector and Gertrude S. Weiss, *Survey of Financial Characteristics of Consumers* (Washington, D.C.: Federal Reserve Board) 1966, p. 96.

Table 4-6. *Percentage of Consumer Units Having Equity in Specified Assets, According to Size of Wealth, 1962*

Wealth Size	Home %	Automobile %	Business and Profession %	Type of Asset Liquid Assets 1 %	Investment Assets 2 %	Miscellaneous Assets 3 %
All units	57	73	17	79	31	8
$1–999	9	74	3	70	4	3
$1,000–4,999	54	76	8	78	14	6
$5,000–9,999	78	77	16	85	30	7
$10,000–24,999	84	82	19	96	42	11
$25,000–49,999	80	88	38	97	64	15
$50,000–99,999	72	89	54	98	89	15
$100,000–199,999	86	93	53	100	93	16
$200,000–499,999	84	84	57	97	95	12
$500,000 and over	81	79	66	100	99	52

1. Checking and savings accounts, savings bonds

2. Mainly marketable securities, investment real estate, mortgages

3. Principally assets held in personal trusts

Source: Abridged from Dorothy S. Projector and Gertrude S. Weiss *Survey of Financial Characteristics of Consumers* Washington, D.C.: Board of Governors of the Federal Reserve System. 1966, p. 110.

highest wealth brackets possess wealth of this type. Therefore, there are major differences not only in the amount of wealth but also in the type of assets at different levels of total wealth.

Table 4-7 further illustrates these contrasts in the type of assets possessed by holders of differential amounts of wealth. This table shows the percentage of total wealth held in each of the six types of assets listed in Table 4-6. Striking contrasts can be observed between the lowest and the highest wealth levels. Among those whose wealth is $999 or less, 82 percent of total wealth is held in an automobile and liquid assets. In comparison, among those whose wealth is $500,000 and over, these assets account for less the 5 percent of total wealth. For the lowest wealth level only 8 percent of total wealth is held in business and professions, investment assets, and miscellaneous assets (principally personal trusts); this figure rises to 91 percent among the most wealthy. Those with wealth holdings ranging from $1,000 to $49,999 have the greatest percentage of their wealth in equity in their home. For those with wealth of $50,000 and above, investments are proportionally the largest single asset.

Table 4-8 further illustrates the concentration of wealth by presenting the mean amount in dollars of equity in specific types of assets. Perhaps the most striking data revealed in the table is the great disparity in the amount of wealth in certain assets between the two highest levels of wealth and those with less wealth. Sharp contrasts can also be seen between the two highest levels themselves. The mean dollar amounts of wealth in the categories of business and profession, investments, and miscellaneous assets (principally personal trusts) increases sharply among those whose total wealth is $200,000–499,999 when this wealth level is compared to those just below. This increase is still greater when this level of total wealth is compared with that above it, composed of consumer units with a total wealth of $500,000 and over. Observe the striking differences between the two highest wealth levels in the mean amount of dollars held in investments and miscellaneous assets. The great concentration of wealth in the United States is again clearly indicated in this table. Note again that Table 4-5 indicates that those with over $500,000 were less than 1 percent of consumer units in 1962, while the lower wealth level ($200,000–499,999) was only 1 percent.

Based on the Projector and Weiss (1966) study and other data pertaining to wealth and its composition in the United States, Turner and Starnes (1976) offer a general overview of the relationship between property differences and social classes. At the bottom of the wealth hierarchy are those whose economic assets are limited to some equity in an automobile and liquid assets. These individuals possessed less than $1,000 in wealth in 1962. Above this bottom rung is the next level in which a majority holds some equity in home ownership. This broad middle range, which constitutes 58 percent of consumer units, held wealth ranging from $1,000 to $24,999 in 1962. Despite differences in wealth levels, a common bond is provided by the fact that approximately half of the wealth of these segments of the population is invested in home ownership. The next wealth level of $25,000 to $49,999 is distinguished from those beneath it by the fact that there is a noticeable decrease in the proportion of wealth in home equity, and an increase in the proportion of total wealth held in equity in a business or profession and investment assets. This level is referred to by Turner and Starnes (1976) as the "gatekeepers" to the real holders of wealth in the United States.

Above $50,000 are the "estate capitalists." It is within these groups that equity is increasingly held in business, trusts and investments. Among the top wealth category,

Table 4-7. *Percentage** Share of Wealth in Specified Form for Consumer Units, According to Size of Wealth, 1962*

Wealth Size	Total Wealth %	Home %	Automobile %	Business and Profession %	Liquid Assets 1 %	Investment Assets 2 %	Miscellaneous Assets 3 %
All Units	100	27	3	18	13	33	5
$1–999	100	10	48	2	34	4	2
$1,000–4,999	100	48	16	3	26	6	1
$5,000–9,999	100	59	8	9	17	6	1
$10,000–24,999	100	55	5	9	16	13	1
$25,000–49,999	100	37	3	19	18	21	2
$50,000–99,999	100	21	2	24	16	36	2
$100,000–199,999	100	17	2	17	14	48	1
$200,000–499,999	100	9	1	24	7	56	3
$500,000 and over	100	4	*	23	4	50	18

**Percentages may not add to 100 due to rounding errors

*Less than ½ of 1 percent

1. Checking and savings accounts, savings bonds
2. Mainly marketable securities, investment real estate, mortgages
3. Principally assets held in personal trusts

Source: Abridged from Dorothy S. Projector and Gertrude S. Weiss *Survey of Financial Characteristics of Consumers,* Washington, D.C.: Board of Governors of the Federal Reserve System. 1966, p. 21.

Table 4-8. *Mean Amount (in dollars) of Equity in Specified Assets for Consumer Units According to Size of Wealth, 1962*

Wealth Size	Total Wealth $	Home $	Automobile $	Business and Profession $	Liquid Assets *1 $	Investment Assets *2 $	Miscellaneous Assets *3 $
All units	20,982	5,653	644	3,881	2,675	7,031	1,116
$1–999	396	40	190	9	134	14	9
$1,000–4,999	2,721	1,298	445	83	701	170	25
$5,000–9,999	7,267	4,260	614	625	1,227	440	100
$10,000–24,999	16,047	8,852	850	1,499	2,624	2,054	168
$25,000–49,999	35,191	12,991	1,134	6,644	6,371	7,518	533
$50,000–99,999	68,980	14,167	1,499	16,719	10,858	24,556	1,181
$100,000–199,999	132,790	22,790	2,232	22,938	18,808	64,127	1,894
$200,000–499,999	300,355	25,889	2,326	72,516	21,007	169,052	9,564
$500,000 and over	1,260,667	56,232	2,679	295,035	46,094	628,271	232,355

*1 Checking and savings accounts, savings bonds

*2 Mainly marketable securities, investment real estate, mortgages

*3 Principally assets held in personal trusts

Source: Abridged from Dorothy S. Projector and Gertrude S. Weiss *Survey of Financial Characteristics of Consumers,* Washington, D.C.: Board of Governors of the Federal Reserve System. 1966, p. 110.

comprised of consumer units holding $500,000 and over, 91.6 percent of wealth is in these three forms. Investments become particularly important above the $100,000 level. Turner and Starnes (1976) note that since such investments are predominantly in owner-ship of corporate stocks, real estate, and mortgages, the property base of the dominant wealth class in the United States is held in ownership of the means of production. Thus, personal wealth merges with control of economic processes and institutions. Comprising 6 percent of all consumer units, those above $50,000 hold 57 percent of the total wealth. They also hold 80 percent of investment wealth, 69 percent of wealth in directly managed business and professions, and 90 percent of wealth in the "miscellaneous" category, which is almost wholly in trusts.

In terms of the conception of social class presented in this book, the distribution of wealth is the most important but not the only factor in class stratification. A more com-plete consideration of the components of social classes also involves a consideration of occupation and education, and the relationship between these factors and wealth.

Table 4-9 shows the distribution of education in the United States in the year 1974. The data show that almost 39 percent of the population has not completed high school, whereas only slightly more than 13 percent has completed four years of college. Although not as skewed as in the case of wealth, the distribution of educational advan-tages also shows that relatively few have attained what is increasingly becoming a mini-mal education for many of the more desirable types of employment.

The relationship between education and yearly and lifetime income is shown in Table 4-10. The data indicate that as educational level increases, both yearly and life-time income increase. The lifetime income for a college graduate is nearly triple that for individuals with fewer than eight years of schooling. The greatest single step increase is between those with some college and those with four or more years of college. This addi-tional level of education yields $4,400 in yearly income and $166,000 in lifetime in-come. As noted in the previous chapter, in addition to increased income, higher educa-

Table 4-9.   *Years of School Completed by Persons 25 Years Old and Over, 1974*

Years of School Completed	Percent Completing %
Elementary School	
0–4 years	4.4
5–7 years	7.6
8 years	10.8
High School	
1–3 years	15.9
4 years	36.1
College	
1–3 years	11.9
4 years or more	13.3

Source: Adapted and abridged from U.S. Bureau of the Census, *Statis-tical Abstract of the United States,* 1975, p. 118.

Table 4-10. *Lifetime* and Mean Income by Years of School Completed, 1972, for Males, Aged 25 to 64*

Years of School Completed	Lifetime Income $	1972 Income $
Elementary School		
Less than 8 years	231,000	6,400
8 years	284,000	7,900
High School		
1–3 years	324,000	9,000
4 years	393,000	10,700
College		
1–3 years	461,000	12,200
4 years	627,000	16,600

*Figures for lifetime income are based on the application of appropriate life tables to arithmetic mean income by age, as obtained for a cross section of population in the year 1972. Figures are based on 1972 dollars.

Source: Adapted and abridged from U.S. Bureau of Census, *Statistical Abstract of the United States,* 1975, p. 123.

tional levels frequently lead to more desirable jobs, which entail the possession of greater authority and of more prestige.

Table 4–11 presents the relationship between occupation and income and years of school completed, for both males and females. The data bear out the discussion in chapter 3 pertaining to the relationship between occupation and the other components of social class. Although the relationships are not perfectly linear, the data for males show that as a man moves from the less skilled and blue-collar occupations to the white-collar and professional occupations, income and education both tend to increase. The same trend is evident for women, although it is not nearly as strong. A noticeable aspect of the data is the striking differences in income between males and females employed in the same occupational category. This disparity will be discussed in further detail in a later chapter that deals with sexual stratification.

PORTRAITS OF SOCIAL CLASSES
IN THE UNITED STATED

A survey of the literature purporting to describe the class structure of the United States shows a lack of consistency with respect to the number of classes that are identified, their names, and their characteristics. Several closely interrelated deficiencies in the current state of scholarly work in the study of stratification are at the root of the lack of more precise and uniform knowledge in this area. Different theories of stratification some-times provide contrasting perspectives which lead to very dissimilar perceptions of the class structure. Class is also conceptualized in very different ways partly because of these more fundamental theoretical differences. The criteria for determining the existence of

Table 4-11. *Median Earnings and Median School Years Completed by Occupation and Sex for the Experienced Civilian Labor Force, 1970*

| | Male | | Female | |
| | Median Earnings (Dollars) | Median School Yrs. Completed | Median Earnings (Dollars) | Median School Yrs. Completed |
Occupation				
Professional, Technical, Kindred	10,617	16.3	6,030	16.1
Managers and Administrators except Farm.	11,012	12.9	5,494	12.6
Sales Workers	8,447	12.7	2,316	12.2
Clerical and Kindred Workers	7,259	12.5	4,228	12.5
Craftsmen and Kindred Workers	8,176	12.0	4,450	12.0
Operatives, except Transport	6,737	11.1	3,634	10.6
Transport equipment operatives	6,923	10.9	2,481	12.0
Laborers, except Farm.	4,614	10.4	2,927	11.0
Farmers and Farm managers	4,869	10.8	2,235	11.5
Service, except priv. household	5,086	11.2	2,323	11.5
Private Household	1,712	9.3	981	11.5

Figures based upon those working median of 50 weeks.
Source: Adapted and abridged from U.S. Department of Commerce, *1970 Census of Population. Occupational Characteristics,* p. 1–11.

classes and the placement of individuals within them varies. The methodology itself, used to measure class, differs. This becomes particularly significant in light of the fact that class divisions and distinctions are sometimes made as much, if not more, on the basis of methodological considerations, as they are on the basis of theory. For example, income distributions may be divided according to the number of individuals in each category, rather than in conjunction with a theory.

Also, due to the differences in the locales of stratification studies (Reissman, 1959: 177–225), care must be exercised in describing the class structure of the United States. Much of the early research on social class structure in the United States dealt with smaller communities. The more recent studies of the class structure on a national level are fragmentary in the scope of their investigations. Factors that are important at the community level often do not exist on the national level, such as widespread personal recognition within the community and high homogeneity of the population. Therefore, careful consideration must be exercised in generalizing from local studies to the national class stratification system.

Despite these problems, enough consensus has been achieved in the literature to allow the class structure of the United States to be described. Notwithstanding some descrepancies, there is general agreement that classes in some way involve, or are based on, occupation, education, income, and wealth. There is also general agreement that classes involve or are closely linked to differential power, privilege, and prestige, although the relative emphasis placed on these three factors differs widely.

The determination of the number of social classes in a given population depends in part on how broadly or narrowly the investigator defines the economic, occupational, and social differences (Sorokin, 1969:272–273). If they are too narrow—say, if economic groupings are differentiated at very small increments of income—then there could be hundreds of "classes." This however would be inaccurate, since the differentiations between classes should be based on fundamental disparities in economic, occupational, and social position. Attention to minute differences tends to obscure similarities of life conditions of the members of the same class, and their dissimilarities from members of other classes.

Although there is a lack of consistency in the literature regarding the number of classes and their sizes, a basic outline of the class structure can be formulated on the basis of various investigations (Kahl, 1960). Both Kahl (1960:184–217) and, more recently, Rossides (1976:23–30), describe a five-class structure of upper, upper-middle, lower-middle, working, and lower classes. Drawing on these two authors, the characteristics of these five classes are summarized as follows:

- *Upper class.* Very high income and great wealth, often going back for several generations. High prestige. Members of this class make fundamental decisions and exert considerable control over the economy and civic affairs. Members of boards of directors of large organizations. Education at elite schools.
- *Upper-middle class.* High incomes. Professionals and high level managers and business people who are just below the very top level of organizational hierarchy. Income derived mainly from occupation. Emphasis on lifelong career. College educated. Own property and have savings.
- *Lower-middle class.* Modest incomes. Lesser professionals, small business, clerical and sales, upper level manual workers. Mainly high school graduates. Some savings. Members emphasize respectability.
- *Working class.* Low incomes. Skilled and semiskilled labor. Some high school or grade school education. Live adequately but on narrow margin. Small or no savings. Little or no hope for advancement in work. Aim at getting by on day to day existence.
- *Lower class.* Poverty income. Unskilled labor. Lowest paying jobs. Irregular work and high unemployment. Grade school or less education. No savings. Considered not respectable by members of other classes.

Rossides (1976:24–25) estimates that the upper class consists of 1 to 3 percent of the population, the upper-middle class 10 to 15 percent, the lower-middle class 30 to 35 percent, the working class 40 to 45 percent, and the lower class 20 to 25 percent.

On the basis of investigations of a number of small communities, W. Lloyd Warner and his associates (Warner, Meeker, and Eells, 1960) maintain that communities in the United States have either five or six social classes. In older communities, the upper class is divided into two segments, the upper-upper and the lower-upper. Membership in the upper-upper class is based on such factors as family lineage and inherited wealth, whereas the lower-upper class is composed of those who have more recently gained wealth.

In newer communities, the upper-upper class has not had time to develop. For an upper-upper class to develop, a community must be large enough that a variety of types of social participation, such as private clubs and choice of marriage partners, can be restricted to the upper-upper class. It is only on this basis that the lower-upper class can be excluded and a separate identity thus created by the upper-upper class.

Warner believes the middle class is also divided into upper and lower levels. The upper level of the middle class is composed of professionals and proprietors, some of whom are typically active in community affairs. The lower-middle class is composed of individuals who principally work in low level white collar positions and own little property.

The lower class is likewise divided into upper and lower levels. The upper-lower class is composed for the most part of semi-skilled and unskilled workers. The lower-lower class is virtually set apart from the rest of the community. They are regarded by others in the community as not respectable, and many receive government support.

Aside from questions of number, size, and difficulties of conceptualization, certain general statements can be made about the nature of social classes. Classes are social worlds with their own particular characteristics. They consist of typical daily experiences, life situations, and cultural expectations. The nature of these social worlds may differ greatly among social classes. Some classes have many advantages whereas others are disadvantaged in various ways. Cultural traditions and style of life may differ radically in different social classes. So also may social affiliations and participation in organizational activities. The relationship of different social classes to legal and law enforcement agencies and to political and educational institutions is often very different.

These social worlds of classes in turn have an influence on the views individuals develop about themselves, others, and society at large. Those in the same social class often have characteristic opinions, viewpoints, and interests that are shared in common and that contrast in varying degrees with those of other social classes. In one way or another, social class position affects the lives of individuals from birth to death.

The following pages present summaries of selected studies of social classes in the United States. These studies illustrate some of the salient features of the major social classes, some of the differences between social classes, and the impact of social class position on the life histories of individuals.

The Lower Classes: W. Lloyd Warner and Associates

The study by W. Lloyd Warner and associates of Yankee City, a New England town of about 17,000 people, provides a portrayal of social classes in a small community (Warner, *et al.,* 1963; Warner and Lunt, 1941; Warner, Meeker, and Eells, 1960). It should be noted that this study was conducted in the 1930s. Despite changes since then, it still graphically portrays many of the important aspects of the lives of people in different classes. The lower class is subdivided into upper and lower levels. The upper-lower class of Yankee City includes 33 percent of the population; approximately 25 percent are in the lower-lower class. Thus, well over half of the community belongs to one of the two lowest classes in the social structure. The upper-lower class is viewed as being on what Warner, *et al.,* refer to as the "Common Man" level; the lower-lower class is set apart as being on a level below that of the Common Man.

Individuals in the upper-lower class are interested in money, but place greater stress on various symbols of status, such as furniture, attractive yards, and a good education for their children. They are regarded by members of other classes in Yankee City as poor, but honest and respectable, members of the community.

The upper-lower class has less economic resources than the lower-middle class. Over 60 percent of those in the labor force are semi-skilled workers, employed in industries such as shoe manufacturing, retail stores, transportation, and the building trades.

Slightly more than half of the houses in which the upper-lower class lives are small dwellings. Significant numbers of these are in medium condition, but this class has double the number of small houses in bad repair than are found in the lower-middle class. Here begins the world of questionable plumbing, floors that are not quite level, leaky roofs, and in some instances, the slight but ever present danger that one's foot may fall through the floor.

Those higher in the class structure view the lower-lower class as not respectable. The latter are regarded as lazy, shiftless, improvident, and unwilling to work. From the frame of reference of the Protestant Ethic and the characterization of middle-class values emphasized by those higher in the class structure in Yankee City, the conduct of the lower-lower class is thus the direct antithesis of virtue. They are also ill regarded because of what are believed by those higher in the class structure to be their low sexual morals.

Almost 80 percent of those in the lower-lower class who work are employed in semi-skilled occupations. This class also has the highest percentage of unskilled workers. Many are employed in shoe and hat factories and in transportation industries in Yankee City. The lower-lower class has the greatest percentage of members working only part time and the greatest percentage of unemployed. About one out of three people in the lower-lower class receive government support; 65 percent of the total number on relief in the city are in this class.

Like the upper-lower class, the lower-class contains a large number of people belonging to ethnic minorities. All the blacks and almost all the Poles and Russians in Yankee City are in the lower-lower class.

Home ownership among the lower-lower class is less than 6 percent, the lowest in Yankee City. This class has the highest percentage of members living in small houses, and the highest percentage living in houses in bad condition.

Members of the lower-lower class are more frequently arrested than are any others in the community. Sixty-five percent of the arrests in Yankee City are from this class. About one quarter of these are below eighteen years of age, and about one third are below twenty-one. This fact indicates that the lower-lower class cannot protect its youth from the police as can those classes that are nearer the top of the class structure.

Most of the high school students from the lower-lower class are enrolled in commercial and general education courses. A larger percentage of youth in this class work than in any other, and a larger percentage go to work before the age of sixteen.

The Lower Blue-Collar Class:
Albert K. Cohen and Harold M. Hodges, Jr.

A study by Cohen and Hodges (1963) gives an interesting and informative portrayal of lower class life. The study focuses on these aspects of the lower blue-collar or "lower-lower" class that are significantly different from other social strata. Data for the study were derived primarily from self-administered questionnaires gathered from approximately 2,600 male heads of families in the San Francisco Peninsula.

Cohen and Hodges (1963) focus on four crucial aspects of the work roles and daily life of what they call the lower-lower class. These basic areas of focus are simplification of the experience world, powerlessness, deprivation, and insecurity.

Simplification of the experience world pertains to the limited range of situations and perspectives to which members of the lower-lower class are typically exposed. The lower blue-collar class work role usually involves a routine activity that does not call for diversification or a response to changing situations. In general, the lower-lower class member's scope of contact with contrasting cultural worlds is limited. His or her vicarious experiences are also relatively restricted due to lack of education and a tendency to limit personal contacts to people from the same background.

People in the lower blue-collar class are relatively powerless in many senses. Their bargaining power is weak because they are easily replaced in the productive process. Their skills confer little prestige. Their access to and control over information affecting their lives is minimal. The work roles of the lower-lower class reflect their relative powerlessness, typically having a narrow range for autonomous decision making.

Deprivation is defined by Cohen and Hodges as "poverty of resources relative to felt needs and levels of aspiration" (1963:305). The lower-lower class is more chronically deprived in this sense than other levels in the class structure. This deprivation is related to the cultural stress placed on self-betterment and upward mobility, and to unfulfilled aspirations relative to the consumption patterns advocated in the mass market. In these areas, the lower blue-collar class is characterized by a general lack of fulfillment of its aspirations.

The insecurity of the lower-lower class is due to irregular and unpredictable occurrences of deprivation. Emergencies such as sickness, disability, injury, or loss of property are particularly calamitous to members in this strata because they lack reserve resources. Their deprivation is further compounded by their lack of knowledge and skills for obtaining assistance, even if assistance is available from public or private organizations.

These four recurrent situations and experiences constitute the effective environment to which those in the lower-lower class must adapt. In order to cope with them, emphasis is placed on the enhancement of power and the reduction of insecurity.

The chief way in which individuals in the lower blue-collar class deal with the difficulties in their environment is by developing a network of social relationships with those in similar circumstances. The principal norm within this network of interpersonal ties is that, insofar as is possible, help should be rendered to others in time of need. If this friendship circle is extensive enough, and if an individual has met previous obligations to others, then he or she can usually obtain sufficient help. In time of trouble or calamity, such as injury, death in the family, unemployment, or problems with law enforcement, someone will be willing to be of assistance. This system of relationships is based on interpersonal ties that are diffuse and reciprocal, rather than on occupational status or achievement in the realm of competition. The lower-lower class person attempts to stay within this network of familiar status equals, and regards those outside its confines as outsiders who are for the most part to be avoided.

Relatives are part of the supporting and protective network of the lower-lower class. Members of this strata interact more with relatives than do individuals of any other strata, both absolutely and in comparison to interactions with other categories of friends such as neighbors, friends from work, or friends they have met elsewhere. Neighbors seem to be of secondary importance to relatives in the social life of the lower blue-collar class. In contrast, this class participates least in voluntary associations, compared to any other strata. Social activities are more restricted in the lower-lower class than in any other social strata, and those ties that do exist are based on kinship and the propinquity of the neighborhood.

Consistent with these findings regarding social relationships and networks, Cohen and Hodges (1963) note that one of the most evident findings of their study is that the typical lower-lower class individual has a distinct preference for the routine, predictable, and familiar. Meeting new people and encountering new situations, forming new social relationships, and interacting with strangers are all undertaken with extreme reluctance. The relative inflexibility of role-taking on the part of the lower blue-collar class member is complementary to the previously noted emphasis on focusing one's social life in interaction with relatives and neighborhood friends, and seldom stepping outside of that circle of familiar faces.

A pessimistic view of the world and a pervasive sense of insecurity were the themes that were most consistently expressed by the lower-lower class members. These attitudes clearly distinguished individuals of this class from others. The world is viewed as an inhospitable place in which misfortune and calamity may occur at any moment. Cohen and Hodges (1963) consider this to be partly a realistic perception of the life situation faced by the lower-lower class and also partly an adaptive perception. Pessimism serves to shield the lower-lower class individual from high expectations that may not be met and from moral criticisms for personal failure to achieve.

Cohen and Hodges (1963) speculate that such a situation creates a vicious circle in which life conditions characterized by powerlessness, deprivation, and insecurity produce a view of the world as bleak and uncertain. This world view in turn influences the adoption of a lifestyle of improvidence that promotes the recurrence of experiences of powerlessness, deprivation, and insecurity, thus confirming the world view of the lower-lower class person. Perception and environment interact and reinforce each other to create a situation that operates to the continued detriment of those in the lower blue-collar class.

The world view of the lower-lower class is reflected in the attitudes of individuals toward others. Lower-lower class members were found to be far more misanthropic than members of other social strata, regarding others in a cynical and distrustful manner. They viewed people as selfish and ready to take advantage of them and others. Consistent with these views, lower-lower class respondents were also more intolerant of social deviants, particularly intolerant of ethnic minorities, and were highly anti-intellectual.

Probably partly due to their views of the world and of others, the lower-lower class individuals tended to emphasize "toughness." They stressed the ability to withstand suffering and troubles, and a general posture of self-assertiveness and defiance.

Lower blue-collar respondents also tended to be more authoritarian than members of other strata. This was manifest in an emphasis on those aspects of authoritarianism that pertain to dominance and submission, the importance of strong leadership, and the necessity of compliance on the part of those in subordinate positions. Cohen and Hodges (1963) speculate that one reason for this orientation is that the role relationships of the lower-lower class, especially at work, usually involve a definite authority structure in which some give orders and others carry them out. Consistent with this emphasis on authority relations, the lower-lower class family often has a patriarchial structure in which men are the head of the family and women are subordinate to them. Thus, for the lower-lower class, more than any other, the social structures and subcultures that constitute their day-to-day environment are significantly cast in an authoritarian mold. This may tend to create the attitudes of authoritarianism characteristic of this class.

The Industrial Worker: Ely Chinoy

In the United States there has traditionally been a strong cultural emphasis on the availability of opportunities for ambitious individuals to achieve advancement and success. The actual degree of openness of the social structure in the United States of course varies from the cultural ideal of equal opportunity. Although opportunities existed in earlier centuries, the growth of large, centralized industry has made it increasingly difficult for individuals starting at the bottom of the structure to achieve significant degrees of upward mobility.

How industrial workers deal with the disparity between the cultural expectations of opportunity and success and the reality of extremely limited avenues of advancement is the topic of Ely Chinoy's study of workers in a large automobile manufacturing plant (1952; 1965). Data for the study was gathered primarily through observation and extensive interviews with sixty-two white male workers. These men were semi-skilled and skilled workers, machine operators, and assembly-line tenders.

Little opportunity for advancement exists within the factory and the workers are very aware of this. Engineering and management positions are almost completely closed to them due to educational and other requirements. Opportunities for movement upward to the position of foreperson are extremely limited and problematical. Advancement from semi-skilled to skilled positions is almost nonexistent. The nature of plant operations and structure is such that hard work, inventiveness, and personal character have little influence on access to what few opportunities for advancement do exist.

Most of the men believe that they have little prospect of shifting to another job. Leaving the plant, however, is a frequent topic of conversation among workers, but is not for the most part either meant or taken seriously.

Chinoy (1952) found that even in the face of these strictures on their realizable aspirations and opportunities, the automobile workers had not abandoned the cultural ethic enjoining continued effort to attain advancement and success. Instead, they transformed the goal of high aspirations and success to conform to the realities of limited achievements and opportunities.

In accordance with the cultural belief regarding the availability of opportunity, some workers take the blame for their lack of success squarely on their own shoulders. This condemnation of self has obvious undesirable effects. As a result, workers develop various constructions of reality to reconcile their less than lofty positions with the success values of society. One such method of coping involves defining the effort to attain the limited goals that can be achieved in their industrial plant as an example of their drive to "get ahead." For example, the smallest wage increase comes to be viewed as an important symbol of the attainment of success values.

Given this dead-end situation, concerns for success are shifted to other avenues, such as job security. Job security becomes equated with advancement, and Chinoy (1952) found that most workers view the two as identical. However, since job security has become collectivized through union efforts toward this end, it does not fulfill the need for individual success strivings. Such needs for individual reaffirmation of success values are partially met through the security attained by the accumulation of personal savings. Public evidence of advancement is realized in the possession and display of material goods. Cars, furniture, television sets, and material possessions in general become evidence of success. Consumption is thus substituted for occupational advancement. Material possessions display one's worth and are symbols of ambition and success.

Industrial workers also reaffirm the cultural traditions of opportunity and advancement by focusing on their children's future. None of those studied by Chinoy wanted their sons to work in a factory, and all believed that if their children manifested the necessary effort and ambition, they could move up in the occupational hierarchy.

The Middle Classes: W. Lloyd Warner and Associates

The middle class in smaller communities is portrayed by Warner and his associates as being divided into two levels, the upper and the lower (Warner, *et al.*, 1963; Warner and Lunt, 1941; Warner, Meeker, and Eells, 1960). The upper-middle class constitutes about 10 percent of the population of Yankee City; the lower-middle class is larger, comprising 28 percent of the total community.

There is a significant difference between these two levels of the middle class. The upper-middle class, along with the two upper classes, constitute the strata above that of the "Common Man." Considerable social distance exists between these classes and those below them.

The upper-middle class is highly respected within the community. This class emphasizes money and comfort. Most members of the upper-middle class try to obtain more money, both for its own value and for the status it brings. They are very much involved in civic affairs and charitable activities, and place emphasis on holding high moral principles. Many members of this class aspire to move into the lower-upper class, and hope that their community activities and good reputation will provide the increased status necessary for upward mobility and entrée into the exclusive cliques and associations of the upper classes. Such is very seldom the case, however.

Most of the upper-middle class who are in the work force are in professional and proprietary occupations. Sixty-three percent are in these types of occupations, as compared to 83 and 86 percent of the upper-upper and lower-upper, respectively. Others are wholesale and retail dealers. The incomes of this class allow them to live comfortably, but are less than that of the upper classes. Most live in middle-sized homes. Almost all the children of this class attend public school; very few go to preparatory schools, as do those in the upper classes.

The lower-middle class, comprising about 28 percent of the population of Yankee City, is characterized as the upper level of the Common Man. Individuals in the lower-middle class tend to view money and high morals as the basic solution to all problems.

The lower-middle class exhibits a definite shift in occupational profile from that of the classes above it. Clerical, rather than professional and proprietary, is the most common occupational category. Almost half are either skilled or semi skilled workers. About twice as many in this class are unemployed than in the upper-middle class. As one descends the social hierarchy, it is also the first class in which a significant number of persons receive government support. Forty-two percent live in small homes.

The lower-middle class also differs significantly from those above it in ethnic composition. This class has more than twice the number of foreign born than are found in the upper-middle class.

The pattern of membership in associations also differs in the lower-middle class from that found in the three higher classes. In general, the lower-middle class is more like the two classes below it with respect to associational membership. In contrast to the classes above it in the social structure, very few members of the lower-middle class belong to charitable associations of social clubs, preferring instead fraternal and auxiliary organizations.

The lower-middle class is also unlike the three classes above it with respect to the educational plans it holds for its young people. The courses taken in high school are designed for immediate use, rather than for college preparation.

The Middle Class: C. Wright Mills

The growth of large numbers of white-collar employees and the decline of the independent entrepreneur is one of the major structural changes of the last century in the United States. The characteristics of the middle class emerging from this social change is the focus of C. Wright Mills, *White Collar* (1956).

Since the beginning of the nineteenth century, the United States' economy has changed from one of small capitalists to one of hired employees. In the early nineteenth century, approximately four-fifths of the labor force were self-employed. By 1870, only one-third were; by 1940 the number of economic entrepreneurs had dropped to about one-fifth. Most of the remaining four-fifths of the labor force earn a living by working for others. Among these are members of what Mills (1956) calls the "new middle class," composed of white-collar people on salary. The salaried white-collar workers who compose the new middle class are located in several social strata, ranging from near the top to near the bottom of society, the greatest concentration being in the lower-middle levels.

The rise of the new middle class represents a shift from ownership of property to occupation as the foundation of stratification. Its chief causes are the development of big business and big government, plus the continued growth of large bureaucratic organizations.

Five types of occupational activity are selected by Mills (1956) as representative of the social and cultural circumstances characteristic of the new middle class of salaried workers. His analysis focuses on managers, professionals, intellectuals, salespeople, and office workers.

The emergence of large organizations has been accompanied by a proliferation of managers. This white-collar occupation has increased in number and importance throughout the social structure. The greater prominence of the manager in organizations means that an increasing number of individuals work and have their lives influenced by the rules of bureaucracy, while at the same time becoming objects of superintendence and manipulation within a hierarchical structure.

Managers have differing responsibilities, depending in part on their place in an organizational structure. They are usually ranked in a hierarchy according to their authority to freely initiate activities and to order the work of others. Each level of manager is accountable to those above it in the hierarchy. Those at the top of the business are responsible to the stockholders, which in practical terms means the small number who hold controlling interests. In government bureaucracies the highest management levels are ultimately responsible to politicians. At these top levels, major decisions are made regarding policy, procedure, and objectives. Middle levels of management are involved primarily in the management of people. It is at this middle level that bureaucratic procedures and styles are most evident.

About half of all managers are forepersons, who represent the bottom stratum of management. The functions of the foreperson have changed drastically since the earlier days of industry. The rise of powerful labor unions has deprived the foreperson of many functions and much of the authority previously delegated to this position. The development of a large cadre of middle-level managers and the need for highly skilled technicians to perform tasks once within the forepersons' domain have also diminished the importance of the foreperson's role. Consistent with the managerial ethos, the role of the foreperson is becoming that of developing and maintaining discipline and loyalty among workers. The abilities to manipulate others and get along with them have replaced knowledge of job skills as the prime qualities desired of forepersons.

According to Mills (1956), the shift from the old to the new middle class condition, namely from that of entrepreneurship to that of salaried employee, has had its greatest impact in the professions. These are the occupations in which specialized and lengthy training is characteristic, and in which the highest developments in the arts and sciences are practiced and applied. In most of the newer professions, many practitioners begin as salaried employees. The older professions, such as law and medicine, which had been primarily composed of self-employed practitioners, have also become bureaucratic, with a supportive corps of subprofessionals and assistants.

Although the old middle-class professional persists, most professionals are now salaried employees. They have increasingly become dependent on new technical machinery and the large organizations that can provide for its use. Professionals today are more often members of a staff in a segment of a large organization in which the conditions and nature of their work are determined by others. Along with these trends, narrow specialization has tended to replace breadth of knowledge and of perspective.

Intellectuals are regarded by Mills (1956) as the most heterogeneous of the major middle class groups. Their social position, background, and style of life differs widely. Because of this diversity in social characteristics, intellectuals must be defined by the functions they perform, which are the creation and distribution of art and ideas.

As in the other occupational activities of the new middle class, intellectuals are increasingly influenced and controlled by bureaucracies. As more and more intellectuals become salaried employees, their general aims and the content of their work come increasingly to be set by the decisions and goals of others. The demands of the mass market are frequently the criteria by which the efforts of intellectuals are shaped and ultimately determined. Many intellectuals are occupied in the role of formulating ideological justifications for the policies and actions of the bureaucratic powers for which they work. All these conditions tend to place restrictions on freedom of thought and expression and to curtail criticism of the existing social order. Large universities are probably the most open environment in which significant numbers of intellectuals are employed.

The practice of salesmanship has changed from an essentially individual and localized activity to a pervasive national enterprise. A nationwide advertising market has emerged, the chief purpose of which is to stimulate desires and the demand for products. Obsolescence of commodities is furthered by various marketing techniques. The appearance of products, whether of automobiles or clothing, is emphasized in terms of current fashion as a means to create a greater turnover of goods. The new is thus continually stressed, with the resultant need to replace what is old and no longer in vogue.

Along with the development of such mass market selling techniques, the practice of selling has been centralized and bureaucratized. The creative salesperson operating individually has been replaced by the sales executive, advertising, and the standardized sales routine that is handed down to the salesperson as the fixed parameters of his or her occupational endeavors. Sales executives and psychologists stress the importance of "personality" in sales. The salesperson's appearance and personality are viewed as instruments to be used in the marketplace for the selling of goods. A superficial politeness and the fixed smile are the media through which salespeople are expected to sell their products.

The growth of centralization characteristic of modern sales and marketing is also a trend in office work generally. The increasing use of office machines has furthered the expansion and specialization of the division of labor. This in turn has prompted greater centralization in the interests of control. The operation of office machinery is a routine job without initiative and diversity. Much of the white-collar machine-operative work in modern offices is very similar in essence to blue-collar factory work. Such office jobs promise no opportunity for advancement. Upward mobility into managerial levels from the operative level is rare.

The modern office is dominated by a managerial cadre, in which both authority and status are vested. The highly compartmentalized and specialized working staff, most engaged in routine kinds of activities, are usually separated from higher executives by the middle levels of management, who act as their immediate supervisors.

The ideal of work as craftsmanship can be compared to the work situation of the typical middle class white-collar worker in the various work situations previously discussed. Craftsmanship has a number of features. Perhaps first and foremost is the idea that the product being made and the process of its completion are of supreme and intrinsic value. No other motive for working needs to exist. The craftsperson clearly sees his or her contribution to the whole product and in this sense is psychologically attached to it. The craftsperson has control over the work situation. The work is of such a nature that self development is attained through its practice. Finally, in the ideal of craftsmanship there is no split between work and leisure. Self-expression and fulfillment are integral parts of the work experience.

Mills (1956) argues that none of the facets of a craft are relevant to the typical middle class white-collar worker today. Craftsmanship is realized by only a few in the trades and professions. In the common situation of modern work, the worker has little control over the process or product of his or her work. Individual creativity is limited or completely stifled by the centrality of decision making and the bureaucratic ethos and its machinery. The worker is psychologically detached from the product, and has no intrinsic involvement in its creation or completion. Under these conditions, work becomes a period of time that must be sacrificed in order to be able to meet the needs of living. Economic rewards have become the principal motive for working. Status and the opportunity for exercising power over others also give meaning to the modern work experience.

Given the limited satisfactions to be derived from work, it becomes primarily a means of providing the economic resources to enjoy life outside of the work situation. Hence, the rise of the mass leisure activities that are a predominant feature of society. Although these activities may provide escape and relaxation, they seldom enlarge emotional or intellectual sensitivities and capacities, nor do they develop the creativity of the individual.

The Upper Classes: W. Lloyd Warner and Associates

Like the lower and middle classes in Yankee City, Warner and his associates believed that the upper class could also be subdivided into upper and lower levels (Warner, *et al.,* 1963; Warner and Lunt, 1941; Warner, Meeker, and Eells, 1960). The most signal feature of the upper class is its division into two segments, the upper-upper class and the lower-upper class. This is a status distinction, based primarily on family history and life style.

The upper-upper class is a social aristocracy. Its superior position is due primarily to the fact that its occupants are from families that have lived in the community for some time and possess a history of wealth and high social standing.

The upper-upper class represents about 1.4 percent of the population of Yankee City. This class has the highest proportion of employable individuals who have never worked. Over 83 percent of those who do hold jobs are employed in professional and proprietary positions. None of the gainfully employed are classified as skilled, semi-skilled or unskilled workers. In terms of ethnic background, all of the members of the upper-upper class are natives or "Yankees." The great majority of Yankees are descendants of British stock, with a few being descendants of non-English societies. A larger percentage of upper-upper class members live in houses classified by the researcher as "large," and a smaller percentage live in houses classified as "medium" or "small," than is true of any other class in Yankee City.

The religious preference of the upper-upper class is primarily Unitarian or Episcopalian. A high percentage of both men and women in this class belong to social clubs. Upper-upper class individuals also belong in significant numbers to associations organized for charitable purposes. Individuals in this class tend to marry within the upper-upper class and to marry at a later age than is characteristic of other classes. Almost all of the children of the upper-upper class are sent to private college-preparatory schools.

The upper-upper class accounts for only one-half of 1 percent of the total arrests in the city. None of these arrests are of individuals below the age of twenty-one years. Interviews indicated that the low arrest rate of juveniles in the upper-upper class is not because these youths behave differently but because they are given greater protection by the upper-upper class environment. The class system also operates in such a way that the illegal activities of upper class youth are usually successfully hidden from the authorities. When this is not the case, social pressures are likely to prevent the police from taking action as they would against middle or lower class youth.

The lower-upper class is immediately below the upper-upper class in the class structure of Yankee City and represents about 1.6 percent of the population. In many of the characteristics considered above, the lower-upper class is quite similar to the upper-upper. However, the lower-upper class lacks a sufficiently long history of upper class position, lifestyle, and family background to belong to the social aristocracy formed by the upper-upper class in Yankee City. Members of the lower-upper class are often as wealthy or wealthier than individuals in the upper-upper class, but their wealth is too new and is not sufficient in itself for acceptance by the social elite. The average income of the lower-upper class is actually larger than that of any class, including the upper-upper.

A signal characteristic of the lower-upper class is a highly unstable situation within the family. Since members of the lower-upper class have usually recently moved upward within the class structure, they lack the support provided by the established extended family characteristic of the upper-upper class. Members of the lower-upper class must learn and adopt standards different from those of their youth, and different from those which their children are exposed to outside the home. Such a situation can also contribute to family conflict and instability.

Members of the lower-upper class read books that accent social climbing more than do members of any other class in Yankee City. One way that such advancement is sometimes achieved for future generations is through young people from wealthy families in this class marrying sons or daughters of the upper-upper class. This event is often boasted about by parents of the lower-upper class children, explained by mothers of the upper-upper class as a result of the "spiritual demands of romantic love," and by friends of the party involved as "a good deal and a fair exchange all the way around for everyone concerned" (Warner, Meeker, and Eells, 1960:12).

The Upper Class: G. William Domhoff

The upper class on the national level has been studied by G. William Domhoff (1967). Social classes are regarded as being based on social interaction, intermarriage, a similarity in income, wealth, and occupation, a sharing of common values and attitudes, and a similarity of lifestyle. Domhoff attempts to demonstrate that such an upper social class exists on the national level in the United States. To document the existence of an upper class, Domhoff used inclusion in Social Registers, attendance at certain private preparatory schools, membership in exclusive gentlemen's clubs, and family or marriage ties as criteria that signified membership in the upper class.

The national upper class is made primarily of successful businessmen and corporation lawyers and their descendants. This upper class became national in scope in the latter part of the nineteenth century, with the development of a nationwide corporate economy, and nationwide transportation and communication networks. The upper class is estimated by Domhoff to comprise about 0.5 percent of the population in the United States.

Various organizations and activities provide the social underpinnings of the upper class in the United States (Domhoff, 1967). Chief among these are private schools, elite universities, gentlemen's clubs, charitable and cultural organizations, and various recreational activities, such as polo and yachting. Its economic base is the holding of corporate stocks and membership on boards of directors of large corporations.

The cohesiveness of the national upper class is indicated by various types of evidence. Attendance at particular private schools and universities, interaction at selected summer resorts, and membership in exclusive gentlemen's clubs reveals a high degree of overlap in participation, which is national in scope. Intermarriage among members of the upper class, as indicated in Social Registers and the social pages of major newspapers, also shows the intercity character of the upper class. Domhoff (1967) cites evidence from other studies that indicate that, when asked, prominent upper class individuals quite frequently state that they know others in similar positions. Interlocking corporation and foundation directorates also indicate the national scope of the upper class in the United States.

For the newly rich, acceptance in the upper class can be obtained primarily for succeeding generations. Such acceptance is gained through participation in charitable and cultural projects, election to an exclusive gentlemen's club, and sending one's children to select private schools.

More than any other occupational and career activity, the members of the upper class are involved in some aspect of business and finance. Many are also involved in legal practice. Some have M.D.'s or Ph.D.'s, or are engaged in other types of professional activity, such as architecture.

Domhoff (1967) maintains that the upper class in the United States is also a governing class:

> . . . a social upper class which owns a disproportionate amount of a country's wealth, receives a disproportionate amount of a country's yearly income, and contributes a disproportionate number of its members to the controlling institutions and key decision-making groups of the country (1967:5).

According to Domhoff, the influence of the governing class is often exercised through the power elite, who are individuals in high level decision-making positions in institutions controlled by the upper class. Not all members of the power elite are members of the upper class. Many are not. What is important is that the upper class has control, in the sense of dominance and authority, over the institutions in which the power elite hold key decision-making positions. In this sense, the power elite are the tool of the upper class and serve their interests. They are often selected by the upper class, if they are not members of it.

The central focus of Domhoff's (1967) investigation is to present evidence to demonstrate the control of the upper class over major institutions. The study illustrates that the upper class is a governing class that overlaps, in terms of membership, and dominates, the power elite. In Domhoff's view the upper class controls the major banks and corporations, which in turn largely determine the economic structure and processes of society. The upper class also controls the foundations, major universities, much of the mass media, and important opinion-forming associations. The executive branch of the federal government is controlled by the upper class, which carries with it dominance over the regulatory agencies, the federal judiciary, the military, the CIA, and the FBI.

The upper class and its power elite do not control the legislative branch of the federal government, most state governments, or most city governments. In these areas they merely exert "influence." Influence, in this sense, does not entail the degree of guidance, direction, and ability to act from a position of authority which are implied when the term "control" is used, as with reference to the major institutions and organizations previously considered. Despite these limitations, Domhoff (1967) considers that the extent of control in major institutional areas qualifies the upper class in the United States to be considered a governing class.

The corporate economy provides an example of the control of the upper class over major institutions in the United States. Substantial evidence indicates that the national economy is controlled by a small number of corporations, insurance companies, and banks. There is general agreement that control of such large businesses is exerted by a board of directors, which makes major decisions on company policy and investments, and selects the individuals responsible for day to day business operations. Domhoff (1967) studied the top twenty industrial corporations, the top fifteen banks, and the top fifteen insurance companies in the United States. Of the 884 individuals on the boards of directors of these fifty organizations, 53 percent were members of the upper class. The largest number of the directors who were not upper class members were hired executives, while another major segment were experts of one type or another, such as engineers or economists. These latter two groups were regarded as trusted employees who were not likely to detract from the control of the economy by upper class members of the boards of directors. Considerable overlap was found in the membership of boards of directors. For example, there is great overlap between banks and insurance companies. Among those on the boards of directors of the twenty large corporations, each individual was on an average of six to seven other boards.

Another indication of control of the economy by the upper class is found in the holding of stocks. After noting the general concentration of wealth in the United States, Domhoff (1967) examines the concentration of stock ownership. Various studies indicate that a very small segment of the population owns approximately three-fourths of the shares of all stocks. Although difficult to document systematically, there are indications that the less than one percent of the population that holds this preponderance of stock ownership are also primarily members of the upper class. Considerable evidence indicates that the biggest shareholders in large corporations generally help to determine both company policies and the personnel in top management positions.

CONCLUSIONS

The previous pages have presented portrayals of the major social classes in the United States, based on research studies by various scholars. The selection by C. Wright Mills*(1963) that follows provides a more macroscopic theoretical context for the consideration of the fundamental nature and basis of class stratification. Mills notes that the distribution of valued things and experiences is the central topic of the study of social stratification, thus stating a basic theme that was also expressed in the previously presented descriptions of social classes. Mills further observes that the chance to obtain such desired values is strongly influenced by four basic factors: occupation, class, status, power. Each of these are interrelated, and their total operation provides the key to understanding inequalities in the distribution of valued things and experiences. These ideas were also stated in varying ways in the previously considered studies of social classes. Mills's analysis thus provides a broad frame of reference within which class structures can be studied and understood.

The next chapters deal with ethnic, sex, and age stratification, respectively. The study of class stratification will again become of major concern thereafter. Classes will be focused on in relation to basic substantive areas, namely the manner in which class position influences attitudes and behavior, the ideologies that support the class structure, consciousness and action based upon class position, and vertical mobility. Class stratification will also be viewed in relation to ethnic, sex, and age strata, both in terms of comparisions among these strata, and in terms of their combinations.

REFERENCES

Centers, Richard. 1949. *The Psychology of Social Classes*. Princeton, N.J.: Princeton University Press.

Chinoy, Ely. 1952. "The Tradition of Opportunity and the Aspirations of Automobile Workers." *American Journal of Sociology* 57 (March): 453–459.

————. 1965. *Automobile Workers and the American Dream*. Boston: Beacon Press.

Cohen, Albert K. and Harold M. Hodges, Jr. 1963."Characteristics of the Lower-Blue-Collar Class."*Social Problems* 10 (Spring): 303–334.

Domhoff, G. William. 1967. *Who Rules America*. Englewood Cliffs, N.J.: Prentice-Hall.

Duberman, Lucile. 1976. *Social Inequality*. Philadelphia: J.B. Lippincott.

Haer, John L. 1957. "Predictive Utility of Five Indices of Social Stratification." *American Sociological Review* 22 (October): 541–546.

Hollingshead, August B. 1971. "Commentary on the 'Indiscriminate State of Social Class Measurement'." *Social Forces* 49 (June): 563–567.

Hollingshead, August B. and Frederick C. Redlich. 1964. *Social Class and Mental Illness*. New York: John Wiley and Sons.

Kahl, Joseph A. 1960. *The American Class Structure*. New York: Rinehart and Company.

Kahl, Joseph A. and James A. Davis. 1955. "A Comparison of Indexes of Socio-Economic Status."*American Sociological Review* 20 (June): 317–325.

Miller, Delbert C. 1977. *Handbook of Research Design and Social Measurement.* New York: David McKay.

Mills, C. Wright. 1956. *White Collar.*New York: Oxford University Press.

—————. 1963. "The Sociology of Stratification." In Irving Louis Horowitz (ed.) *Power, Politics and People.* New York: Ballantine Books. Pp. 305–323.

Projector, Dorothy S. and Gertrude S. Weiss. 1966. *Survey of Financial Characteristics of Consumers.* Federal Reserve Technical Papers. Washington, D.C.: Board of Governors of the Federal Reserve System.

Reissman, Leonard. 1959. *Class in American Society.* Glencoe, Ill.: Free Press.

Roach, Jack L., Llewelyn Gross, Orville Grusslin. 1969. *Social Stratification in the United States.* Englewood Cliffs, N.J.: Prentice-Hall.

Robinson, John P., Robert Athanasiou, Kendra B. Head. 1969. *Measures of Occupational Attitudes and Occupational Characteristics.* Ann Arbor, Mich.: Institute of Social Research.

Rossides, Daniel W. 1976. *The American Class System.* Boston: Houghton Mifflin.

Sorokin, Pitirim A. 1969. *Society Culture and Personality.* New York: Cooper Square.

Turner, Jonathan H. and Charles E. Starnes. 1976. *Inequality: Privilege and Poverty in America.* Pacific Palisades, Calif.: Goodyear Publishing Company.

Warner, W. Lloyd and Paul S. Lunt. 1941. *The Social Life of a Modern Community.* New Haven: Yale University Press.

Warner, W. Lloyd, Marchia Meeker, Kenneth Eells. 1960. *Social Class in America.* New York: Harper and Brothers.

Warner, W. Lloyd, J.O. Low, Paul S. Lunt, Leo Srole. 1963. *Yankee City.* New Haven: Yale University Press.

The Sociology of Stratification

C. Wright Mills

IN NEW York City, some people taxi home at night from Madison Avenue offices to Sutton Place; others leave a factory loft in Brooklyn and subway home to East Harlem. In Detroit there is Grosse Pointe, with environs, and there is Hamtramck, without environs; in a thousand small towns the people live on either side of the railroad track. In Moscow, high party members ride cautiously in black cars to well-policed suburbs; other people walk home from factories to cramped apartments. And in the shadow of swank Washington, D.C., apartment houses, there are the dark alley dwellings.

In almost any community in every nation there is a high and a low, and in many societies, a big in-between.

If we go behind what we can thus casually observe while standing on street corners, and begin seriously to observe in detail the 24-hour cycle of behavior and experience, the 12-month cycle, the life-long biography of people in various cities and nations, we will soon be forced to classify. We might well decide to make our classification of people in terms of the social distribution of valued things and experiences; to find out just which people regularly expect to and do receive how many of the available valued things and experiences, and, on every level, why. Such a classification is the basis of all work in stratification.

In any society of which we know some people seem to get most of such values, some

least, others being in between. The student of stratification is bent on understanding such ranking of people, and in finding out exactly in what respects these ranks differ and why. Each ranking or stratum in a society may be viewed as a stratum by virtue of the fact that all of its members have similar chances to gain the things and experiences that are generally valued, whatever they may be: things like cars, money, toys, houses, etc.; experiences, like being given respect, being educated to certain levels, being treated kindly, etc. To belong to one stratum or to another is to share with the other people in this stratum similar chances to receive such values.

If, again, we go behind these strata of people having similar life-chances, and begin to analyze each stratum and the reasons for its formation and persistence, sooner or later we will come upon at least four factors that seem to be quite important keys to the general phenomena. We call these "dimensions of stratification." Each is a way of ranking people with respect to their different chances to obtain values, and together, if properly understood, they enable us to explain these differing chances. These four dimensions are occupation, class, status and power.

I

By an occupation we understand a set of activities pursued more or less regularly as a major source of income.

From the individual's standpoint, occupational activities refer to types of skill that are marketable. These skills range from arranging mathematical symbols for $1000 a day to arranging dirt with a shovel for $1000 a year.

From the standpoint of society, occupations as activities are functions: they result in certain end products—various goods and services—and are accordingly classified into industrial groups.

As specific activities, occupations thus (1) entail various types and levels of skill, and (2) their exercise fulfills certain functions within an industrial division of labor.

In the United States today the most publicly obvious strata consist of members of similar occupations. However it has been and may now be in other kinds of societies, in contemporary U.S.A. occupations are the most ostensible and the most available "way into" an understanding of stratification. For, most people spend the most alert hours of most of their days in occupational work. What kind of work they do not only monopolizes their wakeful hours of adult life but sets what they can afford to buy: most people who receive any direct income at all do so by virtue of some occupation.

As sources of income, occupations are thus connected with *class* position. Since occupations also normally carry an expected quota of prestige, on and off the job, they are relevant to *status* position. They also involve certain degrees of *power* over other people, directly in terms of the job, and indirectly in other social areas. Occupations are thus tied to class, status, and power as well as to skill and function; to understand the occupations composing any social stratum, we must consider them in terms of each of these interrelated dimensions.

The most decisive occupational shift in the twentieth century has been the decline of the independent entrepreneurs ("the old middle class" of businessmen, farmers, and fee professionals) and the rise of the salaried employees ("the new middle class" of managers and salaried professionals, of office people and sales employees). During the last two generations the old middle class has bounded from 6 to 25 per cent, while the wage workers as a whole have levelled off, in fact declining from 61 to 55 per cent. In the course of the following remarks we will pay brief attention by way of illustration to these three occupational levels in the cities of the United States.

II

"Class situation" in its simplest, objective sense has to do with the amount and source of income. A class is a set of people who share life choices because of their similar class situations.

Today, occupation rather than property is the source of income for most of those who receive any direct income: the possibilities of selling their services in the labor market, rather than of profitably buying and selling their property and its yields, now determine the class-chances of over four fifths of the American people. All the things money can buy and many that men dream about are theirs by virtue of occupational level. In these occupations men work for someone else on someone else's property. This is the clue to many differences between the older, nineteenth century world of the small propertied entrepreneur and the occupational structure of the new society. If the old middle class of free enterprisers once fought big property structures in the name of small, free properties, the new middle class of white-collar employees, like the wage-workers in latter-day capitalism, has been, from the beginning, dependent upon large properties for job security.

Wage-workers in the factory and on the farm are on the propertyless bottom of the occupational structure, depending upon the equipment owned by others, earning wages for the time they spend at work. In terms of property, the white-collar people are *not* "in between Capital and Labor," they are in exactly the same property-class position as the wage-workers. They have no direct fiscal tie to the means of production, no prime claim upon the proceeds from property. Like factory workers—and day laborers for that matter—they work for those who do own such means of livelihood.

Yet if bookkeepers and coal miners, insurance agents and farm laborers, doctors in a clinic and crane operators in an open pit have this condition in common, certainly their class situations are not the same. To understand the variety of modern class positions, we must go beyond the common fact of source of income and consider as well the amount of income.

In the middle thirties the three urban strata, entrepreneurs, white-collar, and wage-workers, formed a distinct scale with respect to median family income: white-collar employees had a median income of $2,008; entrepreneurs, $1,665; urban wage-workers, $1,175. Although the median income of white-collar workers was higher than that of the entrepreneurs, larger proportions of the entrepreneurs received both high-level and low-level incomes. The distribution of their income was spread more than that of the white-collar.

The wartime boom in incomes, in fact, spread the incomes of all occupational groups, but not evenly. The spread occurred mainly among urban entrepreneurs. As an income level, the old middle class in the city is becoming less an evenly graded income group, and more a collection of different strata, with a large proportion of lumpen-bourgeosie who receive very low incomes, and a small, prosperous bourgeoisie with very high incomes.

In the late forties (1948, median family income) the income of all white-collar workers was $4,058, that of all urban wage-workers, $3,317. These averages, however, should not obscure the overlap of specific groups within each stratum: the lower white-collar people—sales-employees and office workers—earned almost the same as skilled workers and foremen,* but more than semiskilled urban wage-workers.

In terms of property white-collar people are in the same position as wage-workers; in terms of occupational income, they are "somewhere in the middle." Once they were considerably above the wage-workers; they have become less so; in the middle of the century they still have an edge but, rather than adding new income distinctions within the new middle-class group, the overall rise in incomes is making the new middle class a more homogeneous income group.

Distributions of property and income are important economically because if they are not wide enough, purchasing power may not be sufficient to take the production that is possible or desirable. Such distributions are also important because they underpin the class structure and thus the chances of the various ranks of the people to obtain desired values. Everything from the chance to stay alive during the first year after birth to the chance to view fine art; the chance to remain healthy and if sick to get well again quickly; the chance to avoid becoming a juvenile delinquent; and very crucially, the chance to complete an intermediary or higher educational grade—these are among the chances that are crucially influenced by one's position in the class structure of a modern society.

These varying, unequal chances are factual probabilities of the class structure. It does not follow from such facts that people in similar class situations will necessarily become conscious of themselves as a class or come to feel that they belong together. Nor does it follow that they will necessarily become aware of any common interests they may objectively share, or that they will become organized in some way, in a movement or in a party, in an attempt to realize such interests. Nor does if follow that they will necessarily become antagonistic to people in other class situations and struggle with them. All these—class-consciousness and awareness of common interests, organizations and class-struggle—have existed in various times and places and, in various forms, do now exist as mental and political fact. But they do not follow logically or historically from the objective fact of class structure. In any given case, whether or not they arise from objective class situations is a matter for fresh empirical study.

III

Prestige involves at least two persons; one to *claim* it and another to *honor* the claim. The bases on which various people raise prestige claims, and the reasons others honor these claims, include property and birth, occupation and education, income and power—in fact almost anything that may invidiously distinguish one person from another. In the status system of a society these claims are organized as rules and expectations which regulate who successfully claims prestige, from whom, in what ways, and on what basis. The level of self-esteem enjoyed by given individuals is more or less set by this status system.

There are, thus, six items to which we must pay attention: From the claimant's side: (1) the status claim, (2) the way in which this claim is

---

*It is impossible to isolate the salaried foremen from the skilled urban wage-workers in these figures. If we could do so, the income of lower white-collar workers would be closer to that of semi-skilled workers.

raised or expressed, (3) the basis on which the claim is raised. And correspondingly—from the bestower's side: (4) the status bestowal or deferences given, (5) the way in which these deferences are given, (6) the basis of the bestowal, which may or may not be the same as the basis on which the claim is raised. An extraordinary range of social phenomena are pointed to by these terms.

Claims for prestige are expressed in all those mannerisms, conventions and ways of consumption that make up the styles of life characterizing people on various status levels. The "things that are done" and the "things that just aren't done" are the status conventions of different strata. Members of higher status groups may dress in distinct ways, follow "fashions" with varying degrees of regularity, eat at certain times and places with certain people. In varying degrees, they maintain an elegance of person and specific modes of address, have dinners together, and are glad to see their sons and daughters intermarry. "Society" in American cities, debutante systems, the management of welfare activities—these often regiment the status activities of upper circles, where exclusiveness, distance, coldness, and condescending benevolence toward outsiders are characteristic.

Claims for prestige and the bestowal of prestige are often based on birth. The Negro child, irrespective of individual "achievement," will not receive the deference which the white child may successfully claim. The immigrant, especially a member of a recent mass immigration, will not be as likely to receive the deference given the Old American, immigrant groups being generally stratified according to how long they, and their forebears, have been in America. Within "the native-born white of native parentage," certain "Old Families" receive more deference than do other families. In each case—race, nationality and family—prestige is based on, or at least limited by, descent, which is perhaps most obviously a basis of prestige at the top and at the bottom of the social ladder. European nobilities and rigidly excluded racial minorities represent the acme of status by descent, the one high, the other low.

Upper-class position typically carries great prestige, all the more so if the source of the money is property. Yet if the possession of wealth in modern industrial societies leads to increased prestige, rich men who are too fresh from lower class levels may experience great difficulty in "buying their ways" into upper-status circles. Often, in fact, impoverished descendants of once high level Old Families receive more deference from more people than do wealthy men without appropriate grandparents. The facts of the *nouveau riche* (high class without high prestige) and the broken-down aristocrat (high prestige without high class) refute the complete identification of upper-prestige and upper-class position, even though, in due course, the broken-down aristocrat often becomes simply broken-down, and the son of the *nouveau riche,* a man of "clean, old wealth." The possession of wealth also allows the purchase of an environment which in time often leads to the development of those "intrinsic" qualities of individuals and families that are required for higher prestige. When we say that American prestige has been fluid, one thing we mean is that high economic class position has led rather quickly to high prestige. A feudal aristocracy, based on old property and long descent, has not existed here. Veblen's *The Theory of the Leisure Class* was focused primarily upon the U.S. post-civil war period and the expressions of prestige claims raised in lavish economic ways by the *nouveau riche* of meat, railroads, and steel.

The prestige of the middle strata in America is based on many principles other than descent and property. The shift to a society of employees had made *occupation* and *education* crucially important. Insofar as occupation determines the level of income, and different styles of life require different income levels, occupation limits the style of life. In a more direct way, different occupations require different levels and types of education, and education also limits the style of life and thus the status successfully claimed.

Some occupations are reserved for members of upper-status levels, others are "beneath their honor." In some societies, in fact, having no work to do brings the highest prestige, prestige being an aspect of property class, the female dependents of high-class husbands becoming specialists in the display of expensive idleness. But only those who do not need to work, yet have more income than those who must, are likely to obtain prestige from idleness. For those for whom work is necessary but not available, "leisure" brings disgrace. And income from property does not always bring more prestige than income from work; the amount and the ways the income is used are more important than its source. A small rentier may not enjoy esteem equal to that of a moderately paid doctor.

Among the employed, those occupations which pay more, involve more mental activities, and some power to supervise others seems to place people on higher prestige levels. But sheer power does not always lend prestige: the political boss gives up prestige, except among his machine members, for power; constitutional monarchs, on the other hand, may gain ceremonial prestige but give up political power. In offices and factories, skilled foremen and office supervisors expect and typically receive an esteem which lifts them above unskilled workers and typists. But the policeman's power to direct street masses does not bring prestige, except among little boys.

The type of education, as well as the amount, is an important basis for prestige: "Finishing schools" and "Prep schools" turn out women and men accomplished in a style of life which guarantees deference in some circles. In others, the amount of intellectual skill acquired through education is a key point for estimation. Yet skill alone is not as uniform a basis for prestige as is skill connected with highly esteemed occupations.

The extent to which claims for prestige are honored and by whom they are honored, may vary widely. Some of those from whom an individual claims prestige may honor his claims, others may not; some deferences that are given may express genuine feelings of esteem; others may be expedient strategies for ulterior ends. A society may, in fact, contain many hierarchies of prestige, each with its own typical bases and areas of bestowal, or one hierarchy in which everyone uniformly "knows his place" and is always in it. It is in the latter that prestige groups are most likely to be uniform and continuous.

Imagine a society in which everyone's prestige is absolutely set and unambivalent; every man's claims for prestige are balanced by the prestige he receives, and both his expression of claims and the ways these claims are honored by others are set forth in understood stereotypes. Moreover, the bases of the claims coincide with the reasons they are honored; those who claim prestige on the specific basis of property or birth are honored because of their property or birth. So

the exact volume and types of deference expected between any two individuals are always known, expected, and given; and each individual's level and type of self-esteem are steady features of his inner life.

Now imagine the opposite society, in which prestige is highly unstable and ambivalent: the individual's claims are not usually honored by others. The way claims are expressed are not understood or acknowledged by those from whom deference is expected, and when others do bestow prestige, they do so unclearly. One man claims prestige on the basis of his income, but even if he is given prestige, it is not because of his income but rather, for example, because of his education or appearance. All the controlling devices by which the volume and type of deference might be directed are out of joint or simply do not exist. So the prestige system is no system, but a maze of misunderstanding, of sudden frustration and sudden indulgence, and the individual, as his self-esteem fluctuates, is under strain and full of anxiety.

American society in the middle of the twentieth century does not fit either of these projections absolutely, but it seems fairly clear that it is closer to the unstable and ambivalent model. This is not to say that there is no prestige system in the United States; given occupational groupings, even though caught in status ambivalence, do enjoy typical levels of prestige. It is to say, however, that the enjoyment of prestige is often disturbed and uneasy, that the basis of prestige, the expressions of prestige claims, and the ways these claims are honored, are now subject to great strain, a strain which often throws men and women into a virtual status panic.

As with income, so with prestige: U.S. white-collar groups are differentiated socially, perhaps more decisively than wage-workers and entrepreneurs. Wage earners certainly do form an income pyramid and a prestige gradation, as do entrepreneurs and rentiers; but the new middle class, in terms of income and prestige, is a superimposed pyramid, reaching from almost the bottom of the first to almost the top of the second.

People in white-collar occupations claim higher prestige than wage-workers, and, as a general rule, can cash in their claims with wage-workers as well as with the anonymous public. This fact has been seized upon, with much justification, as the defining characteristic of the white-collar strata, and although there are definite indications in the United States of a decline in their prestige, still, on a nation-wide basis, the majority of even the lower white-collar employees—office workers and salespeople— enjoy a middle prestige place.

The historic bases for the white-collar employees' prestige, apart from superior income, have included (1) the similarity of their place and type of work to those of the old middle-classes which has permitted them to borrow prestige. (2) As their relations with entrepreneur and with esteemed customer have become more impersonal, they have borrowed prestige from the firm itself. (3) The stylization of their appearance, in particular the fact that most white-collar jobs have permitted the wearing of street clothes on the job, has figured in their prestige claims, as have (4) the skills required in most white-collar jobs, and in many of them the variety of operations performed and the degree of autonomy exercised in deciding work procedures. Furthermore, (5) the time taken to learn these skills and (6) the way in which they have been acquired by formal education and by close contact with the higherups in charge has been important. (7) White-collar employees have monopolized high school education—even in 1940 they had completed 12 grades to the 8 grades for wage-workers and entrepreneurs. They have also (8) enjoyed status by descent: in terms of race, Negro white-collar employees exist only in isolated instances—and, more importantly, in terms of nativity, in 1930 only about 9 per cent of white-collar workers, but 16 percent of free enterprisers and 21 per cent of wage-workers, were foreign born. Finally, as an underlying fact, (9) the limited size of the white-collar group, compared to wage-workers, has led to successful claims to greater prestige.

IV

To be powerful is to be able to realize one's will, even against·the resistance of others. The power position of groups and of individuals typically depends upon factors of class, status, and occupation, often in intricate interrelations.

Given occupations involve specific powers over other people in the actual course of work; but also outside the job area, by virtue of their relations to institutions of property as well as the typical income they afford, occupations lend power. Some occupations require the direct exercise of supervision over other employees and workers, and many white-collar employees are closely attached to this managerial cadre. They are the assistants of authority: the power they exercise is a derived power, but they do exercise it.

Property classes may involve power over job markets and commodity markets, directly and indirectly; they may also support power, because of their property, over the state. As Franz Neumann has neatly indicated, each of these powers may be organized for execution, in employers association, cartel, and pressure group. From the underside of the property situation, propertyless wage workers may have trade unions and consumers co-ops which may be in a struggle with the organized powers of property on each of these three fronts.

When we speak of the power of classes, occupations and status groups, however, we usually refer more or less specifically to political power. This means the power of such groups to influence or to determine the policies and activities of the state. The most direct means of exercising such power and the sign of its existence are organizations, either composed of members of certain strata, or acting in behalf of their interests, or both. The power of various strata often implies a political willfulness, a ''class-consciousness'' on the part of members of these strata. But not always: there can be, as in the case of ''un-organized, grumbling workers,'' a common mentality among those in common strata without organizations. And there can be, as in the case of some ''pressure groups,'' an organization representing the interests of those in similar strata without any common mentality being notable among them.

The accumulation of political power by any stratum is generally dependent upon a triangle of factors: willful mentality, objective opportunity, and the state of organization. The opportunity is limited by the group's structural positions within the stratification of the society; the will is dependent upon the group's awareness of its interests and ways of realizing them. And both structural position and awareness interplay with organizations, which strengthen awareness, and are made politically relevant by structural position.

V

What is at issue in theories of stratification and political power is (1) the objective position of various strata with reference to other strata of modern society, and (2) the political content and direction of their mentalities. Questions concerning either of these issues can be stated in such a way as to allow, and in fact demand, observational answers only if adequate conceptions of stratification and political mentality are clearly set forth.

Often the "mentality" of strata is allowed to take predominance over the objective position.

It is, for example, frequently asserted that "there are no classes in the United States" because "psychology is of the essence of classes" or, as Alfred Bingham has put it, that "class groupings are always nebulous, and in the last analysis only the vague thing called class-consciousness counts." It is said that people in the United States are not aware of themselves as members of classes, do not identify themselves with their appropriate economic level, do not often organize in terms of these brackets or vote along the lines they provide. America, in this reasoning, is a sandheap of "middle-class individuals."

But this is to confuse psychological feelings with other kinds of social and economic reality. The fact that men are not "class conscious" at all times and in all places does not mean that "there are no classes" or that "in America everybody is middle class." The economic and social facts are one thing. Psychological feelings may or may not be associated with them in rationally expected ways. Both are important, and if psychological feelings and political outlooks do not correspond to economic or occupational class, we must try to find out why, rather than throw out the economic baby with the psychological bath, and so fail to understand how either fits into the national tub. No matter what people believe, class structure as an economic arrangement influences their life chances according to their positions in it. If they do not grasp the causes of their conduct this does not mean that the social analyst must ignore or deny them.

If political mentalities are not in line with objectively defined strata, that lack of correspondence is a problem to be explained; in fact, it is the grand problem of the psychology of social strata. The general problem of stratification and political mentality thus has to do with the extent to which the members of objectively defined strata are homogeneous in their political alertness, outlook, and allegiances, and with the degree to which their political mentality and actions are in line with the interests demanded by the juxtaposition of their objective position and their accepted values.

To understand the occupation, class, and status positions of a set of people is not necessarily to know whether or not they (1) will become class-conscious, feeling that they belong together or that they can best realize their rational interests by combining; (2) will have "collective attitudes" of any sort, including those toward themselves, their common situation; (3) will organize themselves, or be open to organization by others, into associations, movements, or political parties; or (4) will become hostile toward other strata and struggle against them. These social, political, and psychological characteristics may or may not occur on the basis of similar objective situations. In any given case, such possibilities must be explored, and "subjective" attributes must *not be used as criteria* for class inclusion, but rather, as Max Weber has made clear, stated as probabilities on the basis of objectively defined situations.

Implicit in this way of stating the issues of stratification lies a model of social movements and political dynamics. The important differences among people are differences that shape their biographies and ideas; within any given stratum, of course, individuals differ, but if their stratum has been adequately understood, we ought to be able to expect certain psychological traits to recur. Our principles of stratification enable us to do this. The probability that people will have a similar mentality and ideology, and that they will join together for action, is increased the more homogeneous they are with respect to class, occupation, and prestige. Other factors do, of course, affect the probability that ideology, organization, and consciousness will occur among those in objectively similar strata. But psychological factors are likely to be associated with *strata,* which consist of people who are characterized by an intersection of the *several* dimensions we have been using: class, occupation, status, and power. The task is to sort out these dimensions of stratification in a systematic way, paying attention to each separately and then to its relation to each of the other dimensions.

VI

The meaning of the term "proletarianized," around which major theories of changes in stratification have revolved, is by no means clear. In the definitions set forth here, however, proletarianization might refer to shifts of "middle-class occupation" toward wage-workers in terms of income, property, skill, prestige or power, irrespective of whether or not the people involved are aware of these changes. Or, the meaning may be in terms of changes in consciousness, outlook, or organized activity. It would be possible, for example, for a segment of people higher in all respects to become virtually identical with wage-workers in income, property, and skill, but to resist becoming like them in prestige claims and to anchor their whole consciousness upon illusory prestige factors. Only by keeping objective position and ideological consciousness separate in analysis can the problem be stated with precision and without unjustifiable assumptions about wage-workers, white-collar workers, and the general psychology of social classes.

When the Marxist, Anton Pannekoek, for example, refuses to include propertyless people of lower income rather than skilled workers in the proletariat, he refers to ideological and prestige factors. He does not go on to refer to the same factors as they operate among the "proletariat," because he holds to what can only be called a metaphysical belief that the proletariat is *destined* to win through to a certain consciousness. Those who see white-collar groups as composing an independent "class," *sui generis,* often use prestige or status as their defining criterion rather than economic level. The Marxian assertion,—for example, L.B. Boudin's,—that salaried employees "are in reality just as much part of the proletariat as the merest day laborer," obviously rests on economic criteria, as is generally recognized when his statement is countered by the assertion that he ignores "important psychological factors."

The Marxist in his expectation assumes *first* that wage-workers, or at least large sections of them, do in fact, or will at any moment, have a socialist consciousness of their revolutionary role in modern history. It assumes, *second,* that the middle classes, or large sections of them, are acquiring this consciousness, and in this respect are becoming like the wage-workers or like what wage-workers are assumed to be. *Third,* it rests this contention primarily upon the assumption that the economic dimension, especially property, of stratification is the key one, and that it is in this dimension that the middle classes are becoming like wage-workers.

But the fact that propertyless employees (both wage-workers and salaried employees) have not automatically assumed any unified political posture clearly means that propertylessness is not the only factor, or even the crucial one, determining inner-consciousness or political will.

Neither white-collar people nor wage-workers in the United States have been or are preoccupied with questions of property. The concentration of property during the last century has been a slow process rather than a sharp break inside the life span of one generation; even the sons and daughters of farmers—among whom the most obvious "expropriation" has gone on—have had their attentions focused on the urban lure rather than on urban propertylessness. As jobholders, moreover, salaried employees have generally, with the rest of the population, experienced a rise in standards of living: propertylessness has certainly not necessarily coincided with pauperization. So the centralization of property with consequent expropriation, has not been widely experienced as "agony" or reacted to by proletarianization, in any psychological sense that may be given these terms.

Objectively, the structural position of the white-collar mass is becoming more and more similar to that of the wage-workers. Both are, of course, propertyless, and their incomes draw closer and closer together. All the factors of their status position, which have enabled white-collar workers to set themselves apart from wage-workers, are now subject to definite decline. Increased rationalization is lowering the skill levels and making their work more and more factory-like. As high-school education becomes more universal among wage-workers, and the skills required for many white-collar tasks become simpler, it is clear that the white-collar job market will include more wage-worker children.

So, in the course of the next generation, a "social class" between lower white-collar and wage-workers will probably be formed, which means, in Weber's terms, that between the two positions there will be a typical job mobility. This will not, of course, involve the professional strata or the higher-managerial employees, but it will include the bulk of the workers in salesroom and office. These shifts in the occupational worlds of the propertyless are more important to them than the existing fact of their propertylessness.

The assumption that political supremacy follows from functional, economic indispensability often underlies theories of the rise to power of one or the other strata in modern society. It is assumed that the class that is indispensable in fulfilling the major functions of the social order will be the next in the sequence of ruling classes. Max Weber in his essay on bureaucracy has made short shrift of this idea: "The ever-increasing 'indispensability' of the officialdom, swollen to millions, is no more decisive for this question [of power] than is the view of some representatives of the proletarian movement that the economic indispensability of the proletarians is decisive for the measure of their social and political power position. If 'indispensability' were decisive, then where slave labor prevailed and where freemen usually abhor work as a dishonor, the 'indispensable' slaves ought to have held the positions of power, for they were at least as indispensable as officials and proletarians are today. Whether the power . . . as such increases cannot be decided a priori from such reasons."

Yet the assumption that it can runs all through most literature on stratification. Just as Marx, seeing the parasitical nature of the capitalist's endeavor, and the real function of work performed by the workers, predicted the workers' rise to power; so James Burnham (and before him Harold Lasswell and John Corbin) assumed that since the new middle class is the carrier of those skills upon which modern society more and more depends, it will inevitably, in the course of time, assume political power. Technical and managerial indispensability is thus confused with the facts of power struggle, and overrides all other sources of power. The deficiency of such arguments must be realized positively: we need to develop and to use a more open and flexible model of the relations of political power and stratification.

Increasingly, class and status situations have been removed from free market forces and the persistence of tradition, and been subject to more formal rules. A government management of the class structure has become a major means of alleviating inequalities and insuring the risks of those in lower-income classes. Not so much free labor markets as the powers of pressure groups now shape the class positions and privileges of various strata in the United States. Hours and wages, vacations, income security through periods of sickness, accidents, unemployment, and old age—these are now subject to many intentional pressures, and, along with tax policies, transfer payments, tariffs, subsidies, price ceilings, wage freezes, et cetera, make up the content of "class fights" in the objective meaning of the phrase.

The "Welfare State" attempts to manage class chances without modifying basic class structure; in its several meanings and types, it favors economic policies designed to redistribute life-risks and life-chances in favor of those in the more exposed class situations, who have the power, or threaten to accumulate the power, to do something about their case.

Labor union, farm bloc, and trade association dominate the political scene of the Welfare State, and contests within and between them increasingly determine the position of various groups. The state, as a descriptive fact, is at the balanced intersection of such pressures, and increasingly the privileges and securities of various occupational strata depend upon the bold means of organized power. Pensions, for example, especially since World War II, have been a major idea in labor union bargaining, and it has been the wage-worker that has had bargaining power. Social insurance to cover work injuries and occupational diseases has gradually been replacing the common law of a century ago, which held the employee at personal fault for work injury and the employer's liability had to be proved in court by a damage suit.

In so far as such laws exist, they legally shape the class chances of the manual worker up to a par with or above other strata. Privileges of status and occupation, as well as income level, have been increasingly subject to the power pressures of union, trade association, and government, and there is every reason to believe that in the future this will be even more the case.

PART III

The Ascribed Hierarchies: Ethnic, Sex, and Age Stratification

INTRODUCING THE ASCRIBED HIERARCHIES: ETHNICITY, SEX AND AGE

CLASS, ETHNIC, sex, and age stratification systems share important characteristics. In each hierarchy, there are unequal distributions of power, privilege, common experiences; prestige; an ideology supporting the system; and a potential for stratum consciousness and stratum action and some form of mobility. There are also great differences between the social class order, as discussed in the last two chapters, and the hierarchies of ethnicity, sex, and age. The next three chapters deal with the special characteristics of these other hierarchies. We present here a general overview of the differences between class inequality and the ascribed, or inherited, inequalities of ethnicity, sex, and age.

CLASS VERSUS THE ASCRIBED HIERARCHIES

Three important distinctions between class stratification and ethnic, sex, and age stratification can be made:

Achieved Versus Ascribed Criteria. Social class is an achieved status. It is determined by criteria such as achievements or accomplishments—what you do, not what you are. Positions in ethnic, sex, and age stratification systems are based on ascribed, hereditary characteristics like skin color or gender—factors determined at birth.

The Clarity of Stratum Boundary Lines. Class boundary lines are fuzzy; it is difficult to say where working-class ends and middle-class begins. Strata within ethnic, sex, and age hierarchies are more clearly delineated: black or white, male or female, old or young.

Potential for Stratum Solidarity and Collective Action. When boundary lines are clear, there is greater potential for shared fate and collective action. Especially in the case of the ethnic hierarchy, certain visible racial groups have developed common feelings of oppression and have pressed for social change.

147

1. Achieved vs. Ascribed Hierarchies

What we have called *social class* is a stratification system based on achievement, in which many individuals move from their class of origin, either rising or falling within the structure. Actually, the term *quasi-achievement* should be used to emphasize that far more than free will and individual effort determine social mobility. Movement up or down a stratification system depends on a complex blend of an individual's inherited advantages, structural opportunities (such as labor market needs), as well as his or her motivation and effort. Persons born in upper-middle or upper-class positions have advantages of inherited wealth, the best education, family connections to aid in securing a first job, and a high degree of parental support for their ambitions. Even with all these advantages, some upper-class people are downwardly mobile, and some people with more modest family advantages are able to reach rather high positions. These kinds of large leaps in mobility are not common. Occupational mobility studies show that children usually rise or fall only one or two occupational levels above or below their parents' levels (Reissman, 1959). For example, the offspring of a blue-collar machinist may very likely become a foreman or salesperson but is far less likely to become a doctor or lawyer. The *number* of persons moving within the stratification system is fairly high, but the extent of their mobility—that is, the distance they move up or down—is only moderate. The fact that individuals can change their economic position, however, makes social class a very different stratification dimension than ethnicity, sex, or age.

In the case of ethnicity (visible minorities), sex, and age, one is born into a particular position that is relatively fixed. One is born white or black, male or female, or in the year 1941 or 1951. Only by extraordinary measures, such as a sex-change operation, can one alter one's gender. Similarly, it is extremely difficult for one to change one's ethnic characteristics such as skin color. Age also is fixed, in two senses. One is born at a particular time and one passes through the life cycle at a fixed rate. Although some sociologists have referred to aging as a form of mobility, it is a mobility over which a person has no control.

The major bases for the unequal distribution of rewards in these ascribed hierarchies are *discrimination* and prejudice, rather than individual achievement. Visible racial minorities, women, and the aged have been defined in negative ways that have excluded them from positions in society that bring honor, power, and prestige. Throughout history, women, blacks, Chicanos, Native Americans, and other minorities have been defined as innately inferior and locked into roles and relationships that often benefit the dominant white male group.

In ethnic, sex, or age stratification systems, can one speak of mobility or social movement at all? Although sex, ethnic, and age changes are difficult if not impossible at the individual level, mobility can be said to occur at the group level. One can speak of the ascendancy of an entire stratum. For example, women and blacks have made some collective gains in power, privilege, and prestige in the last fifteen years. As a result of social protest, laws were changed, resulting in more women and blacks being employed in occupations that involve a high level of authority. Some women and blacks have advanced economically. They have also made advances in their potential to exert power through bloc voting, social protest, and occupancy of policy-making positions. These changes have increased the prestige of women and blacks as a whole. *Collective mobility,* then, can be considered and measured among the ascribed hierarchies.

2. Clarity of Stratum Boundary Lines

Social class strata in the United States have been characterized by vague boundary lines; a moderate amount of social mobility from one stratum to another; and rather low degrees of shared fate. In the United States, it is difficult to find visible criteria that clearly and consistently set apart one class from another. The relatively high wages paid many skilled blue-collar workers equal or exceed those paid to many white-collar workers. The mass consumption of similar styles of clothing and durable goods (such as cars and television sets) and the fact that persons of a fairly wide socio-economic range reside in similar-appearing tract houses also tend to blur class lines.

The unlimited faith in the openness of the American system and the success of some people in moving up within it contribute further to the fluidity of the class system. Many view their present position as only temporary and are therefore not inclined to perceive rigid class divisions or to identify with the class interests of a particular class group.

Ascribed hierarchies are very different in that the stratum boundary lines are quite clear. One can rather easily disguise his or her class position by modes of dress, styles of life, and the acquisition of certain status symbols, but there is rarely a question about whether a person is black or white or male or female. Age involves slightly less visibility; although many people are able to "pass" as older or younger than their chronological age, their "passing age" rarely exceeds a decade (Nelson and Nelson*, 1972).

If the visible differences of ascribed hierarchies were socially neutral and if they had no relationship to the distribution of rewards, there of course would be no problem in stratification. But because institutions, customs, and beliefs are structured to exclude or limit the access of these visible groups, there is indeed a stratification problem. Black Americans in particular have experienced discrimination. When the Constitution was first written, blacks were defined as biologically inferior and were assessed as "three-fifths of a man" for determining the number of congressional seats for each state. Although the extreme racist ideologies that developed during slavery and the era of Jim Crow have been discredited, many white Americans continue to cling to milder versions of inherent black inferiority (Schuman*, 1975).

Because ethnicity and sex are highly visible traits, disadvantages and barriers remain for members of ethnic and sex strata, even after they have achieved socioeconomic success. For example, highly successful black professionals may still have trouble soliciting white clients or moving into white neighborhoods. Women in high-ranking positions of authority may face problems in working with men who cannot accept women as peers or business superiors. In both cases, the social traditions, roles, and beliefs surrounding race and sex are not altered by individual or group achievements.

3. Stratum Solidarity

The clarity of stratum boundary lines, or high visibility, may contribute directly to stratum consciousness. High visibility groups are likely to be discriminated against with great consistency. This very consistency can sow the seeds for feelings of solidarity within a group—feelings such as "we have shared a common oppression" and "we have a common destiny." For example, in the case of blacks, Puerto Ricans, Chicanos, and American Indians, the visibility is high and the discrimination by society severe.

The potential for collective action is further heightened by physical separation, or segregation. Ethnic minorities are highly concentrated geographically—in ghettos, barrios, and reservations. Such communities facilitate the sharing of frustrations and discontents. Thus, collective definitions of oppression often develop when a group is highly concentrated in a geographic community. This is not possible when individuals are widely scattered. Many other factors (discussed in detail in chapter 10) are necessary for stratum consciousness to develop. High visibility and segregated communities are not the only ingredients; rather, they are major contributing factors for stratum consciousness and action when the historical period is ripe.

Group consciousness and collective action are more likely to develop when people cannot move out of inherited, ascribed statuses, such as ethnicity and sex. By contrast, the boundaries of socioeconomic classes are vague and there are numerous opportunities for upward mobility.

> ...There is little impetus for the members of a subordinate class to organize for collective power exertion and class conflict; it is far easier and less costly for these persons, as they rise in status, to move individually into a higher class (Olsen,* 1970:300).

ETHNIC STRATIFICATION VERSUS THE OTHER HIERARCHIES

Ethnic stratification is somewhat unique among the ascribed hierarchies because subjugated members of ethnic strata live in separate and unequal communities. Women, by contrast, are not isolated and living in separate communities. To some extent, age groups are segregated in geographical space (such as schools and retirement communities), but length of stay in the community is more temporary and there is more voluntarism in coming and going. Perhaps an inner-city area in which the poor, white aged are forced to reside (a geriatric ghetto) is most similar to a segregated community.

Separate Nation State. Ethnic groups are the only strata with the potential to carve out their own independent society within an existing nation or society (Lieberson, 1970:173). Obviously, efforts to establish separate nations or political communities on the basis of age or sex would be futile. A crucial dependence exists between the sexes such that neither has the potential for maintaining an enduring society without the other. Efforts to reduce or eliminate stratification along sex lines therefore must occur within the mainstream of society. Ethnic groups, however, have another choice; if discrimination and oppression are so severe that an ethnic group sees little hope of attaining societal rewards, it can choose to disengage from the mainstream and set up a separate society.

In the United States, the very strong traditions of assimilation, the "ethnic melting pot ideology," and individual class mobility have weakened the potential for ethnic separatism. Separatist currents can be documented in this country, however. The Marcus Garvey Movement of the 1920s, which encouraged black Americans to return to Africa to set up a separate nation state, and the more recent Black Muslim movement have attracted large numbers of blacks, if not as joiners, at least as sympathizers. In the 1960s, many blacks expressed

separatist ideas when they exhorted blacks to gain control over their ghetto communities, schools, stores, and banks, and to exert group power. The separatist outlook has always existed throughout the history of blacks in America, although it has been considerably muted by the dominance of the assimilationist ideology.

Native Americans illustrate the most successful example of separate ethnic nations. Historically, there have been two major attempts on the part of the United States government to assimilate American Indians. The Indian Allotment Act of 1884 granted land to individual Indian families, not to tribal communities. Indian families were to be assimilated into white rural communities as independent farmers. In the 1950s, Congress tried to terminate tribal nations or reservation communities. Indians were expected to give up their treaty rights to become individual citizens, paying taxes, buying houses, competing for the same color television sets and cars as everyone else. In both historical instances, Indians strongly resisted assimilation attempts in efforts to preserve their culture and to protect their valuable land base from economic exploitation. Native Americans have been successful in maintaining their legal status as "nations within a nation" (Lurie, 1975).

Other unique characteristics of the ethnic hierarchy will be discussed in more depth in chapter 5, "Ethnic Stratification." The ascribed hierarchies of sex, and age are presented in chapters 6 and 7, "Sex Stratification," and "Age Stratification."

REFERENCES

Leiberson, Stanley. 1970. "Stratification and Ethnic Groups." In Edward O. Lauman (ed.), *Social Stratification: Research and Theory for the 1970s.* Indianapolis: Bobbs-Merrill.
Lurie, Nancy. 1975. "The American Indian: Historical Background." In Norman R. Yetman & C. Hoy Steele (eds.), *Majority and Minority.* Boston: Allyn & Bacon.
Nelson, Elizabeth Ness & Edward E. Nelson. 1974. "Age Passing." Revised copy of a

paper presented at the 67th Annual meeting of the American Sociological Association, 1972. (Included in this volume.)

Olsen, Marvin E. 1970. "Power Perspectives on Stratification and Race Relations." In Marvin E. Olsen (ed.), *Power in Societies.* New York: Macmillan.

Reissman, Leonard. 1959. *Class in American Society.* Glencoe, Ill.: Free Press.

Schuman, Howard. 1975. "Free Will and Determinism in Public Beliefs About Race." In Norman R. Yetman & C. Hoy Steele (eds.), *Majority and Minority.* Boston: Allyn & Bacon.

5

Ethnic Stratification

Edward Ransford

OVER THIRTY years ago, Louis Wirth (1945) defined an ethnic minority as

> . . . a group of people who, because of their physical or cultural characteristics are singled out from others in the society in which they live for differential and unequal treatment and who therefore regard themselves as objects of collective discrimination (Wirth, 1945:347).

In most societies, ethnic groups are found in a hierarchy of power, privilege, and prestige. The hierarchy represents power, privilege, and prestige *institutionalized*. Like all stratification systems, ethnic inequality endures beyond the lifetime of single individuals.

What are the origins of ethnic stratification systems? How do they get started? Donald Noel* (1968) argues that there are three crucial components of ethnic stratification: *ethnocentrism, competition,* and *differential power.* When two distinct ethnic populations come into contact with each other, inequalities or stratified relations are only likely to occur when all three of these variables are operating simultaneously. *Ethnocentrism* means that a group defines their values, institutions, and belief systems as more natural or superior to those of others. Ethnocentrism alone is not enough to set in motion a system of ethnic stratification, but it is a propensity factor. Although Population One may regard the beliefs, knowledge, and social institutions of Population Two as hopelessly backward, this fact in itself may not lead to a system of inequality. In addition, Noel argues, there must be a strong desire for Population One to seize and exploit the resources of Population Two (competition). Typically, this is land or other natural resources. In the conquest of American Indians, for example, the white conquerors were strongly led by one goal; to seize the choice fertile land held by the Indians. A variant of economic competition is that Ethnic Group One may define a goal as desirable while Ethnic Group Two is indifferent to the same goal. In such a case, Group One may

An asterisk (*) accompanying a citation indicates a selection included in this volume.

attempt to exploit the labor of Group Two to maximize goal attainment. For example, black labor became a vital resource in the developing tobacco and cotton plantations.

Yet, ethnic stratification will not be generated until Noel's third condition, that of differential power, occurs. "Without differential power it would simply be impossible for one group to achieve dominance and impose subordination to its will and ideals upon the other[s]" (Noel, 1968:163). Superior organization, technology, and gun power were crucial facts in European colonization, American slavery, and the forcing of Indians on to barren reservations. Noel's thesis is summarized in Figure 5-1.

If one of these three conditions is missing, then something other than ethnic stratification develops. If ethnocentrism is absent, the two populations would be likely to merge (because of cultural similarity) with competition and stratification developing along class rather than ethnic lines. Similarly, if ethnocentrism and competition are present, but a power differential is missing, a kind of structural pluralism may emerge with two closed societies competing for scarce resources but unable to dominate each other.

Noel's theory is one of the clearest and most concise statements of the origins of ethnic stratification. The theory has applicability to ethnic relations in the United States. Belief in cultural superiority, desire for scarce resources and superior power were important facts in the subordination of Indians, blacks, and Mexican Americans. In the United States, ethnic minorities can be: (1) racial groups, such as blacks, who are distinguishable primarily by visible physical criteria; (2) cultural populations, such as American Poles, Irish, Jews, and Italians, who are distinguishable by language, heritage, nationality, or special traditions; and (3) groups, such as American Indians, who are differentiated by both cultural and physical differences. Our primary focus throughout this book is on the visible ethnic minorities (1 and 3) and especially on those minorities that were conquered by force—blacks, Mexican Americans, and Native Americans.

The conquered minorities had qualitatively different experiences in the United States from those of white immigrants, such as the Italians, Irish, and Poles. Indeed, the distinctiveness of these experiences allows us to argue for a separate ethnic hierarchy. The barriers experienced by blacks, Mexican Americans, and native Americans represent far more than social class discrimination. Two schools of thought that describe the unique experiences of conquered minorities are the *caste* and the *conquest-colonial* perspectives.

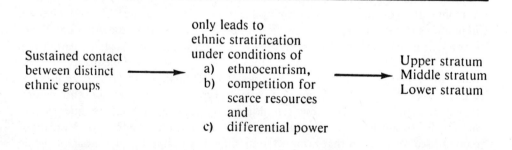

Figure 5-1. *Summary of Noel Thesis: The Origins of Ethnic Stratification.* (Adapted from H. Edward Ransford, *Race and Class in American Society: Black, Chicano, Anglo.* Cambridge, Mass.: Schenkman Publishing Co., 1977, p. 8.)

CASTE

Following conquest, blacks were brought to this country and placed in a system in which they were totally subordinate. Caste stratification is one way to describe that system. Caste connotes a rigid ascriptive form of stratification based on skin color, heredity, or other genetic or physical characteristics. One is born into, lives his or her life, and dies within a caste group, with no chance of ever leaving it.

Ethnic caste systems usually have three major characteristics: the practice of *endogamy,* in which marriage is allowed only between members of the same caste, never between castes; *rules of etiquette* that specify appropriate deference behavior for members of the subordinate group when they interact with members of the dominant group; and an *ideology* or belief system that justifies the subordination of the lower caste, usually on the grounds that they are less intelligent and incapable of producing a "high culture." In the United States, black-white relations have been described as caste-like. The term also has been applied to the position in American society of Mexican-Americans and Indians (Grebler, Moore, and Guzman, 1970:317–324).

In describing slavery in the United States, van den Berghe (1967) speaks of a horizontal color bar that separated the black and white castes. The caste line resulted in a huge gap in power, wealth, health, status, and general life chances. Even the few blacks who achieved some wealth or occupational position ranked lower than lower-class whites. The *ascribed* system of ethnicity was always more important than the *achieved* system of class.

The Jim Crow laws and caste etiquette were the most dramatic examples of this stratification system. Such laws and customs enforced a systematic separation of the races in all potential situations of close contact: restaurants, schools, drinking fountains, restrooms, and public transportation. Caste rules dictated that black men must never have sexual relations with white women. Violations resulted in black men being lynched and compliant women being exiled. On the other hand, many white men had sexual relations with black women with impunity. Equally repressive were the many informal rules of social etiquette that reinforced black feelings of inferiority. Consider the following description of caste etiquette in the deep South in the 1930s:

> Negroes and whites must not shake hands when they meet; the white man must start the conversation (although the Negro can hint that he wants to talk): the Negro must address the white person as Mr., Mrs. or Miss, but he must never be addressed by these titles himself (Negroes are addressed by their first name or called uncle, aunty, darky, nigger, or in some cases—for politeness sake—may be called by their last name or by such titles as doctor, professor or teacher). The topic of conversations must be limited to specific job matters or to personal niceties (e.g. inquiries after one's health); it must never stray over to bigger matters of politics or economics or to personal matters such as white husband-wife relationships. Negroes should never look into the eyes of white people when they talk to them but generally keep their eyes on the ground or shifting, and their physical posture in front of white people when they talk to them should be humble and self-demeaning (Rose, 1961: 358).

Such caste etiquette is an extreme example of what we are calling unequal cultural privilege in the sense of norms and conventions. Blacks were locked into highly circumscribed roles under a caste system.

The black-white caste system was not fully formed until several decades after the end of slavery. It was legitimized by the famed *Plessy* vs. *Ferguson* decision of the United States Supreme Court some thirty years after the Civil War. That decision legitimized "separate but equal" facilities for blacks and whites. The caste system remained substantially unchallenged between 1890 and 1940. During the 1940s, 1950s, and 1960s, social forces began to chip away at the caste order. The employment of blacks in skilled positions during World War II, the desegregation of the armed forces after World War II, the large-scale migration from the South to urban industrial centers, the 1954 Supreme Court desegregation case, and the increase of black protest and civil rights legislation—all contributed to a weakening of the caste system.

Class within Caste.

As opportunities increased for blacks, some obtained better-paying, skilled, blue-collar and white-collar positions. It was no longer accurate to speak of a horizonal color bar in which all blacks were subordinate to all whites. A dynamic interaction between caste and class was developing.

Lloyd Warner was one of the first social scientists to observe this interaction in a 1941 study (*Deep South*, Davis, *et al.*, 1941). Warner noted that within each caste (of black and white society) a socioecnomonic structure existed, Figure 5–2 shows the caste line as no longer horizontal but slanted, indicating a moderate degree of socioeconomic

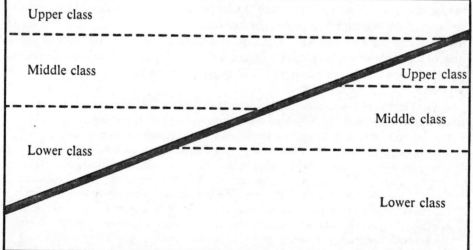

Figure 5-2. *Class and Caste Lines.* (Adapted from *Deep South: A Social-Anthropological Study of Caste and Class,* by Allison Davis, Burleigh B. Gardner, and Mary R. Gardner, p. 10, by permission of The University of Chicago Press. Copyright, 1941, by The University of Chicago.)

differentiation with the black minority (or caste) group. In other words, lower-class blacks were far more disadvantaged in socioeconomic characteristics than lower-class whites; upper-class blacks were more comparable to the white "upper-middle class." Even though the black stratification system is more truncated than the white, it became increasingly possible for some high-achieving blacks to have greater status in the society at large than lower-class whites. However, Warner did not clearly spell out all the possible results of internal differentiation within the black group, leaving significant questions unanswered: To what extent does class achievement override caste position? To what extent does class similarity between blacks and whites break down social-interaction barriers? Does improved socioeconomic status for blacks mean an improved power base?

There seem to be two major ways that social scientists have tried to answer these questions. Some sociologists think that caste stratification is the most accurate way to describe black-white relations in current times. They say that social-class achievement and civil rights gains have not altered the caste order significantly. Howard (1970) writes that "Implicitly, in popular thinking black ancestry constitutes an indelible genetic stain which can never be entirely removed. . . . Any person with known black ancestry is thought of as black, however 'white' he may be phenotypically. . ." (Howard, 1970:7). Other social scientists (and we include ourselves in this second group) think that the caste order has been significantly altered so that terms like "semicaste" are more appropriate for the 1970s and 1980s. In particular, three major changes have occurred: 1) the power potential of blacks has improved; 2) the black middle class has grown; and 3) barriers to social intimacy between blacks and whites have been reduced.

The increase of blacks in decision-making positions, such as supervisor, mayor, senator, and manager, has been apparent. Blacks have also exerted collective power in elections, protests, strikes, and boycotts. The power potential for both individual blacks and blacks as a whole has been increased by recent civil rights laws that attempt to ensure equal employment opportunities and open housing policies.

By a variety of socioeconomic measures, the size of the black middle class has increased significantly in the last fifteen years. For example, recent census data show that the proportion of blacks in white-collar jobs has increased from 16 percent in 1960 to 35 percent in 1977. Depending on one's definition of middle class, somewhere between 25 and 35 percent of blacks are in middle-class occupations and income categories (see chapter 13). Progress, however, has not been the common experience of all American blacks in the past few decades. Some individuals have made dramatic gains, while others are more firmly entrenched in poverty and dependency than ever before. Thus Moynihan speaks of an "up-down" pattern, one segment making gains, another segment slipping further into poverty (Moynihan, 1972).

Survey research data indicate that whites, in current times, are far more willing to interact with blacks in moderately intimate social situations than they were twenty or thirty years ago. For example, the proportion of whites who object to having a black family living next door has decreased from 49 percent in 1950 to 16 percent in 1972 (Hermalin and Farley, 1973:579). Most whites, however, continue to object strongly to the most intimate forms of social interaction such as dating and intermarriage. In short, although there have been substantial changes in the caste order, racism and barriers also persist. It is this mixed profile of change and partial gains for blacks that calls for terms like "semicaste."

The rigidity of caste barriers has also declined significantly for Mexican Americans. Research conducted in Corpus Christi, Texas in the 1920s indicates that there were many caste-like qualities in Anglo-Mexican interaction.

> Mexicans were 'overwhelmingly' laborers in the cotton fields and definitely lower class . . . Mexican Americans went to segregated schools. Restrictive covenant clauses usually confined them to segregated neighborhoods. Discrimination in public accommodations was almost as stringent as it was against Negroes. Mexican Americans were allowed to sit at the drugstore fountain (though not at the tables) while Negroes would not be seated at all. Intermarriage was disparaged and the Anglo member of an intermarrying couple became socially a Mexican (Grebler, Moore and Guzman, 1970:323).

Even so, Mexican-Americans had more escape valves, more inconsistencies of status, and more opportunities for upward mobility than did blacks. Upwardly mobile Mexican-Americans who did not have Indian-like appearances could claim all or predominantly Spanish ancestry in communities where the caste sanctions toward Mexicans were extreme. Further, Mexican Americans in middle-class occupations faced inconsistent caste status, depending on where they lived. San Antonio was seen as a relatively open place for the middle class—a very different milieu from Corpus Christi. As Mexican-Americans have become more urbanized and entered the industrial sector in large numbers, some social scientists have questioned whether the term caste is appropriate for contemporary Anglo-Chicano relations. Penalosa likens present-day Chicanos in southern California to "a European immigrant group of a generation ago such as . . . the Italian-Americans in New York, Boston or San Francisco" (Penalosa, 1971). Regardless of the best term, it can be said with certainty that the rigidity of caste barriers in such areas as intermarriage and equality of employment have diminished consider-

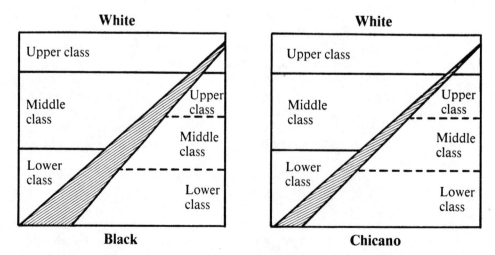

Figure 5-3. *Revised Class Within Caste Model of Stratification.* (Adapted from H. Edward Ransford, *Race and Class in American Society: Black, Chicano, Anglo,* Cambridge, Mass.: Schenkman Publishing Co., 1977, p. 52. Supported by additional data from Davidson and Gaitz, 1975; Mittlebach and Moore, 1968.)

ably. An updated version of the class-within-caste model (for both blacks and Chicanos) is presented in Figure 5–3.

Notice first that the diagonal line has shifted further on its axis (compared with Figure 5–2) indicating the increased size of the middle-class segments of black and Chicano groups. Second, the thickness of the line symbolizes the social distance (or the degree of social intimacy) between castes. It is not of uniform width but is only thick at its lower class end. In other words, lower-class blacks and Chicanos continue to experience much social exclusion. At the middle- and upper-class end of the diagram, the line funnels down to indicate a moderate barrier for middle- and upper-class blacks and an almost permeable barrier for middle-class Chicanos. Middle class blacks may have (if they choose) moderately intimate contact with middle-class whites, and many middle-class Chicanos have been completely assimilated with few barriers to interracial friendships, dating, and marriage.

THE CONQUEST-COLONIAL PERSPECTIVE

The conquest-colonial perspective on ethnic stratification makes a distinction between minorities that voluntarily immigrated and the minorities that were conquered or colonized. Robert Blauner* (1972), for example, maintains that white ethnics (such as the Irish, Italians, and Poles) had a very different experience from the colonized groups because they voluntarily entered the country; were a part of the free labor market; and were able to maintain control over the cultural traditions and institutions of their ethnic communities. White ethnics had economic and political control over a viable community, which was able to bargain for political favors and provide a way station between immigrant arrival and assimilation into the larger society. Accordingly, the white ethnic experience fits an immigration model in which each succeeding generation made more gains in class position and assimilation, and each newly arriving immigrant group took the bottom position and forced the then lowest groups up a notch.

In contrast to the immigration model, blacks, Chicanos, and American Indians experienced colonialism within the United States. Colonization means that an ethnic group undergoes three kinds of domination:

1. Entry into the larger society is forced, either in the sense that a foreign ethnic group is conquered and transported to the dominant society for their slave labor (Africans), or in the sense that ethnic groups already settled in the country are conquered within the boundaries of that country (Mexicans in the Southwest; Indians throughout the United States).
2. The ethnic minority is forced into unfree labor contracts such as slavery and peonage.
3. The culture of the colonized group is destroyed or transformed (Blauner, 1972).

The colonized minorities, then, are not the last arrivals in an immigrant mobility cycle—they have experienced a qualitatively different set of social forces. Although the historical circumstances are quite different for each, blacks, Chicanos, and native Americans faced the following common factors:

Forced Entry and Conquest.

All three groups entered into relationships with whites through force and violence rather than choice. For example, large numbers of Mexicans were settled in (what is now) Texas, New Mexico, and California, in the period between 1800–1900. Mexicans lost their land base because of the war between the United States and Mexico, annexation, land purchases, and the inundation of white settlers. Relations between Mexicans and Anglos in Texas were especially hostile and marked with violence. Joan Moore notes that in South Texas, "violence continued in organized fashion well into the twentieth century with armed clashes involving the northern Mexican guerilleros and the U.S. army" (Moore, 1970).

Systems of Inequality.

Following conquest, each of the three groups experienced *systems* of power inequality referred to as "internal colonialism." "caste stratification," or "paternalistic" race relations (Blauner, 1972; van den Berghe, 1967; Dollard, 1957). For example, blacks were totally controlled and forced to stay "in their place" by the slavery system and by Jim Crow laws.

The Bureau of Indian Affairs represented a highly paternalistic system of control over native Americans. In tracing the evolution of the relationship between Indians and the United States Government, it was decided in 1862 to designate the members of Indian tribes as "wards" of the Indian Bureau rather than to let them be considered as sovereign or independent enemies. "Unfortunately, and without ever really having legal sanction, the term 'ward' took on administrative connotations by which the Bureau exercised incredible control over the lives and property of individuals, much as a guardian would act for minors or helplessly retarded children" (Lurie, 1975:178).

American Indians experienced a unique kind of paternalism as wards of the government, administered by their guardian, the Bureau of Indian Affairs. Much has been written about the paternalism of the Bureau. One of the more caustic accounts is found in Edgar S. Cahn's *Our Brother's Keeper*:

> From birth to death his home, his land, his reservation, his schools, his jobs, the stores where he shops, the tribal council that governs him, the opportunities available to him, the way in which he spends his money, disposes of his property, and even the way in which he provides for his heirs after death—are all determined by the Bureau of Indian Affairs acting as the agent of the United States Government (Cahn, 1969:5).

So anxious are American Indians to protect their land and traditions that they have militantly opposed any action to do away with the BIA. Though the Bureau has taken advantage of Indians again and again, the alternative—termination of this trusteeship and protective arrangement—is far less desirable. In those instances in which termination has occurred, Indians have lost all their land, their special services and institutions, and have become individual welfare cases. For example, with termination, Indian land comes under state and local property taxes. Indians are unable to pay the taxes and their land is absorbed or sold at public auctions. The BIA system may exploit, but it provides services and continues to exist because it is the lesser of two evils.

Limited Employment Opportunities.

Blacks, Chicanos, American Indians, and Asians worked under forced labor systems as slaves, coolies, or peons. Even within nonagricultural sectors, colonized minorities were concentrated in unskilled jobs, such as building railroads, in ". . . industries that were essential to the early development of a national capitalist economy, but which were primarily prerequisites of industrial development rather than industries with any dynamic future" (Blauner, 1972:63). The colonized minorities provided cheap, marginal labor for the industrializing economy.

In contrast, white ethnics had far greater access to manufacturing industries. Even though they held unskilled jobs, they were a part of the dynamic, expanding industrial enterprise of the late 1800s and early 1900s. To be sure, certain white immigrant groups experienced a great deal of discrimination. Often they were viewed as peasants, ". . . unwashed, uneducated, uncouth, as culturally inferior" (Rose, 1973:15). Widespread exploitation took place in textile towns and "company stores." As unskilled factory workers and laborers, however, they had a chance to rise, in time, to semiskilled and skilled positions (Blauner, 1972:63).

Economic Tension between White Ethnics and the Colonized Minorities.

In some cases, white European immigrants directly blocked the opportunities for mobility of the colonized minorities in the industrial sector. Discrimination on the part of white ethnics toward colonized minorities was more a function of economic threat than racial prejudice.

This phenomenon is most clearly explained by the model of a split labor market. Bonacich distinguishes between three classes in the industrial sector; business, higher paid labor, and cheap labor. In order to maximize profits and minimize labor costs, the business class may attempt to introduce cheap labor such as the colonized minorities "as strikebreakers or as replacements to undercut a labor force trying to improve its bargaining position with business" (Bonacich, 1972:553). Higher paid labor (white ethnics) is greatly threatened by the possible use of cheaper labor and does everything possible to block entry of the cheaper labor stratum. Asian Americans (Chinese, Japanese, and Filipinos) for example, were imported to build railroads and to work as farm laborers. As long as they did not directly compete for jobs with the white working class, there was very little racial tension. Only when Chinese and Japanese workers acquired land and began to enter occupations and work for lower wages, did racial hostility increase. In the 1870s, there were serious economic crises following the gold rush that intensified the competition for jobs. White workers expressed extreme antagonism toward Asian competitors ("Yellow Peril") and were instrumental in pressuring politicians to enact immigration restriction policies ("The Acts of Oriental Exclusion"). The split labor market theory has also been used to explain the exclusion of blacks and Chicanos from many skilled labor unions.

Control of Minority Communities.

The ghettos, barrios, and reservations of our nation have been controlled and manipulated by white officials and their agents. Conquest and forced labor systems weakened the potential of colonized groups to develop separate communities that might have resisted white domination. "Culture and social organization are important as vessels of a people's autonomy and integrity; when cultures are whole and vigorous, conquest, penetration, and certain modes of control are more readily resisted" (Blauner, 1972:67). For the most part, blacks have not owned ghetto institutions (the black church is a notable exception). Absentee landlords, nonresident merchants, white police, and welfare officials generally have controlled the lives of blacks and Chicanos living in the inner city. The Bureau of Indian Affairs has exercised extreme control over the economic development, land sales, and education of Indians. The external control of the communities of conquered or colonized minorities contrasts sharply with the relatively autonomous white-ethnic enclaves (Blauner, 1972:51–81).

Reduced Social Mobility Due to Skin Color.

Blacks, Chicanos, and American Indians are visible minorities. When there are stereotypes of inferiority attached to particular ethnic groups and these groups are physically visible, their mobility in society is greatly reduced. Black Americans in particular have been locked out by physical visibility and by the stigma attached to their color.

Semicolonial Groups: Asians and Puerto Ricans

The experience of Asian Americans and Puerto Ricans can be conceptualized as semicolonial in the sense that these groups had both colonial and immigration experiences. For example, although many Chinese chose to enter the United States for a period of debt servitude, others were "shanghaied" or pressed into service (Blauner, 1972:54). Asians were largely excluded from industrial manufacturing jobs in the late 1800s and early 1900s and thus resemble blacks and Chicanos as an unfree labor force. But Asians were not conquered by force and did not experience an attack on their culture to the same degree that blacks, Chicanos, and Native Americans did. Asian minority communities provided more alternatives to a white-dominated market; they developed many exclusive ethnic small businesses and credit associations.

The Puerto Rican experience represents another mixed case of colonialism and immigration. For five hundred years, Puerto Rico was a Spanish colony. "Spanish dominance . . . established and maintained to the end of the nineteenth century the Spanish language, the Roman Catholic Church, and a civil and military administration" (Marden and Meyer, 1978:262). In 1898, Puerto Rico became an American Possession. American corporate businessmen were highly involved in Puerto Rico's economy in the 1920s and 1930s. Puerto Rico became increasingly dependent on mainland business capital. For example, in 1930 American businessmen had absentee control of 60 percent of all sugar production, 31 percent of the fruit production, 50 percent of public utilities, and 100 percent of the steamship lines (Diffie and Diffie, 1931:135). There were clear elements of colonial domination and control during this period.

More recently, Puerto Rico has moved toward greater autonomy. Today the island is classified as a Free Associated State, which means it is a part of the United States but has a good deal of autonomy from the United States government.

Puerto Ricans immigrated to the United States mainland as early as 1900, but large scale migration (especially to New York) occurred after World War II. At first glance, the migration patterns of Puerto Ricans may appear similar to that of white ethnics. It is true that both Puerto Ricans and white ethnics voluntarily immigrated to the East coast of the United States in search of better economic opportunities. Puerto Rican migration, however, was quite different from that of white ethnics. Fitzpatrick (1968) notes these unique features of Puerto Rican immigration:

- Puerto Ricans are Spanish speaking and from a different cultural background, yet they are United States citizens.
- They are the first group of immigrants to bring with them a tradition of intermarriage between people of widely different color (mixes of Spanish, Indian, and African people).
- They are Catholic migrants but they have not had a native clergy to accompany them.
- They are usually visible by skin color.
- They arrived in New York at a time when automation was eliminating thousands of unskilled and semi-skilled positions, thus greatly reducing their chances for employment.
- With air travel time of but three hours between New York and the Island, there is a feeling among many Puerto Ricans that one can always return to the Island if life becomes too harsh in the big city.

Currently, Puerto Ricans can be classified as a disadvantaged minority group. Their socioeconomic characteristics are very similar to blacks and Mexican Americans. In the mid 1970s in New York City, 48 percent of Puerto Ricans earned less than $7,000 a year compared with 48 percent of blacks. For both groups (New York City) the proportion on welfare is approximately one-third (Time, 1978:55, 58). The median income of Puerto Rican males nationwide was $8,051 compared with $7,708 for Mexican American males (Bureau of Census, Series P–20 #38, 1978). The high school drop out rate for Puerto Ricans is high and violent crime and drug use are common among the young. Historically, then, the Puerto Rican experience can best be described as semi-colonial but by contemporary socioeconomic measures Puerto Ricans are most like the colonized minorities.

Drawing from this discussion on conquest and colonialism, an ethnic stratification order in the United States would look like that shown in Figure 5–4. Descending the scale in Figure 5–4, we find increasing degrees of political powerlessness, economic oppression, and social exclusion. White ethnics experienced high degrees of prejudice and discrimination but, with each generation, they also experienced steady class mobility. Voluntary immigration, greater employment opportunities in the manufacturing sector, relatively autonomous ethnic communities that could preserve ethnic culture, and low physical visibility allowed white ethnics to be assimilated rather rapidly. The colonized minorities, in contrast, were conquered, excluded from the free labor market and the manufacturing sector, lived in controlled communities with few cultural institutions to resist discrimination, and were far more visible by facial features and skin color. Asian Americans and Puerto Ricans are placed in between white ethnics

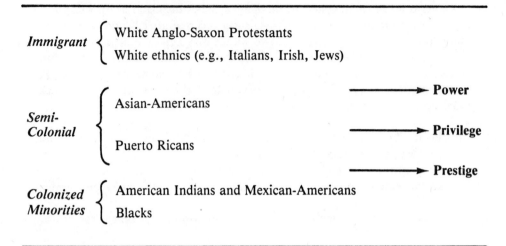

Figure 5-4. *Stratification Order in the United States.*

and the colonized minorities since in both groups there was a mix of immigration and colonial characteristics. Asians are higher than Puerto Ricans on many socioeconomic measures and are therefore placed closer to white ethnics; Puerto Ricans are placed closer to blacks, Chicanos, and Native Americans because their occupation, education, and income profiles more closely resemble the colonized groups.

Dominant White Stratum or Power Elite?

The conquest-colonial model emphasizes, above all, power inequality as the essential fact of an ethnic stratification order. From the initial conquest of an ethnic population, to caste and colonial systems of labor exploitation, to the manipulation of minority communities, a white power stratum has controlled the life chances and destinies of black and brown people. Moreover, the degree of power held by a given ethnic group directly affects its access to privilege and prestige. That is, power, the most central variable in ethnic stratification, determines the amount of social honor and economic privilege that a given ethnic group will enjoy (Olsen*, 1970:300).

It is important, however, to clarify several points dealing with the dispersal of power in the white population and in the minorities. Who has the power in this country? A widely held theory is that a small group of men at the top of major institutions make things move. C. Wright Mills (1972) argues that at the highest levels of the political, economic, and military hierarchies, a small elite group has an inordinate amount of control over the destinies of individual citizens *of all races*. "For they are in command of the major hierarchies and major organizations of modern society. They rule the big corporations. They run the machinery of the state and claim its prerogatives. They direct the military establishment" (Mills, 1972:278).

From this power elite model, it would seem inappropriate to refer to a "dominant white group" since some whites (i.e., Mills's elite) have far more control over the stratification system than rank-and-file whites. One could even argue that the white and minority masses are equally dominated by a powerful few. However, a much larger group of whites than a power elite have controlled the destinies of black, Chicano, and Native American people. Systems of racial inequality initiated by a small group of powerful whites allowed for a wide dispersal of authority such that the middle class, working class, and even to some degree, poor whites helped to perpetuate the racial order. Consider C. Van Woodward's statement about the extent to which Jim Crow laws operated in Southern society:

> The Jim Crow laws put the authority of the state or city in the voice of the streetcar conductor, the railway brakeman, the bus driver, the theater usher and also into the voice of the hoodlums of the public parks and playgrounds. They gave free rein and the majesty of the law to mass aggressions that might otherwise have been curbed, blunted or deflected (Woodward, 1957:93).

More currently, many whites of modest status and economic attainment have prevented black encroachment in their trade unions. Indeed, it is commonly noted that the white working class has perpetuated the discrimination norms of the old caste order. This is because the white working class, more than any other strata in society, faces the greatest status threat as well as economic competition from the upwardly mobile black population. Those holding a colonial perspective also emphasize the fact that white agents of powerful ruling groups (for example, the white police) enforce the system of inequality (Blauner, 1972). Thus, large numbers of whites, far in excess of the power elite, have been and continue to be involved in racial discrimination.

To refer to the white population as dominant in power and to the conquered minority populations as subordinate in power is only partially accurate, however. One exception worth noting is that some segments of the white majority have identified with the ethnic liberation movements and actively participated in them. (One of the major support groups in Cesar Chavez's farm-worker movement is white and middle class, for example.) The white majority group, then, cannot be viewed as one homogeneous oppressor. Another very important fact is that, increasingly, some members of the minority populations have attained middle-class status or influential political office and, in consequence, have more personal influence and control than some whites. Therefore, not all whites are dominant over all blacks.

Two Kinds of Power

If power is defined as control over major institutions and in particular control over the economy, then few minority persons possess such top power. Even at upper-middle levels of institutional power (for example, mayors or senators) whites have far more representation and influence than minority people. However, if power is thought of in more individual terms as the probability of exerting control over one's own life, then middle-class blacks often have more control than working and lower-class whites.

Middle-class blacks, in contrast to lower-class whites, typically have more money, influence within the context of their occupation, knowledge of redress channels when they face inequalities, and generally better life chances. The terminology of dominant and subordinate racial strata completely ignores this possibility.

In the preceding discussion, we explored two models of ethnic stratification, caste and conquest-colonial and related ethnicity to the unequal distribution of power in society. Another important meaning of low position in the ethnic hierarchy is that blacks, Chicanos, American Indians, and Puerto Ricans have lacked access to the comforts, services, material ends, and education enjoyed by the dominant group. They have not had the same privileges—the same rights, advantages, services, and immunities—as white Americans. The next section deals with how ethnic stratification can be viewed as an unequal distribution of privileges.

ETHNIC STRATIFICATION AND PRIVILEGE

A number of studies (Pinkney, 1975; Clark, 1964; Blau and Duncan, 1967; Pettigrew, 1964) have shown that blacks, Chicanos, and American Indians (in contrast to whites) have less chance of:

- surviving the first year of life and living to a healthy old age.
- receiving a quality education in their neighborhood.
- receiving good medical and dental care.
- growing up in a neighborhood relatively free of violence, drugs, and delinquent gangs.
- completing four years of college.
- receiving the same income as whites even after achieving the same education.
- avoiding an arrest record.

Obviously some of these inequities are linked to income and may also be shared with low-income whites. However, many involve a combination of ethnic and economic discrimination. That is, ethnicity (black, Chicano, and Indian) and low class position together mean a far greater reduction of life chances than does low class position alone.

Unequal privilege also encompasses various forms of discrimination because discrimination is the denial of opportunity and equal access to society's benefits. Recently there has developed an important distinction between individual and institutional discrimination.

Individual vs. Institutional Discrimination

Until quite recently, ethnic discrimination has been conceptualized largely in psychological terms to mean that prejudiced individuals exclude racial and ethnic minorities. From this viewpoint, discrimination is ultimately a function of a prejudiced actor. An employer, for example, may not hire blacks, Puerto Ricans, and Chicanos because he or she believes them to be lazy and inefficient workers. This expression of prejudice in discriminatory behavior is certainly one reason that racial minorities have fewer privileges.

However, another important component of discrimination and privilege is found in *system patterns* that exclude minorities irrespective of the behavior of prejudiced individuals. *Institutional discrimination* refers to inequalities rooted in society that have little relation to racial or ethnic prejudice of individuals. This type of discrimination involves policies or practices that appear to be neutral in their effect on minority individuals or groups, but which have harmful consequences. For example, the rate of unemployment among minority persons has risen recently. This rise is not due to an increase in personal prejudice, but rather due to these economic and historical factors: (1) minority persons have only recently entered the skilled job market, have the least seniority, and are first to be laid off in hard economic times; and (2) the pace of automation is accelerating to such a degree that minority groups and other workers without special skills are displaced first. Neither of these economic trends is predicated on any personal bigotry; minority persons are excluded because of impersonal, structural processes.

Both individual and institutional discrimination have had debilitating effects on racial minorities. Although blacks and Chicanos have made gains in the last fifteen years (see chapter 13), current census reports reveal that a great deal of racial inequality remains in our society. For example, Table 5-1 shows that the proportion of black families with incomes under $4,000, in 1974 is three times higher than that of white families. Only 19 percent of black families were earning incomes over $15,000, as compared with more than twice that proportion, or 42 percent, of white families. Similarly, in 1976, 26.5 percent of Mexican American families were living below the poverty level, while only 25 percent of the families were earning over $15,000 (Bureau of Census, Series P-20, No. 310).

Table 5-2 shows the unemployment rates in 1974 for blacks and whites of different sex and age levels. For every category of age and sex, the black unemployment rate is roughly twice the white rate. Note the incredibly high unemployment rate for sixteen-

Table 5-1. *Race and Family Income in 1974 (Adjusted for price changes in 1974 dollars.)*

Income	Black	White
Under $4,000	23%	7%
$15,000 and over	19%	42%

Source: Current Population Reports, Series P-23, No. 54, Bureau of the Census; adapted from Table 11, p. 27.

Table 5-2. *Unemployment Rates by Race, Controlling for Sex and Age (1974)*

	Black	White
Total, all ages, both sexes	10.4%	5.0%
Men, 20 years and over	7.3	3.5
Women, 20 years and over	8.7	5.0
Both sexes, 16 to 19 years	34.9	14.0

Source: Current Population Reports, Series P-23, No. 54, Bureau of the Census; adapted from Table 39, p. 65.

to nineteen-year-old blacks (34.9 percent) compared with the much lower rate for young whites (14 percent).

Not only are there disparities in income and employment but quality of life differs as well. Blacks are much more likely than whites to be the victims of violent crimes (rape, robbery, assault). This is especially true at low socioeconomic levels. The victimization rate in 1973 was 63 per 1,000 population for low-income blacks, compared with 46 for low-income whites (Bureau of Census, Series P–23, No. 54).

The Minority Community and the Distribution of Privileges

As previously noted, ethnic stratification is somewhat unique among the ascribed hierarchies in that minorities are highly concentrated in geographical space. Blacks and Mexican Americans are typically concentrated in inner-city ghettos and barrios. Approximately one-half of all Native Americans live on isolated reservations. Much of the stratification literature portrays minority communities as pathological, teeming with frustration and discontent. Residence in these communities reduces the chances for a person to acquire the services, comforts, quality education, positive self-image, and other benefits that we are calling privileges. Recent research, however, indicates that the minority community also provides adaptations, positive functions, and resources to off-set discrimination. In all likelihood the minority community provides both negative and positive features. To strive for a balanced presentation, we will review the literature of both views.

Disadvantages of the Minority Community

Ghettos, barrios, and Indian reservations are separate and unequal geographical communities. They are externally controlled (to some degree), economically exploited, and have separate, usually inferior, institutions. Low ethnic position is linked to reduced privileges through the minority community. Studies have shown that in barrios and ghettos (in contrast to white suburban or urban areas) residents pay more for the same consumer goods yet receive lower-quality goods, such as repossessed furniture sold as new and rancid meat sold as fresh (Sturdivant and Wilhelm, 1968; Caplovitz, 1963). Residents of ghettos and barrios are more likely to experience demeaning encounters with authority (such as being stopped, searched, and questioned by police), and the probability of ghetto residents having an arrest record is far higher (Kerner Report, 1968:299–322). With regard to educational opportunity, segregated ghetto, barrio, and Bureau of Indian Affairs schools are notorious as nonlearning environments. Large classes, inexperienced teachers, the rigid use of culturally biased IQ Tests, and low teacher expectations for success are often-mentioned drawbacks (Clark, 1964; Mercer, 1972). Recent studies of educational tracking—the placement of students into separate groups according to presumed ability—indicate that students in low-ability groups often receive a qualitatively different and generally inferior education. Since verbal test scores are the main criteria for track assignments, lower-class black and Mexican-American children, who come from homes where a black dialect or Spanish are commonly spoken, are most likely to be assigned to a low-ability track. Once placed in such a track, the chances of upward mobility into a college-bound group are practically nil. Studies find a caste-like rigidity in terms of movement up or down (Schafer, Olexa and Polk,* 1970; Lauter and Howe, 1972). The differences in achievement and IQ between black and white students is very small when they first begin school. But the longer black children remain in ghetto schools, the greater the gap grows until by high school graduation the gap is so large that many blacks are eliminated from the achievement race for good jobs and a college education (Clark, 1964). That is, attendance at a ghetto or barrio school often represents a cumulative loss of privileges.

In short, ghettos and barrios can be seen as somewhat separate, closed worlds with day-to-day direct exploitation as well as long-standing and cumulative training for failure, as in segregated schools.

Positive Aspects of the Minority Community

The minority community can also be viewed in a more positive light. Ethnic persons living side by side and facing high degrees of discrimination have developed extraordinary adaptations, cultural innovations, and insulation mechanisms to combat discrimination. These adaptations result in privileges such as self-esteem and economic independence.

1. Life Style Alternatives. A participant-observation study by Hannerz (1969) found a variety of adaptive life styles among lower-class blacks in a Washington, D.C., ghetto. Lower-class black males who are denied status and male ego satisfaction provided by steady employment and support of their dependents may attain respect and status through a unique definition of *ghetto-specific masculinity.* "The male-female relationship in its ghetto-specific forms is influenced not only by what the male cannot do but also by what he does instead" (Hannerz, 1969:79). Ghetto-specific masculinity involves "sexual exploits, toughness, an ability to command respect, personal appearance with an emphasis on male clothing fashions, liquor consumption and verbal ability" (Hannerz, 1969:79). Among streetcorner men, who are often assumed to be lacking in confidence and self-worth, Hannerz finds an alternative life style that provides for triumph and dominance.

Even when blacks face overwhelming structural barriers (racism, unemployment, a welfare system that excludes the black male from the family unit) and are accordingly in a very depressed niche in the race-class hierarchies, there still is "space" left for cultural innovation. Too often sociologists have ignored the creative responses of the black community to its circumstances. The concept of community plays heavily in this interpretation. We are not talking about individual adaptations; rather, we are noting the cultural adaptations that occur when there is a community of people who share similar problems and have intense interaction with each other.

Although ghetto-specific masculinity may contribute to the personality integration and self-esteem of low-income black males, it also may have negative consequences. There may be conflicts between mainstream and ghetto-specific values, especially in marital relations. Often a wife judges her husband in terms of the mainstream values of providing for the family and of sexual fidelity. When her husband spends much of his time and money on peer-group activities, she becomes dissatisfied with his performance as household provider. Some couples do come to terms with the contradictions between mainstream and ghetto values of masculinity. They work out compromises between these two life styles. For example, a wife may overlook occasional sexual unfaithfulness if the husband is discreet and continues to make economic contributions to the household. Hannerz also points out that ghetto-specific masculinity is most ardently practiced among younger men, and it becomes increasingly maladaptive as a life style as a man grows older.

> Particularly for older men ghetto-specific masculinity is difficult; if a man has not by then managed to make the transition to a more mainstream-like male role, middle age may meet him well on the road downhill to alcoholism, isolation, and poor health, while his ability to live up to his role, with sex, toughness, and all, becomes progressively more impaired (Hannerz, 1969:87).

Ghetto-specific masculinity can be functional or dysfunctional. For younger men facing extreme race and class discrimination, it provides a kind of "short-run strategy" or coping mechanism. But it also introduces its own problems. Males highly involved in ghetto-specific masculinity may have more difficulty becoming bicultural, that is, able to play successfully both mainstream and ghetto-specific roles. The young person will not be prepared for life outside the ghetto. Ghetto masculinity provides a system of rewards and satisfactions only within the ghetto.

2. *Ethnic Enterprise.* The development and ownership of small businesses within a minority community provides one of the most important adaptations that a minority can make. Through ethnic enterprise, a minority group gains the privilege of autonomy and no longer has to compete in the white labor market. The minority group frees itself of discriminatory loan agencies and exploitive hiring practices. Small business enterprises in ethnic enclaves also mean that profits flow back into the minority community and are invested in services and additional businesses, which further benefit the community. Because Japanese- and Chinese-Americans have not experienced the system of total control that blacks did under slavery or that Indians did under the Bureau of Indian Affairs, Asian communities in America have been relatively autonomous, allowing for the development of small business activities.

A fascinating analysis of ethnic enterprise is Ivan Light's (1973) comparative research on the propensity of Japanese, Chinese, and blacks to develop small businesses in their ethnic communities. Japanese, Chinese, and black Americans have all faced extreme labor-market discrimination. Why did the Chinese and Japanese develop a strong business class whereas blacks did not? Light rejects the simplistic explanation that certain ethnic groups have more entrepreneurial drive than others. Rather, he searches for the complex historical, structural, and cultural factors that promoted ethnic enterprise among Chinese- and Japanese-Americans and decreased the propensity among black Americans.

The cultural tradition of rotating credit associations may help to explain why small businesses characterize certain ethnic communities. Rotating credit associations combine funds and rotate these pooled funds among a membership group. The importance of these associations is substantial because they free ethnic minorities from dependence upon white credit associations in small-scale capital formation.

Strong traditions of rotating credit associations exist among immigrants to the United States from southern China and Japan. Although discrimination against these groups was often extreme, it was not of a kind that destroyed the cultural traits of the group. Rotating credit, a cultural trait that survived, was widely practiced among the Japanese in Hawaii, northern California, and the Pacific Northwest.

Anthropological research also has found evidence of rotating credit associations in many parts of Africa, "including West Africa from which the progenitors of American Negroes were abducted as slaves" (Light, 1973:30). Especially among the Yoruba of Nigeria strong traditions of rotating credit existed. Africans who were sold to slave-owners in the West Indies continued to practice this form of ethnic enterprise. African slaves brought to the United States did not continue this cultural practice, however. Light and others (Elkins, 1959, for example), argue that the American slave system did not allow African cultural traits to be carried over, whereas the Caribbean slave system did. The white elite of the Caribbean system were more hospitable to the perpetuation of African cultural traditions such as the *esusu,* or Nigerian version of rotating credit. With a shortage of whites to administer the slave system, West Indian slaveholders had to allow blacks a considerable degree of economic independence. In fact, since many were absentee landowners, the European slaveholders depended to some extent on blacks working out their own subsistence economy. "To support themselves, slaves were customarily and typically provided with plots of land on which to grow their own subsistence" (Light, 1973:38). The great leeway accorded to slaves in the organization of their subsistence economy contrasts sharply with slavery in the United States. Slaves here were totally controlled and never given anything close to the rights of self-maintenance found among Caribbean blacks.

If American slavery destroyed the esusu practice of rotating credit while Caribbean slavery allowed it to continue, then one might expect that blacks who immigrated to this country from the Caribbean, and who therefore did not experience United States slavery, would establish associations of rotating credit. This is indeed the case. Blacks from the West Indies, who immigrated to the United States from 1900 to 1924, "distinguished themselves from Native born Negroes by their remarkable propensity to operate small business enterprises" (Light, 1973:33). Unfortunately, the majority of blacks in the United States did not share this cultural heritage with West Indies blacks. In sum, black Americans did not develop a strong class of independent merchants in part because the West African cultural tradition of rotating credit was destroyed by the milieu of total control and dependency of United States slavery.

Summary and Discussion of the Ethnic Community

Consideration of the positive aspects of the minority community leads to an interesting revision of the caste and conquest-colonial models discussed earlier in this section. Visible ethnic minorities, and especially those conquered by force, have experienced extreme degrees of political powerlessness, economic exploitation, and social exclusion. Yet even the most totally controlled minorities have not reacted by passively complying. Rather, we find a variety of adaptations and cultural innovations.

> It is certainly not likely that black people in America have adapted to circumstances as boxed-in individuals or couples. With a structurally segregated and rather uniformly depressed group such as this, it seems more likely that there has been a hot house atmosphere for new collective adaptations (Hannerz, 1969:77).

To some extent, the minority community represents an extension of dominant-group controls and discrimination; at the same time it provides cultural innovations and adaptations. Figure 5-5 indicates that ethnic stratification should be viewed as a dynamic interaction between subordination efforts of the dominant group and cultural innovations that develop within the minority community to cope with white discrimination and control mechanisms.

Much sociological research has tended to ignore the creative responses of the minority community. Lower-class, unemployed blacks are often seen as totally lacking in self-esteem and power over their lives. The minority community is viewed as a wasteland

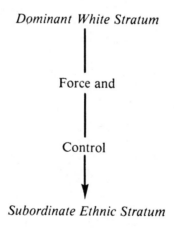

Dominant White Stratum

Force and

Control

Subordinate Ethnic Stratum

A. Minority community discrimination and unequal opportunity are further institutionalized in the minority community with separate and inferior institutions that limit access to privileges (e.g., unequal education, housing, legal and medical opportunities).

B. Minority community reacts with adaptations, coping mechanisms, and innovations such as "ghetto-specific masculinity" and ethnic enterprise.

Figure 5-5. *Two Sides of the Minority Community.*

of pathologies and deficits rather than a community with integrity and with positive functions of its own (Horton, 1966; Baratz and Baratz, 1970).

At a more theoretical level, much research has approached ethnic subordination from a *structural* viewpoint alone—emphasizing, for example, power inequality and institutional discrimination. But there is a *cultural* level of analysis as well.

Minority persons in a community setting generate their own unique culture—a shared set of traditions, meanings, norms, and values. Not all cultural adaptations are functional; we have discussed the positive and negative sides of ghetto-specific masculinity. But many of these adaptations allow minority persons to better cope with structural discrimination. This interaction between structural and cultural levels of analysis provides a far more complete and valid understanding of ethnic stratification.

In the preceding section, we have focused on ethnic stratification as unequal privilege. But low position on the ethnic hierarchy also means that blacks, Chicanos, and Native Americans are assigned a low degree of social honor, or prestige, in American society. The next section deals with ethnic stratification from the viewpoint of unequal prestige.

ETHNICITY AND PRESTIGE

One major reason for the low prestige position of blacks, Mexican-Americans, and Native Americans is that these groups have had the least access to occupations that command high prestige. Until very recently, many of these minority persons have been employed in the most exhausting, dirty, and routine kinds of jobs. The low degree of social honor assigned to blacks, Chicanos, and Indians is more than the result of occupational position, however. As conquered minorities experiencing highly subordinate positions, stereotypes of inferiority developed in part to justify the on-going exploitation. For example, under slavery and the post-Civil War and Jim Crow laws, blacks were regarded as "immature, irresponsible, unintelligent, physically strong, happy-go-lucky, musically gifted, grown-up children" (van den Berghe, 1967:82). At the time of westward settlement and conquest, Indians had a reputation for treachery and savagery (Grebler, *et al.*, 1970:44). Later, under Bureau of Indian Affairs control, Indians were stereotyped as docile, unambitious, and prone to alcoholism (Cahn, 1969). Simmons reports that the majority of Anglos have viewed Mexican-Americans as "physically unclean with tendencies toward drunkenness and other criminal behavior." As workers, they have been stereotyped as "improvident, undependable, childlike, and indolent" (Padilla and Ruiz, 1976:112; Simmons, 1961:289–292).

Although surveys show drastic shifts in white attitudes, some significant residues of belief in inferiority no doubt remain. Even the question of inherited or genetic racial differences has not been laid to rest. Current opinion polls of white attitudes show that there is only a small proportion believing that blacks have less native intelligence than whites (Morris and Jeffries, 1967; Schuman,* 1975). In 1969, however, Arthur Jensen, an educational psychologist, resurrected the genetic argument by reporting that racial differences in IQ scores—notably in conceptual and reasoning abilities—were due to inherited differences. The failure of contemporary education programs such as Headstart to bring lasting gains in academic performance was explained in part by the lower genetic potential of blacks. Although the Jensen report has come under devasting criticism in recent years (Deutsch, 1969; Stinchcombe, 1969), it is likely that some people have been influenced by it and hold onto beliefs in racial inferiority. However, some may hesitate to use a genetic explanation for racial differences in today's relatively tolerant climate of race relations. It is more fashionable today to use terms like "cultural deprivation"; or to say that blacks, Chicanos, and Indians are in lower positions or score lower on IQ tests because they come from a depressed environment. A cultural deprivation rationale is no different in its consequences than a genetic explanation; both positions view blacks (or Chicanos or Indians) as having certain deficits.

Even though most white Americans reject the view that blacks are genetically inferior, many "explain" the lower position of blacks in society by saying that blacks simply have not tried hard enough, that they lack motivation (Schuman, 1975). This reasoning places "the whole burden of black disadvantage on blacks themselves" (Schuman, 1975:379).

Further, although many whites may not have well-defined negative beliefs about minority persons, they may hold a vague feeling of difference. This attitude has been detected in studies of social distance in which whites were asked the degree of intimacy they would allow ethnic groups (Banton, 1960; Bogardus, 1928). Although most whites show no objection at all to working side by side with blacks on the job or having a black family move next door, they do raise strong objections to interracial dating or marriage. At the level of intimate interaction, blacks, Chicanos, and Native Americans continue to face social exclusion. Of the three conquered minorities, blacks face the most social barriers (Davidson and Gaitz, 1973).

Very few studies have asked minority groups to report their stereotypes about whites. No doubt, many minority persons hold stereotypes about whites—that they are materialistic, scheming, individualistic, lacking soul, cold, and inhumane. The very paucity of such studies indicates that the prestige of a minority group is measured only from the perspective of the (white) group in power. The group in control also controls the criteria of admission to prestigious positions.

Shifting Prestige Rankings

Since the Civil Rights Movement, larger numbers of blacks are moving into high-prestige occupations in business, law, medicine, government, and the military. The prestige inherent in such occupational positions should help to override negative evaluations based on race.

However, it is still quite likely that persons with unequal profiles of prestige, such as a black doctor, will receive inconsistent treatment by majority group members. A black doctor in a large hospital may receive exactly the same respect and prestige for his or her occupational competence as a white doctor, but when the black doctor leaves the hospital setting he or she may experience discrimination when trying to move into an upper-class neighborhood or join a select social club. In some situations, then, a person is rewarded for his or her achieved position (such as doctor), while in others he or she is defined first according to ascribed status, such as race. The high-achieving minority person may face constantly shifting prestige as he or she moves from one situation to another.

CONCLUSIONS

The major task of this chapter has been to relate ethnicity to the rewards of power, privilege, and prestige. Two theoretical perspectives—caste and conquest-colonialism—were summarized to distinguish clearly the conquered racial minorities (blacks, Chicanos, Native Americans) from white immigrant groups.

Distinctions were made between individual and institutional discrimination. Positive and negative aspects of minority community life were discussed. White discrimination is amplified and extended in the minority community but the community also provides alternatives to white discrimination and a white-controlled marketplace.

The conquered minorities also have been characterized by low prestige or social honor in American society, not only because they have occupied low-prestige occupations, but also because entire ethnic minorities have been stigmatized as inferior. Middle-class blacks, Chicanos, and Indians escape some of these negative judgments, but they are likely to experience shifting prestige evaluations as they move through social situations that alternately reward their high-achieved rank and their low-ascribed rank.

A theme emphasized throughout this chapter is that ethnic subordination is far more than class subordination. Poverty, slavery, and early lack of access to industrial jobs are important facts in explaining racial oppression and colonialism in America. But in addition, the conquered minorities occupy a low position on a *separate* ethnic hierarchy because of a combination of these non-economic factors:

1. High visibility (especially blacks)
2. Conquered status and long-lasting paternalistic relationship with the white majority
3. Relatively powerless communities controlled and manipulated by white society
4. Highly crystallized racist ideologies of inferiority (especially blacks)
5. Pronounced cultural differences (especially Chicanos and Indians).

REFERENCES

Banton, Michael. 1960. "Social Distance: A New Appreciation." *The Sociological Review,* December, 1960.

Baratz, Stephen, S. & Joan C. Baratz. 1970. "Early Childhood Intervention: The Social Science Base of Institutional Racism." *Harvard Educational Review* 40 (Winter): 29–50.

Blau, Peter M. & Otis Dudley Duncan. 1967. *The American Occupational Structure.* New York: John Wiley & Sons.

Blauner, Robert T. 1972. "Colonized and Immigrant Minorities." In Robert T. Blauner (ed.), *Racial Oppression in America.* New York: Harper & Row.

Bogardus, Emory S. 1928. *Immigration and Race Attitudes.* Indianapolis: D.C. Heath.

Bonacich, Edna. 1972. "A Theory of Ethnic Antagonism: The Split Labor Market." *American Sociological Review* 37 (October): 547–559.

Bureau of the Census. 1975. *Current Population Reports,* Series P–23, No. 54.

_____. 1977. *Current Population Reports,* Series P–20, No. 310: 10–11.

_____. 1978. *Current Population Reports,* Series P-20, No. 38.

Cahn, Edgar S. 1969. *Our Brothers Keeper.* New York: World Publishing Co.

Caplovitz, David. 1963. *The Poor Pay More.* New York: The Free Press.

Clark, Kenneth. 1964. *Dark Ghetto.* New York: Harper & Row.

Davidson, Chandler & Charles M. Gaitz. 1973. "Ethnic Attitudes as a Basis for Minority Coopera-tion in a Southwestern Metropolis." *Social Science Quarterly* 53 (March): 738–748.

Davis, Allison, Burleigh R. Gardner & Mary R. Gardner. 1941. *Deep South.* Chicago: University of Chicago Press.

Deutsch, Martin. 1969. "Happenings on the Way Back to the Forum: Social Science, IQ, and Race Differences Revisited." *Harvard Educational Review* 39 (Summer): 523–557.

Diffie, W. Bailey & Justin Whitfield Diffie. 1931. *Porto Rico: A Broken Pledge.* New York: Vanguard Press.

Dollard, John. 1957. *Caste and Class in a Southern Town.* New York: Doubleday.

Elkins, Stanley M. 1959. *Slavery: A Problem in American Institutional and Intellectual Life.* Chicago: University of Chicago Press.

Fitzpatrick, Joseph W. 1968. "Puerto Ricans in Perspective: The Meaning of Migration to the Mainland." *International Migration Review* v.2 (Spring): 7–19.

Grebler, Leo, Joan Moore, & Ralph Guzman. 1970. *The Mexican American People.* New York: Free Press.

Hannerz, Ulf. 1969. *Soulside.* New York: Columbia University Press.

Hermalin, Albert I. & Reynolds Farley. 1973. "The Potential for Residental Integration in Cities and Suburbs: Implicatons for the Busing Controversy." *American Sociological Review* 38 (October): 595–610.

Horton, John, 1966. "Order and Conflict Theories of Social Problems as Competing Ideologies. " *American Journal of Sociology* 71 (May): 701–713.

Howard, John R. 1970. *Awakening Minorities.* Trans-Action Books. Chicago: Aldine Publishing Co.

Jensen, Arthur R. 1969. "How Much Can We Boost IQ and Scholastic Achievement?" *Harvard Educational Review* 39 (Winter): 1–123.

Kerner, Otto. 1968. *Report of the National Advisory Commission on Civil Disorders.* New York: Bantam.

Kramer, Judith R. 1970. *The American Minority Community.* Scranton: Thomas Y. Crowell.

Lauter, Paul & Florence Howe. 1972. "How the School System Is Rigged for Failure." In Robert Lejeune (ed.), *Class And Conflict in American Society.* Chicago: Rand McNally.

Lieberson, Stanley, 1970. "Stratification and Ethnic Groups." In Edward O. Lauman (ed.), *Social Stratification: Research and Theory for the 1970s.* Indianapolis: Bobbs-Merrill.

Light, Ivan. 1973. *Ethnic Enterprise.* Berkeley: University of California Press.

Lurie, Nancy. 1975. "The American Indian: Historical Background." In Norman R. Yetman & C. Hoy Steele (eds.), *Majority and Minority.* Boston: Allyn and Bacon.

Marden, Charles F. & Gladys Meyer. 1978. *Minorities in American Society.* New York: D. Van Nostrand Company.

Mercer, Jane R. 1972. "IQ: The Lethal Label." *Psychology Today* 6 (September): 44–47 and 95–97.

Mills, C. Wright. 1972. "The Higher Circles." In Paul Blumberg (ed.), *The Impact of Social Class.* New York: Thomas Y. Crowell.

Mittlebach, Frank G. & Joan W. Moore. 1968. "Ethnic Endogamy: The Case of Mexican Americans." *American Journal of Sociology* 74 (July): 50–62.

Moore, Joan W. 1970. "Colonialism: The Case of the Mexican Americans." *Social Problems* 17 (Spring): 463–472.

Morris, Richard T. & Vincent Jeffries. 1967. *The White Reaction Study.* Institute of Government and Public Affairs. University of California, Los Angeles.

Moynihan, Daniel P. 1972. "The Schism in Black America." *The Public Interest* 27 (Spring): 3–24.

Nelson, Elizabeth & Edward E. Nelson. 1972. "Passing in the Age Stratification System." Paper presented at the 67th Annual meeting of the American Sociological Association.

Noel, Donald. 1968. "A Theory of the Origins of Ethnic Stratification." *Social Problems* 16 (Fall): 157–172.

Olsen, Marvin E. 1970. "Power Perspectives on Stratification and Race Relations." In Marvin E. Olsen (ed.), *Power in Societies.* New York: Macmillan.

Padilla, Amado M. & Rene A. Ruiz. 1976. "Prejudice and Discrimination." In Carrol R. Hernandez, Marsha J. Haug, Nathaniel N. Wagner (eds.), *Chicanos: Social and Psychological Perspectives.* St. Louis: C.V. Mosby.

Penalosa, Fernando. 1971. "The Changing Mexican American in Southern California." In Norman R. Yetman and C. Hoy Steele (eds.), *Majority and Minority.* Boston: Allyn & Bacon.

Pettigrew, Thomas F. 1964. *A Profile of the Negro American.* New York: D. van Nostrand.

Pickney, Alphonso. 1975. *Black Americans.* Englewood Cliffs, N.J.: Prentice-Hall.

Ransford, H. Edward. 1977. *Race and Class in American Society: Black, Chicano, Anglo.* Cambridge, Mass.: Schenkman Publishing Co.

Reissman, Leonard. 1959. *Class in American Society.* Glenview, Ill.: Free Press.

Rose, Arnold M. 1961. "Race and Ethnic Relations." In Robert K. Merton & Robert A. Nisbet (eds.), *Contempory Social Problems.* New York: Harcourt Brace.

Rose, Peter I. 1973. Review Essay on White Ethnics in *Contemporary Sociology: A Journal of Reviews* (2): 14–17.

Rosenberg, Morris & Roberta G. Simmons. 1971. *Black and White Self Esteem: The Urban School Child.* Arnold M. & Caroline Rose Monograph Series, American Sociological Association.

Schafer, Walter E., Carol Olexa & Kenneth Polk. 1970. "Programmed for Social Class: Tracking in the High School." *Transaction* (October): 39–46, 63.

Schuman, Howard. 1975. "Free Will and Determinism in Public Beliefs About Race." In Norman R. Yetman & C. Hoy Steele (eds.), *Majority and Minority.* Boston: Allyn and Bacon.

Simmons, Ozzie G. 1961. "The Mutual Images and Expectations of Anglo-Americans and Mexican Americans." *Daedalus* 90 (2): 286–299.

Stinchcombe, Arthur L. 1969. "Environment: The Cumulation of Effects Is Yet to be Understood." *Harvard Educational Review* 39 (Summer): 511–522.

Sturdivant, Frederick D. & Walter T. Wilhelm. 1968. "Poverty Minorites and Consumer Exploitation." *Social Science Quarterly* 49 (December): 643–650.

Time. 1978. "It's Your Turn in the Sun," Vol. 112 (Oct, 16): 48–61.

van den Berghe, Pierre L. 1967. *Race and Racism.* New York: John Wiley & Sons.

Warren, Donald I. & Patrick Easto. 1972. "White Stratification Theory and Black Reality: A Neglected Problem of American Sociology.' Paper presented at the 67th annual meeting of the American Sociological Association.

Wirth, Louis. 1945. "The Problem of Minority Groups." In Ralph Linton (ed.), *The Science of Man in the World Crisis.* New York: Columbia University Press.

Woodward, C. Vann. 1957. *The Strange Career of Jim Crow.* New York: Oxford University Press.

Yetman, Norman R. & C. Hoy Steele (eds.). 1975. *Majority and Minority: The Dynamics of Racial and Ethnic Realtions.* Boston: Allyn and Bacon.

Ethnocentrism, competition, and differential power provide the necessary and sufficient bases for constructing a theory of the origin of ethnic stratification. The essence of the theory is that ethnic stratification will emerge when distinct ethnic groups are brought into sustained contact only if the groups are characterized by a high degree of ethnocentrism, competition, and differential power. Competition provides the motivation for stratification; ethnocentrism channels the competition along ethnic lines; and the power differential determines whether either group will be able to subordinate the other. The theory is initially tested via application to the emergence of slavery in seventeenth century America. The outcome encourages further testing of the theory.

A Theory of the Origin of Ethnic Stratification*

Donald L. Noel

WHILE A great deal has been written about the nature and consequences of ethnic stratification, there have been few theoretical or empirical contributions regarding the causes of ethnic stratification.[1] It is the purpose of this paper to state a theory of the origin of ethnic stratification and then test it by applying the theory to an analysis of the origin of slavery in the United States. A number of recent contributions have clarified our knowledge of early Negro-white stratification[2]

but there has been no attempt to analyze slavery's origin from the standpoint of a general theoretical framework. The present attempt focuses upon ethnocentrism, competition, and differential power as the key variables which together constitute the necessary and sufficient basis for the emergence and initial stabilization of ethnic stratification.

Ethnic stratification is, of course, only one type of stratification. Social stratification as a generic form of social organization is a structure of social inequality manifested via differences in prestige, power, and/or economic rewards. Ethnic stratification is a system of stratification wherein some relatively fixed group membership (e.g., race, religion, or nationality) is utilized as a major criterion for assigning social positions with their attendant differential rewards.

Prior to the emergence of ethnic stratification there must be a period of recurrent or continuous contact between the members of two or more distinct ethnic groups. This contact is an obvious requisite of ethnic stratification, but it is equally a requisite of equalitarian intergroup relations. Hence, intergroup contact is assumed as given and not treated as a theoretical element because in itself it does not provide a basis for predicting whether ethnic relations will be equalitarian or inequalitarian (i.e., stratified). Distinct

*The present paper attempts only to explain the *origin* of ethnic stratification. The author and Ernest Barth have essayed a more general statement which answers a number of sociological questions in addition to that of origin in their article on "Conceptual Frameworks for the Analysis of Race Relations: An Evaluation," *Social Forces,* 50 (March, 1972), pp. 333-348. Donald Noel is Professor and former chairperson, department of Sociology, University of Wisconsin–Milwaukee. From "A Theory of the Origins of Ethnic Stratification," *Social Problems,* 16:2 (Fall, 1968), 157-172. Reprinted by permission of The Society For The Study of Social Problems and the author.

1. The same observation regarding social stratification in general has recently been made by Gerhard Lenski, *Power and Privilege,* New York: McGraw-Hill, 1966, p. ix.

2. See Joseph Boskin, "Race Relations in Seventeenth Century America: The Problem of the Origins of Negro Slavery," *Sociology and Social Research,* 49 (July, 1965), pp. 446-455, including references cited therein; and David B. Davis, *The Problem of Slavery in Western Culture,* Ithaca: Cornell U., 1966.

ethnic groups can interact and form a stable pattern of relations without super-subordination.[3] Factors such as the nature of the groups prior to contact, the agents of contact, and the objectives of the contacting parties affect the likelihood of an equalitarian or inequalitarian outcome but only as they are expressed through the necessary and sufficient variables.[4]

THE THEORY AND ITS ELEMENTS

In contrast to intergroup contact *per se,* the presence of ethnocentrism, competition, and differential power provides a firm basis for predicting the emergence of ethnic stratification. Conversely, the absence of any one or more of these three elements means that ethnic stratification will not emerge. This is the essence of our theory. Each of the three elements is a variable but for present purposes they will be treated as attributes because our knowledge is not sufficiently precise to allow us to say what degrees of ethnocentrism, competition, and differential power are necessary to generate ethnic stratification. Recognition of the crucial importance of the three may stimulate greater efforts to precisely measure each of them. We shall examine each in turn.

Ethnocentrism is a universal characteristic of autonomous societies or ethnic groups. As introduced by Sumner the concept refers to that ". . . view of things in which one's own group is the center of everything, and all others are scaled and rated with reference to it."[5] From this perspective the values of the in-group are equated with abstract, universal standards of morality and the practices of the in-group are exalted as better or more "natural" than those of any out-group. Such an orientation is essentially a matter of in-group glorification and not of hostility toward any specific out-group. Nevertheless, an inevitable consequence of ethnocentrism is the rejection or downgrading of all out-groups to a greater or lesser degree as a function of the extent to which they differ from the in-group. The greater the difference the lower will be the relative rank of any given out-group, but any difference at all is grounds for negative evaluation.[6] Hence, English and Canadian immigrants rank very high relative to other out-groups in American society *but* they still rank below old American WASPs.[7]

Ethnocentrism is expressed in a variety of ways including mythology, condescension, and a double standard of morality in social relations. Becker has labeled this double standard a "dual ethic" in which in-group standards apply only to transactions with members of the in-group.[8] The outsider is viewed as fair game. Hence, intergroup economic relations are characterized by exploitation. Similarly, sexual relations between members of different groups are commonplace even when intermarriage is rare or prohibited entirely. The practice of endogamy is itself a manifestation of and, simultaneously, a means of reinforcing

3. A classic example is provided by Ethel John Lindgren, "An Example of Culture Contact Without Conflict: Reindeer Tungus and Cossacks of Northwest Manchuria," *American Anthropologist,* 40 (October–December, 1938), pp. 605–621.

4. The relevance of precontact and of the nature and objectives of the contacting agents for the course of intergroup relations has been discussed by various scholars including Edward B. Reuter in his editor's "Introduction" to *Race and Culture Contacts,* New York: McGraw-Hill, 1934, pp. 1–18; and Clarence E. Glick, "Social Roles and Types in Race Relations," in Andrew W. Lind, editor, *Race Relations in World Perspective,* Honolulu: U. of Hawaii, 1955, pp. 239–262.

5. William G. Sumner, *Folkways,* Boston: Ginn, 1940, p. 13. The essence of ethnocentrism is well conveyed by Catton's observation that "Ethnocentrism makes us see out-group behavior as deviation from in-group mores rather than as adherence to out-group mores." William R. Catton, Jr., "The Development of Sociological Thought" in Robert E. L. Faris, editor, *Handbook of Modern Sociology,* Chicago: Rand McNally, 1964, p. 930.

6. Williams observes that "in various *particular* ways an out-group may be seen as superior" insofar as its members excel in performance vis-a-vis certain norms that the two groups hold in common (e.g., sobriety or craftsmanship in the production of a particular commodity). Robin M. Williams, Jr., *Strangers Next Door,* Englewood Cliffs, N.J.: Prentice-Hall, 1964, p. 22 (emphasis added). A similar point is made by Marc J. Swartz, "Negative Ethnocentrism," *Journal of Conflict Resolution,* 5 (March, 1961), pp. 75–81. It is highly unlikely, however, that the out-group will be so consistently objectively superior in the realm of shared values as to be seen as generally superior to the in-group unless the in-group is subordinate to or highly dependent upon the out-group.

7. Emory S. Bogardus, *Social Distance,* Yellow Springs: Antioch, 1959.

8. Howard P. Becker, *Man in Reciprocity,* New York: Praeger, 1956, Ch. 15.

ethnocentrism. Endogamy is, indeed, an indication that ethnocentrism is present in sufficient degree for ethnic stratification to emerge.[9]

Insofar as distinct ethnic groups maintain their autonomy, mutual ethnocentrism will be preserved. Thus Indians in the Americas did not automatically surrender their ethnocentrism in the face of European technological and scientific superiority. Indeed, if the cultural strengths (including technology) of the out-group are not relevant to the values and goals of the in-group they will, by the very nature of ethnocentrism, be negatively defined. This is well illustrated in the reply (allegedly) addressed to the Virginia Commission in 1744 when it offered to educate six Indian youths at William and Mary:

> Several of our young people were formerly brought up at Colleges of the Northern Provinces; they were instructed in all your sciences; but when they came back to us, they were bad runners, ignorant of every means of living in the woods, unable to bear either cold or hunger, knew neither how to build a cabin, take a deer, or kill an enemy, spoke our language imperfectly, were therefore neither fit for hunters, warriors, or counsellors; they were totally good for nothing. We are, however, not the less obliged by your kind offer, though we decline accepting it; and to show our grateful Sense of it, if the Gentlemen of Virginia will send us a Dozen of their Sons we will take great care of their education, instruct them in all we know, and make Men of them.[10]

Ethnocentrism in itself need not lead to either interethnic conflict or ethnic stratification,

however. The Tungus and Cossacks have lived in peace as politically independent but economically interdependent societies for several centuries. The groups remain racially and culturally dissimilar and each is characterized by a general ethnocentric preference for the in-group. This conflict potential is neutralized by mutual respect and admission by each that the other is superior in certain specific respects, by the existence of some shared values and interests, and by the absence of competition due to economic complementarity and low population density.[11]

The presence of competition, structured along ethnic lines, is an additional prerequisite for the emergence of ethnic stratification. Antonovsky has suggested that a discriminatory system of social relations requires both shared goals and scarcity of rewards,[12] and competition here refers to the interaction between two or more social units striving to achieve *the same scarce goal* (e.g., land or prestige). In the absence of shared goals members of the various ethnic groups involved in the contact situation would have, in the extreme case, mutually exclusive or nonoverlapping value hierarchies. If one group is not striving for a given goal, this reduces the likelihood of discrimination partly because members of that group are unlikely to be perceived as competitors for the goal. In addition, the indifference of one group toward the goal in effect reduces scarcity—i.e., fewer seekers enhance the probability of goal attainment by any one seeker. However, if the goal is still defined as scarce by members of one group they may seek to establish ethnic stratification in order to effectively exploit the labor of the indifferent group and thereby maximize goal attainment. In such a situation the labor (or other utility) of the indifferent group may be said to be the real object of competition. In any event the perceived scarcity of a socially valued goal is crucial and will stimulate the emergence of ethnic stratification *unless* each group perceives the other as: 1) disinterested in the relevant goal, *and* 2) nonutilitarian with respect to its own attainment of the goal.

9. Endogamy is an overly stringent index of the degree of ethnocentrism essential to ethnic stratification and is not itself a prerequisite of the emergence of ethnic stratification. However, where endogamy does not precede ethnic stratification, it is a seemingly invariable consequence. Compare this position with that of Charles Wagley and Marvin Harris who treat ethnocentrism and endogamy as independent structural requisites of intergroup hostility and conflict. See *Minorities in the New World,* New York: Columbia, 1958, pp. 256–263.

10. Quoted in T. Walter Wallbank and Alastair M. Taylor, *Civilization: Past and Present,* Chicago: Scott, Foresman, 1949, rev. ed., Vol. 1, pp. 559–560. The offer and counter-offer also provide an excellent illustration of mutual ethnocentrism.

11. Lindgren, *op. cit.*

12. Aaron Antonovsky, ''The Social Meaning of Discrimination,'' *Phylon,* 21 (Spring, 1960), pp. 81–95.

In actuality the various goals of two groups involved in stable, complex interaction will invariably overlap to some degree and hence the likelihood of ethnic stratification is a function of the arena of competition. The arena includes the shared object(s) sought, the terms of the competition, and the relative adaptability of the groups involved.[13] Regarding the objects (or goals) of competition the greater the number of objects subject to competition, the more intense the competition. Moreover, as Wagley and Harris observe, "It is important to know the objects of competition, for it would seem that the more vital or valuable the resource over which there is competition, the more intense is the conflict between the groups."[14] Barring total annihilation of one of the groups, these points can be extended to state that the more intense the competition or conflict the greater the likelihood—other things being equal—that it will culminate in a system of ethnic stratification. In other words, the number and significance of the scarce, common goals sought determine the degree of competition which in turn significantly affects the probability that ethnic stratification will emerge.

The terms of the competition may greatly alter the probability of ethnic stratification, however, regardless of the intensity of the competition. The retention of a set of values or rules which effectively regulates—or moderates—ethnic interrelations is of particularly crucial significance. If a framework of regulative values fails to emerge, or breaks down, each group may seek to deny the other(s) the right to compete with the result that overt conflict emerges and culminates in annihilation, expulsion, or total subjugation of the less powerful group. If, in contrast, regulative values develop and are retained, competition

even for vital goals need not result in ethnic stratification—or at least the span of stratification may be considerably constricted.[15]

Even where the groups involved are quite dissimilar culturally, the sharing of certain crucial values (e.g., religion or freedom, individualism, and equality) may be significant in preventing ethnic stratification. This appears to have been one factor in the enduring harmonious relations between the Cossacks and the Tungus. The influence of the regulative values upon the span of ethnic stratification is well illustrated by Tannenbaum's thesis regarding the differences between North American and Latin American slavery.[16] In the absence of a tradition of slavery the English had no established code prescribing the rights and duties of slaves and the racist ideology which evolved achieved its ultimate expression in the Dred Scott decision of 1857. This decision was highly consistent with the then widely held belief that the Negro "had no rights which the white man was bound to respect. . . ." By contrast the Iberian code accorded certain rights to the Latin American slave (including the right to own property and to purchase his freedom) which greatly restricted the extent of inequality between free man and slave.[17]

In addition to the regulative values, the structural opportunities for or barriers to upward mobility which are present in the society may affect the emergence and span of ethnic stratification. Social structural barriers such as a static, nonexpanding economy are a significant part of the terms of competition and they may be more

13. This analysis of the arena of competition is a modification of the analysis by Wagley and Harris, *op. cit.*, esp. pp. 263–264. These authors limit the concept "arena" to the objects sought *and* the regulative values which determine opportunity to compete and then partly confound their components by including the regulative values, along with adaptive capacity and the instruments necessary to compete, as part of the "terms" of competition.

14. *Ibid.*, p. 263. They suggest that competition for scarce subsistence goals will produce more intense conflict than competition for prestige symbols or other culturally defined goals.

15. Discussing the ideological aspect of intergroup relations, Wagley and Harris note that equalitarian creeds have generally not been effective in *preventing* ethnic stratification. *Ibid.*, pp. 280 ff. The operation of ethnocentrism makes it very easy for the boundaries of the in-group to become the boundaries of adherence to group values.

16. Frank Tannenbaum, *Slave and Citizen: The Negro in the Americas*, New York: Random House, 1963.

17. *Ibid.*, esp. pp. 49 ff. Marvin Harris has criticized Tannenbaum's thesis arguing that the rights prescribed by the Iberian code were largely illusory and that there is no certainty that *slaves* were treated better in Latin America. Harris in turn provides a functional (economic necessity) explanation for the historical difference in treatment of *free* Negroes in the two continents. See Marvin Harris, *Patterns of Race in the Americas*, New York: Walker, 1964, esp. Chs. 6 and 7.

decisive than the regulative values as regards the duration of the system. Finally, along with the goals and the terms of competition, the relative adaptive capacity of the groups involved is an aspect of competition which significantly affects the emergence of ethnic stratification.

Wagley and Harris assume that ethnic stratification is given and focus their analysis on the adaptive capacity of *the minority group* in terms of its effect upon the span and the duration of ethnic stratification. Thus they view adaptive capacity as:

> those elements of a minority's cultural heritage which provide it with a basis for competing more or less effectively with the dominant group, which afford protection against exploitation, which stimulate or retard its adaptation to the total social environment, and which facilitate or hinder its upward advance through the socio-economic hierarchy.[18]

We shall apply the concept to an earlier point in the intergroup process—i.e., prior to the emergence of ethnic stratification—by broadening it to refer to those aspects of any ethnic group's sociocultural heritage which affect its adjustment to a given social and physical environment. The group with the greater adaptive capacity is apt to emerge as the dominant group[19] while the other groups are subordinated to a greater or lesser degree —i.e., the span of the stratification system will be great or slight—dependent upon the extent of their adaptive capacity relative to that of the emergent dominant group.

The duration, as well as the origin and span, of ethnic stratification will be markedly influenced by adaptive capacity. Once a people have become a minority, flexibility on their part is essential if they are to efficiently adjust and effectively compete within the established system of ethnic stratification and thereby facilitate achievement of equality. Sociocultural patterns are invariably altered by changing life conditions. However, groups vary in the alacrity with which

they respond to changing conditions. A flexible minority group may facilitate the achievement of equality or even dominance by readily accepting modifications of their heritage which will promote efficient adaptation to their subordination *and* to subsequent changes in life conditions.

Competition and ethnocentrism do not provide a sufficient explanation for the emergence of ethnic stratification. Highly ethnocentric groups involved in competition for vital objects will not generate ethnic stratification *unless* they are of such unequal power that one is able to impose its will upon the other.[20] Inequality of power is the defining characteristic of dominant and minority groups, and Lenski maintains that differential power is the foundation element in the genesis of any stratification system.[21] In any event differential power is absolutely essential to the emergence of ethnic stratification and the greater the differential the greater the span and durability of the system, other things being equal.

Technically, power is a component of adaptive capacity as Wagley and Harris imply in their definition by referring to "protection against exploitation." Nevertheless, differential power exerts an effect independent of adaptive capacity in general and is of such crucial relevance for ethnic stratification as to warrant its being singled out as a third major causal variable. The necessity of treating it as a distinct variable is amply demonstrated by consideration of those historical cases where one group has the greater adaptive capacity in general but is subordinated because another group has greater (military) power. The Dravidians overrun by the Aryans in ancient India and the Manchu conquest of China are illustrative cases.[22]

Unless the ethnic groups involved are unequal in power, intergroup relations will be

---

18.   Wagley and Harris, *op. cit.,* p. 264.

19.   This point is explicitly made by Tamotsu Shibutani and Kian M. Kwan, *Ethnic Stratification: A Comparative Approach,* New York: Macmillan, 1965, p. 147; see also Ch. 9.

20.   This point is made by Antonovsky, *op. cit.,* esp. p. 82, and implied by Wagley and Harris in their discussion of the role of the state in the formation of minority groups, *op. cit.,* esp. pp. 240–244. Stanley Lieberson's recent modification of Park's cycle theory of race relations also emphasizes the importance of differential power as a determinant of the outcome of intergroup contacts. See "A Societal Theory of Race and Ethnic Relations," *American Sociological Review,* 26 (December, 1961), pp. 902–910.

21.   Lenski, *op. cit.,* esp. Ch. 3.

22.   See Wallbank and Taylor, *op. cit.,* p. 95; and Shibutani and Kwan, *op. cit.,* pp. 129–130.

characterized by conflict, symbiosis, or a pluralist equilibrium. Given intergroup competition, however, symbiosis is unlikely and conflict and pluralism are inevitably unstable. Any slight change in the existing balance of power may be sufficient to establish the temporary dominance of one group and this can be utilized to allow the emerging dominant group to perpetuate and enhance its position.[23] Once dominance is established the group in power takes all necessary steps to restrict the now subordinated groups, thereby hampering their effectiveness as competitors,[24] and to institutionalize the emerging distribution of rewards and opportunities. Hence, since power tends to beget power, a slight initial alteration in the distribution of power can become the basis of a stable inequalitarian system.

We have now elaborated the central concepts and propositions of a theory of the emergence and initial stabilization of ethnic stratification. The theory can be summarized as follows. When distinct ethnic groups are brought into sustained contact (via migration, the emergence and expansion of the state, or internal differentiation of a previously homogeneous group), ethnic stratification will invariably follow if—and only if—the groups are characterized by a significant degree of ethnocentrism, competition, *and* differential power. Without ethnocentrism the groups would quickly merge and competition would not be structured along ethnic lines. Without competition there would be no motivation or rationale for instituting stratification along ethnic lines. Without differential power it would simply be impossible for one group to achieve dominance and impose subordination to its will and ideals upon the other(s).

The necessity of differential power is incontestable but it could be argued that either competition or ethnocentrism is dispensable. For

example, perhaps extreme ethnocentrism independent of competition is sufficient motive for seeking to impose ethnic stratification. Certainly ethnocentrism could encourage efforts to promote continued sharp differentiation, but it would not by itself motivate stratification unless we assume the existence of a *need* for dominance or aggression. Conversely, given sociocultural differences, one group may be better prepared for and therefore able to more effectively exploit a given environment. Hence, this group would become economically dominant and might then perceive and pursue the advantages (especially economic) of ethnic stratification quite independent of ethnocentrism. On the other hand, while differential power and competition alone are clearly sufficient to generate stratification, a low degree of ethnocentrism could readily forestall *ethnic* stratification by permitting assimilation and thereby eliminating differential adaptive capacity. Ethnocentrism undeniably heightens awareness of ethnicity and thereby promotes the formation and retention of ethnic competition, but the crucial question is whether or not some specified degree of ethnocentrism is *essential* to the emergence of ethnic stratification. Since autonomous ethnic groups are invariably ethnocentric, the answer awaits more precise measures of ethnocentrism which will allow us to test hypotheses specifying the necessary degree of ethnocentrism.[25]

Given the present state of knowledge it seems advisable to retain both competition and ethnocentrism, as well as differential power, as integral elements of the theory. Our next objective, then, is to provide an initial test of the theory by applying it to an analysis of the genesis of slavery in the seventeenth century mainland North American colonies.

THE ORIGIN OF
AMERICAN SLAVERY

There is a growing consensus among historians of slavery in the United States that Negroes were not initially slaves but that they were gradually

23. See *ibid.*, esp. Chs. 6, 9, and 12; and Richard A. Schermerhorn, *Society and Power*, New York: Random House, 1961, pp. 18–26.

24. Shibutani and Kwan observe that dominance rests upon victory in the competitive process and that competition between groups is eliminated or greatly reduced once a system of ethnic stratification is stabilized, *op. cit.*, pp. 146 and 235, and Ch. 12. The extent to which competition is actually stifled is highly variable, however, as Wagley and Harris note in their discussion of minority adaptive capacity and the terms of competition, *op. cit.*, pp. 263 ff.

25. The issue is further complicated by the fact that the necessary degree of any one of the three elements may vary as a function of the other two.

reduced to a position of chattel slavery over several decades.[26] The historical record regarding their initial status is so vague and incomplete, however, that it is impossible to assert with finality that their status was initially no different from that of non-Negro indentured servants.[27] Moreover, while there is agreement that the statutory establishment of slavery was not widespread until the 1660's, there is disagreement regarding slavery's emergence in actual practice. The Handlins maintain that "The status of Negroes was that of servants; and so they were identified and treated down to the 1660's."[28] Degler and Jordan argue that this conclusion is not adequately documented and cite evidence indicating that some Negroes were slaves as early as 1640.[29]

Our central concern is to relate existing historical research to the theory elaborated above, *not* to attempt original historical research intended to resolve the controversy regarding the nature and extent of the initial status differences (if any) between white and Negro bondsmen. However, two findings emerging from the controversy are basic to our concern: 1) although the terms servant and slave were frequently used interchangeably, whites were never slaves in the sense of serving for life and conveying a like obligation to their offspring; and 2) many Negroes were not slaves in this sense at least as late as the

1660's. Concomitantly with the Negroes' descent to slavery, white servants gained increasingly liberal terms of indenture and, ultimately, freedom. The origin of slavery for the one group and the growth of freedom for the other are explicable in terms of our theory as a function of differences in ethnocentrism, the arena of competition, and power vis-a-vis the dominant group or class.[30]

Degler argues that the status of the Negro evolved in a framework of discrimination and, therefore, "The important point is not the evolution of the legal status of the slave, but the fact that discriminatory legislation regarding the Negro long preceded any legal definition of slavery."[31] The first question then becomes one of explaining this differential treatment which foreshadowed the descent to slavery. A major element in the answer is implied by the Handlins' observation that "The rudeness of the Negroes' manners, the strangeness of their languages, the difficulty of communicating to them English notions of morality and proper behavior occasioned sporadic laws to regulate their conduct."[32] By itself this implies a contradiction of their basic thesis that Negro and white indentured servants were treated similarly prior to 1660. They maintain, however, that there was nothing unique nor decisive in this differential treatment of Negroes, for such was also accorded various Caucasian outgroups in this period.[33] While Jordan dismisses the Handlins' evidence as largely irrelevant to the point and Degler feels that it is insufficient, Degler acknowledges that "Even Irishmen, who were white, Christian, and European, were held to be literally 'beyond the Pale,' and some were

26.   The main relevant references in the recent literature include Carl N. Degler, *Out of Our Past*, New York: Harper and Row, 1959 and "Slavery and the Genesis of American Race Prejudice," *Comparative Studies in Society and History*, 2 (October, 1959), pp. 49–66; Stanley M. Elkins, *Slavery: A Problem in American Institutional and Intellectual Life*, Chicago: U. of Chicago, 1959; Oscar and Mary F. Handlin, "Origins of the Southern Labor System," *William and Mary Quarterly*, 3rd Series, 7 (April, 1950) pp. 199–222; and Winthrop D. Jordan, "Modern Tensions and the Origins of American Slavery," *The Journal of Southern History*, 28 (February, 1962), pp. 18–30, and *White over Black*, Chapel-Hill: U. of North Carolina, 1968. See also Boskin, *op. cit.*, and "Comment" and "Reply" by the Handlins and Degler in the cited volume of *Comparative Studies. . .*, pp. 488–495.

27.   Jordan, *The Journal. . .*, p. 22.

28.   Handlin and Handlin, *op. cit.*, p. 203.

29.   Degler, *Comparative Studies. . .*, pp. 52–56 and Jordan, *The Journal. . .*, pp. 23–27 and *White over Black*, pp. 73–74. Also see Elkins, *op. cit.*, pp. 38–42 (esp. fns. 16 and 19).

30.   Our primary concern is with the emergence of Negro slavery but the theory also explains how white bondsmen avoided slavery. Their position vis-à-vis the dominant English was characterized by a different "value" of at least two of the key variables.

31.   Degler, *Out of Our Past*, p. 35. Bear in mind, however, that slavery was not initially institutionalized in law or in the mores.

32.   Handlin and Handlin, *op. cit.*, pp. 208–209.

33.   *Ibid.* They note that "It is not necessary to resort to racialist assumptions to account for such measures; . . . [for immigrants in a strange environment] longed . . . for the company of familiar men and singled out to be welcomed those who were most like themselves." See pp. 207–211 and 214.

even referred to as 'slaves'."[34] Nevertheless, Degler contends that the overall evidence justifies his conclusion that Negroes were generally accorded a lower position than any white, bound or free.

That the English made status distinctions between various out-groups is precisely what one would expect, however, given the nature of ethnocentrism. The degree of ethnocentric rejection is primarily a function of the degree of difference, and Negroes were markedly different from the dominant English in color, nationality, language, religion, and other aspects of culture.[35] The differential treatment of Negroes was by no means entirely due to a specifically anti-Negro *color* prejudice. Indeed, color was not initially the most important factor in determining the relative status of Negroes; rather, the fact that they were non-Christian was of major significance.[36] Although beginning to lose its preeminence, religion was still the central institution of society in the seventeenth century and religious prejudice toward non-Christians or heathens was widespread. The priority of religious over color prejudice is amply demonstrated by analysis of the early laws and court decisions pertaining to Negro-white sexual relations. These sources explicitly reveal greater concern with Christian-non-Christian than with white-Negro unions.[37] During and after the 1660's laws regulating racial intermarriage arose but for some time their emphasis was generally, if not inevitably, upon religion, nationality, or some basis of differentiation other than race *per se*. For example, a Maryland law of 1681 described marriages of white women with Negroes as lascivious and "to

the disgrace not only of the English but also [sic] of many *other Christian* Nations."[38] Moreover, the laws against Negro-white marriage seem to have been rooted much more in economic considerations than they were in any concern for white racial purity.[39] In short, it was not a simple color prejudice but a marked degree of ethnocentricism, rooted in a multitude of salient differences, which combined with competition and differential power to reduce Negroes to the status of slaves.[40]

Degler has noted that Negroes initially lacked a status in North America and thus almost any kind of status could have been worked out.[41] Given a different competitive arena, a more favorable status blurring the sharp ethnic distinctions could have evolved. However, as the demand for labor in an expanding economy began to exceed the supply, interest in lengthening the term of indenture arose.[42] This narrow economic explanation of the origin of slavery has been challenged on the grounds that slavery

34. Jordan, *The Journal...*, esp. pp. 27 (fn. 29) and 29 (fn. 34); and Delger, *Out of Our Past*, p. 30.

35. Only the aboriginal Indians were different from the English colonists to a comparable degree and they were likewise severely dealt with via a policy of exclusion and annihilation after attempts at enslavement failed. See Boskin, *op. cit.*, p. 453; and Jordan, *White over Black*, pp. 85–92.

36. The priority of religious over racial prejudice and discrimination in the early seventeenth century is noted in *ibid.*, pp. 97–98 and by Edgar J. McManus, *A History of Negro Slavery in New York,* Syracuse: Syracuse U., 1966, esp. pp. 11–12.

37. Jordan, *The Journal...*, p. 28 and *White Over Black*, pp. 78–80.

38. Quoted in *ibid.*, pp. 79–80 (emphasis added). Also see pp. 93–97, however, where Jordan stresses the necessity of carefully interpreting the label "Christian."

39. See Handlin and Handlin, *op. cit.*, pp. 213–216; and W. D. Zabel, "Interracial Marriage and the Law," *The Atlantic* (October, 1965), pp. 75–79.

40. The distinction between ethnocentrism (the rejection of out-groups *in general* as a function of in-group glorification) and prejudice (hostility toward the members of a *specific* group because they are members of that group) is crucial to the controversy regarding the direction of causality between discrimination, slavery, and prejudice. Undoubtedly these variables are mutually causal to some extent but Harris, *op. cit.*, esp. pp. 67–70, presents evidence that prejudice is primarily a consequence and is of minor importance as a cause of slavery.

41. Degler, *Comparative Studies...*, p. 51. See also Boskin, *op. cit.*, pp. 449 and 454 (esp. fn. 14); Elkins, *op. cit.*, pp. 39–42 (esp. fn. 16); and Kenneth M. Stampp, *The Peculiar Institution,* New York: Knopf, 1956, p. 21. The original indeterminacy of the Negroes' status is reminiscent of Blumer's "sense of group position" theory of prejudice and, in light of Blumer's theory, is consistent with the belief that there was no widespread prejudice toward Negroes prior to the institutionalization of slavery. See Herbert Blumer, "Race Prejudice as a Sense of Group Position," *Pacific Sociological Review*, 1 (Spring, 1958), pp. 3–7.

42. Handlin and Handlin, *op. cit.*, p. 210. Differential power made this tactic as suitable to the situation of Negro bondsmen as it was unsuitable in regard to white bondsmen.

appeared equally early in the Northern colonies although there were too few Negroes there to be of economic significance.[43] This seemingly decisive point is largely mitigated by two considerations.

First, in the other colonies it was precisely *the few* who did own slaves who were not only motivated by vested interests but were also the men of means and local power most able to secure a firm legal basis for slavery.[44] The distribution of power and motivation was undoubtedly similar and led to the same consequences in New England. For the individual retainer of Negro servants the factual and legal redefinition of Negroes as chattel constitutes a vital economic interest whether or not the number of slaves is sufficient to vitally affect the economy of the colony. Our knowledge of the role of the elite in the establishment of community mores suggests that this constitutes at least a partial explanation of the Northern laws.[45] In addition, the markedly smaller number of Negroes in the North might account for the fact that "although enactments in the Northern colonies recognized the legality of lifetime servitude, no effort was made to require all Negroes to be placed in that condition."[46] We surmise that the laws were passed at the behest of a few powerful individuals who had relatively many Negro servants and were indifferent to the status of Negroes in general so long as their own vested interests were protected.

The explanation of the more all-encompassing laws of the Southern colonies is rooted in the greater homogeneity of interests of the Southern elite. In contrast to the Northern situation, the men of power in the Southern colonies were predominantly planters who were unified in their need for large numbers of slaves. The margin of profit in agricultural production for the commercial market was such that the small landholder could not compete and the costs of training and the limitations on control (by the planter) which were associated with indentured labor made profitable exploitation of such labor increasingly difficult.[47] Hence, it was not the need for labor *per se* which was critical for the establishment of the comprehensive Southern slave system but rather the requirements of the emerging economic system for a particular kind of labor. In short, the Southern power elite uniformly needed slave labor while only certain men of power shared this need in the North and hence the latter advocated slave laws but lacked the power (or did not feel the need) to secure the all-encompassing laws characteristic of the Southern colonies.

There is a second major consideration in explaining the existence of Northern slavery. Men do not compete only for economic ends. They also compete for prestige and many lesser objects, and there is ample basis for suggesting that prestige competition was a significant factor in the institutionalization of slavery, North and South. Degler calls attention to the prestige motive when he discusses the efforts to establish a feudal aristocracy in seventeenth century New York, Maryland, and the Carolinas. He concludes that these efforts failed because the manor was "dependent upon the scarcity of land."[48] The failure of feudal aristocracy in no way denies the fundamental human desire for success or prestige. Indeed, this failure opened the society. It emphasized success and mobility for "it meant that wealth, rather than family or tradition, would be the primary determinant of social stratification."[49] Although the

---

43.   Degler acknowledges that the importance of perpetuating a labor force indispensable to the economy later became a crucial support of slavery but he denies that the need for labor explains the origin of slavery. His explanation stresses prior discrimination which, in the terms of the present theory, was rooted in ethnocentrism and differential power. See *Comparative Studies. . . ,* including the "Reply" to the Handlins' "Comment;" and *Out of Our Past,* pp. 35–38 and 162–168.

44.   Elkins, *op. cit.,* pp. 45 (esp. fn. 26) and 48.

45.   Historical precedent is provided by the finding that "The vagrancy laws emerged in order to provide the powerful landowners with a ready supply of cheap labor." See William J. Chambliss, "A Sociological Analysis of the Law of Vagrancy," *Social Problems,* 12 (Summer, 1964), pp. 67–77. Jordan, *White over Black,* pp. 67 and 69, provides evidence that the economic advantages of slavery were clearly perceived in the Northern colonies.

46.   Elkins, *op. cit.,* p. 41 (fn. 19).

47.   By the 1680's "The point had clearly passed when white servants could realistically, on any long-term apraisal, be considered preferable to Negro slaves." *Ibid.,* p. 48.

48.   Degler, *Out of Our Past,* p. 3. Also see Hubert M. Blalock, Jr., *Toward a Theory of Minority Group Relations,* New York: Wiley, 1967, pp. 44–48.

49.   Degler, *Out of Our Past,* p. 5; see also pp. 45–50. Elkins, *op. cit.,* esp. pp. 43–44, also notes the early emphasis on personal success and mobility.

stress was on economic success, there were other gains associated with slavery to console those who did not achieve wealth. The desire for social prestige derivable from "membership in a superior caste" undoubtedly provided motivation and support for slavery among both Northern and Southern white, slaveholders and nonslaveholders.[50]

The prestige advantage of slavery would have been partially undercut, especially for nonslaveholders, by enslavement of white bondsmen, but it is doubtful that this was a significant factor in their successfully eluding hereditary bondage. Rather the differential treatment of white and Negro bondsmen, ultimately indisputable and probably present from the very beginning, is largely attributable to differences in ethnocentrism and relative power. There was little or no ethnocentric rejection of the majority of white bondsmen during the seventeenth century because most of them were English.[51] Moreover, even the detested Irish and other non-English white servants were culturally and physically much more similar to the English planters than were the Africans. Hence, the planters clearly preferred white bondsmen until the advantages of slavery became increasingly apparent in the latter half of the seventeenth century.[52]

The increasing demand for labor after the mid-seventeenth century had divergent consequences for whites and blacks. The colonists became increasingly concerned to encourage immigration by counteracting " the widespread reports in England and Scotland that servants were harshly treated and bound in perpetual slavery" and by enacting "legislation designed to improve servants' conditions and to enlarge the

prospect of a meaningful release, a release that was not the start of a new period of servitude, but of life as a freeman and landowner."[53] These improvements curtailed the exploitation of white servants without directly affecting the status of the Africans.

> Farthest removed from the English, least desired, [the Negro] communicated with no friends who might be deterred from following. *Since his coming was involuntary, nothing that happened to him would increase or decrease his numbers.* To raise the status of Europeans by shortening their terms would ultimately increase the available hands by inducing their compatriots to emigrate; to reduce the Negro's term would produce an immediate loss and no ultimate gain. By mid century the servitude of Negroes seems generally lengthier than that of whites; and thereafter, the consciousness dawns that the blacks will toil for the whole of their lives . . . [54]

The planters and emerging agrarian capitalism were unconstrained in a planter-dominated society with no traditional institutions to exert limits. In this context even the common law tradition helped promote slavery.[55]

Ethnocentrism set the Negroes apart but their almost total lack of power and effective spokesmen, in contrast to white indentured servants, was decisive in their enslavement. Harris speaks directly to the issue and underscores the significance of (organized) power for the emergence of slavery.

> The facts of life in the New World were such . . . that Negroes, being the most defenseless of all the immigrant groups, were discriminated against and exploited more than any others. . . . Judging from the very nasty treatment suffered by white indentured servants, it was obviously not sentiment which prevented the Virginia planters from enslaving their fellow Englishmen. They undoubtedly would have

50. Stampp, *op. cit.*, pp. 29–33, esp. 32–33. Also see J. D. B. DeBow, "The Interest in Slavery of the Southern Non-Slaveholder," reprinted in Eric L. McKitrick, editor, *Slavery Defended: The Views of the Old South*, Englewood Cliffs, N.J.: Prentice-Hall, 1963, pp. 169–177.

51. Stampp, *op. cit.*, p. 16; and Degler, *Out of Our Past*, pp. 50–51. Consistent with the nature of ethnocentrism, "The Irish and other aliens, less desirable, at first received longer terms. But the realization that such discrimination retarded 'the peopling of the country' led to an extension of the identical privilege to all Christians." Handlin and Handlin, *op. cit.*, pp. 210–211.

52. Elkins, *op. cit.*, pp. 40 and 48; and Handlin and Handlin, *op. cit.*, pp. 207–208.

53. *Ibid.*, p. 210.

54. *Ibid.*, p. 211 (emphasis added). That the need for labor led to improvements in the status of white servants seems very likely but Degler in *Comparative Studies . . .* effectively challenges some of the variety of evidence presented by the Handlins, *op. cit.*, pp. 210 and 213–214 and "Comment."

55. Elkins, *op. cit.*, pp. 38 (fn. 14), 42 (fn. 22), 43 and 49–52; and Jordan, *White over Black*, pp. 49–51.

done so had they been able to get away with it. But such a policy was out of the question as long as there was a King and a Parliament in England.[56]

The Negroes, in short, did not have any organized external government capable of influencing the situation in their favor.[57] Moreover, "there was no one in England or in the colonies to pressure for the curtailment of the Negro's servitude or to fight for his future."[58]

The Negroes' capacity to adapt to the situation and effectively protect in their own behalf was greatly hampered by their cultural diversity and lack of unification. They did not think of themselves as "a kind." They did not subjectively share a common identity and thus they lacked the group solidarity necessary to effectively "act as a unit in competition with other groups."[59] Consciousness of shared fate is essential to effective unified action but it generally develops only gradually as the members of a particular social category realize that they are being treated alike despite their differences. "People who find themselves set apart eventually come to recognize their common interests," but for those who share a subordinate position common identification usually emerges only after "repeated experiences of denial and humiliation."[60] The absence of a shared identification among seventeenth century Negroes reflected the absence of a shared heritage from which to construct identity, draw strength, and organize protest. Hence, Negroes were easily enslaved and reduced to the status of chattel. This point merits elaboration.

We have defined adaptive capacity in terms of a group's sociocultural heritage as it affects adjustment to the environment. Efficient adaptation may require the members of a group to modify or discard a great deal of their heritage. A number of factors, including ethnocentrism and the centrality of the values and social structures requiring modification, affect willingness to alter an established way of life.[61] Even given a high degree of willingness, however, many groups simply have not possessed the cultural complexity or social structural similarity to the dominant group necessary to efficient adaptation. Many Brazilian and United States Indian tribes, for example, simply have not had the knowledge (e.g., of writing, money, markets, etc.) or the structural similarity to their conquerors (e.g., as regards the division of labor) necessary to protect themselves from exploitation and to achieve a viable status in an emerging multi-ethnic society.[62]

By comparison with most New World Indians the sociocultural heritage of the Africans was remarkably favorable to efficient adaptation.[63] However, the discriminatory framework within which white-Negro relations developed in the seventeenth century ultimately far outweighed the cultural advantages of the Negroes vis-a-vis the Indians in the race for status.[64] The Negroes from any given culture were widely dispersed and their capacity to adapt *as a group* was thereby shattered. Like the Negroes, the Indians were diverse culturally but they retained their cultural heritage and social solidarity, and they were more likely to resist slavery because of the much greater probability of reunion with their people following escape. Hence, Negroes were preferred over Indians as slaves both because their cultural background had better prepared them for the slave's role in the plantation system (thus enhancing the profits of the planters) and because they lacked the continuing cultural and group support which enabled the Indians to effectively resist

56.   Harris, *op. cit.*, pp. 69–70.

57.   The effectiveness of intervention by an external government is illustrated by the halting of the Indian emigration to South Africa in the 1860's as a means of protesting "the indignities to which indentured 'coolies' were subjected in Natal, ..." See Pierre L. van den Berghe, *South Africa, A Study in Conflict*, Middletown: Wesleyan U., 1965, p. 250.

58.   Boskin, *op. cit.*, p. 448. Also see Stampp, *op. cit.*, p. 22; and Elkins, *op. cit.*, pp. 49–52.

59.   Shibutani and Kwan, *op. cit.*, p. 42. See also William O. Brown, "Race Consciousness Among South African Natives," *American Journal of Sociology*, 40 (March, 1935), pp. 569–581.

60.   Shibutani and Kwan, *op. cit.*, Ch. 8, esp. pp. 202 and 212.

61.   See the discussions in Brewton Berry, *Race and Ethnic Relations*, Boston: Houghton Mifflin, 1965, 3rd ed., esp. pp. 147–149; Shibutani and Kwan, *op. cit.*, esp. pp. 217f; and Wagley and Harris, *op. cit.*, pp. 40–44.

62.   *Ibid.*, pp. 15–86 and 265–268.

63.   *Ibid.*, p. 269, Harris, *op. cit.*, p. 14; and Stampp, *op. cit.*, pp. 13 and 23.

64.   The Indians were also discriminated against but to a much lesser extent. The reasons for this differential are discussed by Jordan, *White over Black*, pp. 89–90; and Stampp, *op. cit.*, pp. 23–24.

slavery.[65] By the time the Africans acquired the dominant English culture and social patterns *and* a sense of shared fate, their inability to work out a more favorable adaptation was assured by the now established distribution of power and by the socialization processes facilitating acceptance of the role of slave.[66]

CONCLUSION

We conclude that ethnocentrism, competition, and differential power provide a comprehensive explanation of the origin of slavery in the seventeenth century English colonies. The Negroes were clearly more different from the English colonists than any other group (*except* the Indians) by almost any criterion, physical or cultural that might be selected as a basis of social differentiation. Hence, the Negroes were the object of a relatively intense ethnocentric rejection from the beginning. The opportunity for great mobility characteristic of a frontier society created an arena of competition which dovetailed with this ethnocentrism. Labor, utilized to achieve wealth, and prestige were the primary object of this competition. These goals were particularly manifest in the Southern colonies, but our analysis provides a rationale for the operation of the same goals as sources of motivation to institutionalize slavery in the Northern colonies also.

The terms of the competition for the Negro's labor are implicit in the evolving pattern of differential treatment of white and Negro bondsmen prior to slavery and in the precarious position of free Negroes. As slavery became insti-

tutionalized the moral, religious, and legal values of the society were increasingly integrated to form a highly consistent complex which acknowledged no evil in "the peculiar institution."[67] Simultaneously, Negroes were denied any opportunity to escape their position of lifetime, inheritable servitude. Only by the grace of a generous master, not by any act of his own, could a slave achieve freedom and, moreover, there were "various legal strictures aimed at impeding or discouraging the process of private manumission."[68] The rigidity of "the peculiar institution" was fixed before the Negroes acquired sufficient common culture, sense of shared fate, and identity to be able to effectively challenge the system. This lack of unity was a major determinant of the Africans' poor adaptive capacity as a group. They lacked the social solidarity and common cultural resources essential to organized resistance and thus in the absence of intervention by a powerful external ally they were highly vulnerable to exploitation.

The operation of the three key factors is well summarized by Stampp:

> Neither the provisions of their charters nor the policy of the English government limited the power of colonial legislatures to control Negro labor as they saw fit. . . . Their unprotected condition encouraged the trend toward special treatment, and their physical and cultural differences provided handy excuses to justify it. . . . [t]he landholders' growing appreciation of the advantages of slavery over the older forms of servitude gave a powerful impetus to the growth of the new labor system.[69]

In short, the present theory stresses that *given* ethnocentrism, the Negroes' lack of power, and the dynamic arena of competition in which they were located, their ultimate enslavement was inevitable. The next task is to test the theory further, incorporating modifications as necessary, by analyzing subsequent accommodations in the pattern of race relations in the United States and by analyzing the emergence of various patterns of ethnic stratification in other places and eras.

65. Harris, *op. cit.*, pp. 14–16, an otherwise excellent summary of the factors favoring the enslavement of Negroes rather than Indians, overlooks the role of sociocultural support. The importance of this support is clearly illustrated by the South African policy of importing Asians in preference to the native Africans who strenuously resisted enslavement and forced labor. Shibutani and Kwan, *op. cit.*, p. 126. Sociocultural unity was also a significant factor in the greater threat of revolt posed by the Helots in Sparta as compared to the heterogeneous slaves in Athens. Alvin W. Gouldner, *Enter Plato,* New York: Basic Books, 1965, p. 32.

66. Shibutani and Kwan, *op. cit.*, esp. Chs. 10–12. Stampp observes that the plantation trained Negroes to be slaves, not free men, *op. cit.*, p. 12. Similarly, Wagley and Harris note that the Negroes were poorly prepared for survival in a free-market economic system even when they were emancipated, *op. cit.*, p. 269.

67. Davis asserts that while slavery has always been a source of tension, "in Western culture it was associated with certain religious and philosophical doctrines that gave it the highest sanction." *Op. cit.*, p. ix.

68. Wagley and Harris, *op. cit.*, p. 124.

69. Stampp, *op. cit.*, p. 22.

Power Perspectives on Stratification and Race Relations

Marvin E. Olsen

A CONCERN with the exercise of power has not been prevalent in most sociological writings on either social stratification or race relations. Within the past few years, however, a growing number of sociologists have begun to argue that neither phenomenon can be understood fully unless power is seen as the crucial determining factor. *The twin themes that link together stratification and race relations are inequality and conflict, both of which are direct outcomes of power exertion.* This essay will therefore examine first stratification and then race relations from a power perspective, treating both processes as manifestations of the distribution and use of power in societies. Most of the readings in this section are based on the United States, but this represents only the limited nature of the current literature, not a restriction on either theoretical perspective.

The dominant figure in the development of a power perspective on social stratification was of course Karl Marx, whose conception of social classes as based on varying relations to the means of economic production has influenced social scientists—and political activists—for a hundred years. As suggested in a previous essay, however, his "theory of social classes" was perhaps more a sophisticated definitional linkage than an adequate explanation of social stratification. We may therefore reject many aspects of this theory as too

narrowly conceived and oversimplified, but nevertheless retain his basic emphasis on power in society as the major determinant of stratification.

Max Weber attempted to broaden Marx's power perspective on stratification, and at the same time relate it more directly to individuals.[1] He argued that the distribution and use of social power typically produces three different kinds of inequality—that is, three distinct yet interrelated dimensions of stratification. These are (a) economic class differences, as determined by individuals' varying "life chances" in the economic marketplace (both productive and consumptive), (b) prestige status distinctions, growing out of common life styles and consequent shared values, and (c) party organization, resulting from efforts of people to exert collective influence on community and societal decision makers. Because of Weber's focus on stratification as a power process, and also because of his recognition that stratification in modern societies is usually multidimensional (rather than unidimensional in the Marxian sense), his essay has become a classic in stratification theory. Unfortunately, however, it gave much more attention to observable expressions of inequality than to underlying causal dynamics, and thus diverted many later sociologists away from the task of formulating a general power theory of stratification.

1. Max Weber, "Class Status and Party," in *From Max Weber*, edited and translated by H. H. Gerth and C. Wright Mills (New York: Oxford University Press, 1958), Chap. 7.

Two contemporary writers have recently taken up the theoretical challenge laid down by Marx and Weber, however. Ralf Dahrendorf has critically analyzed Marx's theory of social classes, rejecting much of it but retaining its essential concern with power, as exercised in authority structures within industrialized societies.[2] He claims that in goal-oriented (or "imperatively coordinated") associations in modern societies, formal authority becomes the predominant type of power—at least from a sociological perspective. The separation between those who do and those who do not exercise authority in these organizations makes the members socially unequal, thus providing a potential basis for the formation of social classes with conflicting interests. Dahrendorf's thesis can be criticized as too limited on at least four counts: (a) he does not deal at all with other types of power such as force or dominance; (b) he insists that within any organization there can be only two classes, which seems unrealistic; (c) he discusses only formal organizations, and does not expand his theory to the total society; and (d) he fails to account for the origins of formal authority structures within organizations. Hence we must look elsewhere for a general power theory of stratification in society.

For this theory, we turn to the writings of Gerhard Lenski.[3] He has outlined a broad theory of social stratification that treats power as the crucial variable, and has also attempted to evaluate this theory by examining both preindustrialized and industrialized societies. The general theory can be expressed in a number of propositions derived from his writing:

1. The basic components of all social stratification are power, privilege (access to desired goods, services, activities, or social positions—of which wealth is an important but not the only indicator), and prestige (favorable evaluation by others, in such forms as recognition, esteem, and honor). Although in reality all three components are highly interrelated, for analytical purposes they must be at least partially distinguished.

2. *In all societies beyond the bare subsistence level, power determines the distribution of nearly all privileges,* both economic and noneconomic. Altruism may occasionally affect the allocation of some privileges, but for the most part the acquisition of privileges is an outcome of the exercise of power in social life.

3. In turn, *most prestige is gained directly from the possession of privileges and indirectly from the exertion of power,* at least in postsubsistence societies. Other factors (not specified by the theory) may sometimes increase an actor's prestige, but these are usually quite minor.

4. Cultural and personal values determine which particular kinds of privileges and prestige various persons will seek, but in general all people normally attempt to exercise as much power as possible and to transform this power into valued privileges and prestige.

5. For a variety of social, psychological, and cultural reasons, power—and hence also privileges and prestige—tends to be unequally distributed within any society. Inequality is not a theoretical imperative, but rather an empirical reality.

6. Once the exercise of power has resulted in the acquisition of some amounts of privilege and prestige, these can in turn be employed as resources for exerting additional power and hence gaining more privileges and prestige. Because these factors are so highly interrelated in social life, any one of them can often be transformed into another in a circular process.

7. At any given time, numerous discrepancies may exist among an actor's power, privileges, and prestige, but most actors will try to keep them in at least rough balance as far as possible—that is, to avoid severe status inconsistency. Hence in the long run a major change in any one of the three factors will eventually tend to result in changes in the other two also.

8. Through a variety of means, social actors normally attempt to protect and retain whatever valued power, privileges, and prestige they presently enjoy, and to pass them on to their children or other heirs. The techniques employed in these endeavors range from power conflicts with others to the creation of organizational struc-

2. Ralf Dahrendorf, *Class and Class Conflict in Industrial Societies* (Stanford, Calif.: Stanford University Press, 1957).

3. Gerhard E. Lenski, *Power and Privilege: A Theory of Social Stratification* (New York: McGraw-Hill Book Co., 1966).

tures to the formulation of legitimizing ideologies.

9.   The resulting patterns of organized and perpetuated social inequality constitute societal systems of stratification.

Lenski has amassed a considerable amount of empirical evidence to illustrate and support this general theory, and makes a compelling argument for its essential validity. At the same time, however, he readily admits that it is far from being a complete explanation of all stratification, and that it requires much additional elaboration and specification. Among the numerous theoretical questions remaining to be answered are these:

1.   What sources of power (that is, resources bases) are particularly significant for acquiring privileges and prestige? Lenski gives primary attention to material technology, political authority, and occupational positions, but also notes that economic systems should be given more extensive consideration in future studies.

2.   How do force, dominance, and authority differ from one another in producing social stratification, for what reasons do each of these three kinds of power become unequally distributed in a society, and through what specific actions or mechanisms is each type of power transformed into privileges and prestige? Lenski provides extensive descriptive data relevant to these questions, but has not yet attempted to answer them with general theoretical propositions.

3.   Under what conditions does the basic process of power→ privilege→ prestige become either reversed, with prestige and/or privilege being used as resources for power exertion, or else blocked, so that power wielding does not lead to the acquisition of privileges or prestige? The general theory allows for these alternative processes, but does not specify why or when they might occur.

4.   What effects do cultural values and similar factors have on the distribution of privilege and prestige in a society? More specifically, as demands increase for greater economic, political, and social equality among all members of a society, will moral values ever override existing power conditions? Very little is presently known about these processes.

5.   Finally, in what ways might this power theory of stratification be combined with some form of functional theory, which sees unequal distribution of socioeconomic benefits as an outgrowth of the differing contributions made by various occupational and other roles to the welfare of the total society? Lenski has attempted to synthesize the power and functional theories, but his solution is historical rather than theoretical in nature. If functional theory can be stated in terms of demand and supply in the job market, as suggested by Richard Simpson,[4] it might then be seen as one mechanism through which individuals utilize power resources (in this case, job skills) to gain desired privileges and prestige (such as income and occupational status).

Beyond these concerns with the causes of social stratification is the equally challenging question of how and why various social classes exercise power in society. If we define *a social class as a population of people who share roughly similar amounts of power, (and hence also privileges and prestige) on one or more stratification dimensions,* and who are delineated from other classes by some type of social boundary, we are then immediately alerted to look for the ways in which various classes exercise power. In response to Marx, much of the sociological discussion on this topic has centered on the present role and future fate of the ''working class'' as compared with the ''middle class.'' All observers seem to agree that in Western societies the ''working class'' has not achieved the organizational unity or capability for exerting power that Marx envisioned, with the result that there have been no major class revolutions in which the ''working class'' sought to gain control of an entire society. (There have been revolutions, of course, but even in Communist countries these have been primarily conflicts among elite classes, not ''workers' revolts.'')

Social scientists often disagree, however, concerning current trends and future possibilities in power relationships among classes in contemporary industrialized societies. Perhaps the majority of writers see the ''working class'' as slowly being absorbed into and merged with the ''middle class,'' to form a vast ''middle mass'' containing numerous internal status gradations

4.   Richard L. Simpson, ''A Modification of the Functional Theory of Stratification,'' *Social Forces,* December 1956, pp. 132–137.

but no divisive class boundaries. Other writers, however, argue that even though the economic standards of living of the "working" and "middle" classes may be constantly improving, both classes are nevertheless being steadily "proletarianized" as they increasingly lose the ability to exercise any significant influence in political processes. These two sets of observations are not entirely incompatible, as long as we conceive of social stratification as multidimensional, so that any particular class might simultaneously be rising on one dimension but declining on another. These are fascinating questions for debate, and they perhaps help us gain greater insight into the dynamics of contempory class struggles, but at the present time sociology can provide very little empirical evidence with which to resolve the debate.

Directly related to these questions about class conflict is the topic of race relations. In a broad sense, racial inequality is one particular type (or dimension) of social stratification, involving social categorization of people on the basis of minor physical characteristics and discriminatory actions by persons in one such category (or "class" or "caste") toward the members of another less powerful category (or "class" or "caste"). From this perspective, the general power theory of stratification sketched above is fully as applicable to racial stratification as to economic, political, or any other kind of inequality. Thus *differential privileges and prestige enjoyed by various "racial classes" can be seen as direct outcomes of unequal power distribution and use,* whereas racial discrimination and segregation can be viewed as techniques used by members of more powerful racial categories to subordinate and control less powerful racial categories.

There is, however, one crucial difference between socioeconomic and racial classes in modern societies. The boundaries of socioeconomic classes are usually quite vague in definition and variable in practice, so that it is relatively easy for many individuals to move from one class to another—that is, to be socially mobile. To the extent that numerous opportunities for individual mobility do occur in a society, there is little impetus for the members of a subordinate class to organize for collective power exertion and class conflict; it is far easier and less costly for these

persons, as they rise in status, to move individually into a higher class. This is not possible with racial classes, though, unless by chance one happens to have mixed ancestry that results in "passable" physical characteristics (e.g., relatively light skin color). For most members of a subordinate racial category there is no possibility of upward individual social mobility into a more desirable racial category, since they cannot change their physical appearance. As a result, class organization, collective power exertion, and class conflict may become prominent social processes in race relations.

Stanley Lieberson has used a power perspective to develop a set of theoretical propositions explaining the broad historical dynamics of racial and ethnic social inequality.[5] He places the roots of racial and ethnic stratification in initial contacts—often resulting from military conquest or voluntary or involuntary migration—between two (or more) populations that differ in physical and/or cultural characteristics. In most cases, one of these populations will be able to exercise more power than the other, because of superior technology and wealth or greater numbers or more unified social organization. Depending on the relative power of the migrant population in relation to the indigenous population, differing patterns of racial and ethnic inequality and conflict will then tend to develop.

The history of race relations in the United States fits this theoretical model quite closely. A population of physically identifiable but relatively powerless people was brought to this society and forced by the more powerful indigenous population to become totally subordinate in terms of power, privileges, and prestige. For 250 years the control of blacks by whites was so complete that the prevailing pattern of race relations was largely "paternalistic" in nature. As described by Pierre van den Berghe,[6] a paternalistic pattern of race relations is characterized by rigid racial class barriers with no possibility of upward

5. Stanley Lieberson, "A Societal Theory of Race and Ethnic Relations," *American Sociological Review*, Vol. 26, December 1961, pp. 902–910.
6. Pierre L. van den Berghe, *Race and Racism: A Comparative Perspective* (New York: John Wiley and Sons, 1967).

mobility, extreme social distance but little physical separation between members of these racial populations, relegation of the subordinate population to the lowest occupational and other roles, paternalistic behavior by members of the dominant class, and acquiesence by those in the subordinate racial category to their positions in society. Because of its total control, the dominant racial class has little need to employ formal methods of discrimination or to enforce physical segregation; most members of the subordinate racial population "stay in their place" voluntarily because they have no opportunity to do anything else and because they have been taught since childhood that servitude is their proper role in life.

This paternalistic pattern may give way to a more "competitive" type of race relations, however, as a society becomes more industrialized and urbanized, as slavery is declared illegal, and as members of the subordinate class become more physically mobile and slowly gain education, occupational skills, and wealth.[7] In place of wholly superordinate and wholly subordinate racial populations, two parallel racial categories develop, each having its own organizational structure, division of labor, and socioeconomic status gradations. The formerly dominant population may continue to enjoy numerous advantages in power, privilege, and prestige for a long period of time, but it no longer totally controls the previously subordinate racial population. The old patterns of paternalism and voluntary subservience give way to competition and conflict between the two racial categories, as the subordinate one struggles to increase its share of power, privilege, and prestige in society. Race relations are no longer static and "peaceful"; dynamic conflict and change now prevail.

In an effort to maintain as much of its previous control as possible, the dominant racial class often resorts to elaborate methods of legal and formal discrimination, physical segregation, disenfranchisement, and even violence toward the subordinate racial class. These techniques were not widely used in the United States until the late 1800's, but as many writers have documented, the Civil War, Reconstruction, and expanding

7. *Ibid.*

industrialization and urbanization largely destroyed the old southern paternalistic pattern of race relations between 1860 and 1890. Formal discrimination and segregation did not appear immediately, however, since during the Reconstruction period the North forced the South to grant Negroes many rights and benefits. Even after the northern troops withdrew during the 1870's there was less open discrimination and segregation in the South than in the North; the southern landed aristocracy attempted instead to reimpose the old paternalistic pattern that did not require these formal means of social control. But during the period between 1880 and 1910 they gradually lost power to the emerging industrialists and growing urban (white) "middle class."

As these new factions gained economic and political power in the South, and as Negroes began to assert the legal rights given them by the federal government, race relations moved from a paternalistic to a competitive pattern. Paternalism based on stable plantation life no longer provided an adequate means by which whites could control blacks, so formal discrimination and physical segregation were increasingly employed as methods of social control. Almost all southern "Jim Crow" laws and the devious restrictions on Negro voting, for instance, were enacted in the South between 1890 and 1910. To those persons who maintain that racial discrimination and segregation cannot be changed through legislation, the obvious rebuttal is that these practices were initiated through political action and hence can be altered in the same manner. The imposition of formal discrimination and segregation against blacks was more protracted in the North than in the South, and did not rely as heavily on legislation, but the basic process and consequent results have been much the same. *As race relations shifted from a paternalistic to a competitive pattern in all parts of the United States during the late 1800's and early 1900's, whites used their superior power resources to force discrimination and segregation upon blacks, in an attempt to retain for themselves as much privilege and prestige in society as possible.*

If racial inequality is in fact largely a consequence of power exertion by whites, it then follows that *blacks seeking to change the situation so as to gain greater equality of privileges and pres-*

tige must in turn exercise power against the dominant whites. This idea may appear to be so self-evident that it hardly needs mentioning, yet not until the late 1950's did large numbers of blacks (and white sympathizers) begin to apply it systematically in an effort to promote widespread social change. Numerous individuals and organizations, both black and white, had of course been trying to combat racism in the United States for many decades prior to that, but for the most part they had relied on an educational rather than an "action" approach. Some of the more blatant aspects of white racism were reduced through extensive educational programs in the schools and through the mass media, but all too frequently the underlying patterns of power exertion did not change significantly; they merely became more covert and subtle.

Part of the reason for this failure was that none of the educational campaigns were ever extensive or intensive enough to reach large numbers of people for sustained periods of time. Perhaps more important, though, is the fact—demonstrated in numerous social psychological experiments—that it is extremely difficult or impossible to alter deep-seated attitudes such as racial prejudice unless the surrounding social environment is also changed. And any major change in the structure of society inevitably requires the exercise of power. When social patterns of discrimination and segregation are eliminated, however, attitudes of racial prejudice often disappear quite rapidly even without purposeful educational programs.[8]

How can a subordinate racial population such as Negroes in the United States effectively wield power to bring about major alterations in patterns of social organization? We cannot here begin to trace the history of the recent civil rights struggle in this society, but we can outline the general process through which successful change efforts frequently occur. Let us call it a "power and conflict" approach to achieving racial equality. This process can be divided into five major

stages, though in practice they usually merge and overlap: organization, power exertion, confrontation, social change, and attitude change.

The initial stage of *organization* is necessary to bring together sufficient resources—including participants, finances, leaders, communication channels, and operational procedures—for generating an effective power base from which to act. Isolated individual members of the subordinate racial class can rarely wield enough power to affect significantly the established organizational structures and control mechanisms of the dominant class. But through the collective actions of many individuals, an adequate foundation of power can be created. These organizational activities must center in and be controlled by the black community itself, although they can always utilize support from sympathetic whites as long as these persons do not attempt to control the black organizations.

The second stage of *power exertion* can be opened as soon as sufficient organizational resources have been acquired. These power actions can take innumerable specific forms—economic, political, legal, physical, and moral—but their goal is always to put pressures on the white community and create tensions and conflicts. If these pressures and conflicts are unfocused (as in many protest parades) or indiscriminate (as in a riot), they will have relatively little effect on the white community, and may invoke retaliation or suppression. To be effective, they must be aimed directly at those persons and organizations that Herbert Blumer calls "key functionaries"—actors in critical positions who are capable of exerting power and effecting change in the white community.[9] They may be elected officials or legislators or business executives or organizational officers or school administrators or police commissioners or religious leaders, depending on the immediate goals of the black movement. These persons may or may not be sympathetic with the goals of the blacks, but that is irrelevant. The important factor is whether the blacks can locate those points at which the key

8. A number of social scientific studies supporting this generalization are summarized by Earl Raab and Seymour Martin Lipset in "The Prejudiced Society," in Earl Raab, editor, *American Race Relations Today* (Garden City, N.Y.: Doubleday and Co., 1962), pp. 29–55.

9. Herbert Blumer, "Social Science and the Desegregation Process," *The Annals of the American Academy of Political and Social Science*, Vol. 304, March 1956, pp. 137–143.

functionaries are vulnerable to outside influences, and then apply sufficient pressures to force the key functionaries to deal with them.

The third stage of *confrontation* is the crucial aspect of this process. The white key functionaries must agree to meet and negotiate with the black leaders, not to build "goodwill" but to resolve the threatening conflicts. Out of this process of give-and-take bargaining between equally powerful antagonists can come, through compromises on both sides, agreements that will produce significant social changes. Lewis Killian and Charles Grigg have described this process of confrontation in a passage that bears repetition:

The establishing of communication between whites and Negroes in no way means that conflict has been terminated. It does not even mean that a minimum of consensus has been reached on the issue involved. It is more likely to signify that the white men of power have found the conflict so costly that they wish to limit it, moving it from the streets, the stores, and the courtroom into the conference room. In actuality the white and the Negro leaders gathered around the conference table do not constitute a biracial team. They are two "truce teams" representing the still antagonistic parties to a conflict. Realism demands that they concentrate not on their points of agreement but on the issues which underlie the conflict. Limitation of the conflict will result from the strategic use of threats and the reciprocal assessment of the balance of power. . . .[10]

The fourth stage of *social change* begins when the agreements reached through negotiation are put into practice by the key functionaries. This may take the form of new legislation, new organizational policies, new operating rules and regulations, or new behavioral practices. The significant feature here is that these broad social changes are being implemented by those persons in the white community who can exercise sufficient power to ensure their success. As these changes take effect, they will simultaneously (a) open new job, housing, educational, and other opportunities to blacks, and (b) alter the social environments of many whites and stimulate the creation of new kinds of social relationships between blacks and whites.

The final state in this over-all process is widespread *attitude change* among whites, as they discard their old attitudes of racial prejudice. In numerous situations it has been found that when whites enter into cooperative, equal-status relationships with blacks—whether at work, in their neighborhood, in recreation, or in school—prejudicial attitudes very quickly disappear. And the longer and more intense these relationships, the more likely the participants are to develop positive attitudes not only towards each other personally, but towards all members of the other race in all situations.[11]

Awareness and utilization of this "power and conflict" approach to racial struggles have been developing among black leaders in the United States since the late 1950's, and it is the basic theme underlying the "Black Power" movement. Black people are seeking to utilize power to change the society toward greater racial equality and increased privileges and prestige for all members of the black community—which may or may not involve racial integration. To do this, they must create viable social organizations that will enable them to exert effective power, both within their own community and throughout the total society. In the words of Stokely Carmichael and Charles Hamilton: "The goal of black self-determination and black self-identify—'Black Power'—is full participation in the decision making processes affecting the lives of black people. . . ."[12]

10.   Lewis Killian and Charles Grigg, *Racial Crisis in America: Leadership in Conflict* (Englewood Cliffs, N.J.: Prentice-Hall, 1964), p. 135.

11.   Raab and Lipset, *Ibid.*

12.   Stokely Carmichael and Charles Hamilton, *Black Power: The Politics of Liberation in America* (New York: Vintage Books, 1967), p. 47.

6

Sexual Stratification

Edward Ransford

AS WITH ethnic identity, one's sex may independently determine access to power, prestige, and privilege. A woman may be in an advantaged position in all the other hierarchies (she may be white, young, and wealthy), but be denied a management position because of her sex. And women who do reach positions of responsibility in organizations still face inequities related to their sex. For example, one study shows that women in positions to exercise authority actually face more inequities in the availability of information needed to perform their jobs, respect from other workers, and job strain than do women lower in the organizational hierarchy (Miller,* *et al.*, 1975).

SEXUAL STRATIFICATION EXPLAINED BY
CONFLICT THEORY

Why does sexual stratification exist? Why have men in most societies dominated women and had a far greater share of resources, life chances, and social honor than women? One of the most forthright explanations in the conflict tradition comes from Randall Collins * (1971). Drawing from Freud's insight that many human social arrangements can be explained by sexual and aggressive motives, Collins (1975) proposes that sexual stratification derives from two facts:

1. Human beings have strong drives for sexual gratification. Although animals also have sexual drives, they are confined to a limited (estrous) period. Human beings are unique in the pervasiveness of their sexual behavior (Collins, 1975:229).
2. "Males on the average are bigger and stronger than females, in the human species. Women are also made physically vulnerable by bearing and caring for children" (Collins, 1975:230).

An asterisk (*) accompanying a citation indicates a selection that is included in this volume.

The conflict approach suggests that people take advantage of these inequalities in resources. That is, men have tended to dominate women and have delveloped ideologies to justify this dominance. Or, as Collins puts it, "Men will generally be the sexual aggressors and women will be the sexual prizes for men" (Collins, 1975:230). Therefore, without consideration of other variables, generally superior male size and strength determines the historically predominant pattern of male dominance, according to the conflict theorist. The following statement by Collins shows the strong emphasis on conflict and coercion in his thinking about sexual stratification.

> Since members of the bigger sex can force themselves on the smaller sex, the former can satisfy their sexual drives at will whereas the latter have sex forced upon them at times they may not want it.
> Unattractive males can force themselves on attractive females, but unattractive females can rarely do the reverse . . . the element of coercion is potentially present in every sexual encounter and this has shaped the fundamental features of the woman's role. Sexual repression has been a basic female tactic in this situation of struggle among unequals in physical strength (Collins, 1975:231).

Figure 6–1 compares Collins's conflict theory of sexual stratification with the conflict theory of Marxian economics. As Figure 6–1 illustrates, both systems of stratification involve force. In class stratification, ownership of the means of production allows one class to wield coercive power in order to exploit the labor of another class. In sexual stratification, the greater average size and strength of males allows them to coerce the other sex in order to be sexually gratified. If the theory were left at this level, it could be seen as a greatly oversimplified statement of male-female inequality. But Collins* adds greater sophistication and theoretical strength to the model by including two important specifying factors—factors that can greatly improve the position of women and, to a certain degree, override the simple fact of male size and strength.

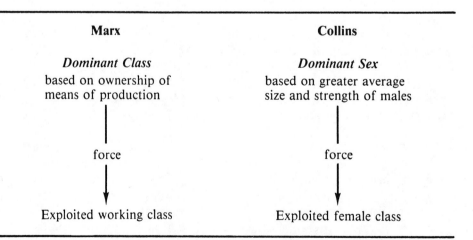

Figure 6–1. *Comparison of Marx's Class Theory and Collins's Sexual Stratification Theory*

First, societies differ in the way force is organized. If the state can intervene on the woman's behalf, the balance of power between the sexes is affected. In societies where the physical violence against women is not condoned, women have more rights and protection such as laws against wife beatings, rape, cruel punishment, and the right to seek divorce.

Second, in societies in which women can achieve economic resources (by owning property or entering the labor market), there is a major shift in the balance of sexual power. Working women with independent incomes and women who own property have more power and autonomy because they are less dependent, or not at all dependent, on men to support them.

The simple formula of male force and coercion in Figure 6–1 is expanded into a more complex model in Figure 6–2. In Figure 6–2, physical size and strength only are the primary determinants of sexual stratification when the state organization of force is weak and women are excluded from participation in the marketplace. Conversely, in a system in which women participate in the market economy and the state grants basic rights and immunities for women, male force has much less salience for sexual stratification. In this latter case, "B" and "C" offset "A" of Figure 6–2 in determining the degree of sexual stratification.

Sexual Stratification in Different Societies.   Collins traces variations in sexual stratification through four societies, from the simplest to the most complex.

In *low-technology tribal societies,* all stratification systems are feeble. For example, in hunting and gathering societies that operate at a bare level of subsistence, women are not forced to do a disproportionate amount of the work; all members of a society must work to survive. There is little or no economic surplus to divide unequally between men and women. Men dominate women by sheer size and strength to some slight degree, but they cannot set down a permanent power structure since the social group migrates constantly.

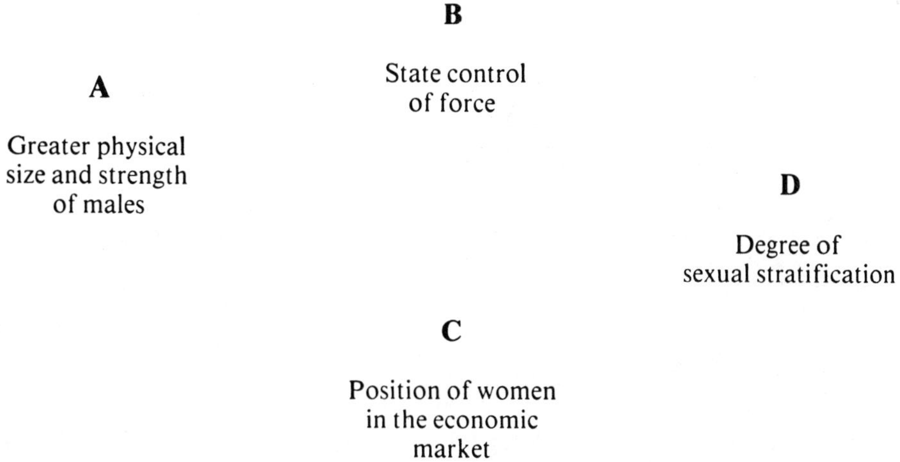

B

State control
of force

A

Greater physical
size and strength
of males

D

Degree of
sexual stratification

C

Position of women
in the economic
market

Figure 6–2.   *Main Factors in Collins's Model of Sexual Stratification*

In the more complex society of *fortified households,* men maximize their control over women. There are higher degrees of economic production in such a society, but the economy is totally controlled by males. Further, each household is like an independent armed unit. The control of force has not yet been monopolized by the state. The concentration of force and of economic resources in the hands of private household heads (that is men) gives them complete control over women. Women are viewed as property and frequently used to cement inter-household alliances. The giving of women in marriage is the main gift exchange system. As a result, female chastity is highly valued. A chaste woman may elicit higher prestige, but she remains a powerless pawn in economic exchanges.

Private households in a market economy is the label Collins uses to describe societies characterized by early industrialization and the development of a centralized bureaucratic state. The first approximation of these structures can be found in cities of the Roman Empire. More current examples are found in the Victorian period of Europe and the United States. The state attains a monopoly on the use of force and violence. No longer are women under the absolute rule of the male household head. Women can appeal to the state (police force) in violent marital disputes. In some societies of this type women have the right to initiate divorce. "With the development of police forces, rapes could be punished by an impersonal agency, and women no longer needed to rely on the force of their sexual owners for protection" (Collins, 1975:246). Norms against adultery are applied to men as well as women; there is some decline of the double standard. Yet even with these improvements in the women's position, she remains essentially powerless in the economic system. Although women on occasion inherit property or participate in the labor force, men continue to control property and monopolize the choice jobs.

Collins maintains that once women had experienced such a *partial* improvement in their position in society, they developed a strategy of using their sexuality in exchange for wealth. For example, to maximize her bargaining power, a woman must be at the same time attractive and inaccessible. Although romantic idealization and coquetry give the woman some degree of bargaining power, she pays a heavy price for this kind of feminine role:

> Prudery . . . and romantic idealization gave women not only a status sphere of their own and a certain amount of control over men, but a great deal of minor deference in the form of polite gestures like hat doffing, door-holding, and hand kissing. But it was basically a strategy of only partly raising an inferior position within the existing order, as women remained confined to the roles of self-decoration and home services: the Southern Belle who gets the most gallant compliments pays for it by being locked in the role of mindless femininity (Collins, 1975:247).

In a society with an *affluent market economy*, such as contemporary United States, the position of women greatly improves. Women often participate in the economic marketplace, and the state organization of force brings new rights and protections for women, such as abortion rights and the right to obtain credit in her name. Working women especially have their own resources. As single women, they are not dependent on men for economic support; as married women, they have more influence and autonomy in the family setting. Freed of the many economic bases for marriage, a more equalitarian bargaining develops between the sexes. Society places more emphasis on personal compatibility, sexual attractiveness, and emotional support; and both male and female can use these resources (Collins, 1975:250).

Using the scheme in Figure 6–2, both the state monopoly of force (B) and the economic market position of women (C) have improved to such a degree that male physical size and strength (A) greatly recedes in importance. Even so, male force survives in advanced market economies. In contemporary courtship, Collins maintains that women may allow themselves to be subject to force after a provisional bargain is made in which the male attains sexual favors in exchange for long-range commitments such as marriage or engagement. Further, among employed women one can see a survival of male dominance. Consider, for example, how women are distributed across occupations in the advanced industrial United States. Typically, women work in occupations in which they receive orders from men and give orders only to other women or to children. Women are highly concentrated in clerical work, elementary school teaching, and nursing. Women who move up in the organizational hierarchy still tend to be in positions in which they give orders only to women or children, such as the head of a secretarial pool (Collins, 1971:5). Only in the last few years have women moved into administrative and managerial positions in which some of their subordinates are men.

Autonomy versus Power.   Here, it is important to distinguish between power and autonomy. Power is the ability to exert control over others. Autonomy is the ability to control one's own life, free of external domination. Collins seems to be saying that under the structural conditions of an advanced market economy, women make large gains in personal autonomy, yet they still have very little control over the lives of men (Collins, 1971). Further, women have not filled the positions that have the greatest impact on societal decisions (Schlegel, 1977:8–9). In many organizations, men continue to block the entry of women to important positions. Thus, the conditions favorable to women in an advanced market economy are not sufficient to increase their *power* on a large scale. Direct challenges to entrenched male power such as the feminist movement and Affirmative Action seem to be essential for a redistribution of power by gender.

Other Conflict Approaches to Sexual Stratification

The theory by Collins outlined above is not the only interpretation of sexual stratification by a conflict theorist. Other theorists, writing in a more Marxian tradition, argue that sexual stratification is the outcome of certain *economic* facts: control over property, the means of production, and the distribution of goods (Schlegel, 1977; Friedl, 1975; Leacock, 1972). Throughout history men have controlled these economic factors. Friedl (1975) points out that control over the *distribution* of goods is the crucial economic fact. Men have had greater power because more often they have controlled the exchange of the group's surplus with other societies. In part, this is true because men have controlled hunting and warfare activities—activities that take them beyond the confines of the local group. Sexual stratification of society is most likely to occur when women's work is directed inward toward the family unit, while men's work is directed outward toward trade and distribution outside the domestic group (Schlegel, 1977:11, Leacock, 1972).

With the development of industrial capitalism and a decline in the need for manual labor requiring strength, Marx predicted that women would become a major part of the industrial labor force. Marx and Engels also believed that as industrial capitalism progressed, there would be a decline in sexual stratification because economic class divisions (bourgeoisie and proletariat) would become so pronounced that they would override sex and ethnic distinctions. Men and women would join together as a part of a commonly oppressed working class (Marx and Engels, 1958:35–36).

Advanced industrial capitalism has not brought men and women workers together into a common working-class coalition (Szymanski, 1974). The Marxist prediction has not been realized. Contemporary Marxist theory instead maintains that sexist ideologies and the concentration of women (and racial minorities) in poorly paid jobs results in direct profits for employers and keeps the working-class splintered and unorganized. "By paying blacks and women less than whites and males, super profits are realized" (Szymanski, 1974:707). Note that sexual stratification is seen as the result (almost as a by-product) of economic conditions; the gains from profits and a divided working class are viewed as causes of continued sexual stratification. There is no unique sexual component to the theory in the same sense that Collins's male force and sexual gratification are components.

Margaret Polatnick* (1973–1974) stresses unequal power as the basis of sex stratification. She gives particular attention to the nonworking woman with child-rearing responsibilities as the source of a woman's powerless position. It is to men's advantage that women are assigned child-rearing responsibility since childrearing will not get a person ahead in the world nor will it even earn power within the family (Polatnick,* 1973–74:60). Because childrearing is so totally time-consuming, it limits one's capacity to engage in any other activity, particularly breadwinning activity. Breadwinners earn money and money is the source of power in a household. As Hill and Becker state, "Money belongs to him who earns it, not her who spends it since he who earns it may withhold it" (Hill and Becker, 1955:790).

A woman who devotes all her energies to childrearing does not have power in the larger society because she is separated from occupational positions that grant power. Occupational achievement is perhaps the major source of prestige and power in society. Even in relatively low-status occupations, a person gains power in the sense of organizational experience, social contacts, and feelings of independence and competence in the world (Polatnick,* 1973–74:62).

A conflict perspective on sexual stratification emphasizes the potential for group consciousness to develop and lead to organized action. In contrast to ethnic minorities, women are a numerical majority in the population. Although the potential for numerical strength is certainly present for women, Rossi (1969) notes that this is offset by the fact that women are not concentrated in ghettos or enclaves, and shared consciousness is far more difficult when a subordinated group is widely dispersed throughout the population. Another major difference that also tends to hinder the development of solidarity and power is that most women live in intimate relationships with men through marriage. Since most women value emotional support from their husbands and stability in their marriages, they may hesitate to assert a militant feminist position for fear of threatening family security. These are important factors that mute the potential for organized action on the part of women.

The Functional Perspective on Sexual Stratification

A very different view of sexual stratification emerges from the functional perspective. The division of male and female roles is not so much a case of unequal power and coercion as it is a natural and necessary division of labor. Sexual stratification is necessary for family organization and the integration of the larger society. The differentiation between men as breadwinners and women as housewives contributes to family cohesion, role clarity, and the accomplishment of important societal tasks. The functional theorist would further argue that the family is an institution that makes vital contributions to the integration of society by providing for the care, survival, and socialization of children and by regulating the sex drive. Since women bear and nurse children, it is natural that they are tied especially to roles of childrearing and to occupations that involve child care, such as elementary school teaching.

Talcott Parsons, a functional theorist, presents one of the clearest statements of the functions of the family and the woman's role in that family. Basic to his thesis is the observation that economic and kinship bonds were undone by industrialization. In the pre-industrial rural family, the wife was highly involved in economic production. Industrialization removed the woman from any active role in the production process. In industrialized societies, the work environment and the home are separated. This does not mean that the nuclear, industrial family is a less important institution in modern society. On the contrary, Parsons argues that the nuclear family in an industrialized society is more vital than ever. The family is more specialized and the society is "dependent more exclusively on it for the performance of certain of its vital functions" (Parsons and Bales, 1955:3–9).

Parsons maintains that the home may offer an escape from the tensions of the job. In urban industrial societies, the family may be the only group from which a person gains a sense of solidarity, trust, affection, and acceptance apart from achievements (Skolnick, 1973:113). The woman's role in such a family is nurturant and expressive. The wife follows a domestic role of raising the children and providing emotional support while the husband goes out into the competitive world to play an instrumental role as breadwinner.

The "Parsons' ideal family" has been criticized recently by many writers. One major criticism is that any deviation from these family patterns "implies social disorganization, or personal psychopathology rather than an alternative life style" (Skolnick, 1973:113). Even more important as a criticism, the functional perspective does not view sexual stratification as an autonomous hierarchy since the woman's position is invariably related to the family unit. She is not seen as having a separate stratification position apart from that of the male breadwinner.

SEXUAL STRATIFICATION AND
UNEQUAL PRIVILEGE

Women are severely limited in their access to economic rewards, services, rights, and immunities. In working-class families especially, women have very little room for independent action without the consent of their husbands (Komarovsky, 1967).

Income is an important variable to consider when discussing the concept of privilege because many services, rights, and immunities are purchased. There are striking differences in the median incomes of men and women (*see* Table 6-1).

At every level of education, women have much lower incomes than men who have achieved the same educational level. For example, the median income for women completing four years of college is $10,357, compared with the much higher male income of $17,188. At the lowest level of education (fewer than eight years), average female income is only 63 percent of average male income; at the highest level of education (four or more years of college) the gender gap is even greater—average female income is only 60 percent of average male income. Table 6-1 also reveals that a *female graduate makes less on the average than a male high school dropout.* Of course, some of this income gap can be explained by factors other than discrimination—the kinds of occupations men and women hold and absences for child care. But a number of studies have indicated that when all income-relevant factors are held constant, there is still a significant income differential between men and women in the same occupational levels and this remaining gap is believed to be a result of sex discrimination (Trieman and Terrell, 1975). (For further discussion of this point, see chapter 8, ''Independent Effects.'')

Most women in the occupational force are confined to a relatively few low-to-middle status occupation categories. There are many explanations for the exclusion of women from the best-paying and most prestigious jobs (Shortridge, 1975). For example, some employers believe that women have higher absentee and turnover rates because of

Table 6-1.   *Median Income of Women and Men by Educational Attainment: 1974*

	Women	Men	(Year-Round, Full-Time Workers) Ratio of Women to Men
Elementary:			
"less than" 8 years	$ 5,022	$ 7,912	.63
8 years	5,606	9,891	.57
High School:			
1-3 years	5,919	11,225	.53
4 years	7,150	12,642	.57
College: 1-3 years	8,072	13,718	.59
4 years or more	10,357	17,188	.60

Source: Current Population Reports, Special Studies, Series P-23, No. 58. ''A Statistical Portrait of Women in the U.S.,'' April 1976. Adapted from Table 10-2, p. 48.

maternity and child-care responsibilities. As a result, they are reluctant to hire, train, and promote women. The Department of Labor has found these beliefs to be inaccurate: "Women workers have favorable records of attendance and labor turnover when compared with men employed at similar job levels and under similar circumstances" (Department of Labor, 1960). Despite this objective evidence, many employers continue to accept the idea that women have high turnover and absentee rates.

The Nondivision of Household Labor and Privilege

Privilege involves not only access to the good things in life, but also immunity from the unpleasant things in life. Much of household labor may be considered unpleasant. Household labor—laundry, cleaning, errands and child care—is a never-ending activity involving some very unpleasant, dirty, and monotonous jobs. Such work is often described as "mindless," encouraging many wives simply to "tune out" (Berk, *et al.*, 1976:33). Rarely is housework described as a source of fulfillment or satisfaction. (One exception is Lopata's (1971:35) finding that housewives enjoy the "freedom from constraining supervision" in their home work.)

With recent developments, such as the increase in the number of working women and the rise of the feminist movement, one gets the impression that there has been a more equitable division of household labor. The mass media have had a number of articles on two-career families and 50/50 marriages. Such articles suggest that the drudgery of household labor is more and more being shared equally by husband and wife.

A recent study by Berk, *et al.* (1976) challenges this equity assumption. To capture fully the household division of labor, the study involved a variety of methods: a one-hour interview with 309 married women; participant-observation in forty households; and a diary of the activities of 158 women covering twenty-four hour periods. (The women were paid for making these detailed accounts.) The study found that women perform 80 to 90 percent of all household labor. Even more provocative was the finding that a woman's contribution to household labor: (1) did not change significantly if she worked full-time outside the home, (2) became only slightly more equal when she was employed in a more prestigious and better-paying job, (3) did not change for older and younger couples, (4) was unaffected by the presence of preschool-age children, (5) and was not affected by the education or income of a couple. That is, even among younger, well-educated, working-wife families, where presumably the goals of feminist equality would be most strongly held, women did the majority of household tasks. Such findings point to a conclusion that career women often are holding down two full-time jobs.

It was also surprising that only 10 percent of the women interviewed expressed overt resentment of the unequal division of household labor. Socialization in part accounts for this absence of anger; many women have been conditioned from childhood to accept the inevitability of domestic work. And, all the other family members have been socialized to expect her to take this role.

The study also showed that although household labor is held in very low esteem by society, some women prefer it to the alternative of highly alienating jobs outside the home. Many women find housework preferable to jobs such as clerk-typist and assembly-line worker. As a housewife, a woman at least retains some control over her labor, by regulating the speed and order with which she performs certain tasks.

Some respondents also mentioned that getting husbands and children to help in household chores was more trouble than it was worth. Husbands and children may resent doing household tasks, or, even more likely, are inexperienced in performing household chores, so the woman does them herself to save time. The overall conclusion of this study is that "married women do most of the household tasks, they do most of the tasks even if they work full time outside the home, and in general they seem pretty much resigned to the situation" (Berk, *et al.*, 1976:37).

Individual and Institutional Sex Discrimination

As with ethnic discrimination, an important distinction can be made between individual and institutional discrimination. Employers who discriminate against women because they believe women to be unfit for the job ("women are too emotional, not physically strong enough, lack the presence to be in supervisory posts") engage in individual discrimination. In many cases, however, women face sexist inequities because of impersonal institutional processes. For example, women are expected to work the same exact hours as men. Yet child care responsibility is also expected to be the job of a woman. Most work organizations do not provide day-care facilities or after school care. Nor do they allow flexibility in work hours that would allow men and women to pick up a child after school.

Both individual and institutional discrimination can be found in some colleges and universities. In 1969, women graduate students at a major university collected a number of statements made by male professors as evidence of sexist beliefs.

> We expect women who come here to be competent, good students; but we don't expect them to be brilliant or original.
> I know you're competent and your thesis advisor knows you're competent. The question in our minds is are you really serious about what you're doing?
> I'm sorry you lost your fellowship. You're getting married aren't you? (Freeman, 1975:194).

Such statements are classic examples of individual prejudice and, if these beliefs are converted into action, of individual discrimination.

Institutional discrimination also exists in universities. Some colleges and universities have had to release junior faculty because of declining student enrollment and inadequate funds. Since women have only recently entered college teaching and research positions in large numbers, some colleges have been forced to lay off women because they have the least seniority. A woman may be laid off not because of individual sexist bigotry, but because of the organizational principle of seniority. Of course, past sexist discrimination based on beliefs that women are less committed or capable (individual discrimination) is one cause for the delayed entry of women into academia. In other words, past *individual* discrimination may interact with present *institutional* discrimination.

Privilege and Socialization

Women have not had access to the same privileges as men because of individual and institutional discrimination and because of traditional gender-role socialization that conditions women to gravitate toward the role of mother and housewife.

Even if all sex discrimination were to end immediately, there would not be a rapid redistribution of women among better-paying, more prestigious occupations. A great many women would continue to choose to be nurses or secretaries rather than doctors or executives.

Ireson (1976) examined the hypothesis that the more traditional a girl's gender-role socialization or the more strongly she experiences pressure for traditionally feminine behavior, the lower her achievement in school is likely to be. Ireson's study involved 3,000 girls in grades seven through twelve from the New York school system. Ireson used a number of measures of gender-role constraint such as: rightness of traditional roles, whether a man should be the family provider and a woman should manage domestic tasks, non-assertive behavior measured by self-reports, and anticipation of an early marriage. As expected, the girls who scored higher in traditional gender-role socialization had lower education and occupation ambitions. Even among girls with high IQ's and well-educated parents, those who expressed traditional gender-role outlooks were lower in anticipated occupational achievement than comparable girls with more liberated outlooks. According to this study, gender-role socialization takes its toll on female achievement even when other factors, such as ability and parental role models, would logically predispose a girl toward high achievement. Gender-role socialization had a more important effect on a girl's achievement orientation as she progressed from early to late adolescence. Among girls in the seventh and eighth grades, there was little relationship between socialization and achievement; but among the eleventh and twelfth graders, the relationship was far stronger. Precisely at the time that young women should be preparing for college and formulating their occupational and educational expectations, gender-role socialization has its most powerful effect in reducing ambition. These studies indicate that the talents of many women remain underdeveloped and underutilized.

In a similar vein, Horner (1972) has advanced the view that capable and highly motivated young women who otherwise would be achievers have a "motive to avoid success." Most women "become anxious about achieving success because they expect negative consequences (such as social rejection and/or feelings of being unfeminine) as a result of succeeding" (Horner, 1972:159). Social stereotypes continue to depict independence, aggressiveness, competition, and intellectual achievement as masculine behavior.

To test the avoidance-of-success hypothesis, Horner administered a Thematic Apperception Test that involved a verbal lead depicting a high level of achievement. Freshman and sophomore college women were asked to respond to this statement: "After the first-term finals, Anne finds herself at the top of her medical school class" (Horner, 1972:161). Male subjects were given the same lead except "John" was substituted for "Anne." More than 90 percent of the men reacted very positively to the male cue, stating, for example, that "John would continue to be successful and a good provider for a future wife.'' But 65 percent of the female subjects expressed great anxiety, confusion, and negativism from the cue about Anne.

> Unusual excellence in women was clearly associated for them with the loss of femininity, social rejection, personal or societal rejection or some combination of the above. . . . There was a typical story, for example, in which Anne deliberately lowers her academic standing the next term and does all she subtly can to help Carl, whose grades come up. She soon drops out of med-school, they marry, and Carl goes to school while she raises their family (Horner, 1972:162–163).

Data for the original study were gathered in 1964. Replication of the study in 1970 by Horner and others using the same methodology showed very little change in the type of response.

The Horner thesis and findings have been challenged. Robbins and Robbins (1973) replicated the study with several methodological refinements and found that in contrast to earlier studies:

1. Female students at Rutgers were much more confident about Anne's chances for success whereas male students at Rutgers expressed more negativism about John's achievement record.
2. There were no differences by sex in terms of fear of success or negativism. The same proportion of males expressed anxiety or negativism about John's achievement as females did about Anne's achievement (44 percent and 48 percent, respectively).

It is difficult to explain the discrepancies between the results of these studies. More refined coding and classification of student responses were used in the later Rutgers research. This could account for the differences. It is also conceivable that women attending certain colleges are more confident about their success goals. That is, there may be pre-selection factors that predispose women of certain backgrounds to attend certain colleges. Fear of success is probably operative in some highly motivated women but such anxieties and fears may be less prevalent than suggested in the original studies by Horner.

These studies indicate that young women may be socialized to avoid high-status occupations. But what of the women who are employed in professional occupations? Even for these women, traditional gender-role socialization has important effects. A study by Paloma and Garland (1971) involved interviews of fifty-three married professional women, all of whom were practicing physicians, professors, or attorneys. Paloma and Garland assert that even high-achieving professional women tolerate domestication to some degree. For professional women, the domestic role competes with a ''pure'' career orientation. For example, the professionals in this study did not have a completely egalitarian marriage: They saw their husbands' jobs as most important, felt that it was appropriate for their job to come second if he were offered a better position in another city, and handled most of the household errands and domestic chores. The interviews also revealed that many of the women viewed their work as a job rather than as a career. They were not eager to have career responsibilities. They prided themselves on balancing their jobs and homemaker roles, and declined promotions or increased career commitments if it interfered with their home life. Finally, most of the respondents felt that they had not personally experienced sex discrimination and minimized the extent of that discrimination in the general marketplace. Traditional gender-role socialization toward the mother-homemaker role is indeed a potent force. The small number of women in this study may not be representative of professional women in general. These data suggest, however, that high achievement in traditionally male occupations does not always erase the effects of gender-role socialization. Rather, these women appear to be striving for a balance between career commitment and the homemaker role.

UNEQUAL PRESTIGE

Women generally have less prestige than men because they are employed in occupations that rank low in social honor. A large proportion of the female labor force is distributed among clerical and secretarial jobs. Although work of this kind is vitally important to the smooth functioning of an organization, such jobs do not require high degrees of creativity, independent decision making, or action. Often, jobs of this kind require an extension of the traditional female role characteristics—physical attractiveness, intuition, and emotional supportiveness. Such work typically requires a woman to be the helper or handmaiden to men.

Women who choose professional careers are granted much greater occupational prestige, but this is often accompanied by role strain as a woman attempts to balance a feminine image with the ambition and assertiveness called for in her job. Women in high positions also have difficulty in gaining the same respect and honor as men in similar positions. A study by Goldberg (1968) asked women college students to read a number of articles on subjects from different fields. The sex of the author of each article was varied by the researchers. Each woman student was asked to evaluate the article for competence, persuasiveness, and other factors. As hypothesized, the identical article received lower ratings when it was connected with a female author. Not only was this true for articles in male-dominated fields such as law, but also in the fields in which women predominated, such as dietetics and elementary school education. Male professionals in the study were perceived to perform better in all fields.

Negative Role Stereotypes and Prestige

The low prestige accorded to women in society is due to more than their position in the occupational structure. Female stereotypes are often very negative. With respect to intellectual abilities, women are stereotyped as scatterbrained, frivolous, shallow, inconsistent, and impractical. In interpersonal relations, women are often viewed as petty, flirty, coy, gossipy, catty, sneaky, fickle, and dependent. In contrast, men are believed to be far more logical, intellectual, rational, and objective (Chafetz, 1974:35–36). As with ethnic stereotypes, women are surrounded by cultural beliefs about their inherent or natural tendencies.

Hunter (1976) points out that contemporary images of women are deeply rooted in historical tradition. In studying the attitudes toward women in Greece and Rome, in the Middle Ages, and in Judeo-Christian tradition, she finds three dominant images of women: as inferior, as evil, and as love objects. The woman in fifth-century Greece was viewed as inferior.

> Hesiod, a major figure in Greek literature, introduced the ever recurring theme of misogyny. His conception of the role of the female sex was purely pragmatic: women were to bear a man's children and nurse him in senility; at any other time they were an expensive nuisance. . . . Athenians excluded women from any political, intellectual, or social life. Shut away in separate quarters, having little contact with anyone outside her own household, the Athenian woman had no legal status, and was for her entire life under the tutelage of her nearest male relative (Hunter, 1976:8).

The chivalric code of love of the Middle Ages idealized women. The woman of that era was "the object of a man's passion and the purifying and elevating force that inspired a man to excellence" (Hunter, 1976:14). The position of a woman that is described here is similar to the one she occupied under the *private household* economy of Collins's analysis. Although women were given a new status in the Middle Ages, they were locked into a passive role. Moreover, if a woman rewarded her gallant suitor, she immediately was charged with sin. "Consummated courtly love implied adultery. Thus, the lady was condemned by the ideas of chivalry to either passivity or sin" (Hunter, 1976:14). Hunter suggests that many of these female images remain embedded in our culture even today.

SUMMARY

Sex can be viewed as one important basis for social stratification. A woman can be privileged on all other stratification dimensions as a white, well-educated young adult, and denied access to certain occupations because of her sex.

A conflict approach stresses power inequality as the basis for male-female stratification. Collins's conflict theory explains how the position of women in a given society is determined by three interacting power variables: 1) male size and strength, 2) the degree to which women participate in the market economy, and 3) the degree to which the state intervenes on the woman's behalf. By contrast, functional theory views male and female roles not as a case of unequal power, but as an important division of labor between the sexes that contributes to societal cohesion.

Women have faced high degrees of both individual and institutional discrimination and, as a result, have limited access to societal privileges such as economic rewards and legal rights. Income disparities are so great between the sexes that female college graduates make less on the average than a male high school dropout. Women are responsible for a disproportionate amount (80 to 90 percent) of household duties and child-care, even when they are working full-time.

Access to privileges is also limited by traditional gender-role socialization. It was shown that young women who subscribed most completely to the traditional female role have lower occupational expectations, even when these young women have high IQ scores and come from well-educated families. Traditional gender-role socialization may deter many capable women from challenging business and professional positions. Among those women who do reach high positions, there still may be residues of traditional gender-role socialization. Female professionals in the Paloma–Garland study (1971) often placed their careers second to their husbands' and to their own roles of wife and homemaker.

Women are accorded far less prestige or social honor than men both because of low occupational positions and because the status of women *per se* has been surrounded by negative cultural stereotypes. In order to eliminate sexual stratification, not only must political and social inequities be challenged but long-standing ideologies of cultural inferiority as well.

REFERENCES

Berk, Sarah Fenstermaker, Richard A. Berk & Catherine White Berheide. 1976. ''The Non-Division of Household Labor.'' Paper read at the Annual Pacific Sociological Association meetings, San Diego, California.

Bureau of the Census, 1976. ''A Statistical Portrait of Women in the U.S.'' *Current Population Reports*. Series P–23, No. 58.

Chafetz, Janet Saltzman. 1974. *Masculine/Feminine or Human? An Overview of the Sociology of Sex Roles*. Itasca, Ill.: Peacock.

Collins, Randall. 1971. ''A Conflict Theory of Sexual Stratification.'' *Social Problems* 19 (Summer): 3–21.

_____. 1975. *''Conflict Sociology.''* New York: Academic Press.

Department of Labor, Women's Bureau Publication. 1960. ''Facts About Women's Absenteeism and Labor Turnover.''

Freeman, Jo. 1975. ''How to Discriminate Against Women Without Really Trying.'' In Jo Freeman (ed.), *Women: A Feminist Perspective*. Palo Alto, Calif.: Mayfield.

Friedl, Ernestine. 1975. *Women and Men: An Anthropologist's View*. New York: Holt, Rinehart and Winston.

Goldberg, Phillip. 1968. ''Are Women Prejudiced Against Women?'' *Transaction* (April): 28–30.

Hill, Reuben & Howard Becker. 1955. *Family, Marriage and Parenthood*. Boston: D. C. Heath.

Horner, Matina. 1972. ''Toward an Understanding of Achievement-Related Conflicts in Women.'' *Journal of Social Issues* 28 (2): 157–175.

Hunter, Jean. 1976. ''Images of Women.'' *Journal of Social Issues* 32 (3): 7–17.

Ireson, Carol J. 1976. ''Effects of Sex Role Socialization on Adolescent Female Achievement.'' Paper presented at the Annual Pacific Sociological Association meetings, San Diego, California.

Komarovsky, Mirra. 1967. *Blue-Collar Marriage*. New York: Vantage.

Leacock, Elanor B. 1972. ''Introduction to the 1972 edition of Engels.'' *Origin of the Family, Private Property and the State*. New York: International Publishers.

Lopata, Helena Z. 1971. *Occupation: Housewife*. New York: Oxford University Press.

Marx, Karl & Frederich Engels. 1958. ''The Communist Manifesto.'' *In Marx and Engels, Selected Works in Two Volumes*. Volume I. Moscow: Foreign Languages Publishing House.

Miller, Jon, Sanford Labovitz & Lincoln Fry. 1975. "Inequities in the Organizational Experiences of Women and Men." *Social Forces* 54 (December): 365–381.

Paloma, Margaret & T. Neal Garland, 1971. "The Married Professional Woman: A Study in the Tolerance of Domestication." *Journal of Marriage and the Family* (August): 531–540.

Parsons, Talcott & Robert F. Bales. 1955. *Family, Socialization and Interaction Process*. New York: Free Press.

Polatnick, Margaret. 1973–74. "Why Men Don't Rear Children." *Berkeley Journal of Sociology* 8: 45–85.

Robbins, Lillian & Edwin Robbins. 1973. "Comment on: Toward an Understanding of Achievement-Related Conflicts in Women." *Journal of Social Issues* 29 (1): 133–137.

Rossi, Alice S. 1969. "Sex Equality: The Beginnings of Ideology." *The Humanist* 29 (Sept.–Oct.): 3–16.

Schlegel, Alice. 1977. *Sexual Stratification: A Cross Cultural View*. New York: Columbia University Press.

Shortridge, Kathleen. 1975. "Working Poor Women." In Jo Freeman (ed.). *Women: A Feminist Perspective*. Palo Alto: Mayfield.

Skolnick, Arlene. 1973. *The Intimate Environment*. Boston: Little, Brown.

Szymanski, Albert. 1974. "Race, Sex and the U.S. Working Class." *Social Problems* 21 (June): 706–725.

Treiman, Donald J. & Kermit Terrell. 1975. "Sex and The Process of Status Attainment: A Comparison of Working Women and Men." *American Sociological Review*. 40 (April): 174–200.

Why Men Don't Rear
Children: A Power Analysis*

*Margaret Polatnick**

INTRODUCTION

THE STARTING point for this paper is a simple fact of contemporary social life: In our society (as in most societies familiar to us), women rather than men have the primary responsibility for rearing children. Of course, fathers are not devoid of obligations vis-à-vis their offspring, but the father who accepts the routine day-do-day responsibility for supervising his children and servicing their needs, at the expense of outside employment and activity,*** is still a rare bird indeed.

In examining why this is so, I plan to steer clear of two potential pitfalls. First, I will make no attempt to unravel historical causes in pursuit of a primeval "first cause." Anthropological evidence

about the origin of male and female behaviors is inconclusive and sheds little light on the contemporary situation, where the conditions of life are substantially different. This paper will deal only with current reasons why men don't rear children.

Second, I have no intention of discussing individuals and their personal motivations. I am treating men as a gender and women as a gender, and my conclusions will be generalizations about groups and group relations.

Now, the choice of who rears a society's children and the implications of that choice for the whole social structure seem to me extremely fruitful subjects for sociological examination. Yet sociologists have shown little inclination to consider the allocation of child-rearing responsibility to women as a matter of social choice. Instead they have been surprisingly willing to lay things at nature's door and ask no more: Men don't rear children because women are the natural rearers of children.

For sociologists, of all people, to rest so content with biological determinist explanations is at best intellectually unproductive and at worst politically suspect. Part I of this paper will discuss in more detail how the use (primarily misuse) of "nature" arguments has obscured the sociological understanding of child-rearing as a social job.

My own explanation for why men don't rear children (Part II of the paper) rests upon a basic premise about male/female relations: In our society (as in most societies familiar to us), men as a gender enjoy a superior power position in relation to women as a gender. That is, they are in

Source: *Berkeley Journal of Sociology*, v. 18(1973-74), pp. 45-85.

Copyright © 1973 by Margaret Polatnick.

*This paper was awarded Honorable Mention in the 1973 Pacific Sociological Association student paper competition.

**Much appreciation for the bloodcurdling critiques of Judie "Tenspeed" Gaffin, "Diesel" Dair Gillespie, Carol "Boss" Hatch, Ann "The Man" Leffler, Elinor "Bulldog" Lerner, Maria "Muscle" Mendes, and "Stompin" Stacey Oliker; much indebtedness to the Women's Movement in general.

***Let this suffice as my definition of child-rearing responsibility, with the qualification that outside employment and activity is possible if children spend part of the day with babysitters, at day-care centers, in school, or alone.

control of the major sources of societal power* (political, economic, social, physical), their superordinate position and the subordinate position of women buttressed by an ideology of male supremacy and female inferiority.** It is not my purpose here to "prove" the existence of an overall power inequality between the sexes. By now there is a sufficient corpus of Women's Liberation literature that documents painstakingly the subordinate status of women in the various spheres of societal life.[2] If every new paper on the sociology of women must prove these fundamental assertions yet again, the field will remain mired in its A B C's.

I am interested instead in demonstrating how the assignment of child-rearing responsibility to women articulates with a general pattern of male domination of our society. My analysis will illuminate and illustrate certain aspects of the gender power dynamic, but those unhappy with the basic premise will simply have to suspend misgivings and come along for the ride.

If, as I will argue, the current allocation of child-rearing responsibility to women must be understood in the context of their subordinate position in society, then two different causal relationships suggest themselves:

1. Because women are the rearers of children, they are a powerless group vis-à-vis men.
2. Because women are a powerless group vis-à-vis men, they are the rearers of children.

The first proposal is of course wholly compatible with a biological determinist position. If those who regard females as the biologically designated rearers of children had at least examined the implications of this "fact" for the overall societal status of women, I would already have

an important ingredient of my "power analysis." Unfortunately, biological determinists have been largely associated with the "different but equal," "complementary," "separate spheres" school of thought about male/female relations, in which power is a foreign concept.

Women's responsibility for child-rearing certainly contributes to their societal powerlessness, but this is only one component of the total "power picture." It will be my contention in Part II of this paper that the second causal relationship is operative as well. Thus, the causal model that will inform my discussion in Part II can be represented best by a feedback arrangement:

Women are a powerless group vis-à-vis men
Women are the rearers of children

My task in the second part of the paper will be to explain, elaborate, and justify this "power analysis."

Two final words of caution are in order. First of all, the subordinate position of women is rooted in multiple causes and reinforced by many different institutions and practices. The causal model above is by no means intended as a complete statement about women's powerlessness; many other variables besides child-rearing responsibility would have to be included in the picture. Freeing women from child-rearing duties would not in and of itself eliminate the power differential between the sexes. For example, if domestic responsibilities didn't bar women from most influential jobs, discrimination in education, training, hiring, and promotion still would. When I isolate the effects of any one variable upon the position of women, keep in mind that there are many other variables left behind.

Second, I will be unable to do justice in this paper to the complexities of social class. The gender dynamic of male superordination/female subordination operates across the entire range of socioeconomic status, but different realities and norms in each socioeconomic group produce variations in the basic pattern. Some of my specific statements, and some of the quotations I use, will be slanted toward middle-class realities. However, the essentials of my argument apply equally well to all social classes.

---

*"The general definition of 'power' is 'a capacity to get things done.' Either resources (rights in things) or authority (rights in persons) increases the ability of a person to do what he decides to do."[1]

**Modern democratic ideology requires that groups be defined as "different" rather than unequal, but the essence of a power relationship shines clearly through most of the basic decrees about male or female natures: women are soft, weak, passive, helpless, compliant, in need of care and protection; men are strong, active, assertive, commanding, suited for leadership and managerial roles.

PART I.
SOCIOLOGISTS
AND THE BIOLOGICAL
IMPERATIVE

There is, to be sure, a strong and fervid insistence on the "maternal instinct," which is popularly supposed to characterize all women equally, and to furnish them with an all-consuming desire for parenthood, regardless of the personal pain, sacrifice, and disadvantage involved. In the absence of all verifiable data, however, it is only common-sense to guard against accepting as a fact of human nature a doctrine which we might well expect to find in use as a means of social control.

Leta S. Hollingworth,
*The American Journal of
Sociology*, 1916[3]

Of all the social "roles"* associated with the female sex, the one most firmly bolstered by references to nature, biology, and anatomy is undoubtedly that of mother. Assumptions that all women are possessed of a maternal instinct, that they innately want to raise children and have the ability to care for them, that children need to be "mothered" by a mother or at least a "mother substitute," or they will suffer from "maternal deprivation," are at the core of both popular and scientific thinking about child-rearing.

The sociological (and psychological) literature is permeated with explicit and implicit statements about the "naturalness" of women rearing children. It is difficult to find a treatment of motherhood that so much as entertains the notion that women's caring for children might be a socially engendered rather than a biologically based activity. When social scientists do feel obliged to offer some evidence for the "naturalness" of mothering behavior, they resort most often to convenient ape analogies, with the underlying premise that "anything primates do is necessary, natural, and desirable in humans."[4]

*The notion of males and females playing different "roles" does not fit well with a power analysis, since it implies a certain voluntarism (actors taking on parts) and ignores power differentials between actors and between "roles." One would not say that black Africans performed "the role" of the colonized, that proletarians are in "the role" of exploited workers.

Even feminist* literature tends to tread lightly when it comes to the subject of motherhood. Old-style feminist writers would typically suggest that women wanting careers could hire babysitters to supervise their children. New-style feminists frequently propose that mothers organize cooperative day-care centers. But challenges to the proposition that children are in any way more the responsibility of females than males are not a common as one might expect.

The corollary to these beliefs about the biological sanctity of motherhood is that there is no such elemental biological connection between father and child. Males are not endowed with a corresponding "paternal instinct," and fatherhood, as "emphasized by Margaret Mead and others, is a 'social invention.'"[5] Leonard Benson, in his comprehensive survey and synthesis of the sociological literature on fathers, finds "the feeling widespread that the basic psychosomatic make-up of men provides them with little aptitude for child-rearing."[6]

Biological Beliefs in
Family Sociology

In examining the literature on the family, one can distinguish two main ways in which the message is conveyed that women are meant to rear children:

1. Constant equation of "mothering" with child-rearing. Without explicitly invoking biology, many family sociologists discuss mothering behavior as if it is an unbreakable rule of nature for females to tend children. Why men don't rear children does not become a conscious question; children are reared by mothers, period. This identity between mother and child-rearer is both:
   a. Linguistic (i.e., use of "maternal care," etc. as generic terms for the child-rearing function).
   b. Conceptual (reflecting the belief that mothers are innately, necessarily the child-rearers).

*The term "feminist" can refer to any advocate of "women's rights" or to a specific ideological camp within the Women's Movement. I am using it only in the former general sense.

2. Explicit biological rationales based on female nature. These consist primarily of:
   a. References to women's specific physiological equipment as determinative of their child-rearing responsibility.
   b. References to more general instinctual or psychosomatic factors as determinative of women's child-rearing responsibility.

(1) Child-Rearer = Mother

The use of terms derived from "mother" to denote caring for children is far too commonplace to require documentation. The activity called "mothering" involves tending children, servicing their needs, and supplying the tender concern vital to healthy personality development. There is no effort to separate these functions semantically from the female person who typically performs them. These things constitute "maternal care," and the implication is that, *ipso facto*, they can only be provided by a female.

Consider the different meanings brought to mind by the following statements: The child was mothered by X; The child was fathered by Y. The first sentence suggests tender loving care, while the second implies mere physical paternity.

In the introduction to their standard anthology on the family, Norman Bell and Ezra Vogel write that "severe personality problems in one spouse may require the wife to become the wage-earner, or may lead the husband to perform most maternal activities."[7] Although "wage-earning" tends to be the job of fathers, the term is not sex-specific. But when a father takes on child-tending responsibilities (because of "severe personality problems" or some other awful eventuality), the job can never be rightfully his, for "pater" just isn't "mater."

So far I have been speaking as if this were all a matter of semantics. But sociologists don't just happen to *say* "mother" for "child-rearer," they *mean* it. Identity in word reflects identity in thought.

The linguistic/conceptual equation of child-rearer and female parent is most pernicious, from a feminist perspective, when it appears in statements about the needs of children. Experts on child development ought to tell us simply that a child needs loving care, but what they proclaim instead is "a child needs a mother."

Let one example suffice: Anna Freud and Dorothy Burlingham, in their study of war-time children's relocation centers, state that a growing child's basic requirements include "intimate interchange of affection with a maternal figure."[8] Are we to conclude that men are incapable of providing this affection? Is their affection biologically not the right sort? Must we refer to those men who do exchange intimate affection with growing children by an exclusively female term?

The term and concept "maternal deprivation" presents similar difficulties. Can a child receive loving care only from a woman? Is it possible for a man to be a "mother substitute"? Are males constitutionally impotent when it comes to "maternal love"?

It might be argued that all these female-specific words for intensive "parenting" are merely *descriptive*, since in the societies familiar to us, women *are* almost exclusively the providers of "maternal care." Nonetheless, there exist a few societies and some individual men in our society that do not conform to this pattern. And the constant use of female terms for the rearing of children becomes obviously *prescriptive*. With messages like this omnipresent—

> . . . when deprived of maternal care, the child's development is almost always retarded—physically, intellectually, and socially . . . [9]

—few mothers will reject the primary parenting role (and few fathers will give them the opportunity to do so). For anyone seeking fresh perspectives on the sexes and the social structure, the very language in which child-rearing is discussed is already blatantly biased. In both the terminology and the thinking of most family sociologists, child-rearing stands defined as inherently women's work.

(2) (a) Wombs and Breasts

One of the ways in which social scientists rationalize their assumption that mothers must be the child-rearers is by reference to women's specific physiology. For instance, in a chapter entitled "Family Organization and Personality

Structure" in Bell and Vogel's anthology, one reads that "the feminine role derives from the woman's biological structure and is related to nurturance of children and the maintenance of a home."[10]

It is certainly indisputable that two fundamental biological factors connect women to children: women bear babies, and they are equipped with breasts to feed infants. Of course, the former function may well become an anachronism at some point in the future,[11] and the latter endowment was undercut some time ago by the advent of the bottle.* However, what I find objectionable is not the existence of these two biological capabilities in women, but the conclusion, blithely drawn by lay people and academics alike, that therefore women have a biologically decreed responsibility to raise and care for children. Where is the compelling logic in either of these connections?:

> Embryos grow in women's bodies, *ergo* women must have primary responsibility for taking care of children.
> Women are able to nurse babies, *ergo* women must have primary responsibility for taking care of children.

Yet sophisticated versions of these same *non sequiturs* roll smoothly from the tongues of reputable social scientists.

With reference to the first of these two assumptions, Ethel Albert has noted that "biological maternity is not correlated very neatly with psychological or social aptitude or liking for motherhood. Having babies is one thing, raising them another."[13] Nonetheless, Erik Erikson informs us that a woman's "somatic design harbors an 'inner space' destined to bear the offspring of chosen men, and with it, a biological, psychological, and ethical commitment to take care of human infancy."[14] Erich Fromm proclaims that the mother/child attachment

> begins before the moment of birth, when mother and child are still one, although they are two. Birth changes the situation in some respects, but not as much as it would appear.

*The rubber nipple was patented in 1845; the first good formula was developed about 1860.[12]

> The child, while now living outside of the womb, is still completely dependent on mother.[15]

Because mother was the one the child depended on in the womb, she must also be the one to meet the infant's needs after birth.

Sometimes the connection is more attenuated, but childbearing still suggests child-rearing. Take Talcott Parsons:

> . . . a certain importance may well attach to the biological fact that, except for relatively rare plural births, it is unusual for human births to the same mother to follow each other at intervals of less than a year with any regularity. It is, we feel, broadly in the first year of life that a critical phase of the socialization process, which requires the most exclusive attention of a certain sort from the mother, takes place.[16]

In other words, nature, by the very spacing of childbirths, has decreed who should attend to infants.

The second physical function in women directly linked to motherhood, producing milk for nursing infants, can easily be broadened into a wider social responsibility for children through a blurring of the two meanings of the term "nurturant." To nurture in the specific sense is to provide food or nourishment, but it also means "to raise or promote the development of; train; educate; rear."[17] Thus, from being the parent endowed with the physical capacity to nurse, the mother becomes, according to Benson's book on *Fatherhood*, "the crucial parent for maintaining the basic essentials of a nurturant family life."[18]

Let's consider a somewhat subtle transition from nursing to "nurturing." Morris Zelditch, Jr., a collaborator with Parsons on *Family, Socialization and Interaction Process*, writes that

> . . . a crucial reference point for differentiation in the family . . . lies in the division of organisms into lactating and nonlactating classes. Only in our own society (so far as I know, that is) have we managed to invent successful bottle-feeding, and this is undoubtedly of importance for our social structure. In other societies necessarily—and in our own for structural reasons which have *not* disappeared with the advent of the bottle—the initial core relation of a family

with children is the mother-child attachment. And it follows from the principles of learning that the gradient of generalization should establish "mother" as the focus of gratification in a diffuse sense, as the source of "security" and "comfort."[19]

The "gradient of generalization" indeed! Mother becomes the source of security and comfort because she *provides* security and comfort: she "cleans and clothes the infant, . . . soothes it with her voice and cuddles it with her body."[20] Who would be the "focus of gratification" if mother merely offered her breast now and then and father provided all the other ingredients of loving care? Wet nurses once fed the infants of mothers who couldn't or wouldn't nurse;* who then was the source of security and comfort?

Zelditch invokes "structural reasons" when he has to explain why bottles haven't freed women from child-rearing responsibility, but otherwise his argument is biological: because mothers produce milk, they are the child-rearers.

The landmark experiments of Harlow and associates with infant monkeys[22] (if I may be permitted to draw upon *reputable* ethology) suggest that the critical aspect of "mothering" is not the providing of food but of warm, comforting physical contact (cuddling, stroking, soothing). This led Harlow to observe that "the American male is physically endowed with all the really essential equipment to compete with the American female on equal terms in . . . the rearing of infants."[23] But this has not caused most sociologists to stop assuming that she who can nurse must also be the nurturant one. Benson concludes his comments on Harlow's work thusly:

Among humans, too, it appears that there are alternatives to the mother's feeding function, but no alternative to the sustained physical presence of a mothering one in the life of the infant. There is no evidence that the father's physical contact with the child provides any special "paternal" quality. . . . [24][!!!]

*According to W. Kessen's study of *The Child:* "Perhaps the most persistent single note in the history of the child is the reluctance of mothers to suckle their babies. The running war between the mother, who does not want to nurse, and the philosopher-psychologists, who insist she must, stretches over two thousand years."[21]

Causal arguments from breast-feeding to child-rearing often have an intervening variable of "convenience": since woman had to be around to breast-feed anyway, it was "convenient" that they take on the other tasks of child care. The question, of course, is convenient for whom? For the mother who doesn't want having children to interfere too much with her activities outside the home? Or for the father who doesn't want having children to interfere too much with *his* activities outside the home? Convenience is a *social* consideration; in many cases it has been "convenient" for humans to circumvent the "givens" of biology. Anyhow, with the easy accessibility in our society of bottles and formulas, such arguments are only of historical interest.

(2) (b) Maternal Instinct

If all biological determinists invoked only wombs and breasts to explain why women are the rearers of children, their position could be easily defeated. However, the more sophisticated "nature" advocates base their arguments upon less clearly defined instinctual or psychosomatic factors. Thus, a "maternal instinct" or something similar predisposes women toward child care, whereas men have no such natural bent. (It might be noted that men also lack a biological "lawyer instinct," "junior executive instinct," "dockworker instinct," etc., yet perform these jobs admirably well.)

Confronting this more general formulation of the biological determinist hypothesis involves us in a classic "nature-nurture" controversy. Such controversies have always been difficult to resolve conclusively in the absence of a feasible, acceptable process for raising "nurture-free" children. In order to demonstrate that certain female and male behaviors are not the result of innate sex differences, one has to pursue two indirect lines of approach. First, one can attempt to prove that there is indeed little rigorous empirical evidence for the "nature" argument. Particularly vulnerable to such scrutiny are the psychologists and psychiatrists who have based their pronouncements about female "nature" almost solely upon subjective clinical experience.

The second line of attack is to accumulate an impressive array of evidence that gender behavior is socially produced. The mere existence of biologically normal individuals who don't conform to expected male/female behavior patterns undermines a strict biological determinist position. However, a more persuasive presentation demands detailed study of the effects of socialization (the inculcation of attitudes and values through formal and informal education processes) and social control (the external enforcement of prescribed behavior through a system of punishments and rewards).*

Another important source of evidence in favor of the social nature of gender behavior is the study of other societies (especially "primitive" ones) in which male/female behaviors are significantly different from or even totally the reverse of our contemporary pattern. And a final promising direction of "nurture" research falls under the rubric "sociology of oppression." The attempt here is to show how the experience of oppression (powerlessness) produces similar behaviors in different "out" groups, fully explainable by their position in the social structure.

All of these lines of investigation can contribute relevant evidence for refuting the biological argument about "maternal" behavior. My purpose here has been simply to map out the *modus operandi* for such a refutation. Thus I will touch only briefly upon some individual points of interest in the "nurture" case.

Here again, the research of Harlow and his co-workers provides a key finding about "mothering" in monkeys (who *can* be raised in "nurture-free" isolation cages). Female monkeys brought up without monkey mothers and without social experience with other monkeys proved to be "totally inadequate" mothers; they "ignored, rejected, and were physically abusive to their infants." The researchers are not willing to discard completely the notion of an innate component to maternal behavior in these monkeys, but they do conclude that "inadequate early social learning can block the expression of the normal maternal pattern."[25]

In his report on *The American Male* (1966), Myron Brenton asserts that, whatever the

maternal propensities of female apes, human maternal behavior must be viewed "in the context of a learning process."

> A woman is, as Morton M. Hunt has pointed out in his balanced exploration of the subject, a human being and is therefore "born almost completely unequipped with rigidly patterned instincts.". . . A human mother . . . must *"learn* how to be kind and loving, and how to want and to care for a child." . . . The learning process . . . begins, as the result of countless cultural clues . . . from infancy on.[26]

Despite these "countless cultural clues," and the overt motherhood training girls receive, many women embark on motherhood with remarkably little knowledge about infant care, but, because it's "their responsibility," they learn fast enough. As Harriet Rheingold has stressed, the infant "teaches [parents] what he needs to have them do for him. He makes them behave in a nurturing fashion."[27] We know which "parent" must attend to the lesson.

There is a prevalent tendency, in "nurture" explanations of female behavior, to stress the effects of socialization (women, because of their training, want to be child-rearers) and to neglect the influence of social controls (women are forced to be childrearers, whether they want to or not). "While affirming the essential nature of woman to be satisfied with maternity and with maternal duties only, society has always taken every precaution to close the avenues to ways of escape therefrom."[28] Two obvious roadblocks are the lack of adequate institutional child-care facilities and the lack of husbands willing to rear children. Even if a husband *is* willing to rear the children, financial considerations militate against such an arrangement. Economic discrimination provides males with a substantial edge in earning power, thus making it difficult to break the pattern of male breadwinner/female childrearer.

The choice for women (to the extent that they have a choice) is thus essentially: (a) have children and rear them,* or (b) don't have children. The latter option has been physically possible for heterosexually active women only since effective birth control became accessible, and is

---

*Under the broad category of social control I would include structural factors (e.g., what options exist for employment, education, living arrangements, etc.) which limit people's possibilities.

*Rich women, of course, can delegate some child-rearing tasks to employees.

still infrequently realized (for reasons of both socialization and social control).

Another weakness in current "sociology of gender" research, as noted by Marcia Millman, is its tendency to focus "heavily on women (the implication being that it has to do only with women) . . . ."[29] Boys, too, undergo a significant learning process about parenthood: they learn that they *don't* have to take care of children. "They see—in their own homes—that fatherhood either assumes narrow dimensions or is more or less irrelevant."[30] "Nurturance," they discover, is not regarded as a suitable ingredient of masculinity or male identity. If they display any fondness for dolls or any "mothering" behavior toward younger children, they are negatively sanctioned. Before long, most boys pick up the appropriate cues about how to act around babies: they become practiced in that clumsy, self-conscious manner of handling infants which insures that some female will quickly step in and take over.

Reflecting the societal estimation of who's going to be doing the job, "parenting" information aimed at males "is remarkably scarce compared to the literature of advice, instruction, and edification for women." As Benson remarks:

Fatherhood is a pastime that does not call for training, discipline, or high-priority effort. Pressures upon men to take stock of themselves as fathers are fitful and unorganized at best.[31]

As for the social advantages to men of avoiding child-rearing responsibility, these will be elaborated in the second part of the paper. All in all, it is hardly a surprise that most males develop neither enthusiasm nor ability for child care.

One can continue indefinitely to demonstrate social factors contributing to the definition of women as child-rearers and men as non-child-rearers, but at what point has one accumulated sufficient evidence to convert a stalwart believer in at least *some* biological basis? Probably never, until biochemists are able to resolve the issue directly.

Be that as it may, the lack of a definitive conclusion to this debate does not constitute a serious stumbling block to my proposed "power analysis." There is certainly enough evidence of a social component to parenting behavior to make a strict biological determinist position disreputable and a "social structure" analysis highly instructive.

A belief that women's responsibility for child-rearing *first arose* as a result of biological factors is not incompatible with a belief that this responsibility is now socially generated and socially alterable. The question of the origin of certain social behaviors can be profitably separated from the question of how and why those behaviors are currently maintained: What are the mechanisms by which the behavior pattern is perpetuated? What interests and uses does that perpetuation serve?*

Explaining mothering versus fathering responsibilities in the context of a whole social system brings into sharper focus how these responsibilities are interrelated with other dimensions of the gender dynamic. Benson, in his overview of the literature on fatherhood, takes occasional account of this theme. On the subject of mothers he says at one point:

"Mothering behavior" is not simply the product of the mother's nature, but is influenced by her relationships with father, her marital frustrations, and by the father's attitudes toward the children. Mothering is as much a function of the woman's position in the family structure as it is an expression of her personality. . . .[34]

---

*This perspective is not very far from the theoretical position of functionalism. Functionalists "interpret data by establishing their consequences for larger structures in which they are implicated."[32] As Alvin Gouldner has pointed out:

The functionalist's emphasis upon studying the *existent* consequences, the ongoing functions or dysfunctions of a social pattern may be better appreciated if it is remembered that this concern developed in a polemic against the earlier anthropological notion of a 'survival.' The survival, of course, was regarded as a custom held to be unexplainable in terms of its existent consequences or utility and which, therefore, had to be understood with reference to its consequences for social arrangements no longer present.[33]

Both feminists and functionalists might wish to show, accordingly, how the pattern of differential parenting responsibilities for males and females ties in to existing institutions, structures, and processes in the society. But the crucial difference between the two perspectives would lie in the value orientation of each toward the integrated, static system such an investigation tends to suggest. One of the main critiques of functionalist analysis has been that it slips imperceptibly into an affirmation of the status quo. Feminist analysis is surely not characterized by *that* shortcoming.

But Benson never develops the full implications of these remarks, because the scope of his thinking (and the thinking in the literature he reviews) is limited by the persistent assumption that child care is inherently the work of women.

For the further purposes of this investigation, then, I will treat the assignment of child-rearing responsibility as the prerogative of society, not biology. Staunch support for biological determinist explanations of gender behaviors can be a convenient rationalization for ignoring their larger social ramifications. By regarding beliefs about proper mother and father duties as ideology rather than eternal verity, I can consider questions of function, utility, purpose, and interest. A number of influential Women's Liberation writings have popularized the policy of viewing personal and social relationships between the sexes as "political"—that is, involving group conflict of interest in which resources of power and leverage are brought to bear.[35] The rest of this paper will be an attempt to apply this framework to the allocation of child-rearing responsibility.

PART II.
SOCIAL ADVANTAGE:
THE POWER ANALYSIS

Having addressed the argument that men don't rear children because of "biology," I can now present and defend the central thesis of this paper: men (as a group) don't rear children because they don't *want* to rear children. (This implies, of course, that they are in a position to enforce their preferences.) It is to men's advantage that women are assigned child-rearing responsibility, and it is in men's interest to keep things that way.

I should emphasize at once that I have no intention of measuring the "inherent worth" of child-rearing as compared to other pursuits. On some "absolute" scale of values, child-rearing would probably rank higher than many a work-world job. But my topic is not "the good life," it is power advantages. Thus my view of child-rearing must be unabashedly pragmatic: Will it get you ahead in the world? Does it even get you power in the family?

I will discuss the undesirability of the child-rearing job under two general categories: (1) the advantages of avoiding childrearing responsibility (which are, primarily, the advantages of breadwinning responsibility); (2) the disadvantages attached to child-rearing responsibility.

BREADWINNING BEATS
CHILD-REARING

Full-time child-rearing responsibility limits one's capacity to engage in most other activities. However, the most important thing, in power terms, that child-rearers can't do is to be the family breadwinner.* This is the job that men prefer as their primary family responsibility. It offers important power advantages over the home-based child-rearing job.

Money, Status, Power

First of all, and of signal importance, breadwinners earn money. "Money is a source of power that supports male dominance in the family. . . . Money belongs to him who earns it, not to her who spends it, since he who earns it may withhold it."[37]

Second, occupational achievement is probably the major source of social status in American society. As Parsons has noted, "In a certain sense the most fundamental basis of the family's status is the occupational status of the husband and father." The wife mother " is excluded from the struggle for power and prestige in the occupational sphere," while the man's breadwinner role "carries with it . . . the primary prestige of achievement, responsibility and authority."[38]

*Many women work during some of the child-rearing years, but if they have husbands, they are very rarely the principal breadwinner. The U.S. Department of Labor reports the following figures for the median percentage of family income earned by wives in 1966:[36]

Family income	Percentage
under $2,000	6.0
$2,000–$2,999	12.2
$3,000–$4,999	14.4
$5,000–$6,999	15.8
$7,000–$9,999	23.0
$10,000–$14,999	28.1
$15,000 and over	22.9

Even if one's occupation ranks very low on prestige and power, there are other tangible and intangible benefits which accrue to wage earners, for example, organizational experience, social contacts, "knowledge of the world," feelings of independence and competence.

Family Power

The resources that breadwinners garner in the outside world do not remain out on the front porch; breadwinner power translates significantly into power within the family. This is in direct contradiction to the notion of "separate spheres": the man reigning supreme in extrafamilial affairs, the woman running the home-front show. (I'll discuss this theme more later.)

The correlation between earning power and family power has been substantiated concretely in a number of studies of family decision making (Blood, 1958; Heer, 1958; Hoffman and Lippitt, 1960; Middleton and Putney, 1960; Nye and Hoffman, 1963).[39] These studies show that the more a man earns, the more family power he wields, and the greater the discrepancy between the status of the husband's and wife's work, the greater the husband's power. When the wife works too, there is a shift toward a more egalitarian balance of power* and more sharing of household burdens.

Lois Hoffman has proposed four explanations for the increased family power of working wives, which convey again some of the power resources connected with breadwinning:

1. Women who work have more control over money, "and this control can be used, implicitly or explicitly, to wield power in the family."
2. "Society attaches greater value to the role of wage earner than to that of housewife and thus legitimizes for both parents the notion that the former should have more power."
3. "An independent supply of money enables the working woman to exert her influence to

---

*This should not imply, however, that women who earn more than their husbands necessarily have superior power, since the subordinate position of women stems from multiple causes.

a greater extent because she is less dependent on her husband and could, if necessary, support herself in the event of the dissolution of the marriage."
4. "Working outside the home provides more social interaction than being a housewife. This interaction has been seen as leading to an increase in the wife's power because of: (a) the development of social skills which are useful in influencing her husband; (b) the development of self-confidence; (c) the greater knowledge of alternative situations that exist in other families; and (d) the more frequent interaction with men, which may result in the feeling that remarriage is feasible."[40]

Not only does the woman's working modify the power relation between husband and wife, it also affects the gender power distribution in the whole family:

> Boys become more dependent and obedient when the mother works, and the masculine side of the family reflects a generally diminished status (L. Hoffman, 1963). By contrast, daughters of working mothers are more independent, self-reliant, aggressive, dominant, and disobedient; in short, they act more like little boys (Siegel, Stolz, et al., 1963).[41]

Power Structure of the "Normal" Family

It is worth noting, in this connection, how sociological definitions of the "normal" family situation and "normal" personality development for sons versus daughters sanction the status quo of male power and female powerlessness. Healthy families are those which produce strong, independent *sons*, ready to take on strong, independent "masculine roles." (Strong, independent daughters are not a goal; they're a symptom of deviance.)

For the proper "masculine" upbringing, boys must have "male role models." What little importance academics have attached to fathers' playing a greater role in child-rearing has been largely motivated by this concern. Boys, brought up by "nurturant" mothers, should have strong male role models available lest they develop "nurturant" personalities. These male role models should be close at hand, but not too actively involved in child-rearing, for

a child whose father performs the mothering functions both tangibly and emotionally while the mother is preoccupied with her career can easily gain a distorted image of masculinity and femininity.[42]

Precisely.

Men Want to Be the Breadwinners

Men have good reason, then, to try to monopolize the job of principal family breadwinner (much as they may appreciate a second income). Husbands' objections to wives' working " . . . stem from feelings that their dominance is undermined when they are not the sole or primary breadwinners."[43] There is also

. . . the feeling of being threatened by women in industry, who are seen as limiting opportunities for men, diminishing the prestige of jobs formerly held only by men, and casting a cold eye on masculine pretensions to vocational superiority.[44]

These feelings are quite justified; as Benson so neatly understates it, "The male fear of competition from women is not based solely on myth."[45]

Where outright forbidding of the wife to work is no longer effective, the continued allocation of child-rearing responsibility to women accomplishes the same end: assuring male domination of the occupational world. Should all other barriers to economic power for women suddenly vanish, child-rearing responsibility would still handicap them hopelessly in economic competition with men.

Of course, children are not just a handy excuse to keep women out of the job market. Most people—male and female—want to have them, and somebody has to rear them. Men naturally prefer that women do it, so that having children need not interfere with their own occupational pursuits.

Since housewife and mother roles are preferred for women, it is considered distasteful and per-

haps dangerous to upgrade their occupational status. Apparently there is a fear of mass defections from maternal responsibility. Perhaps there is also a hidden suspicion that the woman's employment is symptomatic of a subversive attitude toward motherhood.[46]

Both these motives, therefore,—the desire to limit females' occupational activities, and the desire to have children without limiting their own occupational activities—contribute to a male interest in defining child-rearing as exclusively woman's domain. Thus,

. . . there has been consistent social effort to establish as a norm the woman whose vocational proclivities are completely and "naturally" satisfied by childbearing and child-rearing, with the related domestic activities.[47]

One of the controls operating to restrict women's breadwinning activities is the social pressure against mothers who "neglect their children." Where financial need compels mothers with young children to work, their absence from the home is accepted as a "necessary evil." (Welfare departments, however, will generally support mothers of young children without pressuring them to seek work.) In the middle classes, sentiments about male female responsibility are less obscured by immediate economic considerations:

. . . some public disapproval is still directed toward the working mother of young children and the mother who devotes her primary attention to a career; the feeling persists that a mother who creates a full life for herself outside the home may be cheating her children, if not her husband.[48]

Fathers, on the other hand, have public license (in fact, a veritable public duty) to devote primary attention to job or career. Sandra and Daryl Bem have illustrated the existent "double standard" of parental responsibility with the example of a middle-class father who loses his wife:

No matter how much he loved his children, no one would expect him to sacrifice his career in order to stay home with them on a full-time basis—even if he had an independent source of income. No one would charge him with selfishness or lack of parental feeling if he sought professional care for his children during the day.[49]

Men Want Women to Be the Child-Rearers

By propagating the belief that women are the ones who really desire children, men can then invoke a "principle of least interest" that is, because women are "most interested" in children, they must make most of the accommodations and sacrifices required to rear them. Benson says that "fatherhood . . . is less important to men then motherhood is to women, in spite of the fact that maternity causes severe limitations on women's activities."[50] My own version would be that fatherhood is "less important" to men than motherhood is to women *because* child-rearing causes severe limitations on the child-rearer's activities.

In a discussion of barriers to careers for women, Alice Rossi cites some very revealing findings about which sex advocates a more rigid standard of "mothering responsibility":

> On an item reading "Even if a woman has the ability and interest, she should not choose a career field that will be difficult to combine with child-rearing," half of the women but two-thirds of the men agree. Again, although half the women thought it appropriate for a woman to take a part-time job if a child was a preschooler, only onethird of the men approved. A quarter of the men, but only 14% of the women, thought a full-time job should not be taken until the children were "all grown up."[51]

Women too imbibe the ideology of motherhood, but men seem to be its strongest supporters. By insuring that the weight of child-rearing responsibility falls on women's shoulders, they win for themselves the right of "paternal neglect." As Benson observes, "The man can throw himself into his work and still fulfill male obligations at home, mainly because the latter are minimal." Men have "the luxury of more familial disengagement than women"[52]

Of course, men as family breadwinners must shoulder the *financial* burden involved in raising children: they may have to work harder, longer hours, and at jobs they dislike. But even factory workers enjoy set hours, scheduled breaks, vacation days, sick leave, and other union benefits.

To the extent that men *can* select work suited to their interests, abilities, and ambitions, they are in a better position than women arbitrarily assigned to child-rearing. And to the extent that breadwinning gains one the resources discussed earlier (money, status, family power, etc.), financial responsibility is clearly preferable, in power terms, to "mothering" responsibility.

Child-Rearing Responsibility Handicaps Women

From the perspective of women—the more affluent women faced with "mother/career conflict," the poorer women faced with "mother/any job at all conflict"—men possess the enviable option to "have their cake and eat it too": that is, to have children without sacrificing their activities outside the home.

A woman knows that becoming a parent will adversely affect her occupational prospects. "For a period, at least, parenthood means that . . .whatever vocational or professional skills she may possess may become atrophied."[53] During this period of retirement the woman

> . . . becomes isolated and almost totally socially, economically, and emotionally dependent upon her husband . . . . She loses her position, cannot keep up with developments in her field, does not build up seniority . . . . If she returns to work, and most women do, she must begin again at a low-status job and she stays there—underemployed and underpaid.[54]

It is not just during the period of child-rearing that women become economically or professionally disadvantaged vis-à-vis men. Most women's lives have already been constructed in anticipation of that period. "Helpful advice" from family, friends, and guidance counselors, discriminatory practices in the schools and in the job market, steer women toward jobs and interests compatible with a future in child-rearing.

With the assistance of relatives, babysitters, or the few day-care centers that exist, woman can hold certain kinds of jobs while they're raising children (often part-time, generally low-status). Women without husbands, women with pressing financial needs, women who can afford hired help, may work full-time despite the demands of "mothering."* But to an important extent, occupational achievement and child-rearing responsibility are mutually exclusive. A 40-hour work week permits more family involvment than a 72-hour work week did, but it's still difficult to combine with primary responsibility for children (given the lack of institutional assistance). Furthermore, the higher-status professional jobs frequently demand a work-week commitment closer to the 72-hour figure. Men can hold these jobs yet also father families only because they can count on a "helpmeet" to take care of children and home. Without this back-up team of wife/mother's, "something would have to give."

Alice Rossi has suggested that the period of women's lives spent at home rearing children is potentially the peak period for professional accomplishment:

> If we judge from the dozens of researches Harvey Lehman has conducted on the relationship between age and achievement, . . . the most creative work women and men have done in science was completed during the very years contemporary women are urged to remain at home rearing their families. . . . Older women who return to the labor force are an important reservoir for assistants and technicians and the less demanding professions, but only rarely for creative and original contributors to the more demanding professional fields.[56]

The woman who tries to work at home while raising children finds that this is not too practicable a solution. As writer/critic Marya Mannes notes with regard to her own profession:

> The creative woman has no wife to protect her from intrusion. A man at his desk in a room with closed door is a man at work. A woman at a desk in any room is available.[57]

Maintaining the Status Quo

If working hours and career patterns were more flexible, if child-care centers were more widely available, and if "retired mothers" re-entering the work force got special preference rather than unfavorable treatment,* child-rearing wouldn't exact quite so heavy a toll on women's occupational achievement. Because men benefit from the status quo, they ignore, discourage, or actively resist such reform proposals. Alternative arrangements for rearing children, for balancing work commitment with family commitment, are not pressing concerns for men; the structural relegation of women to domestic service suits their interests very well.

Women's responsibility for children in the context of the nuclear family is an important buttress for a male-dominated society. It helps keep women out of the running for economic and political power. As Talcott Parsons states:

> It is, of course, possible for the adult woman to follow the masculine pattern and seek a career in fields of occupational achievement in direct competition with men of her own class. It is, however, notable that in spite of the very great progress of the emancipation of women from the traditional domestic pattern only a very small fraction have gone very far in this direction.** It is also clear that its generalization would only be possible with profound alterations in the structure of the family.[58]

* * * * *

I have chosen to focus upon breadwinning (economic activity) as the most important thing, from a power perspective, that childrearers can't do. However, other activities—educational,*** political, cultural, social, recreational—suffer as well when one's life becomes centered around children and home. The "on call" nature of "mothering" responsibility militates against any kind of sustained, serious commitment to other endeavors. A full-time mother loses

---

*In 1960, 18.6% of mothers with children under six years old were in the labor force in some capacity; 11.4% were working 35 hours or more per week.[55]

*Consider how the re-entry of veterans into the work force is eased by special benefits and preferential treatment.

**One might well inquire what this "very great progress" is, if "only a very small fraction" of women are actually involved.

***Here again, there's been little effort, for the sake of *female* child-rearers, to develop more flexible programs of higher education and professional training.

. . . the growth of competence and resources in the outside world, the community positions which contribute to power in the marriage. The boundaries of her world contract, the possibilities of growth diminish.[59]

While women are occupied with domestic duties, men consolidate their resources in the outside world and their position of command in the family. By the time most women complete their childrearing tenure, they can no longer recoup their power losses.

CHILD-REARING: NOT AN EQUAL SPHERE

By my explicit and implicit comparisons of bread-winning with child-rearing, I have already asserted that the former is the more desirable "sphere" of action. Now I will discuss more directly the disadvantages of the child-rearing job.

Money, Status, Power

Once again, let's begin with the simple but significant matter of money. Money is a prime source of power in American society, and tending one's own children on a full-time basis is not a salaried activity. Margaret Benston has elucidated most effectively the implications of this fact:

> In sheer quantity, household labor, including child care, constitutes a huge amount of socially necessary production. Nevertheless, in a society based on commodity production, it is not usually considered "real work" since it is outside of trade and the market place. . . . In a society in which money determines value, women are a group who work outside the money economy. Their work is not worth money, is therefore valueless, is therefore not even real work. And women themselves, who do this valueless work, can hardly be expected to be worth as much as men, who work for money.[60]

Performing well at the job of child-rearer may be a source of feminine credentials, but it is not a source of social power or status. According to Parsons, of all the possible adult roles for females, "the pattern of domesticity must be

ranked lowest in terms of prestige," although "it offers perhaps the highest level of a certain kind of security."[61] When a woman bears and raises children, therefore, she is fulfilling social expectations and avoiding negative sanctions but she "is not esteemed, in the culture or in the small society of her family, in proportion to her exercise of her 'glory,' childbearing."[62]

The rewards for rearing children are not as tangible as a raise or a promotion, and ready censure awaits any evidence of failure: "if the child goes wrong, mother is usually blamed."[63] Thus the male preference for the breadwinner role may reflect (among other things) an awareness that "it's easier to make money than it is to be a good father. . . . The family is a risky proposition in terms of rewards and self-enhancement."[64]

Family Power

If child-rearers don't accumulate power resources in the outside world, do they at least win some advantage in the family balance of power? I have already cited the evidence that family power is directly related to earning power. Not surprisingly, researchers have also found that the wife's power declines with the arrival of children; an inverse relationship exists between number of children and the wife's power vis-à-vis her husband (Heer, 1958; Blood and Wolfe, 1960; Hoffman and Lippitt, 1960; Campbell, 1967).

There are two major theories of conjugal power which suggest explanations for this effect. Blood and Wolfe's "resource theory" (1960) posits that "power will accrue to the spouse who has the more imposing or relevant resources, and thus has the greater contribution to make to the family."[65] If one considers occupational status and income as the most imposing of resources, then this explanation is little different from the "earning power equals family power" thesis. However, Blood and Wolfe don't illuminate why breadwinning should be a "greater contribution" to the famiy than child-rearing.

David Heer's "exchange value theory" (1963) postulates that "the spouse who could most likely marry another person who would be as desirable as or much more desirable than his (her) present spouse"[66] enjoys the superior power position. When a woman has children and becomes a full-time child-rearer, she grows more dependent on her husband, her opportunities to meet men decrease, and her prospects for remarriage decline. The husband thus possesses the more promising alternatives outside the marriage, and his power increases.

The woman's power is at its lowest point during the "preschool" period, when child-rearing responsibilities are most consuming.

> When her children start school, the mother can be more autonomous and exercise more power because she is better able to handle outside employment; the children can now take care of themselves in many ways and are supervised to a greater extent by the school and other community agencies (Heer, 1963). The mother's gradual resumption of a position of independent influence coincides with her re-emergence from the ceaseless responsibilities of mothering (Blood, 1963), and children do report father as "boss" of the family less often as they grow older (Hess and Torncy, 1962).[67]

Child-Rearing:
Not a Separate Sphere

Despite the empirical evidence that women lose family power when they become mothers, one is still tempted to believe that by leaving child-rearing to women, men have surrendered a significant area of control. This belief is based on the erroneous notion that women preside over child-rearing as a separate sovereign domain. On the contrary, men's authority as family provider/family "head" carries right over into child-rearing matters. Men may have surrendered the regular responsibility and routine decision making, but they retain power where important decisions are concerned (including what the routine will be).

> In a sample of adolescents studied by Charles Bowerman and Glen Elder (1964), the father was reported to be the dominant parent in child-rearing matters as often as the mother, in spite of the fact that mother does most of the actual work; apparently she often finds herself responsible for doing the menial chores without having the stronger voice in "child-rearing policy."[68]

Constantina Safilios-Rothschild (1969) found that American men delegate to their wives many of the minor decisions related to rearing children and running a home—those decisions, the enactment of which involves time-consuming tasks." This suggests to her that

> American husbands do not wish to take on "bothersome" decisions which are not crucial . . . and take too much of the time and energy that they prefer to dedicate to their work or leisure-time activities.[69]

Fathers may default from the daily child-rearing routines, but, much like male principals supervising female teachers, they still tend to wield the ultimate force and the ultimate decision making power. Consider these statements of Benson's on the nature of paternal authority:

> The father as threatener is superimposed upon the mother's more basic pattern and is therefore more likely to appear as a terrorizing intruder, but one who speaks as authority and therefore ought to be obeyed.
> Family members can foresee his judgments and are constrained to act correctly according to their conception of his wishes.
> Even the social pattern that mother establishes is typically legitimized by the larger, more insistent parent lurking in the background. . . . Father is the embodiment of a basic form of social control: coercive power. . . . Father is an agent of both internal and external control, and the child responds to him in terms of both his respect for the man and his respect for the man's power.
> But when order breaks down or is openly challenged the need for a new approach assumes an immediate, deliberative significance, and father is customarily expected to help meet the crisis. In fact, it is common for him to take charge. . . .[70]

Taking care of children, therefore, does not provide women with any real power base. Men can afford to leave child-rearing *responsibility* to women because, given their superior power resources, they are still assured of substantial child-rearing *authority*.

The Nature of the Job

Child-rearing, I have argued, is not a source of money, status, power in the society, or power in the family. The child-rearing job is disadvantageous in terms of these major assets, but there are also drawbacks inherent in the nature of the work itself. The rearing of children "involves long years of exacting labor and self-sacrifice," but

the drudgery, the monotonous labor, and other disagreeable features of child-rearing are minimized by "the social guardians." On the other hand, the joys and compensations of motherhood are magnified and presented to consciousness on every hand. Thus the tendecy is to create an illusion whereby motherhood will appear to consist of compensations only, and thus come to be desired by those for whom the illusion is intended.[71]

The responsibilities of a child-rearer/homemaker are not confined to a 40-hour work week. Margaret Benston estimates that for a married woman with small children (excluding the very rich), "the irreducible minimum of work . . . is probably 70 or 80 hours a week."[72] In addition to the actual hours of work, there is the constant strain of being "on call." Thus, another consideration in why the husband's power is greatest when the children are young "may be the well-described chronic fatigue which affects young mothers with preschoolers."[73]

Furthermore, women are adults (assertions that they have "childlike" natures notwithstanding), and they need adequate adult company to stimulate their mental faculties.

. . . . A lot of women become disheartened because babies and children are not only not interesting to talk to (not everyone thrills at the wonders of da-da-ma-ma talk) but they are generally not empathic, considerate people.[74]

Although interaction with young children is certainly rewarding in many ways, child-rearers can lose touch with the world outside their domestic circle. In addition, American society segregates the worlds of childhood and adulthood; adults who keep close company with children are *déclassé*.

Since the "less-than-idyllic child-rearing part of motherhood remains 'in small print,'"[75] new mothers are often in for some rude shocks. Betty Rollin, in the Skolnick and Skolnick anthology on the family, quotes some mothers interviewed in an Ann Arbor, Michigan study:

Suddenly I had to devote myself to the child totally. I was under the illusion that the baby was going to fit into my life, and I found that I had to switch my life and my schedule to fit *him*. . . .

You never get away from the responsibility. Even when you leave the child with a sitter, you are not out from under the pressure of the responsibility. . . .

I hate ironing their pants and doing their underwear, and they never put their clothes in the laundry basket. . . . Best moment of the day is when all the children are in bed. . . . The worst time of day is 4 P.M., when you have to get dinner started, and the kids are tired, hungry, and crabby—everybody wants to talk to you about *their* day. . . . Your day is only half over.

Once a mother, the responsibility and concern for my children became so encompassing. . . . It took a great deal of will to keep up other parts of my personality. . . .

I had anticipated that the baby would sleep and eat, sleep and eat. Instead, the experience was overwhelming. I really had not thought particularly about what motherhood would mean in a realistic sense. I want to do *other* things, like to become involved in things that are worthwhile—I don't mean women's clubs—but I don't have the physical energy to go out in the evenings. I feel like I'm missing something . . . the experience of being somewhere with people and having them talking about something—something that's going on in the world.[76]

Avoiding the Job

When women are wealthy enough to afford it, they often hire nurses and governesses to relieve them of the more burdensome aspects of child care. They can then enjoy the children's company when they want to, be active mothers when it suits them, but have the constant responsibility and the more unpleasant parts of the job (diapers, tantrums, etc.) off their shoulders.

The relationship between the rich mothers and governess resembles in significant respects the relationship between average father and average mother. The father "hires" the mother (by providing her with support), in the expectation that she will relieve him of the major burdens of child-rearing. (However, even a rich mother is expected to pay a lot more personal attention to her children than any father is.)

From the perspective of an ambitious person, taking fulltime care of your own children is rather like baking your own bread: it might be nice if one had the time, but there are more important things one needs to be doing. Thus you pay for the service of having someone else do it, increasing your financial burden, but freeing yourself of a time-consuming task.

Fathers, with full social support, can buy a significant degree of freedom from direct family responsibility. They have a category of people at hand—women—constrained by social forces to accept that responsibility. Women have no such convenient group to whom they can pass the child-rearing buck. For mothers, the price of escape from child-rearing—financial, social, psychological—is usually too high.

"Motherly Selflessness"

A final relevant feature of the child-rearing job itself is that mothers are obliged to subordinate their personal objectives and practice "selflessness"—putting the needs of others first, devoting themselves to the day-to-day well-being of other family members, loving and giving "unconditionally."* Such domestic service may be deemed virtuous, but it isn't a path to power and success. Males primed for competitive achievement show no eagerness to suppress their personal ambitions and sacrifice their own interests to attend to others' immediate wants.

Furthermore, men desire from women the same services and support, the same ministration to everyday needs, that mothers are supposed to provide for children. ("I want a wife to keep track of the children's doctor and dentist appoint-

ments. And to keep track of mine, too. . . . A wife who will pick up after my children, a wife who will pick up after me."[77]) "Mothering" behavior is not very different from "feminine" behavior. By grooming females for "nurturance," men provide a selfless rearer for their children and an accomodating marriage partner for themselves. Thus:

> Evidence clearly indicates that the wife is more likely than the husband to subordinate her personal desires to family goals (Bowerman, 1957). The woman is called upon to adapt to her husband's life pattern: to the man, his work schedule, where he works, what he does, and to the general proposition that she is a helpmeet. It is the wife, not the husband, who finds marriage accommodation a primary life task (Burgess and Cottrell, 1939). Since we still define the woman as keeper of the family retreat, she develops an accommodative pattern in her relationship with her husband and becomes the expressive, compliant member of the family (Stuckert, 1963).[78]

Several movies and television serials have been constructed around the situation of a father/widower with a son or two, all in need of a "nurturant" woman to take care of them. The fact that children and fathers "compete" for similar services from the mother may explain why the Oedipus Complex is more pronounced than the Electra Complex (if these concepts still have any credibility).[79]

Margaret Adams has discussed the negative effects of this obligatory "selflessness" upon women, under the title of "The Compassion Trap":

> Both family and professional commitments incorporate the insidious notion that the needs of others should be woman's major, if not exclusive, concern. Implicit in the role that derives from this notion is the supposed virtue of subordinating individual needs to the welfare of others and the personal value and supposed reward of vicarious satisfaction from this exercise. . . . Women must abandon the role of the compassionate sibyl who is at everyone's beck and call, because being permanently available to help others keeps women from pursuing their own chosen avocations with the concentration that is essential for their successful completion.[80]

---

*Erich Fromm, in *The Art of Loving*, waxes eloquent about mothers' "unconditional" love.

Men have a stake in insuring that women remain unable to "abandon the role of the compassionate sibyl." They derive double benefit—as husbands wanting wifely services, as fathers wanting child-rearing services—from the "emotional indenture"[81] of women.

More Evidence That Men Don't Want the Job

Despite all the disadvantages of child-rearing responsibility, men often protest that they'd love to be able to stay home with the kids. However, there are two additional sources of evidence that men don't really find the job desirable.

The first relates to the widely noted phenomenon that boys who behave like girls draw stronger negative reactions than girls who behave like boys. A "sissy" playing with dolls elicits unmixed scorn, while an adventurous "tomboy" (as long as she's not too old) gets a certain amount of approval. In over-all social estimation, female activities and traits are not as worthy or desirable as those of males. "The fact that . . . both sexes tend to value men and male characteristics, values, and activities more highly than those of women has been noted by many authorities."[82]

All of this suggests the essential hypocrisy of men who laud female achievements as "different but equal," or who claim they'd gladly switch. Studies have consistently shown that far fewer men than women wish they had been born the opposite sex. The work of women, including most prominently the "nurturing" of children, is socially devalued, and a miniscule number of men have actually taken it on.

The second source of evidence relevant here is the attitude of men toward working with children as a salaried job. The overwhelming majority of people in occupations involving close interaction with children (elementary school teachers,* day-care and nursery school personnel, child welfare workers, etc.) are women. Students of male/female occupational distribution (Bird, 1968; Epstein, 1970) have noted that men monopolize the jobs most desirable in terms of

*The closer children approach to adulthood, the higher the percentage of males teaching them.

prestige, power, and salary, leaving the residue to women. Judging by the statistics, men have not chosen working with children as suitable employment for their sex.

However, as Caroline Bird found in her "Sex Map of the Work World," the "most striking boundary of all is occupational *status.*"[83] Thus, men are willing to enter such "female" fields as children's education at the upper echelons. In 1968, 78% of elementary school *principals* were male.[84] Men dominate the top of the profession of child study[85] and dispense highly professional advice on child-rearing to the actual rearers of children ("Dr. Spock Speaks to Mothers").

Thus, working with children might not be such an unattractive prospect for males, if the rewards (money, status, power) could be made commensurate with their expectations. In fact, there seems to be a current trend toward increased participation of males in elementary education. This development is probably the result of a few different causes: a tight job market; the effect of the draft on male occupational choice; a new concern that men be present in schools as "male role models"[86]; and a general societal shift toward evaluating early childhood as a crucial learning period, and early education as a more important business. If the last factor is the predominant one, then it's possible that the occupation of elementary school teacher could undergo a sex change, with the improvements in salary, benefits, job conditions, etc. that result when males move into female occupations. But even with a radical change in the status of salaried work with children, it is doubtful that unsalaried rearing of children will ever attract many males.

CONCLUSION

The allocation of child-rearing responsibility to women, I have argued, is no sacred fiat of nature, but a social policy which supports male domination in the society and in the family.

Whatever the "intrinsic desirability" of rearing children, the conditions of the job as it's now constituted—no salary, low status, long hours, domestic isolation—mark it as a job for women only. Men, as the superordinate group, don't want child-rearing responsibility, so they assign it to women. Women's functioning as child-rearers reinforces, in turn, their subordinate position. Thus we come back again to the causal model of my Introduction—

Women are the rearers of children

Women are a powerless group vis-à-vis men

—one of the vicious circles which keeps male power intact.

I would very much like to receive feedback from readers. Please write me c/o Sociology Department, U.C. Berkeley, Berkeley, Calif. 94720. Margaret Polatnick.

NOTES

1. Arthur Stinchcombe, *Constructing Social Theories* (New York, 1968), p. 157.
2. See, for example: Caroline Bird, *Born Female;* Cynthia Fuchs Epstein, *Woman's Place;* Kirsten Amundsen, *The Silenced Majority;* Simonde de Beauvoir, *The Second Sex.*
3. Leta S. Hollingworth, "Social Devices for Impelling Women to Bear and Rear Children," *The American Journal of Sociology,* XXII (July, 1916), p. 20.
4. Naomi Weisstein, "Psychology Constructs the Female," in Michele Hoffnung Garskof, *Roles Women Play* (Belmont, Calif., 1971), p. 77.
5. Myron Brenton, *The American Male* (New York, 1966), p. 144.
6. Leonard Benson, *Fatherhood: A Sociological Perspective* (New York, 1968), p. 7.
7. Norman W. Bell & Ezra F. Vogel, eds., *A Modern Introduction to the Family,* Rev. ed. (New York, 1968), p. 32.
8. Anna Freud & Dorothy Burlingham, *Infants Without Families* (New York, 1944), p. ix.
9. John Bowlby, *Maternal Care and Mental Health* (Geneva, 1952), p. 15.
10. Bell & Vogel, *op. cit.,* p. 580.
11. See Shulamith Firestone, *The Dialectic of Sex,* on test-tube babies.
12. Robert F. Winch, *The Modern Family,* Rev. ed. (New York, 1964), p. 451.
13. Ethel Albert, "The Unmothered Woman," in Garskof, *op. cit.,* p. 29.

14. Erik H. Erikson, "Inner and Outer Space: Reflections on Womanhood," in Robert Jay Lifton, ed., *The Woman in America,* 2nd ed. (Boston, 1965), p. 5.
15. Erich Fromm, *The Art of Loving* (New York, 1956), p. 41.
16. Talcott Parsons, Robert F. Bales, *et al., Family, Socialization and Interaction Process* (New York, 1955), p. 18.
17. Webster's New World Dictionary (New York, 1957), p. 1009.
18. Benson, *op. cit.,* p. 249.
19. Parsons, Bales, *et al., op. cit.,* p. 313.
20. Benson, *op. cit.,* p. 65.
21. Quoted in Arlene S. Skolnick & Jerome H. Skolnick, *Family in Transition* (Boston, 1971), p. 12.
22. See bibliography listings under Harry F. Harlow and Bill Seay.
23. Harry F. Harlow, "The Nature of Love," *The American Psychologist,* XIII (Dec., 1958), p. 685.
24. Benson, *loc. cit.*
25. Bill Seay, Bruce K. Alexander, & Harry F. Harlow, "Maternal Behavior of Socially Deprived Rhesus Monkeys," *Journal of Abnormal and Social Psychology,* LXIX (Oct., 1964), p. 353.
26. Brenton, *op. cit.,* pp. 146 & 145.
27. Harriet L. Rheingold, "The Social and Socializing Infant," in David A. Goslin, ed., *Handbook of Socialization Theory and Research* (Chicago, 1969), p. 783.
28. Hollingworth, *op. cit.,* p. 24.
29. Marcia Millman, "Observations on Sex Role Research," *Journal of Marriage and the Family,* XXXIII (Nov., 1971), p. 773.
30. Brenton, *op. cit.,* p. 146.
31. Benson, *op. cit.,* pp. 5–6.
32. Robert K. Merton, *Social Theory and Social Structure* (Glencoe, Ill., 1957), pp. 46–7.
33. Alvin Gouldner, "The Norm of Reciprocity," *American Sociological Review,* XXV (April, 1960), p. 162.
34. Benson, *op. cit.,* p. 120.
35. Kate Millett, *Sexual Politics;* Pat Mainardi, "The Politics of Housework"; Susan Lydon, "The Politics of Orgasm"; Ti-Grace Atkinson, "The Politics of Sexual Intercourse."
36. U.S. Women's Bureau, *1969 Handbook on Women Workers,* p. 35.
37. Reuben Hill & Howard Becker, eds., *Family, Marriage, and Parenthood* (Boston, 1955), p. 790.
38. Talcott Parsons, "Age and Sex in the Social Structure," in Coser, Rose Laub, ed., *The Family: Its Structure and Functions* (New York, 1964), pp. 258, 261–2.

39. For a full report, see Benson, *op. cit.,* pp. 297–305.
40. Lois Wladis Hoffman, "Effects of the Employment of Mothers on Parental Power Relations and the Division of Household Tasks," *Marriage and Family Living,* XXII (Feb., 1960), p. 33.
41. Benson, *op. cit.,* pp. 302–3.
42. Bell & Vogel, *op. cit.,* p. 586.
43. Phyllis Hallenback, "An Analysis of Power Dynamics in Marriage," *Journal of Marriage and the Family,* XXVIII (May, 1966), p. 201.
44. Helen Mayer Hacker, "The New Burdens of Masculinity," *Marriage and Family Living,* XIX (Aug., 1957), p. 232.
45. Benson, *op. cit.,* p. 293.
46. *Ibid.*
47. Hollingworth, *op. cit.,* p. 20
48. Benson, *op. cit.,* p. 292.
49. Sandra L. Bem & Daryl J. Bem, "Training the Woman to Know Her Place," in Garskof, *op. cit.,* p. 94.
50. Benson, *loc. cit.*
51. Alice S. Rossi, "Barriers to the Career Choice of Engineering, Medicine, or Science Among American Women," in Jacquelyn A. Mattfeld & Carol G. Van Aken, eds., *Women and the Scientific Professions* (Cambridge, Mass., 1965), p. 87.
52. Benson, *op. cit.,* pp. 132 & 134.
53. Winch, *op. cit.,* p. 434.
54. Dair L. Gillespie, "Who Has the Power? The Marital Struggle," *Journal of Marriage and the Family,* XXXIII (Aug., 1971), p. 456.
55. U.S. Bureau of the Census, *Statistical Abstract of the U.S.: 1971,* Table 332, and *U.S. Census of Population: 1960, Subject Reports: Families,* Table 11.
56. Rossi, *op. cit.,* pp. 102–3, 107.
57. Quoted in Betty Rollin, "Motherhood: Who Needs It?" in Skolnick & Skolnick, *op. cit.,* p. 352.
58. Parsons, *op. cit.,* pp. 258–9.
59. Gillespie, *loc. cit.*
60. Margaret Benston, "The Political Economy of Women's Liberation," in Garskof, *op. cit.,* p. 196.
61. Parsons, *op. cit.,* p. 261.
62. Judith Long Laws, "A Feminist Review of Marital Adjustment Literature," *Journal of Marriage and the Family,* XXXIII (Aug., 1971), p. 493.
63. Benson, *op. cit.,* p. 12.
64. Brenton, *op. cit.,* p. 133.
65. Benson, *op. cit.,* p. 149.
66. Constantina Safilios-Rothschild, "The Study of Family Power Structure: A Review 1960–1969," *Journal of Marriage and the Family,* XXXII (Nov., 1970), p. 548.
67. Benson, *op. cit.,* p. 152.
68. *Ibid.,* p. 157.
69. Safilios-Rothschild, "Family Sociology or Wives' Family Sociology?" *Journal of Marriage and the Family,* XXXI (May, 1969), p. 297.
70. Benson, *op. cit.,* pp. 14, 18, 50–2, 59.
71. Hollingworth, *op. cit.,* pp. 20–1, 27.
72. Benston, *op. cit.,* p. 199.
73. Hallenbeck, *op. cit.,* p. 201.
74. Rollin, *op. cit.,* p. 353.
75. *Ibid.,* p. 349.
76. *Ibid.*
77. Judy Syfers, "Why I Want a Wife," in *Notes From the Third Year* (New York, 1971), p. 13.
78. Benson, *op. cit.,* pp.134–5.
79. See Firestone, *The Dialectic of Sex,* for an excellent analysis of these Complexes in power terms.
80. Margaret Adams, "The Compassion Trap," *Psychology Today,* V (Nov., 1971), pp. 72, 101.
81. *Ibid.,* p. 100.
82. Jo Freeman, "The Social Construction of the Second Sex," in Garskof, *op. cit.,* p. 126 (references included).
83. Caroline Bird, *Born Female* (New York, 1968), p. 101.
84. Cynthia Fuchs Epstein, *Woman's Place* (Berkeley, Calif., 1971), p. 10.
85. Bird, *op. cit.,* p. 102.
86. See Patricia Sexton, *The Feminized Male.*

7

Age Stratification

Edward Ransford

ALTHOUGH THE study of age groups has long been an important area in sociology, the study of age stratification is very new, beginning in the last few years under the impetus of the works by Riley, Johnson, Foner, and others (Riley, 1971; Riley, Johnson and Foner, 1972; Foner, 1974). Age strata divide people into groups in a manner similar to class strata. An age stratum is composed of people of about the same age who share the attendant life circumstances of that age.

Of crucial importance is the fact that people in different age strata have differential access to power, privilege, and prestige. This fact relates age differences to the broader concept of stratification, or structured inequality. The age stratification differs from other stratification systems in that the distribution of power, privilege, and prestige is curvilinear, not as are class, ethnic, and sex stratification—linear. That is, the very young and the very old are the most powerless and underprivileged age strata, whereas the middle strata—young adults and the middle aged—have the most access to power, privilege, and prestige (see Figure 7–1).

The Life Cycle and Power, Privilege, and Prestige

The curvilinear pattern of the distribution of power, privilege, and prestige in age stratification corresponds to the life cycle (see Figure 7–1). Children have no formal power and few privileges compared to other age groups. Although children are not competent to enter into some of the affairs of adult society (they cannot vote or drive a car), they experience control and domination in many institutional areas where they are competent to have some voice in decision making. For example, in the area of education, children have few choices in the subject matter and the methods by which they are taught. Children are expected to conform to adult-oriented curricula that often do not

An asterisk (˚) accompanying a citation indicates a selection that is included in this volume.

233

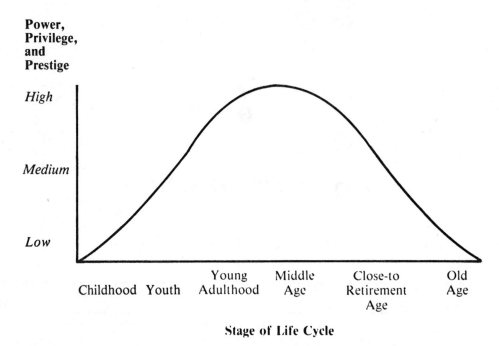

Figure 7-1.   *Distribution of Power, Privilege, and Prestige by Age*

allow for individual developmental patterns or do not fit learning styles and areas of competence. Children often are spoken to in a patronizing manner and experience invasions of privacy. Children daily face groups of powerful adults—teachers, parents, and counselors—who determine their lives and destinies.

> Children have been treated paternally; their conduct has been controlled by parents or others in authority. Such control has been justified in the paternalist view, by the need to protect children from themselves and others. It is argued that children cannot be responsible for their own welfare because by their nature they lack an adequate conception of their present and future interests. They are said to want instant gratification and to be incapable of fully rational decisions (Worsfold, 1974:142).

During adolescence, young people are given increasingly more access to power and privilege. Adolescents are physically larger and stronger and can counter parental force and manipulation with their own strategies. Ultimately, they have the strength and resources to leave the family unit if the home situation becomes intolerable. Although few adolescents run away from home, the fact that some do leave the home illustrates ⋅dramatically their increased independence. More commonly, young people remain in their families and turn to the peer group as a major source of power. As described later in this section, the peer group provides a separate social world with its own norms of achievement and status that increase the autonomy of the adolescent.

Young adults, by securing a job, move into the institutional arena of power and privilege. With a job, a person for the first time can claim a certain amount of authority by virtue of his or her position in an occupational hierarchy. Privileges such as voting, drinking, and property ownership also are granted to the young adult.

Middle-aged persons (of forty to sixty years of age) ordinarily reach the highest point of power and privilege in the life cycle. At this stage in their lives, they usually reach the top positions of their occupation and accordingly command a high degree of legitimate authority over others. They are often accorded special opportunities and deference because of their higher occupational position. It should be pointed out, however, that these generalizations apply mainly to white males in white-collar jobs. Women, minority persons, and blue-collar workers often do not reach a peak of power and privilege in their middle years. These people usually hold jobs with early ceilings such that their earnings, authority, autonomy, and special job privileges are no greater than when they were young adults.

When a person reaches the aged stratum, he or she is stripped of formal power and peak earnings as a result of forced retirement. Older people experience a decline in stratification rewards not only because retirement forces them to sever organizational links and lose the related income, but also because old age *per se* is not highly valued in the contemporary United States. Old age is believed to be associated with a decline in physical attractiveness, energy, good health, sexual prowess, and flexibility in thought. In other cultures, and in other historical periods, age may be associated with positive characteristics such as maturity and wisdom. The status of the aged appears to decline in highly industrialized, technocratic societies in which the types of knowledge and skills needed for occupational success are constantly changing.

A person also loses status as he or she reaches old age simply because of the expectation of fewer years left for life itself.

> The inescapable fact of human mortality forces all other aspects of ranking to fade into lesser significance when evaluated in relation to life itself. Stating it boldly and simply, almost all peoples when asked to rank the dimensions of stratification—income, possessions, education, prestige, political power, honor—would choose extension of life over these other traits (Streib, 1976:162).

In the last years of life, some older people are confined to total institutions such as nursing homes. In a total institution, the individual is isolated from society and from the competing bonds of other institutions or groups (Goffman, 1961). The institution has total control over the individual; every part of his or her life is under surveillance. The person is totally dependent, even for the satisfaction of his or her physical needs. In total institutions, the past statuses of a person are ignored. Positions in which the person had group recognition and personal pride are disregarded. Life in nursing homes usually means an extreme loss of power, autonomy, and self-respect for the aged person.

Age and the Very Rich and Powerful

Generalizations about the loss of prestige, power, and privilege among the aged should be carefully qualified. Although most of the aged experience a decline in one or more of these stratification rewards, there is also a concentration of great wealth and power among a small number of the aged. The average age of the very richest segment of our population is about sixty-five (Louis, 1968). In a capitalistic society, successful persons are able to accumulate great wealth but it usually takes a number of years to do so. People in their fifties, sixties, and seventies have had ample time to reap the rewards of successful investment and capital-building activities.

It is also true that a small segment of the aged hold many of the most important and powerful offices in government. The seniority system practiced in most legislatures and in the United States Congress allows senior state legislators, congressmen, and senators to exercise more than their share of influence. "Inasmuch as elective officials are not subject to any formal retirement process except by the will of the electorate, some aged persons are able to exercise disproportionate power" (Streib, 1976:166). The aged stratum, then, contains extremes of power and wealth. For most aged persons there is a sharp decline in income, prestige, and formal authority, yet a small number of the aged are the richest and most powerful persons in the country.

We have presented a general overview of how age is related to the distribution of power, privilege, and prestige. A more specific discussion of relationships follows. Included will be (1) age stratification between parents and children as an example of the power dimension, (2) the objective loss and perceived loss of privileges among older Americans, and (3) how some of the aged maintain prestige after retirement.

THE PARENT-CHILD RELATIONSHIP AND AGE STRATIFICATION

The Functional Explanation

One of the most basic examples of stratification between age groups is the relationship between parents and children. The functional and conflict schools lead to very different interpretations of this interaction between age strata. To a marked degree, the literature on parent-child interaction has been heavily weighted toward functionalism. Functional theory emphasizes the process of childhood socialization; that is, the process by which a child acquires the culture of a society. The new-born child is often viewed as a "barbarian invader"—a child who is unaware of the sacred traditions and rules of the culture (Linton, 1936). Socialization is first and foremost a study of conformity. The growing child becomes aware of cultural norms and must increasingly conform to these norms to receive positive reinforcement from parents.

In the first stage of socialization, a child learns that not all of his or her actions are received by others in the same way. Even before a child learns verbal language, parents can communicate extreme displeasure by facial expression, tone of voice, and stance. The child values parental approval as a part of his or her gratification package. In order to receive full gratification, a child learns that he or she must maximize certain behaviors and minimize others. This is an extremely important step because the child has "come to care about norms" (Bredemeier and Stephenson, 1962:65). By so doing, a child enters the adult world of "shoulds" and "should nots."

Conformity achieved by parental approval is only the beginning of socialization. Functionalists have borrowed from the symbolic interaction tradition to explain more completely why children conform to societal norms. Drawing from the works of Cooley (1922) and Mead (1934)—well-known interactionists—functionalists explain that culture is internalized at a deeper level when it is connected with self-image and conscience. A child's self-image and conscience (that is, feelings of guilt) develop only through social interaction with other members of society. A girl, for example, begins to see herself (as bright or slow) as she perceives how others define her. This is what Cooley referred to as the "looking-glass self"—the self-image as a reflection of the definitions of others.

The concept of a conscience is closely related. A child is taught certain norms with such consistency and moral overtones that if transgression occurs, he or she feels a sense of discomfort or guilt independent of discovery by others. Mead notes that conscience develops especially as a child "takes the role of the other." For example, a girl stands outside herself and judges her actions according to how she thinks some authority figure would behave in the same situation. If she fails to live up to this role model, she will experience guilt.

Self-image and conscience add a strong additional motivation for conformity in the sense that the child is now conforming to maximize his or her self-image and to avoid guilt. Conformity becomes much more certain if the socializers' criteria can be put inside the child "so that they become the standards by which he assesses himself" (Bredemeier and Stephenson, 1962:67). Functionalism has borrwed interactionist concepts (self image, conscience) but has left out the interactionist emphasis on individual initiative. Interactionists argue that: 1) culture is not deterministic; 2) individuals have some freedom of choice to take on different roles; and 3) culture is often internally inconsistent, allowing for some freedom of choice. In short, interactionists see the likelihood for individuals to innovate within a cultural context.

The result of successful childhood socialization is a young person who has internalized a significant portion of the culture; who will defend widely shared values and beliefs, conform to society's most important norms, and competently play a variety of social roles. From a functional point of view, socialization makes possible an organized society with some degree of value consensus and normative order. Although there is validity to the functional viewpoint on childhood and socialization, there are many omissions.

In the first place, functionalism places all the emphasis on adult values. Children are not seen as having cognitive and emotional capacities of their own. The exercise of parental will is seen as right and legitimate, since parents possess culture or simply have more experience. Under the process of socialization described by functional theory, unequal power and coercion is ignored. Whether or not parents use physical punishment or withhold their love to control their children, in the last analysis they are a more powerful stratum exerting their will on a relatively powerless stratum. Conflict theory, however, tells us that it is rare for one stratum of any hierarchy to control another completely. Rather, certain resources are available to each stratum and a negotiation or struggle is likely as each side attempts to use these resources to further its ends. Following this line of reasoning, "the socialization of the child, even in infancy, is not simply an imposition of the parent's culture . . . upon the child, but a negotiated product which can change as the resources available to the parties change" (Collins, 1975:260).

A Power-Conflict Approach to Age Stratification

A conflict perspective of age stratification views both parents and children as employing age resources in their transactions with one another. Although parents possess most of the power initially, the equation becomes more balanced as children enter their teens. Essentially, parents have resource advantages in 1) being there first and 2) having greater size and strength. Parents have already accumulated benefits and resources that put the younger generation at a disadvantage. Those who hold power (parents) are able to organize behavior and set up communication networks that reinforce and institutionalize their control. Size and strength, Collins's second parental resource, is a rather obvious one; physical punishment of children is often the ultimate technique used to maintain adult control. Physical punishment can always be used as a last resort, but many parents use other control techniques such as withholding of love and control by rewards.

Children also have resources, although they differ greatly by age. A very young child has only his or her attractiveness and the capacity to annoy or pester adults by crying or behaving in obtrusive ways. One of the best resources for children is the "direct pleasure they can give to adults as pets" (Collins, 1975:266). If a child is viewed as cute or clever, he or she can engage in a great deal of manipulation of adults.

Children age six to puberty acquire a new resource—the peer group. Childhood peer groups tend to reduce the dependence of children on adults. The peer group offers emancipation of children from their parents by providing alternative pathways for esteem in the form of prowess in athletics, fighting, and social popularity.

Beyond the age of puberty, children develop considerable resources of their own. Consider the following statement by Collins on the resources of teenage young persons:

> Depending on the individual, many reach the borderline at which they can no longer be physically coerced; all become better in some degree at fighting back or running away. They also begin to acquire full mobility and capacity to support themselves depending on the type of economy. In addition, they become sexually active; in many cases they are at or near their height of sexual attractiveness. Given this shift in the balance of resources, it is not surprising that the teenage years are ones of tremendous conflicts with adults to the extent that the latter do not allow adolescents to be inducted into at least the initial privileges of adult life, but attempt to maintain childhood controls over them (Collins, 1975:274).

Recently, undercurrents of change within the society have been acting to eliminate this power struggle, movements that aim to reduce or at least to question extreme inequality between parents and children. Our culture no longer adheres so strenuously to such maxims as "spare the rod and spoil the child" or "children are to be seen and not heard." Many children today are expected to be independent, innovative, scientifically questioning, logical thinkers in order to function in a fast-changing, complex industrial society. Childrearing experts such as Thomas Gordon encourage parents and children to listen to one another with respect and to work out solutions democratically, solutions that are agreeable to both—the "no win-no lose" method (Gordon, 1970). A Bill of Rights for children has been proposed (Farson,* 1974). There are new laws to protect people who inform government agencies about parental child abuse; there are public and private centers for child protection; and programs aimed at reducing the battered-child syndrome. The issue of children's rights has appeared most recently in divorce court proceedings. Some attorneys argue that children have a right to appear at custody trials, to be represented by their own lawyer, and to state with which parent they would most like to live.

"Alternative" schools and curriculum experts in the field of education have espoused child-oriented (versus adult-oriented) programs in which children help plan and choose areas of study most meaningful to them, and in which parents and teachers are urged to have faith in children's inherent abilities to learn.

Also flourishing, however, are other recent child-rearing techniques that disguise, but are still concerned with, parental control: Dreikurs's advice to parents to allow children to "experience the consequences of their actions" often means that parents manipulate the consequences—for example, by denying food to children who arrive late to the dinner table (Dreikurs, 1964; Brown, 1976).

In many communities, there are enrollment waiting lists for fundamental schools that emphasize the "3 R's" and stringent conformity to adult-made rules. Fundamental schools and parent training courses on "how to get your children to do what you want them to do" indicate that the long-standing system of stratification between parents and children is alive and well; but adult-child relations are coming under greater scrutiny and possibly are leading toward partial equalization.

PRIVILEGE AND THE AGED

As stated earlier, privilege refers to rights, opportunities, services, and immunities accorded to certain strata. Privileges often are closely related to wealth or to class position since they are most easily obtained with money. This is especially true for the aged. At retirement and in the years following, the aged often experience a significant decline in opportunities and services such as health care, adequate housing, legal care, and mobility, primarily because of a loss in income. The income or class position of the aged therefore bears directly on the privileges they enjoy in society.

Income of the Aged

Duberman (1976:271) reports that 54 percent of older couples have incomes that are less than half of what they were when the couples were in their middle years. In 1973, the median income for families in which the head of the household was over sixty-five years old was only $6,435—compared to $13,448 when the family head was fifty-five to sixty-four years old (Bureau of Census, Series P–23, No. 57). Of course the demands on family income may not be as great for an older couple as they are for a middle-aged couple who must make house payments, support children, and so forth. But older people also face expenses peculiar to their stage in the life cycle, such as more frequent medical and dental costs. Even if the family members are in good health, $6,435 is a very low income for these inflationary times. Moreover, this is a median income, which means that 50 percent of all aged families were living on less than $6,435.

Turning to poverty data, we can note that one of every six persons (persons, not families) over sixty-five, or 16 percent, were living below the poverty level in 1973. However, there are major income variations among the aged that are not revealed by this figure. Among aged black persons, 37 percent live in poverty—more than double the 16 percent national average. Women over sixty-five are more likely than men to have incomes below the poverty level—19 percent of women compared to 12 percent of men. Older persons living in non-metropolitan areas were more likely to be classified as poor than metropolitan residents—23 percent compared to 13 percent. (Bureau of Census, Series P–23, No. 57).

One particular category of individuals lives on very low incomes. Persons living alone or with nonfamily members are classified as "unrelated individuals" by the Census Bureau. In 1973, the median income for "unrelated" elderly persons was only $3,087 for men and $2,642 for women. About 75 percent of these persons lived entirely on Social Security income (Bureau of Census, Series P–23, No. 57). The problems of loneliness and isolation, poor diet, and inadequate medical care are especially acute for this segment of the aged population. There has been a large increase in the number of poor elderly persons living alone in the central city areas (see chapter 8 of this text and the article by Clark*, 1971).

The great majority of older people must rely on inadequate Social Security payments and pension plans that too often have a smaller return than the worker anticipated. In some cases, a pension fund has not been carefully managed or in many other cases a firm is no longer in business. A labor department official made these comments about the pension plans of private enterprise:

> In all too many cases the pension promise shrinks to this: If you remain in good health and stay with the same company until you are sixty-five years old, and if the company is still in business, and if your department has not been abolished, and if you haven't been laid off for too long a period, and if there is enough money in the fund, and if that money has been prudently managed, you will get a pension (quoted in Schultz, 1970:39).

How the Aged Perceive Their Loss of Income. Objectively, most of the aged suffer a loss in income; at the subjective level, recent studies indicate that many older people do not feel deprived. Streib (1976) reports that many people say they do not worry more about money after they retire. "In answer to the question 'Do you consider your present income enough to meet your living expenses,' from 60 to 87 percent of the different age cohorts said that it was enough despite the fact that their income was about half its previous level" (Streib, 1976:163). Even in a study of old-age assistance recipients (Tissue, 1972), as many as one-third of the respondents receiving $200 or less a month reported that they had no serious financial problems. (However, many others in this aged poor sample did express economic hardship.)

How is it possible that a significant number of the aged do not feel economically pinched? A number of factors appear to buffer the loss of income and allow many of the aged to define their situations as "getting along quite well."

First, many elderly persons have accumulated goods and possessions that allow them to maintain a particular life style. They own their own homes, have accumulated favorite pieces of furniture, drive their cars less, and in general have fewer consumer needs (Streib, 1976:164).

Second, the ideologies and beliefs surrounding retirement and reduced income do not define either circumstance as social injustice or a violation of civil rights. Rather, retirement seems to be viewed by society as a legitimate form of unemployment, and retirees are expected to get along on less (Kasschau, 1977). Many older people may have internalized these beliefs and consequently reduce their expectations.

Third, there may be a shift in reference groups. Many aged persons no longer compare themselves with employed persons, but on retirement, compare themselves with other retirees. In shifting reference groups, these retired persons may feel relatively well off compared to others in their age stratum.

Finally, aging may be regarded as a kind of career (Bengtson, 1975). Completing small tasks such as trips to the market, or raking the leaves, to the elderly become sources of personality integration and pride. "Meaning is provided by the sense that each day is lived autonomously in the community, with independence, dignity, alertness and control over one's faculties and mobility" (Bengtson, 1975:60).

Health Services and Mobility

Older people also suffer a loss of privileges in the sense of health services and mobility. The aged are much more likely than younger groups to have chronic illnesses such as heart disease, arthritis, or paralysis and, accordingly, may have to curtail drastically such activities as travel or driving a car. The Census Bureau reports that in 1972, 3.5 million persons, or about 18 percent of those sixty-five and over had some kind of limitation on their mobility because of a chronic condition. "About three out of every 10 of these persons had a limitation sufficiently severe to keep them confined to the house, and the remainder, though able to leave the house, needed the assistance of another person or aid such as a wheelchair" (Bureau of Census, Series P–23, No. 57:45).

Although older people are more likely to develop chronic illnesses, they have less money to spend on medical care and nutrition. "Medicare was designed to help older people finance their illnesses and almost everyone over sixty-five is eligible. However, Medicare is useful for short term health care rather than for chronic debilitating illnesses to which the old are more prone" (Duberman, 1976:275).

Older people with more chronic illnesses may have little or no means of transportation to health care facilities and have lower incomes with which to pay for increased health care. Older people with adequate incomes, who are able to live in private retirement communities, may find the near-by medical practices charge much more for services when compared to equivalent care that is available to the general population. For example, doctors and dentists who establish offices adjoining retirement communities may urge elderly patients to undergo surgeries and dental work (full-mouth dentures and gold fillings) that doctors located outside retirement communities seldom recommend for elderly patients. It appears that some medical practices are established in retirement communities to take advantage of the relatively immobile, powerless aged population in much the same way that some merchants establish businesses in ethnic ghettos.

Privilege and the Perception of Discrimination Among the Aged

An important aspect of the concept of privilege is the degree to which the people comprising a statum feel they have been unjustly treated in the distribution of services; that is, the degree to which they perceive discrimination and feel their rights are being violated. In general, older Americans have been much less likely to define their situation as one of exclusion and discrimination and have been less likely to engage in social protest than have ethnic minorities and women. Kasschau (1977) explains why the aged do not feel discriminated against.

First, middle-aged and older persons often try to deny their age and to appear younger (*see* Nelson and Nelson,[*] 1974). "An individual's reluctance to label a particular experience as discriminatory on the basis of his age . . . may simply reflect the individual's reluctance to define himself as old or past the prime of his life" (Kasschau, 1977:731). In many ways this explanation parallels the ethnic literature on passing. For example, Mexican Americans and American Indians who are light-skinned and in other features Caucasian in appearance may attempt to pass or blend into the white majority to escape minority-group stigma and discrimination. Such persons are not likely to be activists in ethnic causes. In a similar way, older Americans may attempt to stay young in appearance and to spend time with a younger age cohort in order to avoid the stigma of being old. This denial of age means that the person avoids all action on behalf of the aged stratum and is likely to deny that high degrees of age discrimination exist.

Second, Kasschau (1977) notes that the legal system has less clearly and consistently defended the civil rights of older Americans than it has those of ethnic minorities. Few laws exist that specifically protect the rights of older Americans, and the few that do exist, such as the Age Discrimination in Employment Act, sanction mandatory retirement, although many older workers strongly oppose mandatory retirement. This law that is designed to protect older workers against discrimination is the same law that also is discriminatory in terms of forced retirement and an individual's right to work. "Such mismatched legal and social definitions of the older Americans' civil rights may discourage older workers from seeking legal recourse for any violation of their civil rights . . ." (Kasschau, 1977:731).

And third, the mass media have paid far less attention to age discrimination than to discrimination based on ethnicity or sex. At the peak of the civil rights movement in the mid-1960s, Americans were dramatically presented the discrepancy between the American creed and the reality of racist, segregationist practices. The march on Washington, the Selma march, firehoses being used to stop civil rights demonstrators—all dramatically etched in the public mind the realities of racial discrimination. For the aged, there are no landmark cases that have captured mass media coverage. The power of the mass media for heightening public awareness of discrimination and for legitimizing efforts to do away with that discrimination has not focused on the aged. For these reasons, the aged have been less likely to define their situation as unjust. Few people today would openly endorse discrimination against blacks or Chicanos, yet many see nothing wrong in a society that persistently favors middle-aged and young adults over youth and the aged (Palmore and Manton, 1973).

AGE STRATIFICATION AND THE MAINTENANCE OF PRESTIGE

Becoming old in the United States generally means experiencing a loss in prestige. The aged "have no place in a society which stresses youth, beauty, skills, talent, work, and ambition" (Duberman, 1976:269). However, Streib (1976) maintains that there are more opportunities for older persons to retain some prestige than to retain power or privilege.

Prestige, or status, is conferred by status groups such as social clubs, fraternities, and other associations. The older person who belongs to such a group does not lose honor simply because he or she is older, retired, or less active in the group. Once a person becomes a group member, he or she retains the affiliation for life. Those people who have attained a high degree of prestige by virtue of educational or occupational achievement also may retain a considerable amount of prestige in their older years. Well-known doctors, judges, lawyers, and professors continue to be recognized by their former occupations and are often given special honors and consultantships.

Another expression of status or prestige is style of life—one's education, tastes, neighborhood, and cultural preferences. Some people can suffer a marked decline in income while retaining the same style of life. They may live in the same neighborhood, have the same friends, and attend the same cultural events (Streib, 1976:165). The ability to retain a degree of social honor or to maintain a life style may be extremely important to the self-image of the older person. When income, power, health, and mobility decline, the ability to retain some social honor may be highly significant for personality integration and a sense of well-being.

Retirement communities may contribute to the continuity of prestige for some of the aged. It has been argued that retirement communities act as a protective shield against loss of status in the society (Streib, 1976:172). The aged may feel some status loss when they are forced to compare themselves with youth or with "productive" members of society in the work world. Retirement communities act as a buffer against such comparisons (Streib, 1976:172).

> Within the retirement community, the residents interact principally with those in the same situation. They do not need to envy those who go off to work each day. They do not need to keep up with younger people who are full of ambition and vigor. They do not need to receive pity when they slow down. They can enjoy leisure without feeling abnormal, for all of the residents are in the same situation. Generally, they have a positive viewpoint of their status, when surrounded by persons who have experienced the same role losses (Streib, 1976:172).

SUMMARY

Age can be viewed as one basis for social stratification. The aged and children in particular have little access to power, privilege, and prestige. Older people and children share an important characteristic: both are judged to be incompetent to run the important affairs of society.

Relations between adults and children are based on structured inequality. Parents, teachers, and other adults have the superior size, strength, organizational resources, and ability to control children. A variety of control techniques are used by parents and teachers from behavior modification and withdrawal of love to physical punishment. But adults are not completely powerful and children are not completely powerless. Collins's (1975) theory of age stratification is important because children as well as adults are seen as having power resources, and the resource equation changes as the child gets older. Adults and children are involved in negotiations and children use the resources available to them. Although adults clearly have a power advantage over young children, the equation becomes much more balanced as children reach their teens.

Some of the aged are very rich and powerful, but forced retirement brings greatly reduced incomes and authority over others to the majority of older people. Old age means reduced levels of power, privilege, and prestige not only because of a loss in financial resources, but also because old age itself is devalued by society. Apart from money and power, the aged are stigmatized in American society because of a presumed loss in competence, energy, and physical attractiveness. Although the aged lose power and income, they may successfully retain some degree of prestige or social honor by continued participation in cliques, clubs, and organizations, or by retaining their life style.

REFERENCES

Bengtson, Vern L. 1975. "The Social and Cultural Contexts of Aging: Implications for Social Policy." Progress Report to National Science Foundation. Los Angeles: Andrus Gerontology Center, University of Southern California.

Bredemeier, Harry C. & Richard M. Stephenson. 1962. *The Analysis of Social Systems.* New York: Holt, Rinehart.

Brown, Catherine Caldwell. 1976. "It Changed My Life." *Psychology Today* (November): 47–57, 108–112.

Bureau of the Census. 1974. "Social and Economic Characteristics of the Older Population, 1974." *Current Population Reports,* Series P-23, No. 57.

Clark, Margaret. 1971 "Patterns of Aging Among the Elderly Poor of the Inner City." *The Gerontologist* (Spring) Part II: 58–65.

Collins, Randall. 1975. *Conflict Sociology.* San Francisco: Academic Press.

Cooley, Charles Horton. 1922. *Human Nature and the Social Order.* New York: Charles Scribner and Sons.

Dreikurs, Rudolph. 1964. *Children: The Challenge.* New York: Hawthorn Books, Inc.

Duberman, Lucile. 1976. *Social Inequality: Class and Caste in America.* Philadelphia: Lippincott.

Farson, Richard. 1974. "Birthrights: A Children's Bill of Rights."*Ms.* 2 (March): 67–69, 71, 94–95.

Foner, Ann. 1974. "Age Stratification and Age Conflict in Political Life." *American Sociological Review* 39 (April): 187–198.

Goffman, Erving. 1961. "On the Characteristics of Total Institutions." In Erving Goffman (ed.), *Asylums.* Garden City, N.Y.: Anchor.

Gordon, Thomas. 1970. P.E.T.: *Parent Effectiveness Training.* Signet.

Kasschau, Patricia. 1977. "Age and Race Discrimination Reported by Middle-Aged and Older Persons." *Social Forces* 55 (March): 728–742.

Linton, Ralph. 1936. *The Study of Man.* New York: Appleton-Century-Crofts.

Louis, Arthur M. 1968. "America's Centimillionaires." *Fortune* 77: 152–157.

Mead, George Herber. 1934. *Mind, Self and Society.* Chicago: University of Chicago Press.

Nelson, E. & E. N. Nelson. 1974. "Age Passing." Revised version of a paper originally presented at the 67th Annual Meeting of the American Sociological Association, 1972. (Included in this volume.)

Palmore, E. B. & K. Manton. 1973. "Ageism Compared to Racism and Sexism." *Journal of Gerontology* 28 (July): 363–96.

Riley, Matilda White. 1971. "Social Gerontology and the Age Stratification of Society." *Gerontologist* 11: 79–87.

Riley, Matilda W., M. Johnson & Ann Foner. 1972. *Aging and Society: A Sociology of Age Stratification,* Volume 3. New York: Russell Sage Foundation.

Schultz, James H. 1970. "Pension Aspects of the Economics of Aging: Present and Future Roles of Private Pensions." Report to the Special Committee on Aging, U. S. Senate, January 1970.

Streib, Gordon F. 1976. "Social Stratification and Aging" in Robert H. Binstock & Ethel Shanas (eds.), *Handbook of Aging and the Social Sciences*. New York: D. Van Nostrand.

Tissue, Thomas. 1972. "Old Age and the Perception of Poverty." *Sociology and Social Research* 56: 331–344.

Worsfold, Victor L. 1974. "A Philosophical Justification for Children's Rights." *Harvard Educational Review.* 44 (February): 142–157.

Social Gerontology and the Age Stratification of Society[1]

Matilda White Riley[2]

ONE DECADE after "the" White House Conference, and on the eve of another, the Gerontological Society and all of us involved in research in this field can survey with satisfaction the amount of information accumulated in these 10 years and the impact of this information upon professional practice, public policy, and popular attitudes. That much remains to be done is patent to all gerontologists, but that the title of this symposium is "Research Goals and Priorities in Gerontology" suggests that we have reached a point where we can pick and choose among alternative strategies.

What we propose as a high priority for the future is a sociology of age stratification. Gerontologists working in the social science fields have amassed a remarkable body of facts on two main topics: being old and growing old.[3] Our immediate aim is not so much to add to these facts and ideas as to look at them from a fresh perspective. This perspective emphasizes not just old age, but all the age strata in the society as a whole; it emphasizes not just aging, but also the societal processes and changes that affect aging and the state of being old.

What do we mean by age *stratification,* which is only now emerging as a new field of sociology? A comparison with the well-established sociology of class stratification is provocative. In that field, two concepts, heuristically stimulating as analogues to our concepts of age strata and aging, have demonstrated their power in explaining diverse social phenomena. These concepts are *social class* (variously defined in terms of inequality of income, prestige, or power) and *social mobility* (consisting of upward or downward movement between lower and higher classes). These concepts of social class and social mobility, which any one of us can grasp intuitively from first-hand experience, have proved scientifically useful in defining and suggesting answers to many important questions. We shall list four sets of these questions briefly, as they may stimulate us to find answers to similar questions in relation to age and aging.

From "Social gerontology and the age stratification of society," by Matilda White Riley, *The Gerontologist,* Spring, 1971, Part I, pp. 79–87. By permission of *The Gerontologist* and the Gerontological Society.

1. Paper presented at a Symposium on Research Goals and Priorities in Gerontology, 23rd Annual Scientific Meeting of Gerontological Society, Toronto, Oct. 23, 1970. A more extensive treatment of this topic is contained in Riley, Johnson, & Foner, A Sociology of Age Stratification (1971). This is the third volume of a series on Aging and society, published by Russell Sage Foundation, under a grant from The Ford Foundation. In addition to the authors of this third volume, the following persons have read earlier versions of this manuscript and made valuable criticisms and suggestions: Beth Hess, Robert K. Merton, Mary E. Moore, M.D. and John W. Riley, Jr.

2. Dept. of Sociology, Rutgers University, 9 Union, New Brunswick, NJ 08903.

3. A team of us at Rutgers required several years to gather, abstract, and organize this impressive body of knowledge before we were able to produce an inventory of research findings, roughly 600 pages of selected social science results, in Riley, Foner, & Associates, 1968.

First, how does an individual's location in the class structure channel his attitudes and the way he behaves? Here there is much evidence that, for example, a person's health, his desire to achieve, his sense of mastery over his own fate, or the way he relates to his family and to his job depend to a considerable extent upon his social class.

Second, how do individuals relate to one another within, and between, classes? Within class lines, many friendships are formed, marriages often take place, and feelings of solidarity tend to be widespread. Between classes, relationships, even if not solidary, are often symbiotic, as people of unlike status live harmoniously in the same society. However, there seems to be greater opportunity between, than within, classes, for cleavage or conflict, as in struggles over economic advantages or clashes in political loyalties.

Third, what difficulties beset the upwardly (or downwardly) mobile individual, and what strains does his mobility impose upon the group (such as his parents of one class) whom he leaves behind and upon the new group (such as his wife's parents of a different class) who must now absorb him?

Fourth, to the extent that answers can be found to these three sets of questions, what is the impact of the observed findings upon the society as a whole? If there are inequalities between classes, for example, what do these portend for the prosperity, the morality, or the stability of the over-all structure of classes? What pressures for societal change are generated by differences, conflicts, or mobility between classes?

The literature on these four aspects of class stratification is impressive, pregnant with insights that might be extended to analyses of kindred phenomena. Our concern is to test the utility of the questions it evokes for understanding old age as just one stratum in a society stratified or differentiated, not by class, but by age. Thus we shall start by thinking of society as divided into strata according to the age of its members. *People* at varying ages differ in their capacity and willingness to perform social roles (of student, spouse, worker, or retiree, for example). Moreover, the age strata differ in the social *roles* members are expected to play and in the rights and privileges accorded to them by society. At any given period of time, old people must live as members of such

a society, finding their place in relation to the other members who are younger than they, and making choices among whatever opportunities are available to them. Over time, not only old people but people of different ages are *all* growing older, moving concurrently through a society which itself is undergoing change.

AGE STRATIFICATION AND THE INDIVIDUAL

To ask our first question, then: how does an individual's location within the changing age structure of a given society influence his behavior and attitudes? (Mannheim, 1952). In the sociological literature generally it has been well established that individuals are conditioned by society. As Robert Merton puts it, "Structure constrains individuals variously situated within it to develop cultural emphases, social behavior patterns and psychological bents" (Merton, 1957). Similarly, it has been well established in the literature of social gerontology that the state of old age reflects the structural context, showing wide variations (as well as some similarities) when primitive and modern societies are contrasted (Simmons, 1960), or even when modern Western nations are compared with one another (Burgess, 1960, Havighurst, Munnichs, Neugarten, & Thomae, 1969; Shanas & associates 1968). But how does it come about that, *within* a given society at any given time, individuals located in *different age strata* differ from one another? How are older individuals set off from the middle-aged and from the young?

The answer to such a question as this involves two distinct dimensions of time: a life course dimension and an historical dimension. These two dimensions can be thought of as coordinates for locating the individual in the age structure of society. On the first dimension, individuals at the *same* stage of the *life* course have much in common. They tend to be alike in biological development, in the kinds of roles they have experienced (such as worker, spouse, parent of dependent child), and in the sheer number of years behind and potential years ahead. People at *different* life course stages tend to differ in these very respects. The rough index of this life course dimension is years of chronological age—we say that a person is aged 20, or in the age category 45 to 60. But chronological age is of interest to us, not intrinsically, but only because it can serve as an approximate indicant of personal (that is biological, psychological, and social) experience—and this experience carries with it varying probabilities of behavior and attitudes. This life course dimension is the familiar one that includes the age-related organic changes affecting physical and mental functioning and that links the biological and the social sciences.

But there is a second time dimension for locating an individual in the age strata that also affects his probability of behaving or thinking in particular ways. This dimension refers to the *period of history* in which he lives. People who were born at the *same* time (referred to as a cohort) share a common historical and environmental past, present, and future. For example, when Americans born in 1910 had reached the age of 30, they had all (in one way or another) experienced World War I and the Great Depression, they were all currently exposed to World War II, and they all confronted the future of the 1940s through the 1970s. People who were born at *different* times (that is different cohorts) have lived through different intervals of history; and even when they encounter the same historical situation, they may, because they differ in age, experience it differently. Thus any one of us—just as we might be ethnocentric—is almost certainly (to add a needed term to our vocabulary) *"cohort-centric."* That is, we view old age, or any other stage of life, from the unique point of historical time at which we ourselves are standing. The rough index of this historical (or environmental) dimension is the date, or the calendar year. Here again our concern is not with dates themselves, but with the particular socio-cultural and environmental events, conditions, and changes to which the individual is exposed at particular periods.

It comes as no surprise, then, that each of the age strata has its own *distinctive sub-culture*. By age differences in sub-culture we mean that a cross-section view of society shows, for myriad characteristics, patterns that are closely related to age. In our own society today, familiar instances of the differing sub-cultures among young, middle-aged, and old include such varied aspects of life as labor force participation, consumer behavior, leisure-time activities, marital status, religious behavior, education, nativity, fertility and childrearing practices, or political attitudes—to name only a few. Such age-related patterns differ from time to time and from place to place, as all the age strata in a society—not the old alone—display differences (or similarities) in behavior and attitudes on the two dimensions of life course and history.

If we want to go beyond a mere description of these age-related sub-cultures, however, we must examine them further, which leads to our next topic.

AGE STRATIFICATION AND SOCIAL RELATIONSHIPS

The second set of questions suggested by the analogy between class stratification and age stratification points to the utility of exploring *relationships* both *between* and *within* age strata. For not only the behavior and attitudes of discrete individuals, but also social relationships—people's positive or negative feelings and actions toward each other—are channeled through the age structure of the particular society. Thus a sociology of age stratification, by investigating these relationships, should help to illuminate the nature of old age.

Many aspects of the cleavages or the bonds *between* old and young, dramatized by philosophers and poets of the ancient past, are still widely discussed today. Is there an inevitable gap between generations? Do the elderly constitute a disadvantaged minority group, regarded with prejudice by the majority? Or do they control important centers of power, refusing to yield to the young? Are old people likely to form political blocs, seeking to solve their own problems with little regard for the rest of society? And, if many conditions foster intergenerational conflict or exploitation, what other conditions foster relationships of harmony or reciprocity?

As a preliminary to addressing such momentous issues, one small illustration of the *sequential relations* among generations within the family will point out the interconnectedness of the age strata. If we start with the elderly generation of parents and their adult offspring, a well-known finding from the gerontological literature reports widespread exchanges of material support. This support varies in amount and kind, ranging from financial contributions and care in illness to baby-sitting and help with housework and home repairs. Contrary to previous notions of an upward flow of contributions *to* older people, the flow of support between aged parents and their adult offspring appears to be two-directional, either from parent to child or from child to parent as need and opportunity dictate (Riley et al., 1968). Indeed (in the United States, at least), the proportions of older people who *give* help to their offspring appear to exceed the proportions who *receive* help from their offspring (Shanas, 1966; Streib, 1965; Streib & Thompson, 1960).

Let us now, however, include in the example still a third generation of the family, for it is our contention that many a commonplace observation about old people can take on new significance through extension to other age strata. Let us move from the flow of material assistance between aged parents and their middle-aged children to the flow between this middle generation and *their* young children. The principle can be illustrated by one small study (Foner, 1969) in which parents of high school students were asked what they would do with money unexpectedly received. Only 2% said they would use it to help their aged parents. But this was not because they would spend it on themselves or save it for their retirement; it was rather because, in the main, they would reserve it to help their children get started in life. Furthermore, the aged generation concurs; they do not expect repayment. The middle generation, then, does not neglect the old because of pre-occupation with their own needs (in fact, they are far readier to offer help than are their aged parents to want or to accept it), but because of their pre-occupation with the needs of their young children. In short, the flow of material support tends to be, not reciprocal, but sequential—with each generation (regardless of its means) attempting to aid the next younger generation.

As such a finding intimates, many middle-aged parents, by investing their resources in the future of their young children, are not only restricting any potential help they might give to the older generation; they are also restricting the accumulation of assets for their own later life. In this example, then, extension of the analysis from the oldest to the youngest generation in the family helps to clarify one aspect of the meaning of old age. Any lack of family support for aged parents now appears, not as willful indifference or neglect, but as an expression of normative agreement among all the generations about the direction in which aid should flow.

Many other conditions of the aged might similarly be better understood against the backdrop of the other strata with whom old people live and relate. Consider the work force data on older men as this might be compared with the differing circumstances of employment of younger people at various periods of history. In the early days of the Industrial Revolution in England, the father (or grandfather), as a skilled workman in his own right, could take his children with him into the factory, himself training the adult sons and supervising the little children throughout the long workday (Smelser, 1968). Thus his authority within the family could penetrate into the workplace, preserving traditional ties among the generations. If such an arrangement encouraged between-strata solidarity, then the subsequent changes in conditions of work may have undermined this basis. More recently, in the United States, quite another set of changes have marked the relative positions of older men and boys in the work force. Between 1900 and 1930, while the majority of older men remained economically active, the proportion of boys aged 10 to 15 who were fully employed declined from 25% to only 6%. Since World War II, as older men have been winnowed from the labor force, boys too are being extruded; the Census no longer counts children under 14 in compiling labor force statistics, and the participation rates of boys from 16 through 19 show slight but consistent declines. Thus older men today live in a society where the situation of both the old and the young must be interpreted in relation to the productivity and economic prestige of men in their middle years (Kalish, 1969).

Such examples suggest a general principle: important increments to gerontological knowledge are obtainable by studying the entire age-differentiated society, not merely the old. The same principle holds when the research focus is on relationships *within* rather than *between* age strata. Here we shall simply allude to the concern of gerontologists with questions of age-similarity as a basis for friendship, or age-homogeneity as a feature of residential settings for older people (Madge, 1969; Riley et al., 1968). It has been shown that, outside of family groups, older people tend (although by no means exclusively) to have friends who are similar to themselves in status characteristics—notably age—that signal mutuality of experiences, tastes, or values. However, as the sociological literature shows (Hess, 1971), such choice of age-mates is only a special case of the widespread phenomenon of homophily (or similarity among friends in status or in values) (Lazersfeld & Merton, 1954).

Age homophily, not only among the old but also at younger age levels, may be especially pronounced in the United States today as a number of factors converge to produce solidarity within age lines. Simply the rapidity of social change, for example, can sharpen the differences among strata and can thereby contribute to a sense of uniqueness among members of each single stratum. The expansion of eduation has extended the social (and often the physical) segregation of age-similars from children in the lower schools to older adolescents and even to young adults in colleges and universities (Parsons & Platt, 1971). Today's middle-aged people, too, many of whom have left the city to rear their children in the suburbs, have experienced long years of age-homogeneous neighborhood settings (Starr, 1971). And old people because of increasing longevity retain larger numbers of their age peers as associates (Spengler, 1969). In many respects, then, we live in an *age-graded* society, with a high potential for strong ties to develop within each age stratum.

However, the possible long-term consequences of such heightened conditions of within-stratum solidarity may be double-edged. On the one hand, homophily may be beneficial to the individuals involved. Age peers have long been recognized as easing the transition from childhood to adulthood (Eisenstadt, 1956); and they may perhaps aid adjustment in old age and at other points of transition in the life course as well. On the other hand, if age peers increasingly turn to each other for aid and comfort, detriments to relationships between strata may ensue as ties between generations may become attenuated or the potential for cleavage or conflict may be increased.

AGING AND COHORT FLOW

It is the third set of questions—those relating to the processes of *mobility* of individuals from one stratum to another—that brings into bold relief certain similarities, but also the essential differences, between class stratification and age stratification.

At points of similarity between the two processes, much can be learned about aging from the rich literature on class mobility. We tend to take aging for granted (much as before the development of physiology as a science, laymen took their bodily functioning for granted). Yet, when aging (social, psychological, and biological) is viewed as mobility through the age strata, it is revealed as a process that entails many of the same tensions and strains as class mobility. Aging individuals must pass through key transition points in the society—from infancy to childhood, for example, from one school grade to the next, from adolescence to adulthood, or from work-life to retirement (Clausen, 1971). And the degree of strain engendered by such transitions depends upon diverse social conditions—upon the continuity or discontinuity in the role sequences (Benedict, 1938); upon how fully institutionalized a particular role may be (Donahue, Orbach, & Pollak, 1960); upon the internal consistency of role expectations, facilities, and sanctions,[4] or upon how effectively people are trained or social-

---

4.   Back (1969) claims ambiguity of retirement which, although socially defined as a right of the individual, offers low rewards and is socially under-valued.

ized at every stage of life (Brim, 1968; Brim & Wheeler, 1966). For example, consider the stress entailed in our society because we crowd formal education almost exclusively into the younger stages of life rather than spreading it over the life course as individuals require it. Since we do not regard students as full-fledged adults, what tensions must be endured by the young person who stays in the role of student beyond adolescence well into adulthood (tensions that are all too evident in universities today)? What difficulties beset the older person if, in order to obtain the further education he needs or desires, he must sacrifice his job? Like social mobility, too, aging places strains not only upon individuals but also upon the groups through which the aging individual passes. Thus a family must regroup itself after the marriage of its youngest child, or a community after the death of an elder statesman. Similarly, group adjustments are necessitated by the advent of new members like the birth of a child into a family, the entry of a new class of children into a school grade, of the move of a widowed old person into the household of her married daughter.

Despite such similarities, however, aging differs from class mobility in certain fundamental respects. Exactly because the analogy breaks down in these respects is age stratification revealed in its full uniqueness and in its intrinsicality to social change. In the first place, mobility across social classes affects only selected individuals, who can move either upward or downward, and who can reverse direction at different stages of life. But mobility through the age strata is, of course, universal, unidirectional, and irreversible. Everybody ages. Everybody changes over his life course as personality develops, experience accumulates, and adjustments are made to new roles. Nobody can ever go back, although individuals may age in different ways and at different rates.

In the second place, knowledgeable as we are about the inevitability of aging, we take much less cognizance of the inexorability of birth and death, and of the endless succession of cohorts (or generations of individuals born at the same time)—for which there is no precise parallel in class mobility. Yet the sociology of age stratification requires examination of the fact that, within a given society, different cohorts can age in differ-

ent ways. Each cohort is tied through its date of birth to societal history. Thus the aging of each new cohort is affected by the special situation of that cohort's particular era in history—by the changing cultural, social, and material conditions in the society and by events in the external environment. While all the members of one particular cohort move together over their life course through the same period of time, the various cohorts in the society can differ because they start at distinct times. Cohorts can also differ markedly in size and in composition (in the proportions of males and females, for example, or of blacks and whites, or of natives and foreign-born).

Consider a few examples of inter-cohort differences in the way people have aged in our own society in the *past*. Epidemiologists tell us that, in comparison with women born a century ago, today's women have experienced menarche at earlier ages and menopause at later ages (National Center for Health Statistics, 1966; Susser, 1969; Tanner, 1962). That is, the period of potential fertility has appreciably lengthened. In practice, however, *recent* cohorts spend fewer years of their lives in child-bearing. Women have telescoped the phase of actual reproduction, having fewer and more closely spaced offspring nowadays than did their mothers or grandmothers (Glick & Parke, 1965). Moreover, the trauma of reproduction have been drastically reduced, as fewer women die in childbirth and fewer of their infants die.

Most striking of all the cohort differences, perhaps, are those in longevity—in the proportions of cohort members who outlive the ills of infancy, who escape maternal deaths and the other mortality risks of young adulthood, and who thus survive into the higher ages of the lifespan. The average lifetime (estimated at only two to three decades among cohorts born in ancient Rome or in medieval Europe) has risen in the United States from four decades among cohorts born in the mid-nineteenth century to an estimated seven decades among those born in the mid-twentieth—a situation apparently unparalleled in human history.[5] The profound implica-

---

5. To be sure, infant deaths weigh heavily in these averages. Moreover, the data are based on hypothetical, rather than true, cohorts. See Riley et al. (1968).

tions of such cohort differences in longevity, can be intimated by just one of the many associated changes, the one called the "revolution in family structure" (Glick & Parke, 1965; Shanas, 1969).[6] The single nuclear household of a century ago (parents and their children, sometimes including a grandparent) has been replaced, because of increased joint survival, by several generations of related nuclear households: the young couple with their dependent children, the middle-aged parents, the aged generation of grandparents, and the great-grandparent who also often survives.

What do such differences between earlier and later cohorts presage for the people who will become old in the *future?* Speculation about many of these differences can prove fruitful of hypotheses. We might speculate, for example, about the extended period of husband-wife relationships in the middle years: the more recent couples have had more time to accumulate assets, or to learn independence from their offspring, or to prepare themselves for retirement. But not all predictions about future implications of cohort differences are entirely speculative, since everybody who will reach 65 during this century or during the early decades of the 21st century is already alive. Much information is already in hand about the size of existing cohorts, for example, or about their place of birth or their educational level. Thus, apart from unforeseeable changes (as through wars, depressions, or major shifts in migration or in values), fair estimates can be made about numerous characteristics of old people at particular dates in the future. The *size* of the aged stratum at the turn of the century will reflect the small numbers of babies in the Depression cohorts; but the size of the aged stratum will predictably increase again in the early decades of the coming century with the influx of the "baby boom" cohorts born after World War II (Spen-

gler, 1969). In respect to *nativity,* the much-studied cohort who had passed age 65 or more by 1960 had contained a sizeable proportion of early immigrants who were largely illiterate and unskilled, whereas the more recent cohorts who will reach old age in subsequent decades contain fewer and better educated immigrants. Or in respect to formal *education,* we know that over 70% of the cohort aged 75 or more in 1960 had had less than 9 years of school, contrasted with only 17% of the cohort aged 25 to 29, who will not reach age 75 before the year 2 005 (Riley et al., 1968). We are aware, also, of many changing societal or environmental conditions, not all of them salutary, that may influence in special ways the future life course of existing cohorts—as, for example, the spread of pollution might have the greatest effect on young cohorts subject to a full lifetime of exposure, or as the increase of smoking among women might bring female death rates more nearly into line with the currently higher male rates. We cannot overestimate the importance of charting such cohort differences for an understanding of old age.

AGE AND SOCIAL CHANGE

We have been discussing the dual processes affecting individuals (or cohorts of individuals) in a society: aging as a social, psychological, and biological process; and the succession of cohorts which do not all age in exactly the same ways. We shall now ask how these processes relate to the macrocosm of the changing society (Ryder, 1965) of which the old people who concern us are one integral part.

Mannheim (1952) once proposed a tantalizing mental experiment. Imagine, he said, a society in which one generation lived on forever, and none followed to replace it. Let us, as social scientists, policy-makers, and professional groups, make such an experiment! If everybody grows old together, what distinctions might remain between old and young? A few moments' thought are enough to suggest the ineluctable connections among the succession of cohorts, aging, and age stratification. For, in contrast to Mannheim's

---

6.   Among couples born a century ago, the last child in the family was married, on the average, at about the same time as the death of one of the parents. But among recent cohorts, husbands and wives typically survive together as two-person families for a good many years after the last child has married and left home. Changes in family structure are associated with changes, not only in longevity, but also in child-bearing and in household living arrangements; see Riley et al., 1968.

imaginary society, our own consists of successive cohorts, each with its own unique life-course pattern. It is clear that these cohorts fit together at any given time to form the age structure of young, middle-aged, and aged strata. And over time, as the particular individuals composing the particular strata are continually moving on and being replaced, the society itself is changing.

Certain connections now become apparent between the flow of cohorts and the age-related societal patterns and changes in individual behaviors, attitudes, and relationships (noted in the first sections of the paper). In the simplest case, because successive cohorts often age in different ways, some of these societal patterns and changes can be viewed as direct reflections of the differing cohorts that comprise the age strata at particular periods. Education is a noteworthy example of the significance of cohort flow for cross-sectional differences among age strata (Riley et al., 1968). The rapid pace of educational advance over the century, leaving its mark on successive cohorts of young people, now sets the age strata clearly apart from one another. And these strata differences in education have incalculable importance for many aspects of behavior and attitude—for prejudice, feelings of powerlessness, narrow ranges of interests and friendships, and the like. Of course, such strata differences do not remain fixed. Not only do new cohorts come along, but society itself can change in its related institutions and practices. The age pattern of education today is a reversal of that in earlier societies where the old were honored for their greater knowledge. If one looks ahead from today's knowledge explosion, the information gap between the very young and even the not-so-young is deepening, creating pressures to change the entire structure of education if people beyond the earliest years are to maintain competitive equality.[7]

In another example, the cross-section age patterns for drinking or smoking have shown a general decline from younger to older strata; and these differences among strata are in part reflec-

tions of the past tendency for each new cohort to espouse these practices to an increasing degree (Riley et al., 1968). Today's younger cohorts, however, may be introducing new habits that could, over the next decades, drastically change the cross-section age pattern. A recent campus interview elicited the student comment, for example, that

> . . . upperclassmen still prefer beer, but a large majority of underclassmen prefer pot. Pot is big in the high schools, and it is very popular with freshmen who just came out of that environment. The trend is definitely away from beer (Cicetti, 1970).

Are these newcomers to the college likely to set the pace for the cohorts that follow?

In such instances, changes in societal age strata can be interpreted as the shifting composite of cohorts who, themselves affected by differing historical backgrounds, have aged in differing ways. In other instances, life course differences among cohorts in one social sphere appear to stimulate further changes in other spheres. For example, far-reaching shifts in the relations between men and women at various ages—the decreasing differentiation between the sexes or the greater freedom of sexual behavior—might be traced in part to a reversal in cohort patterns of female participation in the labor force (Riley et al., 1968, 1971). Many cohorts of women born during the late 19th century showed steadily declining rates of participation over the life course. Following World War II, a new pattern began to emerge, as many married women entered the labor force during their middle years, although work force participation of young women in the child rearing ages remained low. The conjunction of these cohort trends meant that, for a considerable period, it was only the young mothers with little children whose labor force participation was low. This situation may have prompted a classic observation (foreshadowing the full force of the Women's Liberation Movement) that "for the first time in the history of any known society, motherhood has become a full-time occupation for adult women" (Rossi, 1964). Women at other times and places shared motherhood with de-

---

7. If such a change is not effected, we may expect increasing convergence of age and class stratification as education achieves preeminence among the distinguishing criteria of social class.

manding labor in the fields, the factory, or the household.

Can we expect that full-time motherhood is now institutionalized and will persist into the future? If so, we may be victims of our own "cohort-centrism"—one more proof that our understandings of society are influenced by our particular historical background. For this fulltime preoccupation of American mothers with their young children seems already to be eroding as recent cohorts have developed a rather different pattern. Not only have the proportions of married women in the labor force during their middle years more than doubled, but there have been pronounced increases also among young married women, even those with little children (Manpower Report of the President, 1970). Thus it may appear to historians of the future that full-time motherhood was a peculiar phenomenon, existing in American society only for a few decades of the twentieth century. Whatever the future may actually hold, the example begins to suggest how the confluence of cohorts with differing life course patterns in one respect (economic activity of women) can change society in other respects as well. Think, for example, of the mature women who no longer "retire" from major social roles many years before their husbands retire from work. Or think of the young husbands and wives who now share the work of homemaking and infant care. May such changing work habits result in entirely new modes of relationship in the family and—if only because of the widespread unavailability of working wives for daytime activities at home or in the community—in other social institutions?

In addition to the impress of cohort succession upon the history of society, it can sometimes happen that innovations emanating from a single cohort ramify rather quickly through the other age strata, without awaiting the lag over a long series of cohorts. Thus the excessive size of the "baby boom" cohort born after World War II has required drastic adjustments throughout a society unprepared to absorb it—from the initial requirements for obstetrical facilities through the successive pressures on housing, schools, the job market, the marriage market, and so on into the future. Among the many other widely discussed

instances are the increased financial burden borne (through transfer payments) by the remainder of society because so many retired old people have inadequate incomes (Bernstein, 1969; McConnell, 1960); or the potential changes in the ethos surrounding work and leisure as large numbers of old and young no longer participate in the work force (Donahue et al., 1960; Riley, Foner, Hess, & Toby, 1969). It has even been suggested that a completely revolutionary "consciousness," now informing the values and behaviors of many young people, may affect the entire society (Reich, 1970).

To return to the immediate topic of this essay, we offer a special challenge to the oncoming cohorts of social gerontologists—not merely to continue looking for new materials, but also to re-examine and fit together the existing materials in a new way. We suggest a review of old age as one ingredient in the societal macrocosm, inseparable from, and interdependent with, the other age strata. We suggest a review of aging and of the succession of births and deaths as integral parts of societal process and change that follow their own rhythm and that in themselves constitute immanent strains and pressures toward innovation. Such a sociological review can, we submit, help to explain old age and aging and can at the same time suggest potential solutions to some of the problems of great immediate concern.

In sum, the forces of social change, whether through deliberate intervention[8] or as an indirect consequence of existing trends, are not only constantly affecting the aging process, but are also bringing new influences to bear on the situation, on the characteristics of persons who are old, and on the younger age strata with whom old people are interdependent. Discovery and evaluation of the implications for old age of these forces for change constitutes a whole new field of opportunity for social scientists, professional groups, and policy makers in gerontology.

---

8. Many possibilities for intervention in the several professional fields are discussed in the series of essays in Riley, Riley & Johnson, 1969, in which experts discuss the implications of social science knowledge for public policy and professional practice affecting older people.

REFERENCES

Back, K. W. The ambiguity of retirement. In E. W. Busse and E. Pfeiffer (Eds.), *Behavior and adaptation in late life*. Boston: Little, Brown & Co., 1969.

Benedict, R. Continuities and discontinuities in cultural conditioning. *Psychiatry*, 1938, *1*, 161–167. (Reprinted in Kluckhohn, C., Murray, H. A., & Schneider, D. (Eds.), *Personality in nature, society and culture*. New York: Alfred A. Knopf, 1953.

Bernstein, M. C. Aging and the law. In M. W. Riley, J. W. Riley, Jr., & M. E. Johnson (Eds.), *Aging and society*, Vol. 2, *Aging and the professions*. New York: Russell Sage Foundation, 1969.

Brim, O. G., Jr. Adult socialization. In J. A. Clausen (Ed.), *Socialization and society*. Boston: Little, Brown, & Co., 1968.

Brim, O. G., Jr., & Wheeler, S. *Socialization after childhood: Two essays*. New York: John Wiley & Sons, 1966.

Burgess, E. W. (Ed.) *Aging in Western societies*. Chicago: University of Chicago Press, 1960.

Cicetti, F. Campuses revisited: New trend at Seton Hall. *Newark Evening News*, Sept. 30, 1970.

Clausen, J. A. The life course of individuals. In M. W. Riley, M. E. Johnson, & A. Foner, *Aging and society*. Vol. 3, *A sociology of age stratification*. New York: Russell Sage Foundation, 1971.

Donahue, W., Orbach, H. L., & Pollak, O. Retirement: The emerging social pattern. In C. Tibbitts (Ed.), *Handbook of social gerontology*. Chicago: University of Chicago Press, 1960.

Eisenstadt, S. N. *From generation to generation; age groups and social structure*. Free Press: Glencoe, Ill., 1956.

Foner, A. The middle years: Prelude to retirement? PhD dissertation, New York University, 1969.

Glick, P. C., & Parke, R., Jr. New approaches in studying the life cycle of the family. *Demography*, 1965, *2*, 187–202.

Havighurst, R. J., Munnichs, J. M. A., Neugarten, B. L., & Thomae, H. (Eds.), *Adjustment to retirement; a cross-national study*. Assen. The Netherlands: Koninklijke van Gorcum, 1969.

Hess, B. Friendship. In M. W. Riley, M. E. Johnson, & A. Foner. *Aging and society*. Vol. 3, *A sociology of age stratification*. New York: Russell Sage Foundation, 1971.

Kalish, R. A. The old and the new as generation gap allies. *Gerontologist*, 1969, *9*, 83–89.

Lazarsfeld, P. F., & Merton, R. K. Friendship as social process: A substantive and methodological analysis. In M. Berger, T. Abel, & C. H. Page, *Freedom and control in modern society*. New York: D. Van Nostrand Co., 1954.

McConnell, J. W. Aging and the economy. In C. Tibbitts (Ed.), *Handbook of social gerontology*. Chicago: University of Chicago Press, 1960.

Madge, J. Aging and the fields of architecture and planning. In M. W. Riley, J. W. Riley, Jr., & M. E. Johnson (Eds.), *Aging and society*. Vol. 2, *Aging and the professions*. New York: Russell Sage Foundation, 1969.

Mannheim, K. The problem of generations. In P. Kecskemeti (Ed. & Trans.), *Essays on the sociology of knowledge*. London: Routledge & Kegan Paul (1928), 1952.

Manpower Report of the President, Mar., 1970. Washington: Government Printing Office.

Merton, R. K. *Social theory and social structure*. (Rev. Ed.) Glencoe, Ill.: Free Press, 1957.

National Center for Health Statistics. Age and menopause, United States 1960–1962. *Vital and health statistics, 1966*, PHS Pub. No. 1000–Series II, No. 19, Washington: Government Printing Office.

Parsons, T., & Platt, G. M. Higher education and changing socialization. In M. W. Riley, M. E. Johnson, & A. Foner. *Aging and society*, Vol. 3, *A sociology of age stratification*. New York: Russell Sage Foundation, 1971.

Reich, C. Reflections: The greening of America. *New Yorker*, Sept. 26, 1970, 42 ff.

Riley, M. W., Foner, A., & Associates. *Aging and society*. Vol. 1, *An inventory of research findings*. New York: Russell Sage Foundation. 1968.

Riley, M. W., Riley, J. W., Jr. & Johnson, M. E. *Aging and society*, Vol. 2, *Aging and the professions*. New York: Russell Sage Foundation, 1969.

Riley, M. W., Johnson, M. E., & Foner, A. *Aging and society*. Vol. 3, *A sociology of age stratification*. New York: Russell Sage Foundation, 1971.

Riley, M. W., Foner, A., Hess, B., & Toby, M. L. Socialization for the middle and later years. In D. A. Goslin (Ed.), *Handbook of socialization theory and research*. Chicago: Rand McNally, 1969.

Rossi, A. S. Equality between the sexes: An immodest proposal. *Daedalus*, Spring, 1964, 607–652.

Ryder, N. B. The cohort as a concept in the study of social change. *American Sociological Review*, 1965, *30*, 843–861.

Shanas, E., & Associates. Family help patterns and social class in three countries. Paper presented at the meetings of the American Sociological Assn., Miami, 1966.

Shanas, E. *Old people in three industrial societies*. New York: Atherton Press, 1968.

Shanas, E. Living arrangements and housing of old people. In E. W. Busse & E. Pfeiffer (Eds.), *Behavior and adaptation in late life*. Boston: Little, Brown & Co., 1969.

Simmons, L. W. Aging in preindustrial societies. In C. Tibbitts (Ed.), *Handbook of social gerontology*. Chicago: University of Chicago Press, 1960.

Smelser, N. J. Sociological history: The industrial revolution and the British working-class family. In N. J. Smelser (Ed.), *Essays in sociological explanation*. Englewood Cliffs, NJ: Prentice-Hall, 1968.

Spengler, J. J. The aged and public policy. In E. W. Busse & E. Pfeiffer (Eds.), *Behavior and adaptation in late life*. Boston: Little, Brown & Co., 1969.

Starr, B. C. The community. In M. W. Riley, M. E. Johnson, & A. Foner. *Aging and society*. Vol. 3, *A sociology of age stratification*. New York: Russell Sage Foundation, 1971.

Streib, G. F. Intergenerational relations: Perspectives of the two generations on the older parent. *Journal of Marriage & the Family*, 1965, 27, 469–476.

Streib, G. F., & Thompson, W. E. The older person in a family context. In C. Tibbitts (Ed.), *Handbook of social gerontology*. Chicago: University of Chicago Press, 1960.

Susser, M. Aging and the field of public health. In M. W. Riley, J. W. Riley, Jr., & M. E. Johnson (Eds.), *Aging and society*. Vol. 2, *Aging and the professions*. New York: Russell Sage Foundation, 1969.

Tanner, J. M. *Growth at adolescence*. (2nd ed.) Oxford: Blackwell, Davis Co., 1962.

Never before in history have adults had so much "understanding" of children: yet we are farther than ever from knowing how to grow people

Birthrights: A Children's Bill of Rights

Richard Farson

THERE IS no way to have a liberated society until we have liberated our children. And right now our society is organized against them. The ideal child is cute (entertaining to adults), well-behaved (doesn't bother adults), and bright (capable of bringing home report cards the parents can be proud of). Efforts of parents to produce these traits have so inhibited children that neither adults nor children can always see the remarkable potentialities that lie beyond or outside them. Because we have become increasingly alert to the many forms of oppression in our society, we are now seeing, as we have not seen before, the predicament of children: they are powerless, dominated, ignored, invisible. We are beginning to see the necessity for children's liberation.

People are not liberated one by one. They must be liberated as a class. Liberating children, giving them equality and guaranteeing their civil rights, may seem to violate the fairly recent realizations that children are not simply miniature adults, and that childhood is a special time of life, with special qualities and problems. In fact, never before in history have parents and teachers had so much "understanding" of children, or at least of their physical and social development. But the "understanding" has led not to improved conditions for children, but simply to more control of them and consequently more burdensome responsibilities of supervision for parents. So that now the best things that happen between parent and child happen by accident or by surprise, very often breaking all rules in the process. Actually, anyone who isn't bewildered by child-rearing, who doesn't find it an extremely formidable and trying experience, probably has never lived with children.

Moreover, increased understanding and concern has not been coupled with increased rights. As a consequence, children's rights have actually diminished, for we have simply replaced ignorant domination with sophisticated domination. With increased attention to children has come resentment. Our efforts to shape children, to reform them, to fix them, to correct them, to discipline them, to educate them, have led to an obsession with the physical, moral and sexual problems of children; but they have not led to our liking them more, or realizing their potential.

By holding a limited and demeaned view of children and by segregating them almost completely from the adult world, we may be subverting their capacity for genius. It has been pointed out that we no longer have infant and child prodigies—or at least that they are now much rarer than before. In the past, when children were an integral part of the community, they sometimes did show great genius. By the age of 17 months, for example, Louis XIII played the violin. He played tennis when he still slept in a cradle. He was an archer, and played cards and chess, at six. Today we might worry a bit about precocity of that magnitude, but then, people took it for granted. One wonders whether we have sacrificed genius for homogeniety and conformity.

The nuclear family (two adults and their minor children), a completely self-contained unit, not dependent upon the community, is a relatively new development. Child care once was distributed among several adults in an extended family; now it falls entirely on the parent or parents. The children do little for the family, and almost nothing for each other or themselves. Overburdened parents feel an increasing sense of both responsibility and guilt as society's expectations of what families should offer their children rise—and yet the community spends less of its money and energy on aid to children or parents.

Though technically the law no longer regards them as chattels, children are still treated as the private property of their parents. The parent has both the right and the responsibility to control the life of the child.

It will take quite a revolution in our thinking to give some of this control back to the child. Nevertheless, the acceptance of the child's right to self-determination is fundamental. It is the right to a single standard of morals and behavior for children and adults, including behavior decisions close to home. From the earliest signs of competence, children might have, for example, the right to decide for themselves about eating, sleeping, playing, listening, reading, washing, and dressing; the freedom to choose their associates, to decide what life goals they wish to pursue.

Parents may argue that the right to self-determination will bring with it the risk of physical and psychological damage. No doubt some risks are involved. But under present conditions, many children are severely damaged—physically, socially, and emotionally. Compared to the existing system, the risks of harming children by accepting their right to self-determination may be greatly over-rated. Impossible as it seems, it may be that the situations we try hardest to avoid for ourselves and for our children, would be actually the most beneficial to us. One can make a good case for a calamity theory of growth—many of our most eminent people, for instance, have come from the most calamitous early childhood situations. Of course, we don't want calamities to happen to our children, but we can be a bit more relaxed about our protectiveness.

In any event, it's time to admit that no one knows how to grow people.

Since most concerns center on the problems of living with a self-determining child, our first thoughts focus on the home. While liberation cannot be truly accomplished at home—because the home is not separate from the rest of society—the situation illustrates in microcosm the dimensions of the problem as it might exist in society at large.

Take, for example, family mealtimes. No one should be expected to prepare a meal at a special time for children simply because they choose not to eat at the regular hour. However, most children could, with some special arrangement and training, prepare meals for themselves when necessary. Those children whose schedules demand special timetables would receive the same consideration afforded any adult member of the household in similar circumstances—but no more.

Loss of authority over a child in areas such as nutrition does not mean that the child cannot be influenced. In the absence of adult tyranny, adult judgment and information have to be the primary influence and are more likely to be accepted.

Bedtime is a case in point. Most parents know that children enjoy sleeping as much as adults do. Resistance to it comes largely from adult pressures. Because adults' sleeping habits are governed largely by the pressures to engage in productive activity during the daytime hours, we adhere to nighttime sleeping hours. Children, too, must follow daytime hours to fulfill their compulsory attendance in school.

If children came to these conclusions for themselves, by suffering the consequences, they would be capable in the long run of learning, as most adults have, that when we are too tired we pay for it the next day. This would make the ritual of going to bed less of a vehicle through which adults and children express their mutual antagonisms. Believe it or not, bedtime is not a big issue in some homes. Children either go to bed by themselves or they are simply covered up on the spot where they drop off to sleep.

What about other physical dangers, such as children playing where they might injure themselves? The first answer is that of course we cannot risk a child's death. Just as we would pull an adult out of the path of an onrushing car, we would do the same for a child. There is no double standard in an emergency situation.

In fact children are equally concerned about safety—their own and their parents'. They try, for example, to keep their parents from chainsmoking, drinking too much, getting too fat, driving dangerously, or working too hard. While they are seldom successful at this, the point is to recognize the concern and responsibility as mutual.

Life is inevitably risky and almost everyone agrees that it is important that children be given the opportunity to take risks in order to develop, to push their limits, to discover their potential. What we fail to realize is that most of the dangers that children face are "man-made" and that, not recognizing what we've done to ourselves, we've accepted the responsibility to protect our children, by constant supervision, from dangers we've created—backyard pools, electrical sockets, poisons under the sink, and speeding automobiles. Unlike man-made dangers, natural dangers like cliffs and crashing waves usually signal their own warning.

Most sports involve some physical risks, but children *do* climb trees even if falling might hurt them; they ride horses, take gymnastics, and engage in other athletics.

Of course, the elimination of all danger in our society is certainly not a realistic nor desirable goal, but we will have come a long way in making the world safer for children if we can solve the problem of the automobile—the Number One enemy of children. Besides creating a situation requiring constant supervision, automobiles have actually decreased the mobility of children while increasing the mobility of adults. This problem is one of social design, and its solution will require some difficult choices for us in city planning, and the utilization of financial resources. We must build cities with children in mind, and devise transportation systems that work for them. It means reducing our use of and reliance on the automobile. It means reorienting our work, play, family life, and commercial activities so that they are all close to each other, which would have the additional benefit of developing stronger communities, more interpersonal activity and greater involvement.

We must find ways of protecting children as best we can from the lethal dangers, where the first lesson is the last one. In our well-meaning protective attitude, however, we must not include the idea that it is our right to have children and to raise them as we see fit. The 1970 White House Conference on Children held that the rights of parents cannot infringe upon the rights of children, and all of us may soon come to the conclusion that the ability to conceive a child gives no one the right to dominate or to abuse her or him. The decisions about a child's home environment should not belong to the parents alone. Parents will have more responsibility than they have authority. They will have to depend more heavily on judgment, advice, and persuasion.

Given the fact that child-rearing practices differ widely from country to country, it is hard to pinpoint a parent's responsibilities and a child's needs. In some cultures children are wrapped tightly, in others they are always naked; some children have close ties with their father, some do not even know their father; some are exposed to the elements as a test of maturity, some are held and fondled almost constantly.

Despite this diversity, there are certain widely shared, if debatable, views of basic needs. Children need loving care as newborns and in early infancy. They need, for what we would call normal physical growth, certain nutritive elements. For their minds to develop they need stimulation and variation. And as children grow older they need to be with adults with whom they can identify. Despite current convention, however, none of these so-called basics justifies the nuclear family as the only model of family life.

Parenting in the nuclear family is difficult, demanding, restrictive, and expensive. Having children is unbelievably burdensome. It is not just the battered children who grow up in oppressive circumstances, but to some degree *all* children. The degrees of oppression vary, but one kind is universal: that children have no alternative but to live with their parents or be housed by the government in some jail-like alternative. Even when family life is delightful, the child should have other options.

Furthermore, the truth is that more than 60 percent of Americans live in domestic arrangements other than the nuclear family: single people with or without children, married people without children or with stepchildren, couples with grown children, homosexual couples or groups, elderly people living in nursing homes, convicts in prisons, students in residence halls, children living with one parent or in institutions, communal arrangements, and so forth.

Ignoring this reality, we persist in glorifying the nuclear family instead of exploring alternate living arrangements into which the child may fit just as well—or better.

One of the few well-known alternatives which honors the child's right to self-determination is A. S. Neill's Summerhill, an English residential school where the freedom and equality of children is of paramount concern and the children's participation in the government of the institution is fundamental to its operation.

Multiple parenting is the core concept of other alternatives now in practice. It means several adults share childrearing responsibilities through community efforts.

In this country child-care arrangements for "normal" kids present a terrible financial burden, usually to the parent, whereas the state pays for all those incarcerated in reform schools and prisons and the 200,000 children in foster-care programs. The approximately $12,000 a year it costs the state to keep one child in an institution should certainly be enough to pay for many different kinds of state-supported institutions which are not prisons, but offer realistic placement options for those children in most serious difficulty at home.

People who want alternative living arrangements need thoughtfully designed programs which (1) place more choice in the hands of the child, (2) redistribute the costs so that neither the state nor the parents suffer the total burden, (3) make use of previously unused resources, including laypeople and paraprofessionals, teenagers, or retired people, and (4) provide a variety of arrangements for new home environments from which to choose.

Large numbers of people could be involved in a professionally managed membership network, a kind of nongeographic community to which participants pay regular dues. Alternative home environments for children which could be developed by such a network are primarily multifamily communes, child-exchange programs, and children's residences.

The multifamily commune could work if there were an organized network to help with problems of autocratic leadership, to establish standards of sexual behavior and fair distribution of maintenance and other responsibilities before the experiment begins and throughout its life. Obviously children would have to participate fully in all aspects of the communal life.

A second model is child exchange where families would swap children, much like today's foreign-exchange student programs. This program would accommodate children who have created a problem for their parents, or children who would like to have the chance to experience new situations.

The problem with child exchange presently is that it is informal, haphazard, and uncommon. But the need is there. (A man took a newspaper ad offering his child in exchange for another troublesome teenager, and within the first few days he received more than 70 responses.) Within a membership network the exchanges could be arranged at the option of the children as well as the parents, and counseling and contracts would also be introduced to help safeguard the system.

A third possible alternative involves residences operated by children. Organized by the network staff and similar to those now operated by and for the elderly, these would have adults in residence as consultants or in other capacities, but would be, by and large, managed by children functioning in self-determined and self-governing ways. One of the problems is that this plan might seriously reduce children's contact with adults (though the children themselves might be far less age-segregated than they are in schools now). Another is that the financing for children's residences would have to come largely from parents and government, and that might impose parent control. Finally, infant care would require adult legal responsibility. While these problems are challenging, they are not insurmountable.

Another model, not requiring a membership network, is the day-care or day-and-night care facility financed not only by parents but by government, business and industry, and society at large.

Then there are basic changes to be made in our current living facilities. Children are simply not considered important enough by those adults who design the environment. Only in places that are used exclusively by children—classrooms, playgrounds, and the like—do we find facilities built to children's scale.

Consider the daily experiences of small children—taking a shower under an uncontrollable waterfall pouring down from several feet overhead, gripping the edges of a toilet seat that is far too high and too large, standing on tiptoe to reach a cabinet or a sink, trying to see in a mirror so high that it misses them completely. Then they must go out into the world to try to open doors too heavy for them, negotiate stairs too steep, reach food on tables and shelves that are too high, pass through turnstiles that hit them directly in the face, see a film almost totally obscured by the back of the auditorium seat in front of them, get a drink out of a fountain they can't reach, make a phone call from a pay telephone placed at adult height, bang into sharp corners just the height of their heads, and risk their safety in revolving doors. Having physical reminders that there are children in the world would help to make us more alert and attentive toward them, making their lives safer and more interesting. The real advance for children will come when adults recognize them as an integral part of the community, expecting them to be around, naturally looking out for them and scaling conveniences to their size.

We must also find a health-care solution that works—for all members of our society. A child must have the right to obtain medical treatment without parental consent. This doesn't mean that the physician is empowered to dictate the kind of treatment a child receives without having to explain it to the parent, but rather that the child is empowered to deal directly with the physician and to have some freedom and responsibility in the actions taken with respect to her or his own health. (In cases where the children are too young or uncomprehending to seek medical attention on their own they should of course be represented by a parent or advocate.) Minors should be given complete information on their condition and on the procedures that are suggested for their treatment, as well as information on a variety of health problems, notably those of birth control and venereal disease. Adopted children must also have the right to obtain their natural family's medical history.

In health, welfare, and education, a child's ignorance is a strong political ally of adult society, and adults have learned to rely heavily on it. Because children are excluded from almost every institution in our society, they don't know what to do to gain power over their own lives. They are separated from the adult world, barred from important conversations, kept out of the rooms where decisions are made, excluded from social gatherings, dinner parties, and business meetings, and denied access to information about society and themselves.

Student's school records provide a good example of this exclusion. Information—including IQ scores, teachers' or counselors' reports, personality data, and health records—is, in most cases, withheld from both parent and child. The secrecy of this system prohibits the careful evaluation of the information's accuracy. Neither parent nor child—but especially not the child—is usually permitted to challenge it. Even though we evolve and change, these records are cumulative and permanent and there is no practice of their systematic destruction at various points in a person's life. Teachers, police officers (who may be able to use the material against a child or parent), and other enforcers of society's rules have access to the file even if they cannot demonstrate a need for the information. The file is often available for medical or educational research purposes. All this may represent a tremendous threat to individual privacy and to the liberation of the child.

Students are labeled and categorized; the advantaged are secretly placed on tracks toward college or vocational training and others are damaged by derogatory material appearing on their permanent files as the result of temporary anger or prejudice of teachers. The serious flaws of all diagnostic measures recorded in these files, the questionable nature of psychological tests used, the fact that having certain knowledge and therefore certain expectations of children tends to be self-confirming, the way in which test scores prejudice teachers and administrators—all these factors combine to make the keeping of records a capricious and sometimes dangerous procedure.

Children are also systematically denied information in sexual matters. The average child sees literally thousands of filmed and televised murders, yet parents and the media strain to keep sex out of the child's thoughts.

The fact that children want information about sex does not mean they should be able to invade adults' bedrooms. Adults and children alike should have control over their private lives. At this point, however, the privacy that needs protection is the child's. Adults think nothing of entering children's private space (if indeed they have private space); of opening their mail, going through their drawers, interrogating them about associates or activities. As a result, most children have little or no private life.

Subjecting children to such prohibitions and deceptions ultimately threatens our democratic process; above all else, that process requires an independent and informed citizenry. The most potent weapon against tyranny is knowledge that is easily accessible to all. Whenever one group decides what is and what is not desirable

for another to know, whenever a "we-they" condition exists, society becomes vulnerable to totalitarian controls. The acquisition of information by the child causes adults distress for exactly the same reasons; it empowers children, and makes it less easy to control and dominate them.

Our predisposition to ignore children's concerns, deal expeditiously with their questions, and deny them entry into the world of adults, is precisely the reason they tend to remain ignorant, dependent, and impotent. It's time to give up our adult privileges and make room for the autonomous child.

Individual action is vital, but it can never be sufficient. Only concerted action taken on many fronts can enable children to escape their prisons. Either we do this together—or it won't be done at all.

A CHILD'S BILL OF RIGHTS

Richard Farson outlines the specific reforms that he considers essential to the true liberation of all children, including his own.

1. The Right to Self-Determination. *Children should have the right to decide the matters which affect them most directly.* This is the basic right upon which all others depend. Children are now treated as the private property of their parents on the assumption that it is the parents' right and responsibility to control the life of the child. The achievement of children's rights, however, would reduce the need for this control and bring about an end to the double standard of morals and behavior for adults and children.

2. The Right to Alternative Home Environments. *Self-determining children should be able to choose from among a variety of arrangements: residences operated by children, child exchange programs, 24-hour child-care centers, and various kinds of schools and employment opportunities.* Parents are not always good for their children—some people estimate that as many as 4 million children are abused annually in the United States, for instance, and that a half million children run away each year.

3. The Right to Responsive Design. *Society must accommodate itself to children's size and to their need for safe space.* To keep them in their place, we now force children to cope with a world that is either not built to fit them, or is actually designed against them. If the environment were less dangerous for children, there would be less need for constant control and supervision of children by adults.

4. The Right to Information. *A child must have the right to all information ordinarily available to adults—including, and perhaps especially, information that makes adults uncomfortable.*

5. The Right to Educate Oneself. *Children should be free to design their own education, choosing from among many options the kinds of learning experiences they want, including the option not to attend any kind of school.* Compulsory education must be abolished because the enforced threatening quality of education in America has taught children to hate school, to hate the subject matter, and, tragically, to hate themselves. Children are programmed, tracked, and certified in a process of stamping out standardized educated products acceptable to the university, military, business and industry, and community. Education can change only through the achievement of new rights for those exploited and oppressed by it—the children themselves.

6. The Right to Freedom from Physical Punishment. *Children should live free of physical threat from those who are larger and more powerful than they.* Corporal punishment is used impulsively and cruelly in the home, arbitrarily in the school, and sadistically in penal institutions. It does not belong in our repertoire of responses to children.

7. The Right to Sexual Freedom. *Children should have the right to conduct their sexual lives with no more restriction than adults.* Sexual freedom for children must include the right to information about sex, the right to nonsexist education, and the right to all sexual activities that are legal among consenting adults. In fact, children

will be best protected from sexual abuse when they have the right to refuse—but they are now trained *not* to refuse adults, to accept all forms of physical affection, and to mistrust their own reactions to people. They are denied any information about their own sexuality or that of others. We keep them innocent and ignorant and then worry that they will not be able to resist sexual approaches.

8. The Right to Economic Power. *Children should have the right to work, to acquire and manage money, to receive equal pay for equal work, to choose trade apprenticeship as an alternative to school, to gain promotion to leadership positions, to own property, to develop a credit record, to enter into binding contracts, to engage in enterprise, to obtain guaranteed support apart from the family, to achieve financial independence.*

9. The Right to Political Power. *Children should have the vote and be included in the decision-making process.* Eighty million children in the United States need the right to vote because adults do not vote in their behalf. At present they are no one's constituency and legislation reflects that lack of representation. To become a constituency they must have the right to vote.

10. The Right to Justice. *Children must have the guarantee of a fair trial with due process of law, an advocate to protect their rights against the parents as well as the system, and a uniform standard of detention.* Every year a million children get into trouble with the law. One out of every nine children will go through the juvenile court system before the age of 18. At any given time about one hundred thousand children are in some kind of jail. Some are held illegally, many have not committed any kind of crime, most have done nothing that would be considered a crime if done by an adult, and none has been given a fail trial with due process of law. The juvenile justice system was designed to protect children from the harsh treatment of the adult justice system—but it is more unfair, more arbitrary, and more cruel.

PART IV

Relationships Among the Hierarchies with Focus on Correlates, Ideology, Consciousness, and Mobility

---

8

The Prediction of Social Behavior and Attitudes: The Correlates Tradition

Edward Ransford

HOW INDIVIDUALS behave, think, or generally view the world stems in some degree from their location in the social structure. Sociologists regard positions in the social structure as sets of daily experiences and life situations out of which individuals construct orientations toward themselves, others, and society at large. When individuals occupy the same statuses in a social structure, their constructions of reality are likely to be similar. Conversely, when individuals occupy different statuses in the social structure, their views on a variety of issues are likely to differ. This is the most general theoretical perspective that underlies the study of what has traditionally been called the *correlates* of stratification hierarchies. Simply stated, the correlates tradition maintains that certain behavior and attitudes are correlated with particular positions in a hierarchy.

Social class is associated with differences in such diverse aspects of human thought and behavior as types of mental and physical illness, family stability, child-rearing practices, reading habits, sexual behavior, organizational memberships, friendship patterns, average lifetime travel, and political attitudes and participation (Hodges, 1964:130–242; Kahl, 1960:127–220; Reissman, 1959:227–290; Duberman, 1976:115–227).

But social class describes only one important position in the social structure. A person's age, sex, and ethnicity, are equally important in shaping attitudes and behavior. For example, membership in an ethnic group is highly related to political behavior, attitudes toward the police, and feelings of alienation (Kahl and Goering, 1971; Middleton, 1963; Ransford, 1977:107–113). Sex also is an important predictor. For example, sex-role socialization operates as a force independent of class or ethnicity in lowering career expectations (Ireson, 1976).

An asterisk (*) accompanying a citation indicates a selection that is included in this volume.

The correlates tradition is closely linked to the sociological concept of norms. Each position in the social structure carries with it certain normative constraints, that is, certain rules of behavior that carry pressure to conform. The normative assumption is important because it allows us to make predictions about modal behavior. Of course, not all people conform to norms at all times, but there is enough conformity to high-intensity norms to allow for a baseline of expected behavior for fairly accurate predictions. The positions of black, female, upper class, or age thirty-five, all involve social expectations of behavior. Until very recently, for example, most women would not think of taking the initiative in asking men for dates except in rare instances (such as a "ladies choice" dance) or in subpopulations such as prostitutes. To do so would have been a clear violation of the norms surrounding appropriate female behavior.

There also is awareness and concern over age-appropriate behavior at particular points in the life cycle: "She's too young to wear that style of clothing," or "That's a strange thing for a man of his age to say"(Neugarten, *et al.*, 1965:711). A person's age is not a neutral position but is surrounded by many norms specifying appropriate behavior. A wide variety of sanctions (punishments and rewards) are attached to these norms. A middle-aged woman who dresses like an adolescent may experience avoidance and disapproval from friends her own age.

> Age norms and age expectations operate as prods and brakes upon behavior in some instances hastening an event, in others, delaying it. Men and women are aware not only of the social clocks that operate in various areas of their lives but they are aware also of their own timing and readily describe themselves as "early," "late," or "on time" with regard to family and occupational events (Neugarten, *et al,* 1965:711).

Neugarten, *et al.*, interviewed a representative sample of middle-class men and women, aged forty to seventy, asking questions such as, "What do you think is the best age for a man to marry? . . . to finish school?" etc. The results are reproduced in Table 8-1. Note the extremely high consensus as to the appropriate age for a given behavior.

Age can be viewed in other ways besides life-cycle expectations. Political generations is one of the most interesting ways to study the social correlates of age.

> A *political generation* is composed of individuals of approximately the same age who have experienced the same politically relevant events. From these experiences the generation creates certain political attitudes and world views which are in some ways particular to that generation (Jeffries, 1974:121).

Jeffries distinguishes between three political generations of current society: *dissent* (those born between 1943 and 1949), *Cold War* (those born between 1927 and 1942), and *World War II* (those born before 1927). These political generations have very different attitudes toward nuclear war. As expected, the *dissent* generation is most opposed to the use of massive nuclear force (when our national interests are threatened), the *World War II* generation is most in favor of nuclear force, and the *Cold War* generation is intermediate between these extremes (Jeffries, 1974).

A variety of correlates could be linked to class, ethnicity, sex, or age. We will emphasize especially those correlates that relate to inequality of power, privilege, and

Table 8-1. *Consensus in a Middle-Class Middle-Aged Sample Regarding Various Age-Related Characteristics*

	Age Range Designated as Appropriate or Expected	Per Cent Who Concur	
		Men (N = 50)	Women (N = 43)
Best age for a man to marry	20–25	80	90
Best age for a woman to marry	19–24	85	90
When most people should become grandparents	45–50	84	79
Best age for most people to finish school and go to work	20–22	86	82
When most men should be settled on a career	24–26	74	64
When most men hold their top jobs	45–50	71	58
When most people should be ready to retire	60–65	83	86
A young man	18–22	84	83
A middle-aged man	40–50	86	75
An old man	65–75	75	57
A young woman	18–24	89	88
A middle-aged woman	40–50	87	77
An old woman	60–75	83	87
When a man has the most responsibilities	35–50	79	75
When a man accomplishes most	40–50	82	71
The prime of life for a man	35–50	86	80
When a woman has the most responsibilities	25–40	93	91
When a woman accomplishes most	30–45	94	92
A good-looking woman	20–35	92	82

Reprinted from Neugarten, Bernice L., Joan W. Moore, and John C. Lowe, 1965. "Age Norms, Age Constraints, and Adult Socialization." American Journal of Sociology 70 (May): 712. By permission of the University of Chicago Press.

prestige. As a result of reduced power, privilege, and prestige, certain outcomes or correlates can be anticipated. People in disadvantaged race and class positions, for example, are more likely to exhibit feelings of anger over discrimination barriers, psychological symptoms of stress, and feelings of distrust toward public officials. In short, under the correlates tradition, class, age, sex, and ethnicity operate as predictors of individual and group behavior. A position in each of the four hierarchies is seen as a strong causal force that affects a wide variety of outcomes.

Figure 8–1 shows a clear causal direction (from stratification position to outcome) yet, we have used the more conservative term *correlates* as a title for this chapter. A correlation means that there is a statistical association between two variables; it may be an instance of cause and effect, or it may not. The term *correlates* then, is chosen as safest and most appropriate. The majority of the studies reviewed in the following pages, however, infer causation; they imply that position in a stratification hierarchy determines an outcome.

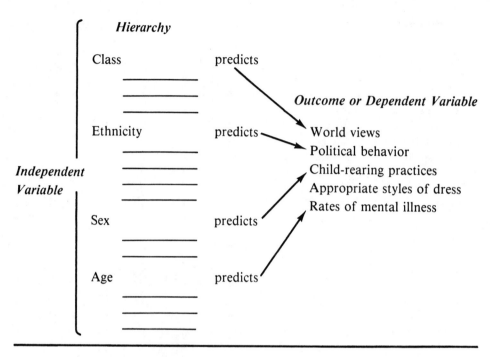

Figure 8-1. *Stratification Position Predicts Outcome*

CORRELATES OF CLASS POSITION

The results of hundreds of studies show that social class has an impact on human behavior and attitudes. Class creates a social world that shapes a person's outlook and values. Political behavior, the frequency and quality of dental care, whether one will complete four years of college, tastes in furniture—all are determined to some degree by class position. This is not to say that individual behavior is rigidly determined by class position; rather, class position creates broad boundaries within which individual action is conducted (Reissman, 1959:228). This notion is illustrated by the research that links class with types and rates of mental illnesses.

Social Class and Mental Illness

Social classes can be viewed as determining environments with different amounts of strain, tension, competition, and isolation that find expression in different rates of mental illness. A landmark study in this area is the Hollingshead and Redlich (1958) research of psychiatric patients in New Haven, Connecticut. Three basic questions guided the research:

1.   How is mental illness distributed by social class?
2.   Is social class related to the severity of psychiatric disorders?
3.   Does social class have anything to do with the treatment of the mentally ill?

A follow-up study conducted ten years later (Myers, Bean, and Pepper, 1968), added a fourth question.

4.   Is social class related to the hospital release-rate of schizophrenic patients?

The data on psychiatric patients was obtained from a variety of treatment centers. This allowed for a study of patients representing a wide range of class origins. The psychiatric population of the study consisted of 1,963 cases. Five social classes were determined from an index of occupation and education. The top class (I) consisted of professionals and business executives with college or postgraduate degrees. Class II could be viewed roughly as upper middle-class, class III as middle-class, class IV as stable working-class, and V as lower class.

The first question of the study, whether mental illness was distributed by social class, was answered with clear results: mental illness is *not* randomly distributed throughout the class structure. Class V had a far higher proportion of mentally ill patients than the other classes. As one descends the class structure, class I, down to stably employed workers, the differences between classes are small. But when one crosses the line from class IV to class V, there is a huge jump in rates of mental illness. In classes I and II combined, there were 556 psychiatric disorders per 100,000 people. In class III the number was 538; class IV showed a slight increase to 642. In class V, the rate dramatically increases to 1,659 disorders per 100,000 people (Harrington, 1966:121).

Not only is the incidence of psychiatric disorders greater in the lower class, but the more severe mental disorders or phychoses also are overrepresented in this stratum. The proportion of schizophrenics and manic depressives was much higher among class V patients. Other studies also have substantiated the correlation between lower-class position and schizophrenia (Farris and Dunham, 1939; Kaplan *et al.*, 1956). (However, these other studies did not show a class link to manic-depressive disorders).

Studies of class correlates ideally should employ a theory that logically links the class environment to the outcome that the researcher has hypothesized. Hollingshead and Redlich did not concern themselves with a theory to explain the connection between class position and schizophrenia, but others have. Two common explanations of why there is greater incidence of mental illness in the lower classes have been asserted: the social isolation theory and the stress factor theory.

The social isolation explanation may derive from the observations of anthropologists. Schizophrenia is almost entirely absent in close-knit folk societies. The absence of schizophrenia has been attributed to the social organization of such societies, which prevents people from withdrawing from social interaction. In other words, meaningful group involvement is believed to prevent persons from withdrawing from reality and creating their own private worlds. In line with this thinking, a study of an urban society found that schizophrenia rates were far higher in the lower-class downtown area of Chicago (Farris and Dunham, 1939). Poverty, of course, was a factor in this study, but the high degree of social isolation and anonymity was even more important. It was an area populated by men without families, men who lived in rooming houses. The social isolation of lower class neighborhoods, just outside the downtown section, was believed to cause psychological withdrawal.

Proponents of the stress factor theory assert that severe mental illness is more likely to occur in the lowest class because the poor are bombarded by stressful life situations. Stress factors common to the lower class are unemployment, poor medical care, family tensions and money worries (Harrington, 1966:123; Kohn, 1968). Stressful situations are likely to arise with more frequency for the poor and to last longer because they lack the money and power to control their environment in the same way that persons in middle and upper classes can (Ryan, 1971:136–173). Of course, stressful situations exist in all class environments, but the poor face more stress inputs per unit of time. Medical, employment, and family tensions that occur sporadically for persons in the middle-class all may be concentrated within a few weeks or a month among members of the lower class (Howell, 1973). Life at the bottom of the class structure is precarious. Schizophrenia is viewed as one outcome of this stress.

The theories of stress and social isolation share one assumption: they both assert that the conditions of social class cause mental illness. Some sociologists have stated a rival hypothesis: that mental illness is greater in the lower class because psychotics drift downward in the class structure (Gibbs, 1962; Antunes, et al., 1974). Those people who are mentally ill (for whatever reason) will become incompetent in a variety of social areas, such as job performance, and, as a result, they will be downwardly mobile. From this view, class has nothing to do with causing mental illness; class is a correlate of mental illness but not its cause. At the time of this writing the debate has not been resolved. Some empirical evidence exists for each position.

The Hollingshead and Redlich study also addressed itself to the question of whether or not psychiatric treatments of the mentally ill vary by class. Again, a strong class relationship was found. Patients from the lower two classes (IV and V) were more likely to receive custodial care, drugs, and shock treatment and not very likely to receive psychotherapy. In the top three classes, psychotherapy was much more common (especially in classes I and II). In trying to find reasons for these differential treatments, the researchers discovered that psychiatrists felt that they had a much more difficult time communicating with the lower-class patients. They were irritated by the values and life styles of some of the class IV and V patients. They resented patients from classes IV and V demanding "quick cures" and authoritarian prescriptions ("Tell me what to do), an approach that is antithetical to the goals of insight therapy. Psychiatrists had a tendency to define lower-class patients as "bad cases" and to suspend their treatment (Hollingshead and Redlich, 1958:344).

A ten-year follow-up of schizophrenic patients (Myers, et al., 1968) in the Hollingshead-Redlich study sample revealed another strong class pattern: the higher the class position, the more likely a patient was to be released to the community. And the lower the class position, the greater the chance that a person remained in the mental hospital.

The study also found, surprisingly, that the higher the social class, the greater the proportion of patients whose mental condition would be considered marginal or impaired after their release. Perhaps there are strong class differences in the ability and willingness of a family to accept a psychiatric patient back into the home. The stigma of mental illness is especially strong in classes IV and V. The working-class family may be less able to offer supervision and care of a patient released to their home because they have smaller houses and less money to provide for home care. On the other hand, upper- and middle-class families are more willing to receive a family member who was hospitalized, and they have greater resources to provide for his or her care. This might explain why more middle- and upper-class schizophrenics, who are relatively poorly adjusted psychologically, are more likely to be discharged from a mental hospital.

In sum, social class is related to the incidence of mental illness, the kind of treatment patients received, and the probability patients have of being released to the community. At every step along the way, the upper classes have greater chance of receiving quality care.

Three other examples of class correlates are briefly summarized to indicate the range of variables with which class is associated.

Correlate: Completion of College.   Higher-status young people are more likely to complete four years of college, even if IQ is accounted for. In fact, some studies show that an upper-class young person with a below-average IQ is as likely to complete college as a very bright young person from a lower-class household (Sewell and Shah, 1967). The upper-status family, school, and neighborhood provide a very supportive environment for college plans. Peer-group support, a high value placed on college education, money, and other resources are all a part of the upper-class environment.

Correlate: Values for Child Behavior.   Middle-class parents give higher priority to values that reflect internal standards of behavior such as self-direction, curiosity, self-control, and consideration for others. Working-class parents give higher priority to values that reflect social conformity such as obedience for boys neatness for girls (Kohn, 1969).

Some of this difference in values is a function of the father's work world. Middle-class jobs encourage more "independent thought, initiative and self direction," whereas working-class jobs involve more routine and conformity to job requirements (Kohn, 1969:139–188).

Correlate: Rates of Delinquency.   Most studies show higher rates of delinquency in the lower and working classes (Nye, Short, and Olsen, 1958; Cohen, 1955). However, official arrest records do not match the self-reported data. Williams and Gold (1972) interviewed 847 teenagers and asked them to report all crimes that they had committed or been part of. A very high proportion (88 percent) admitted committing at least one offense but most of these crimes did not appear in police statistics; in fact, most were not even detected by the police (only 3 percent). There was no significant relationship between class and self-reported crime. If anything, the upper and middle classes in this study were slightly *more* likely to have committed crimes. Upper- and middle-class youth probably have committed crimes with the same frequency as lower-class youth, but are more successful in evading detection and an arrest record. Class is related to officially recorded delinquency but not to self-reported delinquency.

CORRELATES OF MULTIPLE POSITIONS
IN SOCIAL HIERARCHIES

The multiple hierarchy approach opens the door to a much more complex and interesting frame of reference for making stratification predictions. How do the class, ethnic, sex, and age hierarchies interrelate, compete, or combine to influence predicted outcomes or correlates?

Research into the combined effects of stratification positions is one of the most unexplored areas in the field of stratification—a veritable empirical wasteland at the time of this writing. Sizable segments of the population face reinforcing deprivations from low positions in more than one hierarchy, such as old, minority, and poor. Other population segments experience competing tugs or cross-pressures from different stratification positions; for example, the Mexican-American woman facing conflict between the goals of the women's movement and the goals of "la raza," the Mexican-American counterpart of black pride. And, much of our knowledge of stratification is based on research dealing with the outlooks and behavior of one combination group—white males. Little is known about the attitudes and behaviors of other combination groups, such as Mexican-American women or the black aged.

When considering all the combinations of statification positions—such as old, black, middle-class, male or young, lower-class, female, Puerta Ricana—the sheer number of possible combinations becomes a problem. Conceptual leverage is needed to organize the many possibilities. Accordingly, we are advancing a typology to account for the different forms of joint hierarchy effects. A number of specific strategies are discussed in the following pages. All of them are classified as either: (I) Comparisons or (II) Combinations of social hierarchies.

The *Comparisons* section attempts to untangle the effects of ethnicity, class, sex, and age in predicting a dependent variable. Two or more hierarchies are considered but the focus is on assessment of their *separate* effects. For example, if the issue regards health care of the minority poor, one could investigate whether race or class is the more important force in determining the quality of medical care. In this case, two hierarchies are put into competition with one another; we try to determine which hierarchy is a more powerful predictor. We also try to find out if one hierarchy has an independent effect when the effects of another hierarchy are controlled, or held constant.

The *Combinations* section of this chapter deals with the combined effects of two or more stratification positions on various outcomes. Stratification hierarchies are not considered separately, but as they interact to produce an outcome that cannot be explained by either one taken singly. In the example of health care, it is possible that race, class, and age all have an important bearing on the quality of health care, and the combined effect of all three results in unusually poor medical service. The *minority aged poor* may have very special problems in receiving quality medical treatment; their health-care services may be significantly below those received by other combination groups, such as aged white poor.

The joint effects of two or more hierarchies will be discussed under each of the two categories of Comparisons and Combinations. The organization of the typology† is as follows:

I   Comparisons
    A.   Independent Effects
    B.   Relative Effects
II   Combinations
    A.   Multiple Jeopardy/Advantage
    B.   Status Consistency
    C.   Low Ascribed/High Achieved Combinations

I COMPARISONS

A. Independent Effects

One way to consider multiple strata is to find out whether each hierarchy has an independent effect on the outcome (or dependent) variable in question. Let us consider whether race or class has a major effect on an individual's position in society. Here, there has been some debate, to say the least. Does racial position, for example, have an effect on life chances when social class is controlled? Some authors have asserted that race is no longer an independent factor in the determination of power and privilege—that poverty or a low position in the class hierarchy is the only really important dimension. Banfield comments:

> If overnight Negroes turned white most of them would go on living under much the same handicaps for a long time to come. The great majority of *New Whites* would continue working at the same jobs, living in the same neighborhoods and sending their children to the same schools. . . . There would be no sudden mass exodus from the blighted and slum neighborhoods . . . New Whites would go on living in the same neighborhoods for the simple reason that they could not afford to move to better ones (Banfield, 1968:73).

For Banfield, the problem described is not race, but lack of money. From this perspective, race has been less important than class exploitation in the oppression of black Americans. Blacks were subordinated in the United States not so much because of racist beliefs *per se* but because the dominant white class needed a cheap, exploitable labor force.

Another theory that gives more weight to class than race points out that the white working class in northern industrial areas kept blacks out of craft unions not primarily because of racist beliefs but because blacks threatened to produce a split-labor market in which blacks would be hired by white capitalists for less than the wages recently won by whites through unionization (Bonacich, 1972). Some sociologists, then, assert that one's position in the class structure is more important than one's race in determining access to power, privilege, and prestige (Wilson, 1978).

Recent research, however, strongly suggests that race does make an independent contribution to the life chances of an individual. Blau and Duncan (1967), for example,

---

†Some of the logic and terms used in the development of this typology are borrowed from Morris Rosenberg, *The Logic of Survey Analysis*, 1968:160–196.

wanted to see if blacks and whites attained different occupational positions with the following class variables held constant: (1) educational attainment (black college graduates were compared with white college grads); (2) class of origin, measured by father's occupations; and (3) the status of the person's first job (blacks who started low in the occupation hierarchy were compared with whites who started low in the occupational hierarchy). Their findings show dramatically that race has a significant impact on occupational attainment, when class origin and class achievement variables are controlled.

> In sum, Negroes are handicapped by having poorer parents, less education, and inferior early career experiences than whites. Yet even if these handicaps are statistically controlled by asking, in effect, what the achievement of non-whites would be if they had the same origins, the same education and the same first jobs as whites, their occupational chances are still consistently inferior to those of whites. Thus, being a Negro in the United States has independent disadvantageous consequences for several of the factors that directly affect occupational success (Blau and Duncan, 1967:209).

Blau and Duncan used 1960 census data in their analysis. But studies with more recent data support the conclusion that race has an independent effect on socioeconomic returns. When the effects of education, occupation, and region of the country have been removed, there remains an income gap between black and white. This is often referred to as the "cost of being black." In 1969 dollars, the cost of being black was $1,380 in 1959 and $1,647 in 1969 (Johnson and Sell, 1976; Siegal, 1965). Similar analyses have been conducted on Mexican-American workers. Poston and Alvirez* (1973) examined income differences in 1960 between Mexican Americans and Anglos at various levels of educational attainment and for eight occupational categories. Do Anglos have higher incomes than Mexican Americans when the effects of educational attainment and occupational level have been removed? Ethnicity does carry an independent effect. The cost of being Mexican American was slightly more than $900.00. Especially striking were the income differences between Mexican Americans and Anglos at the level of managers, officials, and proprietors. "At every level of educational attainment, save one, the average income of Anglo managers is at least $1,200 more than Mexican American managers, and in the case of those workers with 1–3 years of college, the differential was $2,700" (Poston and Alvirez, 1973: 703). Ethnicity has independent negative consequences on earnings. More recently, Poston, *et al,*. repeated the study with 1970 data to see if there had been changes in the cost of being Mexican American (Poston, Alvirez and Tienda, 1976). They found that the "cost" had actually increased in the ten year period; this was true for younger cohorts of Chicanos as well as older.

The independent effects of sex and class were studied with similar results (Sell and Johnson, 1977). In 1969, the mean income for working men was $9,564; the comparable figure for women was only $4,349. The differential between the average salary for men and the average salary for women was $5,215. A large proportion of this differential (about 73 percent) can be ascribed to the fact that women have lower educational attainment, are employed in lower-paying jobs, and are less likely to work year-round. Nevertheless, there is a remaining male-female difference of $1,429, which is probably a function of sex discrimination. Research supports the view that gender has an effect independent of class position on the life chances of an individual.

B. Relative Effects

If a case can be made for some degree of independence among the four hierarchies, then it makes sense to ask what is the relative importance of one or the other. Which stratification position has the greater (or greatest) effect in predicting the dependent variable?

People charged with implementing social policy frequently base their decisions on the *relative effects* of one social hierarchy over another. Ethnic minorities, women, and, most recently, the aged have developed group consciousness, political lobbies, and protest techniques, causing competition for resources such as political appointments, Affirmative Action commitment, and federal funding. These competing groups must demonstrate to public officials that their inequality or underrepresentation in some employment sector is as great or greater than that of another group.

Let us suppose that a researcher is interested in determining the effects of race and sex on earnings. Does sex discrimination have a greater effect than racial discrimination? The data in Table 8–2 indicate that sex is a more important factor in determining income than is race.

Table 8–2. *Comparison of Mean Earnings by Race and by Sex, 1970*

	Sex		Sex Differences
	Male	Female	
Race			
White	$10,458	$5,280	$5,178
Black	6,404	4,077	2,327
Race differences	4,054	1,203	

Source: U.S. Bureau of the Census; 1970 Subject Reports, "Earnings by Occupation and Education," Final Report PC (2)-88. Data are for year-round workers only. Organization of data into race-sex comparisons taken from Elizabeth M. Almquist, "Untangling the Effects of Race and Sex: The Effects of Race and Sex: The Disadvantaged Status of Black Women," *Social Science Quarterly* 56: 129–142.

However, these are very crude data that need to be standardized on other variables relevant to income. Some of the findings in Table 8–2 may be due to factors such as the age of the worker or region of the country. Almquist (1975) standardized the earnings of the four groups on the variables of age, education, occupation, and region of the country. That is, she statistically removed the effects of all the other variables except the one under consideration. She reports the following gaps in income that remain after standardization:

		Gaps
1.	Black males standardized to white males	$1,772
2.	Black females standardized to white females	$0
3.	White females standardized to white males	$4,570
4.	Black females standardized to black males	$2,501

The income disparities are now much lower because the effects of other variables have been subtracted, leaving the net effects of race and sex. The standardized data make it even more clear that the sex gap (see numbers 3 and 4) exceeds the racial gap (see numbers 1 and 2) in income. Of course, effects of racial discriminaton are still present since the black males earn on the average $1,772 less than white males, but from the standpoint of relative effects, the income differences of the sexes are much greater than the income differences between blacks and whites.

The relative effects of stratification systems also can be tested on a more social-psychological level, using attitude survey data. Recent studies have sought to determine whether class or race is more important as a determinant of friendship. In one study, white respondents were asked: "Who do you think you could more easily become friends with—a Negro with the same education and income as you or a white person with a different education and income than you?" (Cambell, 1971; Ransford, 1977: 145–155). Striking differences were found among whites of different socioeconomic levels (Ransford, 1977). Those in higher occupation, education, and income brackets reported that they could more easily become friends with a black person of the same education and income level than with a white person of a very different level. That is, upper-middle and upper-status whites were more likely to choose friends from the same class, regardless of race. In contrast, whites at the lower levels of the class hierarchy said they would choose a white person of a different socioeconomic status rather than a black person of the same class.

These findings cannot be generalized too much, based as they are on a single question involving a hypothetical situation for most of the respondents. Still, the data encourage the interpretation that, among whites, socioeconomic similarity is far more likely to break down racial barriers to friendship at middle- and upper-class levels than at lower-class levels.

"Ageism Compared to Racism and Sexism," an article by Palmore and Manton* (1973), is the first three-way comparison of age, sex, and race. They asked, "Which is stonger in our society—race, sex, or age inequality?" An inequality index was developed and each of the three variables was paired: white/black, male/female, and under 65/65 and over. Viewing income as the most basic measure of life chances, the following pattern of comparative inequality was found: the male-female comparison produced the greatest income inequality; the black-white comparison produced the least inequality; and the aged-nonaged comparison was intermediate between sex and race in its effects. The article also made comparisons of inequality through time. Between 1950 and 1970 there was a small but clear trend toward greater racial equality in the country. In contrast, sex inequality showed no change through the twenty-year period and age inequality actually worsened.

There are some methodological problems with the Palmore-Manton analysis. It is reasonable to divide race into black/white and sex into male/female categories. But it may be statistically misleading to cut age groups crudely into under 65/over 65 categories. There is a high degree of age discrimination in our society against particular age groups under 65. A fifty-year-old man is replaced as a top manager by a younger person; an attractive forty-five-year-old woman is judged too old to be a receptionist in a law firm; housewives who have stayed home to raise their children find it extremely difficult to reenter the job market in their mid-forties—all are examples of age discrimination among preretirement persons. The Palmore-Manton article completely misses this kind of age inequality by comparing only the under 65/over 65 groups. Despite these problems, the Palmore-Manton piece is a classic first attempt to compare the relative degree of inequality across hierarchies.

II COMBINATIONS

This approach to multiple hierarchy correlates deals with the combined effects of two or more stratification positions. The idea of *unique social space* underlies all discussions in this section. We refer to unique social space as the specialized environment created when class, ethnicity, age, and sex intersect in particular combinations. These combinations determine a person's options, constraints, discrimination battles, and attitudes. A unique social space also has a pattern of social interaction in which individuals interact with one another within a context of common traditions or shared meanings. Consistent with symbolic interaction theory, the members of a unique social space are more likely to interact with each other because they share common symbols, gestures, and life situations. Examples of unique social spaces are the social worlds of *third-generations Japanese Americans* (age combined with ethnicity), *young female Chicanas* (age, sex, and ethnicity), and *wealthy white males* (class, ethnicity, and sex).

The Concept of Unique Social Space

The concept of unique social space derives from Milton Gordon's discussion of *ethclass*. Gordon (1964) made a breakthrough in stratification theory by stating how class and ethnicity might logically combine to predict particular outcomes. His model dealt only with ethnicity and class; he was not concerned (as we are) with the interactions among four hierarchies. Nevertheless, his is one of the clearest statements of combination effects.

Gordon views both class and ethnicity as powerful forces that affect identity, social participation, and cultural behavior (Gordon, 1964). Social class is likely to be more important than ethnicity as a determinant of cultural behavior, life style, and taste. However, if one is considering collective identity—a sense of peoplehood in which common destiny and heritage is shared with a large number of others with the same racial or national descent—ethnicity becomes more salient. When people have *both* class and ethnicity in common, there develops a powerful basis for social interaction.

Class outlooks and ethnic identification often unite or blend into what Gordon calls and ethclass. *Ethclass* is the social space created by the intersection of the ethnic group with the social class. This is illustrated in Figure 8–2, in which four ethnic populations are cross-matched with four social classes. Each block on Figure 8–2 represents a unique social space, a kind of subsociety. According to Gordon, ethnic and class factors combine to affect primary-group participation (such as marriage and close friendship). Following Gordon's logic, working-class Mexican Americans would be more likely to enter into relaxed, trusting relationships with other working-class Mexican Americans than with middle-class Mexican Americans or with working-class Anglos.

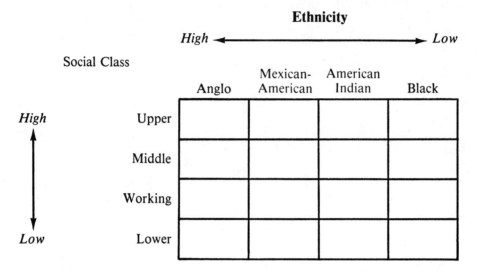

Figure 8-2. *Possible Intersections of Class and Ethnicity to Create a Unique Social Space, or Ethclass*

Gordon hypothesizes that *cultural behavior* is best predicted by class; *sense of people-hood* is most often a reflection of ethnicity; and *participation in primary groups* is confined to ethclass.

Surprisingly, the concept "ethclass" has received very little attention in race or stratification literature in recent years. It becomes evident that ethclass is a provocative concept for analyzing stratification combinations.

Class stratification within the black and Mexican-American populations appears to be developing rapidly at the same time that black pride and "la raza" are producing heightened ethnic identifications. Therefore, a concept that posits that unique social spaces are determined by a blend of race and class has special relevance to the contemporary scene.

Gordon's version of ethclass is confined to the single prediction of primary group participation. We suggest that the concept of an ethclass can be generalized to explain any instance in which the behavior or attitudes of individuals result from the combined effect of ethnicity and social class. The attitudes or actions of an ethclass might be cultural attitudes or political behaviors, as well as the primary-group interaction that Gordon suggests. Our expanded version of the concept means that the values and tastes of individuals are not necessarily due to their social class positions alone. Since blacks, Chicanos, and Native Americans are asserting their cultural uniqueness,as illustrated by "soul," chicanismo, and tribal nationalism, and at the same time are developing varying class interests, it seems likely that distinct blends of ethnicity and class will be reflected in attitudes and values. For example, Ransford considered ethnic-class combinations in analyzing the perception of police force in the East Los Angeles riot of 1970 (Ransford, 1977:113). Reaction varied dramatically by ethclass: whites of all classes perceived that Chicanos were treated fairly by police, whereas blacks, and especially middle-class blacks, believed that Chicanos were usually not treated fairly by the police. The Chicano perception of police force varied greatly by class. Lower-class Chicanos were far more critical of the police than middle-class Chicanos. In other words, for Mexican Americans, as one ascends the class structure, police hostility diminishes; for blacks, police hostility remains high at all class levels and is greatest for middle-class blacks. For whites, *support* for the police is uniformly high at all class levels. Ethnicity and class, then, combine to produce particular ethclass attitudes.

It is interesting that middle-class Mexican Americans expressed far less hostility toward the police than middle-class blacks (22 percent and 67 percent, respectively). Perhaps the middle-class Mexican American can more easily move out of the high-crime rate barrio to the suburbs where contacts with the police are likely to be fewer and more positive. In contrast, middle-class blacks are still racially visible and often live on the periphery of the ghetto, where police stop-and-search procedures are more common. Only by considering the complex blends of ethnicity and class can we understand these differences in attitude.

In sum, ethclass can be viewed as one example of the broader concept of unique social space. Interactions of two or more of any of the four hierarchies will produce unique social spaces. The concept of social space:

- Encompasses not just two (race and class) but four hierarchies (race, class, sex, and age);
- Explains values and attitudes not only as a function of class position, but also as the result of the juncture of two or more hierarchies (police attitudes, above, is an example); and
- Goes beyond predictions of primary-group interaction to predict a variety of behaviors, attitudes, life styles, and achievement opportunities.

Unique social space serves as the backbone concept for the following discussion on multiple jeopardy, status crystallization, and low ascribed/high achieved status sets.

A. Multiple Jeopardy and Multiple Advantage

If each of the four hierarchies of age, race, sex, and class can be individually related to power, privilege, and prestige, then the effect of two or more may compound deprivations or advantages. That is, the social space created by the combination of positions may represent multiple jeopardy or multiple advantage. From this perspective, the idea of structured inequality is expanded from a single-class dimension to an image of society in which there are multiple, stacked layers of inequality that reinforce one another. The multiple-jeopardy perspective leans strongly toward a conflict interpretation of stratification by suggesting that the distribution of power, privilege, and prestige is unjust: certain groups face combined barriers in obtaining the rewards of society. If blacks face institutional discrimination by race and women face institutional discrimination by sex then options for black females especially may be reduced.

Positions in the four hierarchies can also accrue multiple advantages. Upper-class white males in their middle or young adult years have far greater, virtually unencumbered access to power, prestige, and privilege.

Multiple jeopardy (or advantage) refers only to a situation of extremes in a number of disadvantages (or advantages). If we are considering the three hierarchies of class, ethnicity, and sex, then multiple jeopardy would focus only on status combinations that result in disadvantaged positions on all three hierarchies (such as poor, black, and female or low-low-low positions). Similarly the concept of multiple advantage is applied only to status combinations of combined advantage (e.g., upper-class white male or high-high-high positions). Multiple jeopardy does not apply to the mixed types of status combinations. When people face mixed status situations that place them high in one hierarchy, low in others (such as upper-class black male) they do not encounter multiple jeopardy (or advantage) in all areas. They face special circumstances that are discussed later in this chapter.

Sociologists have made few attempts at understanding how structured inequalities reinforce each other. The traditional literature on social class tends to place poverty in the forefront as the most important deprivation while age, sex, and ethnic inequality, if mentioned at all, are seen as adding a small increment of disadvantage to the poverty position. Multiple jeopardy emphasizes that class, ethnicity, sex, and age discrimination may combine to produce unique barriers that cannot be explained by any one of these hierarchies taken singly. But we cannot casually assume that a combination of two low positions leads inevitably to a multiple-jeopardy effect. Multiple jeopardy must be demonstrated statistically or with convincing qualitative description (like case studies or participant observation reports). Some particular combinations of status position may lead to combined disadvantages; others may not. For certain correlates, such as availability of legal aid, race and class may compound the effect; for others, such as medical care, being poor may be the most important circumstance (Bell and Zellman, 1975).

Following is a review of recent studies (many included in this volume) that suggest a multiple-jeopardy effect. The articles reviewed here did not always begin with a multiple-jeopardy theory, but the findings are clearly in this direction. Exceptions to the multiple-jeopardy thesis are included also.

Involuntary Sterilization and Lower-Class Minority Women.

With data obtained from interviews with doctors in several major hospitals, Kistler (1974) found evidence that low-income black and Chicana women particularly have been the victims of involuntary sterilization. Minority women with low incomes often are given misleading information or even coerced into signing sterilization forms during the delivery of a baby. Such practice is an extreme abuse of a woman's legal right to be fully informed about sterilization before opting for an irreversible surgical procedure. Kistler quotes Dr. Juan Nieto on this point:

> What they did to minority group women there, particularly Mexican Americans, really turned me off. They would get a young woman, maybe 19 or 20, who was having a baby and start right in on her in the delivery room, urging that she have her tubes tied . . . Young parents, many of whom barely spoke English, had no idea that the proce-dure that was being urged on them was permanant. They probably thought they could sim-ply have their tubes untied later (quoted in Kistler, 1974:27–28).

The Kistler article agrees with other research that finds lower-class people are much more likely to be intimidated by experts in bureaucratic settings and to lack the information to question the advice of experts (Rainwater, 1974; Howell, 1973). But involuntary sterilizations depict more than a class finding. Doctors may tend to urge sterilization on black, Puerto Rican, and Mexican-American women because it is for these select minority groups that one finds ethnic stereotypes operating. Many low-income minority women are perceived by some middle-class doctors as having too many children, as being promiscuous, or as a drain on welfare rolls and health-care services. A minority woman is much more likely to be treated as part of a statistical category rather than as an individual person when such stereotypes exist in society. Moreover, as the Kistler quote indicates, the lower-class Mexican-American woman who is not fluent in English may easily misunderstand, be uninformed, and therefore vulnerable to deception. Lower class *and* ethnicity contribute to a situation of multiple disadvantage.

The Minority Aged.   The minority aged have been frequently viewed as a classic example of multiple jeopardy. Older blacks, Mexican Americans, and other minority aged persons are often described as having the least access to quality-of-life-resources such as income, housing, and health care (National Urban League, 1964; National Council on Aging, 1972). But there is another very different theory to describe the minority aged. From this second perspective, age has a leveling influence in that inequalities that exist between whites and minority groups decrease from middle to old age (Kent and Hirsch, 1969). Forced retirement, loss of income, a decline in health, and other deprivations actually make older white and minority persons more alike than at any other time in the life cycle. Research by Dowd and Bengtson* (1978) contrasts these two theories (double jeopardy and leveling effect) using a large sample of middle-aged and older blacks, Mexican Americans, and whites.

Support for the multiple-jeopardy hypothesis was found when the income and health of aged people were measured. The average income reported by older black and Mexican American respondents was far below the income of older whites. Further support for multiple jeopardy was given by the finding that blacks and Mexican Americans had a greater decline in income over a thirty-year age span (age forty-five to age seventy-four) than did whites. Similarly, "older minority respondents were significantly more likely to report poorer health than older whites even with the effects of SES, sex, and income held constant" (Dowd and Bengtson,* 1978).

The data also showed some credence for the leveling theory. On a life satisfaction variable (tranquility and optimism), there was a decline in the ethnic difference between blacks and whites with increased age.

A conclusion that one reaches from the Dowd-Bengtson research is that two low positions do not always lead to multiple jeopardy. For certain outcomes (income and health, in this case) a low position on two hierarchies does, indeed, result in special combined deprivations, but for other outcomes such as tranquility, this does not occur.

The topic of double jeopardy and the minority aged is of more than theoretical interest. Jacquelyne Jackson has documented the development of the National Caucus for the Black Aged, an activist group specifically formed to help improve the quality of life for aging blacks (Jackson, 1974). The NCBA was active at the 1971 White House

Conference on Aging. Members of the group felt that aged blacks had pronounced deprivations and special needs and must forge their own policy. To join with the White House Conference on many issues would dilute and weaken their need to develop specialized policy. Thus, groups suffering from double jeopardy may develop a new and formidable basis for activist communities.

Elderly Poor of the Inner City.   Margaret Clark, * in a sensitive article on the aged poor of the inner city, presents another case of the compounding of deprivations (Clark,* 1971). Factors of age, poverty, and the poorest locations of the central city combine in the development of *geriatric ghettos* that have arisen in the last two decades.

The elderly of the inner city are different from other aging groups: "The inner city elderly are both physically and psychologically sicker than their age peers in other groups. They have a harder time surviving—perhaps the hardest of any elderly cohort we know" (Clark,* 1971:59). Clark, whose research describes particularly the white ethnic poor living alone in rented apartments, used open-ended interviews and direct observation. As a more impressionistic study with qualitative data, it cannot be shown conclusively that this is an instance of multiple jeopardy. That is, it cannot be statistically demonstrated that this group faces more deprivations in quality of life than the nonaged poor, the black poor, or the aged poor in rural areas.

The evidence, however, suggests that the central city environment contributes additional deprivations to old age and poverty. For example, as renters in the central city, the aged poor face the worst housing imaginable. "Researchers who visit the inner city poor in their dwellings encounter the most indescribable squalor of flea bag hotels, rodent infested flop-houses, and filthy tenements . . ." (Clark, 1971:61). There are also special problems in seeking intimate interactions within the inner city. Because of the rise in street crimes, such as muggings and assaults, many of the elderly remain isolated and locked in their apartments.

Yet the central city is not a totally dysfunctional environment for the elderly poor. With the reduced agility that accompanies old age, the inner city offers a cluster of resources by which older persons can obtain needed services and thus retain some degree of control and autonomy over their lives (Birren, 1970:36–38). For example, the aged inner-city resident can locate close to cafeterias with discount meals, to a variety of stores, to frequent, regular public transportation, and to medical services. The impersonality and anonymity of the city that contribute to isolation may also promote autonomy and independence. Clark observes,

> The aged themselves value the chance to live with some measure of privacy and autonomy—no matter how dreadful the cost. We suspect that this persistant yearning for privacy is also related to a desire to cloak aging decrements that might put the older person in jeopardy of institutionalization (Clark, 1971:62).

In sum, age combined with poverty and a central city environment present a complex example of stratification interactions. For the most part, it is an example of multiple jeopardy, but not completely so. In one sense, the inner city brings deprivations that push the aged poor farther down the quality-of-life ladder. But the central city also provides the elderly person with access to services and coping mechanisms that allow him or her to cling to the American values of individualism and self-sufficiency.

Education of the American Indian Child.   In chapter 7, we discussed the low position children occupy on the age hierarchy. Children lack privileges, status, and power in a variety of institutions, especially in the educational institution. All children experience a great deal of regimentation and social control within their schools; seldom do they have a major voice in determining the content of material or the method by which it is taught. But lower-class minority children, in particular, face these constraints. Lower-class black, Chicano, and Native American children are more likely to drop out of school and fall further behind at each grade level in their achievments than middle-class white (or middle-class minority) children (Clark, 1965; Cahn, 1969). Unfortunately, the most common explanation for failure has been the lower-class minority environment, otherwise known as "cultural deprivation" theory (Baratz and Baratz, 1970). With slightly different variations for black, Chicano, and Indian children, this explanation says that aspects of a deprived environment, such as apathy, poor nutrition, the attraction of street life, and lack of cognitive interaction between parents and children, cause children to fail. Writing about the education of Mexican American children, Moore notes,

> Federal financial assistance has encouraged Southwestern educators to develop "compensatory education" programs to help Mexican American children compensate for certain inadequacies they display when compared to a "standard middle class child." The idea of "cultural disadvantage" provides a rationale for action to overcome the minority group child's real or assumed deficiencies. It is designed not to change the school but to change the child (Moore, 1970:81).

Only recently have educational institutions, their policies, and their programs been studied in a critical way. These studies have drawn attention to teacher expectations for failure on the part of the child, abuse in the use of IQ tests for classifying minority children, and the negative consequences of "tracking" minority children into slow-learner classes (Mercer, 1972; Schafer, *et al.,* 1970; Rosenthal and Jacobson, 1968). The failure to educate lower-class black, Chicano, and American Indian children is seen by many as not so much a function of a depressed environment as that of an insensitive reaction on the part of educational institutions to children outside the mainstream.

Nowhere is this insensitivity to minority culture more clearly demonstrated than in the education of American Indian children in BIA boarding schools. In 1969, approximately 30 percent of Indian children who attended school, attended boarding schools run by the Bureau of Indian Affairs. Such schools are frequently located a considerable distance from the reservation. "Once in a boarding school, the children are effectively cut off from their families. Parents cannot visit often because of the great distance and because many schools are located where roads are impassable much of the year. . . . Permission to see one's own parents is not a 'right'. It is often granted as a reward for good behavior—or denied as a form of punishment" (Cahn,* 1969:32–33). Edgar Cahn*. describes education as a "forced journey to an alien institution" (Cahn,* 1969:33). In many schools Indian traditions are totally denied; all effort is toward assimilating the child into the mainstream white culture. The more a child persists in maintaining an Indian identity, the more the school becomes an assault on his or her self-worth. Cahn speaks of the cultural casualties of the BIA schools. Indian children who try to maintain their Indian identity become withdrawn and sullen as they realize that their Indian heritage is defined as inferior. Suicide rates among Indian teenagers in Bureau of Indian Affairs boarding schools are far higher than the national average.

As we have seen from this discussion on multiple jeopardy, people who are disadvantaged on two or more hierarchies are likely to suffer markedly—unwanted sterilization (Kistler), poor health and low income (Dowd and Bengtson), loneliness, poor housing, and inadequate diet (Clark), academic failure and forced denial of Indian culture (Cahn). But multiple jeopardy can also lead to special adaptations; under certain conditions, people suffering from combined disadvantages can work out solutions to their situation.

Favorable Effects of Multiple Jeopardy.   Occasionally people occupying a combination of low positions can use multiple jeopardy to their advantage. Epstein reports that some highly successful black women have used their two negatively evaluated statuses of black and female as an impetus for achievement (Epstein, 1973). From interviews with thirty-one black female professionals she found patterns that partly explained their success. In a white professional working environment, a black woman may be seen as lacking the "female deficiencies" attributed to white women. White professional women, for example, still face considerable pressure to marry and to place their career in a secondary position to their husband's. In contrast, black women have not faced the consistent socialization pressure to marry, nor are they as likely as white women to view marriage as a guarantee of economic security. The black professional female, then, is freed from some of the sex-role pressures that may weaken total commitment to a career for some white women. Accordingly, black professional females may be more accepted in the white professional world. A black professional female may create a unique status in the marketplace with few existing stereotypes and no established price. "In this situation the person has a better bargaining position in setting . . . her own worth" (Epstein, 1973:914).

The combined disadvantages of being black and female can actually serve as motivation (Epstein, 1973). Black women were detemined to show that they could succeed. They tried to excel in order to make sure that one could not use incompetence as a reason for discriminating against them.

However, two low-status positions usually lead to combined disadvantages. Black women, as a group, remain at the bottom of the occupational and income ladders. But, there were special background features about the black professionals in the Epstein study. They came from intact families in which the mothers worked as professionals or semi-professionals, and in which the middle-class values of hard work and educational achievement were emphasized above all others. Some black women raised in such supportive environments find their negative status works in positive ways, whereas black women without the advantages of money, good schooling, and a professional-mother role model face the more usual outcome of combined disadvantage.

Multiple Advantages: The White Male Club.   White males in our society are in a position of dual advantage. White males hold 96 percent of the jobs in the United States that pay over $15,000 a year; women and blacks hold the remaining 4 percent (Terry, 1974). Although recent inflation may have changed this statistic somewhat, the relative advantage enjoyed by white males is probably very similar.

Terry (1974) showed that white males dominate the corporate centers of technological power, the military, courts, police, federal, and local governments. In many unions where membership primarily is comprised of women and minority-group members, white males still remain in control. Some have asserted that white women possess inordinate power through control of stocks. However, Terry finds that men carry out 75 percent of all securities transactions. "Women often control stock in name only to suit their husband's tax purposes" (Terry, 1974:71).

Two Forms of Multiple Jeopardy.   Data can reveal multiple jeopardy (or multiple advantage) in two ways, which could be termed the *additive* and the *interaction* patterns. In both patterns, two or more dimensions of inequality (class, ethnicity, sex, age) reinforce one another to produce a severe loss of life chances. In the following hypothetical illustrations, race and class are viewed as variables that affect a person's distrust of the government. The following is an example of an additive pattern:

| | Black | | White | |
	Middle Class	Lower Class	Middle Class	Lower Class
Percent Distrusting Government	30%	50%	10%	30%

It can be seen that class has an effect but so does race. What is especially interesting is that when race and class unite in the combination of "black lower-class" one finds the highest proportion (50 percent) distrusting the government. The black lower-class percentage is the greatest because it represents the sum of race and class operating jointly.† This is called an additive effect.

Race and class can also combine in an interaction pattern as shown below:

| | Black | | White | |
	Middle Class	Lower Class	Middle Class	Lower Class
Percent Distrusting Government	30%	80%	10%	30%

†The reader can actually add up the effects of race and class in the following manner: viewing the white middle class as a baseline (the high end of the race and class hierarchies where one would expect the least distrust of government) one can assess the class effect by comparing middle-class and lower-class whites (20 percent difference) and the effect of race by comparing middle-class whites and middle-class blacks (again, a 20 percent difference). Adding these two effects together gives us 40 percent, and when the 40 percent is added to the baseline of 10, we have the observed 50 percent black lower class combined effect.

In this example, the same combination of "lower-class black" has produced an extremely high percentage of persons distrusting the government. The simplest explanation of this statistical interaction is that something special happens when two variables get together in a particular combination—something above and beyond what would be expected from the additive effects. Blalock (1972) discusses statistical interaction as somewhat analogous to what happens when hydrogen and oxygen are combined to produce water: the result is more than a simple sum of the parts. Though statistical interaction may seem somewhat rare, in the case of race-class combinations it may occur often. Poverty and race frequently combine to form communities of frustration and discontent. Ghettos and barrios usually involve a pile-up of deprivations and lack of redress channels that would result in exceptionally high, nonadditive combinations. If urban renewal programs force low-income ghetto residents to move, create hostile police contacts, result in inadequate city services, and are accompanied by the presence of absentee landlords, these factors may combine to produce uniquely high feelings of distrust toward public officials and the city government (Ransford, 1977:123–127).

The preceding discussion on multiple jeopardy illustrates how individuals or groups can occupy reinforcing positions of advantage or disadvantage. But what of the mixed types? What of the high-low combinations—status sets such as black doctor, female executive, or the person with a high income but low education? The next two sections explore the mixed types, or nonreinforcing, combinations of statuses.

B. Status Consistency

No chapter on status combinations would be complete without a review of the concept *status consistency,* sometimes called *status crystallization.* It would be fair to say that status consistency has dominated "combinations" thought since the mid-1950s. From our point of view, there has been an excessive focus on status crystallization as the single best way to handle combinations of positions and this overemphasis has worked detrimentally for the building of a more general theoretical scheme to handle the many ways that combinations can be viewed (unique social space, multiple jeopardy, etc.).

Status consistency is quite different than the other approaches we have reviewed because it focuses on a horizontal or nonvertical dimension of stratification. That is, the concern is with the consistency *across* various status dimensions.

In Figure 8–3, the cases of status consistency are circled. For example, a high-ranking professional, with a postgraduate degree, high income, and of White Anglo-Saxon heritage has status consistency. An unemployed, high school dropout, low income minority person also has status consistency. Persons would be considered to have status consistency if they were *consistently high, consistently medium,* or *consistently low.* Moreover, people with any of these consistency patterns would be combined into an overall consistency-group on the logic that they all share consistency *across* status dimensions. But many people do not have consistency across status hierarchies. *Status inconsistency* means that a person ranks considerably higher on one dimension of stratification than on another. For example, ministers and college professors usually have incomes that rank far below their occupational prestige and high educational attainment. When the ascribed hierarchies of ethnicity, sex, and age are added to the class variables, many possibilities exist for status inconsistency. Figure 8–4 illustrates status inconsistency in

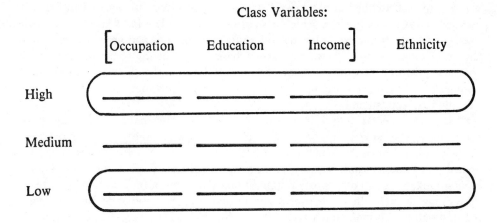

Figure 8-3. *Examples of Status Consistency with Three Class Variables and Ethnicity*

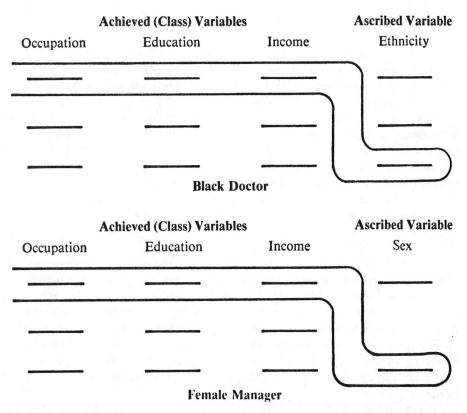

Figure 8-4. *Examples of Status Inconsistency with Three Class Variables and Ethnicity/Sex*

which a mix of ascribed and achieved statuses are involved. In both examples, the ascribed status is low but the achieved statuses are high. The black doctor or female manager are prototypic examples. By conceptualizing persons and groups according to their horizontal consistency, we have a new basis for predicting correlates. Degree of consistency becomes an independent or predictor variable that is related to any of a number of outcomes. For example, do inconsistents express more stress or vote more liberally than consistents?

In 1954, Lenski found that people with large discrepancies in status positions—those who ranked high on some positions and low on others—were more liberal in their political outlooks than those with greater consistency across status ranks. He argued that a status inconsistent man, for example, will act toward others in terms of his highest rank, although others may respond to him in terms of his lowest rank. A black doctor may interact with others in terms of his high achieved rank of doctor, but others may respond to him more in terms of his low ethnic rank. Lenski argues that a status inconsistent person may feel deprived of true worth and, as a result, turn to liberal politics of change that would bring a more equitable flow of resources.

Since Lenski, hundreds of articles on status inconsistency have been published. Status inconsistency has been correlated with every imaginable outcome, from support of George Wallace for president (Eitzen, 1970) to the sighting of UFOs (Warren, 1970).

The Development of a Status Consistency Theory

Underlying many studies of status consistency is the theoretical assumption that it is stressful or uncomfortable to occupy widely disparate positions on different hierarchies. Since each stratification position carries a set of behavioral expectations, the person with disparate statuses is seen as laboring under conflicting expectations (Jackson, 1962; Geshwender, 1967). "Anxiety is produced for all concerned and social relations are hampered and unsatisfying" (Geshwender, 1967:161). Not only is status inconsistency a source of stress and role strain, but also, according to the theory, persons with such profiles of inconsistency will turn to adaptive or stress-reducing responses such as political liberalism, mobility striving, withdrawal, or prejudice.

Since the role strain and stress occasioned by inconsistent status positions could lead to such a wide variety of outcomes it is very difficult to make specific predictions. In an important theoretical contribution that sharpened the inconsistency predictions, Geshwender developed the following line of reasoning:

If income and occupation are viewed as rewards and education as an investment, then persons with high education but low income or low occupational positions can be considered *underrewarded status inconsistents*. They will face distributive injustice—the flow of rewards to them does not equal their investment in education. Such persons are likely to feel anger. These persons are likely to try to move upward in occupational position or income to reduce the dissonance created by their status inconsistency. If attempts at social mobility are blocked because a person is female or black, for example, then she or he is likely to turn toward liberal political action or beliefs that will bring more just rewards.

Geshwender also conceptualizes an *overrewarded status inconsistent*—a person with high occupation or income but low educational attainment. He argues that the reaction to status inconsistency in this case would more likely be guilt rather than anger. "If educational investment is the low dimension, they may either attempt to raise their level of education to one consistent with rewards received or else develop a definition of education as being 'ivory tower' and impractical, which would lead to antiintellectualism" (Geshwender, 1967:171).

Others have linked the combination of high income and low education to right-wing politics. Eitzen found that the supporters of George Wallace were more likely to be high-income status inconsistents (Eitzen, 1970). In such cases, the explanation is not guilt, but rather, perceived threat. The more economically successful members of the white working class especially feel threatened by recent social changes, such as integration of housing and schools. The more affluent working class (high-income status inconsistents) have small, but hard-earned, privileges and economic investments which they are anxious to protect and fearful of losing.

Methodological Problems with Status Inconsistency

Despite a tremendous amount of evidence that status consistency has effects on a variety of outcomes, the concept has been dealt some telling methodological blows in recent years.

> . . . there is no logically conceivable way of isolating the effects of status crystallization from the effects of the socioeconomic variables from which measures of status crystallization are constructed (Hodge and Siegel, 1970:514).

Since occupation, education, income, and ethnicity—variables that make up a status consistency score—are in and of themselves powerful determinants of many correlates, how does one separate the main effects of these variables from their consistency effects?

Hodge and Siegel give an interesting example of this point. A very basic measure of consistency is related to the attitude of powerlessness. To limit the number of possible inconsistency combinations, they worked with only two variables: education and income. Consistency is viewed as high education and high income: inconsistency is seen as high education and low income. It was found that those whose income and educational levels were sharply inconsistent expressed a greater sense of powerlessness than did those with more consistent profiles.

The finding makes a certain amount of sense. Those with high educational investments but low economic rewards supposedly should express a variety of psychological symptoms such as frustration, anger, and powerlessness. The problem with this conclusion is that the relationship between inconsistency and powerlessness could have been caused by income alone. Income alone logically relates to powerlessness since those with lower incomes have fewer resources with which to exert control. Are feelings of powerlessness a function of greater inconsistency or lower income? "We are, then, back in the quandry we started in, *unable to isolate the effects of status consistency from the effects of the status variables which define it*" (Hodge and Siegel, 1970:517; emphasis added).

Most methodologists think that the only way to isolate status inconsistency is to demonstrate a statistical interaction effect. Earlier we noted that statistical interaction occurs when two or more variables in a particular combination produce an effect above and beyond what would be expected from a sum of their individual effects.

When a test of statistical interaction is applied to some long-standing relationships, status consistency as a predictive variable has not fared well. Consider, for example, the widely studied relationship between status inconsistency and political liberalism. The conclusions of a number of studies based on statistical interaction show that most forms of inconsistency have no effect at all on liberal beliefs or behavior (Olsen and Tully, 1972; Broom and Jones, 1970; Lauman and Segal, 1971). Only the combinations of low ascribed rank such as black, and high achieved rank (high education, income, occupation) was significantly related to liberal economic attitudes and Democratic voting (Olsen and Tully, 1972). It seems that status consistency only has predictive clout in determining political behavior when a disadvantaged ascribed position exists in combination with a high achieved position. Inconsistencies among the achieved positions have virtually no effect on political beliefs.

Low ascribed-high achieved is the one form of status inconsistency that has survived the statistical interaction test. It is the one form of inconsistency that most clearly relates to political change. People who attain a high education or occupation but are blocked from certain privileges by an unalterable ascribed status should, indeed, feel stress and anger.

C. Low Ascribed-High Achieved Combinations of Status

Traditional status consistency literature has not taken us far enough in understanding the exact kinds of stress, dissonance, and discrimination battles faced by persons of inconsistent status. In particular, the unique social space of persons with low ascribed-high achieved status has not been adequately developed. Little is known about the discrimination and role stress experienced by blacks, Chicanos, and women who have managed to reach professional and managerial positions traditionally held by whites and males. This section considers the black middle-class and high-achieving women as two examples of low ascribed-high achieved inconsistency.

We posit that minority persons and women who are in middle and upper levels of socio-economic achievement or authority in organizations will:

1. experience strain and residues of race or sex discrimination, and
2. display distinctive attitudes, outlooks, and behaviors, as a result of their low ascribed-high achieved status.

Residues of Sex and Race Discrimination.

High socioeconomic achievement may not override race and sex inequities. For example, a person may experience prestige or social honor due to achieved merit, but also may receive (or *not* receive) social honor due to ascribed position. A male black professional may be recognized and esteemed for competence in his occupation, but when he leaves his office and insulated occupational role, he may be accorded the same low level of prestige faced by less successful blacks. His social honor may constantly shift as he moves from social situations that acknowledge his achieved rank to social situations in which his racial status is most important. This kind of periodic and unpredictable discrimination is unique to the black middle-class experience. Lower-class blacks, concerned with gut issues of poverty and employment, experience a very different kind of discrimination than shifting evaluations of social honor.

In addition to the problem of shifting prestige, the black middle class has difficulty in converting their income into the same privileges that middle-class whites automatically enjoy (Ransford, 1977:84; Lieberson, 1970:180). The black middle class continues to face housing discrimination and often lives in neighborhoods on the periphery of the ghetto. Residents of these neighborhoods may experience some of the same inequalities felt by the poor who live "deeper" in the ghetto. Residents of the "periphery neighborhood" often face inadequate schools, police surveillance, and declining property values as the neighborhood is increasingly defined as "going black" by real estate brokers and developers. Safe neighborhoods that are free of exploitation and full of city services are what middle class blacks find they cannot buy, when most housing that is available to them is located on the edge of the ghetto.

In many organizations, low ascribed-high achieved status inconsistents experience stress and frustration. Strain results when high achieving women or minority persons attempt to "cash in" fully on their achieved rank only to find that they receive fewer rewards, have less chance to be promoted, or are denied access to the same organizational resources as males or white incumbents of the same position. This is somewhat akin to the notion of distributive justice and to Geshwender's "under-rewarded inconsistents," in that the rewards simply do not match the investments.

In sum, low ascribed-high achieved status inconsistents face a special environment of discrimination (a unique social space) that is qualitatively different from the discrimination experienced by minority persons who are in lower positions of organizational hierarchies. Of course, in some organizations it is possible that women or minority persons may be completely respected for their achieved ranks so that their ascribed status becomes insignificant. However, it is more likely that ascribed status continues to make a difference and certain racial and sex barriers persist.

High-Achieving Women.   A study of working women in five organizations illustrates the stress and inequities that often occur with low ascribed-high achieved status inconsistency (Miller, Labovitz, and Fry*, 1975). To our knowledge, none of the status consistency literature deals with gender as an ascribed status; only race, religion, or nationality have been studied. But women in high ranking positions of authority in organizations represent an especially clear example of the "remaining barriers thesis" discussed above. Miller, *et al.,* examined the flow of resources to men and women of different levels of achievement. They found that women employees were more likely to be isolated from networks of interaction than men. Although it might be expected that women who had reached higher positions would be favorably rated, the opposite was found. Women in higher positions of authority, occupational rank, and educational attainment were the most likely to be isolated from professional peers and to receive unfavorable friendship and influence scores. They had less "contact with persons in authority and with individuals who are popular, respected or considered to be influential" (Miller, *et al.,* 1975:366). The higher the rank in the organization, the greater the gap between men and women in terms of isolation from important interaction and resources.

The Miller, *et al.*, study also measured job strain. The measures used were job clarity (whether women were given a clear description of duties and job responsibilities); autonomy (ability to function independently and influence the actions of superiors); progress (knowledge of available opportunities for promotion or advancement), and job tension (pressures created by the work load). The same isolation-from-authority pattern unfolded with the measures of job strain. Women who are ranked high in occupation, education, or authority in the organization express more job strain than men. In sharp contrast, women in lower ranks of the organization (secretaries and typists) reported the *lowest* job strain, lower than men in comparable ranks. Apparently, women lose this benefit when they achieve the highest education, occupation, and authority levels.

The findings of Miller, *et al.*, support the view that high-achieving women occupy a unique social space. High-ranking women in organizations showed a configuration of job strain and isolation that was distinct from all other comparison groups—distinct from high-ranking men, low-ranking women and low-ranking men.

Distinctive Attitudes and Behavior.   People in low-ascribed positions but high-achieved ranks are likely to hold distinctive attitudes and behaviors. The assertion is most clear in the case of high-achieving minorities. As we said before, middle-class blacks are likely to be influenced simultaneously by their race and class positions. The idea that middle-class blacks will show a blend of race and class interests derives from a unique space perspective and is different from much of the traditional literature. The common assumption is that the higher-achieving middle class segment of any minority group detaches itself from its ethnic identification and becomes an undifferentiated part of the white middle class (or at least attempts to do so). This point of view says that the middle-class life style overrides racial identification and ethnic loyalties, that the middle-class black becomes acculturated to the life style of the middle-class white.

This does not seem to be an accurate characterization for large portions of the black middle class. The Civil Rights Movement and the theme of ''Black is Beautiful'' generated new tendencies toward racial identification and militance. The class interests of acquisition, materialism, and career mobility have been combined with or modified by an intense movement of ethnic identification. Sociologists need a model that takes into account the class interests of upwardly mobile minorities as well as the increased ethnic identification of these minorities.

Unique space, or in this case, *ethclass,* is a promising concept for such a model. Ethclass suggests that ethnic identification is a powerful source of collective identity that does not disappear with class mobility. Many blacks, Chicanos, and Native Americans who make subtantial class gains retain a sense of shared fate with their racial brothers and sisters from working- and lower-class origins.

A 1971 study found that middle-class black and white workers are very similar on matters of economic ambition and consumerism. However, the black middle class had not become completely bourgeois or gone through cooptation in a political sense. Rather, stable black workers were found to have a *blend* of materialistic personal ambition, identification with the black masses, and orientation toward militant protest (Kahl and Goering, 1971). These findings encourage the interpretation that the combination of middle class and black leads to a unique set of outlooks.

SUMMARY

In this chapter, we have shown that the correlates tradition can be expanded from the single hierarchy of social class to apply to the multiple hierarchies of class, sex, age, and ethnicity. Although social class is a potent determinant of many outcomes or correlates, consideration of two or more hierarchies as affecting one outcome often adds predictive ability and better theoretical understanding. *Comparisons of social hierarchies* deal especially with the relative importance of class, ethnicity, sex, or age on a given outcome. *Combinations of social hierarchies* stress the concept of unique social space. The idea of a distinctive social world created by the intersection of stratification positions is a core concept that underlies multiple jeopardy and advantage, status inconsistency, and low ascribed-high achieved status sets.

REFERENCES

Almquist, Elizabeth M. 1975. "Untangling the Effects of Race and Sex: The Disadvantaged Status of Black Women." *Social Science Quarterly* 56 (June): 129–142.

Antunes, George, Chad Gordon, Charles Gaitz & Judith Scott. 1974. "Ethnicity, Socioeconomic Status, and the Etiology of Psychological Distress." *Sociology and Social Research* 58 (July): 361–368.

Banfield Edward C. 1968. *The Unheavenly City*. Boston: Little, Brown & Co.

Baratz, Stephen S. & Joan C. Baratz. 1970. "Early Childhood Intervention: The Social Science Base of Institutional Racism." *Harvard Educational Review* 40 (Winter): 29–50.

Bell, Duran & Gail L. Zellman. 1975. "The Significance of Race for Services Delivery to the Elderly." Paper presented at the 28th Annual meeting of the Gerontological Society, Louisville, Kentucky, Oct. 30, 1975.

Birren, James E. 1970. "The Abuse of the Urban Aged." *Psychology Today* 3 (No. 10): 36–38.

Blalock, Hubert M. Jr. 1972. *Social Statistics*. New York: McGraw-Hill.

Blau, Peter M. & Otis Dudley Duncan. 1967. *The American Occupational Structure*. New York: John Wiley & Sons.

Bonacich, Edna. 1972. "A Theory of Ethnic Antagonism: The Split Labor Market." *American Sociological Review* 37 (October): 547–549.

Broom, Leonard & F. Lancaster Jones, 1970. "Status Inconsistency and Political Preference: The Australian Case." *American Sociological Review* 35 (December): 989–1001.

Cahn, Edgar S. 1969. *Our Brother's Keeper*. Washington, D.C.: New Community Press.

Campbell, Angus. 1971. *White Attitudes Toward Black People*. Ann Arbor, Michigan: Institute for Social Research, University of Michigan.

Clark, Kenneth. 1965. *Dark Ghetto*. New York: Harper and Row.

Clark, Margaret. 1971. "Patterns of Aging Among the Elderly Poor of the Inner City." *The Gerontologist* (Spring) Part II.

Cohen, Albert K. 1955. *Delinquent Boys*. Glencoe, Ill.: The Free Press.

Dowd, James J. & Vern L. Bengtson. 1978. "Aging in Minority Populations: An Examination of the Double Jeopardy Hypothesis." *Journal of Gerontology* 33 (May): 427–436.

Duberman, Lucile. 1976. *Social Inequality: Class and Caste in America* New York: J.B. Lippincott Company.

Eitzen, D. Stanley. 1970. "Status Inconsistency and Wallace Supporters in a Midwestern City." *Social Forces* 48 (June): 493–498.

Epstein, Cynthia Fuchs. 1973. "Positive Effects of the Multiple Negative: Explaining the Success of Black Professional Women." *American Journal of Sociology* 78 (January): 912–935.

Farris, Robert E. & Warren H. Dunham. 1939. *Mental Disorders in Urban Areas.* Chicago: University of Chicago Press.

Gerth, H. H. & C. Wright Mills (eds.). 1958. *From Max Weber.* New York: Oxford University Press.

Geshwender, James A. 1967. "Continuities in Theories of Status Consistency and Cognitive Dissonance." *Social Forces* 46 (December): 160–171.

Gibbs, Jack P. 1962. "Rates of Mental Hospitalization: A Study of Societal Reaction to Deviant Behavior." *American Sociological Review* 27: 782–792.

Gordon, Milton. 1964. *Assimilation in American Life.* New York: Oxford University Press.

Harrington, Michael. 1966. *The Other America.* Baltimore: Penguin.

Hodge, Robert W. & Paul M. Siegel. 1970. "Nonvertical Dimensions Of Social Stratification." In Edward O. Lauman, Paul M. Siegel & Robert W. Hodge (eds.), *The Logic of Social Hierarchies.* Chicago: Markham Publishing Co.

Hodges, Harold M. 1964. *Social Stratification.* Cambridge, Mass.: Schenkman Publishing Co.

Hollingshead, August B. & E. C. Redlich. 1958. *Social Class and Mental Illness.* New York: John Wiley and Sons.

Howell, Joseph T. 1973. *Hard Living on Clay Street.* New York: Doubleday Anchor.

Ireson, Carol J. 1976. "Effects of Sex Role Socialization on Adolescent Female Achievement." Paper presented at the Annual Meeting of the Pacific Sociological Association, San Diego, Calif., March 1976.

Jackson, Elton. 1962. "Status Consistency and Symptoms of Stress." *American Sociological Review* 27 (August): 469–480.

Jackson, Jacquelyne Johnson. 1974. "NCBA, Black Aged and Politics." *The Annals* 415 (September): 138–159.

Jeffries, Vincent. 1974. "Political Generations and the Acceptance or Rejection of Nuclear Warfare." *Journal of Social Issues* 30 (No. 3, Part II): 119–136.

Johnson, Michael P. & Ralph R. Sell. 1976. "The Cost of Being Black: A 1970 Update." *American Journal of Sociology* 82 (July): 183–190.

Kahl, Joseph. 1960. *The American Class Structure.* New York: Holt, Rinehart.

Kahl, Joseph A. & John M. Goering. 1971. "Stable Workers, Black and White." *Social Problems* 18 (Winter): 306–318.

Kaplan, Bart, Robert B. Reed, & Wyman Richardson. 1956. "A Comparison of the Incidence of Hospitalized Cases of Psychoses in Two Communities." *American Sociological Review* 21: 472–479.

Kent, Donald P. & Carl Hirsch. 1969. "Differentials in Need and Problem Solving Techniques Among Low Income Negro and White Elderly." Paper presented at the 8th International Congress of Gerontology, Washington, D.C., 1969.

Kistler, Robert. 1974. "Women Pushed Into Sterilization, Doctor Charges." *Los Angeles Times,* December 2.

Kohn, Melvin. 1968. "Social Class and Schizophrenia: A Critical Review." In D. Rosenthal & S. Kety (eds.), *The Transmission of Schizophrenia.* London: Pergamon Press.

——————.1969. *Class and Conformity: A Study in Values.* Illinois: Dorsey Press.

Lauman, Edward O. & David R. Segal. 1971. "Status Inconsistency and Ethnoreligious Group Membership as Determinants of Social Participation and Political Attitudes." *American Journal of Sociology* 77 (July): 33–60.

Lenski, Gerhard. 1954. "Status Crystalization: A Non-Vertical Dimension of Social Status." *American Sociological Review* 19 (August): 405–413.

Lieberson, Stanley. 1970. "Stratification and Ethnic Groups" in Edward O. Laumann (ed.), *Social Stratification: Research and Theory for the 1970s.* Indianapolis: Bobbs-Merrill.

Mercer, Jane. 1972. "IQ: The Lethal Label." *Psychology Today* 6 (September): 44–47; 95–97.

Miller, Jon, Sanford Labovitz, & Lincoln Fry. 1975. "Inequalities in the Organizational Experiences of Women and Men." *Social Forces* 54 (December): 365–381.

Moore, Joan. 1970. *Mexican Americans.* Englewood Cliffs, N.J.: Prentice-Hall.

Myers, Jerome K, Lee L. Bean & Max P. Pepper. 1968. *A Decade Later: A Follow-up of Social Class and Mental Illness.* New York: John Wiley & Sons.

National Council on Aging. 1972. *Triple Jeopardy: Myth or Reality.* Washington, D.C.: NCOA, 1972.

National Urban League. 1964. *Double Jeopardy: The Older Negro in America Today.* New York: National Urban League.

Neugarten, Bernice L., Joan W. Moore & John C. Lowe. 1965. "Age Norms, Age Constraints and Adult Socialization." *American Journal of Sociology* 70 (May): 710–717.

Nye, F. Ivan, James F. Short & U. J. Olson. 1958. "Socioeconomic Status and Delinquent Behavior." in *Family Relationships and Delinquent Behavior.* New York: John Wiley & Sons.

Olsen, Marvin E. & Judy Corder Tully. 1972. "Socioeconomic-Ethnic Status Inconsistency and Preference for Political Change." *American Sociological Review* 37 (October): 560–574.

Palmore, Erdman B. and Kenneth Manton. 1973. "Ageism Compared to Racism and Sexism." *Journal of Gerontology* 28 (No. 3): 363–369.

Poston, Dudley L. & David Alvirez. 1973. "On the Cost of Being a Mexican American Worker: *Social Science Quarterly* 53 (March): 697–709.

Poston, Dudley L., Jr., David Alvirez & Marta Tienda. 1976. "Earning Differences Between Anglo and Mexican American Male Workers in 1960 and 1970: Changes in the Cost of Being Mexican American." *Social Science Quarterly* 57 (December): 618–631.

Rainwater, Lee. 1974. "The Lower Class: Health, Illness, and Medical Institutions." In Lee Rainwater (ed.), *Social Problems and Public Policy.* Chicago: Aldine Publishing Co.

Ransford, H. Edward. 1977. *Race and Class in American Society.* Cambridge, Mass.: Schenkman Publishing Co.

Reissman, Leonard. 1959. Class in American Society, Glencoe, Ill.: The Free Press.

Rosenberg, Morris. 1968. *The Logic of Survey Analysis.* New York: Basic Books.

Rosenthal, R. & L. Jacobson. 1968. *Pygmalian in the Classroom.* New York: Holt, Rinehart and Winston.

Rush, G. B. 1967. "Status Consistency and Right Wing Extremism." *American Sociological Review* 32 (February): 86–92.

Ryan, William. 1971. *Blaming the Victim.* New York: Vintage.

Schafer, Walter E., Carol Olexa & Kenneth Polk. 1970. "Programmed for Social Class: Tracking in the High School." *Transaction* 7 (October): 39–46, 73.

Sell, Ralph R. & Michael P. Johnson. 1977. "Income and Occupational Differences between Men and Women in the United States." *Sociology and Social Research* 62 (October): 1–20.

Sewell, William H. & Vimal P. Shah. 1967. "Socioeconomic Status, Intelligence, and the Attainment of Higher Education." *Sociology of Education* 40: 1–23.

Siegel, Paul M. 1965. "On the Cost of Being a Negro" *Sociological Inquiry* 35 (Winter): 41–57.

Terry, Robert. 1974. "The White Male Club." *Civil Rights Digest* 6 (Spring): 66–77.

U.S. Bureau of the Census. 1970. *Census of Population: 1970,* Subject Reports, "Earnings by Occupation and Education." Final Report PC (2)-88.

Warren, D. I. 1970. "Status Inconsistency Theory and Flying Saucer Sightings." *Science* 170 (Nov. 6): 599–603.

Williams, Jay R. & Gold, Martin. 1972. "From Delinquent Behavior to Official Delinquency." *Social Problems* 20 (2): 209–229.

Wilson, William Julius. 1978. *The Declining Significance of Race.* Chicago: University of Chicago Press.

Ageism Compared to Racism
and Sexism[1]

Erdman B. Palmore and Kenneth Manton

The problem investigated was the relative equal-ity between age, race, and sex groups in terms of income, occupation, weeks worked, and educa-tion. US Census data for 1950-1970 was used. Relative equality was measured by the Equality Index, which is the proportion of two group's percentage distribution which overlap. The main findings in relation to ageism are: (1) lowest equality in education and weeks worked is found between age groups; (2) when two or three of the factors are combined, the effects are generally additive; (3) comparisons between subgroups show that age equality is lower among men and nonwhites than among women and whites; (4) changes since 1950 show nonwhites making small but steady gains, women barely maintaining their lower status, but the aged losing ground in income and education. Various interpretations and explanations for the findings are discussed.

THERE IS a voluminous literature describing the various forms of discrimination and inequalities between blacks and whites in our society (Miller & Fisher, 1970). There is also a growing body of lit-erature describing the various forms of discrimin-ation and inequalities between men and women (de Beauvoir, 1953; Ellis, 1970; Morgan, 1970). Most recently there have developed a few studies

Reprinted by permission of the *Journal of Gerontology;* Erd-man B. Palmore and Kenneth Manton, "Ageism Compared to Racism and Sexism," *Journal of Gerontology,* Vol. 28; No. 3; 1973. Pp 363–369.

1. This is an expanded version of a paper presented at the American Sociological Association meeting in New Orleans, Auguust, 1972. The analysis was supported in part by Grant HD-00668, National Institute of Child Health and Hu-man Development.

describing various forms of discrimination and in-equalities between age groups in our youth-oriented culture (see references in Palmore, 1969; Palmore & Whittington, 1971). This inequality was first called age-ism in 1969 (Butler), and in 1971 President Nixon condemned ageism in the United States at the White House Conference on Aging. These three sets of literature make it clear that the ascribed statuses of race, sex, and age are of fundamental importance in our society, and that they are closely related to the differential dis-tribution of the classic stratification variables: in-come, occupation, and education. This is true de-spite our cultural ideal that all men (and women) are created equal and that all persons should be entitled to equal opportunity regardless of race, sex, or age.

Yet there has been little or no systematic or quantitative attempt to compare the *relative* im-portance of these three kinds of social differentia-tion or to compare the relative amounts of socio-economic inequalities resulting from them. In other words, which is stronger in our society: race, sex, or age inequality? Civil Rights and Black Power leaders assert that racism results in the most serious inequality, while Women's Liberation leaders assert that sexism is a more serious prob-lem. Only a few sociologists have recently become aware of a fact that many gerontologists have long recognized: that ageism may be related to as much inequality as racism or sexism.

The extent to which such socioeconomic in-equalities are directly due to racism, sexism, and ageism, in the sense of conscious political ideol-ogy and discrimination, and the extent to which they are due to institutional discrimination, or to biological and cohort differences will be discussed later. First, we need to examine the quantitative evidence about the relative amounts of these inequalities.

Similarly, we need to analyze the joint or combined effects of two or three of these inequalities. For example, what is the effect of combining ageism and sexism (how do older females compare to younger males on income?); or of combining all three types of differentiation (how do older black females compare to younger white males on income?)? Are the effects of different types of inequality additive or are there more complex interactions?

A third type of analysis shows which subgroups are more affected by race, sex, and age inequality. For example, are younger persons more affected by sex inequality than older persons? Are men more affected by age inequality than women?

The fourth neglected area is the quantitative analysis of trends over time in race, sex, and age inequality. Because of various problems of measuring and comparing different kinds of changes over time in different areas of inequality, most of the trend data have been unsystematic and difficult to compare across time or from one type of inequality to another. A basic sociological question, therefore, is whether or not our society is becoming more or less differentiated by one kind of ascribed status (such as race), but more differentiated by another kind (such as age). Census data changes from 1950 to 1970 will be used to answer this question.

THE MEASURE OF EQUALITY

To answer these question quantitatively, we need to define the concepts of racism, sexism, and ageism, and then to specify the operational indicator used in this analysis. The basic concepts are simple enough: racism, sexism, or ageism are attitudes and behaviors, either individual or institutional, which discriminate against a person because of his or her race, sex, or age. The concept of institutional or structural discrimination is becoming more important as it becomes apparent that much inequality results from the policies and procedures of key institutions in our society (such as segregated schools and compulsory retirement) rather than from consciously biased actions of prejudiced individuals. Indeed, institutional discrimination may well be the primary link between personal ideology and these group inequalities. Institutional discrimination may also change more slowly because it is often associated with basic social values and norms (the neighborhood school, women's place is in the home, retirement at 65).

However, there are complex problems of definition and measurement which make it virtually impossible to directly measure discrimination on a large scale at present. Usually the best we can do is to measure the actual *inequality* between groups and then discuss, on the basis of other evidence, how much of this inequality is due to various forms of prejudice or discrimination, individual or institutional (Blalock, 1967). This will be our procedure. Alternative explanation of the inequality are considered in the discussion section.

The operational measure of equality should be comparable between any two groups (in this case, racial, sexual, or age groups) in terms of any kind of characteristic (in this study we will use primarily income, occupation, and education). Most traditional measures, such as means, medians, and Gini Indexes, cannot be used with ordinal or nominal characteristics such as occupation. Our operational measure, the Equality Index, can precisely measure the amount of equality (or similarity) between any two groups or subgroups in terms of any kind of characteristics (Palmore & Whittington, 1970, 1971).

The Equality Index (EI) is the positive complement of the older index of dissimilarity (Duncan & Duncan, 1955). It may be described in several ways. It is the proportion of two groups' percentage distributions which overlap each other. Or, it is the sum over all categories of the smaller of the two percentages in each category. It can be thought of as the percentage of complete equality, because 100 would mean that there is complete identity between the two percentage distributions, 50 would mean that 50% of the inferior groups would have to move upward to equal the higher group, and 0 would mean that there is no overlap between the two distributions.

The EI is simple to calculate: the percentage of one group in a given category is compared to the percentage of the other group in that category, and the lesser of the two percentages in each comparison are summed. Algebraically, it may be stated as

$$\sum_{i=1}^{N} (a \cdot Xi \div b \cdot Yi),$$

where X_1 = % of one group in i category; Y_1 = % of the other group in i category; a = 1 when X < Y; a = 0 when X > Y; b = 1 when Y < X; and b = 0 when Y > X.

To illustrate, Figure 1 shows graphically the curves of the aged (65 +) and nonaged (25–64) per capita income distributions superimposed upon one another with the area of overlap shaded. The EI is the measure of the shaded overlap area as a percentage of the total area underneath the two curves. Thus, the EI increases if more of the aged shift to the upper end of the distribution, thereby increasing the amount of overlap.

To illustrate how the EI is computed, it can be seen from Figure 1 that the nonaged have smaller percentages compared to the aged in each $1,000 income category below $5,000. These percentages for the nonaged (27.6, 6.2, 5.6, 6.5) are summed and added to the (smaller) percentages of aged in the $1,000 categories above $5,000 (4.9, 3.7, 2.7, 1.9, 1.2, 1.1, and 3.9 above $10,000) for a total EI of 65.3. This means that

the aged had about two-thirds of complete income equality in 1969 compared to the non-aged.

There are several advantages of the EI (and of its complement, the Index of Dissimilarity) over the other measures that have been used to compare equality between groups: it can be used with ordinal or nominal data; it is not subject to the heavy influence of a few extreme cases; it reflects general changes in distributions, such as in range and skewness as well as in central tendency; it is easier to calculate and understand than most other indexes. The EI requires only one step to calculate compared to three steps for the Index of Dissimilarity.

US Census data from 1950 and 1970 were used to compute all the EI in this study. The age categories were 65 and over for the aged and 25–64 for the nonaged. Age 25 was used as the lower limit in order to restrict the analysis to adults, most of whom have completed their education. Race was dichotomized into white and nonwhite. We would have preferred to compare blacks to whites, but the data are not usually available for this comparison. Since more than 92% of nonwhites are blacks, the difference in EI between using nonwhite or blacks is usually less than 2 EI points. The income EI were computed from the percentage distribution of all persons over 25 by per capita income (including those reporting no income).[3] The occupation EI was computed from the percentage distribution of employed persons over 25 in the 12 major census occupational categories. The education EI was computed from the percentage distribution of persons over 25 by the highest year of school completed.

COMPARATIVE INEQUALITY

The answer to the question as to whether there is more race, sex, or age inequality is being examined (Table 1 & Fig. 2). The income EI is lowest

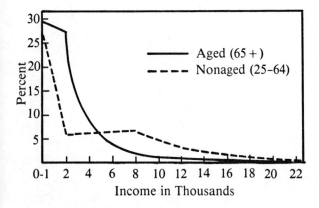

Figure 1. *Percentage Distribution of Aged and Non-aged by Per Capita Income for 1969.*

3. In computing the income EI, all persons with no income or income under $1,000 were combined in one category to eliminate occasional "reversals", i.e., comparisons in which a group with generally higher incomes had a somewhat higher percentage in the no income or the under $500 category than the other group.

Table 1. *Equality Indexes for Race, Sex, and Age Groups (1970).*

Groups	Income EI	Occupation EI	Education EI
Nonwhite/white	83	71	76
Female/male	45	56	91
65+/25–65	65	79*	63

*Estimate for 1970.

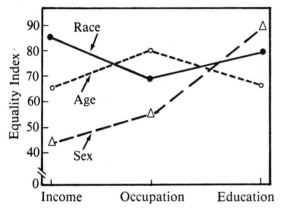

Figure 2. *Equality Profile for Race, Sex, and Age Groups (1970).*

for the sexes (45) and highest for the races (82). The occupation EI (for those employed) also show the least equality between the sexes (56) but most equality between the ages (79). This is somewhat misleading because the majority of the aged are not employed. In terms of weeks worked, the aged have the least equality. The education EI is lowest for the age comparison (63) and highest for the sex comparison (91). To put it another way, age inequality is strongest in education and weeks worked, sex inequality is strongest in income and occupation, and race inequality is second strongest in occupation and education. Thus, one cannot say that any one form of inequality is stronger than the other two in all dimensions. All the EIs show substantial inequalities between each type of group (with the possibile exception of the education EI between the sexes).

Although various explanations of these inequalities will be discussed later, it might be rec-

Table 2. *Equality Indexes Showing Joint Effects of Race, Sex, and Age (1970).*

Groups	Income EI	Occupation EI	Education EI
Nonwhite 65+/ white 25–64	50	47[a]	36
Female 65+/ males 25–64	25	52[a]	67
Nonwhite females/ white males	40	39[a]	77
Nonwhite females 65+/white males 25–64	13	26[a]	40

[a]Estimate for 1970

ognized that cohort differences account for much of the inequality between age groups, especially in education.

Use of the EI also allows us to measure the effects of combining two or three types of discrimination. This is the idea of double jeopardy or triple jeopardy. Thus, the EI comparing older blacks to younger whites (showing the combined effects of age and race) are all at or below the 50% of equality mark (Table 2.) The income EI is particularly low for the combination of the older females compared to younger males (25). Finally, the triple jeopardy of being an older Negro woman results in the lowest equality compared to younger white males. In fact, the income EI for the comparison begins to approach the extreme case of almost no overlap in the two distributions (13). In general, these joint effects appear to be additive regardless of which types of discrimination are combined.

INEQUALITY AMONG SUBGROUPS

The third question we will examine is the extent to which the various racial, sexual, and age subgroups suffer from the various forms of inequality. We will present data only for the income EIs in this section because it can be argued that income is the single most important factor measuring socioeconomic status and life chances.

The race comparisons show that men and the aged are more affected by race inequality than women and the nonaged (Table 3).[4] Sex inequality affects whites and younger persons more than nonwhites and the aged (Table 4). Age inequality has substantially more effect on men than women and somewhat more effect on nonwhites than whites (Table 5). As for whether nonwhite women suffer more from race than sex inequality, the relevant comparison shows that they are much less equal to nonwhite men (61) than to white women (97). The same is true for the occupation comparisons (54 compared to nonwhite men and 71 compared to white women). This indicates that sex inequality has much greater effect than race inequality on black women. Part of the explanation here is that occupational equality between the races has increased faster for women than for men (Palmore & Whittington, 1970).

How can we explain these differential inequalities among these various subgroups? Is there a general principle that would encompass all these differential effects? In an earlier paper we formulated a general principle that does explain most of these differentials: "Greater equality among the inferior category" (Palmore & Whittington, 1970). We argued that this principle holds because there is less room for as much discrepancy in the inferior category compared to the superior category. Thus, race inequality is less among females because females in general have less income and less variation in which inequality could show itself. Similarly, sex inequality is less among nonwhites and among older persons because they have less income. Finally, age inequality is less among women again because they have less income. However, there are two exceptions to this principle related to the decrease in race inequality. Race appears to have somewhat less effect among younger persons presumably because the reduction in race inequality has affected younger persons more than older persons. Similarly, age differences are somewhat greater among blacks than whites, presumably because of the greater progress made by younger blacks.

4.   It may be noted that the total EIs in each column of Table 3 are slightly larger than the age subgroups. This is not an error, but results from the greater equality found in the total groups than in the subgroups. Some of the inequality found in the subgroups is canceled out by combining them into the total groups.

Table 3. *Nonwhite/White Income EI for Sex and Age Sub-Groups (1970).*

	Males	Females	Total
25–64	65	96	81
65+	67	82	76
Total	68	97	83

Table 4. *Female/Male Income EI for Race and Age Sub-Groups (1970).*

	White	Nonwhite	Total
25–64	36	58	39
65+	57	70	59
Total	43	61	45

Table 5. *65+/25–64 Income EI for Race and Sex Sub-Groups (1970).*

	White	Nonwhite	Total
Males	44	45	45
Females	82	62	82
Total	65	57	65

TRENDS IN INEQUALITY

But what about the many revolutionary changes toward equality that are supposed to be taking place in our society—is our society becoming more equalitarian or is it becoming more differentiated by race, sex, and age? The many civil rights laws since 1950 outlawing discrimination by race, sex, or age and the many programs that have been instituted to help bring about more equality to disadvantaged groups would lead one to expect that there should be marked changes toward greater equality. However, there are many delays between the enactment of legislation and the actual accomplishment of the objectives of that legislation.

The race EIs do show modest but clear trends toward greater equality from 1950 to 1970 in income, occupation, and education (Table 6) (for further documentation of this trend in other areas see Palmore & Whittington, 1970). Thus, those who say that race inequality has been get-

Table 6. *Changes in Equality Indexes for Race, Sex, and Age Groups (1970–1950).*

	Income EI	Occupation EI	Education EI
Nonwhite/white	+ 3.5	+ 11.7	+ 13.2
Female/male	+ 1.1	− 1.8	− 3.5
65 + /25–64	− 7.5	− 0.6	− 16.6

ting worse in our country appear to be wrong, at least for the period of 1950–1970. On the other hand, the sex comparisons indicate little or no change, with the occupation and education EIs registering a small decline (negative values in Table 6 indicate a decline in the Equality Index). But the age inequality appears to be getting substantially worse, with the income EI registering a drop of over 7 points and the education EI showing a drop of over 16 points since 1950 (for further documentation of this trend in other areas see Palmore & Whittington, 1971). This rapid drop in the education EI reflects the rapid increase in years of education during this century.

Thus, blacks in our society appear to be making small but substantial gains in most areas, while women are barely maintaining their generally inferior status, and the aged are actually losing ground in income and education.

This is related to cohort differences between age groups (see next section) as well as to difference in militancy and organization of three minority groups and to differences in society's willingness to enact legislation and programs to help achieve equality for these groups. The blacks are undoubtedly better organized than the other two groups, and our government and private groups have instituted some programs to overcome inequality between the sexes. In fact, there is still much disagreement among both men and women as to the proper role for women and the extent to which equality between men and women is desirable. The aged are probably the least organized and, while there appears to be some consensus that some of the aged need assistance in their incomes and medical care there appear to be few who advocate that the aged should have equal income and employment opportunity compared to younger people. Compulsory retirement and other age discrimination is legal and generally ac-

cepted. Few people recognize the magnitude of age inequality in our society. There has been almost no recognition that the relative status of the aged is declining.

DISCUSSION

The patterns of inequality shown in this analysis invite discussion and speculation which could fill several volumes. We will restrict ourselves to a discussion of the validity of the EI as measures of discrimination. It may be argued that the EI of income, occupation, and education are not valid or accurate measures of racism, sexism, and ageism, because there are alternative explanations for the observed socioeconomic differentiation. Let us consider these alternative explanations.

There are a few white supremacists left in academia who argue that the inferior socioeconomic position of blacks is the result of racial genetic inferiority. Similarly, there are male chauvinists who maintain that the inferior position of women is the result of female genetic inferiority (women are weaker or irrational). Suffice it to say that there is an almost unanimous consensus among geneticists and social scientists alike that the known genetic differences between races and sexes are insufficient to explain the inferior positions of blacks and women in our society.

As for the inferior position of the aged, an alternative explanation would be that this results from the physical and mental disabilities of old age. Undoubtedly some of the socioeconomic differences between the aged and nonaged do result from physical and mental decline in old age, but it is difficult to estimate how much can be explained this way. In an attempt to partially control for age-related physical mental declines, we computed the income EI for ages 55–64 compared to ages 65–74, because evidence indicates that there is much less decline between these two 10-year-age groups than between the two 40-year-age groups of 25–64 and 65 + (Riley & Foner, 1968). The result was an increase in the income EI of ten points (70 for the 65 + /25–64 comparison and 80 for the 65–74/55–64 comparison, 1960). Thus, a crude control for physical and mental declines reduces by one-third the total inequality between the aged and nonaged. However, it can be argued that part of even this reduction is due to a reduction in the range of age-related discrimination, because there is considerable discrimination against older workers in the 55–64 age range.

It should be clear that the educational inequality between aged and nonaged and most of their occupational inequality are due to cohort differences rather than to a loss of education or occupational level as persons age. That is, the aged have not lost ground in the sense of an absolute drop in education or occupation, but have been left behind as the educational and occupational levels of younger cohorts have risen. The income inequality between aged and nonaged represent a combination of such cohort differences and of absolute reductions in income as earnings diminish among the aged (partly because of age discrimination in employment). Regardless of the relative importance of these two explanations, the inequality between aged and nonaged remains substantial and has important effects on the socioeconomic status and life style of the aged.

Another alternate explanation would be that blacks, women, and the aged have lower socioeconomic status because more of them prefer less demanding jobs, part-time jobs, or no jobs at all. Although there seems little evidence for this explanation among blacks, it probably has some validity for women and the aged. But this explanation only moves the explanation back one step from current discrimination to earlier differences in socialization and cultural expectations which produce these differential preferences and values. It becomes a moot question as to whether such differences in preferences should be considered to result from earlier discrimination.

A general criticism of the income EI would be that it exaggerates the inequality because it does not take into account the goods and services contributed by whites to blacks, by children to aged parents, and by husbands to wives. The first answer to this argument is that in our society dependence on contributions and charity usually implies an inferior socioeconomic status, even though it is generally assumed that children have some obligation to help support needy parents and that husbands have an obligation to support their wives. Second, the average amount of such contributions for blacks and the aged are relatively small. The amount of income contributed by husbands to their wives is, of course substantial and controlling for marital status by computing the EIs for single persons gives some estimate of the importance of this factor. The occupation EI for single women compared to single men is almost the same as for all women compared to all men (55 for the former, 57 for the latter, 1960). However, the income EI for unattached females compared to unattached males is 37 points higher than that for all women compared to all men (82 for the former, 45 for the latter, 1970). Thus, controlling for marital status has no effect on the occupational differentiation by sex, but it substantially increases income equality among unattached persons. Our marriage institution appears to reinforce dependency of women on men and in this sense perpetuates inequality between the sexes. However, the income EI by sex for single persons is still slightly below the race income EI (83).

A final point: one should distinguish between the descriptive facts of inequality related to race, sex, and age, *versus* value judgments as to whether this inequality is good or bad. This analysis is devoted to clarifying the facts of inequality. We leave to others the controversial task of arguing which aspects are good or bad and what should be done about it.

SUMMARY

The Equality Index was used to measure the equality or inequality between racial, sex, and age groups in terms of income, occupation, weeks worked, and education. The main findings in relation to age are: (1) Age inequality is greatest in education and weeks worked, but least in occupation of those working. Age also produces more income inequality than race. (2) When comparisons are made combining two of the factors, the joint effects are generally additive, with the age-sex combination producing the lowest equality in terms of income. The combination of all three factors produces the lowest equality in both income and occupation. (3) Comparison between subgroups shows that age inequality is greater among men and nonwhites than among women and whites. Most of these subgroup differences are explained by the principle of greater equality among the inferior category, the two exceptions to this principle are related to the increase in race equality. (4) Changes since 1950 show that non-whites are making small but steady gains in all three areas, that women are barely maintaining their generally inferior status, but the aged are actually losing ground in income and education. This was related to cohort differences between the aged and nonaged, to differences in organization and militancy among the three minority groups, and to the difference in public and private programs to overcome inequality between these groups.

REFERENCES

Blalock, H. *Toward a theory of minority-group relations.* Wiley & Sons, New York, 1967.

de Beauvoir, S. *The second sex.* Knopf Publishing Co., New York, 1953.

Butler, R. N. Age-ism: Another form of bigotry. *Geronologist,* 1969, 9, 243–246.

Duncan, O., & Duncan, B. A methodological analysis of segregation indexes. *American Sociological Review,* 1955, 20, 210–217.

Ellis, J. *Revolution of the second sex.* Lancer, New York, 1970.

Miller, E., & Fisher, M. *The Negro in America: A bibliography.* (2nd ed.) Harvard Univ. Press, Cambridge, 1970.

Morgan. R. (Ed.) *Sisterhood is powerful.* Random House, New York, 1970.

Palmore, E. Sociological aspects of aging. In E. Busse & E. Pfeiffer (Eds.), *Behavior and adaptation in late life.* Little, Brown, Boston, 1969.

Palmore, E. Trends in the relative status of the aged. *Social Forces,* 1971, 50, 84–91.

Palmore, E., & Whittington, F. Differential trends toward equality between whites and nonwhites. *Social Forces,* 1970, 49, 108–117.

Riler, M., & Foner, A. *Aging and society.* Russell Sage Foundation, New York, 1968.

Aging in Minority Populations—An Examination of the Double Jeopardy Hypothesis[1]

James J. Dowd and Vern L. Bengtson

The plight of minority aged has been characterized by many as one of double jeopardy: in addition to the disadvantages imposed by their minority group status, the minority aged are said also to experience the devaluation in status associated with old age in our society. Other research has indicated, however, that the gaps between minority and majority individuals tend to decline with age, such that the status disparity between white and minority aged actually may have decreased from middle to old age. To test these competing hypotheses, a series of health, income, life satisfaction, and social participation variables (interaction with family, kin, neighbors, and friends) was examined with data from a large (N=1269) sample of middle-aged and older blacks, Mexican Americans and whites in Los Angeles County. Differences among the three ethnic groups were found which, in some cases, constituted a case of "double jeopardy" for minority aged. On variables measuring life satisfaction or frequency of contact with relatives, however, the extent of ethnic variation declined across age strata, indicating some support for the "age as leveler" hypothesis.

THE PLIGHT of the minority aged has been characterized by many as one of "double jeopardy" or "multiple hazards" (Jackson, 1970; 1971a; National Council on Aging, 1972; National Urban League, 1964; U.S. Senate Special Committee on Aging, 1971). These descriptions refer to the additive negative effects of being old *and* black (or any other racial/ethnic minority) on frequently cited indicators of quality of life, such as income, health, housing, or life satisfaction.

The minority aged are said to bear, in effect, a double burden. Like other older people in industrial societies, they experience the devaluation of old age found in most modern societies (Cowgill & Holmes, 1972). Unlike other older people, however, the minority aged must bear the additional economic, social and psychological burdens of living in a society in which racial equality remains more myth than social policy. It has been noted in this regard that, compared to the white aged, most of the minority aged "are less well educated, have less income, suffer more illnesses and earlier death, have poorer quality housing and less choice as to where they live and where they work, and in general have a less satis-

Reprinted by permission of the *Journal of Gerontology;* James Dowd and Vern L. Bengtson, "Aging in Minority Populations: An examination of the Double Jeopardy Hypothesis," *Journal of Gerontology,* May, 1978.

[1] The development of this paper was supported by grants from RANN program of the National Science Foundation (#APR 75–21178), the UPS Foundation of the United Parcel Service (Vern L. Bengtson. Principal Investigator: Pauline K. Ragan, Project Director), and AOA (#90-A-1010/02), James J. Dowd. Principal Investigator. Thanks also to members of the Community Research Planning Committee (Alicia Noriega and Carnella Barnes, Chairpersons of the Chicano and Black caucuses, respectively). None of these individuals or agencies, however, bears any responsibility for the analyses or interpretations presented here.

fying quality of life'' (U.S. Senate Special Committee on Aging, 1971).

The implications of double jeopardy for both social policy and social gerontological research are many. For social scientists with research interests in the field of gerontology, the awareness of the double jeopardy situation has been reflected in an increased concern with the methodological biases imposed by sample composition and a consequent call for more cross-ethnic research (Ehrlich, 1973; Jackson, 1971b, c; Kalish, 1971; Kent, 1971a, b). By restricting sampling to populations of aging whites, the risk of compositional effects is greatly increased. That is, the varying racial composition of different age strata may confound interpretation of findings should race be related to the dependent variable of interest (Douglas et al., 1974). Rather than continue to *exclude* minority aged from ongoing gerontological research, a growing number of social gerontologists have critized prior research for its failure to *control* for variables such as ethnicity, education, locale of residence and SES (cf., Bengtson et al., 1977; Reynolds & Kalish, 1974).

Related to this methodological issue is the policy issue of whether racial or ethnic identity alone constitutes sufficient basis for differential treatment. Several have argued affirmatively, suggesting that racial contrasts are so great as to require a social policy that reflects those differences (Jackson, 1971b; National Urban League, 1964). The U.S. Senate Special Committee on Aging, (1971) for example, has expressed concern that if the characteristics of the minority aged are indeed different from the general older population, social policy must be modified to reflect such differences. Others have disagreed, noting that while differences among ethnic groups are frequently observed and incontestable, it also is true that the aging individual, regardless of ethnic background, is subject to a variety of influences which cut across racial lines and may mediate or level differences in patterns of aging (Kent & Hirsch, 1969). The relative numbers of minority *aged* having good health and adequate income, for example, may well be less than those of aged whites. If, however, the percentage differences between middle-aged blacks or Mexican Americans and their white counterparts are greater *yet,* a characterization of the minority aged as being in double

jeopardy would be an incomplete description. Viewed from a different perspective, it may also be said that age exerts a *leveling* influence on the ethnic differences found among the younger cohorts.

To address this issue, we will present data on a series of selected dependent variables (ranging from economic and health indicators to social interaction and life satisfaction items) in order to identify the nature of age differences within different ethnic groups. The analysis will focus on the two apparently contradictory perspectives on ethnicity and aging identified above. The first perspective suggests that the minority aged suffer from a double jeopardy, that is, the experience of both race *and* age discrimination combine to make their relative status more problematic than that of either the aged or racial minorities considered separately. The second perspective views *advancing age as a leveler* of racial inequalities that existed in mid-life. To what extent either of these perspectives can be said to characterize the lives of the minority aged is the central question to be answered in this paper.

SAMPLE AND METHODS

The data to be analyzed in this research were collected as part of a larger survey with a probability sample of 1,269 residents of Los Angeles County stratified by age and SES within race groups (see Bengtson et al, 1976). The sampling universe of the research included all black, Mexican American and Anglo residents of Los Angeles County, aged 45 to 74. The sample drawn from this universe was divided into nine age-by-ethnicity cells, formed by the cross-classification of the three ethnic categories and three age strata (45-54, 55-64, and 65-74). The sample design further specified equal distribution within the three race groups between two socioeconomic strata. SES was operationalized using the Duncan Socioeconomic Index; the score of 31 on this index was established as the dividing point between the two strata during the sampling phase.

Respondents were identified through a multistage sampling procedure, the initial stage of which involved screening more than 15,000 households chosen from 184 Census tracts in Los

Angeles County to identify eligible respondents. Final interviews were conducted between July, 1974 and January, 1975 by a team of interviewers matched with the respondents on race/ethnicity. Interviews were conducted either in English or Spanish, depending upon the respondent's preference. Response rates averaged approximately 80% during both screening and final interviewing.

Table 1 presents the final distribution of 1269 respondents by age and ethnicity.

Although the present sample was not part of a longitudinal panel which would ideally be necessary for proper analysis of "leveling" properties of age, the design does facilitate at least an initial investigation of this issue as it allocates cases equally into three age strata and three ethnic groups. Thus, while we cannot follow one birth cohort through time and determine whether increased age "levels" any ethnic variation that may exist, we *can* compare three different age strata and determine the extent of the ethnic variation within each stratum. If the ethnic differences among the 65- 74-year-old individuals are not as great as those among the 45- 54-year-old, there would be an indication that age exerts a leveling influence.

Double jeopardy, on the other hand, would be indicated should the following conditions obtain: (1) significant differences exist between minority and white respondents over 65 on a dependent variable that *favor* the white respondents: (2) within the particular minority group being studied, a significant decline in the dependent variable with increasing age can be observed; and either (3a) significant differences do *not* exist between younger (45–64) minority and white re-

spondents; or (3b) significant differences exist between younger minority and their white counterparts that favor the white respondents but which are not larger than the differences observed between the *older* minority and their white counterparts; or (3c) significant differences exist between *younger* minority and white respondents that favor the *minority* respondents. In other words, a condition of double jeopardy will be said to characterize the minority aged should the relative disadvantages of the minority *aged* vis-à-vis the white aged in any of the dependent measures included here (income, health, life satisfaction, and primary group interaction) be equal to or greater than the relative disadvantage of *middle-aged* minority respondents vis-à-vis middle-aged white respondents.

Measurement

The *dependent* variables chosen for this analysis include: (1) total family income for 1973; (2) self-assessed health; (3) a series of social interaction items (e.g., frequency of interaction with children, grandchildren, friends, and relatives); and (4) two measures of life satisfaction. The two life satisfaction measures were derived from a factor analysis of a battery of 11 items selected primarily from the Philadelphia Geriatric Center Morale Scale (Lawton, 1975). The principal components factor analysis indicated that two factors underlie the 11 life satisfaction items. The construction of these two measures is detailed in Appendix B. Actual items used to measure each of the dependent variables are listed in Appendices A and B.

The analysis that follows will compare *mean* scores for the nine age/race categories studied here on each of the four major dependent variables. F-tests for the significance of any observed differences among means will be conducted for both age and race groups. Rather than presenting separate pair-by-pair comparisons of the age strata or race groups, the F-test allows a more parsimonious, single comparison which addresses the question of whether or not all three age strata of race groups differ among themselves sufficiently to cause one to reject the hypothesis of equal population means (Blalock, 1960).

Table 1. *Sample Composition by Age and Ethnicity.*

| | | Ethnicity | | |
Age	Black	Mexican American	White	Total
45–54	134	146	137	417
55–64	135	149	135	419
65–74	144	154	135	433
Total	413	449	407	1269

In addition to reporting the *simple* means for each of the nine categories of the predictor variables, multiple classification analyses (MCA) will be run to determine the extent of change in the simple means produced when controls are introduced into the analyses. In effect, MCA distinguishes *net* means from simple, or gross, means. In order to preclude attributing to race or age differences that which more accurately should be attributed to the effects of sex or SES, for example, F-tests will be run for the differences in *net* means as well as the differences in gross, or simple, means. Only the uncontrolled, or simple, means are actually presented in the tables, however. The results of the F-tests for differences among controlled (net) means are indicated in Tables 2–5 by astericks. One asterick (located above and to the right of the results of the F-tests for differences among simple means) indicates the probability of Type 1 error to be less than .10; two astericks indicate $p < .05$; and three astericks indicate $p < .001$. In either case, the logic of the analysis remains the same: If the aging process can be said to level in old age the differences found to exist between ethnic groups in middle age, the means (either simple or net) of the white and minority respondents on the dependent variable under consideration should become more similar with older strata. The controls to be entered into the analysis are two variables frequently reported to be distributed differently within different racial/ethnic groups: sex and occupational prestige (SES). Occupational prestige is measured here using Duncan's Socioeconomic Index for all occupations. Respondents are coded according to the occupation they held *most* of their lives. Housewives are coded according to their spouse's occupation. Widowed, separated or divorced women are also coded according to their late/former spouse's occupation unless they have been widowed, separated, or divorced for more than 5 years, in which case their (the respondent's) *current* occupation is used.

Additionally, income and health are included as controls in the analysis of life satisfaction and primary group-interaction; income also is included as a control variable in the analysis of *health;* and, vice versa, the measure of health is entered as a control into the analysis of income. Each of the four control variables utilized here

(sex, occupational prestige, income, and health) was selected because of the differing nature of its distribution by both race and age.

ANALYSIS

When the double jeopardy hypothesis was initially stated by the National Urban League in 1964, the focus of concern was in the areas of income and health. Analyzing the income and health data in the present research, one is led to conclude much as did the National Urban League, viz., in terms of their relative income and health, the minority aged do indeed suffer double jeopardy.

Income

The data presented in Table 2 show that, while the income of both white and minority respondents declines with age, the mean income reported by older black and Mexican American respondents is considerably lower than any other group in the sample (3.49 and 3.36, respectively). Further, the relative *decline* in income between the 30-year age span studied here is much greater for minority respondents than it is for whites. The mean income reported by blacks, for example, declined 55% (7.80 to 3.49) across the three age strata. Mexican Americans showed an even larger drop in mean income, 62%, across the three age strata.

The income of older white respondents, by contrast, decline only 36% (from 10.941 to 6.891). Thus, the rather large income "gap" that exists between middle-aged minority and white respondents, becomes an even larger one among the respondents aged 65 or older. These differences in income cannot be explained merely by invoking the SES, sex, or health differences that exist between white and either Mexican Americans or blacks. Even with these variables held constant, the net incomes of the respondents over 65 (these figures are not included in the tables) are 3.89 for blacks, 3.89 for Mexican Americans, and 5.84 for whites, a finding that remains significant ($p < .001$).

Table 2. *Age and Race Effects on Income and Health*

| Dependent Variable | Age Range | Ethnicity of Respondent | | | F-Test Race Diffs. |
		Black	Mexican American	White	
Income[a]	45–54	7.80	8.87	10.94	$p < .001$***
	55–64	5.75	6.82	9.35	$p < .001$***
	65–74	3.49	3.36	6.89	$p < .001$***
	F-Test Age Diffs.	$p < .001$***	$p < .001$***	$p < .001$***	
Self-assessed health[b]	45–54	3.80	3.86	4.27	$p < .001$
	55–64	3.45	3.48	3.80	$p < .05$
	65–74	3.28	3.11	3.91	$p < .001$***
	F-Test Age Diffs.	$p < .001$	$p < .001$	$p < .001$***	

[a]The income data reported in this table are *not* raw income scores in thousands of dollars but rather the mean score computed from 15 income *categories* (see Appendix A). However, since the categories used here approximate very closely raw income (reported in thousands of dollars), the figures in this table can be interpreted as *estimates* of actual dollar income.

[b]Health data were coded from 1 to 5 with higher scores indicating better health.

Health

In response to the question "In general, would you say your health is very good, good, fair, poor, or very poor?", older minority respondents were significantly more likely to report poorer health than white respondents even with the effects of SES, sex, and income held constant. The differences in health among the three ethnic groups were less apparent among younger respondents, particularly those aged 55 to 64. While the mean health scores of blacks and Mexican Americans across the three age strata dropped, respectively, 13% and 19%, the mean score of white respondents declined less than 9% (from 4.271 to 3.911). As was the case with income, the self-assessed health of whites is greater than that of minority respondents at each age stratum with the greatest disparity occurring among those aged 65 or older.

While it is possible that the poorer health reported by the minority aged may reflect a biogenetical difference between whites and nonwhites that is also manifest in the different life expectancies at birth for each group, the more probable explanation for these health differences is a sociological one. Because of past and present policies of racial discrimination in our society, nonwhites have had less income, inadequate nutrition and, consequently poorer health and a lower life expectancy at birth than whites.

The relative life expectancy of different race or ethnic groups tend to converge, however, as individuals age. Although older blacks and Mexican Americans report poorer health than older white respondents, estimates of the additional life expectancy of persons already 50 years of age differ by less than 3 years for whites and nonwhites (Bengtson et al., 1976). This suggests that while racial discrimination may indeed be largely responsible for the lower life expectancy at birth of blacks and others classified as nonwhite, it does not adequately explain the increased proportions of *older* blacks and Mexican Americans who report their health to be poorer. *Age* discrimination is implicated as well in the health problems experienced by our society's minority aged. Consequently, the descriptive label, double jeopardy, is certainly appropriate when analyzing the health status of older blacks or Mexican Americans.

Life Satisfaction

Life satisfaction is a concept that, while directly affected by both income and health, is related to age in ways that suggest income and health to be only imperfect predictors at best. For, while the transition to old age is generally associated with declines in income and health, life satisfaction—particularly as measured by Tranquility—remains relatively stable over the 30-year span analyzed here.

Considering Tranquility, this pattern of stability is less characteristic of Mexican Americans than it is of either blacks or whites. While the Tranquility scores of black respondents remain virtually the same at each age level and the scores of whites show small *increases* with age, the Tranquility scores reported by Mexican Americans in our sample decline slightly with increasing age (this decline is not statistically significant). Consequently, although the mean level of Tranquility reported by 45- to 54-year-old Mexican Americans is somewhat higher than that reported by whites of similar ages, this pattern is reversed among the older (65–74) respondents. In this oldest age group, Mexican Americans have significantly lower Tranquility scores than either whites or blacks ($p < .05$). However, from our earlier definition, this pattern cannot be said to constitute a case of double jeopardy for the Mexican American respondents, since no statistically significant decline *with age* is observed.

Considering the second measure of life satisfaction included in the present analysis, Optimism, the situation of Mexican Americans *does* meet the definitional criteria for double jeopardy specified earlier. The data in Table 3 show that for Mexican Americans: (1) there is a significant decline in Optimism with age; (2) their Optimism scores in old age are significantly lower ($p < .001$) than the scores of older whites (0.981 vs 1.431); and (3) their dissimilarity from white respondents (as measured by differences in group means) is greater among older respondents than it is among younger respondents. White respondents have higher Optimism scores than Mexican Americans at every age considered here; and the difference in mean scores is greater in old age as whites show a decrease in mean Optimism of only 2% between the youngest and oldest strata, while Mexican Americans evidence a *decline* of 23%.

No such double jeopardy characterizes black respondents on either Tranquility or Optimism. In each case, the differences that exist between *younger* blacks and whites become *smaller* with increasing age. On Tranquility, for example, there is almost no difference between black and white respondents 65 to 74 years old, while a small difference is observed among younger respondents.

Table 3. *Age and Race Effects on Life Satisfaction*

| Dependent Variable | Age Range | Ethnicity of Respondent | | | F-Test Race Diffs. |
		Black	Mexican American	White	
Tranquility	45–54	2.15	2.08	1.95	$p > .10$***[a]
	55–64	2.16	2.08	2.14	$p > .10$
	65–74	2.17	1.93	2.17	$p < .05$*
	F-Test Age Diffs.	$p > .10$*	$p > .10$**	$.10 > p > .05$***	
Optimism	45–54	1.60	1.29	1.47	$p < .01$***
	55–64	1.39	1.25	1.38	$p > .10$
	65–74	1.31	0.98	1.43	$p < .001$***
	F-Test Age Diffs.	$p < .05$	$p < .01$	$p > .10$	

[a]The three asterisks indicate that, when sex, SES, income, and health were controlled, the differences among ethnic groups in the 45–54-age group were found to be significant (p .001). The reader should note that, without controlling on any variables, the ethnic differences were not apparent ($p > .10$), a finding which points to importance of introducing test factors (or controls) into the analysis.

On Optimism, black respondents do evidence a decline with age, although at none of the three age strata studied are the differences between blacks and whites substantially different. This point becomes more clear when one considers the differences in *net* means (not reported in the tables) for black and white respondents after income, SES, health, and sex are held constant. Among the older (65- to 74-year-old) respondents, blacks have a net Optimism score of 1.37 and whites have an almost identical score of 1.38. For blacks, then, particularly on the Tranquility component of life satisfaction the age-as-leveler hypothesis receives moderate support, while the double jeopardy hypothesis is not supported by the data.

Primary Group Interaction

Different measures of primary group interaction are included in the analysis in order to obtain estimates of the degree of social integration and group cohesion of the three ethnic groups under investigation. While primary group interaction may not be as critical an indicator of relative status as income or health, it does indicate a source of reward available to the individual in the course of their daily lives that contributes significantly to overall "*quality* of life." The reliable presence of other people may constitute an important resource that enables the older individual to insulate himself from the breakdown in self-esteem and diminution of skills often associated with the transition to old age in our society.

Primary group interaction was measured here by asking the respondent when was the last time he or she had seen (a) children; (b) grandchildren; (c) other relatives; and (d) friends and neighbors. On the first two measures, frequency of contact with children and grandchildren, the data in Table 4 indicate that, generally, it is the white respondents who report the *lowest* frequency of contact. Mexican Americans at every age report the most frequent contact with their children and grandchildren. Even when controls such as income, occupational prestige (SES), health, and sex are introduced, the unique cultural heritage of Mexican Americans in our society remains very evident in the data as the differences between Mexican Americans and blacks and whites continue to be statistically significant in all but one case. Consequently, when one considers frequency of primary group interaction as an important personal resource, the relatively advantageous position of Mexican American respondents (and, to a lesser extent, black respondents) vis-à-vis white respondents persists into old age.

Table 5 presents the data for the final two measures of primary group interaction, frequency of contact with (a) other Relatives and (b) Friends and Neighbors. Considering the *contact with*

Table 4. *Age and Race Effects on Frequency of Interaction with Children and Grandchildren*

| Dependent Variable | Age Range | Ethnicity of Respondent | | | F-Test Race Diffs. |
		Black	Mexican American	White	
Frequency of Contact w/Children	45–54	4.31	4.56	4.18	.10>p>.05**
	55–64	4.16	4.38	3.94	p<.05
	65–74	3.91	4.25	4.09	.10>p>.05*
	F-Test Age Diffs.	p>.10	.10>p>.05	p>.10	
Frequency of Contact w/Grand-children	45–54	3.99	4.28	3.90	p>.10*
	55–65	4.07	4.44	3.79	p<.001***
	65–74	3.87	4.37	3.76	p<.001***
	F-Test Age Diffs.	p>.10	p>.10	p>.10	

Table 5. *Age and Race Effects on Frequency of Interaction with Relative and Friends*

Dependent Variable	Age Range	Ethnicity of Respondent			F-Test Race Diffs.
		Black	Mexican American	White	
	45–54	3.52	3.53	2.97	$p < .01$***
Frequency	55–64	3.10	3.31	2.74	$p < .01$**
of Contact	65–74	2.80	2.99	2.81	$p > .10$
w/Relatives	F-Test Age Diffs.	$p < .001$*	$p < .01$	$p > .10$	
	45–54	2.32	2.06	2.69	$p < .001$**
Frequency	55–64	2.26	2.04	2.77	$p < .001$***
of Contact	65–74	2.43	2.04	2.98	$p < .001$***
w/Friends	F-Test Age Diffs.	$p > .10$	$p > .10$	$p < .05$**	

relatives variable first, a variation of the age-as-leveler pattern can be identified. In this case, a significant ethnic difference is observed among 45- to 54-year old individuals, although the difference is one which favors the minority respondents. Whites in this age group have significantly lower contact with their relatives than either blacks or Mexican Americans ($p < .01$). This difference becomes smaller with increasing age, however, as the pattern of contact with relatives among minority respondents declines, while the levels of contact reported by whites remains stable across age strata. The result is the *leveling* of ethnic differences in contact with relatives in old age. The F-test for the oldest age group shows no significant ethnic differences either with or without statistical controls. As with the two previously discussed measures of primary group interaction, Mexican Americans report a higher mean frequency of contact with relatives than either blacks or whites at all three age ranges included in the analysis. The extent of this difference among the older respondents, however, is not sufficient to warrant claims of significance.

Focusing attention on the frequency of interaction the individual social actor has with friends, neighbors, or other non-related acquaintances, an interesting shift in the pattern of ethnic differences occurs. Whites report *higher* levels of contact with friends and neighbors than blacks or Mexican Americans at all ages. Further, the dif-

ferences among ethnic groups are significant at each age level *with* the inclusion of control variables ($p < .05$) as well as without controls ($p < .001$).

While the contact with friends and neighbors for white respondents increases in small increments with each age stratum, there are no apparent age differences in contact with friends or neighbors among black and Mexican American respondents. As a result, the differences in old age (over 65) between groups are the most visible of all. We do not characterize the lower contact of the minority aged with friends and neighbors as being a double jeopardy situation, however, for the following reason: for the minority respondents, the observed *lower* interaction on this variable is not explained to even a minimum degree by their *age*. Younger blacks, for example, are not substantially different than older black respondents on this variable. While ethnic differences, then, are certainly present in frequency of contact with friends and neighbors, the lower mean contact reported by the minority aged does not constitute double jeopardy.

The greater frequency of *familial* interaction (i.e., interaction with children, grandchildren, and relatives) among the minority respondents, particularly Mexican Americans, suggests that the primary group needs of the minority aged *are* being satisfied within the extended family. However, the fact that Mexican Americans also report the *least* amount of interaction with nonrelated individuals, such as friends, neighbors, or acquaintances, suggests a certain amount of social isolation for the minority respondents as well.

These data also suggest the possibility that individuals seek, and generally find, an optimum level of social interaction. The need to maintain at least a minimum level of primary group interaction requires the individual to seek new patterns in their social exchange networks should death, for example, steal from them a spouse or relative (cf., Acock et al., 1974). This phenomenon appears particularly salient for white respondents whose interaction with children, grandchildren, and relatives is generally less than either blacks or Mexican Americans yet whose frequency of interaction with friends and neighbors is considerably greater than either Mexican Americans or blacks.

SUMMARY AND CONCLUSION

Utilizing data from a large (N = 1269) multi-stage probability sample of middle-aged and aged blacks, Mexican Americans and Anglos living in Los Angeles County, indicators of relative status and primary group interaction were analyzed to determine the degree and nature of any ethnic variation. It was found, that differences among the three ethnic groups do exist and, in some cases, particularly on income and self-assessed health, constitute a case of double jeopardy for the minority aged.

But while double jeopardy was found to be an accurate characterization of the black and Mexican American aged on several variables, the data also suggest that age exerts a leveling influence on some ethnic variation over time. Variables such as frequency of interaction with relatives as well as, for black respondents, the life satisfaction factors of Tranquility and Optimism all evidence a certain decline in the extent of ethnic variation across age strata. While cross ethnic longitudinal research designs would be necessary to definitively explore the age-as-leveler hypothesis, the present analysis offers some support for the earlier cross-sectional work of Kent (1971a) in this area. His perspective on the issue of the rela-

tionships among ethnicity, age and social problems bears careful consideration:

> . . . The problems older people face are very similiar regardless of ethnic background. This is not to say that the same proportion of each group faces these problems; obviously they do not. The point, however, is that if we concentrate on the group rather than on the problem, we shall be treating symptoms rather than causes.

Put differently, to presume that ethnic differences are alone sufficient to understand the personal and social situation of the aged ignores tremendous variation both *across* ethnic boundaries and *within* ethnic categories (as has been underscored, for example, by Jackson, 1970; 1971a). Data discussed here only partially support those who argue that the world of the minority aged is one of double jeopardy. Differences in old age across race lines on income or health, for example, do suggest that older blacks and Mexican Americans suffer from a double jeopardy. However, on variables measuring frequency of familial contact, the mean figures for black and Mexican American respondents indicates fairly stable interaction—not less—across each age strata. The existence of double jeopardy, therefore, is an empirical, not a logical, question. To assume otherwise would be to ignore the warning of Kent (1971c) that "age may be a great leveler with regard to both racial and social influences. . . ."

REFERENCES

Acock, A. C., Dowd, J. J., & Roberts, W. *The primary group: its rediscovery in contemporary sociology.* General Learning Press, Morristown, NJ, 1974.

Bengtson, V. L., Kasschau, P. L., & Ragan, P. K. The impact of social structure on the aging individual. In J. E. Birren & K. W. Schaie (Eds.), *Handbook of the psychology of aging.* Van Nostrand Rinehold, New York, 1977.

Bengtson, V. L., Cuellar, J., & Ragan, P. K. Stratum contrasts and similarities in attitudes toward death. *Journal of Gerontology,* 1977, *32,* 76–88.

Blalock, H. M. *Social statistics.* McGraw-Hill, New York, 1960.

Cowgill, D. O., & Holmes, L. D. *Aging and modernization.* Appleton-Century-Crofts, New York, 1972.

Douglas, E., Cleveland, W. P., & Maddox, G. L. Political attitudes, age, and aging: A cohort analysis of archival data. *Journal of Gerontology*, 1974, *29*, 666–675.

Ehrlich, I. F. Toward a social profile of the aged black population in the United States: An exploratory study. *Aging & Human Development*, 1973, *4*, 271–276.

Jackson, J. J. Aged Negroes: Their cultural departures from statistical stereotypes and rural-urban differences. *Gerontologist*, 1970, *10*, 14–145.

Jackson, J. J. Compensatory care for the black aged. In *Minority aged in America*, Occasional Paper #10, Institute of Gerontology. Univ. Michigan-Wayne State Univ., Ann Arbor, 1971, 15–23. (a)

Jackson, J. J. Negro aged: Toward needed research in social gerontology. *Gerontologist*, 1971, *11*, 52–57. (b)

Jackson, J. J. Sex and social class variations in black and parent-adult child relationships. *Aging & Human Development*, 1971, *2*, 96–107. (c)

Kalish, R. A. A gerontological look at ethnicity, human capacities and individual adjustment. *Gerontologist*, 1971, *11*, 78–87.

Kent, D. P. Changing welfare to serve minority. In *Minority aged in America*, Occasional Paper #10, Institute of Gerontology. Univ. Michigan-Wayne State Univ., Ann Arbor, 1971, 25–34. (a)

Kent, D. P. The elderly in minority groups: Variant patterns of aging. *Gerontologist*, 1971, *11*, 26–29. (a)

Kent, D. P. The Negro aged. *Gerontologist.* 1971, *11*, 48–51. (c)

Kent, D. P., & Hirsch, C. Differentials in need and problem solving techniques among low income Negro and white elderly. Paper presented at the 8th International Congress of Gerontology, Washington, 1969.

Lawton, M. P. The Philadelphia Geriatric Center morale scale: A revision. *Journal of Gerontology*, 1975, *30*, 85–98.

National Council on Aging *Triple jeopardy: Myth or reality*. National Council on Aging, Washington, 1972.

National Urban League *Double jeopardy, the older Negro in America today*. National urban League, New York, 1964.

Palmore, E., & Manton, K. Ageism compared to racism and sexism. *Journal of Gerontology*, 1973, *28*, 363–369.

Reynolds, D. K., & Kalish, R. A. Anticipation of futurity as a function of ethnicity and age. *Journal of Gerontology*, 1974, *29*, 224–232.

United States Senate, Special Committee on Aging, Lindsay, I. B. *The multiple hazards of age and race: The situation of aged blacks in the United States*, Washington, 1971.

APPENDIX A: OPERATIONALIZATION OF DEPENDENT VARIABLES

A. 1973 Family Income:

"Now, please look at the Income Card and give me the letter of the income group that includes the total income for you (and your spouse) for last year, 1973 (before taxes). That figure should include salaries, wages, dividends, interest, profits, pensions, and support from children and all other income."

```
01.  0       — 1,999 (A)
02.  $ 2,000— 2,999 (B)
03.  $ 3,000— 3,999 (C)
04.  $ 4,000— 4,999 (D)
05.  $ 5,000— 5,999 (E)
06.  $ 6,000— 6,999 (F)
07.  $ 7,000— 7,999 (G)
08.  $ 8,000— 8,999 (H)
09.  $ 9,000— 9,999 (I)
10.  $10,000—10,999 (J)
11.  $11,000—11,999 (K)
12.  $12,000—14,999 (L)
13.  $15,000—19,999 (M)
14.  $20,000—24,999 (N)
15.  $25,000 or over (O)
```

B. Self-Assessed Health:

"In general, would you say your health is . . . very good (5), good (4), fair (3), poor (2) or very poor (1)?"

C. Primary Group Interaction:

1. "When did you last see . . . (a) any of your adult children who do not live with you? . . . (b) any of your grandchildren? . . . (c) any of these (previously specified) relatives?"
   01. more than a year ago
   02. within the last year
   03. within the last month
   02. within the last week
   01. today or yesterday
2. "Now, how often do you visit with *other people*, such as friends, neighbors, or acquaintances:"
   01. less than once a month
   02. at least once a month
   03. at least once a week
   04. daily

APPENDIX B: VARIMAX ROTATED FACTOR MATRIX OF LIFE SATISFACTION ITEMS[a]

	Tranquility[b]	Optimism
1. Do you have a lot to be sad about?	.613	.243
2. Do you feel that life isn't worth living?	.420	.324
3. Do you worry so much that you can't sleep?	.664	.150
4. Do you feel afraid?	.476	.169
5. Do you feel bored?	.576	.208
6. Do you feel lonely these days?	.577	.217
7. Do you get upset easily?	.450	.134
8. Do you feel that things keep getting worse as you get older?	.381	.494
9. Do you feel that you have as much pep as you did last year?	.062	.307
10. As you get older, do you feel less useful?	.221	.697
11. Do you feel that life is hard for you?	.539	.440

[a]Items 1 thru 8, 10 and 11 were all recoded such that positive scores indicate life *satisfaction* not dissatisfaction, and the greater the score, the greater the life satisfaction. A response of "Hardly ever" to item #5 above, for example, is coded to indicate positive life satisfaction.

[b]The indices representing each of the two factors were constructed by repeatedly multiplying the factor-score coefficient of each item by the standardized score corresponding to the appropriate item and then summing the results of these operations for *each* of the variable items. The labels applied to the factor variables, *Tranquility* and *Optimism*, were suggested by a description of the individual variables that loaded highest on the particular factor.

Patterns of Aging Among the Elderly Poor of the Inner City

Margaret Clark[1]

PEOPLE HAVE an enormous ambivalence about cities. As Strauss (1968) has said, the American city evokes strikingly contradictory images, in part because it is a place of such diversity. Extremes of

Reproduction permission, THE GERONTOLOGIST. Margaret Clark, "Patterns of aging among the elderly poor of the inner city." *The Gerontologist*, Spring, 1971, Part II, pages 58–65.

1.   Director of Subcultural Studies, Adult Development Research and Training Program, Langley Porter Neuropsychiatric Institute, and Professor of Anthropology in Residence, University of California, San Francisco, Calif. 94122. The author would like to acknowledge the assistance of Mr. Gerard Brissette in reviewing the literature for this paper.

wealth and poverty, a Babel of tongues and cultures drawn from all over the world, the hundreds of microcosms of specialized occupational groups, the movement and the sheer massiveness of it—all of these contribute to the image of the city as a place of drama, color, excitement, and cosmopolitan vigor on the one hand; and, on the other, as a place to suffer poverty and wretched loneliness, to grow old in despair, and to die without a trace.

As we know, cities in America are housing more and more ethnic minority populations, and more and more aged people as well. These trends are clearly the result of a deterioration of the quality of life in downtown areas. The aged poor, like the ethnic poor, have been unable to "join the flight of younger and affluent families to suburbia to avoid the noise, smog, dirt, social tension and poor housing of the central city" (Birren, 1970). Both groups are held in part by the inexpensive housing; when the slum neighborhoods in which they live are razed, they move on to other tenements, other skid row hotels, other furnished rooms.

This paper will discuss this group of aged people—the poor of the inner city—both in terms of what we already know about them and in terms of the kinds of additional information that would be useful, either in planning for their needs or in understanding more about aging and adaptation to its circumstances.

The aged poor of the inner city have seldom been studied as a discrete group. Most large sample studies of the elderly have concentrated on institutional populations where numbers of older people are readily available. I am using the term "institution" here in its broader sense—to include senior centers, "adult communities" or retirement villages, and "golden age clubs," as well as hospitals and old age homes. Nor have there been small-sample studies done, of the kind usually conducted by urban anthropologists, because the elderly poor in cities are usually white and Euroamerican in ethnicity, they have missed such scholarly attention which has rather been focused on minorities and other exotic groups. Numerous survey studies, however, have spotted the inner-city aged and identified them as a unique group in our aging population (Clark & Anderson 1967; Lowenthal & Berkman, 1967; New York State Department of Mental Hygiene, Mental Research Unit, 1961; Srole, Langner, Michael, Opler, & Rennie, 1962; and others). Suddenly, we have become aware that "geriatric ghettos" have sprung up within the last two decades in the downtown areas of our principal cities.

This phenomenon is relatively new in America. Many factors (historical, economic, and political) can account for this age-specific concentration of people. It is consistent with the general social pattern of the polarization of many low-status groups in our society and their segregation from the mainstream of American life.

Many members of this group are largely "invisible" (Harrington, 1963) and are missed in the standard polls and surveys. We seldom see them on the main arterials of the city; rather, we find them huddled in the city's interstices—in the small side streets and less frequented byways. Their apartments and rooms are in the basements or in the rear of buildings, or in walk-up hotels. They can be found shopping in small neighborhood stores rather than in the large emporiums or supermarkets. They are also invisible because our current culture, with its primary concerns of productivity and profits, has trained us to dismiss such people from our range of perception. Even in studies specifically designed to locate these people and identify their problems, the very techniques of research themselves may be chosen to preserve an emotional distance from the subjects. Simon, Lowenthal, and Epstein (1970) have given an admirably forthright account of the reluctance of researchers to expose themselves to the mental health problems of a sample of such people in San Francisco:

> We suspect that both our research priorities and our choices of procedure may, to some extent, have reflected the stresses generated by our prolonged exposure to human misery and hopelessness. Project psychiatrists who might normally have been absorbed by the analysis of individual life histories resorted to highly complex computer techniques which led them away from the individual. Some social researchers left the project to study less threatening phenomena; others, also usually fascinated by the analysis of life histories, were able to steep themselves in the project but thereafter encountered intractable writing blocks.

Is this hard-core of aging urbanites different from other aging groups? We do know from comparative studies (Lowenthal & Trier, 1967) that the inner-city elderly are, both physically and psychologically, sicker than their age peers in other groups. They have a harder time surviving—perhaps the hardest of any elderly cohort we know. No one lovingly watches over the destinies of these tough survivors. They survive by their wits, like the rats that are often their only company. Whether they are "loners" or elderly couples, they usually are stubbornly trying to maintain the American ethic of individualism and autonomy as primary values in their old age. These were the standards by which they were raised at the turn of the century, and although they know that times have changed, they still cling to the old ideals (Clark & Anderson, 1967). For this fidelity, they pay a high price. Unlike some in the ethno-minority groups (e.g., older Negro women, Oriental grandparents, etc.), the white, impoverished inner-city aged lack the familial supports and the respect of others which sustain the waning powers of those in certain minority groups. Although they are not as isolated from their kind as was once supposed (Rosenberg, 1970; Shanas, Townsend, Wedderburn, Milhoj, & Stehower, 1968; Townsend, 1957), their life-style seems to exemplify isolation, social invisibility, and—above all—grinding poverty.

We need to know more about this group, other than what can be culled here and there from demographic or survey data. We need to know about their patterns of survival in the inner city. How has their poverty affected the process of aging among them? Is this process substantially different from other, more fortunate groups of aged people? We have some indication that the downwardly-mobile, who have slipped into poverty during their later years, fare worse psychologically than those who have endured this condition all their lives (Brill, Weinstein, & Garratt, 1969). However, in contrast, we can also pinpoint a hardy breed of older people who, although not indigenous to the downtown areas, have learned its rules of survival very well.

Certain kinds of popular gerontological research will have little relevance for this group. Retirement studies, for example, will have little bearing on those who think of themselves as simply unemployed or too sick to work. Then, too, studies of special housing for the elderly (Carp, 1966; Rosow, 1964) will have little relevance for those who cannot afford moderate-priced housing.

Above all, we need to know the *experience* of growing old in a geriatric ghetto in terms of the perceptions of those who must live it. We shall never fully understand the experience until we can see it through their eyes and comprehend it on their terms. Accordingly, there is a great need for more phenomenological studies of this group—research that allows subjects to think and act and speak for themselves.

THE CITY AS A PROCESS

To understand the urban aged and their experiences, attention must be given to the city as a social institution that has evolved from the earliest times of human history (Mumford, 1961; Strauss, 1968). Certain districts have always been set aside in cities for special categories of people (traders, foreigners, the military, seats of government, etc.), but rarely have we seen concentrations of old people into certain districts as evidenced today. What are the political, economic, and historical reasons for this phenomenon? Do cross-cultural studies show similar patterns in the large cities of the rest of the world? We do know that, until recently, the large cities of Japan and India were mainly populated by young people who had left their native villages to work in the cities until they could return to the villages for retirement. Are there certain consequences of industrialization and modern technology which make it inevitable that advanced societies will segregate their aged in special residential enclaves, be it somewhere in the inner city or in the outlying suburbs?

Within the last 20 years, as I noted at the beginning of this paper, we have witnessed a decline in the quality of life in American inner-cities. What were at one time stately mansions or respectable middle-class homes are now warrens, teeming with many varieties of the rejected and dispossessed. Certainly, the cheapest housing to be had in any modern city is to be found in these shabby, run-down buildings which often stand directly behind the large office buildings, the splendid hotels, and the gaudy theaters of the main boulevards and thorough fares.

Why do we find large concentrations of old people living here? Are they people who have always lived in these districts but who were left behind in the Great Rush to the Suburbs after the Second World War? Have they been drawn here out of economic necessity or personal choice? Many of us might believe that the last place we would want to grow old in is in the heart of a large

American city in these times. Inflated prices make a mockery of the fixed pension; the law of the inner city can be heartless and unconcerned with the welfare of the feeble and helpless; and in an atmosphere that almost crackles with violence, potential or actual, what chances does an older person have to escape robbery or bodily harm? (he is often, in fact, the ideal victim). Under these circumstances, we ought to be witnessing a concerted effort on the part of the inner-city aged to escape from this trap, but we do not. As it is true of ghetto life everywhere, there is possibly some comfort for the aged urban poor in "being with one's own" and sharing with others a mistrust and fear of others outside the enclave. For most, however, there is nowhere else to go, so they must make the best of it, rationalizing away the real disadvantages and real injustice of their misery. Despite these painful realities (and the need to deny them), we can discern, through reports from the people themselves, that inner-city living is in some ways functional to their survival. Birren (1970) has commented on this fact, pointing out that in modern cities, social resources are more and more scattered. This makes life more complicated for the elderly:

> The mere reduced agility of the aged individual markedly reduces the life space available to him in the cities. It is easier for him if he moves into an older neighborhood with clustered small shops and narrow streets. Paradoxically, it is in the most deteriorated areas of cities that aged persons may live independent lives, piecing together for themselves the combinations of needed services.

One can readily imagine that a move to more comfortable suburban or even rural locales would spell the doom of many who have worked out careful strategies of survival within the limits of the most pitful adversity.

For about 5 years (1959 to 1964), an interdisciplinary research group at Langley Porter Neuropsychiatric Institute in San Francisco studied a large group of aged subjects in various conditions of mental and physical health. Many of these people were from substantial neighborhoods in outlying areas of the city, but an appreciable number comprised a group that could

qualify as inner-city poor aged. From findings on this group[2] I have selected a number of problem areas around which to organize the following discussion. Of particular value are a series of intensive interviews with selected subjects. From their own testimony, we can see how inner-city life is functional and dysfunctional in the following major areas of concern:

Nutrition. The procurement of food, whether nutritious or not, is very important to these informants. References to cafeterias and restaurants are frequent. The corner groceryman takes on an imposing stature in their eyes, for he is both food-supplier and banker, extending credit and cashing the monthly OAS or Social Security checks. An enforced move from one room to another in a different district can be perceived as a catastrophe if the cafeteria that offers cutrate breakfasts is now six rather than two blocks away from home base. The frequency of these references can be misleading, however. Most of the meals are prepared in one's own quarters, often over an electric hot-plate or gasring. Some men even make arrangements with older women in their building to come in and fix meals at a certain rate (four meals a week for a dollar, for example). But even as rare as restaurant visits might be, the references still recur.

In a recent monograph on nutrition and aging (Howell & Loeb, 1969), it was noted:

> A variable that has been considered to be positively related to dietary intake and nutrition in the elderly is social interaction. Although little systematic data have been collected, the evidence does seem to support the general hypothesis.

Within this group, a high level of malnutrition has been related to social isolation, while one study, at least, suggests that eating with others tends to upgrade the nutritional quality of the diet (Schwartz, Henley, & Zeitz, 1964). The many references to public eating places might, therefore, be more related to the need for social interaction (or mental stimulus) than to the needs of nutrition *per se.* Further study is needed to

2. This research was supported in the main by Public Health Service Grant MH-09145.

explore this relationship between eating and sociability. Even the most cursory reflection will suggest that the relationship is not a simple one. Eating alone in a public place can be experienced as a lonelier event than eating at home alone. Idly viewing city life from the windows of a cheap cafeteria might serve only to emphasize how little a role in society one has left. Doubtless, eating out is a complex experience for the aged poor of the inner city, but what little information we have would suggest a positive adaptive relationship between eating and some conviviality.

In response to this suspected need, nutritional planners have set up programs of feeding the urban elderly who are least able to prepare their own meals or go to public dining halls. Meals-on-Wheels, home deliveries of hot meals, have been tried in many cities. A national assessment of these programs would be helpful. Other approaches include shopping services where shopping lists are picked up and groceries delivered to the client's door, or programs where welfare assistants deliver hot meals to clients and eat with them in their quarters. Some church groups and philanthropic organizations which have long been in the business of providing group-nutrition programs for the elderly are beginning to show some interest in smaller, more intimate eating arrangements for their clients as well as providing other amenities for pleasant dining conditions.

Educational programs for better nutrition among the urban poor have not been successful for several reasons. Once again, the targets for such programs are hard to reach, and even where some contact is made, it is unlikely that the programs have substantively changed eating habits. These are particularly resistant among those who have immigrated into the inner city during their maturity from rural or foreign cultures. The former pattern of a substandard diet is not easily replaced, let alone *augmented* with more nutritional foods. As a group, the elderly are the least likely to respond to such suggested changes— even where such changes could easily fit into their meager budgets. Health educators, therefore, need more information about the sociocultural factors that shape the eating patterns of the elderly (Sherwood, 1970).

Shelter. Very few of the central city elderly own their own homes. The older citizen is a renter: 70% of households in New York City with heads 65 and older rent (Cantor, Rosenthal, & Mayer, *n.d.*), while four-fifths of the San Francisco sample discussed here (Clark & Anderson, 1967) were renters. In New York, nearly a fifth of all rental units are occupied by the elderly. Since the average income of the vast majority of these city elderly is woefully low, we need hardly guess at the substandard housing facilities they are forced to live in. Researchers who visit the inner-city poor in their dwellings encounter the most indescribable squalor of flea-bag hotels, rodent-infested flop-houses, and filthy tenements (Bogue, 1963). The aged themselves would be the first to agree with these impressions. In fact, these deplorable housing conditions rank first in their complaints about their lot (despite their equally pressing needs in nutrition), and the search for better living quarters is ceaseless. Subjects talk at length about elaborate searches and "deals"—listening for the dropped cues that might lead to a favorable move, hunting perpetually for slightly better living arrangements. Sometimes blessedly, they come, but not without some further cost in loss of social contacts or old proximity to needed services.

The aged themselves value the chance to live with some measure of privacy and autonomy—no matter how dreadful the cost. We suspect that this persistent yearning for privacy is also related to a desire to cloak aging decrements that might put the older person in jeopardy of institutionalization. Inner-city living requires only the most superficial facade of social regularity to act as passport through a few simple, daily routines and consequently, having "a place of one's own," even in the most turgid of social conditions, can be a positive boost to one's morale. Also, subjects express the feeling that, although they do not care to interact with their neighbors except in the most superficial ways, they consider it a comfort to have someone—*anybody*—near at hand in case of emergencies. One subject from the San Francisco sample was dumbfounded to learn how many friends from his floor in the hotel he had after he was taken to the hospital. People he had hardly spoken to before came and wished him well.

However, when he was discharged, he slipped back into the old patterns of nodding acquaintance and arm's-length relatedness.

There is no doubt that "a place of one's own" is highly functional for the aged and one could wish that every elderly person, not needing institutional care, could enjoy pleasant, adequate housing. In some perverse ways, the highly inadequate housing facilities of the inner city do manage, ultimately to supply some minimal aid to these people in terms of privacy, individual space, and availability of help. Some cities, like Detroit, have experimented with refurbished downtown hotels for the elderly, recognizing the desires of many to live close to the company of others like themselves. As yet, no assessments of these experiments have been published, but the concept is provocative. In fact, the whole commune movement among the young (especially those communes set up in urban settings) might afford some workable models for elderly groups in the city, suffering from their own varieties of rootlessness and anomie. Certainly, most older Americans would not cherish the kind of tribal closeness that the young currently value, but strengthening some communal bonds for the inner-city aged might be as relevant as they appear to be for upper-middle-class groups who move into "retirement communities" (Rosow, 1964, 1967).

Medical Services. There is an illusion in the inner city: there is a belief that medical help is closer than it really is. In fact, the availability of medical help within the inner city may be more distant than in suburban or rural areas (Norman, 1969). A high degree of mobility is necessary to gain transportation to county clinics and many of the poorest elderly—who are often the sickest of all groups of aged—lack both the mobility and the cost of transportation to get to a source of medical help.

The advent of Medicare in 1965 has since helped to alleviate the desperate medical problems of the aged of the inner city to some degree. Unfortunately, the monthly charge (which is matched by the federal government) is still too high for some to pay. Many of this group—especially the male urban nomads—are unaware of these benefits and would even be disinclined to enroll. Their life-style of surly independence from all Establishment doings keeps them on the police-prisoner cycle (Spradley, 1970), rather than on the doctor-patient cycle. The code of the inner city is imbued with a profound mistrust of aid programs, especially when emanating from the federal government. Consequently, a hard kernel of our elderly population, we suspect, is still not reached with these grants-in-aid. An evaluation-research project has been set up in Kansas City to assess the effectiveness of Medicare, but, as of this writing, no public reports had appeared.

Furthermore, we seem to be approaching a new crisis in Medicare. A recent inquiry by a Senate Special Committee on Aging has disclosed that, because of inflation and increased charges, Medicare is now covering only half the medical costs of the aged in the United States (*San Francisco Chronicle*, Jan. 11, 1971). The remainder must be paid by the elderly themselves. Clearly, the current Medicare program, while it has so far been a godsend to many of the elderly poor, is not the final answer.

Various "out-reach" programs attempt to keep in contact with the "hidden" aged with medical needs. Some senior centers or old-age clubs employ volunteers to visit the house-bound regularly and provide for professionals a kind of referral service. The Visiting Nurses' Association and public health nurses are also deeply involved in inner-city health care, and, interestingly, some hospitals have become involved in home-care programs that utilize "flying squads" of physicians and nurses. In San Francisco, for example, a geriatric screening unit at the county hospital now provides on-call services for emergencies, treating patients in a home setting wherever possible (Rypins & Clark, 1968).

Since the concept of switchboard emergency service has gained wide popularity with such groups as potential suicides, persons needing legal aid and minority members who get into trouble, perhaps we might see in the future within every major city a switchboard for the elderly who, by calling one telephone number, can be put into contact with the service personnel appropriate to their needs. Perhaps this might be the best way to reach the hidden isolates of the inner city and bring them the necessary help for their medical problems.

All in all, it is clear that living in the inner city is a disadvantage to the older person when it comes to procuring much-needed medical services. Very often county medical personnel do not even get to see the ailing aged poor until an acute crisis arrives. By this time, proper medical treatment is often too late. New ways of bringing medical care to elderly patients before the crisis-point is reached need to be explored. A few recent reports describe some interesting experimental approaches (Norman, 1969).

Mobility. It is surprising that this very important factor in the life-support of the aged has been overlooked in gerontological studies until quite recent years. In fact, its importance is evident in every dimension of aging we study. It is crucial in medical care (can one meet a clinic appointment?); it is important in nutrition (can one get to a store safely?); or it can be the determining factor of whether one can move to new quarters. It is strongly related to morale and self-esteem, and for the hospitalized elderly, the ability to move about on one's own volition becomes one of their primary expressed needs (Clark & Anderson, 1967). Its importance for the inner-city aged is clear—once an elderly "loner" loses the ability to move about on his own, he becomes dependent on friends and neighbors to supply him his necessities. If he lacks these, then his loss of mobility might well be the precipitating factor that puts him into the hospital (Lowenthal, 1964). Once the power to move about on one's own is lost, the deadly laws of inner-city life take hold. Retaining one's mobility allows for freedom and autonomy; it permits one to remain open to new possibilities and other alternatives in the environment; it allows the older person to reach for the opportunities available in his society. Immobility, on the other hand, is life in an ever-shrinking world, forcing a slow attrition in many other areas of an individual's personal and social system and resulting in an impoverishment of all segments of life.

Urban life has always presented obstacles to the mobility of the elderly: there have always been stairs to climb or impatient bus drivers who refuse to give a helping hand. But within the last 5 years, as civil disorders and street crimes have increased, a sinister, new threat to the mobility of the aged has risen within the city—fears of muggings and assaults which make the elderly prisoners in their own quarters. In a recent Associated Press news release, the Special Senate Committee on Aging reported that these fears are causing "the elderly, in increasing numbers, [to] stay at home behind locked doors after dark and even during some daylight hours" (*New York Times,* Jan. 10, 1971). The report also cites a New York study which showed that of 137 elderly interviewees *all* had been mugged on the streets at least once. The elderly are also reluctant to wait for buses or streetcars anymore. The Committee called this situation a "crisis in mobility," where the old of the inner city "live almost entirely within their own walls, overwhelmed by illness, despair, or fear of crime." Most tragically, this situation seems to be beyond remedy, short of a major roll-back of the social deterioration that has been plaguing all American cities within the past decade. Most interesting is the importance given by the Committee to mobility itself, recognizing it as a key factor in old people's survival.

Social Interaction. Cities have always attracted people who either seek a variety of social contacts or prefer to live aloof from others. This wide spectrum of social opportunities has always been a major appeal of city living. One can seek and find deeply personal friendships or a collection of nodding acquaintances. One can build a large network of close friends or one can move about, nameless, never coming too close to others. The point is: in the city, one is *free to make an individual choice.*

The urban elderly share in these advantages of city life. In this environment, they can control the degree of social interaction they desire. By watching the aged, one can observe the conviviality of some and the solitary habits of others. In the lobbies of the old hotels, one can chat with the day clerk or simply look at TV.

From what we know, the social interaction of the aged poor is simple, seldom intimate, and narrowly circumscribed. One female subject from the San Francisco sample reported that she wanted friends but had trouble making them.

Further, it became evident that her real problem was keeping them. "I met this woman in a cafeteria," she said, "She seemed like such a nice person at first, but then I found out that she drank. I can't stand people who do that." Does this coolness and reserve have any functional value for the aged of the inner city? How much of it is the result of sensory loss which, in their poverty, they cannot buy aids for? In some cases, it appears that social withdrawal is masking psychological impairment of both psychogenic or organic origin. In other cases, especially among those who have slipped into the ghetto late in life from a higher economic status, the aloofness masks the poverty.

It would be especially helpful to know something about the social networks (Bott, 1957; Epstein, 1961) of these people. From the information available, we know they lack personal contact with a variety of other social systems that could be of beneficial help to them. They are, consequently, quite limited in procuring for themselves vital services and must rely on the formal and impersonal systems provided by society for the unfortunate and under-privileged. In fact, is not an essential characteristic of poverty that one be almost entirely dependent on the impersonal patron—the "agency"—for the procurement of vital services?

With loss of employment and decrements in mobility, the aged individual's social world inevitably shrinks. Yet, we know that social interaction and mental stimulus is of great importance in the mental health of the elderly (Goldfarb, 1958, 1964). We also know that sexuality and sexual needs in individuals in their 60s and 70s are far from extinguished (Rubin, 1965). But research on social and particularly sexual needs is very spotty. But do the aged rank this topic as low as do the researchers? It is an open field for the courageous investigator.

In the general area of social interaction, we need some investigation of several questions: What would be the best way to go about improving the scope and quality of social contacts in this group? How successful has the "Senior Center approach" been among them? How can what we have seen to be an understandable fear of strangers be assuaged and new patterns of inter-relationship built?

Symbolic Values. Cities are the repositories of the most potent symbols of our culture—monuments, cathedrals, skyscrapers, government buildings, technological marvels, fantastic merchandise, memorable landmarks. To live in Boston, New York, Washington, or San Francisco is to live within a symbol of the "best" that our culture has produced. All who live in the city, rich and poor alike, can share in these symbolic values and draw some personal pride from an association with them. Here, in the symbolic realm, the egalitarian dreams of our democracy can become actualized for all.

At one time in our cultural history, an identity as a New Yorker represented the height of sophistication and modernity. No matter how poor one was, status as a New Yorker placed one high above the "hicks" and the "rubes." New York seemed to be the hub of America and the whole universe. Is it possible that any of this old pride in city yet remains or that it has any functional value at all for the elderly, regardless of how poor they are? Have the ethnic and political loyalties so polarized the nation that one's identity as the citizen of a famous, particular city is no distinction anymore? Has the new cynicism so corroded all the old value systems that even the aged, who hold on to them with the greatest tenacity, can only let them fall from their hands in disgust?

The whole field of cultural history and its relationship to the aging process has been sadly neglected in gerontological studies. Erikson (1950) has repeatedly urged that studies of identity take into account the intuitive knowledge that everyone's "life is the accidental coincidence of but one life-cycle with but one segment of history." Ways must be found to relate this evolving cultural matrix to the aging patterns of groups of individuals.

CONCLUSION

The position I have taken in this paper is that the urban environment, like any other milieu in which aged individuals find themselves, has great potential for promoting both human misery and human survival. One of the more promising approaches to social planning for the inner-city aged, it seems to me, is to examine the ways in which the aged poor, when faced with basic problems of physical and psychological survival, develop informal structures for their solution. If planned programs can be constructed to emulate or develop these spontaneous arrangements among people, they are more likely to be acceptable and effective. Such approaches require that we know something about subgroups of the urban aged. As Birren (1970) has said, we know that

> a massive effort to make matters better probably would misfire if it followed a simple-minded notion of the poor as a single, self-contained group. It is questionable whether the aged regard themselves or behave as a minority group, or that they cross ethnic, religious and occupational lines to associate with each other.

Insofar as programs to help the inner-city aged are being considered, they should take into account the diversity that is an integral feature of the city.

How much behavioral science can contribute to the plight of the urban aged remains to be seen. It is fairly obvious, however, that studies of the urban aged can contribute a great deal to behavioral science—to our further understanding of the tenacity of human life and of human purpose.

BIBLIOGRAPHY

References Cited:

Birren, J. E. The abuse of the urban aged. Psychology Today, 1970, 3, No. 10, 36–38; 72.

Bogue, D. J. Skid-row in American cities. Community & Family Study Center, University of Chicago, 1963.

Bott, E. Family and social network. London: Tavistock, 1957.

Brill, N. Q., Weinstein, R., & Garratt, J. Poverty and mental illness: Patients' perception of poverty as an etiological factor in their illness. American Journal of Psychiatry, 1969, 125, 1172–1179.

Canton, M., Rosenthal, K., & Mayer, M. The elderly in the rental market of New York City. US Dept of Health, Education, & Welfare, Administration on Aging, Monogr. 26, n.d.

Carp, F. M. A future for the aged: The residents of Victoria Plaza. Austin: University of Texas Press, 1966.

Clark, M., & Anderson, B. G. Culture and aging: An anthropological study of older Americans. Springfield, Ill.: Charles C Thomas, 1967.

Epstein, L. J. The network and urban social organization. Rhodes-Livingstone Institute Journal, 1961, 29, 29–62.

Erikson, E. H., Growth and crises of the "healthy personality." In M. J. E. Senn (Ed.), Symposium on the healthy personality, Suppl. 11 to the Transactions of the 4th conference on Problems of Infancy and Childhood, New York: Josiah Macy, Jr. Foundation, 1950.

Goldfarb, A. Management of aged patients who are mentally ill. Roche Report, 1964, 1, No. 7.

Goldfarb, A. Patterns in planning a psychiatric program for the aged. Bulletin of the New York Academcy of Medicine, 1958, 34 (2nd ser.), 811–822.

Harrington, M. The other America. New York: Macmillan, 1963.

Howell, S. C., & Loeb, M. B. (eds.) Nutrition and aging: A monograph for practitioners. Gerontologist, 1969, 9, No. 3, Pt. 11.

Koller, M. R. Social gerontology. New York: Random House, 1968.

Lowenthal, M. F., & Berkman, P. L. Aging and mental disorder in San Francisco: A social psychiatric study. San Francisco: Jossey-Bass, 1967.

Lowenthal, M. F. Lives in distress: The paths of the elderly to the psychiatric ward. New York: Basic Books, 1964.

Lowenthal, M. F., & Trier, M. The elderly ex-mental patient. International Journal of Psychiatry, 1967, 13, 103–106.

Mumford, L. The city in history: Its origins, its transformations, and its prospects. New York: Harcourt Brace, 1961.

New York State Dept. of Mental Hygiene. Mental Health Research Unit. A mental health survey of older people. Utica, NY: State Hospitals Press, 1960, 1961.

Norman, J. C. (ed.) Medicine in the ghetto. New York: Appleton-Century-Crofts, 1969.

Rosenberg, G. S. The worker grows old: Poverty and isolation in the city. San Francisco: Jossey-Bass, 1970.

Rosow, I. Housing and social integration of the aged, final report of study submitted to the Cleveland Welfare Federation & the Ford Foundation. Cleveland: Western Reserve University, 1964.

Rosow, I. Social integration of the aged. New York: Free Press, 1967.

Rubin, I. Sexual life after sixty. New York: Basic Books, 1965.

Rypins, R. F., & Clark, M. L. A screening project for the geriatric mentally ill. California Medicine, 1968, 109, 273–278.

Schwarz, D., Henley, B., & Zeitz, L. The elderly ambulatory patient: Nursing and psychosocial needs. New York: Macmillan, 1964.

Shanas, E., Townsend, P., Wedderburn, D., Friis, H., Milhoj, P., & Stehouwer, J. Older people in three industrial societies. New York & London: Atherton Press, 1968.

Sherwood, S. Gerontology and the sociology of food and eating. Aging & Human Development, 1970, 1, 61–85.

Simon, A., Lowenthal, M. F., & Epstein, L. J. Crisis and intervention: The fate of the elderly mental patient. San Francisco: Jossey-Bass, 1970.

Spradley, J. P. You owe yourself a drunk: The ethnography of urban nomads. Boston: Little, Brown & Co., 1970.

Srole, L., Langner, T., Michael, S., Opler, M., & Rennie, T. Mental health in the metropolis: The midtown Manhattan Study, Vol. 1. New York: McGraw-Hill, 1962.

Strauss, A. (Ed.) The American city; a sourcebook of urban imagery. Chicago: Aldine, 1968.

Townsend, P. The family life of old people: An inquiry in East London. London: Routledge & Kegan Paul, 1957.

Other Suggested Readings:

Anderson, N. The hobo: The sociology of the homeless. Chicago: Phoenix Books, 1961.

Ben Broek, J. Conference of the law of the poor (University of California, 1966). San Francisco: Chandler, 1966.

Cottrell, F. Life of older people in today's cities. In L. Pastaian & W. Donahue (eds.). Growing old in tomorrow's cities, publication pending.

Dumont, M. P. Tavern culture: The sustenance of homeless men. American Journal of Orthopsychiatry, 1967, 37, 938–946.

Faris, R. E. L., & Dunham, H. W. Mental disorder in urban areas. New York: Hafner, 1960.

Finney, J. C. (Ed.) Culture change, mental health, and poverty. Essays by E. Berne [and others]. Lexington: University of Kentucky, 1969.

Hunter, R. Poverty: Social conscience in the progressive era. New York: Harper Torchbooks, 1965.

Jacobs, P. The permanent paupers. Paper presented at the meeting of the American Orthopsychiatric Assn., Chicago, Mar., 1964.

Madge, J. The elderly in an English city. In L. Pastaian & W. Donahue (eds.). Growing old in tomorrow's cities, publication pending.

Niebanck, P. L. (with the assistance of J. E. Pope) The elderly in older urban areas: Problems of adaptation and the effects of relocation. Institute for Environmental Studies, University of Pennsylvania, 1965.

President's Commission on Income Maintenance Program. Poverty amid plenty: The American Paradox. Washington: US Government Printing Office, 1969.

Riessman, F., Cohen, J., & Pearl, A. (eds.) Mental health of the poor. New York: Free Press of Glencoe, 1964.

Shanas, E. A note on restriction of life space: Attitudes of age cohorts. Journal of Health & Social Behavior, 1968, 9, 86–89.

Townsend, P., & Wedderburn, D. The aged in the welfare state. London: G. Bell & Sons, 1965.

Weinberg, J. The city as a social psychological milieu for older people. In L. Pastaian & W. Donahue (eds.). Growing old in tomorrow's cities, publication pending.

Education As War

Edgar S. Cahn

Education for the American Indian today follows a pattern of "cold war," modeled on a time-tested formula. Its components:

—Promises made and promises broken.

—The long trek from home to the white man's wasteland.

—Unremitting pressure toward total submission, leading to personal, cultural and ethnic annihilation.

PROMISES ARE cheap. A treaty signed a century ago between the United States Government and the Navajo nation included this pledge:

"The United States agrees that for every 30 children . . . who can be induced or compelled to attend school, a house shall be provided and a teacher competent to teach the elementary branches of an English education shall be furnished. . . ."

In 1969, 40,000 Navajos—nearly a third of the entire tribe—are functional illiterates in English.

Rupert Costo, President of the American Indian Historical Society and a chairman of the Cahuilla tribe of California, says Indians have always considered education crucial to their survival. "In our contact with the whites, we have always and without fail asked for one thing. We wanted education. You can examine any treaty, any negotiations with the American whites. The first condition, specifically asked for by the Indian tribes, was education."[1]

In spite of that and in spite of periodic reassertions by the Government of its commitment to education, the product—through BIA-operated boarding schools and day schools and through contract arrangements with local public school districts—is abysmally poor.

The Bureau of Indian Affairs operates 77 boarding schools, scattered throughout the nation, and 147 day schools located on or near reservations. In recent years, the Bureau has sought to transfer much of its responsibility for educating Indian children to local school districts, entering into contracts with the states. In 1969, 57.4 percent of all Indians attending schools were in public schools, attending classes with non-Indians. Two-thirds of the remaining youngsters, or some 35,000 children, are sent to boarding schools. BIA day schools serve only 16,000 children, or about 14 percent of the Indians in school.

In 1966, more than 16,000 Indian children of school age were not attending any school at all.

- *The average educational level for all Indians under federal supervision is five school years.*
- *Dropout rates are twice the national average.*
- *Indian children score consistently lower than white children at every grade level, in both verbal and non-verbal skills according to national tests, administered in 1965. The longer the Indian child stays in school, the further behind he gets.*
- *More than one out of five Indian males (22.3 percent) have less than five years of schooling.*
- *The Cherokees of Oklahoma today have reached an educational level one year behind the state's Negro population of 10 years ago and 2.2 school years behind the Negro population of present-day Oklahoma.*

It is the same bleak story, no matter whether one studies national Indian statistics, a single BIA school, or even the public schools serving Indians and receiving special federal funds. (If any distinction is to be made, the public schools receiving special BIA funds may have done even worse. The BIA has abdicated responsibility—even though its funds and its trust obligations are involved.)

The human needs of children are "swept away when [the Indian child] is put in a BIA boarding school situation, where there might be as many as 100 to 150 other children under the care of a single matron. She is supposed to provide a substitute environment to become a parent-substitute for him."[2]

"I many times stay up late at night holding a girl's head on my lap while she is crying," a boarding school staff member lamented, "but when you have 100 students in a dormitory it is impossible to comfort all those who need comforting."[3]

Senator Walter Mondale of Minnesota, a member of the Senate Indian Education Subcommittee was advised by the BIA recently that "there is one psychologist in the whole BIA [school] system and only two or three social workers." Most counselors and dormitory aides are unprepared for the difficult tasks that face them at Bureau boarding schools. They often perceive their roles as that of guards rather than substitute parents. Those few who are skilled and dedicated have little time to devote to helping the children with special problems, because of overcrowding and understaffing. One boarding school counselor said he spends most of his time retrieving AWOLs, supervising housekeeping and other "general service tasks," but spent *none* of his time counseling—even though he works a 10 to 16 hour day.

"There is a tendency—a pronounced tendency—to "herd" rather than guide. The boys and girls are yelled at, bossed around, chased here and there, told and untold, until it is almost impossible for them to attempt to do anything on their own initiative—except, of course, to run away."[4]

The entire BIA educational system is plagued by mediocrity: an overburdened and sometimes insensitive staff, inadequate physical facilities, out-of-date texts and supplies, little money for innovation. Teachers' salaries are not competitive with the public schools. The pay may be the same, but the BIA hires on a year-round basis requiring 12-months work while public school teachers work about 180 days a year. Educational specialists confirm the observation of a 1966 Presidential Task Force that "too many BIA employees were simply time-servers of mediocre or poor competence who remain indefinitely because they were willing to serve in unattractive posts at low rates of pay for long periods of time."

Teachers who come to the reservation day schools often know little about the children they are going to teach (only one percent of the reservation elementary teachers are Indian). Teacher orientation and training sessions pay scant attention to Indian cultural values or to problems which the teacher may encounter with children who speak little or no English, have different values and know different experiences. Instead, orientation concentrates on housing, pay, and civil service fringe benefits.

Widely publicized innovations and crash programs have slight impact on BIA schools. For example, an experimental program to teach English as a second language was implemented to make it easier for Indian children to learn English, but a national report has shown that the program often is ignored. One teacher left the materials untouched because she "did not believe in the new system of teaching English."

A former Assistant BIA Commissioner of Education, Dr. Carl Marburger, remarked: "The Education Division is isolated from the research, program development, evaluation and dissemination activities in education so that the educators in the Bureau are severely out of touch with the practices in the field."

I was in Alaska," reports Congressman Julia Butler Hansen of Washington, "and I saw 'John and Jane went to the store,' or 'John and Jane had a cow,'" as reading examples in the textbooks. This was the Far North, just below the Arctic Circle. They had never seen a cow and they may never see a cow. . . .

The sterility of the curriculum is typically matched by the bleakness of the facilities. Dr.

Robert Bergman, a child psychiatrist with the Indian Division of the Public Health Service, noted:

> Dormitories are usually large barrack-like structures with no provision for privacy, and usually no space that is each individual's to control as he sees fit. Only occasionally is there opportunity for the children to decide on the decoration of any of their living spaces.

At the Chilocco boarding school in Oklahoma, one dormitory room contained exposed heavy duty electrical wiring at the head of one youngster's bed. A BIA report on conditions at the school admitted, "the possibility of that girl being electrocuted in her sleep was evident." The two-room Gila River Indian Day School in Arizona is a rebuilt garage. It serves 130 children, 60 of them in a room which should hold 29.

A survey of BIA teachers in 1965 revealed that 25 percent would rather be teaching whites than Indians. Still another survey showed that while Indian students saw jobs and college as their long-range educational priorities, their teachers believed an ability to get along and assimilation were more important traits for Indians to absorb.[5]

It was the Indian's great misfortune to be conquered by a people intolerant of cultural diversity. The Indian looked different, spoke a different language, had his own religion and customs; Americans saw him as an anathema and were chagrined when he refused to conform to "civilization." Indian education policies were formulated—in the words of a Commissioner of Indian Affairs—". . . to prepare him for the abolishment of tribal relations, to take his land in severalty and in the sweat of his brow and by the toil of his hands to carve out, as his white brother has done, a home for himself and his family."[6]

THE LONG TREK—FROM HOMELAND TO WASTELAND

The Indian child's trek to school, measured in miles, becomes a Trail of Tears, a form of compulsory and permanent expatriation, especially for the 35,309 children attending BIA boarding schools. In 1968, 9,000 of the children in Indian boarding schools were less than nine years old.

In Alaska, where 15 percent of the national Indian population resides, there are not enough schools, nor is there room for all the Indian children in public schools. As a result, Indian children are shipped as far away as Oklahoma, 6,000 miles from their parents.

Even where the Indian children attend day schools or public schools, the journey can be a rugged one. In Utah, Indian children wake up at 4:30 a.m., walk three to four miles over rough terrain to the bus and then ride 65 miles to the public school. In New Mexico, high school students walk two miles to the bus every day, and then ride 50 miles to school.

Once in a boarding school, the children are effectively cut off from their families. Parents cannot visit often because of the great distance and because many schools are located where roads are impassable for much of the year. Boarding school officials do not offer transportation or accommodations for parents who might want to come. Even when the school is convenient to the reservations, parental visits are discouraged because the children often become hard to manage after parents leave and sometimes run away.

Permission to see one's own parent is not a "right." It is often granted as a reward for good behavior—or denied as a form of punishment. "If [the child] has been a 'problem' (e.g. has run away) parents are often not allowed to take him until he has 'learned his lesson.' This may take up to a month to accomplish."[7]

Education becomes a forced journey to alien institutions: on the Navajo reservation, BIA schools are called "*Washingdoon bi oltka*" which means "Washington's schools." From the Indian's point of view, the public schools seem the longest way from home. The Navajos refer to them as "*Beligaana bi oltka,*" the "little white man's schools."

The journey to school takes on many meanings. But above all it expresses the white man's judgment of rejection and disdain for the child's home and way of life. The message is not subtle. At one boarding school, a child was heard to pray:

> *"Dear Lord, help me not to hate my mother and father."*

At another, a school teacher exclaimed in a fit of anger: "If you want to live in a hogan for the rest of your life just don't bother to study." One student left school precisely because she did want to live in a hogan for the rest of her life.[8]

Boarding schools serve "students with marked educational retardation based on either delayed school entrance or past social and behavioral problems, and . . . students who have unsatisfactory home conditions or social-emotional problems," as well as children who have no schools available near their homes. Poverty is regarded as an unsatisfactory home condition. Many boarding school students are welfare referrals; the schools are used to avoid providing increased family assistance and parents are penalized for being poor by having their children shipped off to distant boarding institutions.

Senator Barry Goldwater showed some understanding of the problem: "I try to picture myself as an Indian parent and try to sense what I might feel when my child was sent to school either close by or many, many miles away to a boarding school, knowing that the child would come back, yes, speaking English but also having forgotten the religion of his tribe, the ancient ways of his tribe. . . ."

The day school is just as explicit a rejection as the boarding school. Its function is to save the child from his own home and family. One school principal states bluntly:

> When the mothers ask me what they can do to help their children, I tell them: 'Don't do anything.'
> It isn't that they should fear authority but that they should respect the authority that is doing things for their own good.[9]

A Pueblo day school teacher expressly rejects the child's home by ruling it off limits professionally:

> My business and my concerns extend only as far as this fence—pointing to the fence around the school—what happens outside of these school grounds is none of my business.[10]

The significance, relevance, and even the existence of the Indian world and its values is systematically denied by school administration. The Indian child is kept in deliberate ignorance of his culture, history and heritage. He is taught, simultaneously, that he should be ashamed of it.

Textbooks, in dealing with the Indian, often are appalling. A history text, recently in use in California public schools, gave this description:

> The Indians who lived in the Stanislaus area were known as the 'Diggers,' although they were the Walla Tribe. They were stupid and lazy and it is said they were given their name because of their habit of digging in the earth. They dug roots for food, and they also dug holes in the ground for shelter. The squaw was required and expected to provide all of the food for her husband and family.[11]

The late Senator Robert F. Kennedy of New York related this experience:

> We were in Idaho the other day and I was asking the superintendent of schools, where they had 80 percent Indian children, whether they taught anything about Indian history or Indian culture. The tribe was a very famous tribe, the Shoshone, which had a considerable history, and he said, 'There isn't any history to this tribe;' this has a tremendous effect on the children. So I asked him if there were any books in the library where all these children could go and read about Indian history, and he said, 'Yes,' and we went to the library. There was only one book and the book was entitled, 'Captive of the Delawares.' It showed a white child being scalped by an Indian.

The teachers are not trained to counteract these distorted accounts of the Indian's history. In California, which has the largest Indian population in the country, teacher training in the colleges devotes "something like six-and-a-half pages of the required reading . . . to . . . Indians, and about five-and-a-half of these six pages are very detrimental to the Indian child."[12]

The Lower Brule Sioux Tribe of South Dakota reports that at their day school "students seldom hear anything about Indian culture or history" and "pride in their heritage is not encouraged." The Mesquakies of Iowa set up an art class in an abandoned farmhouse when the instructors at their day school refused to permit Indian art in the classrooms.

The official business of the school is teaching middle-class values and skills to "culturally deprived children.'' The BIA's *Curriculum Needs of Navajo Pupils* states that the Navajo child:

> Needs to begin to develop knowledge of how the dominant culture is pluralistic, and how these people worked to become the culture which influences the American mainstream of life . . .
>
> Needs to understand that every man is free to rise as high as he is able and willing . . .
>
> Needs assistance with accepting either the role of leader or follower . . .
>
> Needs to understand that work is necessary to exist and succeed . . .

These ''needs'' are defined and centered within the cultural universe of the non-Indian world. The possibility that the Indian child may need an education which helps him function as an Indian, or that Indian parents might want such an education for their children, is not considered.

Instead of family-type cohesion based on respect, the schools encourage market relationships to enforce rules. At one boarding school, a program of ''behavior modification'' has been instituted. A child may earn points for good behavior and use them to purchase items he may want. A can of deodorant sells for 150 to 200 points. A frisbee, a 50-cent toy children toss in the air, goes for 500 points. But a child who maintains a ''perfect'' record can only earn 60 points in any week.

Dr. John Collier Jr., a professor of cultural anthropology at San Francisco State College, reports of children at Chilocco, Oklahoma Boarding School: Pervasive attacks are made against their cultural beliefs . . . teachers advocate the free labor of Navajo girls in their homes, doing laundry, scrubbing floors, etc., all done on students' after-school time, 'to teach them the American way of housekeeping.' ''[13]

When an Eastern Oklahoma public school administrator was asked whether he thought English should be taught as a second language to Indian children, he blindly insisted that ''only 'American' be taught in [the] schools.''[14]

Struggling with English, the Indian child gradually learns how he is regarded: ''dumb Indian.''

In the public schools of today, the Cherokee student is frequently infringed against by the teacher. He is at a linguistic disadvantage in that he possibly hears and speaks only Cherokee at home. Then, when he goes to school, he has to think and talk in English. This is confusing and naturally makes his responses slower than the white student of the same mental ability. This hesitation sometimes gives rise to the oft-heard phrase 'dumb Indian,' when the Indian really is not 'dumb' at all.[15]

The main ''achievement'' of the schools is to provide Indian children with an educational experience designed to root out all traces of their Indian heritage. Some of the methods go back 70 years, as if time stood still for Indian education.

Dr. Bergman made these observations:

> On the theory that 'if the children are allowed to talk Navajo, they won't bother to learn English,' native language is usually forbidden. . . .
>
> In the world of the boarding school not only the Navajo language but almost all things Navajo are rated very low. The children are frequently told not to be like their parents and are often admonished against following the traditions of their people.[16]

The Indian child often encounters discrimination in the public schools. In Oklahoma, Cherokee children have been called ''black rats'' by the teachers.

> A student in Ponca City asks if she has to sit by an Indian. The teacher says, 'No, I know what you mean.' Our girls are called 'squaws.' We are greeted with, 'How.' If it rains, we are asked if we have been dancing. If we get a haircut, we are asked if they can scalp us. Everything we know and cherish is derided and made a butt of jokes.[17]

In Arizona, Indian children so poor that they come to school without breakfast have been made to work for their lunch. In Oklahoma, some children who recently graduated from high school never received their diplomas; they were ashamed to appear at the ceremony because they had no decent clothes to wear, nor could they afford to buy class rings and pictures. Isolated and separate, the Indian public school children stick to themselves, exiles in their native land.

It does not take long for the Indian child to understand the true nature of his journey. That exciting adventure of exploring a new world called "school" quickly becomes perceived as a one-way journey—to a wasteland from which there is no return.

When the Indian child enters school, he appears eager to learn.

An observer's first impressions of the lower elementary grades (Beginners, First, Second, Third) at an Indian Day School are likely to be positive. If the teacher is fairly competent and the class small, the children appear attentive, obedient, and eager to learn.[18]

The children "jump up and answer right away" and "help out each other." They seem "enormously 'teacher oriented' " and say they "like school." Tests show that Indian children appear to achieve satisfactorily until they reach about the fourth grade level. After that, the relationship between teacher and student changes radically. Achievement scores show a steady and progressive decline. "Children of the typical rooms appear shy, withdrawn, stupid and sullen." By the seventh grade "the students have surrounded themselves with a wall of silence that is impenetrable to the outsider. . . ."[19]

Resistance begins when the Indian child is old enough to know he is Indian and conscious enough of the world around him to understand what the school is teaching him about being Indian:

Indian children perceive very early what most whites think of their parents and themselves. Once past the primary grades, they approach each teacher with caution, testing her response to them; if it is negative, they quickly retreat.[20]

Passive resistance and withdrawal express the Indian's silent defiance against overwhelming odds. The Indians "tune out." Teachers rise to meet the challenge; persuasion changes to coercion. At the Lower Brule school in South Dakota, for example, "teachers persist in violating explicit Bureau rules against verbal humiliation and corporal punishment. Tongue lashings are common; order is kept in the primary grade room with the threat, often the reality, of a stick; frequently, primary grade children are forced to sit in a locked closet for punishment. School becomes a terrifying experience as well as a waste of time."[21]

The educator sees the child's behavior as changing. He even has a technical term for it: "The cross-over phenomenon." To the Indian child, it is not he who is changing—but the world into which he was welcomed, and which he entered with joy and trust.

Indian children face unremitting pressure toward submission and toward cultural annihilation. All who pass through the Indian education system become casualties—casualties of education waged as war. The casualties take many forms.

There are the Dead.

Recently, two young boys froze to death while running away from a boarding school. They were trying to get to their homes—50 miles away.

Senator Mondale made this report on the Fort Hall, Idaho Reservation: "The subcommittee was told during its visit to that reservation that the suicide rate among teenagers was perhaps as high as 100 times the national average. No one really knew for certain but everyone could cite examples. We were told that suicides had occurred as early as 10 years of age."

In one school on the Northern Cheyenne Reservation, also in Montana, there were a dozen suicide attempts in 18 months, among fewer than 200 pupils.

There are the Physically Scarred.

At Intermountain Indian School in Utah, "unmanageable" students are regularly handcuffed and beaten. Last Fall, a student thought to be drunk and unmanageable was carted off to jail, where he committed suicide by hanging himself with his sweater. The student was actually having convulsions and needed medical attention. One school employee at Intermountain "dunks the students' head into a toilet bowl which is unfit for even a hand," whenever he suspects them of drinking.[22]

There are the Psychologically Scarred.

There is not one Indian child who has not come home in shame and tears after one of those sessions in which he is taught that his people were dirty, animal-like, something less than a human being.[23]

At a boarding school, a nervous, intense boy rose in the assembly hall and blurted out, "Let's face it, some of us are here because we haven't anywhere else to go."[24]

A Cheyenne girl, when asked why she spent her 'hard-earned' money on liquor, replied,'Because I am a Cheyenne, and that is the way we Cheyennes are.'[25]

The Indian child in the 12th grade has the poorest self-concept of all minority groups tested. Dropouts among Indian children "wander around the reservation for five or six years, just doing unskilled labor, or off the reservation. I do not think anybody has any figures on this. . . ."[26]

A study: "Papago male, age 18, full Indian. Left federal boarding school 9th grade at age 17. He was in some kind of trouble at school. Later, he was sent to the federal camp in the Catalinas. After being discharged he was picked up and [sent] to a federal prison in Colorado."
"Pima boy, age 18, one-half Indian. Left public school 12th grade at age 18. Attendance and grades were poor. Now looking for work."
"Pima boy, age 16, full Indian. Left public school 9th grade at age 15. . . . He is not working. . . ."
"Papago boy, age 16, full Indian. Left public school 8th grade at age 15. Poor grades. Subsequently sent to a reform school, now released."[27]

There are the Casualties Which Mark the Slow But Sure Death of a Culture.

Mrs. Smith was one of the first Indians on her reservation to attend public school. She dropped out before high school graduation. "I didn't like it," she remembers, "and I couldn't speak very good English." She still speaks her native language with older members of her family, but memories of her embarrassment in school made her determined never to teach her own eight children their Indian tongue.[28] An 80-year-old Shoshone Indian, Moroni Timbimboo of Weshakie, Utah, says: "Yes, we still speak in our language. But we had 20 grandchildren and seven great-grandchildren . . . none of them speaking our language no more. They just can't understand what we are talking about."

Recently, when the Minnesota Department of Education as part of an effort to upgrade Indian education tried to find Indians willing to impart some knowledge of their history to school teachers, the Indian parents responded: "How can we? We attended the public school systems and we know nothing about our history or past. What we know we are getting on our own."[29]

Wallace L. Chafe of the Smithsonian Institution says that of about 300 recognizably separate Indian languages and dialects still extant in the United States, only roughly 40 per cent have more than 100 speakers. In the case of about 55 per cent of all these languages, the remaining speakers are of advanced age, "which implies that many of the tongues—each one an irreplaceable miracle no less than the whooping crane—are destined to disappear."

There are the Educationally Scarred.

If the Indian child fails, it is because he is Indian. Failure is expected, and the expectation becomes self-fulfilling. Educators hope to overcome the Indian child's cultural deprivation, but they really don't expect to succeed. Most schools are prepared to pass every Indian child, what they call "social promotions," regardless of his performance. The school insulates itself in this way from taking the blame; failure springs from cultural deprivation—not from the school. When Indian children drop out of school, stumble in learning English or withdraw into themselves, teachers call it "going back to the blanket." The phrase sums up an attitude of disdain and their definition of failure. A study at Pine Ridge Day School in South Dakota characterized the most common teacher attitude as "condescension, sometimes kindly, often well-meant, but always critical."[30] At the Chilocco, Oklahoma boarding school the staff attitude was summed up by one who said: "Well, what can you expect? These are Indian kids."

Educational failure becomes a way of life, and a method of survival.

Roughly half the young Sioux who leave high school very early claim they left because they were unable to conform to school regulations.

What happens to the country boys who remain? Do they 'shape up' and obey the regulations? Do they, even, come to 'believe' in them? We found that most of the older and more experienced youths were, if anything, even more inclined to boast of triumphs over the rules than the younger fellows who had left. Indeed, all but one assured us that they were adept at hookey, and food and car stealing, and that they had frequent surreptitious beer parties and other outlaw enjoyments.[31]

At boarding schools, children sneak out to drink or run away. Some transfer from school to school. School records in Minnesota show that some Indian children have changed schools as many as 13 times, and up to 35 per cent will move during the school year.

The educationally scarred may be the lucky ones. They may be the least damaged. The most frightening casualties are those who have succeeded—and in doing so have lost themselves. Some achievers do make their way back. Sun Chief, a Hopi, tells his story this way:

As I lay on the blanket I thought about my school days and all I had learned. I could talk like a gentleman, read, write, and cipher. I could name all the states of the Union, with the capitals, repeat the names of all the books of the Bible, 100 verses of Scripture, sing more than two dozen hymns, debate, shout football yells, swing my partners, and tell dirty stories by the hour. It was important that I had learned how to get along with the white man. But my experience had taught me that I had a Hopi Spirit Guide, whom I must follow if I wish to live and I want to become a real Hopi again, to sing the old songs and to feel free to make love without the fear of sin or rawhide.[32]

Some are not so lucky. They are lost, sense it—and their words are haunting:

Education . . . it has separated you from your family, your heritage. . . . What more sickening life do you want? So God help me I didn't ask for this. No, I didn't.''[33]

The BIA Education System is not primarily an education system. It is best understood as a major division of the Bureau's own ''military—industrial complex'' which wages unrelenting war upon Indian survival.

Securing Money and Property Becomes an End in Itself; Children Become Merely Means to That End.

A study of the school system on the Pine Ridge Reservation in South Dakota concluded: ''The major exhortation made by an administrator to the education committee of the Tribal Council was 'to twist the parents' arms and get them to make their children come to school.' '' Administrators rewarded teachers with praise for maintaining high attendance, spoke of absent children as money out of their pockets (higher attendance means larger budget allocations and more power), felt threatened when researchers tried to check figures for attendance, and hesitated to suspend children who broke rules with impunity since it would mean fewer children on the school rosters.[34]

The education system does not exist for the sake of the children or the community; sometimes it seems to exist for its own sake, especially where acquisition of property is concerned. A piano at one boarding school is kept locked for fear the children might damage it. Bathrooms at the Pine Ridge school are locked during school hours, for, as the administrator told entering freshmen: ''Once in the morning, once at noon, and after school. Only babies go more often.'' Day school facilities are rarely opened to the community for social affairs. A school official who did open a building one evening, to demonstrate to the community that it was ''their school,'' felt the community showed its basic irresponsibility when minor damage was done to ''his'' building.

In 1953, the BIA started a crash program to provide improved educational opportunities for Navajo Indian children. Between 1953 and 1967, ''supervisory positions in headquarters, area offices, and agencies increased by 112.9 per cent; supervisory positions at BIA schools increased by 144.3 per cent; general administrative and clerical positions at BIA schools increased by 93.8 per cent; while teaching positions increased by only 19.5 per cent.''[35] The staff that implemented the crash program still holds office. Through the flexibility of civil service, the average age of top level (GS-14 and 15) education administrators is 58 years; the median years of BIA experience is 27 years; and of other outside experience only 4½ years.

Non-education activities which serve the bureaucracy's empire-building activities are passed off as educational expenditures. A recent study cites six administrative-type service programs which draw on education program funds. Included in the education budget were such items as maintaining order, resources management, construction of irrigation systems, and federal-aid highway road construction projects. This assessment against education funds amounted to $12,235,000 in 1967, approximately 10 per cent of the total education budget. When confronted with this, Congresswoman Hansen of Washington, chairman of a Congressional Appropriations Subcommittee, raged:

> For the people wanting to economize, they will look at the cost of educating an Indian child as against the cost of educating somebody in the public schools. We are not writing off against the public school budget the administration of the town hall. . . . You see the difficulties you get into. It is going to hurt your education program eventually, because as these increase, this 10 per cent looks very high. . . . The soul of an accountant shouldn't run education. I am going to be very blunt on that.

Recently, the Government Accounting Office reviewed BIA housing construction for school employees undertaken over a seven-year period.[36] In Arizona and New Mexico, the GAO reviewed 752 out of 1,322 units, and concluded that about 350 units costing $5 million were not justified or needed to meet the Bureau's housing requirements. GAO said another 220 units out of 274 constructed at seven school facilities located near communities and costing about $3.2 million also were not justified or needed. Another 130 of 478 units constructed in isolated areas, built at a cost of $1.8 million, also were criticized. GAO concluded, "This [construction] resulted primarily because the Bureau had not administered its employee housing construction program in accordance with the policies and standards established

by the [Bureau of the Budget]." As part of its review, GAO discovered that a considerable number of housing units in different school areas were occupied by BIA employees not connected with the operation of the school and by individuals not employed by the BIA.

Education funds also are spent on supplies which are not needed, wanted or used, which results in the accumulation of inventory as an end in itself.[37] GAO found that Navajo area schools in the Southwest were ordering supplies without reference to stocks on hand. Nine schools had purchased supplies valued at $124,650 in excess of need, enough to last up to 38 years. At six of the schools, 20,883 unused books were in storage, and the purchase of an additional 1,390 books had been approved. GAO found that 3,073 books on hand were not being used because there was no program at the schools requiring them.

The GAO found instances where equipment had been purchased for a school even though serviceable items could have been obtained from other schools.[38] For example, at the Fort Wingate, New Mexico elementary school, 18 sewing machines were stored in a basement, five of them still packed in the manufacturer's shipping cartons. At the Thoreau School in New Mexico, GAO found an overhead projector and a duplicating machine packed in cartons and an order showing that the equipment was purchased two years earlier.

Much equipment on hand was allowed to remain in an unserviceable condition. GAO found that at two schools, "73 equipment items, with recorded values totalling about $11,200 . . . had remained unserviceable for extended periods . . ." up to two years.

The Government Accounting Office's review of BIA school construction showed that large sums had been programmed and expended to repair, improve, and rehabilitate old buildings.[39] Some of these old buildings were demolished a short time later and others are scheduled for demolition in the near future. For example, the BIA spent over $80,000 to repair a boys' dormitory from 1960 through 1964, only to raze the building in 1965. The kitchen-dining hall at Fort Wingate School in New Mexico was repaired for $70,000 during 1960 through 1962. In 1963, the building was abandoned.

Education funds also are siphoned off for capital investment in obsolete plants and obsolete approaches. Despite official policy decisions dating back 40 years to move away from the boarding school concept and toward day schools, the Bureau continues to make large investments in building new boarding schools and rehabilitating old ones, deepening its financial commitment to the boarding school approach. The boarding school program has been under attack since 1928. Yet in 1967 and 1968, half the construction budget went into building new and fixing old boarding school facilities.

The BIA justifies building boarding schools by citing a shortage of access roads in rural areas on the reservations. A separate division of the BIA builds roads, but no effort has been made to coordinate road construction with school location.

Plans are underway to refurbish the dilapidated school of Chemawa, Oregon. The children at Chemawa are shipped there from Alaska because there is no room for them in schools at home. Instead of building more schools in Alaska, the BIA is repairing Chemawa and perpetuating the practice of shipping children 6,000 miles to school.

Recently, the Navajo Tribal Council passed a resolution asking the BIA to build boarding schools nearer to the reservation so that children could be educated closer to home. Two new facilities are now under construction on the reservation. At the same time, the BIA is constructing a new facility at Riverside, California for boarding students, 70 percent of whom are Navajo children from the Southwest.

"As far as construction of schools are [concerned]," a representative of the Navajo tribe reports, " . . . they just build them anywhere they wish. . . . They build these big institutions. . . . There is lots of empty space, so they round up these kids and fill them up. The demand is there, they think that Congress is going to get after them because they don't fill those spaces. And so, Toyci School (Arizona) isn't filled yet, so they are going to come around and take some more of these little bitty ones to fill that school so they can keep the Congress happy."

At the Budget Bureau, former Assistant Commissioner Marburger recalled, "They continually make odious comparisons with local school districts where Indian children are also often receiving an inadequate education without recognizing the formidable additional handicap of isolation, language and family problems of the children in boarding schools."

The BIA per-pupil cost is much higher than the nationwide average of $536 per-pupil. As a result, Bureau officials have been forced to argue that this is not a fair comparison. They have blamed the Indian child, classifying him as "culturally deprived" and therefore in need of special expenditures, like the handicapped and retarded. That rationale shifts the blame for failure to the child. And it avoids any honest examination in terms of expenditures and results.

The Bureau of Indian Affairs continues waging educational war against the Indian children. Its methods haven't changed.

Educational goals are subordinated to the accumulation of power as an end in itself.

Substantive educational policy is consistently subordinated and professional decisions are thwarted and subverted by the overriding concern of the larger bureaucratic establishment. Those who control Indian education policy are neither Indians nor educators. It is the responsibility of non-educators—mostly land administrators—to whom the educators are subject in the BIA line of command. The Assistant Commissioner for Education, second-ranking official within the BIA, does not even control his own line staff. Dr. Marburger, a respected educator, took office in April 1966 and remained only 15 months. He left in frustration after realizing that his policies were not followed down the line, and that he could not even obtain information from the field.

"There was not a flagrant disobedience of orders or anything of the sort," Dr. Marburger said, "but just a failure for things to happen." Personnel decisions, construction and rehabilitation projects and data processing fell under other assistant commissioners or directors, and attempts to bring in new blood or innovate were thwarted by a lack of access and lack of control over personnel. "I would find out that so-and-so had been promoted and I was not aware of it. The channels were there, but it just didn't happen quite that way."

In December 1968, Leon Osview, an educational consultant from Temple University, pointed out that the Assistant Commissioner of Education in the BIA was doomed to failure because at the Washington level he could be overpowered by other assistant commissioners in charge of budget, administration and long range program planning. In the field, he exercises no vertical control over his own education staff. Osview commented, "Under present circumstances I, for example, wouldn't take his job for either love or money. . . . My impression is that the Bureau is spongy enough to absorb almost any amount of criticism."

Osview notes that educational decisions are, in fact, made by non-educators, by administrative officers, and that the decentralized structure of the BIA renders headquarters officials powerless to effect change: "[N]o one is in much doubt that it is the Area Directors who make or break the Bureau."

Purposeful insulation from professional criticism or external review is built in the BIA makeup. The Bureau has built up a series of offensive and defensive weapons to attack or discredit those who are critical of educational performance—and to suppress or render ineffectual both criticism and constructive efforts to improve the educational system—and finally to eliminate clear lines of responsibility and accountability so that it is never possible to affix blame or hold any single official accountable for its failures.

Nowhere has this been better illustrated than in Chilocco, Oklahoma. For years there were rumors of BIA staff members abusing students at the Chilocco boarding school. In late 1968 the BIA sent investigators to the school. They found evidence of criminal malpractice among the teachers and school officials, and reported it to the Interior Department's top official for Indian matters, Theodore Taylor. Taylor asked for a full report.

The report was written, but no action was taken until early April 1969, when the report was leaked to Senator Lee Metcalf of Montana. Metcalf exposed the Chilocco conditions in a Senate floor speech and, at a hearing on April 23, he chided BIA education commissioner Charles Zellers: "It seems you would have done something."

Only after Metcalf's outcry was anything done to alleviate conditions. The school's super-

intendent was suspended. From the time the investigation was ordered, however, retaliatory measures had begun against officials working to change Chilocco. Once out of office, BIA education commissioners have admitted that their proposals for change, their demands for information, and their policy mandates often went nowhere. (A summer 1969 FBI report denied physical abuse at Chilocco.)

Criticism and change is thwarted at the bottom, as well as at the top. A plaintive expression of this frustration came from a teacher in a letter to the late Senator Kennedy:

> Finally, please don't bother to send this letter on to the BIA, as I wrote you last year and the letter came back 'down the line' to the local level, and the very people involved in some of the situations described here evaluated themselves and their programs. The only thing that came out of that were some dark days for me, and a label as a troublemaker.
>
> I'd like to, someday, be able to work my way up to a position where I could change things—that would be hard to do if I'm on my superiors' [black] list. . . ."[40]

Staff members of the Carnegie Cross Cultural Project, examining Indian education in Oklahoma, found themselves subjected to ostracism and professional defamation.

Staff members of Congressmen who are suspected of being critical of the Bureau meet similar obstacles—though they are treated more deferentially. Overt attacks are channeled by the Bureau through tribal spokesmen. In anticipation of a forthcoming congressional field staff trip, officials at the Albuquerque Boarding School hastily purchased and distributed teddy bears and drapes for the children's dormitories.

Today the Bureau seeks to absolve itself from responsibility for failure by contracting out its responsibility to public schools. Under the 1934 Johnson-O'Malley Act the BIA receives funds for the purpose of contracting with the states to provide education for Indian children. The BIA exacts no special commitments in exchange for these funds. The states simply ignore the special needs of Indians while using Indian funds to subsidize the total state school system. In

1968, 57.4 per cent of all school-age Indians attended public schools.

The record of state public schools in educating Indians with special BIA funds is sometimes worse than the BIA's. The BIA points to their failure to show that BIA schools are superior—and indirectly to imply that its failures are the fault of the Indian and not the Bureau. In this manner, the Bureau buys political support from state education agencies permitting its money to be used to subsidize the normal operating costs of the public schools, to increase the state education budget—but not to provide specialized quality education for Indians.

> In New Mexico, neither the Bureau nor the State Board of Education make suggestions as to how the Johnson-O'Malley funds should be used. The local boards . . . spend the money as they wish. The annual reports about Johnson-O'Malley money from the states do not explain how the money is used.[41]

Osview, in examining public school education of Indian children, commented:

> I was shocked to find that BIA does not, apparently as a matter of policy, engage in any *programmatic* co-operation with public school people, of whose desire and willingness to do justice to their Indian students there can be no doubt. BIA knows about Indian children, or if they don't, they should. Public schools don't and can't really be expected to, on their own.

In the BIA's educational operations there is no accountability to the Indian. The Bureau resists at every point any steps which would make Bureau employees and Bureau-paid educators directly accountable to the Indians. In 1968 President Johnson issued a message of Indian Affairs: "I am directing the Secretary of the Interior to establish Indian school boards for Federal Indian schools."

The BIA's response has been to establish education advisory boards. The advisory boards are not elected and they are just that—advisory. They have no power over funding, hiring, or over the general direction of Indian educational policy. Former Assistant Commissioner Marbur-

ger called the advisory boards "a phony . . . like a student council."

Even where there is an Indian school board, it is kept powerless, manipulated by the Bureau school superintendent. Where Indians make up a majority of a school board, as has happened on rare occasions on the Navajo reservation, "the superintendent plays the dominant role and meetings are characterized principally by Navajo acquiescense and very little participation." They are "not aware of their potential responsibilities and areas of influence."[42] This is no accident. Attempts to secure some degree of control and accountability are ignored or are met with swift retaliation.

"Over at Steamboat," relates Annie Wauneka, a Navajo representative, ". . . they had a problem with the Bureau school, and there was certain personnel, the top official, the top echelon which means the superintendent, the principal, and so forth—the community didn't like these individuals. They were unfair to the employees, they were unfair to the community. . . . We have a chapter meeting, and we call this grassroot organization. . . . So, they voted there at the chapter meeting, 171 to 0, none opposed, asking that the responsible people . . . at the area office . . . to transfer these individuals out and replace them with somebody else who they can work with. We were unsuccessful. They said civil service regulations say we can't move these people unless you have facts to show us what is wrong with these people. Well, we are beaten just like on the television, the Indians are always beaten."

Similarly, where Indians are enrolled in state public schools no attempt has been made to give Indians a meaningful voice in the way in which their children are being treated in the public schools. The Bureau takes a hands-off policy.

Robert A. Roessel, Jr., former director of the Rough Rock Demonstration School in Arizona, noted that "on the Navajo reservation . . . public schools which reservationwide enroll over 80 per cent Navajo students are in every instance controlled by school boards whose membership is over 50 per cent non-Indian."

In Oklahoma, one school has a 100 per cent Indian enrollment and a three-man, non-Indian school board. In California, where 80,000 Indians reside and the children attend public schools, there is no Indian representation on the State Advisory Commission on Education.

Such figures indicate the promise of Indian education has not been met after three centuries.

It was in 1792 that Cornplanter, negotiating for the Senecas, asked President George Washington to make education a provision of the peace treaty:

Father, you give us leave to speak our minds concerning the tilling of the ground. We ask you to teach us to plough and to grind corn; that you will send smiths among us, and above all, that you will teach our children to read and to write, and our women to spin and to weave.

That was the first of many requests and many promises. They were not honored then. They are not honored now. The Indians are still waiting.

NOTES

1. *Hearings Before a Special Subcommittee on Indian Education of the Senate Committee on Labor and Public Welfare,* 90 Cong., 1 and 2 sess., Part I, p. 242, January 4, 1968.
2. Statement by Dr. Daniel J. O'Connell, Executive Secretary, National Committee on Mental Health. Indian Education Subcommittee Hearings, 90 Cong. 1 and 2 sess., Part I, p. 53, December 14, 1967. See also Dr. Robert L. Bergman, "A Second Report on the Problems of Boarding Schools," reprinted in the Indian Education Subcommittee Hearings, Part III, p. 1130, March 30, 1968.
3. Statement by Dr. Robert L. Leon, M. D., Professor and Chairman of the Department of Psychiatry, University of Texas Medical School. Indian Education Subcommittee Hearings 90 Cong., 1 and 2 sess., Part V. p. 2152, October 1, 1968.
4. Letter from a boarding school teacher to the late Senator Robert F. Kennedy, Chairman, Indian Education Subcommittee. Indian Education Subcommittee Hearings, 90 Cong., 1 and 2 sess., Part III, p. 1118, March 20, 1968.
5. James Coleman, "Equality of Education Opportunity," quoted by Senator Robert F. Kennedy at Indian Education Subcommittee Hearings, 90

Cong., 1 and 2 sess., Part I, p. 5, December 14, 1967; Abt Associates, Inc., *Systems Analysis Program Development and Cost-Effectiveness Modeling of Indian Education for the Bureau of Indian Affairs,* Sixth Monthly Progress Report, p. 11, December 14, 1967.
6. Brewton Berry, "The Education of American Indians: A Survey of the Literature," prepared for the Indian Education Subcommittee of the Senate Committee on Labor and Public Welfare, 91 Cong., 1 sess., p. 17.
7. Letter from a boarding school teacher to the late Senator Robert F. Kennedy, p. 118.
8. Dr. Robert L. Bergman, "Boarding Schools and Psychological Problems of Indian Children," reprinted in Indian Education Subcommittee Hearings, 90 Cong., 1 and 2 sess., Part IV, p. 1122, April 16, 1968.
9. Murray L. Wax, *et al,* "Formal Education in an American Indian Community," *Social Problems,* Vol. 11, No. 4, Spring 1964, reprinted in Indian Education Subcommittee Hearings, 90 Cong., 1 and 2 sess., Part IV, pp. 1391, 1403, April 16, 1968.
10. Statement by Dr. Alfonso Ortiz, Anthropologist, Princeton University. Indian Education Subcommittee Hearings of the 90 Cong., 1 and 2 sess., Part I, p. 64, December 14, 1967.
11. Statement by Rupert Costo. Indian Education Subcommittee Hearings of the 90 Cong., 1 and 2 sess., Part I, p. 242, January 4, 1968.
12. Statement by David Risling, Jr. Indian Education Subcommittee Hearings of the 90 Cong., 1 and 2 sess., Part I, p. 240, January 4, 1968.
13. Quoted by Senator Walter F. Mondale of Minnesota. Indian Education Subcommittee Hearings of the 90 Cong., 1 and 2 sess., Part V, p. 2133, October 1, 1968.
14. Statement by Mrs. Iola Hayden, Director, Oklahomans for Indian Opportunity. Indian Education Subcommittee Hearings of the 90 Cong., 1 and 2 sess., Part II, p. 587, February 19, 1968.
15. Statement by Louis R. Gourd, Cherokee Indian, Tahlequah, Oklahoma. Indian Education Subcommittee Hearings of the 90 Cong., 1 and 2 sess., Part II, p. 547, February 19, 1968.
16. Bergman, p. 1122.
17. Official release of testimony to be given by William Pensoneau, Vice President, National Indian Youth Council at Indian Education Subcommittee Hearings of the 90 Cong., 1 and 2 sess., February 24, 1968.
18. Wax, *op. cit.,* p. 1397.
19. Robert V. Dumont, Jr. and Murray L. Wax, The Cherokee School Society and the Intercultural

Classroom, reprinted in Indian Education Subcommittee Hearings, 90 Cong., 1 and 2 sess., Part II, p. 890, February 19, 1968.

20. Wax, *op. cit.*, p. 1420.
21. Statement by Lower Brule Sioux Tribe, Lower Brule, South Dakota, Indian Education Subcommittee Hearings before the 90 Cong., 1 and 2 sess., Part I, p. 64, December 14, 1967.
22. Letter from employee of Intermountain School to the Citizens Advocate Center, March 2, 1969.
23. Statement by Rupert Costo. Indian Education Subcommittee Hearings of the 90th Cong., 1 and 2 sess., Part I, p. 243, January 4, 1968.
24. Statement by Dr. Alfonso Ortiz, Anthropologist, Princeton University. Indian Education Subcommittee Hearings of the 90 Cong., 1 and 2 sess., Part I, p. 64, December 14, 1967.
25. *Ibid.*, p. 65.
26. Statement by Fr. John Bryde, S.J., Ph.D., Superintendent, Holy Rosary Mission School, Pine Ridge, South Dakota. Indian Education Subcommittee Hearing of the 90 Cong., 1 and 2 sess., Part I, p. 45, December 14, 1967.
27. William H. Kelly, *A Study of Southern Arizona School-Age Indian Children*, 1966–1967, reprinted in Indian Education Subcommittee Hearings, 90 Cong., 1 and 2 sess., Part III, pp. 1105–1107, March 30, 1968.
28. "You're No Indian—You Talk Too Much," *Northwest Sunday Oregonian Magazine*, November 24, 1968.
29. Statement by Wilfred Antell, Minnesota Department of Education. Indian Education Subcommittee Hearings, 90 Cong., 1 and 2 sess., p. 187, February 19, 1968.
30. Wax, *op. cit.*, p. 1391.
31. Rosalie H. Wax, "The Warrior Reports," *Transaction*, May 1967, reprinted in Indian Education Subcommittee Hearings, 90 Cong., 1 and 2 sess., Part IV, p. 1304, April 16, 1968.
32. Quote by John Belindo, Executive Director, National Congress of American Indians. Indian

Education Subcommittee Hearings of the 90 Cong., 1 and 2 sess., Part I, pp. 221–22, December 15, 1967.
33. Anonymous, *Education.* A theme paper written for an English class at Arizona State University.
34. Wax, "Formal Education in an American Indian Community," pp. 1379–81.
35. "Investigative Report for House Appropriations Subcommittee." Hearings on the Department of the Interior and Related Agencies Appropriations for 1969 before a Subcommittee of the House Committee on Appropriations, 90 Cong., 2 sess., p. 591, February 29, 1968.
36. Comptroller General of the United States, *Report to the Congress: More Precise Planning Initiated in Employee Housing Construction Program, Bureau of Indian Affairs, Department of the Interior*, 1968.
37. Comptroller General of the United States, *Report to the Congress: Improvements Achieved by the Bureau of Indian Affairs in the Management of Supplies*, 1968.
38. Comptroller General of the United States, *Report to the Congress: Need to Improve System for Managing Capitalized Equipment in the Bureau of Indian Affairs*, 1968.
39. Comptroller General of the United States, *Report to the Congress: Proposals for Improving the System for Management of Repairs and Maintenance of Buildings and Utilities*, 1968.
40. Letter from a boarding school teacher to Senator Robert F. Kennedy, *op. cit*
41. Statement by Domingo Montoya, Member, National Indian Education Advisory Committee. Indian Education Subcommittee Hearings, 90 Cong., 1 and 2 sess., Part I, p. 94, December 14, 1967.
42. Statement by Robert A. Roessel, Jr., Director, Rough Rock Demonstration School, Chinle, Arizona. Indian Education Subcommittee Hearings, 90 Cong., 1 and 2 sess., Part I, p. 13, December 14, 1967.

9

Supporting Ideologies

Vincent Jeffries

SYSTEMS OF social inequality are partly maintained by ideas that justfy the unequal distribution of power, privilege, and prestige. For example, class stratification is supported by the belief in an open system in which people who apply themselves can become economically successful. On this basis, the poor can be regarded as inferior and undeserving because they have failed to manifest the necessary effort to change their disadvantaged position (Huber and Form, 1973). Sexual stratification is reinforced and maintained by beliefs such as those that say men are temperamentally unsuited to rear children or to be homemakers, or that women find personal fulfillment only through motherhood (Bem and Bem,* 1972; Polatnick,* 1973–1974). This chapter places stratification systems in a cultural context and examines the manner in which such ideas serve to support and enhance the existing distribution of power, privilege, and prestige. The term *supporting ideologies* is used to refer to the ideas that perform this function.

Ideologies—systems of ideas composed of values, norms, and beliefs—are a general characteristic of social hierarchies. Whether the stratification system is one of class, ethnicity, sex, age, or some other type, a complex of ideas exists to explain, justify, and maintain it. Supporting ideologies are a general attribute of stratification systems and have many of the same characteristics regardless of the particular hierarchy.

All systems of stratification must be justified in some manner (Huber and Form, 1973). Striking inequalities will be accepted if a rationale is provided that makes them appear to be fair. Some degree of acceptance of the existing distribution of rewards is necessary to maintain social stability, and a generally accepted ideology performs this function.

Supporting ideologies help to maintain stratification systems in a variety of ways. For people in favored positions, they provide a justification for their privileges and prerogatives. For people in disadvantaged positions, such ideologies make their lot in life understandable and acceptable. Those in high positions often want the less advantaged

An asterisk (*) accompanying a citation indicates a selection included in this volume.

to be socialized to accept the major tenets of the ideas that justify their lowly positions. If this socialization is not successfully performed, manipulation and coercion of one form or another are necessary to maintain a system of social inequality.

The following pages consider the structure and components of supporting ideologies and the contributions of the conflict, functionalist, and symbolic interactionist theories to an understanding of how supporting ideologies operate in social organization. The content of the ideologies supporting the existing hierarchies of class, ethnic, sex, and age stratification in the United States is then analyzed.

The multiple hierarchy approach provides for the comparative analysis of the attributes of supporting ideologies across hierarchies. It also provides for the analysis of the role of components of these ideologies in maintaining inequality in more than one hierarchy. The multiple hierarchy approach focuses attention on the manner in which ideologies supporting different strata, such as age and sex, may combine in a particular way to produce greater disadvantages for individuals because of their multiple positions in stratification systems.

THE CHARACTERISTICS OF IDEOLOGIES

In the broadest sense, this chapter focuses on the relationship between culture and stratification systems. Attention is centered on how the prevailing cultural patterns influence both the characteristics and the continuance of existing social hierarchies.

Pitirim A. Sorokin (1969) divides culture into three basic components: the ideological, the behavioral, and the material. The ideological refers to the sphere of ideas, in the most universal and inclusive sense. The behavioral components of culture include the totality of actions through which ideas are objectified, conveyed, and socialized. The material components of culture include various physical objects through which ideas are externalized. The emphasis in this chapter is on the ''idea'' component of culture, which is viewed as exerting a high degree of influence on the characteristics of both behavioral and material culture.

The term *ideas* is used here in the broadest sense possible to refer to anything existing in the mind as an object of knowledge or thought. Ideas in this generic sense thus include mental conceptions, notions, or opinions held by the members of a society or group within that society. Four types of ideas are of primary importance to an understanding of the relationship between ideology and social stratification. These types of ideas are values, norms, beliefs, and ideologies.

Values are conceptions of the desirable. A value is a preference, believed to be justified, of what is regarded to be a worthwhile end of human endeavor. Values are in this sense a conception of what it is thought to be proper to want, rather than merely of what may be desired apart from any considerations of propriety (Kluckhohn, 1951). Values do not carry the connotation of obligation, as norms do; but are rather recommended as preferable and worthy. Values define the criteria by which excellence is viewed and social honor is accorded in a society. By implication those not possessing or objectifying dominant values are placed in an unfavorable light. With respect to supporting ideologies, dominant values provide a standard by which individuals and groups can be evaluated. Values thus serve as an ultimate justification for a system of differential ranking and for the superordinate and subordinate social relationships that follow from it (Turner and Starnes, 1976).

Norms are standards of what is viewed as correct or proper; they carry the idea of obligation and oughtness. Norms are enforced by various penalties visited on those who do not conform to them. Penalties vary from extreme forms, such as imprisonment or death, to more intermediary levels, such as exclusion from the group or severe social disapproval, to milder forms of social ostracism, such as being regarded as odd or out of place. There are various types of norms, such as laws and legal statutes, rules and regulations, and norms of a less formal nature, such as commonly accepted mores, traditions, and customs.

Alice Rossi (1969) has noted that inequality can be manifested in several ways, such as through legal statute, corporate or organizational policies, and, most importantly, covert social pressures that restrict the freedom and aspirations of individuals. With respect to supporting ideologies, norms specify standards of conduct and practice that serve to limit the opportunities, advantages, and aspirations of subordinate strata. The normative component of a supporting ideology most directly serves this purpose. Thus, for example, the racial norms of the earlier part of this century in the United States rigidly prescribed that blacks occupy particular jobs and living areas, and behave in a subordinate manner to whites. In a similar vein, the normative system has limited women to particular types of occupations and to traditional roles and modes of conduct.

Beliefs are opinions, expectations, or judgements about some aspects of reality that are accepted as true. They often, but not always, involve a positive or negative evaluation of the object or category about which the belief is held. With respect to supporting ideologies, beliefs that pertain to the presumed negative characteristics of subordinate strata provide a rationale for discriminatory policies. Other beliefs, such as the belief in equality of opportunity in the United States, justify the advantageous position of members of the superordinate strata, and at the same time suggest the inferiority of those in the lower strata.

Gunnar Myrdal (1962) has described how discriminatory norms and negative beliefs interact to support ethnic stratification. Myrdal called this process the "Principle of Cumulation." According to Myrdal, norms of discrimination kept blacks in low standards of living, health, education, manners, and culture. These low standards gave support and credence to negative beliefs about the characteristics of blacks. Thus, norms and negative beliefs reinforced each other. Norms produced characteristics in the subordinate group that seemed to illustrate the validity of the negative beliefs. The manifestation of these characteristics in turn served to support the negative beliefs that were used to justify the discriminatory norms. Thus, a "Principle of Cumulation" exists in which various aspects of the system of inequality reinforce each other. The same relationship between norms and beliefs regarding subordinate strata probably operates in other systems of stratification, particularly those of sex and age, where normative restrictions are far more prevalent and explicit than in the class system.

Ideologies are systems of beliefs, norms, and values that are to some degree coherent and integrated. Any culture contains many identifiable and distinct ideologies. For example, religious denominations espouse systems of ideas that define the ends of human existence, forbidden attitudes and behavior, and various beliefs about God and the supernatural. Supporting ideologies are a specific type of ideology, namely, those that provide a rationale and justification for an existing distribution of power, privilege, and prestige. They include not only those ideas which explicitly refer to social inequality or the presumed inferiority of particular groups, but also the broader systemic web of interrelated ideas that are less overtly linked to the phenomenon of unequal distribution.

For example, Jeffries (1971) has demonstrated that values such as egoism, restricted loyalty, self reliance, and materialism are related to negative beliefs about blacks, though none of these values contains direct reference to blacks or to their position in society. The place of women in society serves to illustrate the nature of a supporting ideology. One value that supports the existing system of sexual stratification defines the most desirable type of family as the traditional family in which the male holds authority in all matters of importance. A norm supporting the existing sex hierarchy is evident in the negative treatment women frequently encounter when entering previously all-male occupations, such as those in the construction industry. An example of beliefs supporting the sexual stratification system is that women are not temperamentally suited for stressful occupations and lack analytical ability. The article by Bem and Bem* (1972) in this section and that by Polatnick* (1973–1974) both describe how these and other beliefs, norms, and values comprise an ideology that helps to keep women in a subordinate position relative to men.

The relationship between components of ideologies that is presented in this book is based on assumptions about the nature of culture and of cultural integration (Albert, 1956; Hoebel, 1958:151–173; Kroeber and Kluckhohn, 1963; Sorokin, 1957). Cultural integration means that culture is not a random conglomeration of meanings, values, material artifacts and behavior patterns, but that to some degree the many components of culture are bound together and integrated into an organic whole. The characteristics of one major aspect of culture, such as its system of art, law, or philosophy, are related to other components of culture and are to some degree interdependent.

The central points around which culture is integrated are certain basic ideas. These ideas pertain to the nature of the external world and of individuals. Every culture selects certain systems of thought, forms of behavior, and material artifacts over others. To the degree that culture is integrated, this selection appears to be made predominantly in accordance with certain highly generalized ideas. The structure of the integration of ideological systems involves a predominant influence of the generalized components over the specific. More often than not, these generalized notions provide the context within which more specific ones are formulated and evaluated (Albert, 1956; Hoebal, 1958; Sorokin, 1957).

Current views among many psychologists about the ideological components of personality approximate the same structure of ideas which was previously described with respect to culture. Psychologists generally agree that personality is integrated. This integration is described as involving some degree of consistency among the component parts of personality, and their arrangement in a hierarchial structure in which certain fundamental and general dispositions are the focal points for the organization of those that are more specific and less stable. Although agreement is less general as to the specific nature of these fundamental dispositions, there is increasing recognition that values are one of the most important focal points for the integration of personality (Allport, 1955:88–93; Krech and Crutchfield, 1948:60–70; Rokeach, 1968, 1974).

In this analysis, values have been defined as generalized and relatively abstract conceptions of the desirable. As such, their points of reference tend to be quite diverse and include a wide range of phenomena. For example, the value of material success can effect such diverse aspects of life as the type of life work one chooses, the number of hours devoted to the job, the way money is spent, choice of friends, the make of auto-mobile one drives, and the neighborhood one selects to live in. Hence, in accordance with the principles of cultural and personality integration that were previously pre-sented, values are considered to be an important factor in influencing and maintaining the more specific norms and beliefs that are a part of supporting ideologies.

On the basis of these models of the systemic nature of ideas, the elements of sup-porting ideologies—values, norms, and beliefs—are considered to have some degree of consistency and interdependence. For example, if women are believed to be emotional, helpless, and unable to make clear analytical decisions, then we would expect that in such a society norms will exist to exclude them from high-level positions in organiza-tions. Similarly, if a society values material success as the prime criteria of personal worth, it is consistent with this value to view the poor as being lazy or having other undesirable characteristics. Thus, the components of ideologies are assumed to consti-tute a loose structure in which the acceptance of one component makes it more likely than not that individuals will hold other components. A conscious awareness on the part of individuals of the logical connection or compatibility between the components of an ideology is not assumed in this model. As noted by Philip Converse (1964), few individ-uals develop such tightly integrated and comprehensive thought systems.

A study by Karen Mason and Larry Bumpass (1975) indicates this same point with regard to the sex role ideology of women. The views about sex roles held by a nationwide sample of women were organized primarily around a conception of the division of labor between men and women. The women in this sample thought the major responsibility of their sex was maintaining the home and caring for their children. A secondary cluster of attitudes pertained to their perception of women's rights in the labor market. Although women in this study held rather traditional views about the division of labor between the sexes, they expressed more egalitarian views on the labor rights issue. On this topic they favored equal opportunity, pay, and working conditions for women in the labor market. Unlike most leaders of the women's movement, to whom these two issues are closely connected, this nationwide sample showed only a weak correlation between these two clusters of attitudes.

An important dimension of the elements of ideological systems that are related to social stratification is the degree to which they explicitly state a subordinate-superordi-nate relationship between various social groupings. For example, the cultural beliefs that blacks have less intelligence than whites, or that women are less emotionally stable than men, clearly define a superordinate-subordinate relationship. Some beliefs, norms, and values do not contain any explicit reference to particular groups, yet may serve to sup-port a given stratification system. Max Weber (1958a) for example, analyzed how the religious ideas of early Protestantism eventually gave rise to a secular work ethic and justification for the distribution of wealth that helped bring into being and later supported the system of class stratification in western capitalist societies. Religious ideas having nothing explicitly to do with stratification thus were part of a supporting ideology. Studies such as those by Feagin* (1972), Huber and Form (1973), and Schuman* (1975) all deal with this same type of phenomenon—ideas that are not explicitly related to superordination-subordination but that serve to maintain and justify stratification systems.

Supporting ideologies are only one part of a vast network of cultural values, norms, and beliefs. Many, if not most, aspects of a culture have nothing to do with maintaining the stratification system. Others in one fashion or another tend to militate against patterned social inequality. For example, Robin Williams (1974) has observed that the main thrust of the culture of the United States is toward humanitarianism, equality, and individual and political freedom. Similarly, Gunnar Myrdal (1962) has identified a complex of values that he calls the "American Creed", which stresses the inherent dignity of all individuals, a moralistic orientation, and belief in the rightness of personal freedom and equality of opportunity.

As will be considered in some detail in chapter 10, various social movements espousing the interests of subordinate strata have typically used these elements of the dominant culture pattern, which are often contrary to those of supporting ideologies, to justify their efforts to change established inequalities in the distribution of power, privilege, and prestige. Any culture is always in a constant state of change, whether it be slow or rapid. One aspect of this change is the relative predominance and adherence to ideologies that support existing systems of stratification, on the one hand, and those that undermine them, on the other hand (Turner and Singleton, 1978).

The influence of supporting ideologies in maintaining stratification systems diminishes when they are often not generally accepted by all segments of a society, particularly by those at the lower levels of the social structure. For example, Joan Huber and William H. Form (1973) found that at poor and middle-income levels blacks are less likely than whites to believe there is opportunity to get ahead and to go to college. Rich whites are more likely to believe in these opportunities than are poor and middle-income whites. Comparing groups in extreme high and low positions, 93 percent of rich whites believe there is plenty of opportunity, as contrasted with only 56 percent of poor blacks with this opinion.

Another issue investigated in this study was belief in equal opportunity. While only 11 percent of poor blacks believe the rich and poor have equal opportunity, 57 percent of rich whites ascribe to this belief. Equal opportunity to attend college is agreed to by 22 percent of poor blacks as opposed to 96 percent of rich whites. Percentages agreeing that the poor are as likely to attend college are 11 percent among poor blacks and 43 percent among rich whites. With regard to legal equality, 46 percent of poor blacks believe the law is fair, as opposed to 75 percent of rich whites.

A similar pattern is observed with respect to political equality. Only 3 percent of poor blacks believe that the poor are able to influence the government as much as the rich, as compared to 55 percent of rich whites. These differences in the acceptance of the legitimacy and openness of the system by different strata are important in the development of stratum consciousness and action among subordinate strata, a topic discussed in detail in chapter 10.

THEORETICAL MODELS IN THE STUDY OF
SUPPORTING IDEOLOGIES

As with other areas in the study of social stratification, the conflict, functionalist, and symbolic interactionist theoretical models provide contrasting but compatible perspectives for examining the nature and role of supporting ideologies. Each theoretical tradition makes particular contributions to the study of supporting ideologies. Hence, this chapter will borrow from each in considering the essential features of the ideologies that help to maintain social stratification.

Several perspectives most associated with the conflict model are stressed. Emphasis is placed on the inequalities and deprivations produced by supporting ideologies. The differing degree of acceptance of these ideologies by various strata is noted. The creation and conscious use of such ideologies by the upper stratum to maintain their position of advantage is also given recognition.

Various perspectives that derive most directly from the functionalist model are also emphasized. Attention is focused on the broad system of ideas—composed of values, norms, and beliefs—which aid in maintaining stratification systems. The systematic analysis of the components of supporting ideologies is stressed. Commonly held cultural values are also emphasized as a key to understanding the nature and maintenance of supporting ideologies.

The importance of the socialization process in the influence that supporting ideologies have on human thought and behavior is of major concern. A focus on the import and dynamics of such socialization is most adequately rendered within the context of symbolic interactionist theory. Symbolic interactionist theory also highlights the interplay between individual personality and the sociocultural, which is basic to understanding why and how supporting ideologies are accepted by some individuals, and rejected by others.

The contrasting perspectives of conflict, functional, and interactionist models are incompatible only if taken as absolutes. The factors and processes that each theoretical tradition stresses are in fact near universal features of social organization, but are variable in the extent of their prevalence. For example, the degree to which functional or conflict theory provides valid insights in the study of a given situation or society can be subjected to empirical investigation (Lenski, 1966; Ossowski, 1963; Van den Berghe, 1963). Take the specific issue of the source of supporting ideologies. On the one hand, supporting ideologies are partly the result of long-term trends in the evolution of ideas and the elaboration of commonly held values, as is emphasized by the functionalist model. On the other hand, they are partly the result of conscious propaganda and manipulation on the part of those espousing the interests of the upper strata, as is emphasized by the conflict model.

The extent to which either of these sources of supporting ideologies may be most influential varies greatly from one society to another. In modern totalitarian states, for example, there is an ability unparalleled in history to espouse an ideology that justifies an existing system, while excluding alternative interpretations. In such cases, a conflict perspective regarding the sources of supporting ideologies is most appropriate. In less rigid societies in which there is freedom of the press and more cultural heterogeneity, a functionalist view of supporting ideologies as deriving from commonly held values and the evolvement of generalized cultural ideas may be closer to the reality of the situation. In either case, however, an absolutist interpretation that entails only one of these viewpoints is incorrect. Both theoretical traditions contain assumptions regarding the source of supporting ideologies that are valid to some degree. Even the most totalitarian society builds the justification for its existence on past cultural traditions, and in this sense, manipulation by the controlling elite and traditional values merge to some degree as explanations. Adolph Hitler and the Nazi party, for example, skillfully built on some of the long-standing cultural traditions of the German people in justifying the policies and actions of the Nazi regime (Shirer, 1960:120–166).

In a similar vein of synthesis, the conflict and functionalist models are most suitable for the analysis of structure and processes at the societal and cultural levels of analysis. Symbolic interactionism complements these more traditional perspectives in the study of social stratification because it concentrates on the ongoing relationship between individuals and the sociocultural, which is fundamental to any study of human behavior.

The following pages contain further elaborations of the conflict, functionalist, and interactionist theoretical traditions as they have been—and can be—applied to the analysis of those ideologies that support systems of social stratification. When viewed in the manner previously suggested, these theoretical models represent elements of a synthesis, rather than incompatible alternatives.

The Conflict Model

From the conflict perspective, supporting ideologies are the ideas that help the upper strata to maintain their position of power and dominance and to exploit and deprive the lower strata. Conflict theorists regard supporting ideologies as primarily the conscious creation of the upper stratum. They are then used as weapons designed to keep subordinate strata quiescent and to forestall and divert the development of true stratum consciousness. For example, from the conflict perspective, the ideology of racism is said to be a weapon used by the upper stratum to keep segments of the lower strata divided and in conflict with each other over ethnic differences. Similarly, the belief in an open society in which anyone who has the ambition and talent can move to the top of the structure is used by those in the upper strata. This belief justifies the position of the upper strata and places the burden for subordinate status on the personal failures of individuals, rather than on the inadequacies of the existing social structure.

The conflict model of stratification views power and the occupancy of key positions in the social structure as prime resources for promulgating an ideology. The upper strata are regarded as being in a unique position to create and maintain a cultural climate favorable to their interests. They control the communication media and major social institutions, such as religion and education, that mold opinions. In many instances, the fusion of structural power and control of cultural content can also mean the ability to limit or virtually eradicate alternative viewpoints that might compete with the ideology supporting the existing distribution of power, privilege, and prestige.

A focus on the role of ideology in establishing and maintaining the interests of the ruling strata is basic to Karl Marx's analysis of class stratification (Marx, 1956; Mills*,

1962). Marx, who represents a classic conflict position in this regard, used the term *ideology* primarily to refer to beliefs and values promulgated by the ruling class to help maintain their dominant position and their control of the production system. According to Marx, the ruling class uses ideas as weapons to divide subordinate classes and keep them from realizing their true interests. The acceptance of these ideologies by members of the subordinate strata was regarded by Marx as a source of "false" class consciousness. Because of supporting ideologies, individuals in subordinate strata fail to see their real interests and identify in some fashion with the ruling stratum. This is in contrast to the effects of "true" class consciousness, in which one's place in the social structure, the exploitive and dehumanizing aspects of the existing system, and the necessity for fundamental structural change, are recognized.

The conflict approach to supporting ideologies is illustrated by Oliver Cromwell Cox's (1959) analysis of the interrelationship between class and race in the southern United States before the Civil Rights Movement. According to Cox, the pattern of race relations in the South was an expression of the economic interests of the ruling class of southern "aristocracy". The economic system was based on worker exploitation that depended "pivotally" on keeping black and white workers divided. By "artfully" playing white workers against black workers, both could be more effectively exploited by the upper strata. Racial ideologies played a key role in this process.

Rather than regarding race prejudice as a basic component of the mores of the South at this time, Cox (1959) views race prejudice as the conscious creation of the white ruling class. This class used its position of power to spread anti-black attitudes among the white masses. Racial beliefs were intentionally created through propaganda to serve the clearly defined purpose of furthering the calculated interests of the white upper strata. According to Cox, millions of dollars were spent by this class to justify and maintain segregation and anti-black attitudes. Race prejudice was used as the ideological mechanism underlying the economic exploitation of both blacks and poor whites. By keeping blacks and whites divided, wages could be kept at a minimal level.

This pattern of race relations in the South emerged from the need of the upper stratum to restore control over its labor supply, control that had been lost with the abolition of slavery after the Civil War. The economically motivated act of maintaining blacks in an exploitable position came first and was based on the use of superior power. The use of propaganda to develop racial prejudice and hatred followed. The end result was to "conceptualize as brutes the human objects of exploitation" (Cox, 1959:475). Blacks thus became isolated from other workers and were defenseless to protect themselves from being used to the economic advantage of the ruling class. Segregation and prohibitions against racial intermarriage were used to prevent any sympathetic contact between blacks and whites, thus helping to maintain the system.

The pattern of a ruling class justifying economic exploitation by a consciously created ideology is regarded by Cox (1959) as not unique to black-white relations in the United States. Rather, it is viewed as characteristic of capitalist societies. Throughout history, rationalizations that were compatible with the prevailing culture have been calculatingly used toward numerous groups to serve the economic interests of the capitalist ruling class. Religious ideas, the Darwinian notion of the "survival of the fittest", and laissez faire individualism have all been employed to justify the placing of various groups in a situation of economic exploitation. For example, the American Indians were defined as heathens who could not be converted to Christianity, and therefore they were removed from their lands and in many instances exterminated. Similarly, the long hours that women and children labored in the factories of Europe were justified by the notion that they were being kept from idleness and the influence of the devil while at the same time paying the price for their sins now, rather than in the hereafter.

The Functionalist Model

The functionalist interpretation of society entails a broad perspective toward the content and function of ideologies supporting existing stratification systems. Rather than focusing primarily on ideas that explicitly justify social inequality, the functionalist approach characteristically places stratification systems in an extensive cultural context and regards them as being maintained by systems of interrelated ideas based on commonly held values. The systemic nature of these ideas is emphasized by functionalists. Highly abstract values that are not explicitly related to stratification are viewed as providing the most general context for its acceptance and justification. Functionalists see supporting ideologies as emerging from historical trends in the evolution of ideas and from the basic social structure of society. Typically, little emphasis is placed on the role of supporting ideologies in benefiting the upper strata and aiding the exploitation of lower strata. Neither is the role of power in disseminating ideas generally credited with much importance.

These characteristics of the functionalist approach are evident in Talcott Parsons's analysis of social stratification (1953). Parsons believes that although differences in the forms of stratification exist, there are certain universal attributes of all stratification systems. Hence, all varieties of stratification can be explained by a single theory.

According to Parsons (1953), social stratification is universal. It finds its source in the basic nature of social interaction. The activity of individuals is directed toward the pursuit of socially desirable goals. In the social context of such goal-oriented activity, not all actions are viewed as equally preferable. Whatever human beings do or possess is evaluated in some ways by other human beings as more or less important and more or less desirable. Social stratification can ultimately be traced back to this process of evaluation, which is basic to all social interaction. Stratification, then, is a system of ranking people according to society's consensus of the relative importance of certain values. Thus, social stratification is both an expression and an implementation of the central values of society, which constitute the ultimate standards on which differential rankings are based.

The process of evaluation is applied to what Parsons (1953) designates as "units". Three basic properties of units about which evaluative judgements can be made are distinguished. Evaluations may involve the basic qualities or characteristics of individuals, such as their sex or ethnicity. The performance of individuals in various activities, such as in their occupation, is a second property of units that may be evaluated. Possessions are also subject to differential evaluation. Possessions can be the material objects individuals own, or the skills they have acquired. Qualities, performances, and possessions are ascribed a meaning and evaluated in accordance with the dominant values of a given society. Hence, the relative importance assigned to different values is fundamental in determining the evaluative ranking of units, which is the basis of all stratification systems.

Parsons (1953) identifies four highly generalized value patterns that exist within every culture. In every society, these values are ranked in some order by consensus of the population. The order given to those alternative values determines the fundamental characteristics of the stratification system. The first of these four basic types of value patterns is universalism. This value places emphasis on efficiency in reaching an objective. Another value pattern pertains to achievement of a set of goals. The main emphasis in this case is on accomplishment. Goals may be specific or quite general and, within broad limits, of an individualized nature. Another value pattern Parsons calls the system-integrative, because it has to do with values that maintain solidarity within the system. Devotion and adherence to the system itself is central in this case. The fourth type of value standard entails values that maintain or regulate changes within the system. In this instance, existing values are judged as most desirable, and priority is given to the maintenance of established traditions.

The relative importance placed on each of these four value standards sets the ultimate criteria for the evaluation of social action as reflected in qualities, performances, and possessions. This is finally reflected in the ranking system that is the basis of social stratification.

According to Parsons (1953), the society of the United States emphasizes universalism and achievement. Parsons (1953) contends that it is principally these commonly held values that support and maintain the existing system of stratification. Within the general context of universalism and achievement, emphasis is placed on productive activity in the economy, the control of possessions through money and activity in the economic market place, and availability of opportunity, as exemplified by the tradition of "equal opportunity". These values are most clearly expressed in the stratification system in the high value placed on occupational status and the monetary earnings derived from it.

The analysis of social stratification by Kingsley Davis and Wilbert E. Moore* (1945) also illustrates many of the tenets and implications of functional theories of stratification with respect to the analysis of supporting ideologies. Along with Parsons, these authors regard cultural values as the primary basis for determining the relative importance of positions in society. For example, in societies in which religious values are paramount, positions associated with religion rank high in importance. The ranking of positions is directly related to the unequal distribution of rewards accorded to different positions. This unequal distribution of rewards assures that vital positions are filled by qualified people and represents an expression of the value consensus of the members of society. Supporting ideologies are thus seen as deeply rooted in the general pattern of cultural integration and as such are closely linked with major value orientations.

The writings of Max Weber (1958a, 1958b, 1964a, 1964b) also place stratification systems within a broad cultural context. Weber's work is most correctly viewed as a synthesis of conflict and functional perspectives (Lenski, 1966:18). It illustrates the functional approach in its stress on the relation between social stratification and a broadly integrated and evolving cultural system of ideas. One perspective from which Weber deals with the relationship between culture and social stratification is through his analysis of the legal and traditional bases for the legitimacy of authority structures. Each of these types of authority (discussed in chapter 2) represents a general system of cultural meanings.

Weber also analyzes the relationship between culture and the maintenance of stratification systems through his study of religious beliefs and values and their relationship to social hierarchies. As noted by Bendix (1962:84, 258), two of Weber's major interests in the sociology of religion center on the effect of religious ideas on economic activities and the relationship between religions and social stratification.

The best known of Weber's studies pertaining to these interests is his analysis of the religious beliefs of Protestantism. Weber observes how Protestant religious ideas influenced changes in the meaning of worldly work and economic activity and eventually contributed to the development of capitalism (Weber, 1958a). Two religious ideas that gained wide currency with the development of Protestantism are regarded as pivotal. These are the Calvinistic doctrine of predestination and the idea of worldly work as the "calling" through which the individual served God and eventually gained eternal salvation. These ideas combined with religious asceticism to produce profound changes in economic activities and structure, and hence in the stratification system.

The doctrine of predestination created extreme anxiety, since it contained as its central notion the idea that there are the elect and the damned, those destined for heaven or hell by God, and that individual action can have no effect on this eternal destiny. The idea of the calling placed service to God squarely in the context of work within the productive system of society, rather than in activities such as prayer and meditation or dedication to the monastic life. One served God and ultimately gained salvation by diligently performing one's worldly duties. Religious emphasis was thus shifted from withdrawal from the world to active engagement with it. Predestination gave impetus to the search for some sign of salvation, while the idea of the calling defined how it was to be achieved. Religious asceticism curbed activities that might detract from worldly work within the productive system, or the wasting of capital that might be accumulated through such activity.

These three religious ideas fused into an ideological system that had profound effects on the development of capitalism and its attendant system of class stratification. Although this system of ideas was profoundly religious in its intent and its manifest content, it had far-reaching implications for economic activity and the economic structure of society. It gave economic activity a religious meaning, which in a deeply religious age constituted a tremendous impetus to worldly activity. As the religious roots of the Protestant Ethic slowly died away, an increasingly secularized work ethic gradually emerged.

In its later secular form the work ethic, which derived from the aforementioned religious beliefs, provided a justification for the pursuit and holding of great wealth, and hence a standard of legitimacy for the capitalist class. Increasingly, the possession of wealth came to be regarded as evidence of a good life and the rewards of God's blessings, which were available to all who were willing to make the necessary effort. At the same time it provided an industrious and dependable work force that diligently labored in the factories and industries of the developing capitalist system of production. Hard work gradually came to be regarded as a virtue, in and of itself, apart from any religious meaning or significance.

Thus, the unequal distribution of power, privilege, and prestige received both justification and general acceptance from the system of beliefs and values that Weber says derived from the teachings of early Protestantism. Weber does not emphasize the view that the ideology known as the Protestant Ethic was a deliberate and conscious creation of the ruling class to enhance their position. Rather, Weber sees the Protestant Ethic as being to some degree the result of a long-term cultural evolution and the integration of ideas. In this sense, Weber's work illustrates a functionalist position on the genesis and nature of supporting ideologies.

The Symbolic Interactionist Model

The symbolic interactionist perspective focuses on the dynamic interplay between individual personality and the sociocultural system. In this context, supporting ideologies are an important part of the effective environment of individuals. The values, norms, and beliefs of society are cultural definitions of reality with which individuals must deal in one manner or another.

The symbolic interactionist approach provides a frame of reference for placing special emphasis on what is perhaps the most powerful force in perpetuating the influence of supporting ideologies from generation to generation. This is socialization. Through internalization in the process of socialization, supporting ideologies become part of the self conception and life organization of the individual. In this sense, they achieve a living existence in the psychic makeup and behavior patterns of many of those who are exposed to them.

One major contribution of the social sciences has been to demonstrate the tremendous power and influence of the socialization process. Even though there is always a degree of individual autonomy and choice, much of what an individual is—how he or she thinks and acts—is largely a product of the continual process of socialization, which takes place throughout the life cycle. Basic definitions of the situation and response patterns are usually formulated in the early years of life. Individuals continually evolve new schemes of life organization based on the interplay between such existing schemes, choices they make, and the characteristics and pressures of the sociocultural environment. Although some of the learning of culture involved in the socialization process takes place through conscious instruction, much is gained through observation and the largely unconscious imitation of others with whom the individual identifies.

The profound influence of ideologies that support stratification systems is derived largely from the fact that they are part of the general culture pattern. They are thus consecrated with the prestige and influence of consensual group opinion. Because of this, they are accepted without question by the vast majority of individuals. In these circumstances, they become a major part of the content of the socialization process, with all of the direct and indirect social pressures toward acceptance and conformity that this entails.

The influence of supporting ideologies on individuals in subordinate strata is of particular interest. Whether the social hierarchy is one of class, ethnicity, sex, or age, those at the bottom are viewed negatively. The cultural definitions may identify the basis of inferiority as biological, inherited, willful, or as some combination of these. Whatever the particular case may be in a given social hierarchy, the social expectations facing those in the lowest levels are not conducive to the full development of whatever capabilities and talents they may possess.

The pervasive influence of supporting ideologies in this respect has been clearly recognized by participants and leaders in social movements seeking to change the existing distribution of power, privilege, and prestige. Hence the development of an ideology to oppose the tenets of prevailing supporting ideologies, and the attempt to build a more positive self-conception. (These features of such movements will be considered in detail in chapter 10.)

Sandra Bem and Daryl Bem* (1972) analyze the influence of ideologies that support sex roles. They note that an "unconscious" ideology that defines a woman's role pervades both the dominant culture and the socialization process. The term *unconscious* is used by Bem and Bem to focus attention on the fact that this ideology—at least until recent years—has been simply taken for granted and not seriously questioned by either men or women. The socialization into traditional sex roles has made it very difficult for women to raise their aspirations and fulfill their creative potential. It has also made it difficult for other lifestyles to emerge with different patterns of male-female and family relationships.

The degree to which individuals in subordinate strata find their lives limited by such socialization is in part a product of their environment, and in part a product of their personality characteristics. Within the latitude allowed by the general social organization, much depends on the more immediate social environment of family and friends. Important also is the life organization that individuals evolve through a series of choices they make throughout their life histories. Some individuals from the lowest strata are able to achieve great eminence, whereas others are handicapped and limited throughout their lives by the implanting of a life organization that reflects the ideology that supports social inequities. By focusing on the individual as an active, choice-making entity, the symbolic interactionist perspective gives further insight into the differential impact of supporting ideologies.

THE MULTIPLE HIERARCHY APPROACH: COMPARISONS

The multiple hierarchy approach provides a basis for the comparative study of supporting ideologies across social hierarchies. A fundamental question posed by the multiple hierarchy approach is: What are the similarities and differences in the content and structure of the ideologies that support different social hierarchies? Another major focus is the degree to which the same cultural values may contribute to the maintenance of more than one hierarchy of stratification.

Although a comprehensive description and analysis of the ideologies that support the existing stratification systems of class, ethnicity, sex, and age is beyond the scope of this work and, to a great extent, of existing empirical research, the following pages will present a partial and tentative formulation of the components and structures of these ideologies. For each social hierarchy, supporting ideologies will be considered in terms of the components of values, norms and beliefs that were previously identified as the basic elements of ideological systems.

The Ideology of Class Stratification

The works of various authors (Feagin*, 1972a; Feagin, 1972b; Huber and Form, 1973; Jeffries and Tygart, 1974; Turner and Starnes, 1976; Williamson, 1974) point to a complex of traditional cultural values that maintain the system of class stratification. Other studies indicate that this same value system may be part of the supporting ideology of ethnic stratification (Adorno, 1950; Evans, 1952; Jeffries and Morris, 1968; Jeffries, 1971; Jeffries, Schweitzer and Morris, 1973; Kaufman, 1957; Silberstein and Seeman, 1959), and of sexual stratification (Ball-Rokeach, 1976). The work of these authors and others has led to the description of a value complex that may be termed the Materialistic Success Ethic. The components of this cluster of values are success striving, work, competition, materialism, self-reliance, and egoism. Each of these values is deeply rooted in the past and present social structure and culture of the United States. Their basic tenets are described below.

Success Striving. In earlier historical periods, the stress on equal opportunity, the opening of new lands, and the development of new forms of wealth and industry gave rise to a situation in which the striving for upward mobility became an obligation to oneself and also to society. Individuals should succeed for themselves, their families, and in order to contribute to the general social welfare. Society emphasized occupational achievement, the amount of money gained from this activity being viewed as a major criterion of both the degree of effort expended and of personal worth. Since World War I, certain changes have taken place in the success ethic. There has been a shift from corporate ownership to managerial positions as the ultimate goal, and more emphasis is placed on education. Despite these developments, the idea of success striving has remained fundamentally the same in stressing the individualistic nature of success and the need for self-improvement as a means for attaining success (Chinoy, 1955; Lynd and Lynd, 1956; Merton, 1961:132–139, 166–170; Potter, 1954; Williams, 1970:454–458; Wyllie, 1954:168–170).

Work. Although it has lost some of its previous emphasis, the value placed on work as an end in itself was one of the basic elements of the culture of the early periods of United States history. The Protestant Ethic, which invested secular occupational activity with religious sanction, a general stress on worldly instrumental activism, and the necessity of work for group survival along the frontier, all found expression in an emphasis on disciplined activity in a regular occupation. Work was considered a means of self-fulfillment and an indication of personal morality. Failure to work in gainful employment was ascribed to laziness or some other fault of character. Today's work ethic still places particular stress on purposeful activity in some gainful occupation, and the self-identity of individuals is closely tied to their occupational status and performance (Laski, 1948:15; Williams, 1970:458–461; Wyllie, 1954:63; Weber, 1958a).

Competition. This value stresses the freedom of individuals to compete with others. Particularly in the nineteenth century, society was viewed as a jungle in which only those most "fit"—that is, individuals who showed the necessary personal qualities and dedication—could survive. Standards of personal excellence are often identified with competitive occupational achievement, and competition is stressed as the credo of the business world. The laissez-faire principle of economic competition in which individuals are expected to struggle with others for material gain, often to the disadvantage of the less successful, continues as a basic expression of this value (Horney, 1937; Lynd and Lynd, 1956).

Self-reliance. The value of self-reliance is strongly emphasized in the culture of the United States and is somewhat unique to this country. The self-made man is a legendary hero and is put forth as the incarnation of the belief that any individual who practices self-discipline and diligence can advance. The rapidly expanding commerce of early America that brought great and numerous economic opportunities, combined with the isolation and necessity for individual initiative and versatility that characterized the frontier, giving rise to the belief in self-help and the ideal of the self-made person. The eighteenth century further emphasized the idea of self-reliance, with cultural heroes such as Nathaniel Ames and Benjamin Franklin providing models of success based on individual initiative. A corollary of the emphasis on self-reliance is the belief that people who do not succeed have only themselves to blame. Thus, public welfare programs should be discouraged or kept at a minimum (Jacob, 1952; Lynd and Lynd, 1956; Sutton, 1962; Wyllie, 1954).

Materialism. Money and property are dominant values in the general culture of the United States. Material success is to be achieved, regardless of the frustrations involved in doing so. The ideology of business expounds materialistic advantages as one of the major achievements of capitalism and as essential to society. Material riches are regarded as fulfilling individual needs, and in this sense materialism is closely linked to individualism. In a study of biographies in popular magazines, Lowenthal (1956) found that whereas the heroes of earlier years were "idols of production", present-day magazine heroes are "idols of consumption," being almost exclusively related to the sphere of leisure time. The advertising media is perhaps the prime exponent of materialistic values of a wide variety, sanctioning drives for material wealth and advancement as acceptable and desirable (Coleman, 1961; Laski, 1948; Merton, 1961; Potter, 1954; Sutton, 1962).

Egoism. Enlightened self-interest is another basic value in the United States. It is widely believed that people are justified in using every opportunity to promote their own welfare, particularly in their economic pursuits. The pursuit of economic self-interest is considered justifiable, irrespective of the effects on others or of the effects on society. Indeed, societal benefits supposedly ultimately derive from the practice of economic self-interest (Jacob, 1952; Laski, 1948; Sutton, 1962).

Recent studies indicate the validity of regarding the components of the Materialistic Success Ethic as a value system, in which the separate values are closely related and tend to reinforce each other (Jeffries, 1968; 1971). Measures of egoism, competition, success striving, self-reliance, and materialism showed consistent and often strong item by item correlations between values. A measure of the value of work was not included in the study.

The ideological system supporting class stratification is characterized by negative beliefs and stereotypes about those at the bottom of the class structure. A study by Joan Huber and William Form (1973) found that 29 percent of middle-income whites expressed the belief that the poor do not want to get ahead, and that 46 percent of rich whites thought the same of the poor. Thirty percent of middle-income whites said they believed the poor do not work as hard, as did 39 percent of rich whites. Personal attributes were identified as a cause for being on relief by 46 percent of poor whites, 59 percent of middle-income whites, and 78 percent of rich whites. At each income level, the percentage of blacks holding negative views of the poor and those on relief was less than that of whites. In a similar vein, a study by Joe Feagin* (1972a) found that in a national sample between 48 and 58 percent considered various individualistic factors as very important reasons for poverty. Among the reasons cited were lack of thrift, effort, ability and talent, loose morals, and drunkenness. When data were summarized with an index, 53 percent scored high in ranking these individualistic factors as explanation of poverty, as opposed to 22 percent who were high in designating structural factors, such as low wages or poor schools, and 18 percent who ranked fatalistic factors such as sickness, physical handicaps, or bad luck as high in importance.

The influence of the complex of values called the Materialistic Success Ethic on such attitudes toward those at the bottom of the class structure is discussed by Joe Feagin (1972b). The findings of this study indicate that many, if not most, of the negative beliefs held about those on welfare are stereotypes, in the sense that they are exaggerated beliefs associated with a given category or group. For example, even though 84 percent of a nationwide sample agreed that "there are too many people receiving welfare money who should be working", available data cited by Feagin indicate that few of those receiving welfare can realistically be considered employable. Similar negative views that are wholly or partially contradicted by available data are presented for a series of other statements regarding welfare recipients.

Feagin (1972b) contends that a value system, comparable to the Materialistic Success Ethic, is linked to the stereotypical beliefs about welfare and welfare recipients. This ideological system includes ideas such as "everyone should work hard and attempt to succeed in competition with others"; "hard work will and should be rewarded"; "economic success is the reward of virtue"; and "poverty or economic failure is the individual's own fault, indicating some inadequacy of character." A generalized tendency to individualize social problems is posited by Feagin as a probable offshoot of this value system. It is easier to regard such problems as stemming from character, rather than from flaws in the structure of society.

The probable relationship between the Materialistic Success Ethic and negative beliefs about the poor was further validated in a study by John Williamson (1974). The results of this research indicate a correlation between adherence to segments of the Materialistic Success Ethic and the perceived work motivation of the poor. Those who scored high on a scale measuring the "Work Ethic" were more likely to view the poor as lacking in motivation to work than were those who did not adhere as strongly to such an emphasis on work. This measure of the "Work Ethic" included questions pertaining to the belief that the paths to success are equally open to everyone; that since opportunity is plentiful those who work hard can go as far as they wish; and that individuals should continue to work even if they inherit enough money to live comfortably. These ideas indicate some degree of comparability to values such as success and work which are part of the Materialistic Success Ethic.

More evidence linking the Materialistic Success Ethic to negative attitudes toward the poor as provided by a study by Vincent Jeffries and Edward Ransford (1971). Their research found that endorsement of the values of egoism, self-reliance, and materialism was related to the belief that most of the poor are "lazy and unwilling to put in an honest day's work" and the belief that the poor "have only themselves to blame" for their position.

Further evidence linking components of the Materialistic Success Ethic to unsympathetic attitudes toward those at the bottom of the class structure is provided by a study by Vincent Jeffries and Clarence Tygart (1974). This investigation showed that among a sample of 321 clergymen of five denominations, adherence to the value of self-reliance was related to negative attitudes toward social welfare. Pastors endorsing the value of self-reliance were less likely to hold the opinion that government should insure adequate incomes, housing, and education for people than were those endorsing the alternative value of collective responsibility. This relationship was considered by the authors to be the result of the generalized orientation of the value of self-reliance, which stresses individual autonomy and responsibility as being beneficial to both the person and society.

Joan Huber and William Form (1973) have commented on the role of various values included in the Materialistic Success Ethic in supporting class and other forms of stratification in the United States. They note that success is strongly emphasized and is defined in terms of materialistic values, such as money or property. The value of work is emphasized as how such success can be achieved. They also note that the idea of equality of opportunity is an important belief which helps to maintain and justify systems of stratification in the United States. The aforementioned values give impetus and social honor to the pursuit of material success and advancement. The belief in equality of opportunity provides both a justification for those who have succeeded and an implicit condemnation of those who have failed and who are in the lower segment of the social structure. To the degree that opportunity is open to all, those who fail to take advantage of it have only themselves to blame for any disadvantages they may suffer due to their social position.

The most comprehensive study dealing with the relationship between culture and the class stratification system of the United States is that of Jonathan Turner and Charles Starnes (1976). The central interest of this investigation is the degree of wealth held by various segments of the population. As considered in some detail in chapter 4, a very small number of people in this country have great wealth, although a large number at the bottom of the class structure have very little. This inequality in the distribution of wealth is perpetuated by what Turner and Starnes call the "wealthfare" and "welfare" systems.

Wealthfare is the system through which privileges are extended to affluent individuals and to large corporations. Several means are used to achieve wealthfare. Various government purchases in the economic market, price supports and regulations in various industries, and export-import policies all tend to benefit the wealthy. Most important, however, are the federal tax laws that favor the wealthy.

Welfare, the system for dealing with the poor, is regarded by Turner and Starnes (1976) as a reflection of the lack of ability on the part of the poor to exert the necessary pressure to bring about a redistribution of income or the rendering of higher benefits. The welfare system also serves the interests of the wealthy by forcing the poor to compete for low paying jobs in a labor market with fluctuating periods of high and low employment.

Both the welfare and wealthfare systems and the social inequalities they entail are legitimated by cultural ideas. Traditional values and beliefs comprise the ideological systems that justify and regulate the inequality of wealth in the United States (Turner and Starnes, 1976). Turner and Starnes (1976) present a systematic view of ideologies which is somewhat similar to that presented earlier in this chapter. Values are defined as generalized and abstract, notions that provide the basic criteria for judging human conduct as desirable or undesirable. These authors regard beliefs as less abstract than values. Beliefs are of two types, evaluative and empirical. Evaluative beliefs are conceptions of what should exist in a specific setting. Empirical beliefs are conceptions of what actually exists. The evaluative beliefs apply the criteria of what should be, which is contained in values, to specific social situations. Values and beliefs are viewed as fitting together into loosely integrated systems, in which the consistencies among ideas are much greater than the inconsistencies.

Nine values that are characteristic of the culture of the United States are identified and described by Turner and Starnes (1976). These values are viewed as providing the source of legitimation for the beliefs and social structure that support and maintain social inequality. These values are activism, achievement, progress, materialism, freedom, individualism, egalitarianism, morality, and humanitarianism.

The value of activism places stress on controlling and manipulating the world through the efficient use of effort and activity. Achievement emphasizes performing to a high standard in competition with others. The value of materialism emphasizes the ability to demonstrate success in competition by the display of material goods and the use of leisure time. Progress as a value stresses the improvement of both the individual and society. The value of freedom emphasizes the desirability of being free from external constraints. Individualism emphasizes such freedom for individuals to pursue material success. Egalitarianism stresses that each individual should have an opportunity to achieve. The value of morality underscores the idea that activities should, whenever possible, be judged as right or wrong. Humanitarianism emphasizes the rendering of charity to those less fortunate, but only if they are not able to be active within the systems, due to misfortune or some other legitimate reason.

Some of the values cited by Turner and Starnes (1976) appear to be somewhat similar or closely related to those included in the Materialistic Success Ethic; one appears to be identical. The value of materialism is a common element in both formulations. The value of achievement in the Turner and Starnes formulation appears to include both success striving and, secondarily, the value of work. Individualism and freedom also appear to bear a close relationship, though certainly not one of identity, to the values of egoism and self-reliance. Thus, even though there are clear differences in the two formulations, they are to some degree comparable in focusing on a somewhat similar core of traditional cultural values.

The wealthfare system, which extends various privileges to the wealthy and corporations, is justified by some of these traditional values and beliefs. Turner and Starnes (1976) believe that these ideas are to some extent maintained and used as propaganda by those espousing the interests of the wealthy. Most relevant in regard to wealthfare are the values of activism, materialism, and progress, which provide impetus and justification for activities directed toward expanding material and capital wealth. The value of morality also plays an important role in the cultural complex supporting wealthfare, because it is used as a reference point to make the above values the only right and desirable alternative.

Turner and Starnes (1976) maintain that the three values of activism, progress, and materialism have spawned the evaluative belief that economic growth and expansion should be continual. This "Growth Ethic" is closely related to two empirical beliefs that justify economic policies that benefit the wealthy. The first of these empirical beliefs is the "National Interest," which says that wealthfare is justified because it performs various functions in the national interest, such as maintaining vital industries and full employment. What Turner and Starnes (1976) call the "Trickle Down" belief provides further support to privileges benefiting the wealthy. In this case, the key idea is that measures to stimulate the economy will eventually benefit the poor and other disadvantaged workers.

Like the wealthfare system, the welfare system is also supported by a system of ideas composed of interrelated values and beliefs. The values of achievement, activism, and materialism are identified by Turner and Starnes (1976) as providing a perspective stressing the desirability of attaining material resources through competitive efforts. Individualism, freedom and equality are values that emphasize the freedom of individuals to seek material success and progress for themselves and society. The value of morality provides the rationale for judgemental views about whether or not individuals take advantage of opportunities to attain material success.

Two evaluative beliefs, the "Work Ethic" and the "Welfare Ethic," provide the concrete application of the above-mentioned value complex to particular social situations (Turner and Starnes, 1976). The Work Ethic says that all individuals who are able to work, particularly men, should do so. Moral worth is determined by hard work. Income should come from work and should be approximately commensurate with the skill and effort to achieve manifested by an individual. The Work Ethic often generates unfavorable views about those who do not work. The harshness of these views is tempered by the value of humanitarianism, which combines with the values underlying the Work Ethic to ultimately shape the nature of the Welfare Ethic.

The central idea of the Welfare Ethic is that no one should receive aid unless they are for some reason unable to work (Turner and Starnes, 1976). To accept welfare under any other conditions is to violate the Work Ethic, and those who do so are morally at fault. Condemnation of the acceptance of welfare is greater among the wealthy and the middle-income levels of society than among the poor, who are the major recipients of welfare. The varying beliefs in different strata about receiving welfare is partly due to the fact that those in higher levels are unlikely to ever be forced to engage in the low-paying, unrewarding, and temporary work that is commonly offered to the poor. Many of the poor do not define such jobs as real jobs, because of their many negative qualities, and so do not perceive any conflict between receiving welfare and the tenets of the Work Ethic and the Welfare Ethic.

The widespread belief in the availability of opportunity for everyone in the United States is noted by Turner and Starnes (1976). Blacks are the only segment of society that perceives significant restrictions of opportunity. This belief in equal opportunity places the responsibility for failure to achieve success squarely on the individual. Such a belief helps to support the existing system, in that it diverts criticism away from the social institutions that help to maintain the prevailing inequalities of income.

The Welfare Ethic and the Work Ethic combine with beliefs such as equal opportunity and individual responsibility to reinforce negative beliefs and stereotypes about the poor. These beliefs in turn reinforce the existing welfare system, which is regarded by Turner and Starnes (1976) as promoting the maintenance of poverty in certain segments of the population of the country.

In a system in which class distinctions are not emphasized by the culture and are somewhat difficult to observe (as is true of the class system of the United States) norms that exert sanctions against subordinate strata are not always readily observed, explicitly expressed, or generally accepted. One area in which formal norms penalize both the middle and the lower classes is the tax structure of the United States. Deductions and exemptions often allow the rich to pay little or no taxes, whereas those lower in the class structure, particularly the middle classes, are taxed for rather sizable portions of their income (Turner and Starnes, 1976). The same advantages to the wealthy are observed in the legal structure. Many offenses are punishable by either a fine or jail sentence, thus allowing those who can afford to pay fines to escape the more severe sanction of the loss of their freedom. Studies on the national (Domhoff, 1967; Mills, 1959) and community levels (Warner, 1941) have indicated that key decision-making positions are usually occupied by members of the upper classes. Requirements of formal education for these positions often serve to further exclude individuals of subordinate strata from decision-making positions.

Figure 9–1 presents a summary of the values, norms, and beliefs discussed in this section as components of the ideology supporting the system of class stratification. Many of the components of this ideology are those identified by Turner and Starnes (1976). The values that they mention that are similar or related to the Materialistic Success Ethic are included in the first group of values cited in Figure 9–1; those that are clearly distinct are listed separately.

The Ideology of Ethnic Stratification

There is a value pattern in the United States that involves the conferring of prestige and privileges on the basis of particularistic group membership, chiefly with

Values
1. Materialistic Success Ethic and related values
2. Other values, including activism, progress, egalitarianism, morality, humanitarianism
Norms
1. Tax structure favoring wealthy
2. Legal structure favoring wealthy
3. Exclusion of poor from key decision-making positions.
4. Governmental economic policies
Beliefs
1. Belief in equal opportunity
2. National Interest, Trickle Down, Growth Ethic, Work Ethic
3. Negative beliefs about the poor

Figure 9-1. *Ideology Supporting the System of Class Stratification*

respect to race, but also with respect to ethnicity and social class (Williams, 1970: 498–500). Although racism and other types of group discrimination do not conform to the main value currents in the United States that stress the dignity of the individual and equality, they are still quite common in established practices and, until the middle of this century, were expressed in laws. Nondiscrimination became the established national policy on a formal level only with the passage of the Civil Rights Act in 1964.

A number of studies have indicated that various components of the Materialistic Success Ethic are related to negative beliefs regarding racial and ethnic minorities. Various studies indicate a relationship between a materialistic value orientation and prejudice toward ethnic minorities (Adorno, *et al.*, 1950; Evans, 1952; Jeffries, 1971). A study by Silberstein and Seeman (1959) indicates a link between success striving and prejudice. Studies by Adorno, *et al.* (1950) and Kaufman (1957) showed that concern with social status, an ideology related to success striving, is predictive of antagonistic attitudes toward ethnic minorities. Adherence to the value of competition is related to negative attitudes toward ethnic minorities (Adorno, *et al.*, 1950; Martin and Westie, 1959), and other studies show that the values of egoism and self-reliance are related to negative views toward ethnic minorities in the United States (Jeffries, 1971; Jeffries and Ransford, 1971; see also Jeffries and Morris, 1968) and in Switzerland (Jeffries, Schweitzer, and Morris, 1973).

The view has been advanced by Jeffries and his associates that this link between the values of egoism, self-reliance, and materialism and negative beliefs about ethnic minorities stems from the nature of these values. In a different way, each value places the self above any other and in this sense is compatible with antagonistic views toward ethnic minorities. Adopting the views previously stated in this chapter that values tend to exert a predominant influence over more specific ideas such as beliefs or attitudes, each of these three values is seen as being likely to give impetus to the holding of negative attitudes. Egoism makes the self the center of attention and hence implies a lack of unity with others. Egoism is thus likely to be linked to a lack of concern for others, a lack of awareness of their needs and grievances, and a tendency to view other people in society only as competitors. The value of self-reliance stresses a sense of detachment from others. Each individual is expected to provide for himself or herself. To render aid to others is considered as possibly harmful to them. Materialism places things before people in the hierarchy of values. And, since material goods are limited, adherence to this value is likely to lead to the view of others as rivals or objects of exploitation.

Negative beliefs about various ethnic groups are part of the prevailing culture, serving to justify and maintain the system of ethnic stratification. Studies conducted over the years have shown a fairly high degree of consistency in a pattern of prejudice and stereotypical beliefs about various ethnic groups (Katz and Braly, 1933; Gilbert, 1951; Ehrlich, 1962; Simpson and Yinger, 1972:109–129). Ehrlich (1962), for example, found a highly consistent pattern of stereotypes of blacks and Jews. Blacks were regarded as irresponsible, lazy, and ignorant, whereas Jews were viewed as a distinctive economic elite. Recent studies that have taken account of long-term trends have indicated a probable decrease in this stereotyping of ethnic minorities in the United States (Simpson and Yinger, 1972:147). For example, Karlius, Coffman, and Walters (1969) compared the tendency to stereotype and the image of minorities held by Princeton University students in the years 1933, 1951, and 1957; they found a generally positive change in the content of stereotypes. The percentage characterizing blacks as ''superstitious'' dropped from 84 percent in 1933 to 13 percent in 1967; for the same period ''lazy'' fell from 75 percent to 26 percent and ''ignorant'' from 38 percent to 11 percent. Another indication of this trend is found in a study of nationwide surveys by Mildred Schwartz (1967). Her analysis of the surveys indicates that the proportion agreeing that blacks are ''as intelligent as white people'' has risen from 42 percent in 1942 to 78 percent in the mid-1960's.

An article by Jonathan Turner and Royce Singleton (1978) details the existence of negative beliefs about blacks from early colonial times to the present. These authors discuss how such ''Dominant'' beliefs about the characteristics of blacks legitimated a social structure that oppressed blacks for centuries in the United States. Although the content of these beliefs has changed considerably, their function in this sense has remained the same. This article is also important because it stresses the major emphasis of this chapter—the need to consider the role of culture in maintaining systems of social inequality.

The article by Howard Schuman* (1975) indicates that the belief in equality of opportunity provides a rationale for negative beliefs about blacks. Survey findings have shown a sizable decrease in recent years of beliefs in the inherent biological superiority of whites over blacks. On the other hand, Schuman found that over half of a nationwide sample of whites believed that the inferior economic and educational position of blacks was due to their lack of motivation or will to advance themselves. Schuman believes that whites tend to hold to the basic idea that individuals are responsible for their actions and that those who really want to get ahead can do so. Therefore, with sufficient effort, inequality can be overcome, whether on an individual or group level. Failure to overcome is regarded as a failure of individual will, rather than as a result of pressures and barriers within the social environment. The same beliefs that stress the opportunities for success, the importance of achieving it, and the fundamentally individualistic nature of the failure to succeed thus appear to have a bearing on justifying both the class and ethnic stratification systems. In the latter case, evidence is available only with respect to blacks, although it is probable that Schuman's findings would also hold with respect to other ethnic groups in a similar social position.

The norms governing relations between blacks and whites have changed drastically in recent decades. At one time relations between blacks and whites were the subject of a rigid normative system of superordination-subordination. For example, in many rural areas of the South blacks were expected to speak with deference to whites, attempt to please them, and to act in a generally subservient manner. Whites were expected to call blacks by their first name and tell rather than ask them what to do (Vander Zanden, 1966:70).

Although this pattern of race relations is no longer prevalent, informal norms of exclusion of blacks still exist, although they appear to be losing acceptance. For example, Schwartz (1967) reports that in 1942 only 30 percent of a national sample of whites felt that schools should be integrated. This figure rose to over 60 percent in the 1960s. Considerably less than half agreed in the 1940s that blacks should have equal job opportunities; these figures increased to over 80 percent in 1963. The percentage who would not mind if a black with the same income and education moved to their neighborhood increased from 35 to 67 percent in a comparable period. Although legal norms of discrimination have been virtually eliminated, various informal norms that limit the aspirations and advancements of blacks still exist. This is also true for other ethnic minorities.

Figure 9–2 presents in summary form the previously discussed elements of the ideology supporting the system of ethnic stratification.

The Ideology of Sex Stratification

The Materialistic Success Ethic probably has some effect on maintaining the subordinate position of women in the system of sexual stratification. Direct empirical evidence of this effect is for the most part lacking, so that any speculation must be regarded as extremely tentative.

The application of the ideology of success to women is somewhat unclear (Huber and Form, 1973). In traditional terms, a woman's social position depends on that of her husband, and her primary tasks are to further her husband's welfare and to care for his children. How success values apply to a woman in this situation is not stated in the prevailing culture. Despite this ambiguity, certain factors suggest the probable importance

---

Values

1. Racism and group superiority
2. Materialistic Success Ethic

Norms

1. Exclusion from various positions, particularly at high levels
2. Informal norms of exclusion from social contact at various levels of social intimacy

Beliefs

1. Belief in equal opportunity
2. *Belief that ethnic minorities who are predominantly on bottom of structure lack motivation
3. Negative beliefs about characteristics of ethnic minorities

---

Figure 9–2. *Ideology Supporting the System of Ethnic Stratification*

of the Materialistic Success Ethnic in the ideology supporting the subordinate position of women in the United States. The monetary holdings of men and women clearly show that men hold most of the wealth in the country (Bernard, 1975). Men make more money than do women (Suter and Miller, 1973). And most women are confined to jobs that involve less decision-making authority and reflect lower prestige (Szymanski, 1974). These aspects of the economic and employment situation of women are complemented by the idea that women's primary place is in the home, and any employment is secondary to the task of caring for the children and, to a lesser extent, their husbands.

Overall, women face a series of barriers to achieving money and an important position in the productive process, which are visible signs of accomplishment according to the value system of the Materialistic Success Ethic. Hence, empirical research would be expected to indicate a relationship between endorsement of components of the Materialistic Success Ethic such as success striving, materialism, self-reliance, and work and acceptance of negative beliefs regarding women. This value system and such beliefs are compatible in the sense that women for the most part fail to measure up to the achievements accorded social honor by this Ethic, and the negative beliefs commonly ascribed to women provide a rationale for their subordinate economic and social position.

Evidence of a possible link between the value of materialism and attitudes toward women is provided by a study by Sandra Ball-Rokeach (1976). This investigation centered on the relationship between values and the receptivity to sexual equality. Values are regarded in this study as a major determinant of both attitudes and behavior. The measure of receptivity to the idea of sexual equality included both attitudes of respondents and reported behavior. One of the value complexes investigated was that of economic values. Ball-Rokeach suggests that high evaluation of economic values in a capitalist society elevates property rights over human rights and competition for material ends over humanistic or social endeavors. Economic values were expected to be associated with low receptivity to sexual equality, given the previously considered orientations associated with them. Economic values were identified as a comfortable life, social recognition, and being clean and polite. Adherence to this complex of values was found to be moderately related to low receptivity to sexual equality. This relationship was stronger among females than among males. The analysis of male-female relationships by Margaret Polatnick* (1973–74) also emphasizes the role of material values in keeping women in a subordinate position to men.

A second complex of values, norms, and beliefs that supports the system of sexual stratification is that linked to the traditional family structure. Such traditional values dictate that husbands are superordinate to their wives and that they control all economic assets, whereas women have the sole responsibility for child-rearing. The article by Polatnick* (1973–74), included in an earlier chapter, describes aspects of this value system, and the manner in which it restricts the aspirations, opportunities, and independence of women, while enhancing those of men.

Another value complex influencing the subordinate position of women is society's highly favorable evaluation of presumably masculine traits. Men are characterized as aggressive, active, and instrumental; men who exhibit these highly valued traits are given privileges and prestige (Weitzman, 1975). Hartley (1959) found that even among young boys there are clear preferences for what are considered to be masculine traits. The boys characterized men as strong, ready to make decisions, capable, exciting, having good ideas, and being the boss in the family.

The basic personality traits of women in the United States are generally character-ized negatively. Women are thought of as emotionally unstable, passive, dependent, in-consistent, emotionally irresponsible, and weak (Weitzman, 1975; Hacker, 1951). A study by Hartley (1959) found that young boys characterized women as being indecisive, afraid of many things, getting tired a lot, people who cannot function in an emergency, and as not very intelligent.

Evidence indicates a fairly high degree of consensus regarding the presumed per-sonality differences between men and women. The unequal evaluation of these traits is also well established. Stereotypic traits assigned to men are more often viewed as socially desirable than stereotypic traits assigned to women (Boverman, et al., 1970; Chafetz, 1974). Interesting evidence of the predominantly negative nature of the attributes char-acteristically assigned to women is provided by a study by Inge Boverman and her asso-ciates (1970). A survey based on questions involving gender-role stereotypes was admin-istered to 79 clinically trained psychologists, psychiatrists, and social workers, 46 of whom were men and 33 of whom were women. The sample was divided into three sub-samples in administering the questionnaire. One subsample was asked to select the attributes on the questionnaire that they felt described a "mature, healthy, socially competent" adult person, without specifying sex. The other two subsamples were asked to describe a male and a female, with these same characteristics.

The results show that the clinicians had different concepts of mental health for men and women. The idea of health for a male did not differ significantly from that ascribed to the idea of a "healthy" adult. The female standard is different, however. Clinicians were less likely to assign traits of the healthy adult to a woman than they were to assign these traits to a man. Thus, a double standard of mental health was revealed. Interestingly enough, there were no significant differences in this regard between male and female clinicians.

The differential evaluation of these concepts of mental health showed in the de-gree of desirability assigned to the traits studied by a sample of college students. On 27 of the 38 stereotypic items, the trait assigned to males was viewed as more socially desir-able, as compared to only 11 items in which the trait assigned to females was seen as most desirable.

The perceptions of the clinicians are viewed by Boverman, et al., (1970) as reflec-tions of the differing behavioral norms assigned to men and women by societal consen-sus. Thus, a notion of mental health that involves the adjustment of the individual to social expectations of necessity involves a double standard of health. For a women to be healthy, from the adjustment viewpoint, she must accept the social expectations for fe-males, even though these expectations include traits that are seen as less desirable by so-ciety. The judgements of the clinicians in the sample reflected the prevailing gender-role stereotypes and the differential evaluation of the traits traditionally assigned to males and females (Boverman, et al., 1970).

Norms tend to restrict the type of employment women may engage in, although norms in this situation appear to be changing somewhat due to legal and other pres-sures. Women have been mainly confined to jobs that involve tasks similar to traditional household work, such as cleaning or sewing; jobs that do not involve strenuous physical activity; routine types of jobs requiring patience; jobs requiring rapid use of the hands and fingers, such as various types of assembly work; those with a welfare orientation, such as social work, and jobs requiring sex appeal (Wilensky, 1968). A study by

Szymanski (1974) compares 1960 and 1970 consensus data and shows that there has been little movement by women during this ten-year period out of the types of occupations cited above.

Another type of discriminatory norm is applied to women in the occupational world. Women in high-level positions are still denied access to aspects of the decision-making process that are open to men holding the same organizational positions. Various studies have also discussed the manner in which norms of interpersonal relations, such as who is able to touch whom and who uses first names with whom, tend to continually place women in a subordinate position relative to that of men (Henley, 1973–74; Henley and Freeman, 1975).

Figure 9–3 summarizes the previously presented elements of the ideology of sexual stratification in the United States.

The Ideology of Age Stratification

In view of a relative lack of research, the discussion of the ideology supporting the disadvantaged position of the aged also must be regarded as highly tentative. The emphasis placed on youth may be one of the prevailing cultural ideas that supports this aspect of the age stratification system. Elizabeth Nelson and Edward Nelson* (1974) have noted that many social scientists have observed a general orientation toward youth in the culture of the United States. The most desirable years of life are believed to be between the ages of about twenty and the late thirties, and a premium is placed on the quality of life viewed as associated with this period. These views are exemplified in what Talcott Parsons (1942) has termed a ''romantic idealization'' of youth that prevails in western societies. Youth is regarded as a period of adventure, excitement, and condoned irresponsibility.

The high value placed on youth is consistent with the general value pattern of western societies as described by Pitirim Sorokin (1957:20–52). In what Sorokin terms the Sensate type of culture that is dominant in this era, the concept of self is based pri-

---

Values

1. Materialistic Success Ethic
2. Emphasis placed on ''male'' characteristics
3. Traditional family ideology

Norms

1. Exclusion from high-level occupational positions
2. Limitations to certain types of occupations
3. Norms of interpersonal relations that reinforce subordinate position of women.
4. Norms defining wife and mother as primary roles of women.

Beliefs

1. Negative beliefs regarding characteristics of women.

Figure 9-3. *Ideology Supporting the System of Sexual Stratification*

marily on physical appearance and the body, and a general emphasis is placed on what is pleasurable to the senses, exciting, and new. Whatever is relatively unchanging, lasting, and pertaining to the inner life, correspondingly is not as highly valued. These value patterns are entirely consistent with a positive evaluation of youth and a negative evaluation of the aged.

The value of work, previously discussed as part of the Materialistic Success Ethic, may also be important in the ideology that supports the system of age stratification and the disadvantaged position of the aged within it. As noted by Talcott Parsons (1942), gainful employment is fundamental to the social status and sense of identity of the average male in the United States. Both self-respect and the respect of others are intimately linked with participation in the productive process. Since most individuals were until recently forced to retire at age sixty-five, and many still face forced retirement at a later age, they are no longer able to behave in a manner consistent with the emphasis on work as a basis of personal prestige and worth. Since many of the aged are reduced to low levels of material living by forced retirement and are denied access to most institutionalized channels of success striving, other elements of the Materialistic Success Ethic may also provide a negative frame of reference for shaping attitudes toward the aged.

Perhaps the primary norm reflective of the ideology of ageism is forced retirement. Given the importance attached to occupation as an aspect of self-identity, and its link to income and all that implies for life style and a sense of personal worth, exclusion from gainful employment must be considered a severe sanction against the aged. For example, studies have shown that morale and a sense of personal well-being are generally higher among the employed than among the retired (Riley and Foner, 1968: 350–351). Age discrimination is also highly prevalent in the employment and promotion practices of many organizations.

An article by Donald McTavish (1971) reviews the findings of various studies that have dealt with a variety of viewpoints and opinions regarding the aged. Although there is some disagreement among scholars and inconsistency in the findings of these studies, the general consensus is that favorable attitudes toward the aged are most prevalent in primitive societies, tend to decrease in modernized societies, and are least favorable in the industrialized nations of the West. Findings gathered in a number of attitude surveys, which are reviewed by McTavish (1971), indicate that between one-fifth and one-third of all respondents agree with relatively negative statements about the aged. The aged are viewed as grouchy, unproductive, mentally slow, less able to learn new things, withdrawn, uninterested in sex, and less likely to participate in a variety of activities. The general view in the literature is that age prejudices exist, and probably for many of the same reasons that other prejudices do.

The recent nationwide survey by the National Council on Aging (1975) further supports these findings. Those under sixty-five years of age have more negative views of the problems of being old than those over sixty-five, indicating that the perceptions of youth and the middle aged about old age are worse than the actual experience. The aged in this study also had negative perceptions of the problems of the aged when asked this question in relation to other aged. In reference to themselves, however, these problems of the aged, such as poor health or loneliness, were not considered as serious in nature. The aged in this study had a very negative view of the problems of being old, although most believed themselves to be exceptions.

In addition to the conditions associated with being old, the survey by the National Council on Aging (1975) also investigated the prevailing views people have about the personal characteristics of the aged and their contributions to society. For the most part there are many negative stereotypes of those people over age sixty-five—they are seen as not very active, open-minded, or adaptable. The composite view appears to be that the aged are nonproductive members of society. The general public also thinks that older people spend far more time at passive sedentary activities than those over sixty-five actually report they do.

Figure 9-4 summarizes the values, norms and beliefs supporting the system of age stratification in the United States.

THE MULTIPLE HIERARCHY APPROACH: COMBINATIONS

Elements of ideologies that support different hierarchies may coalesce in a manner to produce increased disadvantages and barriers for particular social groups. Such a situation produces a unique set of cultural meanings that apply to a segment of society characterized by its dual position in two or more social hierarchies.

Increasing attention has been paid to the particular ideological complex surrounding age and sex. The elements of the ideology of age stratification that stress the desirability of youthfulness, and those elements of the ideology of sexual stratification, which emphasize physical attractiveness as one of the primary attributes of women, combine to disadvantage the middle-aged, and older women. This age-sex ideology has been analyzed by Susan Sontag* (1972), by Bell (1970), and by Sommers (1974). These authors have observed a "double standard" of aging in our society, in which advancing years are defined and evaluated more negatively for women than they are for men. The society in the United States, as in other industrialized societies, places great emphasis on "youth" as the most desirable and attractive stage of life. This general valuation falls unequally on men and women, however. Society defines women as "old" ten to fifteen years sooner than it does men. This produces psychological, interpersonal, and economic disadvantages for women.

The differential view of the aging of men and women is related to the structure and ideology of sexual stratification. The culture defines one of the primary assets of women as physical appearance and attractiveness. Motherhood is a major role assigned

---

Values

1. Emphasis on youth
2. Materialistic Success Ethic

Norms

1. Forced retirement
2. Norms of discrimination in employment

Beliefs

1. Negative beliefs about the aged.

Figure 9-4. *Ideology Supporting the System of Age Stratification*

to women by the traditional culture (Polatnick*, 1973–1974). For men, on the other hand, society emphasizes attributes such as personality, intelligence, earning power, and position in the community. Even though men often are more desirable in terms of these qualities in the middle and later years of their lives, women's culturally defined attributes of being a physically attractive partner and mother decrease the older she becomes.

These ideas regarding age and sex are undoubtedly particular expressions of a much more generalized complex of ideas that Pitirim A. Sorokin (1957) has noted are characteristic of the "Sensate" culture that is dominant in contemporary Western civilization. The emphasis on the physical appearance and sexuality of women is just one expression of a highly generalized cultural emphasis on the physical, material aspects of existence. Similarly, the role of occupational success and wealth in the cultural evaluation of middle-aged and older men also is a manifestation of a more generalized materialism which, Sorokin has observed, is characteristic of the mentality of a Sensate culture.

Several disadvantageous effects for women of this ideology of a double standard of aging may be observed. For example, there are differing cultural expectations for women regarding marriage. In the market of close interpersonal relations and marriage, a primary asset of women is culturally defined as physical appearance and attractiveness. Men can marry women much younger than they are; but social disapproval is usually incurred if women marry men more than a few years younger than they are. Middle-aged men looking for marriage partners tend to marry younger women, thereby limiting the opportunities of the divorced or widowed woman in choosing another marital partner. Thus, it has been estimated that even though three-fourths of divorced men remarry, only about two-thirds of divorced women do.

Another affect of the combined sex and age ideology is in the employment of middle-aged or older women. In many occupations, a premium is placed on young women who fall within the cultural definition of physical attractiveness. Women returning to the labor market after a divorce or after their children no longer need continual supervision are thus placed at a disadvantage in finding satisfactory employment. These inequities in employment opportunities are carried over into smaller Social Security payments for women when they reach retirement age. The article by Susan Sontag* (1972) included in this chapter details many other personal and social disadvantages suffered by women as a result of the prevailing ideological complex pertaining to sex and age.

A similar situation of ideological combination appears also to exist with respect to the combination of blackness and low-class status. The previously discussed article by Howard Schuman* (1975) indicates that negative beliefs regarding the poor are in a sense superimposed on the residue of diminishing negative stereotypes and beliefs of racial inferiority regarding blacks. Thus, in this case, ideologies supporting the class and ethnic hierarchies combine to disadvantage lower class blacks.

CONCLUSION

This chapter has discussed the characteristics and functions of the ideologies supporting the major systems of social stratification in the United States. Common elements characterize the supporting ideologies of the class, ethnic, sex, and age hierarchies. On the level of beliefs, each ideology has a set of negative beliefs pertaining to members of the subordinate strata. Because negative characteristics are presumed to be either inherent or matters of personal failure, those in lower strata are regarded as inferior individuals who are unable or unwilling to manifest qualities that would enable them to participate more fully and adequately in society, and in doing so raise their social position. These cultural beliefs contained within the supporting ideologies are widely held and highly persistent in time, although some change has been noted in the case of negative beliefs about ethnic groups—which is probably paralleled to some degree by a change in negative beliefs about women.

Each ideology supporting a stratification system includes a system of norms. Particularly in the case of ethnic, sex, and age stratification, these norms tend to confine and limit the aspirations and opportunities of members of subordinate strata. The norms supporting the ethnic and sex hierarchies, especially the former, have undergone vast changes in recent decades. This is primarily due to the fact that the social movements espousing equality for subordinate strata have emphasized changing norms, particularly legal statutes, to increase opportunities for upward mobility and full participation in various segments of society. It is much easier to change regressive and restricting norms through the use of the legal apparatus than it is to change the values and beliefs that less obviously support structured inequality. Thus, the changes in the character of supporting ideologies in recent years have been primarily at the normative level, especially with respect to formal norms of one type or another, such as laws or organizational policies.

Much further research is needed in the area of prevailing cultural values and how they serve to support existing systems of social stratification. Limited evidence was presented linking the complex of values termed the Materialistic Success Ethic with negative beliefs toward the poor and toward blacks. The relationship of other values to social inequality was also considered. At this time, there appears to be almost no empirical evidence linking cultural values with support of the sex and age hierarchies. In lieu of such evidence, what may best be regarded as tentative hypotheses were presented in this regard.

It is perhaps in the area of values that the most fundamental cultural changes are involved, given that values tend to be highly general and thus applicable to a wide range of groups and social phenomena. If certain key values support systems of social inequality, then the empirical validation of their identity and functioning in broader ideologies is an important contribution that the social sciences could make toward fashioning a more egalitarian and just social system.

REFERENCES

Adorno, T. W., Else Frenkel-Brunswick, Daniel J. Levinson, R. Newitt Sanford. 1950. *The Authoritarian Personality*. New York: Harper and Row.

Albert, Ethel M. 1956. "The Classification of Values: A Method and Illustration." *American Anthropologist* 58 (April): 221–248.

Allport, Gordon W. 1955. *Becoming: Basic Considerations for a Psychology of Personality*. New Haven: Yale University Press.

Ball-Rokeach, Sandra J. 1976. "Receptivity to Sexual Equality." *Pacific Sociological Review* 19 (October): 519–540.

Bell, Inge Powell. 1970. "The Double Standard." *Trans Action* 8 (November-December): 75–80.

Bem, Sandra L. and Daryl J. Bem. 1972. "Homogenizing the American Woman: The Power of an Unconscious Ideology." Unpublished Paper. Revision version of a paper originally published in Daryl J. Bem *Beliefs, Attitudes and Human Affairs* 1970. Belmont, California: Brooks/Cole.

Bendix, Reinhard. 1962. *Max Weber.* New York: Doubleday.

Bernard, Shirley. 1975. "Women's Economic Status: Some Cliches and Some Facts." in Jo Freeman (ed.) *Women: A Feminist Perspective.* Palo Alta, Calif.: Mayfield.

Boverman, Inge K., Donald M. Boverman, Frank E. Clarkson, Paul S. Rosenkrantz, Susan R. Vogel. 1970. "Sex-Role Stereotypes and Clinical Judgements of Mental Health." *Journal of Consulting and Clinical Psychology* 34 (February): 1–7.

Chafetz, Janet Saltzman. 1974. *Masculine/Feminine or Human?* Itasca, Ill.: F.E. Peacock Publishers.

Chinoy, Ely. 1955. *Automobile Workers and the American Dream.* Garden City, N.Y.: Doubleday.

Coleman, Lee. 1961. "What is an American? A Study of Alleged American Traits." *Social Forces* 19 (May): 492–499.

Converse, Philip E. 1964. "The Nature of Belief Systems in Mass Publics." in David E. Apter (ed.). *Ideology and Discontent.* New York: Free Press, 206–261.

Cox, Oliver Cromwell. 1959. *Caste, Class and Race.* New York: Monthly Review Press.

Davis, Kingsley and Wilbert E. Moore. 1945. "Some Principles of Stratification." *American Sociological Review* 10 (1945): 242–249.

Domhoff, G. William. 1967. *Who Rules America.* Englewood Cliffs, N.J.: Prentice-Hall.

Ehrlich, Howard J. 1962. "Stereotyping and Negro-Jewish Stereotypes." *Social Forces* 41 (December): 171–176.

Evans, Richard I. 1952. "Personal Values as Factors in Anti-Semitism." *Journal of Abnormal and Social Psychology* 47 (October): 749–756.

Feagin, Joe R. 1972a. "God Helps Those Who Help Themselves." *Psychology Today* 6 (November): 101.

_____. 1972b. "America's Welfare Stereotypes." *Social Science Quarterly* 52 (March): 921–933.

Gilbert, G. M. 1951. "Stereotype Persistence and Change among College Students." *Journal of Abnormal and Social Psychology* 46 (April): 245–254.

Hacker, Helen Mayer. 1951. "Women as a Minority Group." *Social Forces* 30 (October): 60–69.

Hartley, Ruth E. 1959. "Sex Role Pressures and the Socialization of the Male Child." *Psychological Reports* 5: 457–468.

Henley, Nancy M. 1973–74. "Power, Sex and Non Verbal Communication." *Berkeley Journal of Sociology* 18: 1–26.

Henley, Nancy and Jo Freeman. 1975. "The Sexual Politics of Interpersonal Behavior." in Jo Freeman (ed.) *Women: A Feminist Perspective* Palo Alta, Calif.: Mayfield Publishing Company.

Hoebel, E. Adamson. 1958. *Man in the Primitive World.* New York: McGraw-Hill.

Horney, Karen. 1937. *The Neurotic Personality of Our Time* New York: W.W. Norton and Company.

Huber, Joan and William H. Form. 1973. *Income and Ideology.* New York: Free Press.

Jacob, Philip E. 1952. *Changing Values in College.* New York: Harper and Brothers.

Jeffries, Vincent. 1968. *Cultural Values and Antagonism Toward Negroes.* Unpublished Ph.D. Dissertation, University of California, Los Angeles.

_____. 1971. "Cultural Sources of Solidarity and Antagonism Toward Blacks." *Social Science Quarterly* 51 (March): 860–872.

Jeffries, Vincent and Richard T. Morris. 1968. "Altruism, Egoism, and Antagonism Toward Negroes." *Social Science Quarterly* 49 (December): 697–709.

Jeffries, Vincent and Edward Ransford. 1971. "The Ideological Sources of Solidarity and Antagonism: An Empirical Test of Continuities in the History of Social Thought." Unpublished paper presented at the American Sociological Association Convention in Denver, Colorado. August.

Jeffries, Vincent, David R. Schweitzer, Richard T. Morris. 1973. "Values, Authoritarianism, and. Antagonism Toward Ethnic Minorities." *Pacific Sociological Review* 16 (July): 357–376.

Jeffries, Vincent and Clarence E. Tygart. 1974. "The Influence of Theology, Denomination, and Values upon the Positions of Clergy on Social Issues." *Journal for the Scientific Study of Religion* 13 (September): 309–324.

Karlius, Marvin, Thomas L. Coffman, Gary Walters. 1969. "On the Fading of Social Stereotypes: Studies in Three Generations of College Students." *Journal of Personality and Social Psychology* (September): 1–16.

Katz, Daniel and Kenneth W. Braly. 1933. "Verbal Stereotypes and Racial Prejudice." in Eleanor E. Maccoby, Theodore M. Newcomb, Eugene L. Hartley (eds.) *Readings in Social Psychology* New York: Holt, Rinehart and Winston.

Kaufman, Walter C. 1957. "Status, Authoritarianism, and Anti-Semitism." *American Journal of Sociology* 22 (January): 379–382.

Kluckhohn, Clyde. 1951. "Values and Value-Orientations in the Theory of Action: An Exploration in Definition and Classification." in Talcott Parsons and Edward A. Shils (eds.) *Toward a General Theory of Action* New York: Harper Torchbooks. 388–433.

Krech, David and Richard S. Crutchfield. 1948. *Theory and Problems of Social Psychology*. New York: McGraw-Hill.

Kroeber, A. and C. Kluckhohn. 1963. *Culture*. Vintage Books.

Laski, Harold M. 1948. *The American Democracy*. New York: Vicking Press.

Lenski, Gerhard E. 1966. *Power and Privileges*. New York: McGraw-Hill.

Lowenthal, Leo. 1956. "Biographies in Popular Magazines." in William Peterson (ed.) *American Social Patterns*. New York: Doubleday.

Lynd, Robert S. and Helen Merrell Lynd. 1956. *Middletown* New York: Harcourt, Brace and Company.

Martin, James G. and Frank R. Westie. 1959. "The Tolerant Personality." *America Sociological Review* 24 (August): 521–528.

Marx, Karl 1956. *Selected Writings in Sociology and Social Philosophy*. T. B. Bottomore and Maximilien Rubel (eds.) New York: McGraw-Hill.

Mason, Karen Oppenheim and Larry L. Bumpass. 1975. "U.S. Women's Sex-Role Ideology, 1970" *American Journal of Sociology* 80 (March): 1212–1219.

McTavish, Donald G. 1971. "Perceptions of Old People: A Review of Research Methodologies and Findings." *The Gerontologist* Winter: 90–108.

Merton, Robert K. 1961. *Social Theory and Social Structure*. Glencoe, Ill.: Free Press.

Miller, Jon, Sanford Labovitz, Lincoln Fry. 1975. "Differences in the Organizational Experiences of Women and Men: Resources, Vested Interests and Discrimination." *Social Forces* 54 (December): 365–381.

Mills, C. Wright. 1959. *Power Elite*. New York: Oxford University Press.

_____. 1962. *The Marxists*. New York: Dell Publishing Co.

Myrdal, Gunnar. 1962. *An American Dilemna*. New York: Harper and Row.

National Council on Aging. 1975. *Perspective on Aging* 4 (March/April): 3–6, 13–15, 16, 18.

Nelson, Elizabeth Ness and Edward E. Nelson. 1974. "Age 'Passing'." Unpublished paper presented at the Annual Meeting of the American Sociological Association. August, 1972.

Ossowski, Stanislaw. 1963. *Class Structure in the Social Consciousness*. New York: Free Press.

Parsons, Talcott. 1942. "Age and Sex in the Social Structure of the United States." *American Sociological Review* 7 (1942): 604–616.

_____. 1953. "A Revised Analytical Approach to the Theory of Social Stratification." in Rinehard Bendix and Seymour Martin Lipset. *Class, Status and Power*. Glencoe, Ill.: Free Press.

Polatnick, Margaret. 1973–1974. "Why Men Don't Rear Children: A Power Analysis." *Berkeley Journal of Sociology* 18: 45–86.

Potter, David M. 1954. *People of Plenty*. Chicago: University of Chicago Press.

Riley, Matilda White and Anne Fonner. 1968. *Aging and Society*. New York: Russell Gage Foundation.

Rokeach, Milton. 1968. "A Theory of Organization and Change within Value-Attitude Systems." *Journal of Social Issues* 24 (January): 13–33.

_____. 1973. *The Nature of Human Values*. New York: Free Press.

Rossi, Alice S. 1969. "Sex Equality: The Beginnings of Ideology." *The Humanist* 29 (September/October): 3–16.

Schuman, Howard. 1975. "Free Will and Determinism in Public Beliefs about Race." in Norman R. Yetman and C. Hoy Steele (eds.) *Majority and Minority*. Boston: Allyn and Bacon; pp. 375–380.

Schwartz, Mildred A. 1967. *Trends in White Attitudes Toward Negroes*. National Opinion Research Center: University of Chicago.

Shirer, William L. 1960. *The Rise and Fall of the Third Reich*. Greenwich, Conn.: Fawcett Publications.

Silberstein, Fred B. and Melvin Seeman. 1959. "Social Mobility and Prejudice." *American Journal of Sociology* 63 (November): 258–264.

Simpson, George Eaton and J. Milton Yinger. 1972. *Racial and Cultural Minorities*. New York: Harper and Row.

Sommers, Tish. 1974. "The Compounding Impact of Age." *Civil Rights Digest*.

Sontag, Susan. 1972. "The Double Standard of Aging." *Saturday Review* (September): 119–126.

Sorokin, Pitirim A. 1957. *Social and Cultural Dynamics*. Boston, Massachusetts: Porter Sargent.

_____. 1969. *Society, Culture and Personality*. New York: Cooper Square.

Suter, Larry E. and Herman P. Miller. 1973. "Income Differences Between Men and Career Women." *American Journal of Sociology* 78 (January): 962–974.

Sutton, Francis X. 1962. *The American Business Creed*. New York: Schocken Books.

Szymanski, Albert. 1974. "Race, Sex and the U.S. Working Class." *Social Problems* 21 (June): 706–725.

Turner, Jonathan H. and Royce Singleton, Jr. 1978. "A Theory of Ethnic Oppression: Toward a Reintegration of Cultural and Structural Concepts in Ethnic Relations Theory." *Social Forces* 56 (June): 1001–1018.

Turner, Jonathan H. and Charles E. Starnes. 1976. *Inequality: Privilege and Poverty in America*. Pacific Palisades, California: Goodyear.

Van den Berghe, Pierre L. 1963. "Dialectic and Functionalism." *American Sociological Review* 28 (October): 695–704.

Vander Zanden, James W. 1966. *American Minority Relations*. New York: Ronald Press Company.

Warner, W. Lloyd and Paul S. Lunt. 1941. *The Social Life of a Modern Community*. New Haven. Yale University Press.

Weber, Max. 1958a. *The Protestant Ethic*. New York: Charles Schribner's Sons.

_____. 1958b. *The Religion of India*. New York: Free Press.

_____. 1964a. *The Sociology of Religion*. Boston: Beacon Press.

_____. 1964b. *The Religion of China*. New York: Free Press.

Weitzman, Lenore J. 1975. "Sex-Role Socialization." in Jo Freeman *Women: A Feminist Perspective*. Palo Alto, Calif.: Mayfield.

Wilensky, L. 1968. "Women's Work, Economic Growth, Ideology and Structure." *Industrial Relations* 7: 235–258.

Williams, Robin M., Jr. 1970. *American Society*. New York: Alfred A. Knopf.

Williamson, John B. 1974. "Beliefs About the Motivation of the Poor and Attitudes Toward Poverty Policy." *Social Problems* 21 (June): 634–647.

Wyllie, Irvin G. 1954. *The Self-Made Man in America*. Brunswick, N.J.: Rutgers University Press.

God Helps Those Who Help Themselves

Joe R. Feagin

JUST A decade ago, the affluent society received some shocking news. Michael Harrington announced in *The Other America* that right here in the richest country in the world were some 40-million poor people. Two years later, in his State-of-the-Union message, President Johnson declared war on poverty. He said that the per-capita income of some 35 million Americans in 1962 had been only $590, compared to a national average of $1,900. By 1968, according to the Census Bureau, the number of people classified as poor had dropped to 25.4 million—13 percent of the population, down from 22 percent in 1961. Since 1968, the figure has changed very little. Recent estimates place the proportion of poor people in the country at 10 to 15 percent; the Census Bureau report for 1971 was that 25.6-million people had incomes below the Government's poverty line, which last year was $4,137 for an urban family of four. Of course, a higher poverty line would put even more people in the poverty category.

Cries. Both Richard Nixon and George McGovern firmly oppose poverty. As far as I know, every political candidate now running for office stands with them on that. But there is far less agreement on how poverty should be eradicated. Workfare, welfare, a guaranteed annual wage, income redistribution, in-kind subsidies —the mention of any of these plans by anyone is sure to call forth loud cries of outrage from someone.

Why is the elimination of poverty such a controversial issue? The United States has been called the most reluctant of all welfare states. Is it, and if so, why? These are important questions, and social scientists have done a good deal of theorizing on them, although not much research. Some argue that the traditional ethic of rugged individualism began to give way, three or four decades ago, to a more socially oriented system of values. Others argue that economic individualism and the Protestant ethic still dominate the beliefs of most Americans. For instance, Robin Williams, a prominent sociologist from Cornell, recently wrote:

"The belief that virtue will be rewarded and that success attends upon effort dies hard, and in our culture failure is still more likely to be charged to defect of character than to blind fate, capricious accident, or impersonalized social and economic forces."

Credo. Williams is correct, Horatio Alger may have a shadowy twin. Alongside the self-made rags-to-riches folk hero may slouch a self-made folk villain: the lazy, irresponsible poor man. He is a fellow toward whom many are unwilling to extend a helping hand, as I discovered in an extensive opinion survey.

The first aim of the survey, conducted in the spring of 1969, was to investigate American attitudes toward poverty and the poor, with special attention to the strength of economic individualism and the Protestant ethic. I also assessed attitudes toward traditional welfare programs such as Aid to Families with Dependent Children (AFDC) and toward three newer proposals: a guaranteed-job plan, a guaranteed-income plan, and an equal-income plan. The subjects were 1,017 adults from all part of the United States, randomly selected to represent a cross-section of demographic groups. The Opinion Research Corporation in Princeton, New Jersey, conducted the interviews, which averaged 45 minutes each.

The results of the opinion survey show that a majority of Americans, in 1969, held poor people themselves responsible for poverty and were correspondingly reluctant to support new programs aimed at eradicating poverty. Within certain groups, however—particularly blacks, Jews, the young and the poor—a substantial number of persons favored new anti-poverty measures. These same persons tended to blame poverty on the social and economic system or on other external factors rather than on the poor themselves.

Characteristics.   When the average American thinks of a poor person, what comes to mind? To find out, I used this question: "If you were asked to describe a typical poor person in this area, how would you do it?" As expected, many respondents mentioned more than one characteristic. By far the most frequent were shortages of material goods: clothing (mentioned by 28 percent of the respondents), housing (27 percent), money (25 percent), and food (23 percent). A smaller number spontaneously mentioned such character traits as laziness (18 percent), wastefulness (seven percent), and loose morals (five percent). Although some gave answers that might reflect a victimization approach to poverty, such as inadequate education (18 percent) and unemployment (10 percent), the majority refrained from a comment on the *causes* of poverty in reply to this question.

Cut-off.   A second question assessed agreement with the poverty-line definition in use by Federal agencies in the late 1960s, which was just over $3,500 for an urban family of four. Each person was asked whether he considered an average family of four in his or her area as poor or not poor if it had an income of $3,500 a year. Four fifths of the respondents answered that such a family was poor. In fact, more than half of the sample agreed that a family was poor even if its income was $4,500. Surprisingly, most people think the official poverty line is by no means too high.

The respondents also agreed with then-current Government estimates of the percentage of Americans who were poor. Recent estimates vary between 10 percent and 15 percent. Almost half our respondents guessed that 10 percent to 20 percent of the population were poor; another fifth estimated the figure at five percent to 10 percent. So the five percent-to-20 percent range seemed right to almost two thirds of the sample. (Only two percent of the respondents said that poverty is practically nonexistent in the United States, while 18 percent said they thought *half or more* of the American people were poor. The rest were not sure.)

Causes.   A major objective of the survey was to examine beliefs about the causes of poverty in America. To assess the extent to which the individualistic view of poverty (as well as alternative interpretations) is still prevalent, respondents were asked to evaluate the importance of a list of "reasons some people give to explain why there are poor people in this country."

1. Lack of thrift and proper money management by poor people.
2. Lack of effort by the poor themselves.
3. Lack of ability and talent among poor people.
4. Loose morals and drunkenness.
5. Sickness and physical handicaps.
6. Low wages in some businesses and industries.
7. Failure of society to provide good schools for many Americans.
8. Prejudice and discrimination against Negroes.
9. Failure of private industry to provide enough jobs.
10. Being taken advantage of by rich people.
11. Just bad luck.

Most of the items were paraphrases of explanations given during a set of two dozen pretest interviews; the rest were taken from public discussions of poverty. The answers fell into three general categories: *individualistic explanations,* which placed responsibility for poverty squarely on the shoulders of poor people themselves; *structural explanations,* which blamed external social and economic forces; and *fatalistic explanations,* which laid poverty to illness, bad luck, and such. The 11 items are listed in order of the importance the respondents attached to them. About half the sample said that lack of thrift, lack of effort, and loose morals on the part of poor people—individualistic factors—are *very* important reasons for poverty. The respondents gave less emphasis, on the average, to structural factors: 42 percent said that low wages were a very important reason for poverty, but only 18 percent stressed exploitation by the rich. The importance attributed to what I have termed fatalistic factors varied greatly. Only eight percent of the respondents emphasized the role of just plain bad luck in poverty, while more than half said that lack of ability and talent were very important factors.

Control.   Using these 11 items, I devised three exploratory indexes to facilitate subsequent analysis. The three items that locate responsibility for poverty in the character of poor persons themselves (items one, two and four) make up the individualistic-factors index. The five that relate poverty to aspects of the economic or social system beyond the control of the poor (items six through 10) are the structural-factors index. The three remaining items (three, five and 11), which cite nonstructural factors more or less outside the control of individuals, are the fatalistic-factors index. The validity of these three indexes can be seen:

1.   in their face validity with items grouped according to the locus of responsibility for poverty, and
2.   in the positive intercorrelations I generally found between items and between items and the indexes.

While just over half of the respondents ranked high on the individualistic-factors index, only one fifth of the respondents scored high on the other two. The index with the highest proportion falling in the "not important at all" category (18 percent) was the structural-factors index. On the average, then, individualistic factors were considered much more important than were structural or fatalistic factors in explaining why there are still poor people. This confirms the picture gained from looking at the individual items.

Charity.   And yet, although it is clear that an individualistic, blame-the-poor view of pov-

erty is firmly entrenched in the American value system, structural interpretations may be gaining ground. Some limited evidence in favor of this theory is offered by comparing these findings to those of a survey of American attitudes conducted in 1945. That survey, done by the Office of Pubilc Opinion Research at Princeton University with a nationwide sample of about the same size, included an open-end question that asked "why some of the people are always poor." The answers strongly emphasized lack of effort and initiative, mismanagement, poor character, and related ideas. Relatively few even mentioned such societal factors as lack of jobs and educational opportunities, low wages, or exploitation by the rest of the society.

Another bit of support for the theory that structural explanations of poverty may be gaining ground turned up when I analyzed the 1969 survey data by socioeconomic and demographic groups. Groups with the largest concentrations of persons who gave high priority to individualistic explanations of poverty were:

1.   white Protestants and Catholics,
2.   residents of Southern and North Central regions,
3.   the over-50 age group,
4.   the middle-income group,
5.   groups with middle levels of education.

Strongholds of structuralism were:

1.   black Protestants and Jews,
2.   the under-30 age group,
3.   the poor,
4.   the less-well-educated.

Limited support for the longitudinal shift can be seen in these differentials between younger and older Americans. Yet I do not want to over-stress the up swing in structural explanations of poverty, only to suggest that a trend may exist.

Creeds.   The data on socioreligious groups deserves special comment, because religious background has been considered a very important source of individualistic perspectives by prominent social scientists, such as Max Weber in his book *The Protestant Ethic and the Spirit of Capitalism.* Inspired by Weber, Gerhard Lenski, in his 1961 study of Detroit religionists, found that

Reasons for Poverty Selected by Americans in National Survey.	Very Important, Percent	Somewhat Important, Percent	Not Important, Percent
1 Lack of thrift and proper money management by poor people.	58	30	11
2 Lack of effort by the poor themselves.	55	33	9
3 Lack of ability and talent among poor people.	52	33	12
4 Loose morals and drunkenness.	48	31	17
5 Sickness and physical handicaps.	46	39	14
6 Low wages in some businesses and industries.	42	35	20
7 Failure of society to provide good schools for many Americans.	36	25	34
8 Prejudice and discrimination against Negroes.	33	37	26
9 Failure of private industry to provide enough jobs.	27	36	31
10 Being taken advantage of by rich people.	18	30	45
11 Just bad luck.	8	27	60

Americans' Explanations of Poverty.

Importance	Individualistic, Percent	Structural, Percent	Fatalistic, Percent
low	7	18	11
medium	40	60	71
high	53	22	18

Explanations of Poverty by Different Groups.	Individualistic Explanations, Percent	Fatalistic Explanations, Percent	Structural Explanations, Percent
Socioreligious Group			
white Protestant (N = 538)	59	17	15
white Catholic (N = 213)	53	21	19
black Protestant (N = 108)	47	26	57
Jewish (N = 26)	35	12	39
Race			
white (N = 830)	56	18	17
black (N = 120)	45	25	54
other (N = 45)	24	15	28
Region			
Northeast (N = 239)	42	16	21
North Central (N = 287)	58	18	18
South (N = 296)	61	21	24
West (N = 181)	46	18	26
Age			
under 30 (N = 229)	42	9	25
thirty to 49 (N = 373)	50	18	21
over 50 (N = 401)	62	24	21
Family Income			
under $4,000 (N = 271)	51	25	28
four-thousand to $5,999 (N = 155)	57	18	20
six-thousand to $9,999 (N = 279)	55	18	23
over $10,000 (N = 284)	50	12	16
Education			
sixth grade or less (N = 108)	52	31	24
seventh to 11th grade (N = 341)	60	21	25
twelfth grade (N = 319)	54	16	21
some college (N = 324)	42	12	18

white Protestants and Jews were more individualistic and competition-oriented than white Catholics or black Protestants, who tended to have more collective, security-oriented attitudes. My data only partially confirm Lenski's conclusions. White Protestants did stress individualistic explanations of poverty more than white Catholics did, but only slightly more. Both groups stressed individualism more than black Protestants did, but again the differences were modest. Jewish respondents, though, were the least likely of all four groups to emphasize individualistic factors. And they scored second to blacks, well above white Catholics and white Protestants, in rating structural factors "very important."

Although the number of Jews in the sample is small, and one should not lean too heavily on these figures, their responses are interesting. While Jewish Americans may well place great stress on individual effort and personal morality in getting ahead, as Lenski's Detroit data suggest, when they view economic failure they are less likely than other whites to emphasize individualistic factors, and more likely to emphasize weaknesses in the system, such as discrimination and lack of job opportunities—perhaps because of their own historical and personal experience in trying to move up within the American system. Moreover, the black Protestants in the sample were by far the most likely to stress the importance of structural factors. These findings suggest that minority status explains more of the variations in attitudes toward poverty than does religion, and that the famous Protestant-Catholic cleavage is no longer very important.

Concepts. A second major objective of the survey was to find out how Americans felt about welfare and welfare recipients. We asked the respondents in our sample to evaluate seven statements about public-assistance programs and recipients.

The statements:

1. There are too many people receiving welfare money who should be working.
2. Many people getting welfare are *not* honest about their need.
3. Many women getting welfare money are having illegitimate babies to increase the money they get.
4. Generally speaking, we are spending too *little* money on welfare programs in this country.
5. Most people on welfare who can work try to find jobs so they can support themselves.
6. One of the main troubles with welfare is that it doesn't give people enough money to get along on.
7. A lot of people are moving to this state from other states just to get welfare money here.

American Attitudes Toward Welfare and Welfare Recipients.	Agree, Percent	Disagree, Percent	Uncertain, Percent
1 There are too many people receiving welfare money who should be working.	84	11	5
2 Many people getting welfare are *not* honest about their need.	71	17	12
3 Many women getting welfare money are having illegitimate babies to increase the money they get.	61	23	16
4 Generally speaking, we are spending too *little* money on welfare programs in this country.	34	54	13
5 Most people on welfare who can work try to find jobs so they can support themselves.	43	49	8
6 One of the main troubles with welfare is that it doesn't give people enough money to get along on.	45	43	12
7 A lot of people are moving to this state from other states just to get welfare money here.	41	31	28

Antiwelfarism Among Different Groups.	High Antiwelfarism
Socioreligious Group	
white Protestant	41
white Catholic	41
Jewish	35
black Protestant	12
Race	
white	41
black	12
other nonwhite	15
Region	
Northeast	40
North Central	37
South	34
West	30
Age	
under 30	30
thirty to 49	36
over 50	39
Family Income	
Under $4,000	26
four thousand to $5,999	35
six thousand to $9,999	40
over $10,000	43
Education	
sixth grade or less	30
seventh to 11th grade	37
twelfth grade	37
some college or more	35

In every case but one (item six), a plurality took an antiwelfare position. Also in every case but one (item seven), the number of persons who replied that they weren't sure was small. This is rather remarkable, since *all* the antiwelfare positions are questionable and many are demonstrably false.

To illustrate, take two of the more specific statements: item three and item seven. Item three not only suggests that welfare mothers are cheating by having illegitimate babies just to increase payments, but it tends to be linked to the view that most welfare children are illegitimate. Data on Aid-to-Families-with-Dependent-Children (AFDC) programs show otherwise. Most children born out of wedlock (at least 80 percent of them) do not receive welfare. Also, only three out of 10 children on welfare are illegitimate, according to

a 1969 survey of AFDC families in all states. Moreover, a recent study in Utah found that 90 percent of the illegitimate children on welfare had been born *before* their families went on relief. In addition, as a welfare booklet published by the state of Utah explains, a mother of two at that time (1967) got $5 a day for all expenses. Another child would increase her grant by a whopping 70 cents a day. In *no* state would the increase in payments cover the cost of having and caring for an additional child.

Cases. Before the late 1960s, the view expressed in item seven—about moving from state to state to get welfare money—was especially ludicrous, because every state had a residence requirement of between one and five years for its welfare programs. A 1968 Supreme Court decision had the effect of outlawing residence requirements, but it does not seem to have been followed by widespread relocation. For example, an Illinois study of AFDC cases during 1969 showed that 96 percent of current recipients had lived in Illinois for at least a year before receiving aid, and three fourths had lived in the state for more than five years.

A 1966 New York City survey showed that three fourths of the recipients had lived in the city for at least a decade; many had been born there. In Los Angeles County, the average length of residence for mothers on welfare was found to be 14 years. In general, welfare recipients are not *recent* interstate migrants.

Credit. If most of these generalizations about welfare recipients are gross exaggerations at best, how do we explain their popularity? As a first step toward an answer, I examined the demographic and attitudinal correlates of antiwelfare beliefs. By scoring each person's responses to the statements about welfare and summing the scores, I created an antiwelfare index. A typical high-antiwelfare person took an antiwelfare position on five statements and was uncertain about the other two. A typical low-antiwelfare person gave prowelfare answers to five items and was uncertain about the other two. In the sample taken as a whole, 36 percent scored high on antiwelfarism, 40 percent scored medium, and 25 percent scored low.

There was a lot of variation in antiwelfarism from one demographic group to another. There was no difference at all between white Protestants and white Catholics: 41 percent of each group were highly antiwelfare. Jewish respondents scored somewhat lower, and black Protestants much lower—only 12 percent were highly antiwelfare. Antiwelfarism increased systematically with age, from 30 percent in the under-30 group to 39 percent in the over-50 group.

Curve.   Income   and   education   were related to antiwelfarism in slightly different ways. The higher a person's income, the more likely he was to take an unfavorable view of welfare. For education, the curve was U-shaped. Respondents with a sixth-grade education or less were the least antiwelfare; those with seventh to 12th grade educations were the most antiwelfare. The college-educated were in the middle—but they were only slightly less antiwelfare than those at middle levels.

This finding deals something of a blow to the idea that education elevates one's critical capacities, since it is clear that a large number of well-educated Americans accept many myths and misconceptions about welfare.

The groups with the largest proportions scoring high on antiwelfarism are roughly the same as the groups most likely to explain poverty by referring to such individual characteristics as laziness. The high antiwelfare groups included:

1. white Protestants and Catholics,
2. residents of the Northeast and North Central regions,
3. the over-50 group,
4. high-income groups,
5. the groups with middle levels of education.

I ran some correlation studies to test the hypothesis that the more individualistic a person's explanations of poverty are, the more likely the person is to be against welfare and against those who receive it. High scores on the antiwelfare index turned out to be strongly correlated with high scores on the individualistic-factors index. Of those who thought individualistic explanations of poverty were very important, 45 percent

were highly antiwelfare and only 15 percent were low. Structural explanations of poverty and antiwelfarism showed the reverse relationship. Only 18 percent of those who held the system responsible for poverty were highly antiwelfare; 40 percent of them were prowelfare.

Concern.   The third objective of the survey was to assess opinions on how to get rid of poverty. What sort of antipoverty program, if any, do Americans favor?

As a preliminary, I should mention that only 10 percent of the sample were optimistic about the nation's ability to eradicate poverty. Asked whether poverty will ever be done away with in this country, 80 percent said no and another 10 percent weren't sure. Yet three fourths of the respondents said they favored "an all-out Federal effort to get rid of poverty." Apparently ending poverty is like finding truth—an unattainable but worthy goal.

The Nixon Administration at times has urged that private industry assume some, if not all, of the antipoverty burden. However, when the nationwide sample was asked in 1969 whether private industry or the Federal Government should be mainly responsible for anti-poverty programs, only 12 percent of the respondents favored private industry acting alone. Forty-one percent replied that the programs should be Federal in the main, while 34 percent took a "both, equally" position. The rest were not sure. More recently, a 1972 follow-up survey by the Opinion Research Corporation asked the same question and revealed no significant shifts in these proportions. In view of this enthusiasm for a Federal antipoverty effort, I was surprised that so few persons turned out to be familiar with the war-on-poverty programs in operation at the time. Head Start and the Job Corps, especially, had received a great deal of publicity by the spring of 1969, the time of the survey. But only two thirds said yes when they were asked if they had even *heard* about Federal programs set up to help the poor during the last few years. And only a quarter could come reasonably close to naming one. Most said they couldn't think of any at the moment, or could name only a local welfare or charity program.

American Attitudes Toward Antipoverty Proposals.	Favor, Percent	Oppose, Percent	Not Sure, Percent
guaranteed jobs (with higher taxes)	64 (35)	26	10
guaranteed income ($3,000)	30	61	10
equal income ($10,000)	13	80	7

Attitudes of Different Groups Toward Antipoverty Proposals.	Guaranteed Jobs	In Favor Guaranteed Income ($3,000)	Equal Income ($10,000)
Socioreligious Groups			
white Protestant	58	25	9
white Catholic	67	26	17
black Protestant	83	59	25
Jewish	73	46	4
Race			
white	61	26	11
black	84	57	27
other nonwhite	79	32	22
Region			
Northeast	71	29	16
North Central	57	24	14
South	66	34	13
West	64	37	8
Age			
under 30	66	35	11
thirty to 49	66	29	15
over 50	62	29	13
Family Income			
under $4,000	69	39	14
four thousand to $5,999	68	30	17
six thousand to $9,999	66	30	16
over $10,000	57	23	7
Education			
sixth grade or less	71	38	24
seventh to 11th grade	73	36	17
twelfth grade	63	25	12
some college or more	49	25	3

Create. Turing from the present to the future, I inquired about the three possible remedies for poverty that the Federal Government might undertake: a guaranteed-job plan, a guaranteed-income plan, and a more radical equal-income plan.

At first, the largest number seemed to favor guaranteed jobs. The item was phrased: "Some people have proposed that the Federal Government guarantee a job to every American who wants to work even if it means creating a lot of public jobs like during the Depression. Would you favor or oppose such a job-guarantee plan?" Nearly two thirds said they would favor it. But that group was cut in half by a follow-up question intended to measure commitment: "Would you favor new Government programs to provide jobs, even if it means that your own taxes would be increased a good bit?'' Workfare, yes. Workfare with higher taxes, no.

Only 30 percent of the sample favored the second proposal, a guaranteed income of $3,000 for every American family. Sixty-one percent opposed the guaranteed-income plan. Asked to explain their opposition, some said merely that they did not like handouts and give-aways. Others spoke in individualistic terms: people would stop working, not work very hard, become dependent on the Government, lose their ambition and motivation, waste the money. A very small part of the opposed group said they voted no because they thought $3,000 was not enough or because such a program should be run by the state or city instead of by the Federal Government.

Note too that this $3,000 level is well below what most of these same respondents consider the poverty line.

More recently, in a 1972 follow-up survey the Opinion Research Corporation found that support for both the guaranteed-job and guaranteed-income approaches had increased:

	1969		1972	
	Favor	Oppose	Favor	Oppose
guaranteed job	64%	26%	72%	20%
guaranteed income	30%	61%	38%	50%

Those favoring the guaranteed-job approach increased from nearly two thirds to almost three quarters, while those supporting the minimum income program grew from 30 percent to 38 percent (with those firmly opposed dropping precipitously). Slowly growing support for these programs now seems apparent.

The most radical proposal—complete income redistribution—was roundly rejected in the 1969 poll. The suggestion that ''every family in this country should receive the same income, about $10,000 a year or so,'' was opposed by 80 percent of the respondents. The few who favored it usually explained their response in egalitarian

terms: things should be more equal, people could live better, poverty would be eliminated. Those who opposed the plan tended to give individualistic explanations: people should work for a living, they should get what they work for, the proposal is communistic. However, a few more persons might have supported this option had the question been phrased in terms of *work* requirements.

As might be expected from earlier findings, the socioreligious groups that most strongly supported guaranteed jobs and a guaranteed income were black Protestants and Jews. On the equal-income plan, the lack of support from Jews is surprising, considering their tendency to favor the other two plans.

White Catholics were somewhat more collectivistic than white Protestants in their responses to all three proposals, as might be predicted on the basis of Lenski's Detroit study.

As before, racial group was significantly associated with the respondents' attitudes. Blacks were most likely to favor all three plans, other nonwhites were next, whites were most opposed. Income and support for two of the proposals were inversely related: the poorer the respondent, the more likely he was to favor them. And the liberating effects of a college education were again strikingly absent. The more formal education, the less the support for all plans.

To summarize, groups with the greatest tendency to favor the proposals included:

1. black Protestants and Jews,
2. low-income groups, and
3. those with least formal education.

Is there a relationship between attitudes toward poverty and attitudes toward these three antipoverty proposals? Are those who believe that the causes of poverty are most in line with individualism also those who reject extension of the welfare state? Yes. Persons who scored high on the individualistic-factors index generally were less likely to support the proposals than those who scored low. The opposite pattern held for those who emphasized structural or fatalistic explanations of poverty. The relationship between high scores on the structural-factors index and support for the three programs was particularly strong.

Relationship Between One's Explanation of Poverty and His Attitude Toward Antipoverty Proposals.		In Favor (Percent)	
Explanations	Guaranteed Jobs	Guaranteed Income ($3,000)	Equal Income ($10,000)
Individualistic			
low	74	38	15
medium	61	32	14
high	66	27	12
Structural			
low	49	15	8
medium	62	28	11
high	84	48	24
Fatalistic			
low	54	24	8
medium	64	30	13
high	74	35	18

Credence. Taken as a whole, the survey data confirm that Americans are dragging their feet on the road toward welfare-statism, and that their reluctance is closely related to strong beliefs about the meaning of economic failure. Persons who hold a man responsible for his own poverty, giving little credence to social or economic factors, also tend to have negative attitudes toward existing welfare programs and to oppose new anti-poverty proposals.

As long as large numbers of Americans attribute social problems to the character defects of individuals, massive economic reform will be extraordinarily difficult. Individualistic interpretations of poverty mesh well with conservative attempts to maintain the status quo. Indeed, major improvements in the American economic structure (such as redistribution of income) may require—among other things—a major shift in American attitudes and values.

Just possibly, this critical shift is already under way. Some signs of change can be seen in differences between generations. Although older Americans cling tenaciously to an individualistic view of poverty and of welfare, the young give more stress to structural explanations. Moreover, comparison of the 1969 and 1972 surveys on new antipoverty proposals showed slowly growing support for Federal guaranteed-income and guaranteed-job programs. And significant numbers among nonwhites, Jews, and the poor now emphasize structural explanations and solutions. These groups are a political minority, but their influence is on the rise. In time, their views may prevail—perhaps in less time than we think.

Eight years ago, when Lyndon Johnson asserted that something must be done for the nation's "forgotten fifth," Barry Goldwater replied by suggesting a probe into the attitudes and actions of the poor, which he thought might have something to do with their plight. According to this 1969 survey, a majority of Americans probably agreed, at least on issues related to poverty, yet Goldwater was overwhelmingly defeated in November. But the issues did not die. Indeed, there's another shot at them this month.

Free Will and Determinism in Public Beliefs about Race

Howard Schuman

THE MOST controversial legacy of the 1968 report of the National Advisory Commission on Civil Disorders was its assertion that "White racism is essentially responsible for the explosive mixture which has been accumulating in our cities. . . ."

To many black Americans this statement seemed painfully obvious, although it was good to hear it said officially by Americans of the commissioners' prestige. Most white Americans, however, did not like being called racists; and even among those who may have felt that the idea behind the words needed saying, there were some who considered "racist" an unnecessarily loaded way of characterizing white beliefs.

The heated discussion over whether most Americans are or are not racists turns out, however, to be largely irrelevant to the way the general white public actually thinks about race today.

Published by permission of Transaction, Inc., from TRANSACTION, Volume 7 #2. Copyright © 1969, by Transaction, Inc. This slightly revised form of the paper ("Free Will and Determinism in Public Beliefs about Race") appeared in *Majority and Minority,* Norman R. Yetman and C. Hoy Steele (eds.), Boston: Allyn and Bacon, Inc., 1975.

Author's note: This is essentially a copy of an article entitled "Sociological Racism," appearing in *Trans-Action,* Vol. 7, No. 2, December, 1969, pp. 44–48. The title used by *Trans-*Action was not the author's, however, and has been corrected here. In addition, several other minor corrections have been made, a table omitted by *Trans-*Action has been restored, and one new paragraph has been added. The latter attempts to take account of an insightful question raised by Guy E. Swanson about an earlier version of this paper. More generally the paper has been influenced by my fruitful collaboration with Angus Campbell on the larger study of which this is one report. The study was financed by the Ford Foundation and carried out through the Survey Research Center of the University of Michigan.

Social scientists take for granted the deterministic assumption common to most science that all events (in this case, human behavior) can be traced to antecedent causes. The scientific debate revolves around which set of determinants "cause" people (for example, people of a particular race) to behave the way they do—primarily, whether heredity or environment or some particular combination of the two is the determining factor in some aspect of human behavior. In this sense, current social science thinking and older theories of racism are both deterministic. But the main premise of the average white American is that people are free to do as they will. The logic of causal inquiry, we will see, plays little or no part in public thinking about white and black differences in status and achievement.

THE DECLINE IN POPULAR RACISM

"White racism" is nowhere defined in the Kerner Commission Report, but the term racism is generally taken to refer to the belief that there are clearly distinguishable human races; that these races differ not only in superficial physical characteristics, but also innately in important psychological traits; and finally that the differences are such that one race (almost always one's own) can be said to be superior to another. More simply, white racism is the belief that white people are *inherently* superior to Negroes in significant ways, but that the reverse is not true.

Questions designed to tap white racism have been asked in national surveys for the past 25 years. The major finding of these surveys has been a dramatic *decrease* in beliefs in white racial superiority over Negroes. The most relevant and consistently measured topic has been white beliefs about racial differences in intelligence. In 1942 a National Opinion Research Center survey asked respondents: "In general, do you think Negroes are as intelligent as white people—that is, can they learn just as well if they are given the same education?" Only 42 percent of a national sample of white Americans said they believed Negroes to be as intelligent as whites. Later surveys, however, showed a continuing rise in the belief in equal intelligence, so that by 1956, 78 percent of a NORC national sample answered the same question in the affirmative. The percentage seemed to stabilize at that point and more recent surveys have continued to show that about four out of five white Americans reject the notion that white people are born with higher mental capacity than Negroes.[1]

The comparatively rapid decline of racist beliefs in this key area, the relatively small proportion of whites who still hold such beliefs, and the fact that the holdouts are disproportionately from the old South, all suggest that racism—at least in the more open forms that can be measured in surveys—is a minor and disappearing phenomenon in this country. This, of course, implies little or nothing about the disappearance of discrimination or racial hostility or other aspects of black-white inequality in America. It merely indicates that attempts to buttress anti-Negro feeling with beliefs about biological racial inferiority are no longer much resorted to by white Americans.

Social scientists tend to see in these opinion trends not only the disappearance of "racist" beliefs, but also growing white acceptance of contemporary environmental explanations of the Negro's law status and achievement in America. This tendency assumes a change in public belief paralleling changes in social science itself. The ideas about psychogenetic racial differences that played such a large role in American social science in the early part of the century have gradually been replaced by assumptions of environmental determinism. Some of these environmental expla-

nations focus on the obvious in the American racial structure: segregation, discrimination, and the domination of Negroes by whites. Other explanations emphasize cultural and culturally induced psychological phenomena, such as the burden that lower class or rural background places on the ability to compete for urban middle-class rewards; the assumed disruptive effects of family instability and lack of successful male models; the disabling experience of growing up in a minority in a society where one's ethnic identity is both permanently fixed and negatively evaluated by the majority. Whatever the particular environmental theory, however, the important point is that an explanatory social science looks for causal variables that are independent of, yet can be said to produce, the "facts" that need explaining.

WHAT THE PUBLIC ACTUALLY BELIEVES

Projection of the logic of science onto the thinking of the general public, however, leads to paradoxical results. For it is clear that although most of the American public reject racist beliefs, unlike social scientists they do not emphasize environmental explanations of racial differences. In the study "Racial Attitudes in Fifteen American Cities," directed by Angus Campbell and myself, the following question was asked early in 1968 of a probability sample of 2,584 urban white Americans: "On the average, Negroes in this city have worse jobs, education, and housing than white people. Do you think this is due mainly to Negroes having been discriminated against, or mainly due to something about Negroes themselves?"[2]

1. These figures are reported in Mildred A. Schwartz. *Trends in White Attitudes Toward Negroes,* National Opinion Research Center, Chicago, 1967.

2. For a general report of the study and a more detailed description of the sample, see Angus Campbell and Howard Schuman, "Racial Attitudes in Fifteen American Cities," in *Supplemental Studies for the National Advisory Commission on Civil Disorders,* July, 1968, U.S. Government Printing Office, Washington, D.C. (Reprinted by Frederick A. Praeger, Publishers, New York, 1968, and by the Institute for Social Research, Ann Arbor, 1969.) The sample discussed here is of the white population, ages 16–69, in the combined 15 cities. The cities are: Baltimore, Boston, Brooklyn, Chicago, Cincinnati, Cleveland, Detroit, Gary, Milwaukee, Newark, Philadelphia, Pittsburgh, San Francisco, St. Louis, and Washington. Results from two suburban areas (around Cleveland and Detroit) are essentially the same.

More than half the sample—54 percent—believes that the inferior economic and educational status of Negroes is due mainly to Negroes themselves. (See Table, Question A.) Only 19 percent places the blame mainly on discrimination, while another 19 percent sees the cause as a mixture of discrimination and "Negroes themselves." It is interesting to note that 4 percent of the sample spontaneously denied the initial assumption of the question, claiming that in their city Negroes have jobs, education, and housing equal to or better than that of whites. This is another indication of how misleading it is for social scientists to assume public knowledge and acceptance of the findings of social science—in this case descriptive findings rather than explanatory ones. Finally, 4 percent of the sample gave "don't know" answers to the question.

The term "discriminated against" was used in the question as a simple way of representing certain environmental causes of Negro behavior, but it may have failed to provide sufficient opportunity for other environmental views, such as the stress on Negro lower-class background. However, a general follow-up question (discussed further below) encouraged respondents to explain their ideas in their own words, and another 18 percent could be identified as giving some sort of apparent environmental explanation, principally the lower education of Negroes, although lower education was already built into the question as part of the problem to be explained. It may well be that many whites giving this answer would attribute the cause of low education to Negroes themselves, but even if we assume an emphasis on environment in this response and add this 18 percent to the 19 percent who mentioned discrimination explicitly, we still find only 37 percent of the total sample attributing Negro disadvantage to causes outside Negroes themselves. More than half the sample places the responsibility for Negro disadvantage mainly or entirely on Negroes.

Somewhat similar results are reported from a July 1968 Gallup Opinion Survey with a national sample. The Gallup question reads: "Who do you think is *more* to blame for the present conditions in which Negroes find themselves—white people, or Negroes themselves?" Only 24 percent of the white population blamed "itself"; 54 percent blamed "Negroes themselves"; and 22 percent had no opinion.

Our results appear at first to contradict the NORC trends that show a sharp drop in white beliefs in Negro racial inferiority in intelligence. If Negro problems are attributed mainly to "something about Negroes themselves," doesn't this imply a racist explanation? The answer may be yes to the scientific determinist, but it is not necessarily yes to the general public.

The situation is considerably clarified by the follow-up questions we asked of the 73 percent of the sample (1,886 cases) who attributed lower Negro achievements to Negroes themsleves or to a mixture of Negroes themselves and discrimination. We inquired first, "What is it about Negroes themselves that makes them have worse jobs, education, and housing?" and recorded the responses *verbatim*. (See Table, Question B.) No matter what the answer, we then asked: "Do you think Negroes are just born that way and can't be changed, or that changes in the Negro are possible?" Skipping over the free answer question for the moment, we found to our surprise that whatever the faults Negroes were seen as having, only 8 percent of the respondents saw these limitations as inborn and unchangeable, while 88 percent believed "changes in the Negro are possible." (See Table, Question C.)

We thus find that a considerable portion of the white urban population belives that the source of Negro hardships lies within Negroes themselves, but denies that this source is inborn and unchangeable. The white public therefore appears simultaneously to accept and to reject racist beliefs.

"THEY DON'T TRY"

The resolution of this paradox is suggested by the free answers to the question: "What is it about Negroes themselves that makes them have worse jobs, education and housing?" These answers were coded into the most meaningful categories inherent in the data, with the following results: Only 8 percent of those asked the question speak in terms that imply or strongly suggest biological or genetic differences—e.g., "low mental ability," "low morals"—between Negroes and

Questions and Responses Bearing on Free Will and Determinism

A. "On the average, Negroes in this city have worse jobs, education, and housing than white people. Do you think this is due mainly to Negroes having been discriminated against, or mainly due to something about Negroes themselves?"

	Percents	
Mainly due to discrimination	19	
Mainly due to Negroes themselves	54	
A mixture of both	19	
Denied Negroes have worse jobs, education, and housing—refused question	4	
Don't know	4	
	100	(2,584 cases)

B. "What is it about Negroes themselves that makes them have worse jobs, education, and housing?" (Asked only of those replying "mainly Negroes themselves" or "mixture" to Question A.)

	Percents	
Responses that suggest genetic explanations of Negro disadvantage (e.g., "low mental ability")	8	
Responses that may indicate environmental explanations (other than discrimination) of Negro disadvantage (e.g., "lack of education")	25	
Responses that suggest lack of motivation as explanation of Negro disadvantage—not indication of genetic or environmental cause	57	
Don't know, not ascertained	10	
	100	(1,886 cases)

C. "Do you think Negroes are just born that way and can't change, or that changes in the Negro are possible?" (Asked only of those asked Question B.)

	Percents	
Born that way and can't be changed	8	
Changes are possible	88	
Don't know	4	
	100	(1,886 cases)

whites, and the number mentioning low intelligence as such is even smaller. This certainly does not contradict the NORC trend data presented earlier, but only accentuates it. Answers that lean in an environmental direction—e.g., "lack of education," "poverty cycle," but *not* "discrimination"—are given by a somewhat larger portion (25 percent) of the follow-up sample. By far the largest category of response, however, does not point clearly in either a genetic *or* an environmental direction, but is best termed "lack of motivation"; 57 percent of those attributing Negro problems to Negroes themselves give such a

response clearly, and another 10 percent offer related responses having much the same implication. Some examples from the interviews of "lack of motivation" responses are the following:

Well, they don't try to better themselves. I've come up through the ranks. I've worked at just about everything. And now I'm at a job where I'm happy and just about making top money. And they can do the same. Get out and look.

They have the same advantages the whites have but don't use them. They quit school. They quit work.

They pity themselves too much. We have Negro friends from the service; one is a hard worker and he has made something of himself. Many don't try to better themselves.

Responses like these outnumber responses focusing on mental or other lack of capacity by about seven to one.

We now have three interlocking clues to the kinds of reasoning about racial differences that most white Americans are engaged in. First, the cause of low Negro status is perceived to lie mainly within Negroes themselves, rather than in the external constraints imposed by American social structure or by the prejudice of white Americans. Second, this internal factor is seen as a matter of motivation or will, not as a matter of capacity or ability. And third, it is not seen as either immutable or ineluctable, but rather as something that can readily be changed.

Changed by whom? For much of the white public, the implicit answer is: by individual Negroes themselves. Evidently a great many white Americans believe in a naive form of free will. Negroes can get ahead at any time, whites feel, simply by setting their sights higher and putting their shoulders to the wheel. The philosophical problem of free will is rarely mentioned, to be sure, but free will is clearly what the general public takes to be an explanation of how individual men and entire ethnic groups can, do, and should achieve success in America.

FREE WILL AND ITS BASIS

There is really nothing surprising in public commitment to the assumption of free will. It must in some form be built into every society, since elders and authorities usually feel it necessary to impress upon children and citizens that they are responsible for their own actions. While it may be that a person fails to live up to an important social norm only because of the way he was brought up or only because of the way his endocrine system functions, others in the society will not wish him to attribute his deviant behavior too easily to such causes. They will want him to hold himself responsible for his actions, and to believe that he can change if he wants to and tries hard enough.

Beyond this universal social need to hold individuals responsible for their actions, in America the emphasis on free will has an additional and very powerful cultural source in the belief that each immigrant group has started at the bottom and proceeded by ambition and effort alone to work its way toward the top. The second, third, or n-th generation descendants of immigrants are usually ready to recount vivid tales of ancestral initiative and industry. Told that Negroes have come from unskilled backgrounds, lack capital and connections, face prejudice and discrimination, many a white American will assert with pride that all this was true of his own parents as well, or of his grandparents, or of at least an uncle or two. He will point out that despite tremendous obstacles his forebears succeeded in America, and that is exactly why they now have their house in the suburbs, their children in college, and the respect of their neighbors. He will assure the listener that Negroes can do as much at any point if only they will exert the effort.

This explanation of why white Americans succeed and black Americans do not, while apparently satisfactory to the white public, will be dissatisfying to the social scientist. It explains nothing about how a motivational difference between white and black Americans, if indeed there is one, has come about. To get at deeper public explanations, social scientists can of course formulate more survey questions for the general population. By pushing a good deal we may force some respondents to assert a genetic-like explanation ("they must be born that way"), others to opt for a family structure explanation ("I guess it's the way their mothers and fathers brought them up"), and so forth. But such responses to probes are given mainly to satisfy the pressure of the interviewer—not because the average respondent himself feels that an explanation assuming free will leaves anything to be desired.

There may be a still more basic paradox underlying the oversimplification of public beliefs about race. In the struggle against earlier public conceptions of Negro inferiority, Negro leaders and white social scientists understandably stressed the essential similarity of Negroes and whites. Discrimination and lack of opportunity were presented as the primary, if not only, barriers to racial equality in achievement: remove these barriers, the implication went, and black performance will automatically and quickly equal that of whites. Insofar as the public accepted this not very subtle view of black disadvantage, it looked for immediate results wherever equality of opportunity began to be approximated. In a sense, the average white person could say: "All right, Negroes have the same potential as whites. But then they should do as well in school, have no higher crime rate, achieve as well occupationally. If many continue to behave in undesirable ways and it is not because of lack of potential, then it must be lack of will, lack of desire." Given the invisibility of much discrimination, and the difficulty of appreciating its long-term psychological effects, the simplistic social science emphasis on immediate discrimination as the sole cause of black disadvantage leads to the simplistic free will interpretations of the public.

THE TERMS OF PUBLIC DISCUSSION TODAY

Our findings make it clear that much of the white public not only does not think in scientific terms about race; it does not even think in psuedoscientific terms. Whites do not look for deeper causes of black-white inequality because they assume this inequality can be overcome at any time by the very people suffering from it. Arguments over types of determinism are really irrelevant to this substantial part of the public, for they feel quite comfortable in thinking about race in the same simple free will terms that they use in thinking about individuals: those who really want to get ahead can do so.

Thus from one standpoint—certainly the black standpoint—the phrase "white racism" appears wholly appropriate. Most white Americans may not be racists in the more technical sense, but nothing said above suggests that they are willing to accept past or present responsibility for prejudice, discrimination, and general inequality in the spread of opportunities. In espousing free will, white Americans deny the reality of the problems faced by black Americans and thus place the whole burden of black disadvantage on blacks themselves. The distinctions concerning the definition of racism made here are, from such a standpoint, distinctions that do not make much of a difference.

In addressing white Americans today, however, it may be essential to take account of exactly the distinction drawn here between deterministic and free will viewpoints. What is more true, and more useful, to realize about the white American public than its supposed racist beliefs is the limited and naive perspective from which it views race and race relations. White Americans are, of course, caught up in their own lives and see the world from their own personal and limited perspective. Not having experienced the world as black Americans have—a self-evident but nonetheless overwhelmingly important fact—the average white American simply has no conception of how heavily public institutions, values, and actions press down upon black Americans and work to convince them that no matter how great their efforts they will not be rewarded in American society. Most of all, white Americans do not understand that individual free will operates and has its beneficial effects only within institutional contexts that give it efficacy and purpose.

Homogenizing the American Woman: The Power of an Unconscious Ideology[1]

Sandra L. Bem and Daryl J. Bem
Department of Psychology
Stanford University

IN THE beginning God created the heaven and the earth. . . . And God said, Let us make man in our image, after our likeness; and let him have dominion over the fish of the sea, and over the fowl of the air, and over the cattle, and over all the earth. . . . And the rib, which the Lord God had taken from man, made he a woman and brought her unto the man. . . . And the Lord God said unto the woman, What is this that thou has done? And the woman said, The serpent beguiled me, and I did eat. . . . Unto the woman God said, I will greatly multiply thy sorrow and thy conception; in sorrow thou shalt bring forth children; and thy desire shall be to thy husband, and he shall rule over thee. (Gen. 1, 2, 3)

There is a moral to that story. St. Paul spells it out even more clearly.

For a man. . . . is the image and glory of God; but the woman is the glory of the man. For the man is not of the woman, but the woman of the man. Neither was the man created for the woman, but the woman for the man. (1 Cor. 11)

Let the woman learn in silence with all subjection. But I suffer not a woman to teach, nor to usurp authority over the man, but to be in si-

lence. For Adam was first formed and then Eve. And Adam was not deceived, but the woman, being deceived, was in the transgression. Notwithstanding, she shall be saved in childbearing, if they continue in faith and charity and holiness with sobriety. (1 Tim. 2)

Now one should not assume that only Chistians have this kind of rich heritage of ideology about women. So consider now, the morning prayer of the Orthodox Jew:

Blessed art Thou, oh Lord our God, King of the Universe, that I was not born a gentile.
Blessed art Thou, oh Lord our God, King of the Universe, that I was not born a slave.
Blessed art Thou, oh Lord our God, King of the Universe, that I was not born a woman.

Or, consider the Koran, the sacred text of Islam:

Men are superior to women on account of the qualities in which God had given them pre-eminence.

Because they think they sense a decline in feminine "faith, charity, and holiness with sobriety," many people today jump to the conclusion that the ideology expressed in these passages is a relic of the past. Not so, of course. It has simply been obscured by an equalitarian veneer, and the same ideology has now become unconscious. That

[1]October, 1972 Copyright © 1972 by Sandra Bem and Daryl J. Bem. Reprinted by permission of the authors. An earlier version of this paper appeared in *Beliefs, Attitudes and Human Affairs* by Daryl J. Bem. Brooks/Cole:1970

is, we remain unaware of it because alternative beliefs and attitudes about women, until very recently, have gone unimagined. We are very much like the fish who is unaware of the fact that his environment is wet. After all, what else could it be? Such is the nature of all unconscious ideologies in a society. Such, in particular, is the nature of America's ideology about women.

What we should like to do in this paper is to discuss today's version of this same ideology.

* * *

When a baby boy is born, it is difficult to predict what he will be doing 25 years later. We can't say whether he will be an artist, a doctor, a lawyer, a college professor, or a bricklayer, because he will be permitted to develop and fulfill his own unique potential—particularly, of course, if he happens to be white and middle class. But if that same newborn child happens to be a girl, we can predict with almost complete confidence how she is likely to be spending her time some 25 years later. Why can we do that? Because her individuality doesn't have to be considered. Her individuality is irrelevant. Time studies have shown that she will spend the equivalent of a full working day, 7.1 hours, in preparing meals, cleaning house, laundering, mending, shopping and doing other household tasks. In other words, 43% of her waking time will be spent in activity that would command an hourly wage on the open market well below the federally set minimum for menial industrial work.

Of course, the point really is not how little she would earn if she did these things in someone else's home. She will be doing them in her own home for free. The point is that this use of time is virtually the same for homemakers with college degrees and for homemakers with less than a grade school education, for women married to professional men and for women married to blue-collar workers. Actually, that's understating it slightly. What the time study really showed was that college-educated women spend slightly *more* time cleaning their houses than their less educated counterparts!

Of course, it is not simply the full-time homemaker whose unique identity has been rendered largely irrelevant. Of the 31 million women

who work outside the home in our society, 78% end up in dead-end jobs as clerical workers, service workers, factory workers, or sales clerks, compared to a comparable figure of 40% for men. Only 15% of all women workers in our society are classified by the Labor Department as professional or technical workers, and even this figure is misleading—for the single, poorly-paid occupation of non-college teacher absorbs half of these women, and the occupation of nurse absorbs an additional quarter. In other words, the two jobs of teacher and nurse absorb three-quarters of all women classified in our society as technical or professional. That means, then, that fewer than 5% of all professional women—fewer than 1% of all women workers—fill those positions which to most Americans connote "professional": Physician, lawyer, engineer, scientist, college professor, journalist, writer, and so forth.

Even an I.Q. in the genius range does not guarantee that a woman's unique potential will find expression. There was a famous study of over 1300 boys and girls whose I.Q.'s averaged 151 (Terman & Oden, 1959). When the study began in the early 1900's, these highly gifted youngsters were only ten years old, and their careers have been followed ever since. Where are they today? 86% of the men have now achieved prominence in professional and managerial occupations. In contrast, only a minority of the women were even employed. Of those who were, 37% were nurses, librarians, social workers, and non-college teachers. An additional 26% were secretaries, stenographers, bookkeepers, and office workers! Only 11% entered the higher professions of law, medicine, college teaching, engineering, science, economics, and the like. And even at age 44, well after all their children had gone to school, 61% of these highly gifted women remained full-time homemakers. Talent, education, ability, interests, motivations: all irrelevant. In our society, being female uniquely qualifies an individual for domestic work—either by itself or in conjunction with typing, teaching, nursing or (most often) unskilled labor. It is this homogenization of America's women which is the major consequence of our society's sex-role ideology.

It is true, of course, that most women have several hours of leisure time every day. And it is here, we are often told, that each women can express her unique identity. Thus, politically interested women can join the League of Women Voters. Women with humane interests can become part-time Gray Ladies. Women who love music can raise money for the symphony. Protestant women play Canasta; Jewish women play Mah Jongg; brighter women of all denominations and faculty wives play bridge.

But politically interested *men* serve in legislatures. *Men* with humane interests become physicians or clinical psychologists. *Men* who love music play in the symphony. In other words, why should a woman's unique identity determine only the periphery of her life rather than its central core?

Why? Why nurse rather than physician, secretary rather than executive, stewardess rather than pilot? Why faculty wife rather than faculty? Why doctor's mother rather than doctor? There are three basic answers to this question: (1) Discrimination; (2) Sex-role conditioning; and (3) The presumed incompatibility of family and career.

DISCRIMINATION

In 1968, the median income of full-time women workers was approximately $4500. The comparable figure for men was $3000 higher. Moreover, the gap is widening. Ten years ago, women earned 64% of what men did; that percentage has now shrunk to 58%. Today, a female college graduate working full-time can expect to earn less per year than a male high school dropout.

There are two reasons for this pay differential. First, in every category of occupation, women are employed in the lesser-skilled, lower-paid positions. Even in the clerical field, where 73% of the workers are women, females are relegated to the lowest status positions and hence earn only 65% of what male clerical workers earn. The second reason for this pay differential is discrimination in its purest form: unequal pay for equal work. According to a survey of 206 companies in 1970, female college graduates were offered jobs which paid $43 per month less than those offered to their male counterparts in the same college major.

New laws should begin to correct both of these situations. The Equal Pay Act of 1963 prohibits employers from discriminating on the basis of sex in the payment of wages for equal work. In a landmark ruling on May 18, 1970, the U.S. Supreme Court ordered that $250,000 in back pay be paid to women employed by a single New Jersey glass company. This decision followed a two-year court battle by the Labor Department after it found that the company was paying men selector-packers 21.5 cents more per hour than women doing the same work. In a similar case, the Eighth Circuit Court of Appeals ordered a major can company to pay more than $100,000 in back wages to women doing equal work. According to the Labor Department, an estimated $17-million is owed to women in back pay. Since that estimate was made, a 1972 amendment extended the Act to cover executive, administrative and professional employees as well.

But to enjoy equal pay, women must also have access to equal jobs. Title VII of the 1964 Civil Rights Act prohibits discrimination in employment on the basis of race, color, religion, national origin—and sex. Although the sex provision was treated as a joke at the time (and was originally introduced by a Southern Congressman in an attempt to defeat the bill), the Equal Employment Opportunities Commission discovered in its first year of operation that 40% or more of the complaints warranting investigation charged discrimination on the basis of sex (Bird, 1969).

Title VII has served as one of the most effective instruments in helping to achieve sex equality in the world of work. According to a report by the E.E.O.C., nearly 6,000 charges of sex discrimination were filed with that agency in 1971 alone, a 62% increase over the previous year.

But the most significant legislative breakthrough in the area of sex equality was the passage of the Equal Rights Amendment by both houses of Congress in 1972. The ERA simply states that "Equality of rights under the law shall not be denied or abridged by the United States or by any state on account of sex." This amendment had been introduced into every session of Congress since 1923, and its passage now is clearly an indication of the changing role of the American woman. All of the various ramifications are hard to predict, but it is clear that it will have profound consequences in private as well as public life.

Many Americans assume that the recent drive for equality between the sexes is primarily for the benefit of the middle-class woman who wants to seek self-fulfillment in a professional career. But in many ways, it is the woman in more modest circumstances, the woman who *must* work for economic reasons, who stands to benefit most from the removal of discriminatory barriers. It is *she* who is hardest hit by unequal pay; it is *she* who so desperately needs adequate day-care facilities; it is *her* job which is often dead-ended while her male colleagues in the factory get trained and promoted into the skilled craft jobs. And if both she and her husband work at unfulfilling jobs eight hours a day just to make an adequate income, it is still *she* who carries the additional burden of domestic chores when they return home.

We think it is important to emphasize these points at the outset, for we have chosen to focus our remarks in this particular paper on those fortunate men and women who can afford the luxury of pursuing self-fulfillment through the world of work and career. But every societal reform advocated by the new feminist movement, whether it be the Equal Rights Amendment, the establishment of child-care centers, or basic changes in America's sex-role ideology, will affect the lives of men and women in every economic circumstance. Nevertheless, it is still economic discrimination which hits hardest at the largest group of women, and it is here that the drive for equality can be most successfully launched with legislative and judical tools.

SEX-ROLE
CONDITIONING

But even if all discrimination were to end tomorrow, nothing very drastic would change. For job discrimination is only part of the problem. It does impede women who choose to become lawyers or managers or physicians. But it does not, by itself, help us to understand why so many women "choose" to be secretaries or nurses rather than executives or physicians: why only 3% of 9th grade girls as compared to 25% of the boys "choose" careers in science or engineering; or

why 63% of America's married women "choose" not to work at all. It certainly doesn't explain those young women whose vision of the future includes only marriage, children, and living happily ever after; who may, at some point, "choose" to take a job, but who almost never "choose" to pursue a career. Discrimination frustrates choices already made. Something more pernicious perverts the motivation to choose.

That "something" is an unconscious ideology about the nature of the female sex, an ideology which constricts the emerging self-image of the female child and the nature of her aspirations from the very beginning; an ideology which leads even those Americans who agree that a black skin should not uniquely qualify *its* owner for a janitorial or domestic service to act as if the possession of a uterus uniquely qualifies *its* owner for precisely such service.

Consider, for example, the 1968 student rebellion at Columbia University. Students from the radical Left took over some administration buildings in the name of equalitarian ideals which they accused the university of flouting. Here were the most militant spokesmen one could hope to find in the cause of equalitarian ideals. But no sooner had they occupied the buildings than the male militants blandly turned to their sisters-in-arms and assigned them the task of preparing the food, while they—the menfolk—would presumably plan future strategy. The reply these males received was the reply that they deserved—we will leave that to your imagination—and the fact that domestic tasks behind the barricades were desegregated across the sex line that day is an everlasting tribute to the class consciousness of these ladies of the Left. And it was really on that day that the campus women's liberation movement got its start—when radical women finally realized that they were never going to get to make revolution, only coffee.

But these conscious co-eds are not typical, for the unconscious assumptions about a woman's "natural" talents (or lack of them) are at least as prevalent among women as they are among men. A psychologist named Phillip Goldberg (1968) demonstrated this by asking female college students to rate a number of professional articles from each of six fields. The articles were collated into two equal sets of booklets, and the names of the authors were changed so that the identical article was attributed to a male author (e.g., John T. McKay) in one booklet and to a female author (e.g., Joan T. McKay) in the other booklet. Each student was asked to read the articles in her booklet and to rate them for value, competence, persuasiveness, writing style, and so forth.

As he had anticipated, Goldberg found that the identical article received significantly lower ratings when it was attributed to a female author than when it was attributed to a male author. He had predicted this result for articles from professional fields generally considered the province of men, like law or city planning, but to his surprise, these women also downgraded articles from the fields of dietetics and elementary school education when they were attributed to female authors. In other words, these students rated the male authors as better at everything, agreeing with Aristotle that "we should regard the female nature as afflicted with a natural defectiveness." Such is the nature of America's unconscious ideology about women.

When does this ideology begin to affect the life of a young girl? Research now tells us that from the day a newborn child is dressed in pink, she is given "special" treatment. Perhaps because they are thought to be more fragile, six-month-old infant girls are actually touched, spoken to, and hovered over more by their mothers while they are playing than are infant boys (Goldberg & Lewis, 1969). One study even showed that when mothers and babies are still in the hospital, mothers smile at, talk to, and touch their female infants more than their male infants at two days of age (Thoman, Leiderman, & Olson, 1972). Differential treatment can't begin much earlier than that.

As children begin to read, the storybook characters become the images and the models that little boys and little girls aspire to become. What kind of role does the female play in the world of children's literature? The fact is that there aren't even very many females in that world. One survey (Fisher, 1970) found that five times as many males as females appear in the titles of children's books: the fantasy world of Doctor Seuss is almost entirely male; even animals and machines are represented as male. When females do appear, they are noteworthy primarily for what they do *not* do.

They do not drive cars, and they seldom even ride bicycles. In one story in which a girl does ride a bicycle, it's a two-seater. Guess where the girl is seated! Boys in these stories climb trees and fish and roll in the leaves and skate. Girls watch, fall down, and get dizzy. Girls are never doctors, and although they may be nurses or librarians or teachers, they are never principals. There seemed to be only one children's book about mothers who work, and it concludes that what mothers love "best of all" is "being your very own Mommy and coming home to you." And although this is no doubt true of many daddies as well, no book about working fathers has ever found it necessary to apologize for working in quite the same way.

As children grow older, more explicit sex-role training is introduced. Boys are encouraged to take more of an interest in mathematics and science. Boys, not girls, are usually given chemistry sets and microscopes for Christmas. Moreover, all children quickly learn that mommy is proud to be a moron when it comes to math and science, whereas daddy is a little ashamed if he doesn't know all about such things. When a young boy returns from school all excited about biology, he is almost certain to be encouraged to think of becoming a physician. A girl with similar enthusiasm is usually told that she might want to consider nurse's training later on, so she can have "an interesting job to fall back upon in case —God forbid—she ever needs to support herself." A very different kind of encouragement. And any girl who doggedly persists in her enthusiasm for science is likely to find her parents as horrified by the prospect of a permanent love affair with physics as they would be either by the prospect of an interracial marriage or, horror of horrors, no marriage at all. Indeed, our graduate women report that their families seem convinced that the menopause must come at age 23.

These socialization practices take their toll. When they apply for college, boys and girls are about equal on verbal aptitude tests, but boys score significantly higher on mathematical aptitude tests—about 60 points higher on the College Board Exams, for example (Brown, 1965). Moreover, for those who are convinced that this is due to female hormones, it is relevant to know that girls improve their mathematical performance if the problems are simply reworded so that they deal with cooking and gardening, even though the abstract reasoning required for solution remains exactly the same (Milton, 1958). That's not hormones! Clearly, what has been undermined is not a woman's mathematical ability, but rather her confidence in that ability.

But these effects in mathematics and science are only part of the story. The most conspicuous outcome of all is that the majority of America's women become full-time homemakers. And of those who do work, nearly 80% end up in dead-end jobs as clerical workers, service workers, factory workers or sales clerks. Again, it is this "homogenization" of America's women which is the major consequence of America's sex-role ideology.

The important point is not that the role of homemaker is necessarily inferior, but rather that our society is managing to consign a large segment of its population to the role of homemaker—either with or without a dead-end job—solely on the basis of sex just as inexorably as it has in the past consigned the individual with a black skin to the role of janitor or domestic. The important point is that in spite of their unique identities, the majority of American women end up in virtually the *same* role.

The socialization of the American male has closed off certain options for him, too. Men are discouraged from developing certain desirable traits such as tenderness and sensitivity, just as surely as women are discouraged from being assertive and, alas, "too bright." Young boys are encouraged to be incompetent at cooking and certainly child care, just as surely as young girls are urged to be incompetent at math and science. The elimination of sex-role stereotyping implies that each individual would be encouraged to "do his own thing." Men and women would no longer be stereotyped by society's definitions of masculine and feminine. If sensitivity, emotionality, and warmth are desirable *human* characteristics, then they are desirable for men as well as for women. If independence, assertiveness, and serious intellectual commitment are desirable *human* characteristics, then they are desirable for women as well as for men. Thus, we are not implying that men have all the goodies and that women can obtain self-fulfillment by acting like men. That is hardly the utopia implied by today's

feminist movement. Rather, we envision a society which raises its children so flexibly and with sufficient respect for the integrity of individual uniqueness that some men might emerge with the motivation, the ability, and the opportunity to stay home and raise children without bearing the stigma of being peculiar. Indeed, if homemaking is as glamorous as women's magazines and television commercials would have us believe, then men, too, should have that option. And even if homemaking isn't all that glamorous, it would probably still be more fulfilling for some men than the jobs in which they now find themselves forced because of their role as breadwinner. Thus, it is true that a man's options are also limited by our society's sex-role ideology, but as the "predictability test" reveals, it is still the women in our society whose identity is rendered irrelevant by America's socialization practices.

Further Psychological Barriers

But what of the woman who arrives at age 21 still motivated to be challenged and fulfilled by a growing career? Is she free to choose a career if she cares to do so? Or is there something standing even in her way?

There is. Even the woman who has managed to finesse society's attempt to rob her of her career motivations is likely to find herself blocked by society's trump card: the feeling that one cannot have a career and be a successful woman simultaneously. A competent and motivated woman is thus caught in a double-bind which few men have ever faced. She must worry not only about failure, but also about success.

This conflict was strikingly revealed in a study which required college women to complete the following story: "After first-term finals, Anne finds herself at the top of her medical-school class" (Horner, 1969). The stories were then examined for concern about the negative consequences of success. The women in this study all had high intellectual ability and histories of academic success. They were the very women who could have successful careers. And yet, over two-thirds of their stories revealed a clear-cut inability to cope with the concept of a feminine, yet career-oriented, woman.

The most common "fear-of-success" stories showed fears of social rejection as a result of success. The women in this group showed anxiety about becoming unpopular, unmarriageable, and lonely:

> Anne starts proclaiming her surprise and joy. Her fellow classmates are so disgusted with her behavior that they jump on her in a body and beat her. She is maimed for life.
>
> Anne is an acn faced bookworm. . . . She studies twelve hours a day, and lives at home to save money. "Well, it certainly paid off. All the Friday and Saturday nights without dates, fun—I'll be the best women doctor alive." And yet a twinge of sadness comes through—she wonders what she really has. . . .
>
> Anne doesn't want to be number one in her class. . . . She feels she shouldn't rank so high because of social reasons. She drops to ninth and then marries the boy who graduates number one.

In the second "fear-of-success" category were stories in which the women seemed concerned about definitions of womanhood. These stories expressed guilt and despair over success and doubts about their femininity and normality:

> Unfortunately Anne no longer feels so certain that she really wants to be a doctor. She is worried about herself and wonders if perhaps she is not normal. . . . Anne decides not to continue with her medical work but to take courses that have deeper personal meaning for her.
>
> Anne feels guilty. . . . She will finally have a nervous breakdown and quit medical school and marry a successful young doctor.

A third group of stories could not even face up to the conflict between having a career and being a woman. These stories simply denied the possibility that any woman could be so successful:

> Anne is a code name for a nonexistent person created by a group of med students. They take turns writing for Anne. . . .
>
> Anne is really happy she's on top, though Tom is higher than she—though that's as it should be. Anne doesn't mind Tom winning.
>
> Anne is talking to her counselor. Counselor says she will make a fine nurse.

By way of contrast, here is a typical story written not about Anne, but about John:

> John has worked very hard and his long hours of study have paid off . . . He is thinking about his girl, Cheri, whom he will marry at the end of med school. He realizes he can give her all the things she desires after he becomes established. He will go on in med school and be successful in the long run.

Nevertheless, there were a few women in the study who welcomed the prospect of success:

> Anne is quite a lady—not only is she top academically, but she is liked and admired by her fellow students—quite a trick in a man-dominated field. She is brilliant—but she is also a woman. She will continue to be at or near the top. And . . . always a lady.

Hopefully the day is approaching when as many "Anne" stories as "John" stories will have happy endings. But notice that even this story finds it necessary to affirm repeatedly that femininity is not necessarily destroyed by accomplishment. One would never encounter a comparable story written about John who, although brilliant and at the top of his class, is "still a man, still a man, still a man."

It seems unlikely that anyone in our society would view these "fear-of-success" stories as portraits of mental health. But even our concept of mental health has been distorted by America's sex-role stereotypes. Here we must indict our own profession of psychology. A recent survey of seventy-nine clinically-trained psychologists, psychiatrists, and social workers, both male and female, revealed a double standard of mental health (Broverman, Broverman, Clarkson, Rosenkrantz, & Vogel, 1970). That is, even professional clinicians have two different concepts of mental health, one for men and one for women; and these concepts parallel the sex-role stereotypes prevalent in our society. Thus, according to these clinicians, a woman is to be regarded as healthier and more mature if she is: more submissive, less independent, less adventurous, more easily influenced, less aggressive, less competitive, more excitable in minor crises, more susceptible to hurt feelings, more emotional, more conceited about her appearance, less objective, and more antagonistic toward math and science! But this was the very same description which these clinicians used to characterize an unhealthy, immature man or an unhealthy, immature adult (sex unspecified)! The equation is clear: Mature woman equals immature adult.

Given this concept of a mature woman, is it any wonder that few women ever aspire toward challenging and fulfilling careers? In order to have a career, a woman will probably need to become relatively more dominant, independent, adventurous, aggressive, competitive, and objective, and relatively less excitable, emotional and conceited than our ideal of femininity requires. If she were a man (or an adult, sex unspecified), these would all be considered positive traits. But because she is a woman, these same traits will bring her disapproval. She must then either be strong enough to have her "femininity" questioned; or she must behave in the prescribed feminine manner and accept second-class status, as an adult and as a professional.

And, of course, should a woman faced with this conflict seek professional help, hoping to summon the strength she will need to pursue her career goals, the advice she is likely to receive will be of virtually no use. For, as this study reveals, even professional counselors have been contaminated by the sex-role ideology.

It is frequently argued that a 21-year-old woman is perfectly free to choose a career if she cares to do so. No one is standing in her way. But this argument conveniently overlooks the fact that our society has spent 20 years carefully marking the woman's ballot for her, and so it has nothing to lose in that 21st year by pretending to let her cast it for the alternative of her choice. Society has controlled not her alternatives (although discrimination does do that), but more importantly, it has controlled her motivation to choose any but one of those alternatives. The so-called "freedom-to-choose" is illusory, and it cannot be invoked to justify a society which controls the woman's motivation to choose.

Biological Considerations

Up to this point, we have argued that the differing life patterns of men and women in our society can be chiefly accounted for by cultural conditioning. The most common counter argument to this view, of course, is the biological one. The biological argument suggests that there may really be inborn differences between men and women in, say, independence or mathematical ability. Or that there may be biological factors beyond the fact that women can become pregnant and nurse children which uniquely dictate that they, but not men, should stay home all day and shun serious outside commitment. What this argument suggests is that maybe female hormones really are responsible somehow. One difficulty with this argument, of course, is that female hormones would have to be different in the Soviet Union, where one-third of the engineers and 75% of the physicians are women (Dodge, 1966). In America, by way of contrast, women constitute less than 1% of the engineers and only 7% of the physicians. Female physiology *is* different, and it may account for some of the psychological differences between the sexes, but America's sex-role ideology still seems primarily responsible for the fact that so few women emerge from childhood with the motivation to seek out any role beyond the one that our society dictates.

But even if there really were biological differences between the sexes along these lines, the biological argument would still be irrelevant. The reason can best be illustrated with an analogy.

Suppose that every black American boy were to be socialized to become a jazz musician on the assumption that he has a "natural" talent in that direction; or suppose that parents and counselors should subtly discourage him from other pursuits because it is considered "inappropriate" for black men to become physicians or physicists. Most Americans would disapprove. But suppose that it *could* be demonstrated that black Americans, *on the average,* did possess an inborn better sense of rhythm than white Americans. Would *that* justify ignoring the unique characteristics of a *particular* black youngster from the very beginning and specifically socializing him to become a musician? We don't think so. Similarly, as long as woman's socialization does not nurture her uniqueness, but treats her only as a member of a group on the basis of some assumed *average* characteristic, she will not be prepared to realize her own potential in the way that the values of individuality and self-fulfillment imply that she should.

THE PRESUMED INCOMPATIBILITY OF FAMILY AND CAREER

If we were to ask the average American woman why she is not pursuing a full-time career, she would probably not say that discrimination had discouraged her; nor would she be likely to recognize the pervasive effects of her own sex-role conditioning. What she probably would say is that a career, no matter how desirable, is simply incompatible with the role of wife and mother.

As recently as the turn of the century, and in less technological societies today, this incompatibility between career and family was, in fact, decisive. Women died in their forties and they were pregnant or nursing during most of their adult lives. Moreover, the work that a less technological society requires places a premium on mobility and physical strength, neither of which a pregnant woman has a great deal of. Thus, the historical division of labor between the sexes—the man away at work and the woman at home with the children—was a biological necessity. Today it is not.

Today, the work that our technological society requires is primarily mental in nature; women have virtually complete control over their reproductive lives; and most important of all, the average American woman now lives to age 74 and has her last child before age 30. This means that by the time a woman is 35 or so, her children all have more important things to do with their daytime hours than spend them entertaining some adult woman who has nothing fulfilling to do during the entire second half of her life span.

But social forms have a way of outliving the necessities which gave rise to them. And today's female adolescent continues to plan for a 19th century life style in a 20th century world. A Gallup poll has found that young women give no thought whatever to life after forty (Gallup & Hill, 1962). They plan to graduate from high school, perhaps go to college, and then get married. Period!

The Woman As Wife

At some level, of course, this kind of planning is "realistic." Because most women do grow up to be wives and mothers, and because, for many women, this means that they will be leaving the labor force during the child-rearing years, a career is not really feasible. After all, a career involves long-term commitment and perhaps some sacrifice on the part of the family. Furthermore, as every "successful" woman knows, a wife's appropriate role is to encourage her husband in *his* career. The "good" wife puts her husband through school, endures the family's early financial difficulties without a whimper, and, if her husband's career should suddenly dictate a move to another city, she sees to it that the transition is accomplished as painlessly as possible. The good wife is selfless. And to be seriously concerned about one's own career is selfish—if one is female, that is. With these kinds of constraints imposed upon the work life of the married woman, perhaps it would be "unrealistic" for her to seriously aspire toward a career rather than a job.

There is some evidence of discontent among these "selfless" women, however. A 1962 Gallup poll (Gallop & Hill, 1962) revealed that only 10% of American women would want their daughters to live their lives the way they did. These mothers wanted their daughters to get more education and to marry later. And a 1970 study of women married to top Chicago-area business and professional men (Ringo, 1970) revealed that if these women could live their lives over again, they would pursue careers.

Accordingly, the traditional conception of the husband-wife relationship is now being challenged, not so much because of this widespread discontent among older, married women, but because it violates two of the most basic values of today's college generation. These values concern personal growth, on the one hand, and interpersonal relationships on the other. The first of these emphasizes individuality and self-fulfillment; the second stresses openness, honesty, and equality in all human relationships.

Because they see the traditional male-female relationship as incompatible with these basic values, today's young people are experimenting with alternatives to the traditional marriage pattern. Although a few are testing out ideas like communal living, most seem to be searching for satisfactory modifications of the husband-wife relationship, either in or out of the context of marriage. An increasing number of young people claim to be seeking fully equalitarian relationships and they cite examples like the following:

> Both my wife and I earned college degrees in our respective disciplines. I turned down a superior job offer in Oregon and accepted a slightly less desirable position in New York where my wife would have more opportunities for part-time work in her specialty. Although I would have preferred to live in a suburb, we purchased a home near my wife's job so that she could have an office at home where she could be when the children returned from school. Because my wife earns a good salary, she can easily afford to pay a housekeeper to do her major household chores. My wife and I share all other tasks around the house equally. For example, she cooks the meals, but I do the laundry for her and help her with many of her other household tasks.

Without questioning the basic happiness of such a marriage or its appropriateness for many couples, we can legitimately ask if such a marriage is, in fact, an instance of interpersonal equality. Have all the hidden assumptions about the woman's "natural" role really been eliminated? Have our visionary students really exorcised the traditional ideology as they claim? There is a very simple test. If the marriage is truly equalitarian, then its description should retain the same flavor and tone even if the roles of the husband and wife were to be reversed:

> Both my husband and I earned college degrees in our respective disciplines. I turned down a superior job offer in Oregon and accepted a slightly less desirable position in New York where my husband would have more opportunities for part-time work in his speciality. Although I would have preferred to live in a suburb, we purchased a home near my husband's job so that he could have an office at home where he would be when the children returned from school. Because my husband earns a good salary, he can easily afford to pay a housekeeper to do his major household chores. My husband and I share all other tasks around the house equally. For example, he cooks the meals, but I do the laundry for him and help him with many of his other household tasks.

Somehow it sounds different, yet only the pronouns have been changed to protect the powerful! Certainly no one would ever mistake the marriage *just* described as equalitarian or even very desirable, and thus it becomes apparent that the ideology about the woman's "natural" place unconsciously permeates the entire fabric of such "pseudo-equalitarian" marriages. It is true the wife gains some measure of equality when she can have a career rather than have a job and when her career can influence the final place of residence. But why is it the unquestioned assumption that the husband's career solely determines the initial set of alternatives that are to be considered? Why is it the wife who automatically seeks the part-time position? Why is it *her* housekeeper rather than *their* housekeeper? Why *her* household tasks? And so forth throughout the entire relationship.

The important point is not that such marriages are bad or that their basic assumptions of inequality produce unhappy, frustrated women. Quite the contrary. It is the very happiness of the wives in such marriages that reveals society's smashing success in socializing its women. It is a measure of the distance our society must yet traverse toward the goal of full equality that such marriages are widely characterized as utopian and fully equalitarian. It is a mark of how well the woman has been kept in her place that the husband in such a marriage is almost always idolized by women, including his wife. Why? Because he "permits her" to squeeze a career into the interstices of their marriage as long as his own career is not unduly inconvenienced. Thus is the white man blessed for exercising his power benignly while his "natural" right to that power forever remains unquestioned. Such is the subtlety of America's ideology about women.

In fact, however, even these "benign" inequities are now being challenged. More and more young couples really are entering marriages of full equality, marriages in which both partners pursue careers or outside commitments which carry equal weight when all important decisions are to be made, marriages in which both husband and wife accept some compromise in the growth of their respective careers for their mutual partnership. Certainly such marriages have more tactical difficulties than more traditional ones: It is simply more difficult to coordinate two independent lives rather than one-and-a-half. The point is that it is not possible to predict ahead of time *on the basis of sex,* who will be doing the compromising at any given point of decision.

It should be clear that the man or woman who places career above all else ought not to enter an equalitarian marriage. The man would do better to marry a traditional wife, a wife who will make whatever sacrifices his career necessitates. The woman who places career above all else would be better—in our present society—to remain single. For an equalitarian marriage is not designed for extra efficiency, but for double fulfillment.

The Woman As Mother

In all marriages, whether traditional, pseudo-equalitarian or fully-equalitarian, the real question surrounding a mother's career will probably continue to be the well-being of the children. All parents want to be certain that they are doing the very best for their children and that they are not depriving them in any important way, either materially or psychologically. What this has meant recently in most families that could afford it was that mother would devote herself to the children on a full-time basis. Women have been convinced—by their mothers and by the so-called experts—that there is something wrong with them if they even want to do otherwise.

For example, according to Dr. Spock (1963), any women who finds full-time motherhood unfulfilling is showing "a residue of difficult relationships in her own childhood." If a vacation doesn't solve the problem, then she is probably having emotional problems which can be relieved "through regular counseling in a family social agency, or if severe, through psychiatric treatment . . . Any mother of a pre-school child who is considering a job should discuss the issue with a social worker before making her decision." The message is clear: If you don't feel that your two-year-old is a stimulating, full-time, companion, then you are probably neurotic.

In fact, research does not support the view that children suffer in any way when mother works. Although it came as a surprise to most re-searchers in the area, maternal employment in and of itself does not seem to have any negative effects on the children; and part-time work actually seems to benefit the children. Children of working mothers are no more likely than children of non-working mothers to be delinquent or nervous or withdrawn or antisocial; they are no more likely to show neurotic symptoms; they are no more likely to perform poorly in school; and they are no more likely to feel deprived of their mothers' love. Daughters of working mothers are more likely to want to work themselves, and, when asked to name the one woman in the world that they most admire, daughters of working mothers are more likely to name their own mothers! (Nye & Hoffman, 1963). This is one finding that we wish every working woman in America could hear, because the other thing that is true of almost every working mother is that she *thinks* she is hurting her children and she feels guilty. In fact, research has shown that the worst mothers are those who would like to work, but who stay home out of a sense of duty (Yarrow, Scott, de Leeuw, & Heinig, 1962). The major conclusion from all the research is really this: What matters is the quality of a mother's relationship with her children, not the time of day it happens to be administered. This conclusion should come as no surprise; successful fathers have been demonstrating it for years. Some fathers are great, some fathers stink, and they're all at work at least eight hours a day.

Similarly, it is true that the quality of substitute care that children receive while their parents are at work also matters. Young children do need security; and research has shown that it is not good to have a constant turnover of parent-substitutes, a rapid succession of changing baby-sitters or housekeepers (Maccoby, 1958). Clearly, this is why the establishment of child care centers is vitally important at the moment. This is why virtually every woman's group in the country, no matter how conservative or how radical, is in agreement on this one issue: that child care centers ought to be available to those who need them.

Once again, it is relevant to emphasize that child care centers, like the other reforms advocated, are not merely for the benefit of middle-class women who wish to pursue professional careers. Of the 31 million women in the labor force, nearly 40% of them are working mothers. In 1960, mothers constituted more than one-third of the total woman labor force. In March, 1971, more than 1 out of 3 working mothers (4.3 million of them) had children under 6 years of age, and about half of these had children under 3 years of age. And most of these women in the labor force—like most men—work because they cannot afford to do otherwise. Moreover, they cannot currently deduct the full costs of child care as a business expense as the executive can often deduct an expensive car. At the moment, the majority of these working women must simply "make do" with whatever child care arrangements they can manage. Only 6% of their children under 6 years of age currently receive group care in child care centers. *This* is why child-care centers are a central issue of the new feminist movement. This is why they are not just an additional luxury for the middle-class family with a woman who wants to pursue a professional career.

But even the woman who is educationally and economically in a position to pursue a career must feel free to utilize these alternative arrangements for child care. For once again, America's sex-role ideology intrudes. Many people still assume that if a woman wants a full-time career, then children must be unimportant to her. But of course, no one makes this assumption about her husband. No one assumes that a father's interest in his career necessarily precludes a deep and abiding affection for his children or a vital interest in their development. Once again, America applies a double standard of judgment. Suppose that a father of small children suddenly lost his wife. No matter how much he loved his children, no one would expect him to sacrifice his career in order to stay home with them on a full-time basis—even if he had an independent source of income. No one would charge him with selfishness or lack of parental feeling if he sought professional care for his children during the day.

It is here that full equality between husband and wife assumes its ultimate importance. The fully equalitarian marriage abolishes this double standard and extends the same freedom to the mother. The equalitarian marriage provides the framework for both husband and wife to pursue careers which are challenging and fulfilling and, at the same time, to participate equally in the pleasures and responsibilities of child-rearing. Indeed, it is the equalitarian marriage which has the potential of giving children the love and concern of two parents rather than one. And it is the equalitarian marriage which has the most potential for giving parents the challenge and fulfillment of two worlds—family and career—rather than one.

In addition to providing this potential for equalized child care, a truly equalitarian marriage embraces a more general division of labor which satisfies what we like to call "the roommate test." That is, the labor is divided just as it is when two men or two women room together in college or set up a bachelor apartment together. Errands and domestic chores are assigned by preference, agreement, flipping a coin, alternated, given to hired help, or—perhaps most often the case—left undone.

It is significant that today's young people, so many of whom live precisely this way prior to marriage, find this kind of arrangement within marriage so foreign to their thinking. Consider an analogy. Suppose that a white male college student decided to room or set up a bachelor apartment with a black male friend. Surely the typical white student would not blithely assume that his black roommate was to handle all the domestic chores. Nor would his conscience allow him to do so even in the unlikely event that his roommate would say: "No, that's okay. I like doing housework. I'd be happy to do it." We suspect that the typical white student would still not be comfortable if he took advantage of this offer because he and America have finally realized that he would be taking advantage of the fact that such a roommate had been socialized by our society to be "happy" with such obvious inequity. But change this hypothetical black roommate to a female marriage partner, and somehow the student's conscience goes to sleep. At most it is quickly tranquilized by the comforting thought that "she is happiest when she is ironing for her loved one." Such is the power of an unconscious ideology.

Of course, it may well be that she *is* happiest when she is ironing for her loved one.

Such, indeed, is the power of an unconscious ideology.

REFERENCES

Bird, C. *Born female: the high cost of keeping women down*. New York: Pocket Books, 1969

Broverman, I. K., Broverman, D. M., Clarkson, F. E, Rosenkrantz, P. S., & Vogel, S. R. Sex-role stereotypes and clinical judgments of mental health. *Journal of Consulting and Clinical Psychology*, 1970, *34*, 1–7.

Brown, R. *Social psychology*. New York: Free Press, 1965.

Dodge, N. D. *Women in the Soviet economy*. Baltimore: Johns Hopkins Press, 1966.

Fisher, E. The second sex, junior division. *The New York Times Book Review*, May, 1970.

Gallup, G., & Hill, E. The American woman. *The Saturday Evening Post*, Dec. 22, 1962, pp. 15–32.

Goldberg, P. Are women prejudiced against women? *Transaction*, April, 1968, *5*, 28–30.

Goldberg, S., & Lewis, M. Play behavior in the year-old infant: early sex differences. *Child Development*, 1969, *40*, 21–31.

Horner, M. S. Fail: bright women. *Psychology Today*, November, 1969.

Maccoby, E. E. Effects upon children on their mothers' outside employment. In *Work in the lives of married women*. New York: Columbia University Press, 1958.

Milton, G. A. Sex differences in problem solving as a function of role appropriateness of the problem content. *Psychological Reports*, 1959, *5*, 705–708.

Nye, F. I., & Hoffman, L. W. *The employed mother in America*. Chicago: Rand McNally, 1963.

Ringo, M. The well-placed wife. Unpublished manuscript, John Paisios & Associates, 332 South Michigan Ave., Chicago, Illinois. 60604.

Spock, B. Should mothers work? *Ladies' Home Journal*, February, 1963.

Terman, L. M., & Oden, M. H. *Genetic studies of genius, V. The gifted group at mid-life: Thirty-five years' follow-up of the superior child*. Stanford, California: Stanford University Press, 1959.

Thoman, E. B., Leiderman, P. H., & Olson, J. P. Neonate-mother interaction during breast feeding. *Developmental Psychology*, 1972, *6*, 110–118.

U.S. Department of Labor, Wage and Labor Standards Administration, Women's Bureau. Fact sheet on the earnings gap, February, 1970.

U.S. Department of Labor, Wage and Labor Standards Administration, Women's Bureau. *Handbook on women workers*, 1969. Bulletin 294.

Yarrow, M. R., Scott, P., de Leeuw, L., & Heinig, D. Child-rearing in families of working and non-working mothers. *Sociometry*, 1962, *25*, 122–140.

The Double Standard of Aging

Susan Sontag

"HOW OLD are you?" The person asking the question is anybody. The respondent is a woman, a woman "of a certain age," as the French say discreetly. That age might be anywhere from her early twenties to her late fifties. If the question is impersonal—routine information requested when she applies for a driver's license, a credit card, a passport—she will probably force herself to answer truthfully. Filling out a marriage license application, if her future husband is even slightly her junior, she may long to subtract a few years; probably she won't. Competing for a job, her chances often partly depend on being the "right age," and if hers isn't right, she will lie if she

Reprinted by permission of *Saturday Review*. Copyright © 1972 *Saturday Review*. From *Saturday Review*, September 23, 1972

thinks she can get away with it. Making her first visit to a new doctor, perhaps feeling particularly vulnerable at the moment she's asked, she will probably hurry through the correct answer. But if the question is only what people call personal—if she's asked by a new friend, a casual acquaintance, a neighbor's child, a coworker in an office, store, factory—her response is harder to predict. She may side-step the question with a joke or refuse it with playful indignation. "Don't you know you're not supposed to ask a woman her age?" Or, hesitating a moment, embarrassed but defiant, she may tell the truth. Or she may lie. But neither truth, evasion, nor lie relieves the unpleasantness of that question. For a woman to be obliged to state her age, after "a certain age," is always a miniature ordeal.

If the question comes from a woman, she will feel less threatened than if it comes from a man. Other women are, after all, comrades in sharing the same potential for humiliation. She will be less arch, less coy. But she probably still dislikes answering and may not tell the truth. Bureaucratic formalities excepted, whoever asks a woman this question—after "a certain age"—is ignoring a taboo and possibly being impolite or downright hostile. Almost everyone acknowledges that once she passes an age that is, actually, quite young, a woman's exact age ceases to be a legitimate target of curiosity. After childhood the year of a woman's birth becomes her secret, her private property. It is something of a dirty secret. To answer truthfully is always indiscreet.

The discomfort a woman feels each time she tells her age is quite independent of the anxious awareness of human mortality that everyone has, from time to time. There is a normal sense in which nobody, men and women alike, relishes growing older. After thirty-five any mention of one's age carries with it the reminder that one is probably closer to the end of one's life than to the beginning. There is nothing unreasonable in that anxiety. Nor is there any abnormality in the anguish and anger that people who are really old, in their seventies and eighties, feel about the implacable waning of their powers, physical and mental. Advanced age is undeniably a trial, however stoically it may be endured. It is a shipwreck, no matter with what courage elderly people insist

on continuing the voyage. But the objective, sacred pain of old age is of another order than the subjective, profane pain of aging. Old age is a genuine ordeal, one that men and women undergo in a similar way. Growing older is mainly an ordeal of the imagination—a moral disease, a social pathology—intrinsic to which is the fact that it afflicts women much more than men. It is particularly women who experience growing older (everything that comes *before* one is actually old) with such distaste and even shame.

The emotional privileges this society confers upon youth stir up some anxiety about getting older in everybody. All modern urbanized societies—unlike tribal, rural societies—condescend to the values of maturity and heap honors on the joys of youth. This revaluation of the life cycle in favor of the young brilliantly serves a secular society whose idols are ever-increasing industrial productivity and the unlimited cannibalization of nature. Such a society must create a new sense of the rhythms of life in order to incite people to buy more, to consume and throw away faster. People let the direct awareness they have of their needs, of what really gives them pleasure, be overruled by commercialized *images* of happiness and personal well-being; and, in this imagery designed to stimulate ever more avid levels of consumption, the most popular metaphor for happiness is "youth." (I would insist that it is a metaphor, not a literal description. Youth is a metaphor for energy, restless mobility, appetite: for the state of "wanting.") This equating of well-being with youth makes everyone naggingly aware of exact age—one's own and that of other people. In primitive and premodern societies people attach much less importance to dates. When lives are divided into long periods with stable responsibilities and steady ideals (and hypocrisies), the exact number of years someone has lived becomes a trivial fact; there is hardly any reason to mention, even to know, the year in which one was born. Most people in nonindustrial societies are not sure exactly how old they are. People in industrial societies are haunted by numbers. They take an almost obsessional interest in keeping the score card of aging, convinced that anything above a low total is some kind of bad news. In an era in which people actually live longer and longer, what now amounts to the latter *two-thirds* of everyone's life is shadowed by a poignant apprehension of unremitting loss.

The prestige of youth afflicts everyone in this society to some degree. Men, too, are prone to periodic bouts of depression about aging—for instance, when feeling insecure or unfulfilled or insufficiently rewarded in their jobs. But men rarely panic about aging in the way women often do. Getting older is less profoundly wounding for a man, for in addition to the propaganda for youth that puts both men and women on the defensive as they age, there is a double standard about aging that denounces women with special severity. Society is much more permissive about aging in men, as it is more tolerant of the sexual infidelities of husbands. Men are "allowed" to age, without penalty, in several ways that women are not.

This society offers even fewer rewards for aging to women than it does to men. Being physically attractive counts much more in a woman's life than in a man's, but beauty, identified, as it is for women, with youthfulness, does not stand up well to age. Exceptional mental powers can increase with age, but women are rarely encouraged to develop their minds above dilettante standards. Because the wisdom considered the special province of women is "eternal," an age-old, intuitive knowledge about the emotions to which a repertoire of facts, worldly experience, and the methods of rational analysis have nothing to contribute, living a long time does not promise women an increase in wisdom either. The private skills expected of women are exercised early and, with the exception of a talent for making love, are not the kind that enlarge with experience. "Masculinity" is identified with competence, autonomy, self-control—qualities which the disappearance of youth does not threaten. Competence in most of the activities expected from men, physical sports excepted, increases with age. "Femininity" is identified with incompetence, helplessness, passivity, noncompetitiveness, being nice. Age does not improve these qualities.

Middle-class men feel diminished by aging, even while still young, if they have not yet shown distinction in their careers or made a lot of money. (And any tendencies they have toward hypochondria will get worse in middle age, focusing with particular nervousness on the specter of heart attacks and the loss of virility.) Their aging crisis is linked to that terrible pressure on men to be "successful" that precisely defines their membership in the middle class. Women rarely feel anxious about their age because they haven't succeeded at something. The work that women do outside the home rarely counts as a form of achievement, only as a way of earning money; most employment available to women mainly exploits the training they have been receiving since early childhood to be servile, to be both supportive and parasitical, to be unadventurous. They can have menial, low-skilled jobs in light industries, which offer as feeble a criterion of success as housekeeping. They can be secretaries, clerks, sales personnel, maids, research assistants, waitresses, social workers, prostitutes, nurses, teachers, telephone operators—public transcriptions of the servicing and nurturing roles that women have in family life. Women fill very few executive posts, are rarely found suitable for large corporate or political responsibilities, and form only a tiny contingent in the liberal professions (apart from teaching). They are virtually barred from jobs that involve an expert, intimate relation with machines or an aggressive use of the body, or that carry any physical risk or sense of adventure. The jobs this society deems appropriate to women are auxiliary, "calm" activities that do not compete with, but aid, what men do. Besides being less well paid, most work women do has a lower ceiling of advancement and gives meager outlet to normal wishes to be powerful. All outstanding work by women in this society is voluntary; most women are too inhibited by the social disapproval attached to their being ambitious and aggressive. Inevitably, women are exempted from the dreary panic of middle-aged men whose "achievements" seem paltry, who feel stuck on the job ladder or fear being pushed off it by someone younger. But they are also denied most of the real satisfactions that men derive from work—satisfactions that often do increase with age.

The double standard about aging shows up most brutally in the conventions of sexual feeling, which presuppose a disparity between men and women that operates permanently to women's disadvantage. In the accepted course of events a woman anywhere from her late teens through her middle twenties can expect to attract a man more or less her own age. (Ideally, he should be at least slightly older.) They marry and raise a family. But if her husband starts an affair after some years of marriage, he customarily does so with a woman much younger than his wife. Suppose, when both husband and wife are already in their late forties or early fifties, they divorce. The husband has an excellent chance of getting married again, probably to a younger woman. His ex-wife finds it difficult to remarry. Attracting a second husband younger than herself is improbable; even to find someone her own age she has to be lucky, and she will probably have to settle for a man considerably older than herself, in his sixties or seventies. Women become sexually ineligible much earlier than men do. A man, even an ugly man, can remain eligible well into old age. He is an acceptable mate for a young, attractive woman. Women, even good-looking women, become ineligible (except as partners of very old men) at a much younger age.

Thus, for most women, aging means a humiliating process of gradual sexual disqualification. Since women are considered maximally eligible in early youth, after which their sexual value drops steadily, even young women feel themselves in a desperate race against the calendar. They are old as soon as they are no longer very young. In late adolescence some girls are already worrying about getting married. Boys and young men have little reason to anticipate trouble because of aging. What makes men desirable to women is by no means tied to youth. On the contrary, getting older tends (for several decades) to operate in men's favor, since their value as lovers and husbands is set more by what they do than how they look. Many men have more success romantically at forty than they did at twenty or twenty-five; fame, money, and, above all, power are sexually enhancing. (A woman who has won power in a competitive profession or business career is considered less, rather than more, desirable. Most men confess themselves intimidated or turned off sexually by such a woman, obviously because she is harder to treat as just a sexual "object.") As they age, men may start feeling anxious about actual sexual performance, worry-

ing about a loss of sexual vigor or even impotence, but their sexual eligibility is not abridged simply by getting older. Men stay sexually eligible as long as they can make love. Women are at a disadvantage because their sexual candidacy depends on meeting certain much stricter "conditions" related to looks and age.

Since women are imagined to have much more limited sexual lives than men do, a woman who has never married is pitied. She was not found acceptable, and it is assumed that her life continues to confirm her unacceptability. Her presumed lack of sexual opportunity is embarrassing. A man who remains a bachelor is judged much less crudely. It is assumed that he, at any age, still has a sexual life—or the chance of one. For men there is no destiny equivalent to the humiliating condition of being an old maid, a spinster. "Mr.," a cover from infancy to senility, precisely exempts men from the stigma that attaches to any woman, no longer young, who is still "Miss." (That women are divided into "Miss" and "Mrs.," which calls unrelenting attention to the situation of each woman with respect to marriage, reflects the belief that being single or married is much more decisive for a woman than it is for a man.)

For a woman who is no longer very young, there is certainly some relief when she has finally been able to marry. Marriage soothes the sharpest pain she feels about the passing years. But her anxiety never subsides completely, for she knows that should she re-enter the sexual market at a later date—because of divorce, or the death of her husband, or the need for erotic adventure—she must do so under a handicap far greater than any man of her age (*whatever* her age may be) and regardless of how good-looking she is. Her achievements, if she has a career, are no asset. The calendar is the final arbiter.

To be sure, the calendar is subject to some variations from country to country. In Spain, Portugal, and the Latin American countries, the age at which most women are ruled physically undesirable comes earlier than in the United States. In France it is somewhat later. French conventions of sexual feeling make a quasi-official place for the woman between thirty-five and forty-five. Her role is to initiate an inexperienced or timid young man, after which she is, of course, replaced by a young girl. (Colette's novella *Chéri* is the best-known account in fiction of such a love affair: biographies of Balzac relate a well-documented example from real life.) This sexual myth does make turning forty somewhat easier for French women. But there is no difference in any of these countries in the basic attitudes that disqualify women sexually much earlier than men.

Aging also varies according to social class. Poor people look old much earlier in their lives than do rich people. But anxiety about aging is certainly more common, and more acute, among middle-class and rich women than among working-class women. Economically disadvantaged women in this society are more fatalistic about aging: they can't afford to fight the cosmetic battle as long or as tenaciously. Indeed, nothing so clearly indicates the fictional nature of this crisis than the fact that women who keep their youthful appearance the longest—women who lead unstrenuous, physically sheltered lives, who eat balanced meals, who can afford good medical care, who have few or no children—are those who feel the defeat of age most keenly. Aging is much more a social judgment than a biological eventuality. Far more extensive than the hard sense of loss suffered during menopause (which, with increased longevity, tends to arrive later and later) is the depression about aging, which may not be set off by any real event in a woman's life, but is a recurrent state of "possession" of her imagination, ordained by society—that is, ordained by the way this society limits how women feel free to imagine themselves.

There is a model account of the aging crisis in Richard Strauss's sentimental-ironic opera *Der Rosenkavalier,* whose heroine is a wealthy and glamorous married woman who decides to renounce romance. After a night with her adoring young lover, the Marschallin has a sudden, unexpected confrontation with herself. It is toward the end of Act I; Octavian has just left. Alone in her bedroom she sits at her dressing table, as she does every morning. It is the daily ritual of self-appraisal practiced by every woman. She looks at herself and, appalled, begins to weep. Her youth is over. Note that the Marschallin does not discover, looking in the mirror, that she is ugly. She is as beautiful as ever. The Marschallin's discovery is moral—that is, it is a discovery of her imagina-tion; it is nothing she actually *sees*. Nevertheless, her discovery is no less devastating. Bravely, she makes her painful, gallant decision. She will arrange for her beloved Octavian to fall in love with a girl his own age. She must be realistic. She is no longer eligible. She is now "the old Marschallin."

Strauss wrote the opera in 1910. Contemporary operagoers are rather shocked when they discover that the libretto indicates that the Marschallin is all of thirty-four years old; today the role is generally sung by a soprano well into her forties or in her fifties. Acted by an attractive singer of thirty-four, the Marschallin's sorrow would seem merely neurotic, or even ridiculous. Few women today think of themselves as old, wholly disqualified from romance, at thirty-four. The age of retirement has moved up, in line with the sharp rise in life expectancy for everybody in the last few generations. The *form* in which women experience their lives remains unchanged. A moment approaches inexorably when they must resign themselves to being "too old." And that moment is invariably—objectively—premature.

In earlier generations the renunciation came even sooner. Fifty years ago a woman of forty was not just aging but old, finished. No struggle was even possible. Today, the surrender to aging no longer has a fixed date. The aging crisis (I am speaking only of women in affluent countries) starts earlier but lasts longer; it is diffused over most of a woman's life. A woman hardly has to be anything like what would reasonably be considered old to worry about her age, to start lying (or being tempted to lie).

The crises can come at any time. Their schedule depends on a blend of personal ("neurotic") vulnerability and the swing of social mores. Some women don't have their first crisis until thirty. No one escapes a sickening shock upon turning forty. Each birthday, but especially those ushering in a new decade—for round numbers have a special authority—sounds a new defeat. There is almost as much pain in the anticipation as in the reality. Twenty-nine has become a queasy age ever since the official end of youth crept forward, about a generation ago, to thirty. Being thirty-nine is also hard; a whole year in which to meditate in glum astonishment that one stands on the threshhold of middle age. The frontiers are arbitrary, but not any less vivid for that.

Although a woman on her fortieth birthday is hardly different from what she was when she was still thirty-nine, the day seems like a turning point. But long before actually becoming a woman of forty, she has been steeling herself against the depression she will feel. One of the greatest tragedies of each woman's life is simply getting older; it is certainly the *longest* tragedy.

Aging is a movable doom. It is a crisis that never exhausts itself, because the anxiety is never really used up. Being a crisis of the imagination rather than of "real life," it has the habit of repeating itself again and again. The territory of aging (as opposed to actual old age) has no fixed boundaries. Up to a point it can be defined as one wants. Entering each decade—after the initial shock is absorbed—an endearing, desperate impulse of survival helps many women to stretch the boundaries to the decade following. In late adolescence thirty seems the end of life. At thirty, one pushes the sentence forward to forty. At forty, one still gives oneself ten more years.

I remember my closest friend in college sobbing on the day she turned twenty-one. "The best part of my life is over. I'm not young any more." She was a senior, nearing graduation. I was a precocious freshman, just sixteen. Mystified, I tried lamely to comfort her, saying that I didn't think twenty-one was *so* old. Actually, I didn't understand at all what could be demoralizing about turning twenty-one. To me, it meant only something good: being in charge of oneself, being free. At sixteen I was too young to have noticed, and become confused by, the peculiarly loose, ambivalent way in which this society demands that one stop thinking of oneself as a girl and start thinking of oneself as a woman. (In America that demand can now be put off to the age of thirty, even beyond.) But even if I thought her distress was absurd, I must have been aware that it would not simply be absurd but quite unthinkable in a *boy* turning twenty-one. Only women worry about age with that degree of inanity and pathos. And, of course, as with all crises that are inauthentic and therefore repeat themselves compulsively (because the danger is largely fictive, a poison in the imagination), this friend of mine went on having the same crisis over and over, each time as if for the first time.

I also came to her thirtieth birthday party. A veteran of many love affairs, she had spent most of her twenties living abroad and had just returned to the United States. She had been good-looking when I first knew her; now she was beautiful. I teased her about the tears she had shed over being twenty-one. She laughed and claimed not to remember. But thirty, she said ruefully, that really is the end. Soon after, she married. My friend is now forty-four. While no longer what people call beautiful, she is striking-looking, charming, and vital. She teaches elementary school; her husband, who is twenty years older than she, is a part-time merchant seaman. They have one child, now nine years old. Sometimes when her husband is away, she takes a lover. She told me recently that forty was the most upsetting birthday of all (I wasn't at that one), and although she has only a few years left, she means to enjoy them while they last. She has become one of those women who seize every excuse offered in any conversation for mentioning how old they really are in a spirit of bravado compounded with self-pity that is not too different from the mood of women who regularly lie about their age. But she is actually fretting much less about aging than she was two decades ago. Having a child and having one rather late, past the age of thirty, has certainly helped to reconcile her to her age. At fifty, I suspect, she will be ever more valiantly postponing the age of resignation.

My friend is one of the more fortunate, sturdier casualties of the aging crisis. Most women are not as spirited, nor as innocently comic in their suffering. But almost all women endure some version of this suffering: A recurrent seizure of the imagination that usually begins quite young, in which they project themselves into a calculation of loss. The rules of this society are cruel to women. Brought up to be never fully adult, women are deemed obsolete earlier than men. In fact, most women don't become relatively free and expressive sexually until their thirties. (Women mature sexually this late, certainly much later than men, not for innate biological reasons but because this culture retards women. Denied most outlets for sexual energy permitted to men, it takes many women *that* long to wear out some of their inhibitions.) The time at which they start being disqualified as sexually attractive persons is just when they have grown up sexually. The double standard about aging cheats women of those years, between thirty-five and fifty, likely to be the best of their sexual life.

That women expect to be flattered often by men, and the extent to which their self-confidence depends on this flattery, reflects how deeply women are psychologically weakened by this double standard. Added on to the pressure felt by everybody in this society to look young as long as possible are the values of "femininity," which specifically identify sexual attractiveness in women with youth. The desire to be the "right age" has a special urgency for a woman it never has for a man. A much greater part of her self-esteem and pleasure in life is threatened when she ceases to be young. Most men experience getting older with regret, apprehension. But most women experience it even more painfully: with shame. Aging is a man's destiny, something that must happen because he is a human being. For a woman, aging is not only her destiny. Because she is that more *narrowly* defined kind of human being, a woman, it is also her vulnerability.

To be a woman is to be an actress. Being feminine is a kind of theater, with its appropriate costumes, *decor,* lighting, and stylized gestures. From early childhood on, girls are trained to care in a pathologically exaggerated way about their appearance and are profoundly mutilated (to the extent of being unfitted for first-class adulthood) by the extent of the stress put on presenting themselves as physically attractive objects. Women look in the mirror more frequently than men do. It is, virtually, their duty to look at themselves—to look often. Indeed, a woman who is not narcissistic is considered unfeminine. And a woman who spends literally *most* of her time caring for, and making purchases to flatter, her physical appearance is not regarded in this society as what she is: a kind of moral idiot. She is thought to be quite normal and is envied by other women whose time is mostly used up at jobs or caring for large families. The display of narcissism goes on all the time. It is expected that women will disappear several times in an evening—at a restaurant, at a party, during a theater intermission, in the course of a social visit—simply to check their appearance, to see that nothing has gone wrong with their make-up and hairstyling, to make sure that their clothes are not spotted or too wrinkled or not hanging properly.

It is even acceptable to perform this activity in public. At the table in a restaurant, over coffee, a woman sometimes opens a compact mirror and touches up her make-up and hair without embarrassment in front of her husband or her friends.

All this behavior, which is written off as normal "vanity" in women, would seem ludicrous in a man. Women are more vain than men because of the relentless pressure on women to maintain their appearance at a certain high standard. What makes the pressure even more burdensome is that there are actually several standards. Men present themselves as face-and-body, a physical whole. Women are split, as men are not, into a body and a face—each judged by somewhat different standards. What is important for a face is that it be beautiful. What is important for a body is two things, which may even be (depending on fashion and taste) somewhat incompatible: first, that it be desirable and, second, that it be beautiful. Men usually feel sexually attracted to women much more because of their bodies than their faces. The traits that arouse desire—such as fleshiness—don't always match those that fashion decrees as beautiful. (For instance, the ideal woman's body promoted in advertising in recent years is extremely thin: the kind of body that looks more desirable clothed than naked.) But women's concern with their appearance is not simply geared to arousing desire in men. It also aims at fabricating a certain image by which, as a more indirect way of arousing desire, women state their value. A woman's value lies in the way she *represents* herself, which is much more by her face than her body. In defiance of the laws of simple sexual attraction, women do not devote most of their attention to their bodies. The well-known "normal" narcissism that women display—the amount of time they spend before the mirror—is used primarily in caring for the face and hair.

Women do not simply have faces, as men do; they are identified with their faces. Men have a naturalistic relation to their faces. *Certainly* they care whether they are good-looking or not. They suffer over acne, protruding ears, tiny eyes; they hate getting bald. But there is a much wider latitude in what is esthetically acceptable in a man's face than what is in a woman's. A man's face is defined as something he basically doesn't need to tamper with; all he has to do is keep it clean. He can avail himself of the options for ornament supplied by nature: a beard, a mustache, longer or shorter hair. But he is not supposed to disguise himself. What he is "really" like is supposed to show. A man lives through his face; it records the progressive stages of his life. And since he doesn't tamper with his face, it is not separate from but is completed by his body—which is judged attractive by the impression it gives of virility and energy. By contrast, a woman's face is potentially separate from her body. She does not treat it naturalistically. A woman's face is the canvas upon which she paints a revised, corrected portrait of herself. One of the rules of this creation is that the face *not* show what she doesn't want it to show. Her face is an emblem, an icon, a flag. How she arranges her hair, the type of make-up she uses, the quality of her complexion—all these are signs, not of what she is "really" like, but of how she asks to be treated by others, especially men. They establish her status as an "object."

For the normal changes that age inscribes on every human face, women are much more heavily penalized than men. Even in early adolescence, girls are cautioned to protect their faces against wear and tear. Mothers tell their daughters (but not their sons): You look ugly when you cry. Stop worrying. Don't read too much. Crying, frowning, squinting, even laughing—all these human activities make "lines." The same usage of the face in men is judged quite positively. In a man's face lines are taken to be signs of "character." They indicate emotional strength, maturity—qualities far more esteemed in men than in women. (They show he has "lived.") Even scars are often not felt to be unattractive; they too can add "character" to a man's face. But lines of aging, any scar, even a small birthmark on a woman's face, are always regarded as unfortunate blemishes. In effect, people take character in men to be different from what constitutes character in women. A woman's character is thought to be innate, static—not the product of her experience,

her years, her actions. A woman's face is prized so far as it remains unchanged by (or conceals the traces of) her emotions, her physical risk-taking. Ideally, it is supposed to be a mask—immutable, unmarked. The model woman's face is Garbo's. Because women are identified with their faces much more than men are, and the ideal woman's face is one that is "perfect," it seems a calamity when a woman has a disfiguring accident. A broken nose or a scar or a burn mark, no more than regrettable for a man, is a terrible psychological wound to a woman; objectively, it diminishes her value. (As is well known, most clients for plastic surgery are women.)

Both sexes aspire to a physical ideal, but what is expected of boys and what is expected of girls involves a very different moral relation to the self. Boys are encouraged to *develop* their bodies, to regard the body as an instrument to be improved. They invent their masculine selves largely through exercise and sport, which harden the body and strengthen competitive feelings; clothes are of only secondary help in making their bodies attractive. Girls are not particularly encouraged to develop their bodies through any activity, strenuous or not; and physical strength and endurance are hardly valued at all. The invention of the feminine self proceeds mainly through clothes and other signs that testify to the very effort of girls to look attractive, to their commitment to please. When boys become men, they may go on (especially if they have sedentary jobs) practicing a sport or doing exercises for a while. Mostly they leave their appearance alone, having been trained to accept more or less what nature has handed out to them. (Men may start doing exercises again in their forties to lose weight, but for reasons of health—there is an epidemic fear of heart attacks among the middle-aged in rich countries—not for cosmetic reasons.) As one of the norms of "femininity" in this society is being preoccupied with one's physical appearance, so "masculinity" means *not* caring very much about one's looks.

This society allows men to have a much more affirmative relation to their bodies than women have. Men are more "at home" in their bodies, whether they treat them casually or use them aggressively. A man's body is defined as a strong body. It contains no contradiction between what is felt to be attractive and what is practical.

A woman's body, so far as it is considered attractive, is defined as a fragile, light body. (Thus, women worry more than men do about being overweight.) When they do exercises, women avoid the ones that develop the muscles, particularly those in the upper arms. Being "feminine" means looking physically weak, frail. Thus, the ideal woman's body is one that is not of much practical use in the hard work of this world, and one that must continually be "defended." Women do not develop their bodies, as men do. After a woman's body has reached its sexually acceptable form by late adolescence, most further development is viewed as negative. And it is thought irresponsible for women to do what is normal for men: simply leave their appearance alone. During early youth they are likely to come as close as they ever will to the ideal image—slim figure, smooth firm skin, light musculature, graceful movements. Their task is to try to maintain that image, unchanged, as long as possible. Improvement as such is not the task. Women care for their bodies—against toughening, coarsening, getting fat. They *conserve* them. (Perhaps the fact that women in modern societies tend to have a more conservative political outlook than men originates in their profoundly conservative relation to their bodies.)

In the life of women in this society the period of pride, of natural honesty, of unself-conscious flourishing is brief. Once past youth women are condemned to inventing (and maintaining) themselves against the inroads of age. Most of the physical qualities regarded as attractive in women deteriorate much earlier in life than those defined as "male." Indeed, they perish fairly soon in the normal sequence of body transformation. The "feminine" is smooth, rounded, hairless, unlined, soft, unmuscled—the look of the very young; characteristics of the weak, of the vulnerable; eunuch traits, as Germaine Greer has pointed out. Actually, there are only a few years—late adolescence, early twenties—in which this look is physiologically natural, in which it can be had without touching-up and covering-up. After that, women enlist in a quixotic enterprise, trying to close the gap between the imagery put forth by society (concerning what is attractive in a woman) and the evolving facts of nature.

Women have a more intimate relation to aging than men do, simply because one of the accepted "women's" occupations is taking pains to keep one's face and body from showing the signs of growing older. Women's sexual validity depends, up to a certain point, on how well they stand off these natural changes. After late adolescense women become the caretakers of their bodies and faces, pursuing an essentially defensive strategy, a holding operation. A vast array of products in jars and tubes, a branch of surgery, and armies of hairdressers, masseuses, diet counselors, and other professionals exist to stave off, or mask, developments that are entirely normal biologically. Large amounts of women's energies are diverted into this passionate, corrupting effort to defeat nature: to maintain an ideal, static appearance against the progress of age. The collapse of the project is only a matter of time. Inevitably, a woman's physical appearance develops beyond its youthful form. No matter how exotic the creams or how strict the diets, one cannot indefinitely keep the face unlined, the waist slim. Bearing children takes its toll: the torso becomes thicker; the skin is stretched. There is no way to keep certain lines from appearing, in one's midtwenties, around the eyes and mouth. From about thirty on, the skin gradually loses its tonus. In women this perfectly natural process is regarded as a humiliating defeat, while nobody finds anything remarkably unattractive in the equivalent physical changes in men. Men are "allowed" to look older without sexual penalty.

Thus, the reason that women experience aging with more pain than men is not simply that they care more than men about how they look. Men also care about their looks and want to be attractive, but since the business of men is mainly being and doing, rather than appearing, the standards for appearance are much less exacting. The standards for what is attractive in a man are permissive; they conform to what is possible or "natural" to most men throughout most of their lives. The standards for women's appearance go against nature, and to come anywhere near approximating them takes considerable effort and time. Women must try to be beautiful. At the least, they are under heavy social pressure not to be ugly. A woman's fortunes depend, far more than a man's, on being at least "acceptable" looking. Men are not subject to this pressure. Good looks in a man is a bonus, not a psychological necessity for maintaining normal self-esteem.

Behind the fact that women are more severely penalized than men are for aging is the fact that people, in this culture at least, are simply less tolerant of ugliness in women than in men. An ugly woman is never merely repulsive. Ugliness in a woman is felt by everyone, men as well as women, to be faintly embarrassing. And many features or blemishes that count as ugly in a woman's face would be quite tolerable on the face of a man. This is not, I would insist, just because the esthetic standards for men and women are different. It is rather because the esthetic standards for women are much higher, and narrower, than those proposed for men.

Beauty, women's business in this society, is the theater of their enslavement. Only one standard of female beauty is sanctioned: the *girl*. The great advantage men have is that our culture allows two standards of male beauty: the *boy* and the *man*. The beauty of a boy resembles the beauty of a girl. In both sexes it is a fragile kind of beauty and flourishes naturally only in the early part of the life-cycle. Happily, men are able to accept themselves under another standard of good looks—heavier, rougher, more thickly built. A man does not grieve when he loses the smooth, unlined hairless skin of a boy. For he has only exchanged one form of attractiveness for another: the darker skin of a man's face, roughened by daily shaving, showing the marks of emotion and the normal lines of age. There is no equivalent of this second standard for women. The single standard of beauty for women dictates that they must go on having clear skin. Every wrinkle, every line, every grey hair, is a defeat. No wonder that no boy minds becoming a man, while even the passage from girlhood to early womanhood is experienced by many women as their downfall, for all women are trained to want to continue looking like girls.

This is not to say there are no beautiful women. But the standard of beauty in a woman of any age is how far she retains, or how she manages to simulate, the appearance of youth. The exceptional woman in her sixties who is beautiful certainly owes a large debt to her genes. Delayed aging, like good looks, tends to run in families.

But nature rarely offers enough to meet this culture's standards. Most of the women who successfully delay the appearance of age are rich, with unlimited leisure to devote to nurturing along nature's gifts. Often they are actresses. (That is, highly paid professionals at doing what all women are taught to practice as amateurs.) Such women as Mae West, Dietrich, Stella Adler, Dolores Del Rio, do not challenge the rule about the relation between beauty and age in women. They are admired precisely because they *are* exceptions, because they have managed (at least so it seems in photographs) to outwit nature. Such miracles, exceptions made by nature (with the help of art and social privilege), only confirm the rule, because what make these women seem beautiful to us is precisely that they do not look their real age. Society allows no place in our imagination for a beautiful old woman who does look like an old woman—a woman who might be like Picasso at the age of ninety, being photographed outdoors on his estate in the south of France, wearing only shorts and sandals. No one imagines such a woman exists. Even the special exceptions—Mae West & Co.—are always photographed indoors, cleverly lit, from the most flattering angle and fully, artfully clothed. The implication is they would not stand a closer scrutiny. The idea of an old woman in a bathing suit being attractive, or even just acceptable looking, is inconceivable. An older woman is, by definition, sexually repulsive—unless, in fact, she doesn't look old at all. The body of an old woman, unlike that of an old man, is always understood as a body that can no longer be shown, offered, unveiled. At best, it may appear in costume. People still feel uneasy, thinking about what they might see if her mask dropped, if she took off her clothes.

Thus, the point for women of dressing up, applying make-up, dyeing their hair, going on crash diets, and getting face-lifts is not just to be attractive. They are ways of defending themselves against a profound level of disapproval directed toward women, a disapproval that can take the form of aversion. The double standard about aging converts the life of women into an inexorable march toward a condition in which they are not just unattractive, but disgusting. The profoundest terror of a woman's life is the moment represented in a statue by Rodin called *Old Age:*

a naked old woman, seated, pathetically contemplates her flat, pendulous, ruined body. Aging in women is a process of becoming obscene sexually, for the flabby bosom, wrinkled neck, spotted hands, thinning white hair, waistless torso, and veined legs of an old woman are felt to be obscene. In our direst moments of the imagination, this transformation can take place with dismaying speed—as in the end of *Lost Horizon,* when the beautiful young girl is carried by her lover out of Shangri-La and, within minutes, turns into a withered, repulsive crone. There is no equivalent nightmare about men. This is why, however much a man may care about his appearance, that caring can never acquire the same desperateness it often does for women. When men dress according to fashion or now even use cosmetics, they do not expect from clothes and make-up what women do. A face-lotion or perfume or deodorant or hairspray, used by a man, is not part of a disguise. Men, as men, do not feel the need to disguise themselves to fend off morally disapproved signs of aging, to outwit premature sexual obsolescence, to cover up aging as obscenity. Men are not subject to the barely concealed revulsion expressed in this culture against the female body—except in its smooth, youthful, firm, odorless, blemish-free form.

One of the attitudes that punish women most severely is the visceral horror felt at aging female flesh. It reveals a radical fear of women installed deep in this culture, a demonology of women that has crystallized in such mythic caricatures as the vixen, the virago, the vamp, and the witch. Several centuries of witch-phobia, during which one of the cruelest extermination programs in Western history was carried out, suggest something of the extremity of this fear. That old women are repulsive is one of the most profound esthetic and erotic feelings in our culture. Women share it as much as men do. (Oppressors, as a rule, deny oppressed people their own "native" standards of beauty. And the oppressed end up being convinced that they *are* ugly.) How women are psychologically damaged by this misogynistic idea of what is beautiful parallels the way in which blacks have been deformed in a society that has up to now defined beautiful as white. Psychological tests made on young black children in the United States some years ago showed how

early and how thoroughly they incorporate the white standard of good looks. Virtually all the children expressed fantasies that indicated they considered black people to be ugly, funny looking, dirty, brutish. A similar kind of self-hatred infects most women. Like men, they find old age in women "uglier" than old age in men.

This esthetic taboo functions, in sexual attitudes, as a racial taboo. In this society most people feel an involuntary recoil of the flesh when imagining a middle-aged woman making love with a young man—exactly as many whites flinch viscerally at the thought of a white woman in bed with a black man. The banal drama of a man of fifty who leaves a wife of forty-five for a girlfriend of twenty-eight contains no strictly sexual outrage, whatever sympathy people may have for the abandoned wife. On the contrary. Everyone "understands." Everyone knows that men like girls, that young women often want middle-aged men. But no one "understands" the reverse situation. A woman of forty-five who leaves a husband of fifty for a lover of twenty-eight is the makings of a social and sexual scandal at a deep level of feeling. No one takes exception to a romantic couple in which the man is twenty years or more the woman's senior. The movies pair Joanne Dru and John Wayne, Marilyn Monroe and Joseph Cotten, Audrey Hepburn and Cary Grant, Jane Fonda and Yves Montand, Catherine Deneuve and Marcello Mastroianni; as in actual life, these are perfectly plausible, appealing couples. When the age difference runs the other way, people are puzzled and embarrassed and simply shocked. (Remember Joan Crawford and Cliff Robertson in *Autumn Leaves?* But so troubling is this kind of love story that it rarely figues in the movies, and then only as the melancholy history of a failure.) The usual view of why a woman of forty and a boy of twenty, or a woman of fifty and a man of thirty, marry is that the man is seeking a mother, not a wife; no one believes the marriage will last. For a woman to respond erotically and romantically to a man who, in terms of his age, could be her father is considered normal. A man who falls in love with a woman who, however attractive she may be, is old enough to be his mother is thought to be extremely neurotic (victim of an "Oedipal fixation" is the fashionable tag), if not mildly contemptible.

The wider the gap in age between partners in a couple, the more obvious is the prejudice against women. When old men, such as Justice Douglas, Picasso, Strom Thurmond, Onassis, Chaplin, and Pablo Casals, take brides thirty, forty, fifty years younger than themselves, it strikes people as remarkable, perhaps an exaggeration—but still plausible. To explain such a match, people enviously attribute some special virility and charm to the man. Though he can't be handsome, he is famous; and his fame is understood as having boosted his attractiveness to women. People imagine that his young wife, respectful of her elderly husband's attainments, is happy to become his helper. For the man a late marriage is always good public relations. It adds to the impression that, despite his advanced age, he is still to be reckoned with; it is the sign of a continuing vitality presumed to be available as well to his art, business activity, or political career. But an elderly woman who married a young man would be greeted quite differently. She would have broken a fierce taboo, and she would get no credit for her courage. Far from being admired for her vitality, she would probably be condemned as predatory, willfull, selfish, exhibitionistic. At the same time she would be pitied, since such a marriage would be taken as evidence that she was in her dotage. If she had a conventional career or were in business or held public office, she would quickly suffer from the current of disapproval. Her very credibility as a professional would decline, since people would suspect her young husband might have an undue influence on her. Her "respectability" would certainly be compromised. Indeed, the well-known old women I can think of who dared such unions, if only at the end of their lives—George Eliot, Colette, Edith Piaf—have all belonged to that category of people, creative artists and entertainers, who have special license from society to behave scandalously. It is thought to be a scandal for a woman to ignore that she is old and therefore too ugly for a young man. Her looks and a certain physical condition determine a woman's desirability, not her talents or her needs. Women are not supposed to be "potent." A marriage between an old woman and a young man subverts the very ground rule of relations between the two sexes, that is: whatever the variety of appearances,

men remain dominant. Their claims come first. Women are supposed to be the associates and companions of men, not their full equals—and never their superiors. Women are to remain in the state of a permanent "minority."

The convention that wives should be younger than their husbands powerfully enforces the "minority" status of women, since being senior in age always carries with it, in any relationship, a certain amount of power and authority. There are no laws on the matter, of course. The convention is obeyed because to do otherwise makes one feel as if one is doing something ugly or in bad taste. Everyone feels intuitively the esthetic rightness of a marriage in which the man is older than the woman, which means that any marriage in which the woman is older creates a dubious or less gratifying mental picture. Everyone is addicted to the visual pleasure that women give by meeting certain esthetic requirements from which men are exempted, which keeps women working at staying youthful-looking while men are left free to age. On a deeper level everyone finds the signs of old age in women esthetically offensive, which conditions one to feel automatically repelled by the prospect of an elderly woman marrying a much younger man. The situation in which women are kept minors for life is largely organized by such conformist, unreflective preferences. But taste is not free, and its judgments are never merely "natural." Rules of taste enforce structures of power. The revulsion against aging in women is the cutting edge of a whole set of oppressive structures (often masked as gallantries) that keep women in their place.

The ideal state proposed for women is docility, which means not being fully grown up. Most of what is cherished as typically "feminine" is simply behavior that is childish, immature, weak. To offer so low and demeaning a standard of fulfillment in itself constitutes oppression in an acute form—a sort of moral neo-colonialism. But women are not simply condescended to by the values that secure the dominance of men. They are repudiated. Perhaps because of having been their oppressors for so long, few men really *like* women (though they love individual women), and few men ever feel really comfortable or at ease in women's company. This malaise arises because relations between the two sexes are rife with hypocrisy, as men manage to love those they dominate and therefore don't respect. Oppressors always try to justify their privileges and brutalities by imagining that those they oppress belong to a lower order of civilization or are less than fully "human." Deprived of part of their ordinary human dignity, the oppressed take on certain "demonic" traits. The oppressions of large groups have to be anchored deep in the psyche, continually renewed by partly unconscious fears and taboos, by a sense of the obscene. Thus, women arouse not only desire and affection in men but aversion as well. Women are thoroughly domesticated familiars. But, at certain times and in certain situations, they become alien, untouchable. The aversion men feel, so much of which is covered over, is felt most frankly, with least inhibition, toward the type of woman who is most taboo "esthetically," a woman who has become—with the natural changes brought about by aging—obscene.

Nothing more clearly demonstrates the vulnerability of women than the special pain, confusion, and bad faith with which they experience getting older. And in the struggle that some women are waging on behalf of all women to be treated (and treat themselves) as full human beings—not "only" as women—one of the earliest results to be hoped for is that women become aware, indignantly aware, of the double standard about aging from which they suffer so harshly.

It is understandable that women often succumb to the temptation to lie about their age. Given society's double standard, to question a woman about her age is indeed often an aggressive act, a trap. Lying is an elementary means of self-defense, a way of scrambling out of the trap, at least temporarily. To expect a woman, after "a certain age," to tell exactly how old she is—when she has a chance, either through the generosity of nature or the cleverness of art, to pass for being somewhat younger than she actually is—is like expecting a landowner to admit that the estate he has put up for sale is actually worth less than the buyer is prepared to pay. The double standard about aging sets women up as property, as objects whose value depreciates rapidly with the march of the calendar.

The prejudices that mount against women as they grow older are an important arm of the male privilege. It is the present unequal distribution of adult roles between the two sexes that gives men a freedom to age denied to women. Men actively administer the double standard about aging because the "masculine" role awards them the initiative in courtship. Men choose; women are chosen. So men choose younger women. But although this system of inequality is operated by men, it could not work if women themselves did not acquiesce in it. Women reinforce it powerfully with their complacency, with their anguish, with their lies.

Not only do women lie more than men do about their age but men forgive them for it, thereby confirming their own superiority. A man who lies about his age is thought to be weak, "unmanly." A woman who lies about her age is behaving in a quite acceptable, "feminine" way. Petty lying is viewed by men with indulgence, one of a number of patronizing allowances made for women. It has the same moral unimportance as the fact that women are often late for appointments. Women are not expected to be truthful, or punctual, or expert in handling and repairing machines, or frugal, or physically brave. They are expected to be second-class adults, whose natural state is that of a grateful dependence on men. And so they often are, since that is what they are brought up to be. So far as women heed the stereotypes of "feminine" behavior, they *cannot* behave as fully responsible, independent adults.

Most women share the contempt for women expressed in the double standard about aging—to such a degree that they take their lack of self-respect for granted. Women have been accustomed so long to the protection of their masks, their smiles, their endearing lies. Without this protection, they know, they would be more vulnerable. But in protecting themselves as women, they betray themselves as adults. The model corruption in a woman's life is denying her age. She symbolically accedes to all those myths that furnish women with their imprisoning securities and privileges, that create their genuine oppression, that inspire their real discontent. Each time a woman lies about her age she becomes an accomplice in her own underdevelopment as a human being.

Women have another option. They can aspire to be wise, not merely nice; to be competent, not merely helpful; to be strong, not merely graceful; to be ambitious for themselves, not merely for themselves in relation to men and children. They can let themselves age naturally and without embarrassment, actively protesting and disobeying the conventions that stem from this society's double standard about aging. Instead of being girls, girls as long as possible, who then age humiliatingly into middle-aged women and then obscenely into old women, they can become women much earlier—and remain active adults, enjoying the long, erotic career of which women are capable, far longer. Women should allow their faces to show the lives they have lived. Women should tell the truth.

10

Stratum Consciousness and Stratum Action: Theoretical Perspectives and Applications

Vincent Jeffries

STRATUM CONSCIOUSNESS and action are important topics because they determine change within stratification systems and thus affect the whole of society and culture. The analysis of stratum consciousness and action rests upon some of the same assumptions regarding the relationships between social structure and individual attitudes and behavior that were discussed in chapter 8. Those people who occupy similar positions in a hierarchical structure share the same experiences, situations, and social expectations. As a result, they share certain real interests. Under the appropriate conditions, they may develop a sense of shared aspirations and grievances regarding their place in the distributive system of society. Their concern often leads to social and political activity directed toward changing the existing distribution of power, privilege, and prestige.

The multiple hierarchy approach expands the study of stratum consciousness and action beyond the traditional focus upon class stratification. In the last fifteen years, the society of the United States has been characterized by instances of consciousness, protests, and social movements based on hierarchical affiliations other than that of class. In the light of events such as the black and women's movements of recent years, a strictly class model of consciousness and action is too limited an explanation of the relationship between social strata and historical change.

The multiple hierarchy approach to social stratification explores the impact of particular combinations of hierarchical positions on stratum consciousness and action in its development, extent, and form. Since individuals simultaneously occupy positions in diverse strata, a coalescence of two or more positions may produce unique influences upon group and individual consciousness. For example, the status of low-income,

An asterisk (*) accompanying a citation indicates a selection that is included in this volume.

unskilled worker combined with that of member of an ethnic minority may produce life experiences and social pressure that cannot be understood by examining either position in isolation from the other. Numerous distinct social worlds are created by the juncture of multiple hierarchical positions, and each social world has its own impact on stratum consciousness and action.

Another major focus of the multiple hierarchy approach is the comparative analysis across different strata of the conditions facilitating or retarding the development of stratum consciousness and action. As with any comparative analysis, the consideration of similarities and differences among several cases provides for the development of greater understanding and more soundly based theory.

MAJOR THEORETICAL APPROACHES TO THE STUDY OF STRATUM CONSCIOUSNESS AND ACTION

Conflict, functional, and symbolic interactionist theories each contribute to an understanding of stratum consciousness and action. Each model focuses attention on particular factors that are fundamental to this area öf study, thus furnishing a more extensive and rigorous perspective than that given by any one of them taken singly.

The conflict model emphasizes the distribution of power, the structural sources of discontent and conflict, and the nature and process of the development of stratum consciousness and action. The functional perspective highlights the role of commonly held values in both retarding and accelerating the spread of consciousness and action. The symbolic interaction model focuses most directly on the interplay between individuals and the socio-cultural system that is the essence of the dynamic evolvement of consciousness and action. The following section of this chapter provides descriptions of substantive events and processes to which these models can be applied.

The Conflict Model

The writings of Karl Marx (1956; Mills*, 1962:81–95) laid the foundation for the study of stratum consciousness and action. In Marx's view, class strata were of overwhelming importance in determining both characteristics of social structure and the direction of social change. Marx's theory presents a classic conflict model in which both individual and social development and progress are achieved through a process of conflict, specifically through class conflict. Conflict is both the cause and the effect of the development of class consciousness, which, according to Marxian theory, finally brings about the concerted action necessary for major social change.

The fundamental source of conflict lies in the productive system of society. The class that controls the economic system seeks to use it to its own advantage, thus creating a contradiction between possible progress and the existing system of class relations. The productive system, as expressed in the class structure, comes to stand in opposition to both social progress and the development of individual potential. Values that are inimical to the unfolding of human potential, such as striving for money and power, come to dominate the culture. These values to some extent are created and disseminated by the superordinate class in order to maintain the existing system of production. Work within the productive process increasingly becomes a monotonous, pervasive, and dehumanizing experience. The social structure and culture thus come to be separated from true human needs and social progress.

Under these conditions conflict develops between those owning the means of production and those who have only their labor to sell, the subordinate classes. Sporadic conflicts become more frequent and generalized and gradually a group consciousness develops among members of the subordinate strata.

Marx envisioned class consciousness emerging from the increasing deprivations produced by the system of production and labor in capitalist societies, just as it had emerged for the same fundamental reasons in the previous feudal society. The essence of these deprivations, Marx believed, was the alienation produced by the capitalist system of production and labor (Mills*, 1962; Fromm, 1963). This alienation involves a separation of individuals from their true selves, from experiences necessary for personal development and fulfillment, and from other individuals.

Marx believed that individuals should be able to develop a sense of identity and achieve self-actualization through participation in the productive processes of society. But in societies in which the economic structure is controlled by a particular class and used for its members' narrowly conceived interests, such opportunities do not generally exist. Work becomes simply a means to survive and provide for the necessities of life. For example, under capitalism the subordinate working class has no control over the productive process and labors long hours, often in prison-like conditions. A sense of powerlessness and lack of control over their lives comes to pervade the consciousness of workers. Individuals become alienated from their work in the sense that it becomes a necessary means to continued existence rather than an end in itself that contributes to human development. Basic human needs are thus not fulfilled.

Alienation also involves a feeling of separation of individuals from other individuals. When the pursuit of money and material advancement are dominant goals, human beings become divided from each other. Individuals become objects to be used for personal gain and advancement, rather than ends in themselves.

This alienation from work and from others also constitutes alienation from the self. This is because what Marx believed to be the basic and true human needs of self-realization through work, and of solidary relations with others, are suppressed and denied by the existing social structure. Individuals are thus separated from their real natures, and false needs, such as money, take the place of true needs. These fundamental deprivations are perceived and their sources realized through the development of class consciousness. With the development of consciousness, an aggregate of individuals occupying the same position in relation to the means of production, a class "in-itself," is gradually transformed into a self-conscious, politically oriented action group, a class "for-itself." Class consciousness contains a number of elements. Perhaps the most basic factor is a sense of group identity. Deprivations and grievances once regarded as individualized are seen as shared by others in a similar social position. Individuals in subordinate strata gradually develop a sense of group identity and bonds of unity centered around an awareness of themselves as a social class. A corollary of this sense of in-group solidarity is a recognition of the existence and nature of other classes. The superordinate class controlling the means of production comes to be regarded as illegitimate and unjust. This class is increasingly viewed as opposed to the true interests of individuals and the welfare of society as a whole. Finally, class consciousness involves a recognition of the necessity of collective political and social action to change the existing use of productive forces and the social relations that are its structural reflection.

Marx believed that the development of class consciousness by the subordinate strata and the eventual ascension of this strata to a position of control over the means of production was an inevitable historical process. In the nineteenth century, this struggle was between the bourgeoisie who dominated the class structure of capitalist society and the wage workers, or proletariat. In this cycle, the ascendant class's interests are originally compatible with social progress since they center on a fuller use and expansion of the productive forces of society. Upon assuming control of the productive system, they instead seek to retard social progress, to maintain control over the economic sector, and to exploit the subordinate classes to further their own class interests.

Marx believed that the revolution of the proletariat, which he thought would occur in all capitalist societies, would break this historical cycle of dominance and exploitation of one class over the rest of society. This would occur because the ideological content of the class consciousness of the proletariat would contain unique elements previously absent in the consciousness of ascendant classes. The key to this transformation lay in the hitherto absent knowledge on the part of the ascendant class of the necessity of destroying the institution of private property and building a new social structure. In this future society, the control of the means of production would not be monopolized by any particular group, and the productive processes would be used for the good of all. The new social structure that emerged would give rise to values consistent with the unfolding of true human needs, Hence, those basic needs relating to personal development through work and solidary relations with others could be more fully realized.

Although Marx's frame of reference was limited to the class hierarchy, its basic orientation has far wider applicability. Many of the fundamental Marxian concepts have direct relevance to ethnic, sex, and age consciousness and action. Figure 10–1 presents a basic model, derived from Marx's writings, which can be applied to these other stratification systems. Previous chapters of this book have dealt with inequalities in power, privilege, and prestige in ethnic, sex, and age hierarchies. Other concepts relating to stratification, such as alienation and consciousness, also can be viewed in a much broader context than that of the system of production and class relations to which they are so closely tied in Marx's writings. For example, women experience alienation due to the limits placed on them by rigidly defined traditional sex roles. Blacks face high degrees of powerlessness by being largely confined to communities controlled in many aspects by the white power structure. The following section illustrates this condition of blacks in the South during the early years of the Civil Rights Movement. Similarly, forced retirement of the aged is directly relevant to the Marxian notion of deprivation of creative expression and development through participation in the productive process.

A significant extension and elaboration of the Marxian concept of class consciousness is the selection by Richard T. Morris and Raymond J. Murphy* (1966) included in this chapter. The article presents a paradigm for the study of stratum consciousness and action that can be applied to any stratification hierarchy. Class is regarded as simply one

I: BASIC SOCIAL AND CULTURAL CONDITIONS

Dominant Culture	Stratification	Nature of Work
1. Superordinate strata control most channels of communication and opinion formation.	1. Unequal distribution of power. Members of one stratum have control over the lives of other strata.	1. Lack of opportunity for fulfillment through participation in productive process.
2. Values antithetical to human and social development are emphasized.	2. Unequal distribution of privilege.	2. Stratum of workers faces highly repetitive and segmented work routines.
	3. Unequal distribution of prestige.	3. Stratum of workers does not receive full value for what they produce.
	4. Social structure prohibits both societal and individual progress and development.	

II: SUBJECTIVE EFFECTS

1. Alienation

   a) sense of separation from work.

   b) sense of separation from others.

   c) sense of separation from self.

2. Sense of powerlessness.

3. Stratum Consciousness

   a) consciousness of common group membership.

   b) awareness of other strata.

   c) sense of injustice.

   d) anger over the distribution of rewards.

   e) recognition of need for change.

III: STRATUM ACTION

1. Collective efforts to bring a redistribution of power, privilege, and prestige.

2. Alternative group structures develop.

3. Development and dissemination of an ideology of protest.

Figure 10-1. *Marxian Conflict Model*

kind of strata, its importance relative to others being a question for empirical investigation.

Six basic stages in the development of stratum consciousness and action are discussed by Morris and Murphy*. The first stage is that in which people do not perceive the existence of stratification phenomena. When this is the case, consciousness has not developed in any form. In the second stage, that of *status awareness,* there is recognition of the existence of stratification in the form of a continuous range of gradations from low to high. There are, however, no clearly delineated strata that are perceived at this rudi-mentary level of consciousness.

In the third stage, *stratum awareness,* discrete categories rather than a continuum are perceived. The self and others can be placed in these ranked levels. This level of con-sciousness is limited to the ability of individuals to place themselves and others in given strata, and makes no assumptions regarding membership identification, interaction pat-terns, or commitment to an ideology. Studies indicate that this level is most character-istic of the class consciousness of the majority of people in the United States. Stratum awareness is also the level of consciousness that is probably most characteristic of age stratification in the United States today. Most people readily perceive differences in age strata, such as youth or middle age, but with some exceptions, age groups have not developed consciousness in the sense of a feeling of belonging or a commitment to a common ideology.

In the fourth stage, *stratum affiliation,* the membership properties of a group of interacting individuals begin to emerge. A feeling of belonging and identification and the presence of commonly accepted norms, sentiments, and activities, are characteristic of this stage. The fifth stage, *stratum consciousness,* adds to the aforementioned dimen-sions that of identification with or commitment to the interests, aims, and goals of the stratum. Finally, the stage of *stratum action* refers to behavior in support of the ideology and interests of the stratum.

These latter stages of consiousness and the presence of action are most applicable to an analysis of sex and ethnicity in the United States today, and particularly to the experience of blacks. Increasing numbers of women and most blacks probably share a consciousness of kind and sense of collective experience due to their respective stratum positions. At the level of stratum action there are numerous groups and organizations representing the interests of these strata. Examples of the stratum consciousness and action of women and blacks are provided in the next section of this chapter.

Of course not every member of a stratum exhibits the same degree of stratum con-sciousness. For example, some women may not view sex differences in a stratification sense; others are highly aware of these differences and devote their lives to concerted stratum action. One reason for these differences in levels of consciousness is that society consists of a complex of strata, groups, and subcultures. Position in any one stratum is rarely so important that it overrides all other influences. Position in any stratum is also not uniform, in the sense that other key social positions differ among the members of a given stratum. For example, in a given ethnic group there are differences in class, age, and sex positions that exert pressures and influences quite apart from those of ethnicity. By conceptualizing society as composed of various strata, with individuals occupying positions simultaneously in these strata, the multiple hierarchy model shows how the coalescence of stratum positions may either retard, or further, the development of consciousness and action in given segments of the population. For example, the article by Nieto* (1974) indicates how ethnic status both shapes and limits the development of consciousness and action among Chicana women; the article by Ransford* (1977) examines how the combined statuses of lower class and black increase consciousness and readiness for stratum action. The effect of combinations of positions on stratum con-sciousness and action will be dealt with in some detail in the next chapter.

The Functional Model

Functional theories emphasize the role of commonly held values in fostering and maintaining the integration of society. This focus offers insights into certain fundamental questions regarding the effects of such values on stratum consciousness and action.

In certain instances, a value consensus that is widespread may retard the emergence of consciousness and action. For example, the previous chapter detailed the manner in which prevailing values, norms, and beliefs help to maintain the systems of class and age stratification. As will be considered in this chapter and in the selection by Trela* (1973), there is but sporadic and limited consciousness and action relative to either of these hierarchies. Studies by Feagin* (1972), Trela* (1973), and Nelson and Nelson* (1972) indicate that one of the principal reasons for this appears to be a general consensus on certain values. Individualistic values are important in retarding consciousness with respect to both class and age stratification. Also significant with respect to class stratification is the belief in the existence of equal opportunity, while the cultural emphasis on youth appears to be a factor in preventing a further development of age consciousness.

Commonly held values may also contribute to the spread of stratum consciousness and the realization of the social programs linked with such consciousness. When those espousing a new consciousness are able to show its consistency with commonly held values, people are more easily convinced of the necessity for action or change. For example, it is detailed in the next section how values stressing equality of opportunity and the dignity of all people, which are an integral part of the culture of the United States, played a part in the development and spread of the Civil Rights Movement among both blacks and whites.

The functional approach also focuses attention on the extent to which the system's performance, by adequately meeting basic human needs and providing justice and opportunity for individuals, may retard the development of consciousness and action. To the extent that institutional policies and performance reflect the common will and serve the common good, and to the extent that the position of individuals in society is determined by their talents and application, it is relatively unlikely that a general desire for change will arise.

The Symbolic Interactionist Model

Since symbolic interactionist theory focuses so directly on the dynamic relationship between individuals and their socio-cultural environment, it is particularly suited to providing specific insights into the basic processes involved in the development of stratum consciousness and action. This is because their emergence entails, in the most general sense, a continued and shifting interplay between individuals and the existing social organization, both of which are constantly changing in reaction to each other.

This perspective captures the essence of the development of stratum consciousness and action, in which ideas and behavior patterns initially held by only a small minority gradually spread to become part of the general culture pattern and eventually may become institutionalized in various ways. This occurs partly through numerous changes in attitude and behavior which bring about changes on the sociocultural level, which then reflect back on individual consciousness as a stimulant to further modification of attitudes, or to a greater resistance to such changes. For example, as described in the next section, when a black woman refused to give up her seat on a bus to a white person in 1955 in Montgomery, Alabama, her action set off a long series of actions and reactions that fundamentally changed many aspects of relations between blacks and whites throughout the United States.

An adequate frame of reference for the study of stratum consciousness and action entails both a recognition of the distinctiveness of individual and sociocultural structures and processes and of the continual interplay between the two. The individual level of analysis focuses most directly on the beliefs and values of individuals and how they are influenced by the prevailing social and cultural environment. An example for this can be seen in the changes of self-conception that accompany contact with consciousness-raising groups, as considered in more detail in the next section, and in the selection by Micossi* (1970). Conversely, the sociocultural level of analysis focuses on the formation, structure, and interrelationships among social groups, the creation of new ideologies on the cultural level, and the role of aggregate individual activity in contributing to social and cultural change. Examples of these social and cultural phenomena can be seen in the formation and rapid expansion of groups in the black and women's movements which are discussed in the next section.

A consideration of the dimension of meaning at both the individual and cultural levels, and the causal interplay between the two, is basic to any adequate understanding of stratum consciousness and action. The development of stratum consciousness involves a fundamental redefinition of the situation in which previously accepted meanings are rejected and new interpretations of reality are developed. The next section and the selection by Micossi* (1970) contain a detailed analysis of how situations are redefined by individuals within the context of a highly supportive social environment. The basic importance of meanings is further illustrated at the cultural level of analysis with respect to the ideologies of social movements. As stratum consciousness and action develop, a new subculture that entails the rejection of traditional meanings and their replacement with new definitions of the situation is created. These new meanings may gradually become manifest, in one form or another, throughout society. This is aptly illustrated in the brief description of the spread of the early Civil Rights Movement in the South, which is included in the next section.

From a symbolic interactionist perspective, the relationship between individuals and their social and cultural environment is viewed as being a two-sided process in which mutual influence and selection is continually taking place. The organization of individual personalities is continually evolving as a result of both individual choices and changes which take place in society and culture. Interaction with others can be a great stimulus to personal change, if such interaction involves contact with new meanings. Conversely, society and culture are in some measure the product of the ideas and behavior of individuals, who continually shape and change the nature of social structures and cultural expectations by their adherence to, or deviance from, dominant traditions and practices.

The process of the emergence and development of consciousness and action may be viewed within the above context. In terms of the impact of individual choice and action, individuals continually make choices within the sometimes wide ranges provided by their cultural environment. Thus, the new meanings contained in an ideology of stratum consciousness are confronted by the systems of meanings characteristic of given individual personalities. Their acceptance or rejection is strongly influenced by the content of the meanings that are central to the ongoing life organization of the individual.

On the other hand, with respect to the impact of society and culture on the individual, cultural meanings are invested with varying degrees of pressure to conform. This is true both with respect to the impact of previous socialization, and with respect to the more direct group pressures and social sanctions that are applied when consensual definitions are ignored or violated. The recognition of such group pressures is important in understanding both the resistance to the ideas contained in a developing stratum consciousness, and the adoption of these ideas.

BASIC CHARACTERISTICS AND PROCESSES OF STRATUM CONSCIOUSNESS AND ACTION

This section considers some of the basic elements and processes of stratum consciousness and action. Five topics are analyzed: the conditions under which stratum consciousness and action originate; the social psychological processes that influence changes in the conception of self as stratum consciousness and action develop; group structure and dynamics; the role of ideology; and how the powerless exert power. The previously considered perspectives of conflict, functional, and symbolic interactionist theory can be selectively applied to these topics, thus placing them in a broader context of understanding, while at the same time illustrating the importance of these models for illuminating the study of stratum consciousness and action.

The Origins of Stratum Consciousness and Action

Certain social and cultural factors appear to facilitate the development of stratum consciousness and action. The emergence of mass protests in the 1950s among blacks in the United States illustrates the conditions and processes attendant to the early stages of stratum consciousness and action.

The Civil Rights Movement is often considered to have begun in December, 1955 in Montgomery, Alabama, when Rosa Parks, a black woman, refused to give her seat on a city bus to a white person. Mrs. Parks was arrested for violating the Jim Crow law that stipulated blacks must surrender their seats to whites on a crowded bus. That night hundreds of black sympathizers met in a church to develop an action strategy. The Montgomery bus boycott, in which blacks refused to ride city buses, resulted from that meeting. A protracted struggle ensued in which Martin Luther King, Jr., emerged as a leader of the movement for black liberation (King, 1960).

When Rosa Parks made her individual stand, an available community of discontent, ready for mobilization, already seemed to exist. The mood of blacks in the United States in the mid-1950s was ripe for an emerging stratum consciousness and action, so that any of several incidents could have triggered a common consciousness and action. When individuals occupy similar positions in similar strata in the social structure, their views of reality are likely to be similar. Thus, particular incidents can bring out common responses in large numbers of individuals. Several social forces seem especially relevant to this emergence of stratum consciousness and action.

James Davies's (1962) theory of revolution suggests some of the reasons why a readiness for stratum consciousness and action existed among blacks at the time of the Montgomery boycott and thereafter. Davies has proposed that consciousness and action are manifested not when living conditions are objectively bad, nor when they are good, but rather when there is some major opening of the structure that produces rising expectations followed by a sharp cutback or reduction of opportunity. Davies believes that this surge of expectations for economic and social betterment followed by a reversal produces an intolerable "want-get gap" that results in a readiness for mobilization in mass protests and rebellion.

Several historical facts of the black experience in the United States fit the theory proposed by Davies. During World War II, blacks were hired for the first time for skilled jobs in large numbers to meet the economic needs of a war time economy (Oberschall, 1973:205). The necessity of operating factories twenty-four hours a day for the war effort superseded traditional racial roles and prejudice. Racial ideologies that said blacks could not handle skilled positions were undermined by their job performances during this period. Following World War II, however, many of the skilled job opportunities for blacks disappeared as the economy returned to peace-time levels of production. As in the Davies theory, hopes and aspirations among blacks for better job opportunities had sharply increased during World War II, only to be deflated after the war by a frustrating return to discrimination in hiring practices.

The Supreme Court decision of 1954 (*Brown* v. *Board of Education, Topeka, Kansas*) ordered school integration in the South "with all deliberate speed" and more broadly undercut the whole premise of Jim Crow laws by ruling that the doctrine of "separate but equal" was unconstitutional. The *Brown* decision appeared to be the beginning of a new era in race relations. However, Jim Crow laws and segregated schools continued into the 1950s and 1960s. Five years following the order, only a handful of schools had complied with the court order (Oberschall, 1973:206–207). Thus, once again aspirations for a new racial and social order rose and then fell sharply.

Another important factor in the development of stratum consciousness and action is the existence of an ideological basis and justification for organized protest. In many cases, general ideologies (systems of values, norms, and beliefs) that are an integral part of long-standing cultural patterns contain ideas readily linked with the goals and aspirations of subordinate strata. Other things being equal, subordinate strata are more likely to protest their position when they believe they have the right to be equal. When a traditional ideology of a society stresses equal opportunity for all, individual achievement rather than family of birth, and dignity of all people, the stage is set for discontent and protest if this ideology is not completely realized. For example, Gunnar Myrdal (1962) refers to the "American Creed" to designate the tradition of equality, inherent dignity of all individuals, and rights of liberty which are part of the cultural heritage of the United States. These values have frequently been cited in one manner or another by advocates of both the black and women's movements.

Myrdal (1962) believes that a basic conflict both in the cultural system and in individual consciences exists between the American Creed and a wide variety of prejudicial beliefs and discriminating practices directed against blacks in the United States. The valuations contained in the American Creed are for the most part quite general, whereas the valuations pertaining to relations between blacks and whites are quite specific. Since prejudice and discrimination are inconsistent with the American Creed, a dilemma is created. Myrdal believes that there is a strain toward consistency, and because people in the United States are fundamentally moralistic and rationalistic, this inconsistency will eventually resolve itself in accordance with the values of the American Creed.

The American Creed has long been part of the cultural heritage of the United States, but the discrepancy between ideological ideals and racial prejudice and discrimination was especially salient just prior to the Civil Rights Movement. World War II highlighted the fact that a black soldier could fight and give his life for the country, yet could not attend the same school, work in the same kind of job, or even eat in the same restaurants as white members of society. Some have also speculated that the discrepancy between ideals and practice was exacerbated with the large-scale introduction of television. For the first time blacks were constantly exposed to a style of life and level of affluence that were effectively denied to them by racial barriers.

Factors that are conducive to the development of stratum consciousness and action are only one side of the coin. It is important to know that there are several social conditions that may prevent or retard the development of stratum consciousness and action. Perhaps the most basic of these is that the system may be so repressive that all attempts at social change are met by vastly superior force. For example, a fully developed and public stratum consciousness and large scale collective action could not emerge among blacks in the South during the period from 1890–1940 because violence and terrorism were too frequently used to keep blacks in a subordinate position. Further, the social and cultural system was so closed and repressive that it was difficult for aspirations for a better life and a new social order to develop on a large scale among blacks.

Even when force and repression are absent, other factors may keep consciousness and action from developing on a wide scale. The case of the aged in the United States is illustrative of this point. James Trela* (1973) maintains that there are three basic conditions for the development of consciousness and action among the aged. First, age must become the basis of a sense of identity and shared disadvantages due to a common age status. Second, there must be an ideology that focuses on pertinent issues, creates discontent, and places collective interests ahead of personal ones. Third, a means of effective political organization must be available. Trela further observes that the negative cultural definitions regarding aging and the perceived legitimacy of the political system are two major factors militating against the emergence of stratum consciousness and action among the aged.

Various barriers to consciousness and action among the aged have also been noted by Patricia Kasschau (1977) in a study comparing age and race discrimination. This study shows that the aged are much less sensitive to prejudice and discrimination against them than are ethnic minorities and women. The aged appear to reluctantly accept forced retirement as legitimate, describing it as "unfortunate" and "inevitable" rather than as "unjust" or "discriminatory." Further, although it is very difficult for individuals to deny their ethnic or sex status, this is not the case with their age status. Individuals move into this status gradually, and many try to deny their own aging. Stratum consciousness of the aged is also retarded because the mass media devote considerably less attention to age discrimination than to discrimination based on race or sex.

Social Psychological Processes: The Transformation of Self-Conception and Image of Society

Stratum consciousness and action are developed partly through the rejection of accepted cultural meanings and the establishment of new definitions of the self and society. Previously held assumptions regarding the nature and capabilities of the self are rejected and new conceptions of the self are formed. At the same time, the image of society and its relation to the self tends to be fundamentally altered. Commonly accepted definitions which are part of the general social and cultural milieu are rejected and replaced by conceptions of reality that are linked to the gradually emerging ideology of the subordinate stratum.

For some individuals, the redefinition of self accompanying the development of stratum consciousness can be fundamental in character. Previously unquestioned cultural assumptions regarding the self are critically examined. Thus begins the often painful and difficult process of discarding feelings of worthlessness and dependency and gradually building a new conception of one's self as independent, positive, and capable. For example, the "Black is Beautiful" aspect of the black movement for equality and consciousness-raising groups in the women's movement was oriented toward rejecting negative definitions of the self that are contained in the dominant culture, and formulating a new positive self-conception. The perception of the source of many personal problems and feelings of inadequacy thus is shifted from an individual to a societal level. What were previously thought of as individual failings come to be regarded as social and cultural in derivation.

The development of stratum consciousness also entails a number of fundamental changes in how individuals view the structure and nature of society and their place in it. Prevailing social arrangements and traditions are redefined as obstacles to individual and societal progress. A sense of group consciousness and an awareness that common problems are shared by members of the stratum develop. Individuals further evolve a view of society as composed of strata, rather than of continuous categories or of groups with differentiated functions but no hierarchial arrangement. A definite stratification perspective emerges in which power, privilege, and prestige are recognized as unequally distributed and one's position within the subordinate strata is clearly recognized. The advantages accrued by the superordinate strata in the social structure come to be clearly perceived. Out of these changed perceptions of society emerge an awareness of the necessity for collective societal action on behalf of the interests and ideology of the stratum.

These basic changes in attitude appear to take place more readily within a social environment highly conducive to the abandonment of old meanings and the acceptance of new definitions of the situation. For example, Freeman (1975:116–119) has noted the important role of consciousness-raising groups in the process of individual attitude change in the women's liberation movement. These groups provide an intimate, intense, and highly supportive social environment. Under these conditions, group discussion and collective opinion can produce fundamental changes in the self-conceptions of the participants and their views of society. The article by Micossi* (1970) describes this process through which women in consciousness-raising groups gradually come to see themselves and society differently.

Group Structure and Dynamics

At the same time that changes in attitude toward self and society take place on an individual level, changes take place on the level of society and culture as stratum consciousness and action begin to become more widespread. Groups that represent the interests and ideology of the subordinate strata come into being and begin to espouse new meanings, which are often in contradiction with established values, norms, and beliefs.

The term "Mushroom Effect" is used by Freeman (1975:147–169) to describe the rapid growth of groups that began about 1970 within the women's liberation movement. From the base formed by the National Organization for Women (NOW) and the "small groups" (consciousness-raising or rap groups), the sudden growth of the women's movement brought in so many new people that existing organizations could not adequately assimilate them. Hence, there was a rapid nationwide proliferation in the number and type of groups that espoused the interests and ideology of the women's movement. Various authors have described a similar process of organizational development and evolution within the Civil Rights Movement and later within the black liberation movement in the United States (Lomax, 1963; Oberschall, 1973:204–241).

When stratum consciousness and action have developed to the degree cited in the previous cases, a major social movement exists. An essential characteristic of social movements is the intention to bring about change in both the pattern of human relations and in major social institutions (Heberle, 1951:6). The structure of social movements is a kind of "social collective" constituted by various groups, only some of which are formally organized (Heberle, 1951:8). For example, the multitude of groups in the women's liberation movement described by Freeman (1975:71–169) represent a wide variety of organizations with differing structures, goals, and tactics, and a somewhat amorphous and changing relationship to each other. While possessing some continuity, the membership of social movements constantly changes and is loosely defined. The degree of commitment to the ideology and activities of any social movement varies greatly among individuals (Killian, 1964:440–446).

Social movements are of various types. The focus in this book is on movements that find their primary impetus in stratum interests in the sense that they are directed toward changing the balance of power, privilege, and prestige in society. Some movements may attract individuals primarily from one stratum but do not focus on stratum interests. For example, the anti–war movement of the 1960s and early 1970s, while involving mostly young people, was not primarily based on age stratum interests. In contrast, the recent movements of blacks and women are principally focused upon stratum interests.

The Role of Ideology

The previous chapter considered in some detail the nature of ideologies that serve to support existing systems of stratification. Similar systems of ideas, which may be referred to as "protest" ideologies to distinguish them from ideologies that support stratification systems, are an integral aspect of a developing stratum consciousness and action. The bonds of unity within the amorphous and shifting social collective that constitute a major social movement are based on the ideology of the movement. Ideology in this case refers to the whole complex of ideas that is characteristic of a given movement. More specifically, ideologies include values, norms, and beliefs. The ideology gives a movement its particular character and identity and defines its purposes and goals.

Cooperative activity is possible because individuals share common perspectives. The term *consensus* has been used to refer to these shared assumptions that are the basis of group activity in social life. People from diverse backgrounds and with differing viewpoints can engage in cooperative enterprises if a consensus upon certain perspectives exists among them. If there is no consensus, cooperative activity is impossible (Shibutani, 1961:140–148).

The ideology of a social movement defines the points of consensus among its members. Particularly important in this regard are what Heberle (1951:23–32) has called the "constitutive ideas" within the broader ideology. These are ideas that are considered as most essential within the movement; that is, they are the consensual ideas. As such, they are the basis of group cohesion and solidarity. Constitutive ideas usually focus on three main problems: the final goals or ends of a movement, as expressed in its social philosophy; the manner in which goals are to be attained; and a justification for the activities of the movement (Heberle, 1951:24). The broader ideology also contains other ideas not considered essential and not generally agreed on. As noted by Morris and Murphy* (1966), stratum linked ideologies involve some statement of goals and means that are directed toward maintaining and improving the position of a given social stratum. Stratum ideologies also describe the existing position of a stratum within a stratification system; interpret and evaluate the present position of a stratum; propose action to change and improve the present position; and propose the desirable future position or role of the stratum.

Within most large scale social movements, various groups usually promulgate both their specific ideology and the constitutive ideas of the broader movement. For example, this can be seen in the following brief statement of the protest ideology of the Gray Panthers, an action oriented group whose primary purpose is to combat prejudice and discrimination based on age.

WHAT WE WANT

1. To develop a new and positive self-awareness in our culture which can regard the total life span as a continuing process in maturity and fulfillment.
2. To strive for new options for life styles for older and younger people that will challenge the present paternalism in our institutions and culture, and to help eliminate the poverty and powerlessness in which most older and younger people are forced to live, and to change society's destructive attitudes about aging.

3. To make responsible use of our freedom to bring about social change, to develop a list of priorities among social issues, and to struggle non-violently for social change which will bring greater human freedom, justice, dignity and peace.

4. To build a new power base in our society uniting presently disenfranchised and oppressed groups, realizing the common qualities and concerns of age and youth working in coalition with other movements with similar goals and principles.

5. To reinforce and support each other in our quest for liberation and to celebrate our shared humanity.

The constitutive ideas and the broader protest ideology redefine many established traditions and norms within the general culture. The development of stratum consciousness, to the point of goals which involve major changes in the pattern of interpersonal and intergroup relations and the institutions of society, constitutes the formulation of a new system of meanings, which is often contradictory to the prevailing culture. The spread of such ideas can be likened to the introduction of drops of a colored liquid into a pool of clear water. In varying intensities and hues, the color gradually spreads throughout the pool, being more visible and having greater effects in some areas than in others. Thus, the impact of the general ideology of the women's movement can be seen in such diverse areas as equal wages for women, relations between husbands and wives, and the increasing use of *chairperson* and *Ms.* rather than *chairman* and *Miss* or *Mrs.* The nature and number of the ideas associated with a movement that ultimately are adopted varies greatly from one segment of society to another. Each social group is a particular subculture, which because of its basic characteristics produces certain pressures and predispositions in its members to respond favorably or unfavorably to a given ideology, and to the practices and social changes it advocates.

How the Powerless Exert Power

The ultimate aim of stratum consciousness and action is to influence the distribution of power, privilege, and prestige. This can be accomplished by putting pressure on those in power so that they will act in favor of the interests of the subordinate strata or by changing their views so they will voluntarily act in this manner. Ideally, representatives of the subordinate strata will achieve positions of power at some future date. As discussed in chapter 3, with control of such decision-making positions changes can be made through legislative and legal processes which can, in time, fundamentally alter both the privileges and the prestige of members of the previously subordinate strata.

How is it possible for subordinate groups to exert pressure for change and what are their sources of power? Killian and Grigg's (1964) account of interracial conflict in the South during the Civil Rights struggle is instructive in this regard. The basic thesis of their study is that blacks needed to force an entrenched white leadership to listen and to act in order to remove the underlying causes of inequality. At that time, communication and negotiation between white and black leaders was effective only within the context of a conflict situation. Demonstrations, sit-ins, and boycotts by blacks in communities throughout the South marked the opening stages of social change in the Civil Rights era. In order to be successful, a rather large proportion of rank and file blacks had to be involved in the protests. Often these nonviolent demonstrations were met with violent opposition by segregationist elements in the local population and from surrounding counties.

These confrontations provided the impetus for a long process of negotiations (Killian and Grigg, 1964). Such confrontations often received the attention of the national media, which gave extremely unfavorable publicity about the city in which they occurred. Black protestors demonstrated their ability to invoke the sanction of notoriety on the community as national newspaper, radio, and television coverage portrayed mob violence on the city's main streets. The disorders alone did not coerce the white leaders, but they did highlight the disjunction of the American Creed and segregationist practices to both a United States and an international audience. This unfavorable publicity created moral pressures to correct the injustices against blacks.

The next stage in this conflict process focuses on the most powerful group of whites in the community, who are usually the business leaders. These economic elites gradually became aware that continued protests could be very harmful to the city's industrial growth. However, white leaders never initiated action to bring about desegregation, except in response to pressure from the black community. Further, white leaders in the South made it quite clear that they were only incidentally concerned with segregation as a moral issue. Their principal concern was the image of their community as it affected their economic interests. The white leaders had the power to activate the police and subdue the black protestors by force, but only at a price they did not care to pay; namely, that extremely repressive measures would result in even more bad publicity and possible intervention by federal troops. Accordingly, white leaders agreed to meet with black leaders to discuss their demands.

The typical result of these meetings was that some establishment around which confrontation had erupted would be changed in some manner. For example, a restaurant was desegregated or blacks were given a certain number of jobs in specific stores. The victory, however, was often token, hardly making a dent in the overall segregated system. Killian and Grigg (1964) note that black leaders could not rest on their laurels, but had to follow each token victory with new demands and the intensification of the conflict. A dialectical process took place in the Civil Rights Movement in which demands constantly alternated with conflict, temporary consensus, new demands, and new conflict.

Killian and Grigg's (1964) study illustrates a number of points about the exercise of power by subordinate strata. First, in a situation in which conflict is not totally repressed by force, a group with developing stratum consciousness needs to induce "creative tension" by making inequities extremely visible. Typically, this has been accomplished with demonstrations, sit-ins, boycotts, and by attracting the attention of the mass media. Visibility is far more effective when it illustrates ideological contradictions, such as discrepancies between the traditional and widely endorsed value of equal opportunity and discrimination according to race and sex.

Second, a broader base of sympathizers than the immediate protesting group needs to be reached. For example, the Killian and Grigg (1964) study showed that effective pressure for change began to occur when the conflict caused notoriety and began to attract a wider base of support, both within and outside of the local communities. Similarly, the movement of farm workers led by Cesar Chavez became successful only when a broader base was created as white middle-class sympathizers and clergy joined the boy-cott of selected products.

Third, economic elites and politically powerful elites must enter the negotiations with subordinate strata in order to achieve meaningful results. The group with emerging stratum consciousness must have enough power to persuade such elites that it is in their vested interests to negotiate for change.

Fourth, one-time confrontations or the passage of a particular law does not usually bring about significant change in the system. A constant process of conflict, carried on over a relatively long period of time, is necessary to bring about major social changes.

SUMMARY

This chapter provided an introduction to the study of stratum consciousness and action. These topics were analyzed from the perspectives of conflict, functionalist, and symbolic interactionist theories. Each of these perspectives makes its own unique contribution to understanding these phenomena.

The second half of this chapter examined five basic aspects of stratum conscious-ness and action: the conditions under which stratum consciousness and action develop, social psychological processes that influence changes in self conception, group structure and dynamics, the role of ideology, and how the powerless exert power. This discussion also served as illustrative material to which the three theoretical perspectives can be applied.

The following chapter continues the analyses of stratum consciousness and action with a review and discussion of studies of class consciousness in the United States. The multiple hierarchy approach to stratum consciousness and action is also considered through comparisons across hierarchies and through the analysis of combinations of positions.

REFERENCES

Davies, James C. 1962. "Towards a Theory of Revolution." *American Sociological Review,* 27 (February): 5–19.

Feagin, Joe R. 1972. "God Helps Those Who Help Themselves." *Psychology Today* 6 (November): 101.

Freeman, Jo. 1975. *The Politics of Women's Liberation.* New York: David McKay.

Fromm, Erich. 1963. *Marx's Concept of Man.* New York: Frederick Ungar Publishing Company.

Heberle, Rudolf. 1951. *Social Movements.* New York: Appleton-Century-Crofts.

Kasschau, Patricia L. 1977. "Age and Race Discrimination Reported by Middle-Aged and Older Persons." *Social Forces* 55 (March): 728–742.

Killian, Lewis M. 1964. "Social Movements" in Robert E. L. Faris (ed.) *Handbook of Modern Sociology.* Chicago: Rand McNally, pp. 426–455.

Killian, Lewis and Charles Grigg. 1964. *Racial Crisis in America.* Englewood Cliffs, N.J.: Prentice-Hall.

King, Martin Luther, Jr. 1960. *Stride Toward Freedom.* New York: Ballatine Books.

Lomax, Louis E. 1963. *The Negro Revolt.* New York: Signet.

Marx, Karl. 1956. Karl *Marx: Selected Writings in Sociology and Social Philosophy.* New York: McGraw-Hill.

Micossi, Anita Lynn. 1970. "Conversion to Women's Lib." *Trans-Action* 8 (November/December): 82–90.

Mills, C. Wright, 1962. "Inventory of Ideas" in *The Marxists.* New York: Dell: 81–95.

Morris, Richard T. and Raymond J. Murphy. 1966. "A Paradigm for the Study of Class Consciousness." *Sociology and Social Research* 50 (April): 298–313.

Myrdal, Gunnar. 1962. *An American Dilemma.* New York: Harper and Row.

Nelson, Elizabeth Ness and Edward E. Nelson. 1974. "Age 'Passing.'" Unpublished paper presented at the annual meeting of the American Sociological Association, August, 1972.

Nieto, Consuelo. 1974. "The Chicano and the Women's Rights Movement." *Civil Rights Digest* 6 (Spring): 36–42.

Oberschall, Anthony. 1973. *Social Conflict and Social Movements.* Englewood Cliffs, N.J.: Prentice-Hall.

Ransford, H. Edward. 1977. "Stratum Solidarity in a Period After the Watts Riot." In H. Edward Ransford *Race and Class in American Society: Black, Chicano and Anglo.* Cambridge, Mass.: Schenkman: 136–144.

Shibutani, Tamotsu. 1961. *Society and Personality.* Englewood Cliffs, N.J.: Prentice-Hall.

Trela, James A. 1973. "Old Age and Collective Political Action." Unpublished paper presented at the annual meeting of the Gerontological Society. Miami, Florida, November: 5–9.

A Paradigm for the Study of Class Consciousness

Richard T. Morris and Raymond J. Murphy

Abstract

The concept of class consciousness has been used to refer to a variety of subjective dispositions from the general ability to perceive a stratification hierarchy to the dedicated pursuit of an ideology expressed in terms of collective mass action. Such disparate definitions are reflected in an equally varied array of techniques for identifying class conscious persons. This major purpose of this paper is to present an analytical scheme which affords a systematic way of comparing the various types of subjective perceptions and identifications in a stratified society.

THE STUDY of class consciousness is certainly at the core of stratification theory and research. In fact, the very term "social class" is often based on an assumption of the presence of class consciousness. MacIver and Page, for example, insist that "Whatever objective criteria we use, we do not have a social class unless consciousness is present. If white collar workers, for example, do not regard themselves as belonging to the same class as industrial workers, then they do not together form one social class."[1] It is generally agreed that without such consciousness or awareness on the part of the members of a society we are dealing only with "statistical classes" or strata.[2]

Reprinted by permission of SOCIOLOGY AND SOCIAL RESEARCH: An International Journal, 50 (April, 1966). "A Paradigm for the Study of Class Consciousness," by Richard T. Morris and Raymond J. Murphy.

Yet, despite the central importance of stratification as a field of study in sociology[3] and despite the central position of class consciousness in the study of stratification, there is a great deal of vagueness, unclarity, and disagreement as to what class consciousness is as a theoretical construct, and as to how it can be measured empirically. It is the purpose of this paper to propose a paradigm for the study of this basic sociological idea, and to outline several of the major theoretical and methodological positions on the definitions and measurement of class consciousness.

Through the use of the paradigm the authors attempt to bring some order to the definitional phase of the problem and to pose some very tentative hypotheses about the formation of class consciousness, its determinants and its results.[4] The paradigm has three uses: (1) first as a classification scheme for variant definitions and research methodologies already employed in this area; (2) second, as a set of social-psychological propositions about the way in which class consciousness develops in an individual member or group in a society; and (3) third, a set of propositions about the way in which class consciousness develops, can be made to develop, or can be impeded, in a society.

The paradigm can be most readily presented as a social-psychological model. The first ingredient necessary for class consciousness in an individual is some sort of perception of differences in status, of a status range or hierarchy in his society. It is possible that some people do not perceive any stratification phenomena in their view of society, but rather assume and operate as though all individuals or groups are equal in

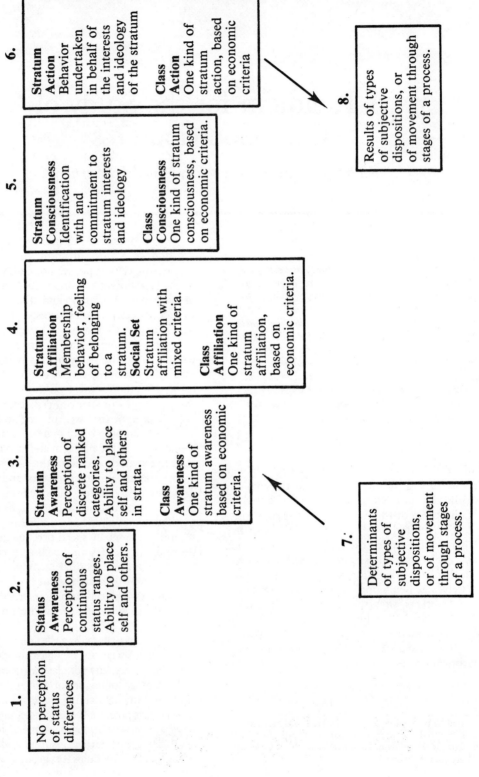

1.

No perception of status differences

2.

Status Awareness
Perception of continuous status ranges. Ability to place self and others.

3.

Stratum Awareness
Perception of discrete ranked categories. Ability to place self and others in strata.

Class Awareness
One kind of stratum awareness based on economic criteria.

4.

Stratum Affiliation
Membership behavior, feeling of belonging to a stratum.
Social Set
Stratum affiliation with mixed criteria.

Class Affiliation
One kind of stratum affiliation, based on economic criteria.

5.

Stratum Consciousness
Identification with and commitment to stratum interests and ideology

Class Consciousness
One kind of stratum consciousness, based on economic criteria.

6.

Stratum Action
Behavior undertaken in behalf of the interests and ideology of the stratum

Class Action
One kind of stratum action, based on economic criteria

7.

Determinants of types of subjective dispositions, or of movement through stages of a process.

8.

Results of types of subjective dispositions, or of movement through stages of a process.

A Paradigm for the Study of Class Consciousness

value. Although we would expect this situation to be rare, we have designated Box 1 of the paradigm to represent this lack of status perception.

Once status differences are perceived, they can take the form of a continuous range of gradations from high to low prestige. (In all of the discussion which follows, our usage of the term status refers to positions arranged in a rank order of evaluation, not simply any position defined by a role). Some students of stratification maintain that this is the perception of most Americans. The equalitarian value system of this country, the lack of a feudal past, the relative absence of the more obvious symbols of class distinction (titles, dress, manners, etc.), the high rate of mobility, abundant economy, and other factors are thought to contribute to a perception of the stratification structure as a more or less complete series (or several parallel series) of status positions hierarchically ordered, but without clear dividing points, or strata.[5] The perception of this hierarchy, and the ability on the part of members of a society to place self and others on this kind of status continuum we should like to term "status awareness" (Box 2). According to this definition, the usual occupational rating scales, even though they may show a great deal of consistency, are not evidences of class consciousness, but of uniformity in status awareness.[6]

It is also possible that people in a society, when they perceive status differences, see discrete categories instead of a continuum of status positions. Such categories are also ordered in a hierarchy of evaluation. The practice of perceiving self and others in ranked categories of status we will term "stratum awareness" (Box 3).[7]

The most commonly perceived strata in industrial societies are probably those based upon the criteria of educational attainment, occupation, economic rewards and life style, religious affiliation, political orientation, genealogical, ethnic, and racial ancestry. In our view, class is a particular kind of stratum based upon the exclusively economic criteria of ownership and control of goods and services as expressed in the operation of the market economy.[8] The perception of such economic strata, and the ability to place self and others in them we will term class awareness, which is but one kind of stratum awareness.

It could be argued, as illustrated at the beginning of this paper, that class cannot exist without class awareness, i.e., that economic strata without stratum awareness on the part of the members of society cannot be called classes, but must be termed strata. We have chosen, however, in order to make the terminology consistent, and in order to be able to talk about other kinds of strata (racial, religious, etc.), with or without stratum awareness, to speak of class in these terms also. Objectively described economic strata are herein called classes; classes may or may not be accompanied by class awareness on the part of members of society.

A number of theoretical approaches and empirical findings relate to this type of stratification perception.[9] In these approaches the investigators use the term "class consciousness" to refer to our definition of class awareness. They seem to assume that if class consciousness is present in society, the best way to find out about its extent and other properties is to ask the members of society directly what their perceptions of class are. The problem is usually investigated in one of two ways: (1) The respondent is asked to comment about the structure of the community or society, so as to reveal his perceptions, if any, of the stratification dimension, or, (2) he is asked the direct question, "What class are you in?" In this latter technique, the structural category is supplied by the investigator and the respondent is asked to fit himself (and sometimes others) into this structure. There are a number of variations in technique, the study may be made nationally, or within a community; the investigator may ask a random sample of members or use judges to make placements of others; the number and names of classes may be specified in advance by the investigator, or the information may be drawn from the opinions of the respondents in order not to prestructure their perceptions.[10] In all of these techniques, however, the assumption seems to be that unless and until a number of the members of a community or society, especially important members, e.g., community leaders, are able to say that there are classes, are able to say how many there are, what the names of the classes are and are able to place themselves and others in these classes, class consciousness does not exist. According to these writers, class consciousness is present in the society to the degree that there is a common perception of such ranked categories.

Both the ability to perceive strata and the number of strata perceived seem to be a function of the positional location of the individual in his social and occupational spheres. Popitz has shown that in Germany, for example, the socioeconomic position of the individual plays an important role in determining whether he perceives society as a status or stratum arrangement.[11] Similarly, Hoggart describes the image of the British working class member as a dichotomous one, with little propensity to view society as composed of a series of infinitely graded statuses.[12] Dahrendorf suggests that these differing models of society distinguished by individuals represent a commitment to ideology. Those with a perception of status gradations represent an ideology of satisfaction and conservatism, while those who see society stratified into discrete strata (the dichotomous image) are more likely to be dissatisfied and express a wish for change in the *status quo*.[13]

It should be noted again at this point that we still are not talking about or defining class consciousness. Most of the studies referred to above are, from our point of view, studies of stratum awareness (or sometimes class awareness) rather than of class consciousness. They are basically measures of the ability of members of a society or community to place themselves and others into a set of categories; they say nothing at all of membership identification, interaction patterns, or commitment to an ideology, as criteria.[14]

Moving on to Box 4 of the paradigm, it may be proposed that the next step in the development of stratum consciousness is the emergence of group membership properties. The category (whether it be racial, economic, religious, etc.) takes on the characteristics of a *group* (or a series of related groups) of interacting individuals who share feelings of belonging, identification with and practice of common norms, expectations, sentiments and activities.[15] This feeling of belonging and the participant behavior which it induces we will term stratum affiliation. As before, we consider class affiliation as one kind of stratum affiliation, based solely on economic criteria. Many investigators use the term "class consciousness" to refer to our definition of class af-

filiation. They seem to assume that individual perception of structure is not a sufficient indicator of class consciousness, but that group membership behavior must be added. It is not enough to perceive class differences, the members of a society must act in accordance with this perception by maintaining patterns of association and dissociation, inclusion and exclusion, in their daily lives. The outstanding proponents of this view are, of course, W. Lloyd Warner and his associates.[16] Although the precise methodology may be rather unclear at times, the general procedure seems to be to combine measures of stratum awareness with an analysis of the actual interaction patterns of the members of a community, such as organizational memberships, attendance at social gatherings and events, intermarriage and dating regularities, and the like. Again, although there are variations in technique, the studies are usually carried out in small communities, but may be investigated in a large metropolis;[17] or on an intercommunity, national or even international level.[18] The investigators may use a combination of ratings by judges, comments from community members, organizational membership lists, "blue books" of various kinds, sociometric techniques, and other methods to arrive at the composition of classes. The investigator who supplies class names to his respondents may "synthetically" arrive at the membership variable by asking respondents to list the organizations they belong to. He then classifies as class consciousness those individuals who identify with a class category and who belong to an organization (usually economic or political) thought by the investigator to be class linked. For example, those who check "working class" from a list of classes and who belong to labor unions may be classified by the researcher as class conscious. "Inappropriate" group memberships serve to identify the nonclass conscious or the "false" class conscious.[19] In all of these techniques there seems to be the assumption that in a society, or a community, class consciousness is expressed through differential interaction patterns and identification and membership in groups reflecting some order of social evaluation, from high to low prestige. The degree of class consciousness varies with the clarity of the differential interaction patterns, e.g., exclusion and inclusion, and with the clarity of and agreement upon, the prestige ranking of these groups.[20] Anderson and Davidson make explicit this meaning of class and class consciousness:

[a self-conscious class] means a social group distinguishable from all other groups by the intimacy of its relationships, aware of its distinction and regardful of its position in the social scale, resisting intrusion from below, fearful of intrusion from above, having a like scale of living, its individual members 'going with' and intermarrying in the group, sharing group rituals and ceremonies, possessing a sense of 'belonging' and for the most part not expecting and perhaps not eager to alter its status. . . . When such a group acquires a sense of permanence, continuing through successive generations, it may be considered a 'class'. When this class becomes aware of its distinct character, develops a ritual and ceremony of membership and class taboos, and is regardful of itself as a distinct entity in the community, then it may be said to have acquired 'class consciousness.'[21]

It should be noted that not all group or organizational affiliation is stratum affiliation and that stratum awareness seems logically to be a necessary precondition for stratum affiliation. In other words, the groups or membership units have to be stratified subjectively, have to be seen by the members of society as ordered in a hierarchy of evaluation before we can speak of stratum affiliation, as distinct from group affiliation. Again, there are many varieties of stratum affiliation: racial stratum affiliation; occupational stratum affiliation; religious stratum affiliation, and class affiliation. Perhaps the most commonly discussed stratum affiliation in American sociology is the community set portrayed by Warner and others. Although these are usually called social classes in the literature, we prefer the term "social set" to refer to these strata made up of mixed criteria, usually genealogy, life style, geographical location, as well as income, and restrict the use of the term class affiliation to mean membership in and identification with exclusively economic strata. The existence of social sets in a community, or in society generally, does not necessarily imply or mean that there is class consciousness or even class affiliation in that community or society. In fact, the existence of

such sets may be a factor precluding or impeding the development of class affiliation, particularly in the sense that any affiliation with stratum groups other than economic may indicate a higher priority of other values and a more meaningful identification with noneconomic aspects of social life. Thus Weber explains the lack of class antagonism and consciousness in the American South by pointing to the importance of the racial affiliation dimension in stratifying the population along noneconomic lines.[22] To speak properly of class affiliation, the stratum criterion must be exclusively economic;[23] to speak properly of class consciousness there must be a commitment to an ideology.

Stratum consciousness (Box 5) is identification with, or commitment to, the interests and ideology of the stratum. It is not enough to perceive the stratification system as being divided into strata and to be able to place self and others in it. It is not enough to feel and behave as a member of the stratum. There must be a knowledge of and a commitment to the interests, aims, and goals of the stratum before we can speak about the presence of stratum consciousness. Again, as above, we consider class consciousness as one kind of stratum consciousness, based solely on economic criteria. Many investigators seem to agree with this definition, and assume that class consciousness is not merely a matter of perception of structure or of group membership and prestige arrangements. They argue that it is essential to the very idea of class consciousness that some sort of commitment to class interest or ideology be present, together with participation in a program of action to forward these interests in the name of the class. Class consciousness often represents a political awareness and orientation. As C. Wright Mills puts it:

Class consciousness has always been understood as a political consciousness of one's own rational class interests and their opposition to the interests of other classes. Economic potentiality becomes politically realized: 'a class in itself' becomes a 'class for itself.' Thus for class consciousness there must be (1) a rational awareness and identification with one's own class interests; (2) an awareness of and rejection of other class interests as illegitimate; and (3) an awareness of and a readiness to use collective political means to the collective political end of realizing one's political interests.[24]

This approach is one which most closely articulates with that of Marx in its emphasis on class action and conflicting interests as essential components of a "mature" class consciousness. Proponents of this orientation, too, place greater stress on structural factors producing class differences. Instead of focusing primarily on the subjective perception of classes or strata and from such psychological data investigating or deducing structural correlates, these investigators analyze broad socioeconomic trends in the structure and analyze or deduce their psychological expression or consequences. Lockwood, for example, analyzes the psychological and behavioral resistance of the British "black-coated" worker to the Labor party in terms of broad historical trends in the work situation, the status structure of British society, and the changing pattern of economic rewards in the English labor force.[25] Similarly, Mills investigates the "social-historical" structure of the United States to account for the apolitical mentality of the white-collar class.[26] A parallel, though usually less broad approach involves the study of the political economic, of social reform attitudes or behavior of individuals located at different points in the social structure, e.g., in different occupations, in unions vs. management positions, at different income levels, in different political parties.[27] Here a typical finding and conclusion might be that if members of unions or those in unskilled occupations favored economic reforms, while those in managerial or professional occupations did not, this is prima facie evidence of class consciousness. In such investigations frequently the respondent is not asked to describe his subjective views about stratification, nor is he required to place himself or others in the system. Rather, he is asked to supply information on his objective status (e.g., occupation, income, education) and asked for his attitudes about political and/or economic issues or for his voting preferences. Thus Glanz, for example, classifies his respondents as class conscious if they are business or white collar people who say they owe allegiance to business (rather than to labor) and if their responses to six attitude items, derived from AFL-CIO and NAM statements show a "business

orientation." In such investigations, then, the researcher rather than the respondent, describes on the existence of and expression of class consciousness.[28]

The ideological approach to the study of class consciousness varies in its theoretical assumptions as well as in its techniques. Some theorists maintain that true class consciousness (as opposed to false) must involve a revolutionary ideology, a clear idea of an enemy class and the desire to destroy it as a necessary part of the action program for the class.[29] This view, of course, stems from the writings of Marx who defined classes as economic groups in opposition: "Individuals form a class only insofar as they are engaged in a common struggle with another class."[30] Others do not hold that revolutionary action or the ideology of inevitable class war are essential, but rather insist that class conscious persons are those who have internalized the interests and aims of their class, and are fully committed to their achievement. Weber seems to have taken this position with regard to property classes:

> The differentiation of classes on the basis of property alone is not 'dynamic' that is, it does not necessarily result in class struggle or class revolutions. It is not uncommon for very strongly privileged property classes such as slave owners, to exist side by side with such far less privileged groups as peasants or even outcasts without any class struggle. There may even be ties of solidarity between privilaged property classes and unfree elements.[31]

Another point about which opinions may differ concerns whether or not real as opposed to intended or hypothetical action must be demonstrated before class consciousness can be said to exist. The proper aim of action also may be disputed. For the more orthodox Marxist, economic issues may be paramount and only political action directed to changes in the basic economic issues may be viewed as indicative of true class consciousness. Others might view actions aimed at "exclusion of undesirables" or aims of union organizations to increase bargaining strengths as indicative of class consciousness.

In the face of these disagreements, in order to provide for a more flexible use of the concept with strata other than classes, we have chosen to use a rather broad definition of the content of the ideology or interests of the stratum. Very generally, by ideology we refer to any set of programmatic goals which involve the use of any means to ensure the maintenance, protection, or improvement of the position of a particular stratum relative to other strata.

More specifically, in order to separate stratum ideology from more general stratum attitudes or values for operational purposes (e.g., middle class values vs. middle class ideology), it may be proposed tentatively that stratum ideology must include the following component elements: (a) an understanding of the present position of the stratum in relation to other strata (e.g., higher, lower, exploited, in power, out of power, superior, inferior, elect, despised, etc.); (b) an explanation or rationale accounting for the present position (e.g., God's will, the nature of man or society, the machinations of another stratum, historical accident, inevitable evolution, etc.); (c) an evaluation or justification of the present position (e.g., legitimate, illegitimate, justified, unfair, intolerable, functionally necessary, threatened, promising, etc.); (d) a proposal of action to be taken in order to maintain, protect, or improve the present position (e.g. political activity, cooperation or conflict with other strata, economic changes, passive acceptance or resistance, educational improvement, legal or illegal action, etc.); and (e) a statement of a desirable ultimate future position and role for the stratum (e.g., as co-equals, as the only existing stratum, national or international betterment, amalgamation, disappearance, a return to the past position, etc).

It is implied in the present discussion that, similar to stratum affiliation, it is possible to discover many varieties of *stratum consciousness,* of which class consciousness is but one type. We can speak of race strata consciousness, occupational strata consciousness, religious strata consciousness, etc., to the extent that the groupings are stratified and the members are identified with and committed to the ideology of the stratum.

An old problem in the literature on class consciousness concerns the issue of whether or not class action is an essential ingredient in consciousness. This difficulty rests in part with the problem of differentiating commitment from activity. It is possible to imagine individuals who are sympathetic to the causes of their class, but who are unable or unwilling to act in its behalf. Is the person who "mans the barricades" more class conscious than the one who wishes him well in his fight? This issue has methodological consequences for us in that it raises the question (almost as ancient in our literature) as to whether attitudes are a form of behavior. Does the respondent who expresses discontent in his replies to an attitude scale, have as much class consciousness as the person who indicates membership participation and activity with others in the cause of his class? We have chosen to separate the concept of class action from class consciousness in the belief that it makes sense, that it is theoretically useful to speak of class consciousness with or without class action on the part of individual members, and that the separation clarifies the nature of class action itself.

Stratum action (Box 6) is behavior undertaken by an individual or group on behalf of the interests of the stratum. This implies that class consciousness (awareness and commitment to the interests) is logically a necessary precondition for class action. By action we mean some form of overt behavior explicitly motivated by what are thought to be class (or stratum) interests on the part of the participants. This may mean proseletyzing friends, distributing propaganda, organizing and joining in strikes, supporting political candidates, boycotting stores, "sit in" demonstrations, participating in passive resistance programs, etc. In each case, the behavior must, according to our definition, be based upon and directed toward the satisfaction or resolution of class (or other stratum) interests. Not all behavior that looks like class or stratum action actually is. Studies which correlate voting behavior with occupation, or attitudes toward picketing with union membership usually have *not* by our definition, demonstrated the presence of class action (or in many cases class consciousness) for two reasons: (1) There is no demonstration that the behavior is based on and motivated by an awareness of and commitment to class or stratum. (2) A set of attitudes or predispositions to act in a hypothetical situation do not constitute action *per se* (although they may be useful devices for predicting potential actors). It is true, that in actual tactics, a person may become engaged in class or stratum action without being class conscious, and he may find out "why" his actions were significant at a later date, e.g., in a well-organized student riot. Subjectively, the person is not engaged in class action, if he goes along for the excitement, the satisfaction of a personal interest or motive (e.g., a share of the rewards of looting), or simply because he happened to be present when the activity was taking place and he is forced to "choose sides."[32] From the point of view of the group organizing the riot, it may well be class action perhaps consciously involving the use of "dupes" to swell the ranks of participants. Here again, we can speak of a variety of *stratum actions* insofar as persons engage in behavior directed toward the achievement of stratum interests.

The remaining elements of the paradigm involve the determinants and results of being in a given box, i.e., having a certain subjective disposition (perception, attitude, behavior) at a given point in time, or in moving as part of a process from one box to another.

It is impossible within the limits of this discussion to do more than make a bare and merely suggestive list of possible determinants of the predominant mode of stratum attitude or behavior in a given society, group, or individual, or of the determinants which facilitate or deter the movement from one type of stratum attitude to another.

The first problem is whether or not in a given society the attitudes toward economic strata (or classes) are more highly developed or salient than attitudes toward other kinds of strata or status hierarchies, e.g., racial, religious, kinship, age, etc. Davis and Moore, and Parsons, among others, seem to agree that the salient criteria for stratification are closely related to the predominant value system of the society. As values change, the importance of various stratification (according to new, or newly important) criteria may emerge. In other words, differential evaluation by economic criteria may become less important or irrelevant, as the value system changes in certain ways. In addition to value determinants, there are structural determinants, e.g., a compression of the range of economic differences, a mixture of racial characteristics, or universal compulsory education through college, which may make certain stratification systems less important,

irrelevant, or impossible to apply. There of course may be discrepancies between the rates of change of value determinants and structural determinants, e.g., the need for artificial labelling of some Jews in Nazi Germany; the difficulty in shifting from a racial stratification system to an economic stratification system in some African nations.

The second problem, given the relative salience of various social hierarchies, is the extent to which these systems are seen as continuous ranges or as vertical arrangements of discrete categories. In our terminology, is there status awareness or stratum awareness among the various hierarchies? Class awareness cannot exist unless the economic criterion is salient, and is used in such a way as to create discrete categories. The chief determinants of perceptive posture in this sense are probably social psychological and structural. The concepts of ambiguity tolerance, rites of passage, role clarity, stereotype, the embedding process are relevant here. The structural determinants may involve such factors as availability of knowledge about, or visibility of, criteria, the degree of demarcation and formalization of symbols of achieved or ascribed rank, the overlap and discrepancy of multiple, coexistent status hierarchies. It is possible that within this list of determinants, for example, we might find reasons why income and occupation are seen as continuous status ranges in our society, why education, and race are divided into discrete stratum categories, and why ownership vs. nonownership is very difficult to use as a criterion at all.

The third problem, given salience of criteria and the perception of strata, is whether or not the strata take on group characteristics. The determinants of the transformation of a collectivity into a group, such as the emergence of interaction patterns, norms, division of labor, roles, etc. are too complex—and at the same time too familiar—to be described here. Suffice to say that many of the preconditions for the formation of classes as groups which were suggested by Marx are still applicable, e.g., communication, interaction, organization, common experience, leadership.

The fourth problem, once the stratum becomes a group, whether it be an economic group, an occupational group, a racial group, or an educational group, is to establish the extent to which the stratum is committed to some ideology or programmatic goal of action. The determinants of the establishment of an ideology have been outlined by Marx and include such elements as a sense of injustice, unwarranted deprivation, dissatisfaction with the system, placement of blame, loyalty and responsibility to group goals, overthrow as the only successful solution. Viewed from the top, we might add such elements as fear of losing identity, protection against intrusion from below, fear of failing, desire to maintain position for next generation, desire to expand or gain more control, and the like. Propaganda, education, a rationale and explication of present conditions, goals and appropriate action are important factors—such determinants should help explain the development of ideologies in professionalization, unionization, or the action programs of racial organizations.

The final problem, once the goals have been set and organized action proposed, is to estabish the conditions under which such action is actually carried out.

Again, within these limits we can only suggest such broad factors as financing, leadership, organization, pressure or aid from the outside, critical incidents, etc.

In closing we would like to summarize what seem to us to be the major contributions of the paradigm to the study of subjective aspects of stratification and to pose some of the questions which the scheme has raised as we have worked on it. The model's most apparent use is in conceptual clarification, both in the differentiation between class consciousness and other types of consciousness, and between class consciousness and other types of subjective perception and identification. While our particular definition of class consciousness may seem unduly restricted to some, particularly since the empirical facts of American life seem to preclude its existence, this narrowness may prevent us from trying to fit a Marxian concept developed to explain 19th Century European social structure to the 20th Century conditions of highly bureaucratized society. If Weber's analytical distinction among class, status, and power have any heuristic significance at all, and the majority of sociologists seem to think they do, then it behooves us to carry out these distinctions in matters of the subjective meanings of stratification. In our distinction between stratum consciousness and class consciousness we have at-

tempted to follow out the implications of this distinction.

Another contribution of the paradigm, as we see it, is its use as an orientation to the analysis of the subjective aspects of social stratification. As has already been suggested, the paradigm can be used as a model for investigating the development of differing states of subjective awareness concerning stratification phenomena. The implication here is that class consciousness (or any other form of stratum consciousness) is a *processual* emergent and that it must be studied in a dynamic framework, either historical or biographical, rather than as a characteristic which is either present or absent among a population at a given time.[33]

A third potentially useful function of the paradigm is in the application as a framework for the comparative analysis of differing kinds of awareness and commitment to social groups or categories which exhibit rank characteristics. We have called attention to the fact that class consciousness is but one kind of stratum consciousness which may be expressed by the members of a society. The paradigm is constructed in such a manner as to invite the analysis of different types of perception and commitment, i.e., those related to racial characteristics, occupational groups, religious denominations, age groups, educational attainment, etc. It would seem to us fruitful for those interested in race relations, for example, to use the paradigm as a model for the study of the development (or disappearance) of race consciousness in a population. Furthermore, many of the studies which have been made of the development of racial prejudice should be classifiable in terms of our categories. The examination of such material might well suggest underlying similarities in the process of perception and identification with race and class. Such comparisons have often been impeded in the past because we have lacked a framework for including both kinds of interests and due to increasing specialization of fields within sociology and social psychology we have had little opportunity to exchange views. A comparative study of subjective perceptions might lead us to ask (and hopefully to answer) such questions as: Under what, if any, conditions does race consciousness lead to class consciousness? Does a preoccupation with race inhibit a commitment to class ideology? Are there "functional equivalents'' for class consciousness in a society?[34]

The paradigm is a suggestion for a way of bringing some order to a field of inquiry which continues to fascinate, but which, unfortunately, is still accurately described by Morris Ginsberg's conclusion of 1937:

The psychology of class differentiation has not been studied with sufficient thoroughness and there is as yet no generally accepted technique for the observation, analysis, and record of the behavior of groups in relation to one another. Accordingly it is extremely difficult to say what exactly one is conscious of when one is class conscious.[35]

NOTES

1. Robert M. MacIver & Charles H. Page, *Society* (New York: Rinehart, 1949), 350.

2. See for example, Gerhard Lenski, "American Social Classes: Statistical Strata of Social Groups?", *American Journal of Sociology,* 58 (September, 1952), 139–44; Richard T. Morris, "Social Stratification," in Leonard Broom & Phillip Selznick, *Sociology,* (Evanston: Row, Peterson, 1958), 165–88; Hans Speier, "Social Stratification in the Urban Community," *American Sociological Review,* 1 (April, 1936), 192–202.

3. The subject of stratification is included routinely in introductory text books; a number of specialized texts and readers have appeared in recent years; a special issue of *The American Journal of Sociology* published in 1953 listed a bibliography of 333 items dealing with the topic, 58, (January, 1953), 391–418). See also Richard L. Simpson, "Expanding and Declining Fields in American Sociology," *American Sociological Review,* 26 (June, 1961), 458–66.

4. For a somewhat parallel discussion of class consciousness and related types of awareness, see Milton M. Gordon, "A System of Social Class Analysis," *The Drew University Bulletin,* 39 (August, 1951), 1–19.

5. See Stanley Hetzler, "An Investigation of the Distinctiveness of Social Classes," *American Sociological Review,* 18 (October, 1953), 493–97, and William F. Kenkel, *An Experimental Analysis of Social Stratification in Columbus, Ohio,* unpublished Ph.D. dissertation, Department of Sociology, The Ohio State University, 1952, summarized in John F. Cuber & William F. Kenkel, *Social Stratification,* (New York: Appleton-Century-Crofts, 1954), 132–56.

6. For an excellent summary and analysis of the NORC occupational prestige material, see Albert J. Reiss, *Occupational and Social Status* (New York: The Free Press, a Division of the Macmillan Co., 1962).

7. We could also speak of *situs awareness,* the ability to place self and others into discrete categories which are not differentially evaluated. See Richard T. Morris & Raymond J. Murphy, "The Situs Dimension in Occupational Structure," *American Sociological Review,* 24 (April, 1959), 231–39.

8. We have chosen to take this restricted economic definition of class in order to avoid confusion with other kinds of strata, also to avoid contradiction with the large, established body of literature which uses the term in the economic sense, e.g., Marx, Weber, Schumpter, etc.

9. The "functionalist" school of stratification would presumably fit into this category. See Kingsley Davis, "Conceptual Analysis of Stratification," *American Sociological Review,* 7 (June, 1942), 309–21, Kingsley Davis and Wilbert E. Moore, "Some Principles of Stratification," *American Sociological Review,* 10 (April, 1945), 242–49 and Talcott Parsons, "An Analytical Approach to the Theory of Social Stratification," in *Essays in Sociological Theory: Pure and Applied,* (New York: The Free Press, a Division of the Macmillan Co., 1949), 166–84, for representative examples.

10. For examples of this methodology see Richard Centers, *The Psychology of Social Class,* (Princeton: Princeton University Press, 1949), Neal Gross, "Social Class Identification in the Urban Community," *American Sociological Review,* 18 (August, 1953), 398–404, Harold F. Kaufman, *Prestige Classes in a New York Rural Community,* (Ithaca: Cornell University Agricultural Experiment Station, Memoir 260, March 1944), and F. M. Martin, "Some Subjective Aspects of Social Stratification," in D. V. Glass (Ed.), New York: The Free Press, a Division of the Macmillan Co., 1954), 51–75.

11. Heinrich Popitz *et al.,* Das Gesellschaftsbild des Arbeiters, (Tubingen, 1957), 237, 252, quoted in Rolf Dahrendorf, *Class and Class Conflict in Industrial Society,* (Stanford: Stanford University Press, 1959), 283–84.

12. Richard Hoggart, *The Uses of Literacy,* (Boston: Beacon Press, 1961), esp. 62–77.

13. Rolf Dahrendorf, *op. cit.,* 284.

14. A number of different criteria are used or discov-

ered in these studies. "Class" may refer to occupational strata, ethnic strata, educational strata, as well as to economic strata. Some of these studies demonstrate that people are thinking in terms of class simply by supplying the word to them, without specifying what they or the investigator means by it. See Neal Gross, *op. cit.*

15. Our meaning of the concept "group" here is similar to that employed by Smith: "A unit consisting of a plural number of organisms (agents) who have collective perception of their unity and who have the ability to act, or who are acting, in a unitary manner toward the environment." M. Smith, "Social Situation, Social Behavior, Social Group," *Psychological Review,* 52, (1945), 224–29.

16. See especially, W. Lloyd Warner & Paul S. Lunt, *The Social Life of a Modern Community,* (New York: Yale University Press, 1941), 81–126; W. Lloyd Warner and Associates, *Democracy in Jonesville,* (New York: Harper, 1949); and W. Lloyd Warner, Marchia Meeker, & Kenneth Eells, *Social Class in America,* (Chicago: Science Research Associates, 1949).

17. See the study of the upper class in Philadelphia by, E. Digby Baltzell, *Philadelphia Gentlemen,* (New York: The Free Press, a Division of the Macmillan Co., 1958), and the journalistic but relevant work by Cleveland Amory, especially *The Proper Bostonians,* (New York: Dutton, 1947).

18. See for example, Thomas Bottomore "Social Stratification in Voluntary Organizations," & Rosalind C. Chambers, "A Study of Three Voluntary Organizations," both in D. V. Glass, *op cit.,* 349–406.

19. This logic is followed (along with a measure of allegiance) by Oscar Glantz in "Class Consciousness and Political Solidarity," *American Sociological Review,* 23 (August, 1958), 375–83. See also, Richard Centers *op cit.*

20. A closely related approach is the subcultural view which assumes that classes are composed of groupings of the population with different ways of life, values, behavior patterns, norms, and the like. See Milton M. Gordon, "The Concept of Sub-Culture and Its Application," *Social Forces* 26 (October, 1947), 40–42 and Joseph A. Kahl, *The American Class Structure,* (New York: Rinehart, 1957), esp. Ch. VII, "Classes as Ideal Types: Emergent Values," 184–220.

21. H. Dewey Anderson & Percy E. Davidson, *Ballots and the Democratic Class Struggle* (Stanford: Stanford University Press, 1943), 211–12.

22. Max Weber, "Social Stratification and Class Structure," in Weber, *The Theory of Social and Economic Organization* (Parsons & Henderson Tr.) (New York: The Free Press, a Division of the Macmillan Co., 1947), 425–26.

23. See the distinction drawn between competitive class feeling and "corporate class consciousness" by MacIver and Page, *op. cit.,* 359–60, for a similar view.

24. C. Wright Mills, *White Collar* (New York: Oxford University Press, 1951), 325.

25. David Lockwood, *The Blackcoated Worker* (London: George Allen & Unwin, 1958).

26. C. Wright Mills, *op. cit.*

27. For an example of this kind of analysis, see Angus Campbell, *et. al., The American Voter* (New York: John Wiley and Sons, 1960), esp. Ch. 13, "The Role of Social Class," 333–80. See also, Bernard R. Berelson, Paul F. Lazarsfeld, and William N. McPhee, *Voting* (Chicago: University of Chicago Press, 1954), 56–60.

28. Oscar Glantz, *op. cit.*

29. See, for example, Nikolai Bukharin, *Historical Materialism* (New York: International Publishers, 1925): "A class interest arises when it places one class in opposition to another. The class struggle arises when it throws one class into active conflict with the other.", 297.

30. Karl Marx & Friedrich Engels, *The German Ideology* (London: Lawrence & Wishart, 1939), II, 59.

31. Max Weber, *op. cit.*

32. An interesting example of this involuntary involvement in collective behavior is provided by Alfred McClung Lee & Norman D. Humphrey, *Race Riot* (New York: Dryden Press, 1943).

33. See Rudolph Heberle "Recovery of Class Theory" and Robert A. Nisbet "The Decline and Fall of Social Class," *Pacific Sociological Review,* 2, (Spring, 1959), 11–24.

34. The recent study of the Muslim movement in the United States by E. U. Essien-Udom is most suggestive of the relationship between race consciousness and class awareness. It is the author's hypothesis that the lower class urban Negro has become estranged both from the white society and the middle-class Negro group. "This estrangement suggests the beginning of class consciousness and conflict among the Negro masses, directed not against whites, but against the Negro middle and upper classes." See E. U. Essien-Udom, *Black Nationalism* (Chicago: University of Chicago Press, 1962), esp. 326–39.

35. Morris Ginsberg, "Class Consciousness," in Edwin R. A. Seligman & Alvin Johnson (eds.), *The Encyclopedia of the Social Sciences* (New York: The Macmillan Co., 1937), Vol III, 538.

Conversion to Women's Lib

Anita Lynn Micossi

THE IMAGE of woman in art and literature reflects the general image of woman in society; at once debased and unreasonably glorified. Unlike the blacks, who until recently were all but invisible in Western art and literature, women are nearly ubiquitous. But when men write of women they are usually either looking down to the whore or up to the goddess—rarely across to another human being. And when she writes about herself the view is much the same: she's either apologizing for her weakness or exalting some "natural" triumph like the "maternal instinct."

But between the Madonna and the harlot is a vast middle ground where humans realize most of their "humanness," and this is what concerns those who wish to expose the mythology of woman; in particular this is what concerns today's movement for Women's Liberation. In sifting through the layers of fantasy and fiction, Women's Liberation has uncovered the intangibles of this oppressive condition as well as material evidence. And in trying to relate these discoveries to others it has found that understanding the woman's predicament demands new concepts and analyses. Accordingly, Women's Liberation has developed an elaborate philosophy to define and articulate its insights. Of course, not all women who identify with Women's Liberation wholeheartedly subscribe to all its views, but many do, and of the women in the movement whom I talked with, all do. As will doubtless be apparent, I, too, subscribe to the beliefs and outlook of Women's Liberation, but my aim here is not to make any converts. It is rather to describe who

gets converted to Women's Lib and how and why. First, though, a word about what it is they get converted to.

Briefly, the basic assertion of the Movement is that a problem exists and that it is social in character. The problem is the general oppression of all women, and this oppression is seen as qualitatively different from the dismal (to some) "human condition." Although the consequences of the oppression are peculiar to women, it resembles the dilemma of all subjugated groups and has a dual nature: first, structural and material discrimination, with its economic, social, legal, and cultural forms, and second, the subjective and psychological participation of women in their own abuse. The subjective aspect is the result of the material condition and reinforces it: a condition of slavery preceded the "happy slave mentality."

From this common belief, modern feminists take off in various directions. Some elaborate the problem in Marxist analyses. Others take a more moderate stance. But whatever the political style, the essential point remains consistent and universal: a woman faces unique obstacles in realizing her full human worth, and these obstacles are rooted in the depths of her consciousness as well as in the society around her.

THE BACKGROUND

Who are the converts? Based on my own participation in the Women's Liberation movement over the past year and on a series of biographical interviews I recently conducted in and around an urban university community, I can say that they are a disparate group. My own subjects came from working-class, middle-class and upper-class backgrounds; their ages went from 19 to 41; they were married, single and divorced; they were with and without children of various age levels; and they were of different religious and ethnic origins. I found them strikingly similar in only two ways: all are Caucasian and all have at least some college education. This probably reflects more the bias of the movement than of my sampling. Although the message is rapidly spreading throughout the country, the origins and continuing centers of Women's Liberation activity are in large urban and university areas. Nevertheless, on the chance that my own sample was too constricted, I worked with another woman, Diane D'Agostino, who, using similar techniques, talked with feminists in groups and with interests different from my ten subjects.

What are some of the conditions that predispose a woman to conversion to Women's Lib? Each biography is a unique account of how and when self-images and levels of self-consciousness matured. Not only do these psychological developments occur at different points in the biographies of different individuals but the order in which they appear varies. For example, some of the women grew up with a political problem-solving perspective. Others had long experienced all the preconditions for conversion, except for a political perspective, which they didn't acquire until college. But this is an idiosyncratic matter of timing. That apart, I believe I can describe the conditions that are both necessary and sufficient for conversion to the beliefs and perspective of Women's Lib.

The first is that a woman must have alternative modes of self-expression and self-esteem beyond the prescribed female sex role. As Betty Friedan, Simone de Beauvoir and others have described it, this traditional role labels the female as inherently passive, weak-willed, frivolous, irrational, emotional, intellectually and physically inferior and dependent. With these imputed characteristics, self-fulfillment can only come with nurturing, motherhood and domesticity. The "traditional woman" gives of herself to the exclusion of personal ambition, desire or need.

The potential convert to Women's Liberation must recognize that there are other alternatives to self-fulfillment than this. Among all the women I interviewed, these other alternatives were available because they all had intelligence, higher education and exposure to upwardly mobile goal orientations. Most had parents who encouraged careers and advanced schooling. One woman was "treated like a son" by her father who was a lawyer and who expected his girl to be like him and have a "public world." Another woman, the second oldest sibling with two brothers, "was definitely my father's favorite, and he encouraged me to be a doctor." This encouragement of ambition and success, clearly antithetical to the traditional role, expanded the range of possibilities for these women in their own minds despite conflicting pressures from school, the media, relatives and the parents themselves to conform to the Feminine Mystique.

Some women were influenced by the example of others who had rejected the constricting image of womanhood in their own lives. One woman describes reading Simone de Beauvoir at age 16 and becoming then and there committed to the feminist perspective. Another grew up with idols like Margaret Sanger, who proved that a woman could do and be more than a mother and domestic. Many others flatly denounced the model of the traditional female closest to them.

- I became committed to a career at an early age because I didn't want to be like my mother.
- I identified with my father [a Ph.D. in physics] because my mother was regarded as the family idiot.
- I associate going crazy with not having a career or meaningful project. Mother had a breakdown and was institutionalized.

These women, even at a very early age, sensed their mothers' dissatisfaction and associated it with their uninspiring lives as housewives. The closest alternative model was the father with his career, his "public world."

Displays of intelligence and academic achievement opened up additional options. One woman was highly precocious as a child, and her parents indulged her interests in books and poetry while letting her out of household chores. Another joined an "anticlique clique" of intellectuals in high school, disdaining the social life of adolescents where girls are expected to play dumb. For several women, intelligence and scholarly excellence became the principal measures of self-esteem, to the exclusion of other "more female" measures like sexiness, popularity and clothes. They rarely if ever played dumb for the sake of appearing more "feminine."

This kind of evidence raises the possibility that significant alternatives to the traditional role of women may be available only to those with an achievement-oriented class background and with access to educational institutions that will develop and affirm their intelligence. If true, this would of course mean that lower-class women are unlikely prospects for conversion. The demands of the black movement, however, have shown that such middle-class values have indeed filtered down into the lower class, although the avenues of realizing these goals have yet to be sufficiently opened. But if and when equal advantage and access are extended to poor and minority groups, then lower-class women will also be exposed to the contradictions of a society that "educates" their minds while encouraging only mindless sorts of self-fulfillment.

Once a woman has a notion, however vague and unarticulated, that housewife-motherhood is not the sole measure of her being, she still needs to see and feel the *discrepancies* between her actual circumstances and her potential, her aspirations and her self-image. This can come about in a number of ways, but a fairly common pattern is that of a woman, aged 40, who had performed brilliantly throughout high school and college and who got most of her self-esteem from personal achievements. She married and felt obliged "as a good wife" to have a child even though she had begun graduate school. Forced into a conventional feminine role which was out of phase with her ambitions and intellectual pursuits, she felt "trapped and suffocated." This resulted in guilt and anxiety about conflicting expectations.

Another woman voices a complaint common to females in New Left politics: "Women get fucked over in the movement." She described the incongruence between the humane and egalitarian programs espoused by male leaders and their actual treatment of "movement chicks." While expected to do the political "shit work," these girls are systematically excluded from policy decision making and strategy planning. Like their housewife counterparts, they are forced into a supportive and passive position vis a vis the male leadership.

Not only do women sense discrepancies between what they know they can do and what others will actually allow them to do, they also sense the injustices caused by arbitrarily assigning sex role obligations and attributes:

> I realized in high school that something was amiss and that "equality" was in fact unilateral giving.
>
> My mother put me in a double bind with her contradictory advice: "You're inferior, but do it anyway." To me this meant, "make up for it" [her inferiority].
>
> It always freaked me out that I would have to change *my* name when I got married. I was surprised to find out that taking one's husband's name was only a custom and not necessarily legal. I don't think many people are aware of that.
>
> I used to wish that I'd been born a man or a moron. An intelligent woman is a contradiction in terms and creates situations very painful to live with.

This last remark is typical. The woman grew up with conflicting and, in a sense, mutually exclusive images of herself. On the one hand, she used her mind and was praised for it. On the other, she was taught that women are by nature passive, inferior and intellectually feeble. When people address only the latter image, this woman has sound reason to feel pushed and hauled between her felt potential and the acceptable means of realizing it. Such women may not doubt their intelligence (any more so than a man), but they are made to doubt the legitimacy of having and showing that intelligence.

The tension and frustration that arise out of felt discrepancies are a very common predicament. Almost all women, be they housewives or workers in a discriminatory job market, feel at one time or another disillusioned and unhappy. What sets Women's Liberation converts apart is their definitions of the problem and their ways of dealing with it. Which brings us to the third precondition of conversion: political problem-solving perspective.

There are many perspectives from which to define a problem, among them the psychiatric, the political, the technological-scientific and the religious. The belief system of Women's Liberation locates the source of problems in the social structure and wishes to change the system as its solution. This kind of program is inherently political. And for an individual to get behind this particular political view she must have some knowledge of, if not experience with, the potential of political solutions in general. It's not surprising then that the Women's Liberation Movement grew up around university centers, where we find high concentrations of political activity, at least in the past decade.

Few of the women I talked with came from homes where there was a lot of heavy political interest. The more frequent pattern is a political "awakening" after the individual has left home for college. Getting out from under parental control permits exploring and experimenting with new ideas. Some women describe being politically "awakened" in activist confrontation, others in discussions of radical thought. One older woman didn't become educated in politics until after she married an active Socialist. Several women talked about involvement at an earlier age, but usually in spite of, rather than because of, parents' involvement or apathy:

> My father, being a diplomat, implicitly supported U.S. imperialism. . . . At age 16 I became a Socialist . . . and engaged my parents in political arguments at every meal. I was known as the high school iconoclast. . . . My battles were essentially over school issues like anti-dress legislation. I fought this because the dress laws were directed primarily against lower-class girls in the school who didn't conform to middle-class standards.

Only one woman came from an "activist" home. And her political manner of solving problems was evident as early as grammar school:

> I was disliked by my teachers and regarded as a trouble-maker. . . . I remember leading a strike against singing Christmas carols in class. After all, it was an all-Jewish school.

The political outlook with its notions of power, dissent, rights and tactics might seem to be readily available only to the highly educated and informed. This implies that the Women's Liberation movement can only appeal to an educated elite who have access to this perspective directly. Indeed, research shows that education is positively correlated with political participation. However, while direct experience with the approach may be essential for early converts, once there is a solid base of the committed, the active political education of others is possible. And already we see the movement reaching out to be the politically isolated, like suburban housewives, not only to "raise consciousness" but to educate those women to the mode of problem solving as well.

NONCONFORMITY

A fourth predisposing condition is a biographical *pattern of defiance* vis-a-vis tradition. Among all the women I interviewed, alternative frameworks and models emerged which enlarged their view and allowed them to reject orthodox behavior. An excellent illustration is provided by a woman who grew up in Utah in a very religious and authoritarian Mormon family. She didn't know any "troublemakers" or deviants who might have encouraged her to rebel, and all her siblings were obedient and faithful. But she had since earliest childhood immersed herself in a private world of books. The exposure to alternative symbolic and moral orders in these books and the critical spirit engendered by reading undermined the legitimacy of Mormonism for her and prompted her to reject it. "[The] rejection of Mormonism gave me moral courage to reject other things I thought were foolish," and she describes her subsequent nonconformity and beatnik life style.

Another woman had a scholarly grandfather who never had to work and was instead indulged by the family to pursue his studies. With him as a model she soon realized that her intellectual activity was far more important than any household responsibilities. So when all the other women at home were doing chores she withdrew to read and write poetry. She saw the usual preoccupations of a young girl like sewing, cooking and housekeeping as stupid wastes of time and refused to have any part of it.

The alternative frames of reference are quite varied in the sample, though books and an intellectual environment outside the home are most often named. The targets of defiance include most of the cherished bastions of orthodoxy from religion (no one is any longer a believer, though most had been raised with a faith) to sex (none of the single girls are virgins, and the divorced ones freely take lovers) to drugs (almost everyone has experimented with illegal drugs). I should add, however, that the people these women associate with now do not judge their behavior as deviant. Nevertheless, the women themselves are perfectly aware that their life styles do offend "general community standards." This is dramatized by how they relate to their parents and relatives, "guardians of the old values." Some simply keep their activities hidden; others describe the "training in tolerance" that they have subjected their parents to ("if you want to see me at all, you'll have to take me as I am").

There are a number of possible explanations for this pattern of defiance. An obvious one is the role of college life in encouraging experimentation and tolerating rebelliousness. However, most of the women were pretty defiant before coming to college. As a matter of fact, almost all felt some degree of contempt for "acceptable" behavior by the time they were adolescents. The libertarian university environment simply allowed the fuller expression of prior inclinations.

Another explanation is the lack of parental control. But such control was overwhelming in some cases, while totally absent or ineffective in others. A third conceivable explanation is the bravado of youth in general and of this generation in particular. Yet I talked with individuals from three generations and discovered that although the youngest women are the most anti-traditional in acts of daring characteristic of youth today (for example, drugs) all of the women regardless of age have to some extent rejected certain traditional practices and mores of the society.

CONVERSION

Although various other social situations may serve as the medium of conversion, the most common is the small group. Quite often, a significant event or encounter in the individual's life will intensify her feelings of anxiety and frustration and move her to join a group. It might be the birth of a child, job discrimination, divorce, social or physical dislocation or a particular book.

Often organized through a local office, these groups of about ten meet once a week at a private home. Someone who has already experienced conversion is usually present, but her leadership position is minimized. The idea is for spontaneous discussion to carry the group to a natural and unmanipulated awakening.

The first step is the articulation of the problem. Participants share anecdotes about their own encounters with discrimination and relate their vague feelings of discrepancy. In these conversations the problem becomes defined as social rather than personal:

> Talking with other women made me realize that it wasn't me personally, but me as a woman.
> The group facilitated the externalization of my individual anxieties onto the situation.
> One can transfer the fault from oneself to the situation, and this can be accomplished alone on an "intellectual level," but to make that feeling "real" one needs a group. . . . Collective awareness is necessary for the transformation of individual problems into social issues.

Once the problem has been articulated and defined, the group begins to explore its character. Props may be used to expose subtleties and clarify its peculiar features: books, articles, movies, statistical reports, advertising layouts—anything that reinforces the belief system, either explicitly or by parading the Feminine Mystique in some offensive way. In this way, the sex role is revealed as an arbitrary and impersonal pattern of constraints, obligations and "privileges." How and why it is oppressive, individually and collectively, is unmasked. Although each small group makes the discovery on its own, there is a rhetoric—the language of Women's Liberation—common to each cell. Women eagerly adopt it because it describes vividly feelings which have remained buried and unspoken for such a long time. The rhetoric is important also because it puts the problem in a social context and in doing so provides a basis for collective mobilization. For example, many women when they first probe their discontent in the small group characterize the men around them as "somehow unfair" or "vaguely condescending" or "selfish and unresponsive." The vocabulary of Women's Liberation labels this behavior as "chauvinistic" and indicative of a general belief by men in their innate superiority. It interprets the oppression of an individual woman by an individual man in a larger social and psychological context. In this way, a personally hopeless and isolated situation is identified with collective struggle. It's not surprising that newcomers frequently sense an invigorating optimism after their first few meetings.

As the problem is considered in increasing detail and complexity, the actual "change in consciousness" gradually occurs. In essence this means a process of discernible, if uneven, increase in self-awareness. Minor setbacks may occur, usually when group reinforcement is absent, but although the process of self-awareness may have to be repeated, it's never entirely reversible: once a woman has adopted a new perspective and absorbed a new vocabulary, even her disavowal of it is defined in its very terms. Regression or backsliding is then seen as a "female cop-out."

The new self-awareness usually produces striking insights, some indication that a change in perspective has occurred. Domestic tasks, for example, traditionally accepted as "women's work," come to be seen as "slave labor." "Chivalrous concessions" are now perceived as part of a game in which the woman must eventually pay up—usually with herself. As one woman remembers:

I was asked out on a date by this friend of mine. It may sound trivial, but I haven't been on a real, prearranged formal type date in two or three years. Well, he blew my mind. Picked me up, brought me flowers, put on my coat, opened doors—the whole scene. What knocked me out was that several years ago I really dug this sort of attention from a strange guy. It made me feel all soft and helpless. But when it happened the other night it put me uptight. I really felt like it was a conspiracy. I kept waiting for his hand to find my knee or something. I guess I was overreacting because he was a nice fellow, and I knew I could handle anything he tried. But the whole evening brought home to me all the games and undercurrents of dating. He's supposed to do a,b,c. In return you're expected to give into his advances, or you're a bitch. I flashed on all those painful "kiss-at-the-front-door" scenes. Even if he's a creep you are somehow cheating him if you don't pay up at the end of the evening.

Once a woman becomes aware of the nature of the traditional role, she cannot act as before.

And this is a painful jolt for the converted woman. The extent to which our lives are played out through sex roles is considerable. And when suddenly a woman invalidates these roles for herself she becomes disoriented, and normal interaction is disrupted. Her identity must be reconstituted, new forms of action constructed and people and objects in her environment reassessed.

Accompanying a rise in self-awareness, therefore, is a process of redefinition of self, significant others and society, all of which complement and reinforce her fresh perceptions of reality. A prime target for reevaluation is the convert's own past. For example:

I've always been a superior student, and for years teachers and counselors have supported my fantasies that I was "meant for something important." But this image was always ambivalent. Sure, I was good. But my education and future didn't have the urgency attached to it that the futures of men around me did. My parents considered it a self-indulgent luxury, and I began to feel guilty about my ambitions. I remember my father being disappointed—almost angry!—with me for taking advanced courses in science and math in high school instead of more "useful" things like typing and shorthand. I was hurt and confused by his attitude. I shrugged it off as part of his general hostility to intellectualism. But as I look back to those dinner table fights it all begins to make sense. He pulled the same thing on my younger sister. But now that my younger brother is in high school you should see his appreciation of physics and trig!

At the time, this woman felt that her ambitions were perhaps "unnatural," but she now sees her father's lack of positive reinforcement as a prejudice against her sex.

Looking at herself and past in this new way is followed by a rise in self-esteem. A woman begins to like herself more. This happens because the self-hatred that comes with failure and disappointment is hurled outward in a liberating catharsis. Society is held to blame for much of her frustration. And freed from guilt and self-doubt, converts often remark on their "new strength," an exhilarating feeling of "wholeness" or "a greater sense of myself and my potential."

In one of the small groups in which I participate, a young mother described a recent experience at a party:

I was talking about Women's Liberation with one of the other girls, and all of a sudden there was silence in the room, and I became the center of attention. So I started rapping down the position of the movement. The guys made snide remarks, and the women were pretty quiet. Later on some of the women came up to me and said they agreed with a lot of the things I'd said. I guess they were too intimidated to speak up when their men were in hearing distance.

I asked how she felt about being the center of attention in such a hostile situation:

I always felt incompetent about talking on any subject. I never knew enough to hold my own with any confidence. Then I realized that I really had learned a lot about Women's Liberation. Something that interested people. So I had something that I knew about and felt strongly and confident about. I enjoy talking Women's Liberation. Hostile remarks only confirm and strengthen my position.

Concomitant with a reassessment of self is the redefinition of significant others. For example, men are judged first as a class, of unaware and generally belligerent opponents, and then individually according to the flagrancy of their own chauvinism:

When I became conscious I couldn't be friends with men anymore. . . . But I like my husband, although he's hardly liberated.

I think all men are chauvinists; they just display it differently. . . . Each man must become aware of his chauvinism and agree to work on it.

My allies are women, my enemies are men. For men the world is more just, and they just can't understand our problem. I don't trust them.

I don't get along with most men because I don't shuffle anymore.

A striking change in attitude towards other women also occurs. Formerly competitors on the man market, they now are recognized as "sisters" in a common effort:

You shouldn't reject or despise "dragon ladies" but pull them into the struggle—make them aware.

I hadn't any close female friends before. But having an all-women group is good. We can be whole people with one another. . . . and I've become sensitized to women in general as people.

I have greater respect for women. . . . All females are potentially salvageable.

I generally feel better about myself around women. I don't have much self-confidence, so I need to be around people who treat me as an equal. Most men don't.

This increase in esteem for members of one's own sex is a measure of the increase in self-esteem (again, similar to the black experience) and demonstrates how relations with the world reflect one's relations to and image of self.

This point is further illustrated by the way in which society is redefined. On the one hand, institutions such as the university, government, legal system, occupational structure and the church are appraised according to their support of the traditional sex role and their manifestations of discrimination:

I identify more with students than with [male] colleagues. We are both in a system where we don't make the rules and are patronized. (40-year-old professor)

The job market ruins you. It doesn't make any difference if you are charming, attractive and unaggressive. You're damned if you're masculine or feminine. They'll use whatever traits you have to evaluate you negatively.

On the other hand, the cultural ideas for women, marriage and maternity, are demoted from necessary and sufficient to supplementary means of fulfillment:

I used to believe that if a woman wasn't married she wasn't a person. . . . If I had the chance, I wouldn't get married again. (A 41-year-old, twice married)

I always assumed that I would have children. Now I no longer feel that I have to in order to be happy. (25-year-old single student)

How have I changed? I used to think that maybe in a year I will have met the man I am going to marry. He'll know everything about everything I'm interested in. Actually he would be bigger and better than me. I wanted to live vicariously. He would have dark hair and be very handsome—very sexy. All the other women wanted him, but he chose me. The "real one." Always I would say to myself, "Is this him?" This view has only faded over the last ten months. (19-year-old student)

More in this spirit, a Berkeley Women's Liberation position paper comments:

Now, with birth control, higher education for women, and the Movement itself, it's becoming clear that the institution of marriage, like so many others is an anachronism. For the unmarried woman it offers only a sanctioned security and the promise of love. The married woman knows that love is, at its best, an inadequate reward for her unnecessary and bizarre heritage of oppression.

In addition to this qualification of the female role, the converted woman becomes sensitized to any presentations of the cultural ideal in the media. The television situation-comedy isn't funny anymore, but just another example of how the "scatterbrained, whining housewife stereotype" is perpetuated. And the jingle that proclaims "You've come a long way, baby" only intensifies a convert's disgust with the image of woman as sex object and consumer, the final blow coming with the word "baby" and its presumptuous intimacy. Movement women find it difficult to keep a sense of humor in the face of such crass condescension, and the constant insensitivity to them as "human beings" only fires up indignation. As one woman put it:

I can hardly go to a movie anymore. I used to be able to laugh along with the dumb blonde and dizzy housewives. But now it's clear that these ludicrous stereotypes are the justifications men use to keep women down. It's like seeing an old Amos and Andy show. Not so funny anymore.

The complex process of redefinition described here does not occur in a vacuum. As a woman begins to see herself and the world differently, her behavior must change to align with these new images. By the same token, her new behavior modifies the whole character of her relations with others. At first this means disorienta-

tion: the old clues of interaction are gone, and new ones based on mutual agreement haven't yet evolved. A married woman faces the dilemma in perhaps the most acute and continual way. One of the married women I interviewed describes the problems she and her husband have trying to "create new roles for ourselves everyday." She has redefined the husband-wife roles out of the master-slave/provider-nurturer mold. That means an equal sharing of household and child care responsibilities. For a woman trained to cook and clean her way through life and a man trained to bring home the bacon to a spotless domicile and bouncy offspring, this is no small readjustment:

I get angry about feeling "grateful" when D is so "cooperative." ... We fight every week about a woman's thing. I'm getting tired of having to point out to him something that's so obvious to me, like what around the house needs attention.

Division of labor in the house may be a small point on which husband and wife relate. But the disorientation reflected in this attempt to fashion new patterns of behavior is symptomatic of a more pervasive difficulty.

I always felt good about the fact that D and I could relate about anything. But now I feel that there is no way to relate on the women's issues. Fights result from my having a higher level of consciousness about personal things.

She is not exactly the same woman he married, for she sees herself in a radically new way. And the relationship must respond to this or collapse under the strain of unresolved ambiguity. I note with relief, however, that those couples who do take the trouble to carve out new roles are much happier in the long run, since both partners have freer range of expression.

This is an extreme example of how interpersonal relations may be influenced by conversion. More casual relationships feel fewer repercussions. But the comprehensiveness of the perspective affects almost all spheres of almost any relationship.

Since Women's Liberation ideology is still very much a minority position and generally considered deviant, most of the convert's casual social contacts will be with nonsupportive people. In fact, a rather unsavory stereotype has already captured the public imagination, and it is this image more often than not that a movement woman must contend with. The best self-defense in such encounters is for the convert to neutralize these pejorative labels, as well as the abusive labelers. One way of doing so is to deny responsibility by deflecting the blame. For instance, a woman accused of being a "feminist bitch" responds:

You're damn right I'm a bitch. But show me a choice. If a woman doesn't lay down some shit around here, she's going to sit in a passive little heap and get dumped on all the time.

She feels compelled to act in a way—loud, aggressive, domineering—that deviates from expected feminine behavior. But she also feels righteously justified in abrogating responsibility for her actions. Another way of meeting criticism, of course, is to deny its validity. For example, part of the program of Women's Liberation calls for freeing the woman of full-time child care duties by establishing day care collectives. Some critics denounce this as a neglect of duty, selfish at best, "unnatural" at worst. An ordinary woman would be crushed by the intimation that she is being a "bad mother" (an incredibly powerful social control). But the individual with a Liberationist perspective undercuts the label by exposing the tyrannical ideal which demands that she organize her life completely around the lives of others, total neglecting her own needs and desires. She further defuses the label by pointing out the advantages to the child in having several adult role models and numerous playmates at hand. If anything, in her own mind, "deviance" from "maternal norms" makes her a better mother.

Some women under attack may simply appeal to "circumstances." They don't deny that they may be committing injustices, but these, they say, are justifiable. An instance of this is the allegation by some women that all men without reservation are "chauvinist pigs." For the movement it earns a label of "man haters," and for some "innocent" men it may involve such unwarranted punishments as economic reprisals, emotional withdrawals or sexual boycotts. The stereotype doesn't affect those women who really do hate men and for those who don't, they slough off any guilt by seeing the "injury" as justifiable when balanced against men's calculated dehumanization of all females.

Another technique of self-defense is to shift the focus of attention from one's own alleged deviance to that of one's opponents. When a movement woman is called frigid or promiscuous or homosexual, depending on your source, she can and often does counter by playing on the insecurity and guilt of the labelers and claiming that they are only revealing their own sexual inadequacies and disappointments. This usually shuts them up.

After a woman has defined and explored the problem, expanded her level of consciousness and reevaluated her past life and present environment, a fifth and final step in the process of conversion is required: she must actively *display her commitments*. The new way she interacts with others, as elaborated above, is part of this. But some form of collective action is also necessary. Such struggle not only "builds and reinforces consciousness" but also confirms the social nature of the problem. The individual may choose to work within the system or to overthrow it. She may join an organization or "action group" with a specific focus (self-defense, abortion laws, professional discrimination), or her own small group may undertake a project. She may educate and proselytize or engage in mass demonstrations and strikes. Whatever the modus operandi, she will not slip into isolation and "try to make it on my own." That's the kind of "private battle" put down by Women's Liberation as ineffective and self-defeating, for it requires a woman to become a man and fight in his world, on his terms.

The more intensive the interaction with Liberation women and involvement with movement activities, the greater the personal growth and commitment. This boundless character is not surprising when one realizes that, for many adherents, Women's Liberation is not just a political cause but a medium through which they discover and mobilize their human potential—and to this there is no limit.

Old Age and Collective
Political Action

James E. Trela

ABSTRACT

The power of age to compel older individuals to act alike politically has been both discounted and dramatized. The circumstances of collective political action by the aged, however, have not been empirically specified. This paper seeks to identify the requisite conditions of political action and those social-psychological and social structural factors militating against or propitious to the emergence of these conditions. Analysis of the social and political attitudes and behaviors of older people and past old age and other political movements suggest three conditions requisite to the union of age status and political behavior. These include the emergence of: (1) age as a major referent in fixing sociopolitical beliefs, (2) an ideology giving meaning and direction to undifferentiated feelings of discontent, and (3) the means of political organization. Factors propitious to the emergence of these conditions include a strong sense of agelinked deprivation and the age-grading of primary and secondary relations. Factors militating against the emergence of these conditions include the tendency toward rejection of a common identity with age peers and the perceived legitimacy and responsiveness of present political arrangements. Government initiatives and retrenchment are seen as potentially having the greatest impact on the relative balance of these factors.

Reprinted by permission of the author, James E. Trela; "Old Age and Collective Political Action," Paper presented at the Annual meetings of the Gerontological Society, November 5-9, 1973, Miami, Florida.

THE POWER of age to compel older individuals to act together politically has generally been either assumed or denied, and the collective political potential of the aged has been both over dramatized and discounted. On the one hand, we are told that if the aged were to organize they could secure from governments almost anything they might demand and that pension movements of the past were pastoral in comparison to those that may occur in the future (Clague, 1940; Havigurst, 1949). Alternatively, enactment of social security legislation, partially in response to pressures by and on behalf of the aged, and the precipitous decline in Townsend Club membership between 1936 and 1951 are cited as indicators of how easily the momentum of pension movements can be dissipated (Messinger, 1955). The paucity of research focusing on the political life of the aged, however, has not empirically specified conditions conducive to collective political behavior on the part of the aged. This paper seeks to identify the requisite conditions of political action and those social psychological and social structural factors militating against or propitious to the emergence of these conditions.

THE BASIS FOR
CURRENT THINKING

Much of what has been said about the politics of aging has been based upon observations pertaining either to demographic changes in Western societies or to the age-linked problems that older people experience. The former implies that the larger the number of people sharing a particular characteristic, the more potent this characteristic becomes in compelling behavior. While the demographic facts of aging are impressive, the size of a social category has never ensured the ability of members to engage in effective concerted action and cannot be taken as evidence that the aged may act as a political group and become a decisive political constituency.[1] The latter, age-related problems, suggests that in an affluent society, people sharing a significant social status, which is linked to socio-economic, honorific, or legal disadvantage, will grow discontent and act together politically to gain social justice. That social and economic deprivation is not a sufficient condition for collective action, however, has been noted by many. Poverty and hardship, rather than leading people to collective action, most often induces fatalism and despair (Bell, 1962). Or, as Davies (1962) submits (and this may be true for any non-routine political behavior):

> revolutions ordinarily do not occur when a society is generally impoverished—when, evils that seem inevitable are patiently endured . . . because the physical and mental energies of people are totally employed in the process of merely staying alive . . . Enduring poverty makes for concern with one's solitary self or solitary family at best and resignation or mute despair at worst.

Hence, demographic factors and problems associated with aging are not sufficient and perhaps not even necessary considerations in trying to explain or predict the political life of the aged.

THE ESSENTIAL CONDITIONS OF COLLECTIVE POLITICAL ACTION

There is, of course, no simple relationship between a group's objective circumstances and its political life. Marx held that a class's political activity depends upon awareness of its situation and level of political maturity, as well as upon its actual economic position. This, of course, is where the notion of "class consciousness" is important. Such a formulation attempts to take account of the interplay between the real situation of individuals (in Marx's case, their relation to the organization of production), the conceptions which they form of their situation, and the lines of social and political action they see open to them. Marx identified the modern large scale factory as the structual arrangement that would be favorable to the growth of class consciousness, the development of a unifying ideology and the organization of a political movement. Similarly, without necessarily subscribing to a Marxist interpretation of political behavior, it is clear that it is not simply the economic and social conditions of the aged but the subjective experience of these conditions and the structural arrangements shaping that experience which are essential to the understanding of aging and political behavior.

At least three basic conditions must exist before there can be a union of age status and political behavior. First, age must be a salient referent in fixing socio-political beliefs and the aged must become a significant reference category in the political life of older people. This age status consciousness necessarily entails the development of a sense of mutual fate and political efficacy based upon membership in a common age grade. The absence of this condition implies the relative dominance of other statuses and precludes the possibility of political activity based primarily upon age status.

A second factor is an ideology that can transform narrow personal interests into collective interests, give meaning and direction to undifferentiated feelings of discontent and, in fact, create such discontent where it does not exist. For a group to act collectively they need a complex of ideas and beliefs that explain and interpret relevant aspects of life in terms of some commonly held characteristic. Before the aged can assert collective political pressures, there must be a pervasive desire for change to benefit older people and a willingness to actually engage in organized activity designed to secure such change. There must be an ideology which defines such action as *necessary* and *legitimate* political behavior.

Finally, the means of effective political organization must be available. The level of social participation of the aged is the critical factor here. Formal social participation, which permits the development of skills crucial to building a new political organization, is characteristically low among the economically and socially disadvantaged and isolated. The degree of informal social participation is also more restricted. Yet, participation is important if the world outside one's immediate concern is to be meaningful. And, "a political movement, like any other idea, must be diffused and in all likelihood through some of the same processes as other items of diffusion. . . . diffusion studies have shown the crucial importance of a rich social life for early adoption (Pinard, 1967)."

Hence, there are at least three essential sets of questions:

1. Are the aged conscious or aware of the social and political implications of their age status and to what degree and under what circumstances is age a major attitudinal and behavioral referent?
2. Is there an identifiable emergent ideology that gives subjective and perhaps political meaning to the objective conditions of aging.
3. Is there a basis in the formal and informal social relationships of the aged for effective political organizations?

These appear to be the critical conditions that explain the process by which political behavior comes to reflect the objective social and economic circumstances of a social group or category, especially a disadvantaged one. They bear on whether or not the aged are discontent, if and how that discontent is politicized and if and how it is converted into collective action. We must next inquire into the cultural, social-psychological and social structural factors that nurture or preclude their emergence among the aged.

FACILITING CONDITIONS

Observers of political movements have often suggested that a strong sense of social dislocation may be a condition propitious to collective political action. Bell, (1962) for example, notes that "Social tensions are an expression of unfulfilled expectations." Key (1958) submits that "a factor of great significance in the setting of political

movements is an abrupt change for the worse in the status of one group relative to that of other groups in society." Turner and Killian (1957) suggest that "Frustration from recent losses or the experience of improving conditions is more likely to make receptive individuals than long continued frustration." The emphasis in these statements, on abrupt change, a perceived disadvantaged state relative to some other groups, or the frustration of expectations suggests that the concept of relative deprivation captures the dislocative social-psychological experience that may link the objective circumstances of aging to political behavior. A sense of relative deprivation contributes to feelings of alienation from society, creates discontent, and sensitizes individuals to messages that give political meaning to attendant social-psychological stress.

Past and present old age movements suggest the nature of the aging experience that may predispose older people to collective political activity. Holtzman commenting on the Townsend movement suggests;

A significant change occurred, in the composition and character of the dependent aged. Jobs having disappeared, businesses ruined and savings wiped out, an influx of despoiled professional men, retired farmers, skilled workers, and independent businessmen entered the ranks of the aged. These were the people who had attained a high degree of independence and economic security. These new accretions to the ranks of dependent aged represented a sensitive force receptive to protest thinking.

On the McLain movement Pinner (1959) reports:

California's old-age security laws permit some pensioners to enjoy a 'slightly privileged' status, and this group supplies a disproportionate share of members . . . The slightly privileged include modest home owners, people with spouses still living and therefore benefiting from combined grants, and those having allowable additional income. These distinct social and economic advantages facilitate political and social participation in community life. McLain's members tend to be among the slightly privileged: the more deeply involved the member, the more likely he is to share these advantages. Thus the membership is not a movement of the utterly dispossessed . . . The slightly privileged status of the McLain members is consistent with the related conclusion that this group shows a relatively greater amount of status-anxiety. Those who have some hold upon the material foundations of respectability are more likely to sustain the aspiration and resent the loss. McLain's members rate somewhat higher in status-anxiety than do non-member pensioners. This probably reflects a selective factor: strong feelings about loss of status stir resentments which make them more readily available for political participation. In addition, membership in the organization strengthens views about the pension, society, and self which show up as increased concern for social status.

These statements illustrate that the losses of aging, loss of status and economic advantage are dislocative; causing stress or anxiety. Further, concern about these losses may manifest itself in political behavior. When the concept of relative or subjective deprivation is invoked to account for social unrest, it is usually on the basis that a rapid rise in expectations has outpaced actual improvement in objective status. We might infer subjective deprivation among the aged in our culture when they compare their present state with that which has been habitual in the past, or when they compare the present with a less promising and threatening future. In this case perhaps the aged person experiencing a sense of social dislocation is caught between the positive attraction of a social category to which he no longer belongs and one to which he belongs but is negatively valued and materially deprived. It might be anticipated that this contributes to feelings of alienation, raises the salience of age status and sensitizes older individuals to the political environment.

The precise political attitudes and behaviors that may be associated with the dislocation experience are not easily predictable. On the one hand, the various circumstances of discontent may precipitate the withdrawal of psychological affect from political symbols and cause a subsequent weakening of socio-political integration. On the other hand, the basis for all social movements is some form of perceived deprivation suffered simultaneously by a segment of the population (Sherif and Sherif, 1956). In this case

perhaps, dislocation attending aging may raise the salience of age status and render individuals receptive to ideas that purport to explain the conditions of the aged.

But while a sense of social dislocation may be an important factor, it may not be sufficient to generate collective political activity. An additional condition which may operate independently or interact with the social-psychological dislocations of aging, is the age grading of interaction at all levels. Voluntary associations, especially those that are age-graded, are critical, not only because they facilitate intensive interaction within an isolated context but because they are basic to political organization and may be avenues for the redress of grievances. While evidence indicates that some voluntary association activities are reduced in the latter part of life, the proliferation of associations designed exclusively for the aged, at the national, state, and especially the local level, suggests that rather than withdrawal from society's secondary structure older people reorient their associational activities in response to their changing age status. That such associations are playing an increasingly important role in the corporate life of older people complements observations of a simultaneous reduction of intergenerational relations and increasing interaction and solidarity among age peers. (Cumming and Schneider, 1961; Rosow, 1967; Bultena, 1968; Rose, 1962) is consistent with both the disengagement (Cumming and Henry, 1961) and quasi-minority (Barron, 1953) theories of aging; and, is a seminal element in Rose's (1962) conceptualization of the aged as an emergent subculture. Inasmuch as political attitudes and behaviors are learned and legitimized by friends and fellow members of organizations. (Campbell, et al., 1954), increased interaction and communication with age peers in voluntary organizations may be conducive to the development of a viable political life based upon age status. Age homogeneity of the social context may possibly lead to: an ascendency of age status as an attitudinal and behavioral referent and the development of a political ideology, and provide a basis for political organization.[2]

Some form of social distinctiveness is an essential precondition to the formation of any group. Association with age peers in voluntary groups exclusively for the aged is a manifestation of feelings of solidarity among people who share age related characteristics, problems and experiences, on the one hand, and who are subject to exclusion from other parts of society, on the other. Although these associations usually do not profess political goals, the conditions of eligibility for membership underscore differences which distinguish members (and those eligible for membership) from others and represent an implicit statement of common interest. Hence, such associations may increase the salience of age status and promote a sense of common identity, encourage involvement in public affairs, and give orientation to political activity from the perspective of the aged. Each of these contributes to the recognition of common interests and the willingness to pursue these interests in the social and political arena.

It has been repeatedly documented that activity in voluntary associations tends to be associated with an expanded life space in general, as well as with feelings of political efficacy, political consciousness, and involvement in political affairs (Berelson, et al., 1954; Freedman and Axelrod, 1952; Maccoby, 1958; Wright and Hyman, 1958; Sallach, et al., 1972). Members are more likely than persons without memberships to vote, be knowledgeable about social and political affairs, and express political opinions. This is also true of age graded associations which, regardless of their goals, provide a context for discussions and activities of political consequence (Trela, 1971). In some cases, voting and other forms of activity may be encouraged as efforts to influence political processes and decisions. But, even in the absence of activity aimed at influencing political processes, group pressures stimulate political interest and enforce the norm of citizen participation.

While age graded associations are like many organizations that promote involvement, they are also different in that they facilitate contact mostly between age peers. And, for several reasons, this may heighten political consciousness and activity somewhat more than membership in groups that mix generations. This is probably true insofar as homogeneity of the social environment reduces exposure to cross-pressures which cause people to withdraw from social and political involvement. For example, it has been found that members of occupations which guarantee a great deal of in-

group interaction are more politically interested and active than other groups (Lipset, 1963). Because contact with others who share similar life circumstances removes individuals from competing requests for political support and competing interpretations of social and political reality, we may expect those aged who choose to associate with age peers to be highly involved in political affairs. Indeed, some existing evidence suggests that older people in age graded associations are somewhat more likely than those who participate exclusively in mixed generational groups to profess high political interest, discuss politics, argue with others over political issues and engage in other forms of activity (Trela, 1971).

Further, inasmuch as group membership generally provides insight into social and political processes from the perspective of group values, we would expect this also to be true of age graded associations. It would be anticipated that heightened peer contact among people who share similar age related problems would raise the salience of age status in political orientations and foster both a desire for change and a willingness to act together in order to secure such change. What evidence exists suggests that such peer contact is conducive to the development of political self-interest among older people. When compared to aged individuals who participate exclusively in mixed generational groups, members of age graded associations record a higher desire for political change to benefit the aged, greater receptivity to appeals for organized social action, and a greater willingness to actually engage in activity designed to secure change (Trela, 1972). Age graded associations, often as a by-product of other activities, provide both the context in which news stories and politician's speeches are interpreted and a perspective from which various social and political processes are viewed. Members engage in small intimate group discussions which serve to create a climate of opinion, homogenize and crystallize group attitudes, and anchor each person's perceptions and political expectations in his group life. Hence, members are provided with sets of reference points from which they can define political problems confronting them and more clearly identify their interests. The political implications of this seem clear. Age status is given political meaning—that is, age becomes an important attitudinal and behavioral referent and there is a subsequent recognition of mutual interests and needs which may be satisfied through collective social action.

FACTORS MILITATING AGAINST THE EMERGENCE OF THE REQUISITE CONDITIONS

There appear to be two factors militating against the emergence of requisite conditions described earlier: The low cultural value associated with aging and the perceived legitimacy of the political system. First, because of the low cultural value associated with aging, older people, rather than identifying themselves with contemporaries, hold the aged as a negative reference category. Because being old in our society brings low prestige, the aged tend to dissociate themselves from old age and identify themselves with other member and non-membership groups. Blau (1956) found that 60 percent of persons between 65 and 70 years of age labeled themselves as middle rather than old aged. The result of this low sense of identification is that the saliency of other membership groups (or categories) is reflected in social and political behavior. The wealthy older person votes as other wealthy individuals do rather than as an elderly person. Similarly, socio-economic status is a more important factor than age in determining party affiliation (Loether, 1967). Lower income blue-collar persons align themselves with the Democratic Party, while the more affluent are usually Republicans. The degree to which political activity is grounded in statuses other than age indicates the extent to which the aged may be working at political cross-purposes. This is especially notable in rural areas where the aged are over represented and their potential political power is more apparent. Yet they are divided among many, and often opposing interest groups, most of which do not make the welfare of the aged their primary goal (Cottrell, 1960). Hence, that potential has never been realized. Pinner (1959) and his associates found that even the aged in the McLain movement did not display a high level of group identity or consciousness.

Anxiety concerning their status both as aged and as pensioners manifests itself in several ways: the pensioners hesitate to identify themselves with other aged persons; they are reluctant to identify themselves as aged; they prefer to be called 'citizens' rather than 'old' and 'pensioners.' Interviews with signature collectors were rated for manifestations of identification with the aged. Criteria for this rating were the use of the pronoun 'we' as well as other expressions of we-feeling. In only seven (of 42) cases could such manifestations be detected, and even in these they occur only occasionally.

Second, the political system is not seen as indifferent, unresponsive or illegitimate. This robs the aged of a common enemy toward which action can be directed. Important issues which might cause older persons to develop a common political consciousness and guiding ideology are absorbed into the platforms of both political parties. Special interest groups have historically been unsuccessful, especially in the development of third party movements, because they are denied the cohesive effects of issues ignored by the major parties. Parsons' (1949) contention that the aged are isolated from "participation in the most important social structures and interests," including the political arena, does not seem to be borne out. Their integration within the major parties appears to be complete, and their level of political participation is high. In contradistinction, Holtzman (1954) has aptly accounted for the Townsend movement by describing the posture of the Federal Government during the early thirties.

> During the five gravest years of the depression, when the plight of aged citizens had become extremely critical, the national government failed to meet their particular problem . . . In this failure to act lay a major responsibility for the rise of independent action by the aged . . .

Although it was partially the concerted political pressure which the aged were able to bring to bear on officials during the early thirties which originally forced politicians to view their political future in relation to the aged, the momentum of the Townsend movement as an independent political force was neutralized when the Democratic Party developed a social security platform in

1935. The acceptance of a positive role by governments for the protection of the aged resulted in a gradual recession of independent politics.

Campbell (1971) has noted:

> The evidence which national surveys provide us does in fact demonstrate that attitudinal differences between age groups are far less impressive than those within age groups.

Smith (1966), in an examination of the group status of the aged, found that older people themselves are far from any consensus about common needs or goals. When asked whether they would approve of efforts by the aged to act as a bloc, only 40% answered affirmatively. Other research has shown the shared beliefs and expectations preventing this linkage of age and political value. The unwillingness to endorse collective political activity by older people reflects: satisfaction with political affairs and the belief that government programs and benefits are adequate; recognition that resources directed toward the aged must necessarily increase "the burden of other generations;" and attitudes of self-reliance and government activity deemed inappropriate. The latter perhaps reflects a form of conservatism typical of this political cohort (Trela, 1971). While this suggests that older people are politically acquiescent for generational reasons, it is impossible to predict if future cohorts may be more militant.

Even contemporary collective political activity by the aged reflects a state of relative content. Current activity does not call into question the basic structure of society and does not call for a redistribution of income. Rather than radical, they are reformant in nature; seeking, in modest ways, to ameliorate or blunt the excesses of an urban industrial capitalist society. Even the political goals of national organizations of the aged "are not of a kind suitable to redress the monetary and social conditions of the severely disadvantaged aged" (Binstock, 1972).[3] On the McLain movement, Pinner (1959) reports:

> Because of this anxiety over status, with its keynotes of respect and respectability, the pensioners are basically conservative. They are not radicals seeking to espouse new values, but

people who want the means to live according to established social norms.

TIPPING THE BALANCE

While it is not difficult to find evidence suggesting that the three conditions identified earlier are indeed requisite to collective political action by the aged, others may also be important. At present, the considerable political energies of the aged are spent in ways other than in pursuit of their age related self interest. Age is not a salient political referent in most cases, there is no system of beliefs and values which shapes the political life of the aged, and except in some rudimentary forms, the aged have no effective political organization. It is probably true that even if issues and electoral politics were framed in terms of the interest of the aged, and there were clear choices, no cohesive voting bloc would emerge. Moreover, it is difficult to determine whether the facilitating and militating social psychological and structural conditions are in some state of balance or imbalance. It does appear, however, that feelings of social and psychological dislocation, to the degree that they exist, are not on the wane and almost surely the self and imposed segregation of the aged in isolated communities of age peers is on the increase. Similarly, rejection of the label of old is not likely to change, given the values of contemporary American Life. Perhaps the most unpredictable factor is the actual and perceived legitimacy and responsiveness of governmental and political institutions. Indeed the response of political and governmental institutions to the growing and increasingly visible aged population may be the key variable determining the degree to which older people act together politically.

Looking at governmental and political institutions, Cotrell (1966) and others see the possibility of a sustained and successful movement by the aged as minimal. While politicians are not unaware of the potential power of the millions of Americans 65 and over, they seem confident that they cannot be mobilized, except perhaps in support of limited objectives. As evidence of this, Cotrell notes that few of the objectives generally sought by those attempting to improve the conditions of aging have been given high priority in either political party. Furthermore, the decline in support for the Townsend movement has been attributed to a presumed availability and responsiveness of existing institutions of political expression (i.e., the major parties) through which the aged can work to achieve their primary objectives (Holtzman, 1954). Nevertheless, it is clear that national economic and social policy directly or indirectly shapes both the objective conditions of the aged and how those are subjectively perceived. Inflation, for example, insures the progressive impoverishment of the aged. Perhaps, more important, however, government and political parties have begun to increasingly respond to the aged as a category with common interests. It may be expected that this will directly facilitate the ascendary of age status as a socio-political referent and may indirectly exacerbate feelings of status and material dislocation. Older people are told that they are an important constituency—one that is disadvantaged and has been denied social justice. The aged are the object of legislative debate and social policy initiatives. New service programs are developed and aggressively publicized. This must inevitably call attention to the community of interests that older people share, legitimize political demands and raise expectations. Further, older people are increasingly brought together in congregate settings for services. Increased consciousness that deprivations are age linked and shared with others, increased intensive interaction in age segregated contexts, and the possibility of retrenchment by governments, may produce the conditions that facilitate collective political action.

NOTES

1. The size of the aged population is not, of course, without political consequence. First, the greater the number of individuals who share a particular status, the greater the potential for intensive interaction among status similars. Further, if the ability of age to compel political behavior is taken as a given, the number of persons in a group may be related to its power in the political arena.

2. The influence of the social context upon the attitudes and behaviors of individuals is a basic interest of sociology. One dimension of this concern focuses on the relationship between an individual's social characteristics, such as race, religion, sex or marital status, and the presence or absence of these characteristics among those with whom he interacts. It is not simply the individual's social characteristics or the social characteristics of those around him, but the relationship between the two—their concordance or discordance—which is of primal significance. Studies have focused on the relationship between the individual's social characteristics and those of the population by which he is surrounded to explain such widely diverse phenomenon as disturbances in self-esteem, depressive affect and psychosomatic symptoms (M. Rosenberg, 1962); political behavior (Lipset, 1963) and friendship (Rosow, 1967; Blau, 1956; G. Rosenberg, 1970).

3. Just as these observations support the contention that present political arrangements are perceived to be legitimate, they also suggest that old age political movements emerging in this context have a greater probability of success. Interest group politics generally produces involvement within the mainstream of national politics. And, just as radical movements have consistently failed, reform movements often succeed precisely because they operate within the existing political structure, and appear moderate compared with more radical positions (Ash, 1972).

REFERENCES

1. Ash, Roberta *Social Movements in America*. Chicago: Markham Publishing Company, 1972.
2. Barron, Milton "Minority group characteristics of the aged in American society." *Journal of Gerontology*, 1953, 8, 477–481.
3. Bell, Daniel *The End of Ideology*. New York, Collier Books, 1962.
4. Berelson, Bernard, Paul F. Lazarsfeld, and William N. McPhee. *Voting*. Chicago: University of Chicago Press, 1954.
5. Binstock, Robert "Interest-Group Liberalism and the Politics of Aging." *The Gerontologist*, 1972, 12, No. 3, Part I, 265–280.

6. Blau, Zena Smith "Changes in Status and Age Identification." *American Sociological Review,* 1956, 21, 198–203.

7. Bultena, Gordon L. "Age-grading in the social interaction of an elderly male population," *Journal of Gerontology,* 1968, 23, 539–543.

8. Campbell, Angus "Politics through the Life Cycle." *The Gerontologist,* 1971, 11, No. 2, Part I, 112–117.

9. Campbell, Angus, Gerald Curin, and Warren E. Miller, *The Voter Decides.* Evanston, Illinois: Row, Peterson and Company, 1954.

10. Clague, E. "The Aging Population and Programs of Security." *Milbank Memorial Fund Quarterly,* 1940, 18, 345–358.

11. Cottrel, Fred "Governmental Functions and the Politics of Age" in Clark Tibbits (ed.), *Handbook of Social Gerontology.* Chicago: The University of Chicago Press, 1960.

12. Cottrel, Fred "Aging and the Political System" in John C. McKinney and Frank K. DeVyver (ed.), *Aging and Social Policy.* New York: Appleton-Century-Crofts, 1966.

13. Cumming, E. and Henry, W. E. *Growing Old: The Process of Disengagement.* New York: Basic Books 1961.

14. Cumming, E. and Schneider, D. "Sibling solidarity; a property of American kinship." *American Anthropologist,* 1961, 63, 498–507.

15. Davies, James E. "Toward a Theory of Revolution." *American Sociological Review,* 1962, 27.

16. Freedman, Ronald and Axelrod, Morris, 1952 "Who Belongs to what in a Great Metropolis." *Adult Leadership* 1952, 1, 6–9.

17. Havigurst, R. J. "Old Age—An American Problem." *Journal of Gerontology,* 1949, 4, 298–304.

18. Holtzman, Abraham "Analysis of old age politics in the United States," *Journal of Gerontology,* 1954, 9, 56–66.

19. Key, V. O., Jr. *Politics, Parties and Pressure Groups.* New York: Thomas Y. Cowell Company, 1958.

20. Lipset, Seymour Martin *Political Man.* Garden City, New York: Anchor Books, Doubleday and Company, Inc. 1963.

21. Loether, Herman J. *Problems of Aging.* Belmont, California: Dickenson Publishing Company, Inc., 1967.

22. Maccoby, Herbert "The Differential Political Activity of Participants in a Voluntary Association," *American Sociological Review,* 1958, 23, 524–532.

23. Messinger, S. L. "Organizational Transformation: A case study of a declining social movement." *American Sociological Review,* 1955, 20, 3–20.

24. Parsons, Talcott *Essays in Sociological Theory.* Glencoe, Illinois: Free Press, 1954.

25. Pinard, Maurice "Mass society and political movements: a new formulation." *American Journal of Sociology,* 1968, 73, 682–690.

26. Pinner, Frank A. "Theories of Political Participation and Age" in W. Donahue and C. Tibbits (eds.), *Politics of Age.* Ann Arbor: University of Michigan Press, 1962.

27. Rose, Arnold M. "The Subculture of the Aging: A Framework for Research in Social Gerontology." *The Gerontologist,* 1962, 2, 123–127.

28. Rosenberg, George S. *The Worker Grows Old.* San Francisco: Jossey-Bass Publishing Company, 1970.

29. Rosenberg, Morris "The Dissonant Religious Context and Emotional Disturbance." *The American Journal of Sociology,* 1962, LXIII, 1–10.

30. Rosow, Irving *Social Integration of the Aged.* New York: The Free Press, 1967.

31. Sallach, David L., Nicholas Babchuk and Alan Booth "Social Involvement and Political Activity: Another View." *Social Science Quarterly,* 1972, 52, 879–92.

32. Sherif, Muzafer and Sherif, Carolyn W. *An Outline of Social Psychology.* New York: Harper and Brothers, 1956.

33. Smith, Joel "The group status of the aged in an urban social structure" in Ida Harper Simpson and John C. McKinney, (eds.), *Social Aspects of Aging.* Durham, North Carolina: Duke University Press, 1966.

34. Trela, James E. "Some Political Consequences of Senior Center and Other Old Age Group Memberships," *The Gerontologist,* 11, No. 2, Part I, 118–123.

35. Trela, James E. "Age Structure of Voluntary Associations and Activist Self-Interest among the Aged," *The Sociological Quarterly,* 1972, 13, 244–252.

36. Turner, Ralph H. and Lewis M. Killian *Collective Behavior,* Englewood Cliffs: Prentice-Hall, 1957.

37. Wright, Charles R. and Hyman, Herbert H. "Voluntary Association Memberships of American Adults: Evidence from National Sample Surveys," *American Sociological Review,* 1958, 23, 284–294.

11

Stratum Consciousness and Stratum Action: Class Consciousness and the Multiple Hierarchy Approach

Vincent Jeffries

THE TERM *class consciousness* has not been used consistently in the scholarly literature or in the various research studies that have purported to empirically study the existence and extent of class consciousness. How the concept is defined has a distinct bearing on what conclusions may be drawn regarding the nature and extent of class consciousness in the United States. An overview of studies of class consciousness provides a basis for some clarification regarding the differing uses of the concept.

The previous considered paradigm of class consciousness developed by Morris and Murphy* (1966) and similar efforts by other scholars (Lopreato and Hazelrigg, 1972) point to the advisability of viewing class consciousness as a continuum. There is clearly a gradual series of gradations from no discernment of the existence of classes or other strata to a fully developed consciousness manifesting such elements as a sense of group identity, a feeling of separateness from other strata, an ideology linked to stratum interests, and a plan of collective action to attain stratum goals. Such a view is similar to Marx's (1956; Mills*, 1962:81–95) view of consciousness as a developing phenomenon stemming from continued conflict between classes and the alienation of the subordinate strata.

Richard Centers's (1949) study constitutes a landmark in the empirical investigations of class consciousness in the United States. His study, based on a nationwide sample, was one of the earlier analyses of this topic. It provoked considerable interest

An asterisk (*) accompanying a citation indicates a selection that is included in this volume.

462

and controversy and set the tone of many later investigations of class consciousness, particularly for those studies conducted in the decade following.

The core of Centers's (1949) approach was his distinction between "stratum" and "class." A stratum is considered to be an objective socioeconomic grouping that derives from the economic system and is related to the manner in which people make a living. The concept of stratum in Centers's study includes three hierarchies: occupation, which is most emphasized; power, as indicated by the degree of dominance or subordination in occupational positions; and economic level. These separate hierarchies are combined into a single index in some of the analysis. In contrast to stratum, Centers regards a class as subjective and psychologically based. Classes are "psycho-social groupings" that involve a "feeling" of membership based on common interests, attitudes, and behavior. Class consciousness is the sense of affiliation and identification, and the similarity of orientation that are associated with being in a common class.

Centers believes a relationship exists between stratum, class, and class consciousness; he describes this relationship in terms of "interest group" theory. Position in the economic system of society is considered as the source of "attitudes, interests, and values" that reflect the life experiences associated with this position. Similarly, occupancy of a position in the productive process gives rise to consciousness of membership in a social class, based on an awareness that members hold these attitudes, interests, and values in common.

Class consciousness is comprised of class affiliation and politico-economic orientation. The existence of class affiliation was determined in Centers's study by asking respondents the question: "If you were asked to use one of these four names for your social class, which would you say you belonged in: the middle class, lower class, working class or upper class?" (Centers, 1949:76). Class affiliation, or identification, as it is sometimes termed by Centers, was found to be moderately correlated (.47 to .69) with occupational, economic, and power strata. People in higher strata were more likely to identify with the upper class, or particularly with the middle class, than were those in lower strata.

Both stratum position and class affiliation were also correlated with politico-economic orientation, as indicated by six questions pertaining to issues such as government or private ownership of industry, the influence of working people in the government, and the treatment of workers by employers. This politico-economic orientation was viewed by Centers as the second major aspect of class consciousness, in addition to that of class affiliation.

Those in higher strata were more likely to have a conservative politico-economic orientation than were those in lower strata. So were those affiliating with the upper and middle classes, when compared to those affiliating with the working and lower classes. A more detailed breakdown for each class showed that 66 percent of those affiliating with the upper class were conservative or ultraconservative in their politico-economic attitudes, as compared to only 23 percent of those affiliating with the lower class. At the other end of the scale, only 17 percent of the upper class were classified as radical or ultra-radical in their responses, as compared to 46 percent of the lower class. The highest degrees of conservatism or radicalism were evidenced when high class affiliation was combined with high stratum position in the case of conservatism and when low class affiliation combined with low stratum position in the case of radicalism.

Stratum position, class affiliation, and politico-economic orientation were all found to be correlated with political behavior. The incidence of voting Republican increased with higher stratum position, higher class affiliation, and conservative orientation.

Centers's (1949) study was an important contribution because it indicated a clear relation between stratum position in the economic structure and subjective factors such as class affiliation, politico-economic orientation, and political behavior. One problem with the study, however, is that the measure of the components of class consciousness does not adequately allow for a non-class-conscious response. Both the measure of class affiliation and that of politico-economic orientation are structured and tabulated in such a manner that, by simply responding to the questions presented, individuals are placed in some positive category with respect to their class consciousness. The issue of whether they are in fact class conscious in any meaningful sense is not really dealt with.

Of the various criticisms of the work that emerged, the most telling went to the method used to determine class affiliation (Roach, Gross and Gursslin, 1969:360). In the original survey by Centers, 3 percent had identified themselves as upper class, 43 percent as middle class, 51 percent as working class, and 1 percent as lower class. One percent answered ''don't know'' and 1 percent said they did not believe in classes. A study by Neal Gross (1953) examined the extent of discrepancy between responses to an open-ended question with no designation of classes and Centers's question with predetermined categories.

When asked the question using the same categories as in Centers's study, the distribution of responses was somewhat similar to the earlier study. Using an open-ended question that offered no class designations produced very different results, however. Only 46 percent of the respondents answered within Centers's categories, 14 percent thought there were no classes, and 20 percent did not know what class they were in. Another 5 percent would not or could not answer the question. Thus well over one-third of the persons in the survey seemed to have no clear sense of class identification. Gross (1953) raised the critical issue that if class is a feeling of belonging that is part of one's ego, as Centers viewed it, people should be able to verbalize this self-identification without the aid of a set of categories provided by the interviewer. Gross's (1953) study clearly indicates that class identification is heavily influenced by the wording of questions. The findings also illustrate a general lack of clarity that still exists today in the study of class consciousness.

Despite the centrality of the study of consciousness to an understanding of the dynamics of stratification systems, the present state of scholarly endeavors shows a lack of consistency at both the conceptual and empirical levels of analysis (Lopreato and Hazelbrigg, 1972). The various empirical studies of class consciousness exhibit many different conceptualizations of this term and of different operational procedures. Attempts to group these diverse studies together under various designated stages of consciousness, such as those by Morris and Murphy* (1966) and Lopreato and Hazelbrigg (1972), provide a way of making sense out of the existing evidence regarding the nature and extent of class consciousness.

Most of the empirical studies of class consciousness conducted in the United States have involved data that can most properly be categorized as what Morris and Murphy* (1966) refer to as ''class awareness.'' These authors include in this category both those studies in which respondents are asked to comment about the structure of society in such a way that their perception of stratification is revealed and those studies in which respondents are asked directly what class they are in. Many of these studies have not extended their scope much beyond this limit with respect to the elements of class consciousness.

Lopreato and Hazelbrigg (1972) have summarized data from a number of these investigations. A comparison of eight studies in the United States shows that when structured questions are used, almost all respondents (92 percent to 100 percent) are able to place themselves in a class position. Small numbers (1 percent to 5 percent) identify with the upper class, with a similar number identifying with the lower class. When "middle class" and "working class" are the other two categories, between 35 percent and 43 percent place themselves in the middle class and 45 percent to 60 percent select the working class. When middle class is subdivided, such as into "upper" and "lower" middle, the percentages of respondents selecting this category increases, while those selecting the working class decreases. When unstructured questions are used, the proportion placing themselves in one of the aforementioned class categories drops to between 46 percent and 76 percent. The overwhelming majority of those placing themselves in a class still identify with either the middle or working class.

Those studies show that the influence of the wording of questions notwithstanding, most people appear to have some awareness of what class they are in. When questions are worded in a similar manner, the results are somewhat consistent through time. Schreiber and Nygreen (1970) reviewed data pertaining to subjective social class identification in the United States between 1945 and 1968. The vast majority of respondents placed themselves in either the middle or working class; and while there is some fluctuation in the percentages choosing various class affiliations, a geneal stability and uniformity appears to exist.

Class awareness (the ability to place self and others in a hierarchy), although often referred to in the literature as "class consciousness," is only a basic element of a more fully developed consciousness. Class consciousness to Marx (1956; Mills*, 1962:81–95) and Morris and Murphy* (1966), for example, includes a sense of group membership and a commitment to the interests and goals of the class to which one belongs, in addition to class awareness. When consciousness is conceptualized in this manner, there is a paucity of studies of class consciousness in the scholarly literature.

One of the few studies of class consciousness that attempts to encompass most of the aforementioned characteristics was done by Oscar Glantz (1958). Data for the study consist primarily of the responses of a sample of big and small businessmen, and union and nonunion workers. Glantz begins with the position that class is objective in nature, in the sense that is is a characteristic of the social structure. Class consciousness is a perspective that develops out of an awareness of these objective conditions. As such, class consciousness is composed of two principal elements: a sense of allegiance to one's class and an orientation to the interests and values of one's class. Ultimately, class consciousness should lead to political cohesiveness.

To be considered class conscious in the Glantz study, respondents had to manifest both allegiance and orientation. Allegiance, defined as a sense of loyalty and commitment to a particular group, was measured by responses to a question asking whether allegiance was owed to business or labor. Those not choosing one of these groups were considered as "middle of the road" in their allegiance.

Orientation to class interests was measured by agreement or disagreement with six strongly partisan statements taken from the literature of business and labor organizations. The questions dealt with issues such as union bargaining, federal control of utilities, rent control, and excess profit taxes. Orientation was conceived as involving both the acceptance of political and economic values that are class related and the rejection of alternative values consistent with the interests of classes other than the one respondents belonged to on the basis of their objective position. Respondents predominantly favoring either business or labor were classified as oriented in these respective directions, whereas those less consistent were designated as "indeterminate."

The results pertaining to orientation showed that there was a high rate of indeterminate response patterns among small businessmen (60 percent), union workers (53 percent), and nonunion workers (65 percent). Thus none of these groups were predominantly oriented toward the interests of their respective class. This pattern was reversed among big businessmen. Sixty-three percent were business oriented, 2 percent were labor oriented, and only 35 percent were indeterminate.

Class consciousness was defined by Glantz (1958) as being composed of both allegiance and orientation. By these criteria, 40 percent of all big businessmen and 25 percent of all small businessmen in the sample were class conscious. Among wage workers 28 percent of all union workers were class conscious, as were 13 percent of nonunion workers. Thus, the extent of class consciousness was relatively limited in the study sample.

Glantz (1958) next examined the extent to which class consciousness was related to political cohesiveness. Political expressions of class consciousness can be explored in terms of party preference in voting and in terms of a motivational basis for voting preference. In this context, the fundamental problem of the relationship between class consciousness and common action to change or maintain the political system can be analyzed.

Since the Republican party is more aligned with business interests and the Democratic party with labor interests, voting behavior provides an indication of the link between class consciousness and political behavior (Glantz, 1958). Data show a clear relationship between consciousness and voting in the presidential elections of 1948 (Truman versus Dewey) and of 1952 (Eisenhower versus Stevenson). One hundred percent of class-conscious big businessmen voted for the Republican party candidates in both elections. Among big businessmen who were not class conscious, 78 percent voted for the Republican presidential candidate in 1948 and 87 percent in 1952. A similar link between class consciousness and voting along the lines of class interest was also observed among wage workers. The percentage of class-conscious union workers voting for the Democratic presidential candidate was 91 percent in 1948 and 86 percent in 1952. These figures were only 75 percent and 64 percent, for respective years, among non-class conscious union workers, indicating a relationship between class consciousness and partisan voting behavior among union wage workers.

To more adequately establish a causal link between class consciousness and voting behavior, Glantz (1958) asked respondents to state their most important reasons for voting for a candidate in the 1952 presidential election. The effect of consciousness on electoral choice should be evidenced in greater frequency of class linked reasons among the class conscious than among the non-class conscious. Class consciousness was indeed reflected in the kinds of reasons given. Fifty-six percent of class-conscious big business-men said they voted for Republican candidates in 1952 to protest the policies and record of the Democratic party, including among these various "isms of the left." Only 20 per-cent of the non-class conscious big businessmen gave this response. Even though 25 per-cent of the class-conscious big businessmen gave Republican principles and policies as a reason for their voting choice, only 15 percent of the nonclass-consciousness big busi-nessmen did so. Although some of the responses regarding Republican principles and policies appeared somewhat ambiguous, others contained definite class related motives.

This greater prevalence of class-linked motives for voting among the class con-scious was also found among wage workers. For example, 72 percent of class conscious union workers cited Stevenson's and the Democratic party's interest in labor as a reason for their voting choice. The open-ended responses to this question showed a class linked rationale pertaining to the Democratic party and labor. Only 34 percent of other wage workers gave similar responses. Thus, class consciousness was found to be related to po-litical solidarity, both with respect to the choice of candidates in presidential elections and to the motives for such choices.

The limited extent of class consciousness (sense of group membership and com-mitment) beyond the level of class awareness (sense of hierarchial structure and one's place in it) found in the Glantz (1958) study coincides with the findings of Morris and Jeffries (1970). The authors used secondary analysis of data gathered in a sample of 583 white respondents to ascertain the extent of class awareness, class consciousness, and class action, and their interrelationships. Class awareness was measured by choice of affiliation with either the upper, upper-middle, middle, lower-middle, working, or lower class. In addition, respondents were asked whether "class differences are very important in this country" and whether "it is easy to tell who is in what class." Objec-tive class position, as measured separately by income, occupation, and education, was strongly related to class affiliation, but showed no relationship to the other two measures of class awareness. Those in a low objective class position were as likely as those in a high position to see classes as observable or important.

Another element of class consciousness investigated by Morris and Jeffries (1970) was the sense of dissatisfaction with the existing social structure, an idea basic to the Marxian notion of a developed class consciousness. One facet of class dissatisfaction, a sense of being treated unjustly, was expressed in questions pertaining to the beliefs that many people "have things that they don't deserve" and that many people are "trying to get ahead at my expense." Other aspects of class dissatisfaction were a belief in lack of opportunity for mobility and a sense of alienation. When class dissatisfaction was related to the class awareness items and objective class position, a fairly consistent, but for the most part a very weak, pattern emerged. Those lower in the class structure were slightly more dissatisfied, as were those who emphasized the importance and observability of class differences.

Class conflict was indicated by a preference for Lyndon Johnson or Barry Goldwater in the 1964 presidential election. The policies on economic and welfare state issues held by these two candidates were particularly salient for class-related issues and interests. Both objective class position and subjective class affiliation were related to the presidential vote, with those in higher positions generally being more likely than those in lower positions to vote for Goldwater. Those high on the various measures of class dissatisfaction (sense of injustice, lack of opportunity for mobility, alienation) were for the most part slightly less likely to vote for Goldwater.

Although faint patterns of relationships were evident, Morris and Jeffries (1970) concluded that, with the exception of the relationship between objective class position and subjective class affiliation, no strong and consistent relationships existed between class awareness, class dissatisfaction, and class conflict. The study indicated that there was no developed and functioning class consciousness in the United States that would lead to collective political activity directed toward class interests.

The lack of development of class consciousness among the major segments of society is also evidenced in Alfred W. Jones's (1941) study of attitudes toward corporate property in Akron, Ohio, a one-industry town whose economy depended on the rubber industry. The years preceding the study were characterized by an "open, dramatic and bitter struggle between capital and labor" (Jones, 1941:115). Job insecurity, strikes, sit-downs by workers, and incidents of violence were frequent occurrences.

To measure the attitudes of the population, Jones (1941) developed a series of seven stories in which corporate property rights were opposed to various personal rights regarding the livelihood, security, or self-respect of the individual. The reactions of respondents to each of the stories was scored on a five-step scale ranging from unqualified approval to unqualified disapproval of the rights of corporate property. These scores formed the basis of an index ranging from 0 to 32, the high end signifying approval of the rights of corporate property.

Interview schedules were administered to 1,705 persons, including a general random sample drawn from the Akron area and thirteen subsamples of specific occupational groupings such as business leaders, teachers, chemists, female office workers, small merchants, ministers, and both union and nonunion rubber workers. The union rubber workers were actively involved in the previously noted strife between labor and industry.

The results of the study showed that the attitudes of business leaders toward corporate property were quite consistent and closely corresponded to the interests associated with their economic position. The overwhelming majority (89 percent) scored high (29 to 32) on approval of the rights of corporate property with little variation of scores among those interviewed. The next most consistent group was the union rubber workers, although the range of attitudes in this group was less consistent and less extreme than that of the business leaders. Clustering at the other end of the scale from the business leaders, 39 percent of the union rubber workers scored 0 to 3 in approval of corporate property, while 29 percent scored 4 through 7. Other groups of workers were far less likely to manifest attitudes in accordance with their economic position and interests. The other occupational groups in the sample also tended to have a moderate attitude toward corporate property, avoiding either extreme. Such a compromising position was the dominant tone or attitude, in which the traditional claims of both property and of humanitarianism were given somewhat equal emphasis. This "Central Morality" tended to mute attitudes of conflict and cleavage.

The attitudinal trend away from extreme positions and a sense of cleavage was complemented by a whole or partial rejection of the idea of class. Among those higher in status, classes were referred to in such terms as the "rich" and the "poor" or the "successful" and the "unsuccessful." Among those in lower status, class appeared to have a very blurred meaning, and workers made very few references to class. Thus, overall, the group of business leaders was the only segment of the population to be consistent in the expression of attitudes correspondent with the interests inherent in their economic position.

The findings of Glantz (1958) and Jones (1941) that class consciousness is highest among big businessmen are consistent with other studies of the class consciousness of the upper strata. For example, C. Wright Mills (1956) has observed that class consciousness is not equally characteristic of all levels of society in the United States, but rather is most apparent in the upper class. The upper strata of families in towns and cities are aware of belonging to the upper strata, know about each other, and share common traditions.

There also is a certain unity among the power elite on the national level in the United States (Mills, 1956). Members of this elite tend to share social origins and formal educational experiences, and to associate with each other frequently, both socially and in the course of their business and professional lives. The key organizations for maintaining the social networks through which power may be exercised are probably the major corporations, and their boards of directors. Mills (1956) observes that at the higher levels of the economic, political, and military elites there are high degrees of similarity of orientation and willingness to see each other's point of view.

Paul Sweezy (1973) has also noted that there is a national ruling class that has a fairly definite organizational structure and an ideology that it guards and seeks to promulgate and that is supported by a complex network of institutional relations. The study by Domhoff (1967), which was discussed in some detail in chapter 4, also presents considerable evidence indicating concerted action in the service of class interests among the upper class on a national level in the United States.

The relatively low levels of class consciousness found in the previously considered studies appear to be typical of studies that define class consciousness in the more extended manner of Morris and Murphy* (1966) and allow for determining that such consciousness is weak or nonexistent. In general, people in the United States do not evaluate their lives in class terms, and there seems to be little development of class consciousness among most segments of the population (Mills, 1956:324–356; Rossides, 1976:264–266). Exceptions may occur in particular segments of society, such as among the very wealthy and powerful, and among the extremely disadvantaged. This higher level of class consciousness among the disadvantaged will be considered later in the chapter.

REASONS FOR LACK OF CLASS CONSCIOUSNESS

Various reasons for the lack of widespread class consciousness in the United States have been suggested by Morris Rosenberg (1953). Classes are regarded by Rosenberg as objective elements of the social structure. They are separate and discrete groups with differing relationships to ownership of the means of production. Class consciousness is subjective in nature; it pertains to an individual's perception of his or her position in the class structure. According to Rosenberg, for class consciousness to exist there must at least be a correspondence between subjective identification and objective class position, a sense of unity with those in a similar class position, and a sense of separation from those in a different class position.

Rosenberg (1953) attempted to identify the perceptual and structural factors that inhibit the development of class consciousness. Six such factors were identified: the structure of large-scale industry, the political structure, multiple group membership, aspects of the prevailing style of life, prevailing cultural goals, and certain kinds of self-image.

The structure of modern industry inhibits the development of class consciousness. It creates perceptions of unity with some, and of separation from others, based on characteristics of the occupational structure. These lines of unity or separation are different from those based on objective class criteria. This disjunction between the class and the occupational structure derives from several sources, one of which is the structure of power in a typical industrial organization. Orders are usually relayed through a hierarchy with many intermediate levels. Policies originating at the top of an organizational hierarchy are usually implemented by an individual, such as a foreperson, who is actually at the same class level as the worker he or she directs. The organizational structure thus dissipates potential class antagonisms by removing the immediate exercise of authority from the lines of class differences.

The complex and highly segmented division of labor characteristic of modern industry also mitigates against class consciousness (Rosenberg, 1953). The occupational structure promotes a sense of difference among individuals who are objectively in the same social class. For example, white and blue collar workers, who are usually in the same class position in relation to ownership of the means of production, often believe they are very different from each other. Another way in which the structure of modern industry inhibits class consciousness is that people in different classes may develop a sense of unity based on common work experiences or association with a common product. Interpersonal relations within work situations that transcend class lines are an additional circumstance that builds a sense of unity that can take precedence over class consciousness.

A second major factor muting the emergence of class consciousness is that the major political parties in the United States do not explicitly represent the interests of particular classes. This is due in part to territorial political representation whereby candidates become symbols for interclass unity rather than representatives of a given class. Another barrier to class consciousness is the competition for votes. Because candidates must usually appeal to a number of segments of the population, they are unlikely to make narrow appeals directed toward class interests.

A third major obstacle to the emergence of class consciousness is that of multiple group identification. In a complex and heterogeneous society, such as exists in the United States, various group affiliations other than that of class compete for an individual's loyalty and identification. Of particular importance in this regard is racial group identification and unity, which often cuts across and negates a sense of class unity.

Another major set of barriers to class consciousness is viewed by Rosenberg (1953) as aspects of the dominant style of life. One of these has to do with consumption patterns. Rather than polarization in the possession of consumption items, a continuum exists in which differences from one level to the next are slight, with no clear and unequivocal differences among classes. Class distinctions are also obscured by the cultural system. The mass communication media tends to produce a certain similarity of culture and ideology. This works against a sense of difference that might otherwise emerge from varying positions in the class structure.

Certain cultural goals also function in opposition to the development of class consciousness. Unifying goals such as nationalism cut across class lines and lessen the imporance of class differences. Traditional values such as competition and individualism also tend to create rivalries and individualize antagonisms, thus detracting from the sense of commonality necessary for class consciousness.

Under varying conditions, the self-image of individuals can also block the development of class consciousness. One condition occurs when individuals identify with interests associated with some high occupational position to which they aspire in the future. Self-image can also inhibit consciousness when, despite downward mobility, individuals still see themselves as occupants of their former higher position.

THE MULTIPLE HIERARCHY APPROACH TO STRATUM CONSCIOUSNESS AND ACTION: COMBINATIONS

A position in a particular stratum constitutes a social world with its attendant subculture. By virtue of occupying such a position, individuals are likely to have certain experiences and to be faced with particular social expectations. Social contacts with other segments of society are in some instances furthered, in others discouraged. Certain subcultures and the meanings they ascribe to particular situations and events become part of the day-to-day experience of individuals because of their position in a given stratum, even though their awareness of other sets of meanings and subcultures may be severely limited or nonexistent. Characteristic degrees of power, privilege, and prestige are associated with positions in social hierarchies.

The multiple hierarchy approach to stratification deals with the impact of particular combinations of such hierarchial positions on the development and ideological content of stratum consciousness. It also deals with the impact of combinations of positions on the manner and extent of participation in stratum action. When multiple stratification hierarchies exist, distinct social worlds are created by the juncture of two or more stratum positions. Being white and old is quite different from being black and old (Dowd and Bengston*, 1978; Jackson, 1974), and being female and middle-aged is different from being male and middle-aged (Sontag*, 1972). A model of multiple strata provides a perspective for analyzing such particular social and cultural configurations and their effects upon the psyches, behavior patterns, and life histories of individuals. In this sense, the study of the impact of multiple hierarchies on stratum consciousness and action is a variation of the study of correlates of stratification discussed in chapter 8.

Multiple positions can exert varying pressures in regard to stratum consciousness and action. There appear to be three general types in this regard. In some instances, multiple positions coalesce to exert reinforcing pressures that further the development of stratum consciousness and action. In other cases, pressures are conflicting. Membership in one stratum may exert pressures toward increased stratum consciousness and action, while membership in another stratum may exert pressure against the development of consciousness and action. Finally, multiple positions may exert reinforcing pressures toward collective opposition to the development of stratum consciousness and action.

An example of the type of multiple hierarchy combination in which positions reinforce each other in furthering the development of stratum consciousness and action is provided by John Leggett (1964; 1968). Data for this study of the class consciousness of the working class was gathered from a sample of 375 male, blue-collar workers. Both blacks and whites were interviewed. Class consciousness is considered as "a cumulative series of mental states" (Leggett, 1964:228), ranging from verbalization to egalitarianism. The first stage, class "verbalization," was defined as a tendency to discuss topics in class terms. "Skepticism," the next stage, referred to the belief of the respondents that wealth is distributed in this society to benefit those higher up in the class structure. "Militance" was defined as the willingness to engage in action beneficial to one's class; "egalitarianism" referred to support of the redistribution of wealth. Response patterns indicated the validity of regarding these stages as a continuum, and hence, individuals were categorized according to their highest level of consciousness. Those who scored as class conscious on all four measures were termed "militant egalitarians"; those scoring class conscious on all but egalitarianism were termed "militant radicals." At the other end of the continuum, the completely non-class conscious were designated as "class indifferents."

Leggett's (1964; 1968) studies focused directly on the interplay of ethnic and class factors upon class consciousness. Within the working class, Leggett identified "marginal workers," those who belonged to a subordinate racial and ethnic group, generally were unskilled and encountered high degrees of economic insecurity. This group was more class conscious than were the "mainstream" members of the working class in the study. This latter category was comprised of those who belonged to a dominant racial group, were skilled workers, and enjoyed considerable economic security. For example, the unemployed were found to be more class conscious than the employed. Thirty-one percent of the employed were either militant radicals or militant egalitarians. In contrast, 46 percent of the unemployed fell into one of these two categories.

Race also had an effect on class consciousness. Only 22 percent of whites fell in one of the two militant categories, but 59 percent of blacks did. When employment status and race were combined and then compared, a sharp contrast was evident. Among blacks, 57 percent of the employed and 56 percent of the unemployed were militantly class conscious. Among whites, 32 percent of the unemployed were militantly class conscious, as opposed to only 20 percent of employed whites. Membership in a racial minority that encounters considerable discrimination was thus associated with higher levels of class consciousness.

Among unemployed blacks who were also union members, 80 percent were either militant radicals or militant egalitarians. Unstructured interview responses showed blacks to be particularly sensitive to the advantages of the wealthy. Class and racial consciousness were also found to be interrelated. Subordinate racial position appeared to reinforce the development of higher levels of class consciousness among members of the working class.

A similar reinforcing effect between race and working class status was found by Ransford* (1977) in his study of the reactions of blacks to the Watts Riot of 1965 in Los Angeles. This study investigated the separate and combined effects of race and class identification on two measures of racial militance: approval of the Watts Riot and advocacy of racial solutions (acceptance of violence or rejection of integration) as a preferred manner of achieving advancement of the black cause. The results indicate that when race and class consciousness combine, they produce especially militant reactions. Blue-collar black workers who identified strongly with both the interests of the working class and with their race were higher than any other group in approval of the Watts Riot and the endorsement of radical policies.

Both the Leggett (1964; 1968) and Ransford (1977) studies illustrate a particular pattern in which a combination of positions in two hierarchies produces high degrees of stratum consciousness. These studies suggest that in advanced and affluent industrial societies, such as the United States, the higher levels of consciousness and stratum-based action expected by Marx are perhaps most likely to develop when multiple hierarchies combine to produce relatively intense levels of deprivation and discontent.

In some instances, subordinate status may produce conflicting pressures that limit consciousness and action or channel it in particular directions. This pattern of conflicting pressures can be observed in the experience of the Mexican-American woman, who is subject to both sexism and racism. A study by Consuelo Nieto* (1974) points out that Chicana women are faced with a unique cultural emphasis, stressed particularly by the Catholic church, which says that a woman's life should be centered around the family roles of wife and mother. The women's movement is also seen as diverting time and energy from La Raza, the general attempt to improve the position of Chicanos in the United States. These social pressures and cultural heritages produce a particular reaction to the women's liberation movement among Chicana women. Even though many Chicana women support the women's movement with respect to issues bearing on equal pay and job opportunities, they are not willing to press for changes in the subordinate position of females within the family and within the general social structure of Mexican-Americans. Changes in patterns of interaction within the family are for the most part resisted because of the strains or possible rupture of husband-and-wife relationships that they would create. Instead of seeking changes in these areas, Mexican-American women hope that their daughters will not have to face the limitations and restrictions that they have.

A recent article by King (1975) about the relation of black women to the women's movement illustrates this same theme of conflicting pressures with respect to stratum consciousness and action. In a statement representing a frequently voiced argument, the position is taken by King that the interests of the women's movement and the black movement for liberation are incompatible. Race is viewed as the basis of the oppression of the black woman, whereas sexual status is regarded as only intensifying the difficulties of being black. The women's movement is largely an attempt to change traditional sex roles and the concept of femininity. These issues King regards as generally not applicable or relevant to black women. The causes of the black woman's discontent are located in the racial caste system, which is either of little concern to, or is often supported by, white women. Hence, to King, the women's movement has little that is positive to contribute to the struggle for black liberation, but rather constitutes a diversion from the true basis of the problems facing the black woman in the United States.

Two kinds of conflicting pressures are evident in the articles by King (1975) and Nieto* (1974). Both studies cite the belief that efforts to elevate one subordinate status is less important than (or will detract from) the necessity for consciousness and action relative to another subordinate status. The Nieto* (1974) article also reveals that particular subcultural configurations may exert strong pressures against the full development of consciousness and action relative to a given subordinate status. Such traditions both shape and limit the content of stratum consciousness and its expression in social action.

A third major type of pressure exerted by the occupancy of multiple positions is that the social expectations and cultural traditions associated with the positions exert reinforcing pressures against the development of stratum consciousness and action. Ransford (1972), for example, found that whites who were in blue-collar positions or those with less than a high school education were especially antagonistic to both the black and student protest movements. Three explanations were given for this finding. One perspective focuses on the emphasis on conformity and respect for authority that studies have indicated are greatest among the working class. Since both student and black protests are antithetical to such values, working-class white persons should be especially hostile toward these movements. A second perspective centers on the white working-class emphasis on the availability of opportunity for advancement. In light of this belief structure, the white lower class may view the black lower class as undeserving of special advantages, and regard their place at the bottom of the structure as primarily a result of their lack of effort. This view of the United States as a land of opportunity for those willing to work is inconsistent with the criticisms voiced by student protestors. The final explanation advanced by Ransford (1972) points to a sense of powerlessness. A general sense of powerlessness felt by the white working class is compounded by the belief that blacks and students are pushing for changes that are a threat to the working class.

Survey data showed that social class, whether indexed by occupation or education, was related to each of the three perspectives pertaining to authority, opportunity, and powerlessness. The working class were more likely to endorse these beliefs. Social class was related to hostility toward the black and student movements, the working class being the most hostile. Each of the aforementioned belief systems was also associated with hostility toward these movements. Thus, Ransford's (1972) study showed that the combination of white racial status and working class status was related to strong opposition to the demands of blacks and students.

THE MULTIPLE HIERARCHY APPROACH TO STRATUM CONSCIOUSNESS AND ACTION: COMPARISONS

By applying the multiple hierarchy approach, the relationship between social stratification and social change can be seen in broader terms than by focusing on a single stratum. By comparing various strata, similarities and differences of basic processes and structures pertaining to stratum consciousness and action may be observed.

Evidence indicates that class, race, sex, and age constitute major stratification hierarchies in the United States today. Each entails definite inequalities in the distribution of power, privilege, and prestige. Comparisons across these hierarchies also show clear differences in the development and extent of stratum consciousness and action. Both sex and race are the basis of recent and ongoing social movements in the United States. Stratum consciousness and action based primarily on age or class interests have been sporadic and relatively limited.

Although the potential for stratum consciousness and action exists whenever social stratification exists, whether or not stratum consciousness and action develop, and in what form and intensity, is problematic. A detailed and comprehensive analysis of this problem relative to class, race, sex, and age strata in the United States is beyond the scope of this work. A few important areas of comparative analyses across all four hierarchies can be briefly considered, however. These points of comparison are the clarity of boundary lines between strata, the likelihood of the development of a sense of self-identity based on stratum position, and the possibility of mobility from one stratum to another. The type and degree of contact that exists between superordinate and subordinate strata also affords an interesting comparison between the sexual and racial hierarchies.

Boundary lines between strata can differ greatly in terms of the degree to which observable characteristics differentiate the members of one stratum from those of another stratum. When differences are readily observable, daily social interaction usually is more subject to social expectations and pressures that are traditionally linked to given strata positions. Clear boundary lines set strata apart from each other. They emphasize and perpetuate status distinctions and, in this way, encourage stereotypical patterns of interaction. With clear boundaries between strata, interaction is more likely to be confined to one's stratum, and if it does cross stratum lines, to be somewhat circumscribed to particular activities. Stratum position is more likely to become a salient element of self-conception when clear boundary lines exist.

The previously considered factors, which are usually associated with clear boundary lines between strata, are all likely to facilitate greater stratum consciousness. In the case of sex, boundary lines are obvious, being based on readily distinguished physical differences. Boundary lines between ethnic groups vary in their clarity, depending on the group under consideration. Between blacks and whites they are quite clear, and except for a few individual cases, passing from one group to another is not possible. Boundary lines in class and age hierarchies are far more vague. In a society, such as the United States, characterized by credit buying, production for mass consumption, and relative affluence, class differences are not always easily recognizable. There are also various cultural traditions, such as individualism and the belief in social equality, that tend to detract attention from the salience of social classes in the United States (Reissman, 1959:3–34).

There is also considerable vagueness of stratum boundaries in the case of age. With the exception of the teenage years, the attainment of the legal status of adult at eighteen or twenty-one years, and retirement age, age tends to comprise a series of continuous gradations rather than discrete and readily identifiable strata. There are wide individual variations in the physical manifestations of age, and actual age may often be concealed in one way or another (Nelson and Nelson*, 1972).

Stratum consciousness and action are also related to how important stratum position is to the self-conception of the individual. Is a stratum position a major point of reference in the meaning ascribed to the self, or is it relatively low in the individual's sense of identity? The clear boundary lines between black and white strata and male and female strata almost ensure that position in these hierarchies will be essential to the self-conception of individuals. Such a sense of stratum based self-identity can become a basis of consciousness and action if social expectations and definitions exert pressures in this direction, as occurred in women's consciousness-raising groups considered in the previous chapter and in the selection by Micossi* (1970).

Because of the relative indeterminacy of class and age strata in the United States, an individual will be less likely to orient his or her self-conception to position in these strata. For example, race and sex, in contrast to age, are life-long statuses that are relatively difficult to deny (Kasschau, 1977). But individuals gradually pass from one age status to another, and thus can more easily disavow passing to the subordinate status of the aged. As noted by Trela* (1973), one of the major barriers to the development of stratum consciousness among the aged is the tendency to avoid identification of the self as aged. Hence, other statuses become far more important in influencing political affiliation and activities.

The degree of mobility between strata is another point of comparison between social hierarchies with respect to the development of stratum consciousness and action. Lack of mobility is apt to lead to blocked aspirations and a sense of injustice, thus increasing pressures toward the emergence of stratum consciousness and action. Opportunities for mobility in the sexual and racial hierarchies differ from the hierarchies of class and age. Until recently, blacks and women were relatively confined to low status, comparatively powerless occupational positions, and rigid traditional roles that stressed subordination. Class mobility for white males, on the other hand, has been moderately evidenced and is further buttressed by a widespread faith in the openness of society and the possibility of upward mobility for those who merit it by their actions. As noted by both Riley* (1971) and Foner (1974), age mobility is inevitable in the sense that everyone must pass through the life cycle. Thus, a younger generation must eventually come to a position of power, a fact that Foner (1974) believes has tended to mitigate against intergenerational conflicts.

The major social movements of recent years in the United States, those of race and sex, thus possess three characteristics in common. They have occurred where boundary lines between strata are clear, where mobility is limited, and where it is difficult to avoid developing a self-conception in which stratum position is highly salient. In class and age hierarchies, in which these three factors are relatively absent, major movements based on the interests of the subordinate strata have not occurred.

Another possible point of comparison between stratification hierarchies is that of the degree and type of contact between the superordinate and the subordinate strata and its effect upon consciousness and action. The sex hierarchy has several interesting points of comparison with the racial hierarchy of blacks and whites in this regard. The sexual hierarchy frequently coincides with close intimate relationships between men and women. Alice Rossi (1969) has noted that the desire to maintain harmonious husband-wife relationships may tend to retard the development of stratum consciousness among females. Despite this fact, it may also be true that once this consciousness is developed to some degree and expressed, resistance on the part of male superordinates may also be considerably weakened due to the desire to maintain harmonious marital relations.

Studies of interracial contact are relevant to understanding the possible import of the husband-wife relationship for stratum consciousness and action. Studies such as those by Jeffries and Ransford (1969) and Surace and Seeman (1967) have indicated a similarity of perspectives exists between blacks and whites when relatively intimate and friendly social contacts take place between them. Applying this finding to the husband-wife relationship, it might be expected that many men would be somewhat receptive to feminist viewpoints, once expressed with some consistency by their spouses. Marriage provides a readily available channel of communication between the sexes within the context of a relationship in which compromise and openness are at least to some degree stressed as the ideal. Because of this, intersex conflict is not easily compartmentalized and ignored, and is likely to be solved by at least some degree of compromise on the part of the superordinate male partner. The extremely high incidence of close interpersonal relations between males and females may thus partly account for the acceptance by some men of many of the ideas of the women's movement. The various gains made by women in the last years (*Newsweek*, 1976; 1978), have been accompanied by very few instances of street confrontations or violence, such as so frequently occurred during the black movement.

There has been far more resistance and hostility to black efforts toward liberation. Conflict between blacks and whites in the last twenty-five years reached both more general and more extreme levels than that between men and women. Contact patterns between blacks and whites are for the most part considerably different than those between men and women. Their incidence is far less, as is their intimacy. Given that, for the most part, blacks and whites live in separate areas of cities and have relatively little communication, sharp differences in opinion and viewpoint can develop. With little communication and spatial separation, interracial conflict can be rather easily compartmentalized and ignored by the superordinate (white) stratum. Under these conditions, forms of conflict such as riots and other forms of violence more readily emerge as manifestations of consciousness and of stratum action.

SUMMARY

Some of the current issues involved in the conceptualization and study of class consciousness were considered in this chapter. Research studies of class consciousness in the United States were briefly reviewed.

A major theme of the chapter has been that the multiple hierarchy approach contributes an expanded and more sensitive perspective to the study of stratum consciousness and action. A multiple hierarchy model builds on the traditional class perspective and extends it by providing for the analysis of the effects of specific combinations of strata upon stratum consciousness and action. It also allows for the comparative analysis across stratification hierarchies of uniformities and differences in basic structure and processes pertaining to consciousness and action.

The study of stratum consciousness and action constitutes one major approach to the understanding of the relationship between stratification and social and cultural change. Another perspective on the dynamics of stratification systems is found in the study of social mobility, which is the topic of the next two chapters.

REFERENCES

Centers, Richard. 1949. *The Psychology of Social Classes.* Princeton, N.J.: Princeton University Press.

Domhoff, G. William. 1967. *Who Rules America.* Englewood Cliffs, N.J.: Prentice-Hall.

Dowd, J. J. and Vern L. Bengtson. 1978. "Aging in Minority Populations: An Examination of the Double Jeopardy Hypothesis." *Journal of Gerontology* 33 (May):427–436.

Foner, Anne. 1974. "Age Stratification and Age Conflict in Political Life" *American Sociological Review* 39 (April):187–196.

Glantz, Oscar. 1958. "Class Consciousness and Political Solidarity." *American Sociological Review* 23 (August):375–382.

Gross, Neal. 1953. "Social Class Identification in the Urban Community." *American Sociological Review* 18 (August) 398–404.

Jackson, Jacquelyne Johnson. 1974. "NCBA, Black Aged and Politics." *The Annals of the American Academy of Political and Social Sciences* 415 (September):138–159.

Jeffries, Vincent and H. Edward Ransford. 1969. "Interracial Social Contact and Middle Class White Reactions to the Watts Riot" *Social Problems* 16 (Winter):312–324.

Jones, Alfred Winslow. 1941. *Life, Liberty and Property.* Philadelphia: J. B. Lippincott.

Kasschau, Patricia L. 1977. "Age and Race Discrimination Reported by Middle-Aged and Older Persons" *Social Forces* 55 (March):728–742.

King, Mae C. 1975. "Oppression and Power: The Unique Status of the Black Woman in the American Political System" *Social Science Quarterly* 56 (June):117–128.

Leggett, John C. 1964. "Economic Insecurity and Working-Class Consciousness" *American Sociological Review* 29 (April):226–234.

_____. 1968. *Class, Race and Labor.* New York: Oxford University Press.

Lopreato, Joseph and Lawrence E. Hazelrigg. 1972. *Class, Conflict, and Mobility.* San Francisco: Chandler Publishing Company.

Marx, Karl. 1956. *Karl Marx: Selected Writings in Sociology and Social Philosophy.* New York: McGraw Hill.

Micossi, Anita Lynn. 1970. "Conversion to Women's Lib." *Trans-action* 8 (November/December): 82–90.

Mills, C. Wright. 1956. *White Collar.* New York: Oxford University Press.

_____. 1959. *Power Elite.* New York: Oxford.

_____. 1962. "Inventory of Ideas" in *The Marxists.* New York: Dell, 81–95.

Morris, Richard T. and Vincent Jeffries. 1970. "Class Conflict: Forget It!" *Sociology and Social Research* 54 (April), 306–320.

Morris, Richard T. and Raymond J. Murphy. 1966. "A Paradigm for the Study of Class Consciousness." *Sociology and Social Research* 50 (April), 298–313.

Nelson, Elizabeth Ness and Edward E. Nelson. 1974. "Age 'Passing' " Unpublished paper presented at the annual meeting of the American Sociological Association, August, 1972.

Newsweek. 1976. "Women at Work." *Newsweek* 88 (December 6) 68–81.

_____. 1978. "How Men are Changing." *Newsweek* 91 (January 16) 52–61.

Nieto, Consuelo. 1974. "The Chicana and the Women's Rights Movement." *Civil Rights Digest* 6 (Spring):36–42.

Ransford, H. Edward. 1972. "Blue Collar Anger." *American Sociological Review* 37 (June):333–346.

_____. 1977. "Stratum Solidarity in a Period After The Watts Riot" in H. Edward Ransford *Race and Class in American Society: Black, Chicano and Anglo.* Cambridge, Mass.: Schenkman, 136–144.

Reissman, Leonard. 1959. *Class in American Society.* Glencoe, Ill.: The Free Press.

Riley, Matilda White. 1971. "Social Gerontology and the Age Stratification of Society." *The Gerontologist* 11 (Spring, part 1):79–97.

Roach, Jack L., Llewellyn Gross, Orville Gursslin. 1969. *Social Stratification in the United States.* Englewood Cliffs, N.J.: Prentice-Hall.

Rosenberg, Morris. 1953. "Perceptual Obstacles to Class Consciousness" *Social Forces* 32 (October):22–27.

Rossi, Alice S. 1969. "Sex Equality: The Beginnings of Ideology" *The Humanist* 29 (September/October):3–16.

Rossides, Daniel W. 1976. *The American Class System.* Boston: Houghton Mifflin.

Schreiber, E. M. and G. T. Nygreen. 1970. "Subjective Social Class in America: 1945–1968" *Social Forces* 48 (March):348–356.

Sontag, Susan. 1972. "The Double Standard of Aging." *Saturday Review* September 23.

Surace, Samuel J. and Melvin Seeman. 1967. "Some Correlates of Civil Rights Activism." *Social Forces* 46 (December) 197–207.

Sweezy, Paul M. 1973. "The American Ruling Class" in Maurice Zeitlin (ed.) *American Society, Inc.* Chicago: Rand McNally, 356–371.

Trela, James A. 1973. "Old Age and Collective Political Action" Unpublished paper presented at the annual meeting of the Gerontological Society. Miami, Florida, November 5–9.

Stratum Solidarity in a Period Shortly After the Watts Riot

H. Edward Ransford

ONE OF the oldest traditions in stratification the-ory and research is to study not only objective strata but stratum consciousness, that is, percep-tions of a class order and feelings of belongingness or solidarity with persons of a similar position. Thus, Marx felt that the revolution of the prole-tariat would occur only when workers banded together into an organized political group that perceived a common enemy, shared common frustrations, and had a vision of a common des-tiny. For Marx, objective class was not sufficient for predicting political action but, rather, the exploitative and alienating forces of industrial capitalism had to develop into subjective class consciousness (a "class in itself" becomes a "class for itself").

Though there have been a number of stud-ies of class consciousness, there is very little research that considers the dual sources of stratum consciousness and solidarity among racial minor-ities in America. For example, each of the two hierarchies—race and class—that have been dis-cussed in this book, involves differing degrees of subjective identification and feelings of solidarity. A young black worker on an auto assembly line may feel high degrees of both class and race con-sciousness. He may feel underpaid and used as a commodity as he participates in boring, repeti-tive, alienating work. As a result, he may identify with the interest and action (strikes, walk-offs) of other workers. But, in addition, he may see him-self as a part of a racial hierarchy—denied power, achievement, and status because of a powerful white stratum—and, accordingly, feel solidarity with a brotherhood of blacks who face common oppression. The results of being high in both race and class solidarity may lead to a special kind of ethclass militance. Although this general line of reasoning has a strong Marxian overtone, the spe-cific prediction is quite different. Marx predicted that the exploitative and alienating forces of capi-talism would unite workers of all ethnic back-grounds into a common solidary group ready to move against the common enemy. Instead, our prediction assumes that racial solidarity (especi-ally in the 1960s and 1970s) is such a powerful source of allegiance that class interests are not likely to sweep over race, but rather that class and racial identification must merge, blend, and rein-force each other to produce a militant outcome. There are some signs of a growing black working-class militance. Recent auto and postal strikes and walk-offs often involve a disproportionate num-ber of black workers uniting in common cause. One of the few studies on the blend of race and class consciousness as a source of militance is found in John Leggett's *Class, Race and Labor.* He notes that Negro blue-collar workers have faced special race-class barriers that have resulted in greater in-group cohesion.

Working-class membership in a marginal racial (or ethnic) group is another source of class con-sciousness. A racial or ethnic group is marginal when the cultural values of an individual society and/or a dominant class move employers to engage in racial discrimination against marginal workmen both at work and elsewhere. Such discrimination contributes to their job insecurity, social isolation, subcultural homogeneity, intensive interaction within a proletarian-class minority sub-community, and organized protest and class or (class-racial) consciousness.[2]

Said another way, while there have been many forces to weaken and splinter class consciousness and militance among white workers, black workers face an unusual combination of factors that would heighten in-group cohesion and militance.

In the Leggett study, militance was a verbal measure—defined as the predisposition to engage in aggressive action to advance the interests of one's class. White workers were found to be considerably less militant than black workers, particularly than blacks who earned moderate incomes and belonged to unions. Further, racial

managerial position with weak feelings of class consciousness. The following is a cross-tabulation of four variables in the case of blacks to indicate the possibilities. Strong racial (black) identification is indicated by a +; weak racial identification by a −.

Thus, group 1 represents blacks in an objective middle-class position (e.g., white-collar job) who subjectively identify with the working class and who identify with their race. Our discussion of race and class consciousness among blue-collar workers leading to a militant reaction can be formalized by noting that those in group 5 (persons in blue-collar jobs who feel themselves to be a part of the working-class and identify also with the black community) will express the most militant posture in terms of race or class change, while those in group 4 will be least militant in terms of class or race change.

	Blacks Objective Class: Middle			
	1	2	3	4
Subjective Class	working	middle	working	middle
Subjective Racial	+ Black	− Black	+ Black	− Black
Identification	Id	Id	Id	Id
	Objective Class: Working			
	5	6	7	8
Subjective Class	working	middle	working	middle
Subjective Racial	+ Black	− Black	+ Black	− Black
Identification	Id	Id	Id	Id

awareness was shown to accompany class consciousness. This finding is not surprising since conflict frequently occurs along class and race lines simultaneously.

Conceptual Possibilities

Studies of race and class consciousness would most likely involve four variables: race, racial consciousness, objective class, and class consciousness. For example, a person could be black, one who identifies strongly with his race, in a

A Test from Watts Data

In the Watts data, there was an opportunity to test one version of the race-class consciousness theme.* Roughly half of the Watts sample (1965–66) consisted of employed blue-collar workers. The other half were white-collar workers. The study included some questions to tap the

*The sample was composed of 312 black males between the ages of 18 and 65. For further specifications on the sample see H. Edward Ransford, "Skin Color, Life Chances, and Anti-White Attitudes," *Social Problems* 18 (Fall) 1970, 164–179.

newly emerging racial identification of the mid-60s as well as a forced-choice question of class identification. The aim of the study design was to note the separate and combined effects of race and class identification on two measures of racial militance—approval of the Watts riot, and action strategies that should be used to liberate black people.

A special ethclass militance effect is anticipated among these in working-class (blue-collar) positions who identify with both their race and their class. The measure of class identification asked respondents, "which of these four social groups would you say you belong to—middle class, upper class, lower class, working class?" Admittedly, this is a rather crude question. What does it mean when a blue-collar worker identifies himself as "working class" rather than "middle class"? It may simply mean that, when presented with forced choice alternatives, the blue-collar manual worker picks "working class" as the best descriptive label and that's all. We expect, however, that many who choose the working-class label are saying much more: that they feel a greater sense of solidarity with other workers, or identify with the frustrations and common interests of the working man as opposed to owners, professionals, and managers. Almost all of the respondents in the Watts sample identified themselves as either middle class or working class. (The few who called themselves upper class were added to those who identified themselves as middle class and the few who called themselves lower class were added to those who identified themselves as working class) Three items were included to tap black identification: "I look at everything from a Negro point of view," "I feel a sense of pride when new African nations gain their independence," and "I feel a sense of kinship with Negroes in Africa." The last two African items are tapping a little different dimension of black identification than "Negro point of view." Accordingly, we examined their effects separately.

We have anticipated greater militant attitudes and action among blue-collar workers who identify both with their class and their race. As a first test of this idea, Table 1 presents data on approval of the Watts Riot cross-tabulated by subjective identifications for both blue-collar and white-collar workers. For blue-collar workers, both the "Negro point of view" and African

Table 1. *Approval of the Watts Riot by Race and Class Identification Among Blue-Collar and White-Collar Workers*

	Blue-Collar Respondents			
% Approving Watts Riot	working class + Black ID*	working class − Black ID	middle class + Black ID	middle class − Black ID
	N	N	N	N
	73 (34)	44 (59)	67 (10)	30 (37)
% Approving Watts Riot	working + Black ID**	working − Black ID	middle + Black ID	middle − Black ID
	N	N	N	N
	56 (66)	52 (27)	42 (26)	30 (20)
	White-Collar Respondents			
% Approving Watts Riot	working class + Black ID**	working class − Black ID	middle class + Black ID	middle class − Black ID
	N	N	N	N
	47 (15)	44 (10)	28 (36)	19 (32)

*"I look at everything from a Negro point of view"

**African Identification

identification versions of black consciousness are shown; for white-collar workers only the African version is presented (the white-collar case base was too small to claim validity for "Negro point of view").

Focusing first on blue-collar workers (top two-thirds of the Table) we see that race and class consciousness do indeed combine to produce the highest proportion approving the riot—73 percent with the "Negro point of view" item, 56 percent with the African identification item. It is difficult to say whether class or race consciousness is the more powerful predictor of riot militance since racial identification is clearly a stronger force with the "Negro point of view" item while for the African item, class identification is the more important. Note also that the strongest combined effect of race and class consciousness occurs not so much at the high end of identification but at the low end—blue-collar workers who identify themselves as "middle class" and who also score low in racial consciousness are uniquely nonsupportive of the Watts rebellion (30 percent in both cases). What is quite interesting is that the pattern is exactly the same for white-collar workers (except that they more consistently score less militant than blue-collar workers).

Blacks in white-collar positions who identify with the working man are far more militant than those who call themselves middle class. Perhaps these are blacks who themselves have only recently moved up from blue-collar jobs and who retain a strong identification with the black working class.

Action Ideology

When our measure of militant outlook is expanded from riot approval to a more sensitive breakdown of action ideologies we find that the ethclass combination of working-class identification and black identification is only predictive of selective kinds of militant ideology. One of the questions in the Watts data asked respondents to choose among four action strategies to liberate black people. The alternatives ranged from the rather conservative "firm negotiation for equal rights" to the more militant "keep the pressure on with more demonstrations and sit-ins" to two extreme responses, "forget integration and im-

prove the Negro community" and "if whites keep up their discrimination, Negroes should be ready to use violence—non-violence won't do it." It should be recalled that the mid-1960s represented (for blacks) a period of peak support for participation in nonviolent civil rights demonstrations. In such a normative milieu of non-violence, equal opportunity, and integration, those emphasizing the development of a separate black community or a readiness to use violence appear to be opting for more radical alternatives. Accordingly, we judge "demonstrate" to be a normative response and "community" and "violence" to be radical responses of this period. Table 2 shows the effects of race and class consciousness on these four action strategies. What is particularly striking in these data is that the working-class identification in combination with racial identification produces the least support for demonstrations (39 percent blue-collar and 48 percent white-collar) and the most support for violence and internal community change. The pattern is even more pronounced when the "violence" and "community" ideologies are combined into a single "radical group" shown in parenthesis. For example, among blue-collar workers high in race and working-class identification, 58 percent score "radical" while only 23 percent of those low in black identification and who identify themselves as middle class do.* However, when we look at other categories, it appears that "demonstrate" is the more preferred response for them. Especially among white-collar workers, one finds high support for demonstrations and sit-ins. What do all these data mean?

When this analysis is added to the riot approval discussion above, we do find support for the thesis that those identifying jointly with a community of workers and an oppressed racial stratum are likely to hold an especially militant outlook toward social change, an outlook characterized by positive responses to the Watts outbreak (e.g., "I'm glad it happened and I feel proud"), a readiness to use violence if white discrimination persists, and an interest in a strong black community rather than an integrated society.

*The pattern is exactly the same with the "Negro point of view" measure of race consciousness except that violence reaches an even higher 38 percent among blue-collar race-class identifiers.

Table 2. *Four Action Strategies to Liberate Black People by Class and Race Identification (Kinship With Negroes in Africa) Among Blue-Collar and White-Collar Workers*

Subjective Class and Black ID	Action Strategies				
	% Firm Negotiation For Change	% Keep Pressure On With Demonstrations & Sit-ins	% Forget Integration And Change Negro Community		% If Discrimination Continues Violence Will Be Necessary
Blue-Collar Workers					
Working + Black ID	3	39	29	(58)	29
Working − Black ID	3	65	16	(32)	16
Middle + Black ID	9	56	24	(36)	12
Middle − Black ID	5	73	14	(23)	9
White-Collar Workers					
Working + Black ID	5	48	33	(47)	14
Working − Black ID	18	73	9	(9)	0
Middle + Black ID	9	70	16	(21)	5
Middle − Black	17	76	7	(7)	0

NEW DIRECTIONS FOR RACE-CLASS CONSCIOUSNESS RESEARCH

The data in this analysis are crude and of another time period in the black struggle. More sensitive measures of race and class consciousness as well as more current measures of race and class action are needed. For example, the simple class identification question in these data should be greatly expanded to find out the *degree* to which persons feel solidarity with or share common interests with a race or class stratum. Morris and Murphy have developed a breakdown of degrees of stratum consciousness. Their paradigm (reproduced in chapter 10) shows that persons may vary from a complete denial of a stratification order (box 1) to strong feelings of solidarity with a stratum (box 4) to a willingness to engage in action to advance the interests of this stratum (box 6). Minority persons may vary from very low to very high identification with both their race and their class strata. The Murphy-Morris paradigm adds a great deal of leverage to the topic of race and class consciousness. Both the sources and the consequences of such consciousness need to be studied. There is also need for refinement at the action-ideology end of our analysis. For example, the "change the community" alternative of these data appear to be a kind of precursor to the current "black control of black institutions" outlook. Are those high on race and working-class consciousness today especially supportive of this ideology? In these data, there were no measures of *class* action, such as propensity to participate in strikes or walk-offs for higher wages or improved working conditions. Are working-class blacks who score high in both race and class consciousness especially likely to engage in such militant class action? Another intriguing area of study would be the conditions under which race and class conscious conflict, so

that black workers are under the stress of competing loyalties between union interests and racial interests.

In sum, the study of the interaction between race and class consciousness appears to be a neglected and extremely important area for future research.

The Chicana and the Women's Rights Movement— A Perspective

Consuelo Nieto

LIKE THE Adelitas who fought with their men in the Mexican Revolution, Chicanas have joined their brothers to fight for social justice. The Chicana cannot forget the oppression of her people, her *raza*—male and female alike. She fights to preserve her culture and demands the right to be unique in America. Her vision is one of a multicultural society in which one need not surrender to a filtering process and thus melt away to nothingness.

Who is the Chicana? She cannot be defined in precise terms. Her diversity springs from the heritage of the *indio*, the *español*, and the *mestizo*.

The heterogeneous background of her people defies stereotyping. Her roots were planted in this land before the Pilgrims ever boarded the Mayflower. As a bicultural person, she participates in two worlds, integrating her Mexican heritage with that of the majority

society. The Chicana seeks to affirm her identity as a Mexican American and a woman and to define her role within this context.

How does her definition relate to women's rights? How does the women's rights movement affect a Chicana's life? The Chicana shares with all women the universal victimhood of sexism. Yet the Chicana's struggle for personhood must be analyzed with great care and sensitivity. Hers is a struggle against sexism within the context of a racist society. Ignore this factor and it is impossible to understand the Chicana's struggle.

The task facing the Chicana is monumental. On the one hand, she struggles to maintain her identity as a Chicana. On the other hand, her demands for equity as a woman involve fundamental cultural change.

The Chicana shares with all women basic needs that cut across ethnic lines. Yet she has distinctive priorities and approaches, for the Chicana is distinct from the Anglo woman. The Chicana's world, culture, and values do not always parallel those of the Anglo woman.

Many Chicanas support the women's movement as it relates to equity in pay and job opportunities, for instance. Yet for some, particularly the non-activists, the closer the movement comes to their personal lives, the more difficult it becomes to tear themselves away from the kinds of roles they have filled.

The lifestyles of Chicanas span a broad and varied continuum. Education, geography, and socioeconomic living conditions are but a few of the variables which make a difference. The urban, educated, middle class Chicana usually has more alternatives, sophisticated skills, and greater mobility than her sisters in the barrios or the fields.

In the worlds of the barrio and *el campo*, with their limited social options, the role of the woman is often strictly defined. Fewer choices exist. Yet among all groups one finds women who are strong and who have endured.

Traditionally, the Chicana's strength has been exercised in the home where she has been the pillar of family life. It is just this role that has brought her leadership and her abilities to the larger community. The Chicano family is ofttimes an extended one, including grandparents, aunts and uncles, cousins (of all degrees), as well as relatives of spiritual affinity, such as godparents and in-laws.

Chicanas, collectively and individually, have cared for that family. It is the Chicana who goes to her children's school to ask why Juanito cannot read. It is the Chicana who makes the long trip to the social security office to obtain the support needed to keep *viejecita* Carmen going in her one-room apartment when taking in ironing will not do it.

It is *la Chicana* who fights the welfare bureaucracy for her neighbor's family. It is *la Chicana* who, by herself and with her sisters, is developing ways in which the youth of her community can be better cared for when their mothers must leave home to work.

Because life in the poorer barrios is a struggle for survival, the man cannot always participate in such community activities unless they pay a salary. He must provide the material support for his family. This is the tradition. It is in his heart, his conscience.

Chicanas owe much of their freedom to work for their communities to their men. It is the Chicana who often gains and develops those skills and attitudes which provide the basis for the transition of her culture into that of the modern United States. A transition, and yes, even a transformation—but not at the price of dissolving that culture.

Last year I taught an adult education class which included some mothers from the barrio. I'm sure they were not aware of the women's movement per se, but I was amazed at their high degree of interest and concern with the question, "How can I help my daughters so that when they get married they will be able to do things that my husband won't allow me to do?"

None of them thought of trying to change their own lives, because they knew that it was a dead end for them. They would say, "He loves me and I love him. I will accept things as they are for me, but I don't want that for my daughter."

It's not that they didn't view change as personally attractive, but that to demand it would place their family and their home in too much jeopardy. It would mean pulling away from their husbands in a manner that could not be reconciled. And they will not pay that price.

Other women who wanted to enroll in my class could not, because their husbands would not permit them to go out at night or allow them to get involved in activities outside the home during the day. This is not surprising—some Chicanas have many facets of their lives more tightly controlled by their husbands than do their Anglo sisters. For some women of the barrio, their hope is to achieve that measure of control over their own lives which many Anglo women already have.

Similarly, some Chicano men will state that they are fighting for their women, but not for that kind of status and position that would give women equal footing. They are fighting to be able to provide for their women the social and economic status and position that Anglo men have been able to give Anglo women.

THE CHURCH

The role of the Catholic Church in the history of the Chicana is an important one. Not all Chicanos are Catholic, and among those who belong to the Church, not all participate actively. But since the arrival of the Spanish, the values, traditions, and social patterns of the Church have been tightly interwoven in Chicano family life.

The respect accorded the Church by many Chicanos must be not shrugged aside. Many will support or oppose a particular issue simply on the basis of "the Church's position." For these people it is very difficult to assess a "moral" issue outside the pale of Church authority and legitimacy.

For the most part, the Church has assumed a traditional stance toward women. It has clearly defined the woman's role as that of wife and mother, requiring obedience to one's husband.

The words of the apostle Paul have been used to justify this attitude: "As Christ is head of the Church and saves the whole body, so is a husband the head of his wife, and as the Church submits to Christ, so should wives submit to their husbands in everything."

Also:

"A man certainly should not cover his head, since he is the image of God and reflects God's glory; but woman is the reflection of man's glory. For man did not come from woman; no, woman came from man; and man was not created for the sake of woman, but woman was created for the sake of man."

Marianismo (veneration of the Virgin Mary) has had tremendous impact upon the development of the Chicana. Within many Chicano homes, *La Virgen*—under various titles, but especially as *La Virgen de Guadalupe*—has been the ultimate role model for the Chicano woman.

Mary draws her worth and nobility from her relationship to her son, Jesus Christ. She is extolled as mother, as nurturer. She is praised for her endurance of pain and sorrow, her willingness to serve, and her role as teacher of her son's word. She is Queen of the Church.

Some Chicanas are similarly praised as they emulate the sanctified example set by Mary. The woman par excellence is mother and wife. She is to love and support her husband and to nurture and teach her children. Thus may she gain fulfillment as a woman.

For a Chicana bent upon fulfillment of her personhood, this restricted perspective of her role as a woman is not only inadequate but crippling.

Some Chicanas further question the Church's prerogative to make basic decisions unilaterally about women's lives. When the Church speaks out on issues such as divorce, remarriage, and birth control, those Chicanas wonder, "Who can really make these decisions for me? Upon what basis should such choices be made?"

Many Chicanas still have a strong affiliation with the Church and seek its leadership and support as they attempt to work out their lives. Others try to establish their identity as women on their own, yet choose not to break with Church mandates.

Still others find this middle road too difficult. They choose not to work within Church structure and seek their independence totally outside the folds of religion. Chicanas find that to advocate feminist positions frowned upon by the Church often evokes family criticism and pressure. Thus some compromise personal values and feign conformity for the sake of peace within the family.

Concerned leaders within the Church do speak out in behalf of the Chicana's struggle for equity. But this is not the norm. While the Church supports equal pay and better working conditions, it would find it most difficult to deal with the sexism expressed in its own hierarchy or within the family model.

BROTHERS AND SISTERS

Chicanos often question the goals of the women's movement. Some see it as an "Anglo woman's trip," divisive to the cause of *el movimiento*. These men assert the need to respect women; but women's liberation . . . ? "That deals with trivia, minutiae—we all must concentrate on the battle for social justice."

Many of our brothers see the women's movement as another force which will divert support from *la causa*. On a list of priorities, many Chicanos fail to see how the plight of *la mujer* can be of major concern within the context of la raza's problems. They see the women's movement as a vehicle to entrench and strengthen the majority culture's dominance. They are concerned that their sister may be deceived and manipulated. They warn her never to be used as a pawn against her own people.

Yet the Chicana may sometimes ask, "Is it your real fear, my brother, that I be used against our movement? Or is it that I will assume a position, a stance, that you are neither prepared nor willing to deal with?"

Other Chicanos may be more sensitive and try to help their sisters achieve a higher status, but the fact that they too usually limit the aspirations of their sisters is soon evident. They would open the doors to new roles and new alternatives, but on a selective basis. Some support upward mobility for their sisters in the professions, but renege when it comes to equality at home.

A good number of Chicanos fear that in embracing the women's movement their sisters will negate the very heritage they both seek to preserve. The Chicana would ask her brother, "to be a Chicana—proud and strong in my culture—must I be a static being? Does not the role of women change as life changes?"

Too many Chicanos fall into using rhetoric which reinforces stereotypes damaging to both men and women. For example, some overglorify large families. To father and mother such a family is considered "very Chicano." Our numbers will increase, goes the story, as the Anglos decrease. This is "good," because somehow our power as a people will grow as our numbers grow.

It is forgotten that each man and each woman must share in the decision to have children. To limit the size of a family is a personal right. To limit the size of a family does not negate a man's virility or a woman's worth.

Further, although the term "machismo" is correctly denounced by all because it stereotypes the Latin man, chauvinist behavior based on a double standard persists and is praised as "very macho." This behavior does a great disservice to both men and women. Chicano and Chicana alike must each be free to seek their own individual fulfillment. Superficial roles and attitudes should be abandoned. Each must support the other in their struggle for identity and fulfillment.

The pursuit of affirmative action for the Chicana in employment and education is often seen as a threat to Chicanos. Our men have not shared social and economic equality with the men of the majority culture. Gradually, jobs have opened up for minorities on higher rungs of the career ladder. When one opens for a Mexican, it has been assumed that Mexican would be a male.

Now Chicanas are gaining the education and skills to qualify for such jobs. But when a Chicana begins to compete for employment more often than not she is pitted against a Chicano, not an Anglo male or female. The Chicano and the Chicana must both fully understand all the ramifications and subtleties of this process which would divide them against each other. And institutions need to realize their responsibility to provide opportunities for all Chicanos, male and female alike.

Affirmative action is crucial to fighting discrimination. In assessing affirmative action programs, institutions must establish well-defined categories. Minorities cannot be lumped together. Each major ethnic group must be counted separately. Within each group a distinction must be made between male and female.

Statistics quickly dispel the myth that to be a Chicana is an advantage in current affirmative action models. Too often affirmative action for women has been interpreted to mean for Anglo women, while that for minorities has been interpreted to mean for minority males. There must be affirmative action for everyone hitherto excluded.

Chicanos themselves should take an active role in supporting their sisters. Within our own organizations, Chicanos must seek to include women in positions of leadership, not just "decorate" their conferences with them. How often Chicanas have participated in organizations or gone to conferences, only to see their role limited to that of the "behind the scenes" worker or the "lovely lady" introduced at dinner for a round of applause!

The Chicana wants more than that. She wants to be among the major speakers at Chicano conferences and to be involved at policy-making levels. She wants to be supported wholeheartedly in bids for public office.

Too often she hears her brothers say, "We would love to include 'qualified' Chicanas, but where are they?" This question has an all too-familiar ring. It is exactly what Anglos tell us collectively.

And our answer is the same. If we are not "qualified," my brother, what are you doing to help us? What experiences and training are you providing us? What support do you give us that we may become articulate and politically sophisticated, and that we may develop the skills of negotiation and decision-making?

When Chicanos maneuver to open up a position for a Mexican and a highly qualified Chicana is not even considered, another familiar statement is heard.

"The problem," Chicanos say, "is that 'our' community wants a man. 'We' know that a certain woman may be highly competent, but in our tradition we look to the male for leadership. Chicanos respect women and care for women, but leadership is seen as a male role."

First, the Chicana questions the assertion that the Chicano community would not accept a competent female in a leadership position. Second, supposing that such a view were valid, what are the "supportive and understanding" Chicanos actively doing to validate the role of a Chicana as a leader and spokesperson within the community?

DEALING WITH
CONTRADICTIONS

Participation within organizations of the women's rights movement can bring to the Chicana a painful sense of alienation from some women of the majority culture. The Chicana may often feel like a marginal figure. Her Anglo sisters assure her that their struggle unequivocally includes her within its folds.

Yet if she listens carefully, certain contradictions will soon emerge. The Anglo women will help the Chicana by providing a model, a system to emulate. The Anglo will help the Chicana erase those "differences" which separate them. Hence, "We will all be united under the banner of Woman. This will be our first and primary source of identity."

For a Chicana allied with the struggle of her people, such a simplistic approach to her identity is not acceptable. Furthermore, it is difficult for the Chicana to forget that some Anglo women have oppressed her people within this society, and are still not sensitive to minorities or their needs. With Anglo women the Chicana may share a commitment to equality, yet it is very seldom that

she will find with them the camaraderie, the understanding, the sensitivity that she finds with her own people.

Anglo women sensitive to Chicanas as members of a minority must guard against a very basic conceptual mistake. All minorities are not alike. To understand the black woman is not to understand the Chicana. To espouse the cause of minority women, Anglos must recognize our distinctiveness as separate ethnic groups.

For example, in dealing with sex role stereotyping in schools, a multicultural approach should be used. Materials must encompass all groups of women. Women's studies courses should not exclude the unique history of minority women from the curriculum.

And the inclusion of one minority group is not enough. Chicanas know only too well the pain of negation which comes from omission. The affront of exclusion may not be intentional, but to the victim that doesn't matter. The result is the same.

What does it mean to be a Chicana? This question the Chicana alone must answer. Chicanas must not allow their brothers or other women to define their identity. Our brothers are often only too ready to tell "who" we are as Chicanas.

Conversely, some Chicanas seeking fulfillment in *la causa* do not question or challenge the parameters set down for them by Chicanos—or more basically, they do not challenge the males' right to such authority.

Similarly, a woman who has never shared our culture and history cannot fully grasp the measure of our life experiences. She will be unable to set goals, priorities, and expectations for Chicanas.

Chicanas must raise their own level of awareness. Too many do not recognize their repression and the extent of it. Many have come to accept is as the norm rather than as a deviance.

Chicanas also need to deal with their men openly. Perhaps the Chicana has been overly protective of her brothers. Hers is a difficult role. She must be sensitive to his struggle, but not at the cost of her own identity. She must support him as he strives to attain the equality too long denied him, but she too must no longer be denied. To fight and provide for the fulfillment of the

Chicano while denying equality to women does not serve the true aims of *la causa,* and will not liberate our people in the real sense.

What must the Chicana do? First, she must work with her own sisters to define clearly her role, her goals, and her strategies. This, I would suggest, can be done by involvement in one of the many Chicana feminist organizations which are currently emerging.

Second, she must be involved with Chicanos in the Chicano movement. Here the Chicana must sensitize the male to the fact that she, as a women, is oppressed and that he is a part of that oppression. She must reinforce the *carnalismo* (spirit of fraternity) which is theirs, but point out that as long as his status as a man is earned at her expense, he is not truly free.

The Chicana must tell her brother, ''I am not here to emasculate you; I am here to fight with you shoulder to shoulder as an equal. If you can only be free when I take second place to you, then you are not truly free—and I want freedom for you as well as for me.''

A third mandate I would give the Chicana is to participate in the mainstream of the women's rights movement. She is needed here to provide the Chicana perspective as well as to provide support for the activities designed to help all women. Moreover, her unique role as a liaison person is crucial. How tragic it would be if all women did not promote and participate in a valid working coalition to advance our common cause!

Chicanas must avoid a polarization which isolates them from Chicanos as well as other women. They must carefully analyze each situation, as well as the means to reconcile differences. This is not easy—it requires a reservoir of understanding, patience, and commitment. Yet unless it is done, success will not be ours.

Finally, the Chicana must demand that dignity and respect within the women's rights movement which allows her to practice feminism within the context of her own culture. The timing and the choices must be hers. Her models and those of her daughters will be an Alicia Escalante and a Dolores Huerta. Her approaches to feminism must be drawn from her own world, and not be shadowy replicas drawn from Anglo society. The Chicana will fight for her right to uniqueness; she will not be absorbed.

For some it is sufficient to say, ''I am woman.'' For me it must be, ''I am Chicana.''

12

Social Mobility: Traditional Class Approach

Edward Ransford

SOCIAL MOBILITY refers to the movement of individuals or groups—up or down—within a social hierarchy. The study of social mobility is concerned with the dynamics within stratification systems.

Traditionally, the literature on social mobility has focused almost exclusively on class mobility. A society characterized by a high degree of class mobility is one in which many people leave their class of origin and move into higher positions. A high degree of class mobility also means that substantial numbers born into high positions in the class structure fall from those positions, creating vacant statuses at the top. A fluid class structure involves mobility both up and down.

The study of social mobility can reveal, at a more personal level of investigation, hundreds of daily dramas of success and failure as persons attempt to gain greater wealth, status, and power. When studied at a societal level, social mobility is related to the amount of cohesion and conflict within a society as a whole. When racial minorities accept the American ideology of an open class structure but find that their mobility efforts are blocked, conflict, tension, and frustration are likely to result. The protest and militance of ethnic minorities in the 1960s can be interpreted as the result of a discrepancy between an open class ideology and the reality of ethnic barriers of upward mobility.

An asterick (˙) accompanying a citation indicates a selection in this volume.

WHAT IS SOCIAL MOBILITY

A.   Definition of Mobility

Vertical mobility is defined as an increase or decrease in power, privilege, or pres-tige for individuals or for groups.† Mobility can involve gains in one, two, or all three of these resources. Since the resources of power, privilege, and prestige are to a large extent correlated, gains in one resource are often accompanied by gains in the other two. An individual who moves from a middle-management position to a top policy-making posi-tion experiences not only a rise in power but one in prestige and privilege as well. In chapter 3 we noted that power and privilege are especially important stratification variables, and that prestige is largely derived from them. It follows, then, that groups or persons who are upwardly mobile in power and privilege are also likely to experience gains in prestige; increases in prestige alone, however, are less likely to be accompanied by gains in power or privilege. In the middle stages of the black Civil Rights movement, for example, it became apparent to black activists that the reduction of prejudice and negative stereotypes toward black Americans (prestige concerns) was far less important as a strategy for change than were efforts to gain power and equal access to all institutions, or privilege (Olsen,* 1970).

B.   Individual versus Group Mobility

Changes in power, privilege, and prestige (that is, social mobility) can occur for both individuals and groups. *Individual mobility* is usually measured by the distance, up or down, that individuals have moved in the social class structure. Two baselines or starting points are used to measure individual mobility: 1) the first occupation in one's working career or 2) one's class of origin, usually measured by father's occupation. A person who begins his or her career as a plumber and later becomes a doctor has been upwardly mobile. Likewise, if a person of lower-class origins achieves a white-collar man-agerial position, we conclude that upward mobility has taken place. But in both in-stances the mobility is for *single* individuals.

Group mobility is defined as gains or losses in power, privilege, or prestige for an entire group. Often the progress of a group is charted through time. If the gap between average black income and average white income has narrowed in the period 1950 to 1975, then it is concluded that blacks as an aggregate have made gains in the last twenty-five years. Sorokin distinguishes between group and individiual mobility:

> When an individual rises from the rank of office boy to that of president of a business firm, or from the status of a peasant to the position of a noble at the court of the Hapsburgs or Romanoffs, the relative positions of the various social ranks remain unchanged. When a multimillionaire becomes a beggar or a general is demoted to the rank of a captain, he sinks individually. When, however, the entire Romanoff or Hapsburg aristocracy is overthrown by revolutions, its members sink collectively in relation to all the other strata of the Russian or Austrian nation . . . (Sorokin, 1947:405).

†Horizontal mobility—the movement from one occupation to another of equal prestige—also has been identified but is not a topic in this chapter.

Some recent research deals with the group mobility of ethnic minorities and women. No doubt the focus on these groups intensified as a result of the highly visible protest activity of the 1960s and early 1970s. The social movements of this period brought changes in law and in educational and occupational opportunities. Many people are concerned with whether these programs resulted in real gains for the *group*, as opposed to token mobility for a few.

The Ascribed Hierarchies and Passing.   We noted in chapter 5 that individual mobility within the ascribed hierarchies is difficult and only rarely occurs. Since one is born into an ascribed status and that position is somewhat visible and immutable, one has difficulty in moving into a higher stratum or falling into a lower one. However, there is some degree of individual mobility within the age and ethnic hierarchies, which is referred to as *passing*. Middle-aged or older persons who are younger in appearance or behavior, or racial minority persons who are light-skinned enough to appear white, have the option of passing into another stratum. People usually attempt to pass because there are more advantages, privileges, or higher status in the other stratum.

For blacks, passing is only an option for the small proportion with a highly mixed heritage; estimates of the frequency of such passing vary from a few thousands to tens of thousands per year (Simpson and Yinger, 1972:208). Perhaps a higher proportion of Chicanos have physical features that allow them to pass. Historically, upwardly mobile Mexican-Americans who did not have dark skin or an Indian-like appearance could claim all or predominantly Spanish blood in communities where caste sanctions toward Mexicans were extreme. But racial passing may be a very painful step for an individual to take. "There is danger of 'discovery' which might destroy the whole pattern of adjustment. There is the problem of relationship to one's old friends and community. . . . Some persons who pass develop a sense of guilt that they have deserted 'their group' " (Simpson and Yinger, 1972:208).

Age passing probably is much more frequently practiced than race passing. Some people may attempt to pass as older (to buy liquor or to enlist in the armed services), but more people try to pass as younger. Given the low degree of social honor accorded the aged in our society and the value given to youthful life styles, many middle-aged or older persons may try to pass as ten, even fifteen, years younger. Women especially are likely to attempt to pass. "The advantages of passing for younger are greater for women than for men, since youth and beauty are more highly valued in the feminine role" (Nelson & Nelson,* 1974:18).

Passing is an interesting way to conceptualize individual mobility on the ascribed hierarchies. However, it is only in the case of age (and perhaps certain ethnic groups) that passing occurs with enough frequency to be considered essential to the study of social mobility.

Passing does not actually change one's ascribed characteristics (chronological age, gender, or racial ancestry); rather, one "role plays" into another stratum so that the true ascribed characteristics are not visible. To consider "true" ascribed mobility involving large numbers of persons one must turn to group analysis. The basic question asked is whether or not the ascribed group as a collective has made gains in power, privilege, and prestige through time.

C.   Class-Linked versus Nonclass-Linked Mobility

How do individuals and groups make gains in power, privilege, and prestige? There are two basic models for discussing increased mobility.

The first model uses social class variables as an indicator of increased power, privilege, and prestige. If women, ethnic minorities, or the aged make gains in occupation, education, or income, we can assume that gains in power, privilege, and prestige have taken place. For example, if the proportion of blacks in professional jobs has doubled in the last decade, one can infer increased power, privilege, and prestige because professional positions usually involve authority over others, many rights and advantages, and high degrees of social honor. It is conceptually logical to view upward mobility in terms of class gains, and most sociologists have taken this approach.

However, gains or losses in terms of class variables are not the only ways to conceptualize mobility. A second model of social mobility postulates that some forms of mobility connected to ethnicity, sex, and age are not fully explained by class achievement. Women, ethnic minorities, and age groups can move up in power, privilege, and prestige (or fail to do so) quite apart from any changes in occupation, education, and income. Sex, age, and ethnic mobility will be discussed more thoroughly in the next chapter, but here are a few brief examples:

In the case of ethnic minorities, it is quite possible for individuals to make gains in ethnic community prestige distinct from any gains in social class. Civil rights leaders can increase their influence and prestige within the minority community yet remain in the same class position. In fact, if such leaders become too economically successful they may lose trust and rapport with the rank and file. Cesar Chavez holds a great deal of social honor within the Chicano community but would rank very low in socioeconomic achievement. His modest living style has helped to maintain his affinity with the economically poor farm workers.

The concept of privilege has a special meaning in ethnic or sex mobility. Increased privilege can mean an increase in opportunity to pursue any occupation one chooses. Not only have women and minorities been employed in lower occupational positions (reflecting a class dimension) but they also have been confined to positions highly stereotyped by sex and race. In this situation, mobility may be described as movement *out* of sex-linked and race-linked occupations. Many women are entering traditionally male-dominated fields such as business management, medicine, and law. Blacks are moving into a wide variety of managerial, professional, and political positions previously reserved for whites. An exclusive focus on class mobility may completely miss this dimension of increased privilege (increased opportunities) to move out of sex-linked, race-linked occupational roles.

Although class mobility is one of the most direct ways to measure gains or losses in power, privilege, and prestige, ethnic, sex, and age mobility cannot be fully explained by class achievements.

WHAT CAUSES SOCIAL MOBILITY?

A.   Individual Motivation

Most people want to maintain or improve their rank because their social position is related to their evaluation of themselves. As Lipset and Zetterberg (1966) put it:

". . . persons like to protect their class position in order to protect their egos and improve their class position in order to enhance their egos" (Lipset and Zetterberg, 1966:566).

Ego enhancement is but one factor that explains individual motivation. Peer-group and family encouragement also contribute to individual motivation. Researchers have found that only a small proportion of bright (highest IQ quintile) young people from lower-class homes have college aspirations or actually complete college (Kahl, 1957; Sewell and Shah, 1967). Interviews revealed that many young people did not have peer-group and parental support for college plans. The few who were successful found it necessary to drop their peer affiliations and find new friends supportive of their college ambitions. On the other hand, the social world of upper-middle and upper-class young people consistently supports the goal of a college education. In middle- and upper-class culture, the question is not, are you going to college? but, rather, which college? One's individual motivation to achieve within the class structure is highly shaped by significant others; but social class mobility is due to far more than individual motivation and free will. Structural circumstances have to be taken into account.

B. Structural Causes of Social Mobility

During periods of economic expansion, or industrialization, the proportion of professional, technical, and managerial positions often increases and the number of unskilled positions often declines. Many vacant positions that develop in the white-collar ranks can be filled by upwardly mobile sons and daughters of the lower and working classes. More generally, upward mobility depends on the *demands* for performance and skills and on the *supply* of talents. When there is not a large demand for particular skills, an elite or ruling class can supply and monopolize the necessary talent through hereditary lines. But with rapid industrialization and economic expansion, the demands for skills are multiplied so that an elite group cannot supply all the talent. Recruitment from lower strata becomes necessary (Weber, in Gerth and Mills, 1946).

Inkeles (1966) in his discussion of the Soviet society during the 1930s, illustrates how structural changes create social mobility. Although Stalin proclaimed that there were only two classes in the Soviet population (the working class and the peasantry), he in fact set in motion a differential economic reward system to attract the most able to fill managerial, technical, and skilled positions. The expansion of the national economy under industrialization and collectivization programs (called the Five Year Plans) resulted in an enormous shift of the populations into newly created positions. Between 1926 and 1937 the number of managers increased 4.6 times, the number of engineers and architects 7.9 times, and the number of scientific workers 5.9 times. Many opportunities for training for these professions were created in the secondary schools and universities, and training for those already employed in industry was provided. There were also marked changes in mobility for women.

> Throughout the period, women comprised a large part, in some cases over half, of the students at industrial training schools, and as a result they came to represent a significant proportion of the skilled worker in Soviet industry. Their advance in fields requiring higher education was even more impressive. Between 1928 and 1938 the proportion of women in the universities increased from 28 percent to 43 percent . . . (Inkeles, 1966:519).

A virtual mobility escalator was created in the Soviet Union by which thousands of men and women moved into managerial and technical positions and this fact was above and beyond any personal motivation factors.

Mobility due to structural changes can occur for other reasons besides economic expansion. For example, demographic factors can operate to encourage mobility when the higher classes do not reproduce themselves at the same rate as the lower classes, creating a demographic vacuum and a supply of vacant statuses at the top of the class structure (Lipset and Zetterberg, 1966:565).

Large macro processes such as industrialization and demographic vacuums are not the only structural variables that affect mobility rates. One could argue that the public education system in the United States fosters a static class structure. It is widely believed that the American educational system is highly congruent with the ideal of an open-class industrial society—one in which persons achieve positions as a result of hard work, initiative, and ability rather than race, religion, or class. However, some maintain that American public schools actually solidify the existing class divisions. Kenneth Clark says that "American public schools have become significant instruments in the blocking of economic mobility and in the intensification of class distinctions" (Clark, 1968:101). Carnoy argues in the same vein:

> The school system is structured, through its tests, reward system, and required behavior patterns, to allow children of an urban bourgeoisie to do well, and to filter out children of the poor. . . . It is a legitimate institution, accepted by all classes in the society (on the belief that it is genuinely meritocratic), for passing social positions from generation to generation (Carnoy, 1974:323–24).

The practice of "tracking" has been particularly criticized. *Tracking,* or ability grouping, is the practice of separating children into academic groups—such as "slow learner" or "advanced," "college bound" or "vocational"—on the basis of presumed ability. Educators often justify tracking on the grounds that the more able students should not be hampered in their progress by slower students. Educators and others also assume that the less bright will be more comfortable and develop greater self-esteem in a group with similar abilities. However, the critics of tracking note that children are sorted according to the degree to which they match white, middle-class norms. Children placed in a low-ability track receive an inferior education and develop negative images of themselves and the school system.

Schafer, et al.,[*] (1970) traced the influence of class background on tracking assignments in three midwestern high schools. The authors found that both social class and race affected which track a student was placed in "quite apart from either his achievement in junior high or his ability as measured by IQ scores" (Schafer, et al.,[*] 1970:40). Moreover, once students were placed in the college or vocational tracks at the end of the ninth grade, they almost never moved up or down. Even more disturbing was the finding that track assignment was related to subsequent academic performance; those assigned to the college track made gains while those assigned to the lower track deteriorated in academic performance.

In sum, public schools can be viewed as social structures that sort students into "ability grooves" according to standardized criteria and tests weighted toward white, middle-class culture. Through tracking, guidance counseling, and grading, lower-class children may be programmed for academic failure and poor occupational futures. On a broader level, then, tracking in the educational system may reduce social mobility in the larger society.

Stratum consciousness and stratum action can also produce structural mobility. If subjugated groups such as women, minorities, and the aged come together as protesting communities and are successful in reaching centers of power, then new laws and programs are instituted which can greatly increase their mobility opportunities (see chapter 13). In this case, structural mobility occurs not because of industrial expansion or demographic vacuums, but rather because subordinate groups exercise sufficient coercion to force business and political leaders to expand opportunities for a heretofore excluded and powerless group.

C. Ideological Encouragement to Achieve

This is the cultural component of social mobility. Societies vary in the degree to which their norms, beliefs, and values encourage mobility, in the extent to which mobility is believed to be possible and legitimate. Ideological encouragement for social mobility is very high in the United States. The cultural ideology says that anyone with hard work and perseverence can climb from the bottom to the top of the class structure:

> . . . the belief in opportunity is so strongly entrenched in the culture that perhaps most Americans feel not only that each individual has the "right to succeed" but that it is his duty to do so. Thus we are apt to look with disapproval upon those who fail or make no attempt to better themselves (Mayer and Buckley, 1970:137–138).

What are the origins of this "American Dream" ideology? Reissman (1959) suggests that the lack of a *feudal past* and the lack of a *hereditary aristocracy* are important historical factors that set the stage for a stratification system based on equal opportunity and individual achievement. That is, America began the modern era without long-held traditions of hard social divisions tied to land ownership (Reissman, 1959:11). The American Revolution broke the ties of aristocracy. The lack of an hereditary aristocracy means that most Americans have rarely been exposed to the idea that certain individuals should be given respect because of their inherited position or their natural superiority.

Individual motivation and structural opportunities for social mobility may vary, but there is little variance in support for the ideology that success is possible for anyone in America. Much publicized and romanticized tales of actresses and athletes, for example, persuade the population that the American Dream can become reality. The question must be asked, how much social mobility does in fact take place?

HOW MUCH CLASS MOBILITY OCCURS IN AMERICAN SOCIETY?

How open or fluid is American society? Do large numbers rise and fall within the American system? Does the actual extent of social mobility in the United States even come close to the American Dream ideology? People who have sought to answer these questions, for the most part, have used a single measure of mobility: movement within the occupational structure. Proponents of this index argue that occupation is the single best indicator of social class because it is easily obtainable data from surveys or census reports and because occupation has strong linkages with the concepts of power, privilege, and prestige. On the other hand, to rest the whole case of social class mobility on a single measure presents serious problems. For example, persons can be upwardly mobile in economic terms through successful investment or family inheritance and yet remain in the same occupation.

Also, the occupational categories used by the Census Bureau and other data sources are so broad that mobility within a category is not captured. For example, a change from a junior college professor to a university professor would not be recorded as mobility since both jobs are categorized as "professional." Likewise, certain types of prestige mobility within a profession are not recorded. A professor who increases his or her national image with important publications in the field is not separated from the less productive, and less prestigious, professor. Keeping these reservations in mind, we will proceed to answer the question of how much mobility occurs in American society, using the two methodologies of occupational studies: *intergenerational* measures and *intragenerational* measures.

Intergenerational Mobility

This type of mobility compares father's occupational status with son's occupational status. Sons are upwardly mobile if they move to an occupation that carries higher prestige than their father's. A few studies have compared the occupation of women with their father's occupation (Tyree and Treas, 1974; DeJong, *et al.*, 1971), although currently our knowledge of intergenerational mobility is based almost exclusively on father-son comparisons. With the increase of women in the labor force, studies comparing parents' and offsprings' occupations should become more common.

Many of the studies of intergenerational mobility use a numbered occupational hierarchy such as the following:

Nonmanual Labor	1. Professional
	2. Managers
	3. Sales Workers
	4. Clerical
Manual Labor	5. Craftsmen and Foremen
	6. Operatives and other semi-skilled
	7. Unskilled

A large leap in mobility is illustrated by a son in a 1 or 2 occupation whose father worked in a 6 or 7 position. A more modest degree of mobility is exemplified by a discrepancy of one or two levels between father and son. Note the horizontal line separating non-manual and manual occupations. The nonmanual jobs are the white-collar jobs. They are judged to be more prestigeous, freer from routine, more challenging and (with noteable exceptions) better paying.

A variety of studies show that between 65 and 70 percent leave their fathers' occupational level and move either up or down in occupational status. However, most mobile sons do not move great distances up or down the occupational structure. For example, mobile sons of semi-skilled fathers (level 6) tend to become either skilled workers (5) if they move up or unskilled workers (7) if they move down. The same is true of the other categories; most of the movement involves one or two levels. Large leaps in the occupational structure are more rare, although the fact that they are so well publicized in the mass media gives the impression that anyone with a little hard work and initiative can climb from the bottom to the top of the class structure. Actually, ". . . the United States falls somewhere in the middle between a condition of extreme mobility and static rigidity of occupational movement" (Reissman, 1959:315).

Another aspect to this trend of limited mobility is that there is more likely to be mobility *within* blue-collar and white-collar ranks than *between* these ranks. Sons of blue-collar workers are more likely to remain in blue-collar jobs and sons of white-collar workers are more likely to remain in white-collar jobs. The chief barrier to both upward and downward mobility lies between the manual and nonmanual categories. Perhaps this is because different criteria for promotion are used in the blue-collar and white-collar ranks; mobility in blue-collar occupations is based on experience, skill, and youth, whereas mobility in white-collar occupations is determined by a postgraduate or college degree, or other certificates that indicate mastery of highly specialized knowledge. Mobility between manual and nonmanual occupations also may be limited because white-collar workers are not likely to move into manual work. Manual jobs and dirty working conditions may deter the sons of white-collar homes from entering high-paying blue-collar jobs (Glenn, *et al.*, 1974:693). Downwardly mobile sons from high-ranking white-collar origins prefer to remain in the white-collar class, even at the cost of lower income.

> The existence of non-manual jobs requiring little skill and commanding meager salaries like sales clerk or file clerk provides [the] failures from higher white collar origins with opportunities to remain in their parental class, with its status symbols that are so meaningful to them. Hence there are relatively few movements from white collar origins to blue collar destinations (Blau and Duncan, 1967:79).

To illustrate these generalizations of occupational mobility, we have taken a portion of one of the many mobility studies and reproduced the data in Table 12–1.

Table 12–1 compares the destinations of sons of professional fathers and the destinations of sons of fathers engaged in semi-skilled, lower-blue-collar work. How much downward mobility occurs among sons born into privileged circumstances, and how much upward mobility occurs among sons born into unprivileged, lower blue-collar households? Table 12–1 shows about one-third (35 percent) of sons from lower blue-collar households are upwardly mobile into white-collar ranks. It is noteworthy that the

Table 12-1. *Mobility from Father's (or Other Family Head's) Broad Occupation Group to Son's Current Occupation Group, for United States Men in the Experienced Civilian Labor Force, Aged 20 to 64, 1973*

| | Son's Current Occupation | | | | |
	Upper White- Collar	Lower White- Collar	Upper Blue- Collar	Lower Blue- Collar	Farm
Father's Occupation					
Upper White- Collar	59.4	11.4	12.8	15.5	.9
		70.8 percent			
Lower Blue- Collar	22.9	12.1	23.9	40.1	1.0
		35 percent		64 percent	

Note: Broad occupation groups are upper white-collar: professionals, managers and officials, and non-retail sales workers; lower white-collar: proprietors, clerical and retail sales workers; upper blue-collar: craftsmen and foremen; lower blue-collar: service workers, operatives and laborers (nonfarm); farm: farm managers, farm laborers, and foremen.

Adapted from David L. Featherman and Robert M. Hauser, *Opportunity and Change*, p. 89. By permission of the authors and Academic Press. Copyright 1978, Academic Press.

largest proportion of these upwardly mobile sons have penetrated the top upper-white-collar jobs (22.9 percent). This is the success side of the story. On the other hand, a much larger segment of the sons (64 percent) remain in the blue-collar ranks, mainly the lower-blue-collar ranks, indicating a fairly high degree of occupational inheritance. An overwhelming proportion of sons with fathers employed in upper-white-collar work also have some kind of white-collar job (70.8 percent). Moreover, almost 60 percent of these sons stay in upper-white-collar positions. There is a little mobility (downward, in this case) but the more dominant trend, again, is inheritance of occupational position.

Intragenerational Mobility

In studies of intragenerational mobility, the careers of individuals are followed through time, usually by asking men in their prime occupational years to trace their career history from first to present position. Generally, findings from *intra*generational research agree with results of *inter*generational research. "The large majority of all occupational changes within an individual's career result in either maintaining his occupational-prestige level or shifting one step above or below it" (Mayer and Buckley, 1970:141). Although a person may change his or her occupation several times, many of the shifts are of parallel or of equal status. Career studies also show limited movement across the manual/nonmanual line. When the line is crossed, blue-collar workers who reach white-collar jobs usually are salespersons or owners of small businesses, occupations that do not require technical training or advanced degrees (Lipset and Bendix, 1960). When someone moves from a blue-collar to a white-collar job, the economic rewards may be no greater than those of the manual occupation the person has left behind; the gains derived from changing jobs are primarily in prestige and perhaps in autonomy.

SUMMARY

A combination of factors explains the extent of mobility in a given society, at a given historical time. These factors include individual motivation, industrial expansion, birth rates, and the degree to which the educational institution facilitates upward mobility for lower-class youth. Studies cited in this chapter show a moderate amount of social mobility in the United States, as measured by occupational movement. Mobility is far short of the American Dream, but still is noteworthy.

REFERENCES

Blau, Peter M. & Otis Dudley Duncan. 1967. *The American Occupational Structure*. New York: John Wiley & Sons.

Carnoy, Martin. 1974. *Education as Cultural Imperialism*. New York: David McKay.

Clark, Kenneth B. 1968. "Alternative Public School Systems." *Harvard Educational Review* 40 (August): 101.

Dejong, Peter Y., Milton J. Brawer & Robin S. Stanley. 1971. "Patterns of Female Intergenerational Occupational Mobility. A Comparison with Male Patterns of Intergenerational Occupational Mobility." *American Sociological Review* 36 (6): 1033–1042.

Gerth, H. H. & C. Wright Mills (eds.). 1946. *From Max Weber*. New York: Oxford University Press.

Glenn, Norvall D., Adreain A. Ross, & Judy Corder Tully. 1974. "Patterns of Intergenerational Mobility of Females Through Marriage." *American Sociological Review* 39 (October): 683–99.

Inkeles, Alex. 1966. "Social Stratification and Mobility in the Soviet Union." In R. Bendix & S. Lipset (eds.), *Class, Status and Power*. New York: Free Press.

Kahl, Joseph. 1957. *The American Class Structure*. New York: Holt, Rinehart, Winston.

Lipset, Seymour Martin & Reinhard Bendix. 1960. *Social Mobility in Industrial Society*. Berkeley: University of California.

Lipset, Seymour Martin & Hans L. Zetterberg. 1966. "A Theory of Social Mobility." In Reinhard Bendix & Seymour Martin Lipset (eds.), *Class Status and Power*. New York: Free Press.

Mayer, Kurt B. & Walter Buckley. 1970. *Class and Society*. New York: Random House.

Nelson, Elizabeth Ness & Edward E. Nelson. 1974. "Age Passing." Revision of a paper presented at the 67th Annual meeting of the American Sociological Association, 1972.

Olsen, Marvin E. 1970. "Power Perspectives on Stratification and Race Relations." In Marvin E. Olsen (ed.), *Power in Societies*. New York: Macmillan.

Reissman, Leonard. 1959. *Class in American Society*. Glencoe, Ill.: Free Press.

Schafer, Walter E., Carol Olexa & Kenneth Polk. 1970. "Programmed for Social Class: Training in the High School." *Trans-Action* 7 (October): 39–46; and 63.

Sewell, William H. & Vimal P. Shah. 1967. "Socioeconomic Status, Intelligence and the Attainment of Higher Education." *Sociology of Education* (40):1–23.

Simpson, George Eaton & J. Milton Yinger. 1972. *Racial and Cultural Minorities: An Analysis of Prejudice and Discrimination*. New York: Harper & Row.

Sorokin, Pitirim. 1947. *Society, Culture, and Personality*. New York: Harper and Brothers.

Tyree, Andrea & Judith Treas. 1974. "The Occupational and Marital Mobility of Women." *American Sociological Review* 39 (June): 293–302.

Age "Passing"*

Elizabeth Ness Nelson and Edward E. Nelson

ABSTRACT

The biological basis of the age stratification system makes mobility within it an irreversible process as each person grows older with each passing year. However, some individuals can alter the pace of aging, or even reverse it for a time, by a process which is analogous to racial-ethnic "passing." Our culture's emphasis on youth makes it advantageous to try to "pass" as a younger person. As in racial-ethnic passing, physical appearance and social behavior facilitate age passing. The person can also change his age cohort by becoming part of a role that is normally populated by individuals of a different chronological age. An individual may take his age in this role as his new social age if three conditions are fulfilled: (1) the role must be identified with a particular segment of the age stratification system, (2) the role must be a visible and salient part of the individual's life and (3) the role must have a process of aging built into it. For various reasons, passing for younger seems to be more important for women than for men.

Reprinted with permission from the authors, Elizabeth Ness Nelson and Edward E. Nelson, "Age 'Passing'," paper presented at the Annual Meeting of the American Sociological Association, August, 1972.

*This paper is a revised version of a paper presented at the 67th Annual Meeting of the American Sociological Association, August, 1972, in New Orleans, Louisiana. We would like to express our appreciation to Anne Foner, Marilyn Johnson, Maurice N. Richter, Jr., Matilda White Riley, and Melvin Seeman who read and made comments on an earlier draft of this paper. We would also like to express our appreciation to the anonymous reviewers who made helpful suggestions. Of course, the final responsibility for any errors of omission or commission rests with the authors.

IN RECENT years, there has been a growing interest in the age stratification system (see, for example, Neugarten, 1968; Riley, Foner, and Associates, 1968; Riley, Riley and Johnson, 1969; Riley, Johnson and Foner, 1972[1]). Most writers have assumed that aging is a one-way process. The biological basis of the age stratification system, it has been pointed out, makes mobility within it an irreversible process with all individuals growing older with each passing year. As Riley (1971:83) has stated, ". . . mobility through the age strata is, of course, universal, unidirectional, and irreversible. Everybody ages. . . . Nobody can ever go back, although individuals may age in different ways and at different rates."

It is clear that biologically individuals can never "go back." However, the different ways and rates of aging permit an individual to "pass" as a younger or older person. These instances of age mobility are, in many ways, similar to "passing" in the racial-ethnic stratification system (on racial-ethnic passing, see Drake and Cayton 1945; Myrdal, 1962; Berry, 1965; Simpson and Yinger, 1965).

The purpose of this paper is to consider the applicability of the concept of passing to the age stratification system, to discuss the conditions under which one might pass for a younger or older person, and to note the relative importance of age passing for men and women.

VARIATIONS IN THE AGING PROCESS

Although with each passing year, every individual becomes increasingly older in chronological age, individuals vary in the chronological age at which they acquire some of the visible signs of age. For example, menstruation and accompanying physical and emotional signs of female maturity usually begins at 12 to 14 years, but many range from 10 to 18 (Miller, 1967:303).[2] Boys arrive at puberty somewhat later, 14 to 16 years, with individuals varying from 12 to 20 (Miller, 1967:304). The average age at menopause is 47–49 years, but individual women vary from 35 to 55 (Miller, 1967:504). Elderly persons of the same age often have quite different mental and physical capabilities (Riley, Johnson, Foner, 1972:496).

In addition to biological differences, individuals vary in the age at which they assume the social roles associated with age. For example, people in the lower social classes achieve adulthood, in the sense of entering work roles, marrying, and having children, at a younger chronological age than their middle class age-mates (Neugarten, 1968:7). Parsons and Platt (1972) suggest that the extension of formal education to more and more individuals has resulted in a new stage in the life cycle—studentry—which affects the age at which individuals assume adult roles.

There are also notable sex differences in the social definition of age. In our society women are assumed to attain adulthood at an earlier age than men, at least in the sense that they have been permitted to marry without parental consent at an earlier age and they are expected to marry men somewhat older than themselves. Women are also expected to remain younger in appearance and behavior than men, but they may retire on Social Security benefits at an earlier age. (However, this may be ruled unconstitutional under the legislation banning discrimination based on sex.) This is not as paradoxical as it might seem. Females are expected to be more childlike than males. Women are expected to be somewhat childlike even as adults. Therefore, women are adult enough to take on marital and parental roles at younger ages than men, and they are not expected to get much older since they are expected to remain dependent on men throughout their lives.

A COMPARISON OF
RACIAL-ETHNIC AND
AGE PASSING

The differences in biological and social aging permit a certain amount of age mobility which is in many ways similar to passing in the racial-ethnic stratification system. In both racial-ethnic and age stratification, passing is usually a means of individual mobility to a more highly rewarded position in society. Further, racial-ethnic and age passing may occur intentionally or unintentionally (Drake and Cayton, 1945:166; Berry, 1965:391).

Passing may occur in only a few aspects of an individual's life or the new identity may extend to all aspects of life. Negroes have frequently passed as white only to get jobs or attend public events while maintaining their social life in the Negro community (Myrdal, 1962). Others have cut all ties with the Negro community and passed as white in all aspects of their lives. Similarly, age passing may occur only in certain situations or it may be extended to every aspect of life.

The factors that facilitate age passing are also quite similar to the factors related to racial-ethnic passing. For both racial-ethnic and age passing, visible physical characteristics are of crucial importance for permitting one to pass. Cosmetic and clothing manufacturers emphasize this in their advertisements for dishwashing detergents that preserve the youthful appearance of a woman's hands or hair color that "only her hairdresser knows for sure." A person whose face and body do not readily show the wrinkles and bulges associated with passing years can use cosmetics, exercise, even plastic surgery, to maintain the illusion of youth, or at least indefinite age. (For a popular presentation of the variety of ways of preserving youthful appearance, see McGrady, 1968.)

In addition to physical appearance, certain forms of social behavior are associated with racial-ethnic and age passing. Several writers commenting on race relations in the South, have noted that the whole set of caste relations adds a social dimension to passing (Drake and Cayton, 1945: 162–3; Myrdal, 1962:684). In other words, Blacks who pass for whites must learn the language, gestures, and other social customs of whites. Similarly, to successfully pass as a younger person, one must also learn the language, gestures, and other social customs of youth.

However, the analogy between racial-ethnic and age passing is not perfect. There are at least two crucial distinctions that should be made. First, age status is not permanent. Rather it is a natural part of the maturation process. In contrast, ethnicity and race begin at birth with no natural process of change. The distribution of power and social status by age in our society varies within the life cycle of individuals and is curvilinear. Very young children have little power; younger and middle age adults have more power; most of the elderly have little power. As a consequence, most individuals have the opportunity to experience the higher status age characteristic (i.e., young adulthood).[3] All adults have been young, but members of lower status ethnic and racial groups have never possessed the higher status characteristic. The natural process of aging facilitates passing for younger because the individual usually passes as an age which he has already experienced although rapid social change diminishes the ease of remaining the same age. Second, it is important to observe that the relationship between social status and power on the one hand and age on the other hand is not as strong as the relationship between social status and power on the one hand and race and ethnicity on the other hand. Although most old people are not powerful, many of the very powerful positions are held by the old (usually men). Members of lower status ethnic and racial groups are overwhelmingly excluded from the very powerful, highest status, positions.

TYPES OF
AGE PASSING

While the analogy between racial-ethnic and age passing is not perfect, it does suggest that the concept of passing might be fruitfully applied to the age stratification system. Two important questions to consider are: (1) what different types of passing may occur in the age stratification system and (2) under what conditions might one pass for a younger or older person?

One dimension along which age passing may be classified is the intentional/unintentional dimension. Some individuals pass intentionally for younger or older. Various techniques may be used to document the new age. Individuals might make use of various types of documents (e.g., the forged identification card) in their attempt to pass as younger or older. Other individuals might

actually attempt to alter their physical appearance (e.g., plastic surgery, hormone treatments, diet). Still others might attempt to develop patterns of behavior similar to the occupants of the age category of which they want to pass. And, of course, often a combination of these various techniques is used in an attempt to pass.[4]

Other individuals have passed unintentionally for younger or older. For example, we have all read of tragic situations such as a policeman shooting a young child whom he mistook for an adult. Of course, it is often difficult for an observer to decide whether a particular instance of age passing is intentional or unintentional. For example, if a bartender asks to see the identification of a young man or woman who is actually of legal age to drink, this is an instance of age passing. But is it intentional or unintentional?

A second dimension along which age passing may be classified refers to the time duration of the passing. A person who is under the legal age to drink may attempt to pass as 18 in order to drink. However, the time duration of this passing will probably be quite short. Once the individual has passed as 18 in order to drink he may not attempt to pass as older again until a similar situation presents itself in the future. Another individual may attempt to pass as older in order to join the armed services. The time duration of this passing, however, will be quite long. As long as the individual remains in the service he must continue to pass as older. In fact, such age passing will probably continue long after the individual has left the service in order to qualify for pensions.

A further distinction can be made with respect to the various types of age passing. Some individuals pass as older or younger at one point in time and then age year by year. Thus the individual who passed as older in order to join the armed services will each year become one year older. At age 15 he may have passed as 18 in order to join the services; however, at age 20 he will now be passing as 23. On the other hand, some individuals pass as older or younger and then attempt to keep this new age for as long as possible without aging year by year. A humorous example of this type of passing would be Jack Benny who for many years said he was 39.

In the next section we will consider the conditions which facilitate age passing.

CONDITIONS
FACILITATING
AGE PASSING

Although physical appearance and social behavior are crucial for age passing, in order to document one's new age one must also obtain membership in a new age group.[5] Myrdal (1962) notes how racial passing is facilitated by educational attainment or entrance into occupations traditionally considered as white. Watson (1967) stresses the importance of Blacks moving into a white neighborhood in order to pass as white in South Africa. Age passing is similarly facilitated by changing one's age cohort.

Riley, Johnson, and Foner (1972:9) define a cohort as "an aggregate of individuals who were born (or who entered into a particular system) in the same time interval and who age together." In age passing, entering a "particular system" identified with a younger or older age cohort than one's own is the crucial aspect. Thus, to successfully pass as a younger person, in addition to preserving a youthful physical appearance and learning youthful behavior patterns, the individual enters a cohort which is usually populated by individuals of a younger chronological age.

In order to pass in the age stratification system, one changes one's age cohort by entering a role that is *identified with a particular segment of the age stratification system,* i.e., the segment into which one intends to pass. In our society, some social roles are identified with particular segments of the age structure and others are not. For example, formal education maintains a very close relationship between chronological age and grade in school. Many adult roles are not so closely age graded, although in few is age totally irrelevant.

Secondly, the role which one enters must be a social role that *is a visible and salient part of the individual's life* so that a person will be identified by this role. Thus, indirectly the role will indicate his social age. In our culture, one's occupation is one of an individual's most salient roles. From one's occupation others infer what kind of a person he is, and his occupation affects his definition of himself and the style of life he leads. Family roles are also highly salient. Whether one is married or unmarried, parent or childless, is highly visible and influences other aspects of life. The relative salience of particular roles varies by sex and by stage in the life cycle (Riley, Foner, and Associates, 1968:411).

Thirdly, for successful age passing, the new role should be one *that has a process of aging built into it* so that individuals can take their age in this role as their new "social age." For example, formal education provides a process by which individuals age as they pass from grade to grade. Many occupations have an orderly process of aging in the form of promotions or seniority. As a parent, an individual ages as he (she) becomes a parent of a newborn, a toddler, a school child, an adolescent, and finally the parent of a grown child. Some other roles do not provide a process of aging. For example, the citizenship role does not necessarily change with increasing age after adulthood; the friendship role does not provide an orderly process of aging over the duration of the friendship.

The following examples illustrate the process of age passing by changing one's age cohort:

1. One may change one's age cohort by becoming a college student. College attendance is usually identified with the young segment of the population (approximately 18–22). It is a highly visible role since students are not part of the labor force and are often geographically segregated from the rest of the community. College is itself an age stratified organization with freshmen occupying the youngest position and seniors the oldest position. Thus, an individual who enters college can take his age in college as his social age. Often an older person who enters college is treated as a younger person, even if others are aware of his chronological age. (Note also that a youth who enters college at a younger age, may speed up his process of social aging.)

2. A woman could change her age cohort by becoming a mother. The median age of women at the birth of their first child was 21.5 for women born from 1930 to 1939 (Glick and Parke, 1965:190). The mother role is a very salient role for a woman since she must care for the child for an extended period of time. As a mother, a woman becomes identified as a mother of a child of X years rather than a woman of Y years. Pass-

ing for older may occur when teenage girls drop out of school to become wives and mothers.

3. Entering military service may permit one to enter a new age cohort. Men enter the armed forces at a fairly young age (approximately 19). For these individuals, military status is clearly the most visible role in their lives. This visibility is increased by their geographical separation from the civilian population. Finally, the military organization provides an aging process which covers an extended period of time allowing the individual to take his age in the military organization as his social age. This is frequently a case of an individual passing for older, as the young man gives an older age in order to enlist. In some cases, he may maintain this new age in other aspects of life, especially when the military becomes his career and he must maintain this new age legally.

ADVANTAGES OF
PASSING FOR YOUNGER

Although Lenski (1966:406) points out that political power, wealth, and property are under the control of the older members of society, it is commonly observed that much of our culture is oriented toward youth. (It should be noted that many of the relatively few powerful people are old, but, in general, most old people are not powerful.) Numerous social scientists have commented on the high value placed on youth in our society. Sirjamaki (1948:467), writing in 1948, noted, "The best years of life are those of youth, and its qualities are the most desirable." (See also the work of La Barre, 1946). Bell (1970:75), a number of years later, observed that "Nobody in this culture, man or woman, wants to grow old; age is not honored among us." Parsons (1942: 615), as early as 1942, noted that the " . . . romantic idealization of youth patterns seems in different ways to be characteristic of modern western society as a whole." Governmental committees have also pointed to the high valuation of youth in the United States. In a working paper prepared for use by the Special Committee on Aging of the United States Senate (1973:14), the following observation is made: "There is also evidence that, like the corporate world, government

managers also create an environment where young is somehow better than old."[6]

Empirical evidence also supports the contention that youth is highly valued in this society. Peters (1971:73) reports the idealized age in American society to be 25 to 30 years. Another study (Batten, Barton, Durstine, and Osborne, Inc., 1966) indicates that "The 'best years' in one's life are typically thought to occur in the 20's (by subjects under 35) or in the 30's (by subjects 35 +)." (Quoted from a summary by Riley, Foner, and Associates, 1968:309).[7]

In addition to the best years of life being defined relatively young, further evidence indicates that old age is negatively evaluated. Kogan and Wallach (1961:277–278; see also Riley, Foner, and Associates, 1968:309) report that both old and young respondents negatively evaluate old age relative to other ages. However, older respondents give less negative evaluations than the younger respondents. In addition, McTavish (1971:92–93) found that between a fifth and a third of adults in the United States "are willing to agree to relatively negative statements about older people in general."[8]

Two different studies on death indicate the low social value assigned to old people. Sudnow (1967a:38)[9] reports on his observation at two hospitals:

> Currently at County there seems to be a rather strong relationship between the age, social background, and the perceived moral character of patients and the amount of effort that is made to attempt revival when "clinical death signs" are detected (and, for that matter, the amount of effort given to forestalling their appearance in the first place) . . . Generally speaking, the older the patient the more likely is his tentative death taken to constitute pronounceable death. . . . One can observe a direct relationship between the loudness and length of the siren alarm and the considered "social value" of the person being transported. The older the person, the less thorough is the examination he is given; frequently, elderly people are pronounced dead on the basis of only a stethoscopic examination of the heart.

Similar observations are reported by Glaser (1966:77–78)[10] in his study of dying:

Inevitably, a social value is placed on a patient and that value has much to do with the impact on the nurse of his dying and, frequently, on the care he receives. . . . The aged patient has had a full past, has little or no contributing present to family or occupation and has no future worth. As one nurse put it: "Nobody really wanted him to live, because he had nothing more to live for."

It is clear, thus, that the aged are assigned lower social value than younger people and that this has an effect on the health care they receive.

Further evidence indicates that those who identify themselves as old are more likely to be maladjusted than those who define themselves as middle-aged (see Phillips, 1957; see also Blau, 1956, for further analysis of the same data).[11] In other words, not only does society assign low social value to older people, but individuals who define themselves as older are more likely to suffer negative consequences.

Because of the high value placed on youth in this society and because of the relatively lower value placed on old age, it is frequently advantageous for an individual to try to pass as a younger person. Passing for older seems to appear largely in the extremes of the age stratification system, e.g., the adolescent who passes for older in order to get a job, buy liquor, or join the armed forces; or the retired person who wishes to prove he is old enough for Social Security or other pensions.

The advantages of passing as a younger person seem to be greater for females than for males. In the first place, youth and beauty *per se* are more highly valued in the feminine role. For example, it is more advantageous to be a young and beautiful wife than a young, handsome husband; it is more important for the secretary or receptionist to be young and beautiful than for the boss. Not only is it more important for the female to be physically attractive, but the beauty standards for women emphasize the beauty of the young girl rather than the middle-aged woman (see "No More Miss America," in Morgan, 1970:523; see also La Barre, 1946:172). In the ideal woman, our culture values youthful physical features, as well as other qualities which emphasize a childlike nature. Myrdal discussed the similarities in social position of slaves, women, and children (1962: 1073–1078). The requirement that women remain perpetually youthful is frequently decried

by writers on women's liberation (Milett, 1970:54; Morgan, 1970:521–4; Moss, 1970: 170–5).

Numerous writers have commented on what Sontag (1972) calls the "double standard of aging." Sontag (1972:31) summarizes her argument as follows:

> The prestige of youth affects everyone in this society to some degree. Men, too, are prone to periodic bouts of depression about aging. . . . But men rarely panic about aging in the way women often do. . . . there is a double standard about aging that denounces women with special severity. Society is much more permissive about aging in men, as it is more tolerant of the sexual infidelities of husbands. Men are "allowed" to age, without penalty, in several ways that women are not.

Rivers (1973:13) in discussing the application of this double standard in the mass media, makes the following observations:

> One may wonder about the profound effect the media image of middle-aged women has on the *real* middle-aged woman. Society is saying to her over and over and over again that she is only acceptable if she appears young and flawless, a condition that takes the kind of time and money few women have.

Sontag and Rivers, thus, both suggest that youth and beauty *per se* are more highly valued in the feminine role.

Sociologists have also made similar observations on the double standard of aging. Bell (1970:75) comments, "For most purposes, society pictures them [women] as 'old' ten or fifteen years sooner than men." Bell goes on to indicate that "It is surely a truism of our culture that . . . the inevitable physical symptoms of aging make women sexually unattractive much earlier than men."

As evidence for this observation Bell (1970:76) indicates that ". . . the divorced or widowed woman is severely handicapped when it comes to finding another marital partner." Bell cites statistics indicating that three-fourths of divorced men remarry, while only two-thirds of divorced women remarry. Related evidence (Schlesinger, 1968) shows that the age gap between men and women at time of marriage is greater for second and third marriages than it is for first marriages. Benson (1971:313) has restated these findings as follows, " . . . as the age of men at the time of marriage goes up, their brides become increasingly younger than themselves."

Bell cites further indirect evidence for the proposition that youth is more highly valued in women than in men by referring to an analysis of the Directory of the American Psychological Association. Bell (1970:78) indicates that " . . . in the listings of the Directory of the American Psychological Association, women are ten times as likely to omit their age as men."[12]

Because of the emphasis on youthful appearance and behavior for women in our society, we suggest that women may attempt to conceal their chronological age and pass as younger persons more frequently than men. A woman who wants to maintain her youthfulness as long as possible can use a variety of cosmetics, exercise, etc. to give physical evidence of her youthful status, but she also needs social documentation of her youth. She needs a "young" social role. For example, the unmarried are often assumed to be "younger" than married people of the same chronological age. (But to retain unmarried status for too long can be detrimental because of low status of spinsterhood.) The mother of young children is often assumed to be younger than the mother of teenagers. So it is possible that a woman who gets married at 25 and has children in her late twenties and thirties can remain socially younger than her age-mate who married as a teenager and is the mother of teenagers in her thirties. Riley, Johnson, and Foner (1972:414) note, " . . . women with grown children may be marked as middle-aged, and be expected to conduct themselves accordingly, regardless of their chronological age."

Although the appearance of youth may not be as important for men as for women, many men still prefer to remain as young as possible. Often occupational positions place a premium on remaining young, even as one advances in the occupancy hierarchy. Cosmetics, hair coloring, etc., are increasingly used by men in our society.

Nevertheless, for men, passing to a younger age cohort is somewhat less advantageous. Although men increasingly make use of cosmetics, etc., masculine maturity is often associated with economic and social success which is often more important than youthful appearance in assessing a man's social worth. Since a man is not as closely identified with his family, his stage in the family cycle is a less salient social characteristic in fixing his social age. Whereas a woman is likely to be identified by her family role, occupation is often the most salient role in a man's life. Even if a woman achieves occupational success, she may still be identified by her marital status rather than her occupational status. For example, Rose Coser (1971) described a medical faculty party to which she was invited because of her own occupational role, but others at the party insisted on acting as if she were there as someone's wife. It is hard to imagine a similar situation happening to a man. Since advancement in the occupational hierarchy is likely to be accompanied by economic and social success, for men, the advantage of being successful and mature may offset any advantage of being young and less successful.

SUMMARY

The biological basis of the age stratification system makes mobility within it an irreversible process with all individuals growing older with each passing year. However, the high value our culture places on youthfulness provides the motivation for individuals to pass as younger people. Similar to racial-ethnic passing, in age passing the visible physical characteristics are of crucial importance, as well as social characteristics such as language, dress, and youthful behavior. To successfully pass as a younger person, the individual must also "change" his age cohort. That is, he must become identified with an organization or role which is populated by younger people. If this is a salient role in the individual's life, and if this role has a process of aging built into it, a person can take his age in this role as his new age.

The advantages of passing for younger are greater for women than for men, since youth and beauty are more highly valued in the feminine role. Since a woman's most visible role is her family role, the mother of young children can pass as a younger woman than the mother of teenagers. Men may still wish to remain young as long as possible, but the economic and social success which are more likely to occur with maturity are more important than youthful appearance in assessing a man's worth.

Recognition of the possibility of an individual's passing as a younger or older person may allow researchers to explain some unexpected age-related behavior. We might speculate that older people who received their college educations in their middle years might have different attitudes and behavior than their age-mates who received their college educations in their youth. Or the role conflict predicted to occur when older people go to college may not materialize if they get some reward from the opportunity to pass as younger. As another example, some observed sex differences in attitude and behavior may be partly a result of the female's efforts to remain young rather than differences in sex-role definitions.

A consideration of passing as a form of mobility within the age stratification system illustrates the similarities and differences in mobility as it occurs in the different stratification hierarchies (e.g., race, age). In order to describe passing as it relates to age mobility, it was also necessary to consider interrelationships with other stratification hierarchies (e.g., sex). We think that the examination of the interrelationships between positions on various stratification dimensions will be important for the further understanding of social processes as they actually occur in individuals and groups.

NOTES

1. Interest in the age stratification system is, of course, not new. See, for example, the early work by Parsons, 1942; Linton, 1942; Cottrell, 1942; and Eisenstadt, 1956. For an excellent bibliography on the sociology of aging prior to 1959, see Cain, 1959. For a slightly more recent review of the literature, see Cain, 1964.
2. Kinsey (1953:123–4) indicates that the median age at first menstruation is 13.0, while the range is from 9 to 25.
3. Since the earliest age (i.e., childhood) has the lowest status, it is possible to keep certain groups subordinate by identifying them with children. For example, women, Blacks, and colonial people have frequently been identified as child-like.
4. An interesting illustration of intentional passing

is found in the sociological literature. In the 1950's Sullivan, Queen, and Patrick (1958) studied the informal structure of an Air Force basic training unit. They used a form of participant observation in which one of the researchers enlisted in the Air Force without revealing his identity as a researcher. In order to conceal the researcher's identity, he attempted to pass as a 19 year old (his actual age ws 26). The techniques used to pass were diet (the researcher lost 35 pounds), minor surgery,. and a nine month training period in which the researcher learned the expected patterns of behavior of his new role. A comparable example in racial passing would be John Howard Griffin's passing as Black in the South (Griffin: 1962) which involved changing his skin color by use of chemicals and ultraviolet ray, and also involved shaving his hair.

5. In this paper we will focus on obtaining membership in a new age group. There are, of course, other factors facilitating or deterring age passing. Some require legal documentation of age. For example, the fact that there are certain ages at which individuals become legally able to drink, vote, etc., and the fact that there are certain ages at which individuals must retire from their jobs are deterrants to passing. In order to drink or vote before the legal age one must obtain a false identification documenting one's new age. This is not always easy to do. A factor which facilitates passing is the anonymity of urban life. In urban communities the individuals with which one interacts are often strangers or only passing acquaintances. People often interact with each other in only one context so the personal history of individuals, including their ages, is often unknown.

6. This same working paper cites evidence of age discrimination. For example (1973:4),

The Department [of Labor] also investigates firms to see whether they are in compliance with ADEA [Age Discrimination in Employment Act]. More than 6,000 establishments were investigated in 1972 and 36 percent were found in violation of one or more statutory provisions. So far the discrimination practice disclosed most often is illegal advertising. However, a significant number of violations have been found in refusal to hire, discharge because of age, and the existence of promotional bars to workers in the 40 to 64 age category.

7. Riley, Foner, and Associates (1968:309) in reviewing the findings of this study, go on to note, "However, the years selected as 'best' tend to rise by age of the subject; thus, among OP 65 +, over one-fourth select the 40's or 50's, and over one-tenth select the 60's or 70's." Nevertheless, it is

clear that most people tend to define the "best years" as relatively young.

8. However, McTavish does not report the percentage of adults who are willing to make relatively negative statements about younger people. Nevertheless, when considered in light of Kogan and Wallach's findings, it seems reasonable to expect that a smaller percentage would make negative statements about younger people.

9. For a further report on Sudnow's findings, see Sudnow (1967b).

10. For further reports of Glaser's findings, see Glaser and Strauss (1964), Glaser and Strauss (1968).

11. Phillips (1957:213) defines maladjustment as a ". . . patterned lack of alignment between the needs of the individual and the rewards he obtains . . ."

12. Bell (1970:78) also cites a content analysis of fiction in American magazines. "A study of characters in American magazine fiction from 1890 to 1955 found a decline in the number of older women appearing as characters." This is especially interesting since life expectancy was increasing over time. Unfortunately Bell does not indicate whether there was a similar decline in the number of older men appearing as characters.

REFERENCES

Batten, Barton, Durstine, and Osborn, Inc. 1966. Report: An Investigation of People's Feelings on Age. (unpublished)

Bell, I. P. 1970. "The Double Standard." Transaction 8 (November/December): 75–80.

Benson, Leonard. 1971. *The Family Bond—Marriage, Love, and Sex in America.* New York: Random House.

Berry, Brewton. 1965. *Race and Ethnic Relations.* Boston: Houghton Mifflin Company.

Blau, Z. S. 1956. "Changes in Status and Age Identification." *American Sociological Review,* 21 (April): 198–203.

Cain, Leonard D., Jr. 1959. "The Sociology of Aging: A Trend Report and Bibliography." *Current Sociology,* 8 (No.2): 57–133.

——————. 1964. "Life Course and Social Structure." Pp. 272–309 in Robert E. L. Faris (ed.), *Handbook of Modern Sociology.* Chicago: Rand McNally.

Coser, R. L. 1971. "Of Nepotism and Marginality." *The American Sociologist* 6 (August): 259–60.

Cottrell, L. S., Jr. 1942. "The Adjustment of the Individual to His Age and Sex Roles." *American Sociological Review* 7 (October): 617–20.

Drake, St. Clair, and Horace R. Cayton. 1945. *Black Metropolis.* New York: Harcourt, Brace and Company.

Eisenstadt, S. N. 1956. *From Generation to Generation: Age Groups and Social Structure.* Glencoe, Illinois: Free Press.

Glaser, B. G. 1966. "The Social Loss of Aged Dying Patients." *The Gerontologist,* 6 (June): 77–80.

Glaser, Barney G., and Anselm L. Strauss. 1968. *Time for Dying.* Chicago: Aldine.

——————. 1964. "The Social Loss of Dying Patients." *American Journal of Nursing,* 64 (June): 119–21.

Glick, P. C. and R. Parke, Jr. 1965. "New Approaches in Studying the Life Cycle of the Family." *Demography,* 2: 187–202.

Griffin, John Howard. 1962. *Black Like Me.* New York: Signet.

Kinsey, Alfred C., Wardell B. Pomeroy, Clyde E. Martin, and Paul H. Gebhard. 1953. *Sexual Behavior in the Human Female.* Philadelphia: W. B. Saunders.

Kogan, N. and M. A. Wallach. 1961. "Age Changes in Values and Attitudes." *Journal of Gerontology,* 16 (July): 272–80.

La Barre, W. 1946. "Social Cynosure and Social Structure." *Journal of Personality,* 14 (March): 169–83.

Lenski, Gerhard E. 1966. *Power and Privilege: A Theory of Social Stratification.* New York: McGraw-Hill.

Linton, R. 1942. "Age and Sex Categories." *American Sociological Review* 7 (October): 589–603.

McGrady, Patrick M., Jr. 1968. *The Youth Doctors.* New York: Ace Publishing Corporation.

McTavish, D. G. 1971. "Perceptions of Old People: *A Review of Research Methodologies and Findings.*" The Gerontologist, 11 (Winter): 90–101.

Miller, Benjamin F. 1967. *The Complete Medical Guide.* New York: Simon and Schuster.

Millett, Kate. 1970. *Sexual Politics.* Garden City, New York: Doubleday and Company, Inc.

Morgan, Robin (ed.). 1970. *Sisterhood is Powerful, An Anthology of Writings from the Women's Liberation Movement.* New York: Vintage Books.

Moss, Z., 1970. "It Hurts to be Alive and Obsolete: The Aging Woman." Pp. 170–5 in Robin Morgan (ed.), *Sisterhood is Powerful.* New York: Vintage Books.

Myrdal, Gunnar. 1962. *An American Dilemma: The Negro Problem and Modern Democracy.* New York and Evanston: Harper and Row.

Neugarten, B. L., and J. W. Moore. 1968. "The Changing Age-Status System," Pp. 5–21 in Bernice L. Neugarten (ed.), *Middle Age and Aging.* Chicago and London: The University of Chicago Press.

Parsons, T. 1942. "Age and Sex in the Social Structure of the United States." *American Sociological Review* 7 (October): 604–16.

Parsons, T., and G. M. Platt. 1972. "Higher Education and Changing Socialization." Pp. 236–91 in Matilda White Riley, Marilyn E. Johnson and Anne Foner, *A Sociology of Age Stratification,* Volume three of *Aging and Society.* New York: Russell Sage Foundation.

Peters, G. R. 1971. "Self-Conceptions of the Aged, Age Identification, and Aging." *The Gerontologist,* 11 (Winter): 69–73.

Phillips, B. S. 1957. "A Role Theory Approach to Adjustment in Old Age." *American Sociological Review,* 22 (April): 212–7.

Riley, M. W. 1971. "Social Gerontology and the Age Stratification of Society." *The Gerontologist,* 11 (Spring): 79–87.

Riley, Matilda White, Anne Foner, and Associates. 1968. *Aging and Society,* Volume one: *An Inventory of Research Findings.* New York: Russell Sage Foundation.

Riley, Matilda White, John W. Riley, Jr., and Marilyn E. Johnson. 1969. *Aging and Society.* Volume two: *Aging and the Professions.* New York: Russell Sage Foundation.

Riley, Matilda White, Marilyn E. Johnson, and Anne Foner. 1972. *A Sociology of Age Stratification,* Volume three of *Aging and Society.* New York: Russell Sage Foundation.

Rivers, C. 1973. "Why Can't Hollywood See That 35 Is Beautiful, Too?" *The New York Times,* April 1: 13.

Schlesinger, B. 1968. "Remarriage—An Inventory of Findings" *The Family Coordinator,* 17 (October): 248–50.

Simpson, George Eaton, and J. Milton Yinger. 1965. *Racial and Cultural Minorities.* New York, Evanston, and London: Harper and Row.

Sirjamaki, J. 1948. "Cultural Configurations in the American Family." *American Journal of Sociology,* 53 (May): 464–70.

Sontag, S. 1972. "The Double Standard of Aging." *Saturday Review of the Society,* 55 (October): 29–38.

Special Committee on Aging, United States Senate. 1973. *Improving the Age Discrimination Law—*A Working Paper. Washington, D.C.: U.S. Government Printing Office.

Sudnow, David. 1967a. "Dead on Arrival." *Transaction,* 5 (November): 36–43.

——————. 1967b. *Passing On.* Englewood Cliffs, New Jersey: Prentice-Hall.

Sullivan, M. A., Jr., S. A. Queen, and R. C. Patrick, Jr. 1958. "Participant Observation as Employed in the Study of a Military Training Program." *American Sociological Review* 23 (December): 660–7.

Watson, G. 1967. "A Process of Passing for White in South Africa: A Study in Cumulative Ad Hoc-ery." *Canadian Review of Sociology and Anthropology* 4 (August): 141–7.

Programmed for Social Class: Tracking in High School

Walter E. Schafer, Carol Olexa and Kenneth Polk

IF, AS folklore would have it, America is the land of opportunity, offering anyone the chance to raise himself purely on the basis of his or her ability, then education is the key to self-betterment. The spectacular increase in those of us who attend school is often cited as proof of the great scope of opportunity that our society offers: 94 percent of the high school age population was attending school in 1967, as compared to 7 percent in 1890.

Similarly, our educational system is frequently called more democratic than European systems, for instance, which rigidly segregate students by ability early in their lives, often on the basis of nationally administered examinations such as England's "11-plus." The United States, of course, has no official national policy of educational segregation. Our students, too, are tested and retested throughout their lives and put into faster or slower classes or programs on the basis of their presumed ability, but this procedure is carried out in a decentralized fashion that varies between each city or state.

However, many critics of the American practice claim that, no matter how it is carried out, it does not meet the needs of the brighter and duller groups, so much as it solidifies and widens the differences between them. One such critic, the eminent educator Kenneth B. Clark, speculates: "It is conceivable that the detrimental effects of segregation based upon intellect are similar to the known detrimental effects of schools segregated on the basis of class, nationality or race."

Patricia Cayo Sexton notes that school grouping based on presumed ability often reinforces already existing social divisions:

> Children from higher social strata usually enter the "higher quality" groups and those from lower strata the "lower" ones. School decisions about a child's ability will greatly influence the kind and quality of education he receives, as well as his future life, including whether he goes to college, the job he will get, and his feelings about himself and others.

And Arthur Pearl puts it bluntly:

> . . . "special ability classes," "basic track," or "slow learner classes" are various names for another means of systematically denying the poor adequate access to education.

In this article we will examine some evidence bearing on this vital question of whether current educational practices tend to reinforce existing social class divisions. We will also offer an alternative aimed at making our public schools more effective institutions for keeping open the opportunities for social mobility.

EDUCATION EXPLOSION

Since the turn of the century, a number of trends have converged to increase enormously the pressure on American adolescents to graduate from high school: declining opportunity in jobs, the upgrading of educational requirements for job entry, and the diminishing need for teenagers to contribute to family income. While some school systems, especially in the large cities, have adapted to this vast increase in enrollment by creating separate high schools for students with different interests, abilities or occupational goals, most communities have developed comprehensive high schools serving all the youngsters within a neighborhood or community.

In about half the high schools in the United States today, the method for handling these large and varied student populations is through some form of tracking system. Under this arrangement, the entire student body is divided into two or more relatively distinct career lines, or tracks, with such titles as college preparatory, vocational, technical, industrial, business, general, basic and remedial. While students on different tracks may take some courses together in the same classroom, they are usually separated into entirely different courses or different sections of the same course.

School men offer several different justifications for tracking systems. Common to most, however, is the notion that college-bound students are academically more able, learn more rapidly, should not be deterred in their progress by slower, non-college-bound students, and need courses for college preparation which non-college-bound students do not need. By the same token, it is thought that non-college-bound students are less bright, learn more slowly, should not be expected to progress as fast or learn as much as college-bound students, and need only a general education or work-oriented training to prepare themselves for immediate entry into the world of work or a business or vocational school.

In reply, the numerous critics of tracking usually contend that while the college-bound are often encouraged by the tracking system to improve their performance, non-college-bound students, largely as a result of being placed in a lower-rated track, are discouraged from living up to their potential or from showing an interest in academic values. What makes the system especially pernicious, these critics say, is that non-college-bound students more often come from low-income and minority group families. As a result, high schools, through the tracking system, inadvertently close off opportunities for large numbers of students from lower social strata, and thereby contribute to the low achievement, lack of interest, delinquency and rebellion which school men frequently deplore in their noncollege track students.

If these critics are correct, the American comprehensive high school, which is popularly assumed to be the very model of an open and democratic institution, may not really be open and democratic at all. In fact, rather than facilitating equality of educational opportunity, our schools may be subtly denying it, and in the process widening and hardening existing social divisions.

TRACKS AND WHO GETS PUT ON THEM

During the summer of 1964, we collected data from official school transcripts of the recently graduated senior classes of two midwestern three-year high schools. The larger school, located in a predominantly middle-class, academic community of about 70,000, had a graduating class that year of 753 students. The smaller school, with a graduating class of 404, was located nearby in a predominantly working-class, industrial community of about 20,000.

Both schools placed their students into either a college prep or general track. We determined the positions of every student in our sample by whether he took tenth grade English in the college prep or the general section. If he was enrolled in the college prep section, he almost always took other college prep sections or courses, such as advanced mathematics or foreign languages, in which almost all enrollees were also college prep.

Just how students in the two schools were assigned to—or chose—tracks is somewhat of a mystery. When we interviewed people both in the high schools and in their feeder junior highs, we were told that whether a student went into one track or another depended on various factors, such as his own desires and aspirations, teacher advice, achievement test scores, grades, pressure from parents, and counselor assessment of academic promise. One is hard put to say which of these weighs most heavily, but we must note that one team of researchers, Cicourel and Kitsuse, showed in their study of *The Educational Decision-Makers* that assumptions made by counselors

about the character, adjustment and potential of incoming students are vitally important in track assignment.

Whatever the precise dynamics of this decision, the outcome was clear in the schools we studied: socioeconomic and racial background had an effect on which track a student took, quite apart from either his achievement in junior high or his ability as measured by IQ scores. In the smaller, working-class school, 58 percent of the incoming students were assigned to the college prep track; in the larger, middle-class school, 71 percent were placed in the college prep track. And, taking the two schools together, whereas 83 percent of students from white-collar homes were assigned to the college prep track, this was the case with only 48 percent of students from blue-collar homes. The relationship of race to track assignment was even stronger: 71 percent of the whites and only 30 percent of the blacks were assigned to the college prep track. In the two schools studied, the evidence is plain: Children from low income and minority group families more often found themselves in low ability groups and non-college-bound tracks than in high ability groups or college-bound tracks.

Furthermore, this decision-point early in the students' high school careers was of great significance for their futures, since it was virtually irreversible. Only 7 percent of those who began on the college prep track moved down to the noncollege prep track, while only 7 percent of those assigned to the lower, noncollege track, moved up. Clearly, these small figures indicate a high degree of rigid segregation within each of the two schools. In fact, greater mobility between levels has been reported in English secondary modern schools, where streaming—the British term for tracking—is usually thought to be more rigid and fixed than tracking in this country. (It must be remembered, of course, that in England the more rigid break is between secondary modern and grammar schools.)

DIFFERENCES BETWEEN TRACKS

As might be expected from the schoolmen's justification for placing students in separate tracks in the first place, track position is noticeably related to academic performance. Thirty-seven percent of the college prep students graduated in the top quarter of their class (measured by grade point average throughout high school), while a mere 2 percent of the noncollege group achieved the top quarter. By contrast, half the noncollege prep students fell in the lowest quarter, as opposed to only 12 percent of the college prep.

Track position is also strikingly related to whether a student's academic performance improves or deteriorates during high school. The grade point average of all sample students in their ninth year—that is, prior to their being assigned to tracks—was compared with their grade point averages over the next three years. While there was a slight difference in the ninth year between those who would subsequently enter the college and noncollege tracks, this difference had increased by the senior year. This widening gap in academic performance resulted from the fact that a higher percentage of students subsequently placed in the college prep track improved their grade point average by the senior year, while a higher percentage of noncollege prep experienced a decline in grade point average by the time they reached the senior year.

Track position is also related strongly to dropout rate. Four percent of the college prep students dropped out of high school prior to graduation, as opposed to 36 percent of the noncollege group.

Track position is also a good indication of how deeply involved a student will be in school, as measured by participation in extracurricular activities. Out of the 753 seniors in the larger school, a comparatively small number of college prep students—21 percent—did not participate in any activities, while 44 percent took part in three or more such activities. By contrast, 58 percent, or more than half of the noncollege group took part in no extracurricular activities at all, and only 11 percent of this group took part in three or more activities.

Finally, track position is strikingly related to delinquency, both in and out of school. Out of the entire school body of the larger school during the 1963–1964 school year—that is, out of 2,565 boys and girls—just over one-third of the college-bound, as opposed to more than half of the non-college-bound committed one or more violations of school rules. Nineteen percent of the college-

bound, compared with 70 percent of the non-college-bound, committed three or more such violations. During this year, just over one-third of all the college-bound students were suspended for infractions of school rules, while more than half of all the non-college-bound group were suspended.

Furthermore, using juvenile court records, we find that out of the 1964 graduating class in the larger school, 6 percent of the college prep, and 16 percent of the non-college bound groups, were delinquent while in high school. Even though 5 percent of those on the noncollege track had already entered high school with court records, opposed to only 1 percent of the college prep track, still more non-college-bound students became delinquent during high school than did college prep students (11 percent compared with 5 percent). So the relation between track position and delinquency is further supported.

We have seen, then, that when compared with college prep students, noncollege prep students show lower achievement, great deterioration of achievement, less participation in extracurricular activities, a greater tendency to drop out, more misbehavior in school, and more delinquency outside of school. Since students are assigned to different tracks largely on the basis of presumed differences in intellectual ability and inclination for further study, the crucial question is whether assignment to different tracks helped to meet the needs of groups of students who were already different, as many educators would claim, or actually contributed to and reinforced such differences, as critics like Sexton and Pearl contend.

The simplest way to explain the differences we have just seen is to attribute them to characteristics already inherent in the individual students, or—at a more sophisticated level—to students' cultural and educational backgrounds.

It can be argued, for example, that the difference in academic achievement between the college and noncollege groups can be explained by the fact that college prep students are simply brighter; after all, this is one of the reasons they were taken into college prep courses. Others would argue that non-college-bound students do less well in school work because of family background: they more often come from blue-collar homes where less value is placed on grades and college, where books and help in schoolwork are less readily available, and verbal expression limited. Still others would contend that lower track students get lower grades because they performed less well in elementary and junior high, have fallen behind, and probably try less hard.

Fortunately, it was possible with our data to separate out the influence of track position from the other suggested factors of social class background (measured by father's occupation), intelligence (measured by IQ—admittedly not a perfectly acceptable measure), and previous academic performance (measured by grade point average for the last semester of the ninth year). Through use of a weighted percentage technique known as test factor standardization, we found that even when the effects of IQ, social class and previous performance are ruled out, there is still a sizable difference in grade point average between the two tracks. With the influence of the first three factors eliminated we nevertheless find that 30 percent of the college prep, as opposed to a mere 4 percent of the noncollege group attained the top quarter of their class; and that only 12 percent of the college prep, as opposed to 35 percent of the noncollege group, fell into the bottom quarter. These figures, which are similar for boys and girls, further show that track position has an independent effect on academic achievement which is greater than the effect of each of the other three factors—social class, IQ and past performance. In particular, assignment to the noncollege track has a strong negative influence on a student's grades.

Looking at dropout rate, and again controlling for social class background, IQ and past performance, we find that track position in itself has an independent influence which is higher than the effect of any of the other three factors. In other words, even when we rule out the effect of these three factors, non-college-bound students still dropped out in considerably greater proportion than college-bound students (19 percent vs. 4 percent).

WHEN THE
FORECASTERS MAKE
THE WEATHER

So our evidence points to the conclusion that the superior academic performance of the college-bound students, and the inferior performance of the noncollege students is partly caused by the tracking system. Our data do not explain how this happens, but several studies of similar educational arrangements, as well as basic principles of social psychology do provide a number of probable explanations. The first point has to do with the pupil's self-image.

Stigma. Assignment to the lower track in the schools we studied carried with it a strong stigma. As David Mallory was told by an American boy, "Around here you are *nothing* if you're not college prep." A noncollege prep girl in one of the schools we studied told me that she always carried her "general" track books upside down because of the humiliation she felt at being seen with them as she walked through the halls.

The corroding effect of such stigmatizing is well known. As Patricia Sexton has put it, "He [the low track student] is bright enough to catch on very quickly to the fact that he is not considered very bright. He comes to accept this unflattering appraisal because, after all, the school should know."

One ex-delinquent in Washington, D.C. told one of us how the stigma from this low track affected him.

It really don't have to be the tests, but after the tests, there shouldn't be no separation in the classes. Because, as I say again, I felt good when I was with my class, but when they went and separated us—that changed us. That changed our ideas, our thinking, the way we thought about each other and turned us to enemies toward each other—because they said I was dumb and they were smart.

When you first go to junior high school you do feel something inside—it's like ego. You have been from elementary to junior high, you feel great inside. You say, well daggone, I'm going to deal with the *people* here now, I am in junior high school. You get this shirt that says Brown Junior High or whatever the name is and you are proud of that shirt. But then you go up there and the teacher says—"Well, so and so, you're in the basic section, you can't go with the other kids." The devil with the whole thing—you lose—something in you—like it just goes out of you.

Did you think the other guys were smarter than you? Not at first—I used to think I was just as smart as anybody in the school—I knew I was smart. I knew some people were smarter, and I *wanted* to go to school, I wanted to get a diploma and go to college and help people and everything. I stepped into there in junior high—I felt like a fool going to school—I really felt like a fool. *Why?* Because I felt like I wasn't a part of the school. I couldn't get on special patrols, because I wasn't qualified. *What happened between the seventh and ninth grades?* I started losing faith in myself—after the teachers kept downing me. You hear "a guy's in basic section, he's dumb" and all this. Each year—"you're ignorant—you're stupid."

Considerable research shows that such erosion of self-esteem greatly increases the chances of academic failure, as well as dropping out and causing "trouble" both inside and outside of school.

Moreover, this lowered self-image is reinforced by the expectations that others have toward a person in the noncollege group.

The Self-fulfilling Prophecy. A related explanation rich in implications comes from David Hargreaves' *Social Relations in a Secondary School,* a study of the psychological, behavioral and educational consequences of the student's position in the streaming system of an English secondary modern school. In "Lumley School," the students (all boys) were assigned to one of five streams on the basis of ability and achievement, with the score on the "11-plus" examination playing the major role.

Like the schools we studied, students in the different streams were publicly recognized as high or low in status and were fairly rigidly segregated, both formally in different classes and informally in friendship groups. It is quite probable, then, that Hargreaves' explanations for the greater antischool attitudes, animosity toward teachers, academic failure, disruptive behavior and delinquency among the low stream boys apply to the noncollege prep students we studied as well. In fact, the negative effects of the tracking system on non-college-bound students may be even stronger in our two high schools, since the Lumley streaming system was much more open and flexible, with students moving from one stream to another several times during their four-year careers.

STREAMED SCHOOLS

As we noted, a popular explanation for the greater failure and misbehavior among low stream or non-college-bound students is that they come from homes that fail to provide the same skills, ambition or conforming attitude as higher stream or college-bound students. Hargreaves demonstrates that there is some validity to this position: in his study, low stream boys more often came from homes that provided less encouragement for academic achievement and higher level occupations, and that were less oriented to the other values of the school and teachers. Similar differences may have existed among the students we studied, although their effects have been markedly reduced by our control for father's occupation, IQ and previous achievement.

But Hargreaves provides a convincing case for the position that whatever the differences in skills, ambition, selfesteem or educational commitment that the students brought to school, they were magnified by what happened to them in school, largely because low stream boys were the victims of a self-fulfilling prophecy in their relations with teachers, with respect to both academic performance and classroom behavior. Teachers of higher stream boys expected higher performance and got it. Similarly, boys who wore the label of streams "C" or "D" were more likely to be seen by teachers as limited in ability and troublemakers, and were treated accordingly.

> In a streamed school the teacher categorizes the pupils not only in terms of the inferences he makes of the child's class room behavior but also from the child's stream level. It is for this reason that the teacher can rebuke an "A" stream boy for being like a "D" stream boy. The teacher has learned to *expect* certain kinds of behavior from members of different streams. . . . It would be hardly surprising if "good" pupils thus became "better" and the "bad" pupils become "worse." It is, in short, an example of a self-fulfilling prophecy. The negative expectations of the teacher reinforce the negative behavioral tendencies.

A recent study by Rosenthal and Jacobson in an American elementary school lends further evidence to the position that teacher expectations influence student's performance. In this study, the influence is a positive one. Teachers of children randomly assigned to experimental groups were told at the beginning of the year to expect "unusual intellectual" gains, while teachers of the control group children were told nothing. After eight months, and again after two years, the experimental group children, the "intellectual spurters," showed significantly greater gains in IQ and grades. Further, they were rated by the teachers as being significantly more curious, interesting, happy and more likely to succeed in the future. Such findings are consistent with theories of interpersonal influence and with the interactional or labelling view of deviant behavior.

If, as often claimed, American teachers underestimate the learning potential of low track students and expect more negative attitudes and greater trouble from them, it may well be that they partially cause the very failure, alienation, lack of involvement, dropping out and rebellion they are seeking to prevent. As Hargreaves says of Lumley, "It is important to stress that if this effect of categorization is real, it is entirely unintended by the teachers. They do not wish to make low streams more difficult than they are!" Yet the negative self-fulfilling prophecy was probably real, if unintended and unrecognized, in our two schools as well as in Lumley.

Two further consequences of the expectation that students in the noncollege group will learn less well are differences in grading policies and in teacher effectiveness.

Grading Policies.   In the two schools we studied, our interviews strongly hint at the existence of grade ceilings for noncollege prep students and grade floors for college-bound students. That is, by virtue of being located in a college preparatory section or course, college prep students could seldom receive any grade lower than "B" or "C," while students in non-college-bound sections or courses found it difficult to gain any grade higher than "C," even though their objective performance may have been equivalent to a college prep "B." Several teachers explicitly called our attention to this practice, the rationale being that noncollege prep students do not deserve the same objective grade rewards as college prep students, since they "clearly" are less

bright and perform less well. To the extent that grade ceilings do operate for non-college-bound students, the lower grades that result from this policy, almost by definition, can hardly have a beneficial effect on motivation and commitment.

Teaching Effectiveness.   Finally, numerous investigations of ability grouping, as well as the English study by Hargreaves, have reported that teachers of higher ability groups are likely to teach in a more interesting and effective manner than teachers of lower ability groups. Such a difference is predictable from what we know about the effects of reciprocal interaction between teacher and class. Even when the same individual teaches both types of classes in the course of the day, as was the case for most teachers in the two schools in this study, he is likely to be "up" for college prep classes and "down" for noncollege prep classes—and to bring out the same reaction from his students.

A final, and crucial factor that contributes to the poorer performance and lower interest in school of non-college-bound students is the relation between school work and the adult career after school.

Future Payoff.   Non-college-bound students often develop progressively more negative attitudes toward school, especially formal academic work, because they see grades—and indeed school itself—as having little future relevance or payoff. This is not the case for college prep students. For them, grades are a means toward the identifiable and meaningful end of qualifying for college, while among the non-college-bound, grades are seen as far less important for entry into an occupation or a vocational school. This difference in the practical importance of grades is magnified by the perception among non-college-bound students that it is pointless to put much effort into school work, since it will be unrelated to the later world of work anyway. In a study of *Rebellion in a High School* in this country, Arthur Stinchcombe describes the alienation of non-college-bound high school students:

The major practical conclusion of the analysis above is that rebellious behavior is largely a reaction to the school itself and to its promises, not a failure of the family or community. High school students can be motivated to conform by paying them in the realistic coin of future advantage. Except perhaps for pathological cases, any student can be motivated to conform if the school can realistically promise something valuable to him as a reward for working hard. But for a large part of the population, especially the adolescent who will enter the male working class or the female candidates for early marriage, the school has nothing to offer. . . . In order to secure conformity from students, a high school must articulate academic work with careers of students.

Being on the lower track has other negative consequences for the student which go beyond the depressing influence on his academic performance and motivation. We can use the principles just discussed to explain our findings with regard to different rates of participation in school activities and acts of misbehavior.

TRACKS CONFORMITY AND DEVIANCE

For example, the explanations having to do with self-image and the expectations of others suggest that assignment to the non-college-bound track has a dampening effect on commitment to school in general, since it is the school which originally categorized these students as inferior. Thus, assignment to the lower track may be seen as independently contributing to resentment, frustration and hostility in school, leading to lack of involvement in all school activities, and finally ending in active withdrawal. The self-exclusion of the noncollege group from the mainstream of college student life is probably enhanced by intentional or unintentional exclusion by other students and teachers.

Using the same type of reasons, while we cannot prove a definite causal linkage between track position and misbehavior, it seems highly likely that assignment to the noncollege prep track often leads to resentment, declining commitment to school, and rebellion against it, expressed in lack of respect for the school's authority or acts of disobedience against it. As Albert Cohen argued over a decade ago in

Delinquent Boys, delinquency may well be largely a rebellion against the school and its standards by teenagers who feel they cannot get anywhere by attempting to adhere to such standards. Our analysis suggests that a key factor in such rebellion is noncollege prep status in the school's tracking system, with the vicious cycle of low achievement and inferior self-image that go along with it.

This conclusion is further supported by Hargreaves' findings on the effect of streaming at Lumley:

> There is a real sense in which the school can be regarded as a generator of delinquency. Although the aims and efforts of the teachers are directed towards deleting such tendencies, the organization of the school and its influence on subcultural development unintentionally fosters delinquent values. . . . For low stream boys . . . , school simultaneously exposes them to these values and deprives them of status in these terms. It is at this point they may begin to reject the values because they cannot succeed in them. The school provides a mechanism through the streaming system whereby their failure is effected and institutionalized, and also provides a situation in which they can congregate together in low streams.

Hargreaves' last point suggests a very important explanation for the greater degree of deviant behavior among the non-college-bound.

The Student Subculture. Assignment to a lower stream at Lumley meant a boy was immediately immersed in a student subculture that stressed and rewarded antagonistic attitudes and behavior toward teachers and all they stood for. If a boy was assigned to the "A" stream, he was drawn toward the values of teachers, not only by the higher expectations and more positive rewards from the teachers themselves, but from other students as well. The converse was true of lower stream boys, who accorded each other high status for doing the opposite of what teachers wanted. Because of class scheduling, little opportunity developed for interaction and friendship across streams. The result was a progressive polarization and hardening of the high and low stream subcultures between first and fourth years and a progressively greater negative attitude across stream lines, with quite predictable consequences.

> The informal pressures within the low streams tend to work directly against the assumption of the teachers that boys will regard promotion into a higher stream as a desirable goal. The boys from the low streams were very reluctant to ascent to higher streams because their stereotypes of "A" and "B" stream boys were defined in terms of values alien to their own and because promotion would involve rejection by their low stream friends. The teachers were not fully aware that this unwillingness to be promoted to a higher stream led the high informal status boys to depress their performance in examinations. This fear of promotion adds to our list of factors leading to the formation of anti-academic attitudes among low stream boys.

Observations and interviews in the two American schools we studied confirmed a similar polarization and reluctance by noncollege prep students to pursue the academic goals rewarded by teachers and college prep students. Teachers, however, seldom saw the antischool attitudes of noncollege prep students as arising out of the tracking system—or anything else about the school—but out of adverse home influences, limited intelligence or psychological problems.

Implications. These, then, are some of the ways the schools we studied contributed to the greater rates of failure, academic decline, uninvolvement in school activities, misbehavior and delinquency among non-college-bound students. We can only speculate, of course, about the generalization of these findings to other schools. However, there is little reason to think the two schools we studied were unusual or unrepresentative and, despite differences in size and social class composition, the findings are virtually identical in both. To the extent the findings are valid and general, they strongly suggest that, through their tracking system, the schools are partly causing many of the very problems they are trying to solve and are posing an important barrier to equal educational opportunity to lower income and black students, who are disproportionately assigned to the noncollege prep track.

The notion that schools help cause low achievement, deterioration of educational commitment and involvement, the dropout problem, misbehavior and delinquency is foreign and repulsive to many teachers, administrators and parents. Yet our evidence is entirely consistent with Kai Erikson's observation that " . . . deviant forms of conduct often seem to derive nourishment from the very agencies devised to inhibit them."

What, then, are the implications of this study? Some might argue that, despite the negative side effects we have shown, tracking systems are essential for effective teaching, especially for students with high ability, as well as for adjusting students early in their careers to the status levels they will occupy in the adult occupational system. We contend that however reasonable this may sound, the negative effects demonstrated here offset and call into serious question any presumed gains from tracking

Others might contend that the negative outcomes we have documented can be eliminated by raising teachers' expectations of noncollege track students, making concerted efforts to reduce the stigma attached to noncollege classes, assigning good teachers to noncollege track classes, rewarding them for doing an effective job at turning on their students, and developing fair and equitable grading practices in both college prep and noncollege prep classes.

Attractive as they may appear, efforts like these will be fruitless, so long as tracking systems, and indeed schools as we now know them, remain unchanged. What is needed are wholly new, experimental environments of teaching-learning-living, even outside today's public schools, if necessary. Such schools of the future must address themselves to two sets of problems highlighted by our findings: ensuring equality of opportunity for students now "locked out" by tracking, and offering—to all students—a far more fulfilling and satisfying learning process.

One approach to building greater equality of opportunity, as well as fulfillment, into existing or new secondary schools is the New Careers model. This model, which provides for fundamentally different ways of linking up educational and occupational careers, is based on the recognition that present options for entering the world of work are narrowly limited: one acquires a high school diploma and goes to work, or he first goes to college and perhaps then to a graduate or professional school. (Along the way, of course, young men must cope with the draft.)

The New Careers model provides for new options. Here the youth who does not want to attend college or would not qualify according to usual criteria, is given the opportunity to attend high school part time while working in a lower level position in an expanded professional career hierarchy (including such new positions as teacher aide and teacher associate in education). Such a person would then have the options of moving up through progressively more demanding educational and work stages; and moving back and forth between the work place, the high school and then the college. As ideally conceived, this model would allow able and aspiring persons ultimately to progress to the level of the fully certified teacher, nurse, librarian, social worker or public administrator. While the New Careers model has been developed and tried primarily in the human service sector of the economy, we have pointed out elsewhere that it is applicable to the industrial and business sector as well.

This alternative means of linking education with work has a number of advantages: students can try different occupations while still in school; they can earn while studying; they can spend more time outside the four walls of the school, learning what can best be learned in the work place; less stigma will accrue to those not immediately college bound, since they too will have a future; studying and learning will be inherently more relevant because it will relate to a career in which they are actively involved; teachers of such students will be less likely to develop lower expectations because these youth too will have an unlimited, open-ended future; and antischool subcultures will be less likely to develop, since education will not be as negative, frustrating or stigmatizing.

Changes of this kind imply changes in the economy as well and, therefore, are highly complicated and far-reaching. Because of this, they will not occur overnight. But they are possible, through persistent, creative and rigorously evaluated educational, economic and social experimentation.

Whatever the future, we hope teachers, administrators and school boards will take one important message from our findings: what they do to students makes a difference. Through the kind of teaching-learning process they create, the schools can screen out and discourage large numbers of youth, or they can develop new means for serving the interests and futures of the full range of their students.

13

Social Mobility: Multiple Hierarchy Approach

Edward Ransford

MULTIPLE HIERARCHY mobility goes beyond the traditional focus on father-son mobility in the class hierarchy. No longer is just the mobility of white males considered; the mobility of ethnic minorities, women, and the aged are also studied.

Several forms of mobility discussed in this chapter could be labeled either comparisons or combinations, according to the terminology established in chapter 2. *Comparative* mobility deals chiefly with the relative movement of entire groups in different hierarchies. An inquiry about comparative mobility might ask whether blacks or women, as aggregates, have made progress in being hired for better-paid, more prestigious occupations during the last twenty years. *Combinations* mobility focuses on mobility involving a combination of positions in different hierarchies. For example, if the mobility careers or pathways of ascent for black men, black women, white men, and white women are found to be quite distinct from one another, combinations, or the *joint effects,* of sex and race are considered.

COMPARATIVE SOCIAL MOBILITY: BLACKS, CHICANOS, WOMEN, AND THE AGED.

Among blacks, Chicanos, and women there has been an awareness of racist and of sexist inequities and an increase in stratum consciousness and stratum action. The aged have shown the beginnings of this kind of awareness with events such as the White House Conference on Aging in 1970 and the formation of a militant coalition of the young and the old (the Gray Panthers) to protest age discrimination and mandatory retirement.

An asterisk (*) accompanying a citation indicates a selection included in this volume.

One reason for studying social mobility is to assess the effects of these movements. After the dust has settled from protests, riots, legal reforms, and economic changes, one may ask whether there has been tangible progress for blacks? for Chicanos? for women? for the aged?

Here we will concentrate on comparative mobility of two sorts: comparisons that involve the changes of a group through time, and comparisons across the hierarchies. A comparative inquiry might ask not only if blacks have made occupational gains in the last fifteen years, but also whether blacks have made more or less progress than women or than Chicanos.

A. MOBILITY OF BLACKS

Although black Americans often have been associated with poverty or working-class positions, recent data show a substantial and growing black middle class. Farley (1977) suggests four factors that account for these gains. First, after World War I and in even greater numbers after World War II, blacks left the rural South and moved to urban industrial areas with their greater job opportunities. Second, since the 1950s, black demands for civil rights have increased. Third, more liberal court rulings and laws forbid discrimination in many areas of social life. And fourth, prejudiced attitudes of whites toward blacks have declined.

The emergence of a middle class from an oppressed minority group can be an extremely important development for the mobility and progress of that group as a whole. Middle-class black Americans have greater resources to fight discrimination. Middle-class blacks, in comparison with those in poverty circumstances, have greater organizational skills, political and business connections, money, and knowledge of re-dress channels—skills and resources that are vital for breaking down discrimination barriers. In the black Civil Rights Movement, for example, the most involved participants were of middle-class origins (Marx, 1967; Searles and Williams, 1962). Along this line of reasoning one study found that in cities with a more developed black middle class, there is a greater probability of electing a black mayor (Marshall and Meyer, 1975).

Middle-class resources are not always used to improve the status of an ethnic group, however. Many middle-class persons are assimilated into the mainstream, and their new skills and resources do not benefit the oppressed group to which they once belonged. One may frequently hear labels such as "bourgeois" or "Uncle Tom" applied to some successful blacks or "Tio Taco" and "Uncle Tomahawk" applied to some successful Chicanos and Indians (Steiner, 1968:250). A developing middle class within a subjugated ethnic group can either mean better resources and skills to fight discrimination or an increased tendency to assimilate into the cultural mainstream.

The potential of the middle-class segment of an ethnic group to improve the lot of the entire group depends on 1) the strength of ethnic ideologies favoring ethnic solidarity and ethnic involvement and 2) the permeability of the color line, or the ease with which middle-class ethnics can cross the color line to acquire resources and acceptance in the dominant white society.

The following hypothesis about the role of the middle class in ethnic minorities is advanced:

If a rising middle class of an oppressed ethnic minority continues to face color stigma, social exclusion, and discrimination, the rising middle-class segment will often use their resources to attempt to change the system. But if the rising middle class of an oppressed racial minority faces a greatly reduced level of color discrimination, much of the potential for protest will be splintered or drained off.

In chapter 5, for example, we noted that middle-class Chicanos face less ethnic prejudice in such areas as housing, integration, and marriage than do blacks. If the color line is more permeable for middle-class Chicanos, then we would expect less militance from them and more militance from middle-class blacks. This, of course, is an aggregate prediction referring to group probabilities. Some young Chicano individuals are entering professional schools for an expressed purpose of returning to the barrio and making available new channels of legal redress or health care to the Chicano poor. For these highly committed Chicanos, the ideology of their ethnic group would seem to override the possibility of assimilation based on their middle-class status.

Besides the possibility of middle-class skills aiding the group as a whole, there is another important reason to study the growth of the black middle class. Recent accounts on the size of an emerging black middle class may have led to a belief on the part of whites that racial discrimination no longer exists. For example, Wattenberg and Scammon (1973) claim that as of 1970, fully 52 percent of all blacks were in middle-class positions. One can only come to this sort of conclusion by using very low cutting points for "middle-class," such as a family income of $8,000 or higher. But such methodological details usually are not stressed in these reports. An *image* of a fairly large "new" black middle class has been created and whites, as a result, may no longer see a need for special programs for black Americans. "On the contrary, increasing numbers of whites are charging 'reverse discrimination' and are strongly resisting the use of their tax dollars for social programs on behalf of the poor and minorities" (Hill, 1978:1). If many of the accounts on the size of the black middle class are inflated or exaggerated, then it is important to study more carefully the size of this group 1) using a variety of measures and cutting points and 2) noting which segments of the black population have made gains, and which segments have not. This we propose to do in the following pages.

Proportion of Blacks in the Middle Class

Income.   A variety of data from the 1970 census and reports from 1971–1978 samples present evidence for a growing middle class in the black population, particularly outside the South. Although the 1974 median family income for blacks was only $7,808 (compared to the white median of $13,356), 38 percent of all black families earned more than $10,000. In the early 1970s, earning more than $10,000 was often considered the bottom line for middle-class status. By this criterion, about four out of ten black families in the nation were earning a middle income (Bureau of the Census, Series P–23, No. 54). But it can be argued that $10,000 is too low a cutting point. An income near $10,000 for a family of four or more does not stretch very far in the inflationary 1970s. More than $15,000 would seem to be a more solid definition of middle income. In 1974, 19 percent of black families in the nation were making more than $15,000; only

13 percent of black families were making this amount in the South but a much larger 26 percent of families in the North and West were in this category.

What about mobility? Has the middle-income group changed through time? Adjusting for price changes, there has been a definite increase in the black middle class between 1965 and 1974. The proportion of black families in the North and West making more than $15,000 increased from 14 percent in 1965 to 24 percent in 1970 to 26 percent in 1974.

Using a family income of more than $15,000 as a criterion of middle-class status, about one out of five black families in the nation are in the middle income (or higher) category, whereas one out of four black families in the North or West are earning this amount. This is a far cry from Wattenberg and Scammon's statement that 52 percent of all black families are in the middle class. A moderate size black middle-income group exists and appears to be growing rapidly.

The Income Gap.   Recent data show that there has been a slight closing of the income gap when black families as a whole are compared with white families as a whole. In 1947, the average black family income amounted to only 51 percent of the average white family income. By 1975, the gap was 62 percent (Farley, 1977:198). Although the income gap has lessened somewhat through time, the average black family income still is only 62 percent of the average white family income.

There are, however, great variations in the black-white income gap according to region of the country, age of the respondents, and whether one or both spouses worked. If one locates certain subgroups within the general black and white populations, the income gap between black and white is much smaller. In 1970, the income gap was virtually nil between young white and young black families outside the South. ''For these young families, the ratio of Negro to white income was about 96% in 1970, up from 78% in 1959'' (Bureau of Census, Series P–23, no. 39:1–8). However, the income parity among young white and black families outside the South holds true only for families in which both husband and wife worked. Young black families in which *just the husband worked* were making about 75 percent of the income of comparable white families. Consideration of black working wives is crucial for the interpretation of the income parity findings. Young black wives in the North and West earned approximately 30 percent more than their white counterparts; one explanation offered for this differential was that young black wives were more likely to hold a job year round (52 percent of the black wives versus 36 percent of the white wives). For the first time in American history, then, one segment of the black population is earning the same income as a comparable segment of the white population. This segment, however, is very small; young black husband-wife families outside the South accounted for only about 10 percent of all black families in the United States.

Occupation.   Besides income, occupation is a major index of social class. Many would consider it a superior measure to income since it taps economic standing, prestige, and authority over others. The data in Table 13–1 show that substantial differences continue to exist between blacks and whites in the types of occupational positions they hold. About 36 percent of employed blacks are engaged in the most physically exhausting, poorly paid, and least prestigious jobs—service, private household, farm, and

Table 13-1.   *Occupational Distribution of Whites and Blacks, 1977*

	Blacks	Whites
Professional	11.8%	15.5%
Managers and administrators	4.8	11.4
Sales workers	2.6	6.8
Clerical	16.1	18
Craftsmen and foremen	9	13.6
Operatives	20.3	14.7
Laborers	8.3	4.6
Farmers and farmworkers	2.2	3.1
Service (excluding private household)	20.8	11.4
Private household workers	4.2	.9

Source: U.S. Dept. of Labor. Bureau of Labor Statistics, *Employment and Unemployment Trends During 1977.* Special Labor Force Report 211: p. A20.

laboring jobs—almost double the 20 percent for whites. On the other hand, from the perspective of a rising middle class, it can be seen that about 35 percent of all employed blacks are in white collar occupations and another 9 percent in the most challenging and rewarding blue-collar jobs (craftsman and foreman). Forty-four percent of employed blacks, then, are in skilled and white-collar occupations.

Skilled blue-collar and most white-collar jobs provide at least a moderate degree of challenge, financial reward, and status in society. Blacks have made considerable gains in moving into white-collar occupations. A comparison of 1960 and 1977 census data shows the proportion of blacks with white-collar jobs more than doubled in this 17 year time period, from 16 percent to 35 percent.

However, when considering white-collar statistics among minority persons, one should separate data for males and females because data often include many black female clerical workers who have low salaries, little authority over others, and limited opportunities for advancement. For the nation, the 35 percent of blacks in white-collar jobs drops to 26 percent when only black males are considered. Findings on the size of the white-collar stratum, then, are not quite as striking when only black males are considered.

Although the category "white collar occupation" is commonly used, it may be a poor indicator of middle-class status because it includes clerical jobs and excludes craftsmen and foremen with relatively high pay and authority over others. An alternative way to categorize middle-class occupations is to combine the better paying, more prestigious white-collar jobs, such as professional, managerial, and sales (but not clerical), with craftsman-foreman blue-collar jobs. One-third (34 percent) of employed black males are in middle-class occupations by this definition. Twenty-one percent of employed black females are in middle-class occupations when the lowest paid clerical jobs are removed from the white collar category (1977).

The occupation index results in a larger estimate of the size of the black middle class (one-third middle class) compared to the family income index (one-fifth middle class). One reason for this discrepancy is that the occupation data involve only employed persons, whereas the income data include families with very low incomes due to unemployment.

Elected Black Officials. The increase in the number of elected officials can be used as a rough index of an increase in power or influence for a minority group. Beginning in the mid-1960s, there was a tremendous surge in the number of blacks elected to office. In 1975, 3,503 blacks held public office, a very large increase (88 percent) over the 1971 figure of 1,860. In 1975, there were 135 black mayors in the nation, a 67 percent increase from the 81 mayors in 1971. Eleven large metropolitan cities now have black mayors, though more typically, blacks are elected mayors in smaller communities in which the black population is at least 50 percent of the total. There also has been a noticeable increase of black state legislators and executives. In 1964 there were ninety-four state legislators and executives compared to the 1975 figure of 281, a *199 percent* increase (Bureau of Census, Series P–23:No. 54).

The Division in Black America

The data summarized above suggest that a moderate-size middle class and upper-working class group has developed in the black population and is likely to show continued growth in the future. However, a number of recent studies indicate that not all blacks are making progress; one segment of the black population has moved up while another segment has made no gains or has moved down. Many reports present data only for the *total* black population and thus mask these counter-trends.

The downward trend is exemplified by black unemployment rates that have increased in recent years. Usually the black unemployment rate is about twice as high as the white rate. In 1975, the jobless rate for blacks was 1.7 times higher than for whites; but the unemployment rate for blacks increased to 2.3 times higher than for whites in the first half of 1978. This is the largest gap ever recorded in Bureau of Labor statistics (Hill, 1978:14). The trend of an increasing unemployment gap between blacks and whites held true for all subgroups of workers (young, old, male, female). The gap was especially pronounced among black and white teenagers. In 1975, the jobless rate for black teenage males was twice as great as for white teenage males. By 1977, the gap had increased to 2.3 and by 1978, 2.7. This means that in 1978, 37 percent of black teenage males were unemployed compared to 14 percent of white teenage males. This increase in unemployment may be due to a combination of the economic recession of the mid-1970s, the cut-back in poverty and job training funds, and the elimination of certain jobs in efforts to control inflation.

Though the unemployment data show an increase in racial inequality, statistics dealing with the *earnings* of employed persons reveal a trend of greater equality. "In 1969 the (median) earnings of all black workers were 62 percent of the earnings of all white workers. But by 1975, black workers' earnings were three-fourths of white workers'" (Hill, 1978:15).

Given evidence for both gains and losses, what are the social characteristics of those blacks moving up or down? Moynihan (1972) argues that the "schism in black

America" results in part from the black family structure. Blacks living in female-headed families did not make substantial gains in the 1960s, whereas two-parent families did. Blacks under thirty-five years old living in the North or West were far more likely to make gains than middle-aged and older blacks living in the South. Education is highly linked with the up-down pattern. Blacks with any college experience (even one year) made gains in income in recent years as contrasted with the small or non-existent gains made by those with no more than a high school education. In sum, one segment of the black population has made substantial gains in the last fifteen years; another segment has made no gains and remains firmly entrenched in poverty.

The counter-trends in black mobility can be used to support opposite political views. Those arguing that special programs are no longer necessary for blacks can stress the "up" side of the mobility story, while those arguing for new programs to combat the unemployment, hopelessness and despair in inner city areas can stress the "down" side of the trends. Social planners should fully consider these data and not let the rising middle class create an illusion of overall black progress (Hill, 1978).

B. MEXICAN-AMERICAN MOBILITY

Although much data relevant to the mobility patterns of black Americans exists, it is much more difficult to note the progress of Mexican-Americans up or down the class structure in recent decades. The biggest obstacle for the sociologist is the U.S. Census Bureau classification of Mexican-Americans, which has varied with each ten-year census. At first, Mexican-Americans were classified as Caucasians and in no way distinguished from the white population. In 1960, "Spanish surname" was the term used to encompass Mexican-Americans as well as all other Latinos. In 1970, the even broader category "Spanish language/Spanish surname" was used. Only in the most recent census reports (based on 1975–1976 samples) are persons of Mexican origin separated from Cubans, Puerto Ricans, and other Spanish-speaking groups. Because of this diversity of classification, it is impossible to make systematic comparisons through time. We will have to settle for a much less precise overview involving some quantitative data and more general historical and qualitative summaries from several Mexican-American scholars.

From Rural Farm Workers to an Urban Working Class

Mexican-Americans are often depicted as rural, migratory farm laborers. This stereotype of the Mexican-American has probably been reinforced by the widely publicized grape and lettuce boycotts led by the United Farm Workers and Cesar Chavez. Although migratory farm laborers are an extremely important population, especially when considering issues of justice and ethnic solidarity, they are a minority of Mexican-Americans. Most Mexican-Americans are concentrated in urban areas and employed in urban occupations.

The 1970 census shows that nine-tenths of California's "Spanish surname" populations lived in urban areas. The typical occupation of Mexican-Americans is a blue-collar semi-skilled or skilled job in an urban setting, not migratory farm labor. This does

not mean that all discrimination battles have been won, for as Penalosa explains
". . . to assert that Mexican-Americans have largely left behind the problems associated
with migratory agricultural labor is not to say that they have no problems. It is rather
that now their problems have become those of an underprivileged urban minority
group" (Penalosa, 1971:327).

As was true of the black American experience, World War II brought a dramatic
shift from rural to urban occupations for Mexican Americans. During World War II,
young Mexican-Americans gained new skills in the military and in war-production
plants, skills which they transferred to urban industrial jobs when the war ended
(Alvarez,* 1973). World War II also served to highlight the unequal status of Mexican
Americans, who fought and gave their lives in defense of the United States, yet continued to face discrimination as returning civilians.

In urban industrial environments there is typically an emphasis on skill, merit,
and rational efficiency rather than family lineage or race. The rigidity of caste barriers
declines and there are more opportunities for employment. The large-scale migration to
urban industrial areas meant that the Mexican-American population was changing from
a lower ethnic caste to a lower-class group.

Geographical mobility is as important as class mobility when discussing Mexican-
Americans. To move from South Texas to Los Angeles is to change dramatically one's
style of life and life chances (Moore, 1970). South Texas is an area where Mexicans have
always faced the most consistent and rigid racial barriers. In contrast, California (particularly Southern California) is a relatively open society with a larger working and middle
class, a lower degree of traditional Mexican folk-culture, a more highly rationalized economic system, and a more permeable color line for upwardly mobile Chicanos. This
characterization of California, however, must be balanced with the realities of the urban
barrio of East Los Angeles, where one finds a high degree of poverty, tense police-com-
munity relations, and an educational system that fails to educate large numbers of
Chicano children.

The Size of the Mexican-American Middle Class
Compared with the Size of the Black Middle Class

The median income of Mexican American families in 1974 was $9,498 compared
to the median income of white families, which was $13,356 (Bureau of Census, P–20:
No. 290). Forty-seven percent of Mexican American families earned more than $10,000
in 1974 and 20 percent earned more than $15,000 in that year. The median income and
percentages are similar to or greater than that of blacks. (As mentioned earlier, median
black income was $7,808 in 1974; and 19 percent of black families were making more
than $15,000 in 1974.)

Relative sizes and composition of families must be considered in interpreting these
data. Some have suggested that because Mexican-American families are more likely to
remain intact and to have extended family members living together for a long period of
time, they have more potential wage earners than black or, for that matter, Anglo families. The higher median family income of Chicanos, compared to blacks, is probably
caused by the fact that many Chicano families have two or more wage earners.

Occupational data reveal that blacks are represented in higher level occupations than Mexican-Americans. For example, the proportion of black males in professional jobs is about double the proportion of Chicano males in these occupations (see Table 13–2). Also, the proportion of black females in top white-collar positions (professional and managerial) is far higher than the percentage of Mexican-American females in these positions. (These differences are discussed in more detail in Section C of this chapter.)

Using the previously explained occupational index of middle class (professional, managerial, sales, and craftsmen-foremen), about 32 percent of Chicano males are in middle-class occupations versus a slightly higher 34 percent of black males.

The education data reveal the greatest discrepancy between the position of Mexican Americans and blacks in American society. The minimum education required for better paying, more interesting, and more prestigious occupations is completion of high school and at least some college. Table 13–3 shows that higher proportions of young blacks than young Chicanos are high school graduates and have attended college. Only 56 percent of young Chicanos and 59 percent of young Chicanas completed high school. This means that 44 percent of Chicanos and 41 percent of Chicanas are high school dropouts.

Another way to compare Chicanos and blacks is in terms of the number of persons who have earned a Ph.D. degree. The number of Ph.D.'s in a population reflects the degree to which ethnic members have entered the most scientific, technological segments of industrial society. "Comparatively . . . out of a population of twenty-four million there are 2,200 black persons who have earned Ph.D. degrees in all disciplines

Table 13-2.   *Occupations of Mexican-Origin Males, Compared with Occupations of Black Males*

	Mexican American* Males (1976)	Black Males** (1977)
Total white-collar workers	18%	27%
Professional	5.5	10
Managerial	5.6	6
Sales	2	3
Clerical	5	8
Craft	19	15.5
Operatives	29	24
Non-farm laborers	14	14
Service workers	11	16
Farm workers	8	3

Source: U.S. Bureau of Census, *Current Population Reports,* Series P–20, No. 302:10.
**Source:*   U.S. Department of Labor, Bureau of Labor Statistics, Employment and Unemployment Trends During 1977. Special Labor Force Report 212.

Table 13–3. *Educational Attainment of Blacks and Mexican-Americans 20–24 years old (1975), by Sex*

	Black		Mexican-American	
	Male	Female	Male	Female
Completion of high school	72%	75%	56%	59%
One or more years of college	27	29	19	20
College graduate*	9	8	8	5.5

*The percentages for college graduates are calculated for those 25–34 years old.
Source: U.S. Bureau of Census, Series P–20, No. 290:24; Series P–23, No. 54:97.

combined. Among the eight million (approximately) Mexican-Americans there are only 60 who have earned Ph.D. degrees when a similar level of disadvantage would lead us to expect approximately 730'' (Alvarez, 1973:939).

The Chicano Generation.   Alvarez* (1973) speaks of the Chicano generation as the group of Mexican-Americans who were reaching draftable age at the time of the Vietnam War. The majority are sons and daughters of urban working-class parents. Compared with earlier generations of Mexican-Americans, they are more affluent and have the highest aspirations. Middle-class status, however, is escaping them. Although they have achieved higher levels of education than their parents, the occupational structure of the larger society has become so technical, bureaucratized, and professionalized, young Chicanos are being excluded from middle-class positions. Many have been eliminated from entrance into a good four-year college because their barrio high school education is so inferior compared to the education in middle-class Anglo schools. Chicanos also lack the credentials for middle-class status because they have not had separate institutions for higher learning. There are more than 100 black colleges and universities, and although some people question the quality of separate institutions, black colleges have played an important role in certifying large numbers of blacks for middle-class positions.

Large corporations are interested, for the first time, in hiring Spanish-surname persons in order to meet federal Affirmative Action regulations. Chicanos, however, often lack the credentials for obtaining such jobs. "The irony is that as discrimination disappears or is minimized those who have historically suffered most from it continue to suffer its after-effects" (Alvarez, 1973:941). Another circumstance militating against the development of a Chicano middle class is the emigration of technically skilled and educated middle-class persons from Latin American countries to the United States, who are lured by the higher pay of United States corporations. This threatens further to displace opportunities for young Chicanos because United States corporations can meet federal demands by hiring *any* Spanish-surname person. Alvarez concludes that there are substantial barriers for many Chicanos and there is not likely to be a dramatic growth of a middle-class sector in the immediate future.

SUMMARY: MOBILITY OF BLACKS
AND CHICANOS

Solid data show that blacks have made progress in bettering their occupation, education, and income in the last ten to fifteen years. The proportion of blacks in white-collar and craft positions has increased; and when the best paying (excluding clerical) white-collar and craft positions are combined, one-third can be found to hold middle-class positions in the late 1970s. However, a large differential remains between types of employment—one-half of whites are in top white collar or craft positions.

The income of black families has also increased through time. Between 19 and 38 percent of black families were in middle-income positions in 1974, depending on whether one uses the ''over $10,000'' or ''over $15,000'' cutting point. Black family income in the North and West is far higher than in the South. The families showing the greatest gains are young black families in the North and West with two working spouses. The income of these families is now equal to comparable young white families.

Although hard data are lacking, there is some evidence for a growing skilled and white-collar stratum among Mexican-Americans. This has occurred especially since World War II and since Mexican-Americans have become highly urbanized. Chicanos are employed in skilled and white-collar positions in about the same proportion as blacks. However, Chicano males are less likely to be in professional occupations and, as we shall see in the next section on women, Chicanas are *far* less likely to be in upper white-collar positions compared with black females.

A substantially smaller percentage of Chicanos have finished high school or have attended college than blacks. The number of Chicano Ph.D.'s is far fewer than black Ph.D.'s controlling for differences in the size of the two groups.

We could find no comparative data on Chicano versus black elected officials, but simple observation would suggest that there are very few Chicanos elected as senators, mayors, and members of state legislatures. Keeping in mind that the United States population includes about 6 percent Mexican Americans and 12 percent blacks, one might expect that half as many Chicanos would be elected as blacks. This is not the case. In sum, although there have been sweeping changes in the Chicano population since World War II, it appears that blacks have a more developed and influential middle class.

Further Meanings of the Rising Middle Class.

Statistics that show a developing middle class among blacks and Chicanos must be carefully interpreted. They do not mean that society now is as open for the conquered minorities as for the population as a whole. Chicanos and blacks still face many ethnic barriers and must expend more effort to overcome these barriers than their white counterparts. For example:

- Chicano and black families often achieve their middle-class incomes only when both husband and wife work full time, year round. They make the same income as a white family in which only the husband works full time. In short, black and Chicano middle income families often have to invest a much greater household input of time and effort to get the same economic outputs as white middle-class families.

- Recent data suggest that blacks in white-collar positions in organizations are less likely to be promoted into positions of high authority (Kluegel, 1978). Accounting for experience, education and skill, blacks continue to face racial barriers in reaching positions such as manager and district supervisor.
- Black and Chicano professionals entering private practice (medical doctors, veterinarians, dentists and lawyers) are forced into a segregated marketplace with a smaller and poorer clientele from which to draw. The black professional in private practice is missing the more lucrative market place from which the white professional benefits.
- Middle-income blacks often live on the periphery of inner city ghettos. In such areas families have difficulty in converting their middle incomes into the same privileges that the white middle class automatically enjoy. Many "peripheral" neighborhoods have higher crime rates, more police stop-and-search contacts, poorer schools, and economic zone changes (more liquor stores and motels) that detract from the beauty and economic stability of the neighborhood.

C. THE SOCIAL MOBILITY OF WOMEN

Unique features must be considered in the case of female mobility. The tremendous increase in the number of women in the labor force in itself represents a kind of massive movement or mobility that greatly effects household income or mobility of whole families. In 1974, working women represented 46 percent of all women 16 years old and over, a considerable increase from the 1950 participation rate of 34 percent (Bureau of Census, Series P–23, No. 58). The substantial increase in the proportion of women workers included many married women. By contrast, Waldman describes the typical working woman of fifty years ago as single, in her late twenties and from the working class:

> The young woman who entered the work force seldom had any intention of remaining long. As soon as "Mr. Right" came along she handed in her resignation, put the finishing touches on her hope chest, and made her plans for the wedding. After the honeymoon she settled down to devote her life to the physical, intellectual, and spiritual needs of her family. Only the tragedy of penniless widowhood or a broken marriage could drive her back into the labor market. The woman who did not marry was apt to be an object of pity (Peterson, as quoted in Waldman, 1972:31).

In the 1970s, the picture of women in the labor force is very different. Single women no longer predominate; in fact, married women outnumber all other groups of working women. Moreover, a greater proportion of women remain in the labor force for longer periods. It is true that a large proportion of women from the ages of thirty-five to fifty-four enter the labor force for the first time as their children leave home and their home-making responsibilities lessen, but it is also true that an increasing proportion of young women with preschool-age children are now entering the labor force. "The labor force rate for women with children under 6 years was only about 12 percent in 1950, but in 1975 this rate had tripled to about 37 percent" (Bureau of Census, Series P–23, No. 58:26).

Of major significance to a discussion of social mobility is the fact that many women make a crucial contribution to the economic mobility of the whole family unit. The woman's income often makes the difference between poverty or nonpoverty standards of living or, at higher levels, the difference between middle-class privileges or not. Many families can only afford privileges such as a college education for all their children, owning their own home, or purchasing a second car, if the wife contributes to the household income. To "get ahead" is increasingly being defined by many couples as possible only with two full-time working spouses.

Sex-Stereotyped Occupations.   Although more women are entering the labor force than ever before, most women continue to enter highly sex-stereotyped occupations, such as clerical work, elementary school teaching, nursing, and semi-skilled factory work. In general, women's jobs continue to involve three major characteristics: 1) they are jobs that have an early ceiling in pay and promotion; 2) they are jobs in which women are helpers or assistants to men; and 3) they are jobs in which women take orders from men and do not themselves originate orders or make policies. Although there has been a general decrease in manual occupations and a concomitant increase in white-collar and technical jobs, women have entered at the lowest rung of the white-collar hierarchy.

To capture fully the concept of women's mobility through time, three different measures must be used. First, we need a measure that is sensitive to the dispersion of women into a wide variety of occupations; that is, a measure that indicates the degree to which women have broken out of sex-stereotyped occupations. Second, we need to note whether women have increased their numbers in the better-paying, more prestigious, white-collar occupations. Third, we need to know if the income differential between men's and women's earnings has lessened through time.

Are Women Less Concentrated in Sex-Stereotyped Occupations?   The concentration of women in sex-stereotyped occupations has sometimes been likened to occupational "caste." Women have been unable to move out of female-linked jobs. A *caste score* is used to measure the dispersal (or nondispersal) of women across a wide variety of jobs. A recent study employing a caste index found virtually no change between 1940 and 1970 in women's mobility out of occupational castes (Szymanski, 1974). Szymanski also presents caste data for blacks through the same time period and finds that here there has been significant movement out of race-linked occupations for both black males and black females. Blacks are finding opportunities for jobs other than those of laborer, porter, postal employee, domestic worker. "While the caste-like barriers between the races have very significantly lessened in the last 30 years, those between the sexes have been maintained" (Szymanski, 1974:719:20).

It is important to update Szymanski's conclusion. Common observation suggests that small numbers of women are moving into male-dominated occupations. Almost daily, one reads of women in territories that have been considered exclusively male, occupations such as Episcopal priest, architect, construction worker, sheriff, telephone worker, mayor, and state supreme court justice: These cases are extremely important, even though few in number, because they illustrate that the opportunity to move out of sex-linked occupations exists. It probably will be some time before this trend shows up in census data because the small number of women moving into such positions is overwhelmed by the much higher proportions acquiring clerical and other sex-stereotyped jobs.

Women in White-Collar Occupations. To what extent have women increased their proportions in upper white-collar occupations such as professional and managerial jobs? Table 13–4 shows that white females have made only slight gains from 1965 to 1974 in securing upper white-collar jobs. Changes for black women are much more pronounced, however. Although trend comparisons for Mexican-American women are not possible with the 1974 data alone, it is instructive to note that Mexican-American women are much less likely to be in upper white-collar positions than either black or Anglo women. In 1974, only about 6 percent of working Mexican-American women were in professional or managerial jobs compared with 14 percent of black working women and 21 percent of white working women. Conversely, Chicanas are far more likely to be represented in the "operatives" category, which usually refers to poorly paid factory assembly work.

In sum, white woman have made very few aggregate gains between 1965 and 1974; black women have made more pronounced gains (that is, they have come much closer to the position of white women) and Mexican-American women have not had the same success in securing white-collar jobs as black or white women.

Other data show the beginning of a trend of women entering higher political positions. A statistical portrait of women reveals that the number of female candidates for public office has increased (Bureau of Census, Series P–23, No. 58, 1976). The number of women candidates for governor increased from zero in 1972 to three in 1974; for state

Table 13–4. *Employed Women by Occupation: 1965, 1970, and 1974*

	1974			1970		1965	
	White	*Black*	*Mexican-American*	*White*	*Black*	*White*	*Black*
Professional	15.4	11.7	4.5	15	10.8	13.9	8.5
Managers	5.3	2.4	1.6	4.8	1.9	4.9	1.6
Sales	7.4	2.7	4.0	7.7	2.5	8.3	2
Clerical	36.4	24.9	27.5	36.4	20.8	34.7	11.8
Craft	1.6	1.4	1.6	1.2	.8	1.1	.7
Operatives	12.3	17.2	29.3	14.2	17.6	15.3	14.5
Nonfarm labor	1	1.2	1.2	.4	.7	.4	.7
Farm workers	1.5	1.1	4.2	1.8	1.7	2.7	5.5
Service workers	19.2	37.3	26.1	18.7	43.1	18.6	54.8

Source: Adapted from Tables 14–7 and 13–16, U.S. Bureau of Census, *Current Population Reports.* Special Studies, Series P–23, No. 58, "A Statistical Portrait of Women in the U.S."

house of representatives the number of female candidates increased from 741 in 1972 to 989 in 1974. And the number of women seeking state senate positions increased from 101 to 137 in the same period. With respect to *elected* female officials, there was an increase from 441 to 596 (a 35 percent increase) in state legislature positions. There also has been an increase in the proportion of female lawyers. In 1960, only 3.5 percent of all lawyers were women; by 1973, the percentage had risen to 16 (*New York Law Journal,* 1974:1–4).

Female-Male Income Differentials.   The gap between male and female incomes is sizable. In 1974, the median income of full-time, working women was a low $6,772 compared to the male median income of $11,835. Women, on the average, earned only 57 percent of what men earned. In 1970, women earned 59 percent of what men earned; in 1960 they earned 61 percent. The earnings of females relative to males have actually declined through this period.

The income differential between women and men is partly explained by differences in educational attainment, occupation, and work experience. But even when these factors are held constant, a sizable difference remains between male and female earnings. "In both 1970 and 1974 . . . the median income of women college graduates aged 25 and over who worked year-round full time was only about 60 percent of the comparable male median income. In fact, women college graduates had incomes that were, on the average, lower than men with only a high school education" (Bureau of Census, Series P–23, No. 58:45). Even when one holds constant certain occupations that require very high educational attainment and training, an income differential between the sexes still exists. Full-time female engineers, for example, had a median salary of $15,600 in 1974 compared with male engineers whose median salary was $19,500.

Social Mobility through Marriage.   This discussion has dealt with the mobility of women in the labor force. But for the approximate 50 percent of women who are *not* in the labor force, traditional measures of social class position are based on the occupation of the father or the husband of the woman. Women's mobility, then, may be measured either through their own jobs or through their marriages.

> Marriage provides a second kind of occupational achievement for women. The girl whose social position is a reflection of the status of her father grows into the woman, who through her choice of a marital partner, can be ranked as the female half of a couple whose "head" does X in his work (Tyree and Treas, 1974:297).

How does women's marital mobility compare with men's occupational mobility? Women have greater mobility through marriage—both upward and downward—than men do through occupational mobility (Chase, 1975). Further, women are much more likely to cross the boundaries among the major status groupings such as blue-collar and white-collar. The fact that women are more mobile by marriage than men are by occupation is an interesting fact that has wide implications. It indicates that there is more fluidity in the American class structure than was formerly believed when only male data was considered.

There are probably a number of reasons why women are more mobile through marriage than men are through occupations. One interpretation likely to raise the ire of feminists is suggested by Chase (1975). He argues that "some of the endowments and skills such as beauty, good grooming and 'charm' which make women desirable to potential husbands of high status are found in women of low origin status" (Chase, 1975:503). In other words, these resources are probably more randomly distributed throughout the class structure and less tied to status origins. Attributes of physical attractiveness are found among women of both upper- and lower-class origins. In partial support of this hypothesis, Elder (1969) reports that physical attractiveness and good grooming are correlated with female upward mobility. Men, in contrast, depend on attributes for occupational mobility that are tied tightly to their class origins. The resources that men need to move up in occupational status—apprenticeship, money for training, personal contacts—are closely related to their father's position in the class structure. Remember from earlier discussions, that men usually do not move more than one or two occupational steps above or below their father's. Women's mobility by marriage is not so restricted.†

Women are also more likely to be downwardly mobile than men. More women than men move downward across the line dividing manual and non-manual labor (Glenn, et al., 1974). This finding also has far-reaching implications for the interpretation of the overall class structure. The downward mobility of women into blue-collar ranks, for example, would provide a large proportion of working-class offspring with mothers of middle-class origins. Glenn notes that this could inhibit working-class consciousness, decrease blue-collar-white-collar attitudinal differences, and instill aspirations for mobility in working-class daughters and sons (Glenn, et al., 1974:698).

In sum, the marital mobility studies of women point to:

1. A greater overall openness in the class structure. That is, larger numbers of persons are moving up and down than was formerly believed.
2. Downwardly mobile women may provide encouragement to achieve for their working-class sons and daughters.

SUMMARY: MOBILITY OF WOMEN

There has been a dramatic increase in the proportion of women entering the labor force, including women with preschool-age children. Most women continue to enter highly sex-linked occupations, such as clerical work. Group data up to 1974 show no reduction in the concentration of women in certain occupations and no closing of the income gap between men and women. The only encouraging data relate to the greater numbers of black women in professional white-collar positions, and the fact that women as a whole are being elected to public office in greater numbers.

†Note: If women are marrying men of statuses different from their own, then those same men have married women of different class statuses. No one has studied statistically the marital mobility of men. This one-sided concern with women's marital mobility is, in itself, an example of sex stratification.

Turning to the question of comparative mobility across the ascribed hierarchies of ethnicity and sex, we would say that the position of blacks compared to whites has improved significantly while the position of women compared to men has not. In other words, the group mobility of blacks has been greater than the group mobility of women.

MOBILITY TRENDS OF THE AGED

There have been very few studies of changes in the relative status of the aged. One by Palmore and Whittington (1971) cited very discouraging findings on the downward mobility of the aged. Using a variety of measures such as income and health, these researchers concluded that the quality of life for the aged was worse in 1960 than in 1940. The latest census reports are slightly more optimistic, showing a turn-around in the downward mobility of the aged. Still, there remains a great deal of inequality by age.

Income and Age.   Families with heads of household aged sixty-five and over have low incomes compared with all other families. In 1974, the median income of families with heads of household over sixty-five years old was $7,298, compared with the median income for all families of $12,836. In other terms, aged families, on the average, earned (or received in income) only 57 percent of what non-aged families earned.

Of course, these data average all aged families. Black aged families have far lower incomes than white aged families. The white-black income gap has not changed appreciably through time. In 1974, the median income for black aged families was only $4,909 compared to the white median of $7,519 (Bureau of Census, Series P–23, No. 59).

A more realistic view of the relative income status between the aged and non-aged is found by adjusting the income data by the number of persons in the family. Consideration of ''per person'' income for the aged more accurately reflects income status, since the typical aged family does not have as many members as the non-aged family. A comparison of the ''per person'' income for families with heads of household over sixty-five versus per person income for all families reveals a much more favorable position for elderly families. With the adjusted data, the median family income of the aged was 82 percent of that of the non-aged in 1974. Though aged families as a whole appear to be in better shape with the per person correction, this adjustment of family-income data actually increases the gap between the income of aged whites and aged blacks. The income of elderly black families is only one-half as much as the income for elderly families of all races.

To what extent have the aged made gains through time? For elderly families in general there has been some closing of the income gap between 1970 and 1974. The 82 percent income gap between aged and non-aged families is an improvement over the 1970 gap of 77 percent. However, the gap between the white aged and the black aged has not varied between 1970 and 1974. At both times, the black aged were making about 50 percent of what the white aged were making.

The proportion of aged people living in poverty is another index of the relative position of the aged in society. Here the outlook is brighter, at least from the standpoint of mobility. The proportion of the elderly population below the poverty level fell sharply in the fifteen years between 1959 and 1974. In 1974, 16 percent of elderly persons were classified as poor as compared with 35 percent in 1959; for elderly families, the proportion fell from 27 percent in 1959 to 8.5 percent in 1974. Data on elderly blacks also show progress, though there remains a very high percent at the poverty level. Considering all black persons over 65, an incredible 62 percent were living in poverty in 1959 versus 36 percent in 1974 (Bureau of Census, Series P-23, No. 59).

Labor-Force Participation. Although most people retire at age sixty-five, some continue to work part time or even full time. Labor-force participation for elderly men has dropped rapidly during the last twenty-five years, however. In 1950, almost half of all men over sixty-five (46 percent) were in the labor force; by 1960 only 33 percent were working, and in 1975 only 22 percent were in the labor force. If present retirement trends continue, the Bureau of Census estimates that only 16.8 percent of men over sixty-five will be employed by 1990 (Bureau of Census, Series P-23, No. 59). This sharp decrease in employment among men over sixty-five years old can be judged as social progress or as an unnecessary restriction, depending on one's interpretation of why the phenomenon is occuring. For those opposed to mandatory retirement, these statistics suggest an increased tendency of American society to define its older members as non-productive "over-the-hill" citizens by forcing them out of the labor market. Others may interpret the trend of reduced employment of men over sixty-five as reflecting that more men are choosing to retire because they have been given the opportunity to do so with improved pension plans.

Another indicator of socioeconomic position of the aged is educational attainment. Education is related to communication skills, awareness of issues, and participation in the political process. If larger numbers of persons entering the over-sixty-five-stratum have greater educational attainment, then there is an increased potential for a politically active age stratum. The educational attainment of people over sixty-five is considerably below that of adults in general, but the gap has narrowed in the 1970s. For example, in 1952 only 18 percent of persons sixty-five years and older had completed high school (versus 38 percent of those twenty-five to sixty-four years old). By contrast, 1975 statistics show that 35 percent of the aged were high school graduates versus 63 percent of those twenty-five to sixty-four. The aged compared to the non-aged have made relative gains. A ratio or gap of .99 would mean almost equal high school attainment between aged and non-aged; the high school graduation ratio between these groups was .48 in 1952, .56 in 1975 and is estimated to be .67 in 1990 (Bureau of Census, Series P-23, No. 59).

SUMMARY: MOBILITY OF THE AGED

Four important conclusions emerge from data on the mobility of the aged:

1. Median family-income statistics—when adjusted by per person income—show that the income of aged families is about 82 percent of the income of non-aged families. There was a narrowing of the gap between 1970 and 1974 (from .76 to .82). The median family income of aged blacks is only half as much as the median family income of aged whites.

2. The proportion of aged persons living in poverty declined sharply from 35 percent in 1959 to 16 percent in 1974. The proportion of aged blacks living in poverty also showed a sharp decline, from 62 percent in 1959 to 36 percent in 1974, although this still represents more than double the number of whites living in poverty.

3. Statistics on labor-force participation show a drastic decline in the proportion of employed men over sixty-five.

4. The educational attainment of the aged is very slowly coming closer to the attainment of the non-aged, suggesting that there will be a more politically aware and politically active group in the future.

Overall, this summary leaves the reader with a sense of optimism and relief that the aged are not suffering as badly as mass media reports would indicate. However, it should be kept in mind that a median income of $7,298 for aged families means that 50 percent of aged families are subsisting on less the $7,000 a year. For people living on fixed incomes in inflationary times, what appears to be encouraging on paper, according to Census Bureau categories of ''above poverty'' may, in reality, represent a high proportion of elderly citizens eking out a bare subsistence standard of living.

COMBINATIONS MOBILITY

The aggregate mobility of blacks, Chicanos, women, and the aged was discussed in the last section. This section focuses on social mobility that involves a combination of positions in stratification hierarchies. The following discussion describes four types of combinations mobility. The first three are new conceptualizations that have not been widely discussed in the literature.

The Juncture of Occupational Mobility and Sex or Ethnicity: Reversals in Authority

If women move into positions in which some of their subordinates are men or, similarly, if blacks move into positions in which some of their subordinates are whites, then upward mobility represents far more than a simple increase in occupational prestige or income—a combination of class and sex mobility (or class and ethnic mobility) is involved.

In previous chapters, we noted than an unequal distribution of power is at the core of all stratification systems. This can be seen clearly in the distribution of authority by race and by sex within occupations. Traditionally, blacks, Chicanos, and American Indians have been in positions clearly subordinate to whites. Rarely are minority persons in occupations in which they give orders to white subordinates. Women are also disproportionately concentrated in occupations like clerical work, elementary school teaching, and nursing, in which they give orders to other women or to children but never to men. Contrary to these traditions, a new form of mobility has been emerging in recent years, evidenced by some minority persons and some women assuming conventional role relationships of dominance. By *conventional role relationships* we mean complementary roles in which rights, duties, prerogatives, and obligations are clearly spelled out, and where there is clear dominance-submission pattern. Examples would be:

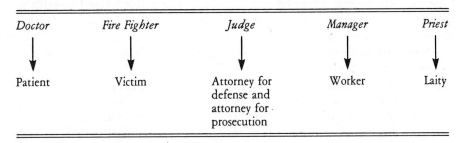

Doctor	Fire Fighter	Judge	Manager	Priest
↓	↓	↓	↓	↓
Patient	Victim	Attorney for defense and attorney for prosecution	Worker	Laity

A black person gains a dominant position in a conventional role relationship by achieving a position in some formal organization such as the government, school, hospital, or military organization. White males do not willingly hand over greater power to minority persons or to women as a matter of course. Rather, women and minorities have fought and collectively pushed for increased racial and sex representation in dominant positions. Such positions, by definition, grant the incumbents a certain amount of legitimate authority.

We maintain that there has been an increase in conventional role relationships in which minority persons or women are dominant and whites or males are subordinate. In quantitative data this change is still on a very small scale and probably would not show up as "significant change" in aggregate census analyses. Yet, in more qualitative terms, a highly visible, though small, number of minority persons and women have moved into occupations of prominance and authority in which some of their subordinates are white or male. One frequently reads about women who have moved into positions such as priest, carpenter, military officer (with authority over men and women), Speaker of the Democratic National Convention, member of the President's Cabinet, member of Congress, airline pilot, and judge. Specific cases are those of Tom Bradley, a black mayor, who is mayor of Los Angeles, and Rose Bird, recently appointed as Chief Justice of the California Supreme Court.

Of course, this kind of mobility could be viewed as another version of class mobility because it deals with occupational movement. However, it can also be considered a form of ethnic or sex mobility because it reverses the basic dimension of power in the ethnic and sex hierarchies. When women become managers of large organizations, they must give orders to both male and female subordinates. For each occurrence of such mobility, a change results in the traditional sex hierarchy—the patterns of dominant, powerful males and subordinate, powerless females is reversed. The movement of women and minorities into dominant role relationships can be seen, then, as a form of multiple-hierarchy mobility on grounds that it is movement that involves both class and ethnicity or both class and sex.

The reader may argue that instances of this kind of race and sex dominance are so rare that only a small number of whites and males directly experience the effects of these new role relationships. However, more and more whites encounter blacks in positions of authority in military institutions, as mayors of their cities, as teachers of their children, as professors in their classes, as police officers giving them tickets. For white people who do not *directly* encounter minority persons in the course of their work or through formal organizations, many *indirectly* experience blacks and women in positions of authority. Almost daily, people are exposed to these new role relationships through the mass media. The increased number of black and female newscasters is an interesting case in point. A good newscaster is articulate, has good presence, and, most important, is *informing* the audience. A subtle power reversal occurs in such a situation when the white (or male) viewer is given information about the world from a black or female newscaster. There is also a prominent reversal of stereotypes in such newscaster-viewer role relationships. The articulate, well-informed black newscaster contrasts sharply with the stereotype of blacks as poorly educated. The woman newscaster who is logical and objective and has a solid grasp of news material is quite different from the stereotype of women as overly emotional, intuitive, and illogical.

Another example of the greater society indirectly experiencing new role relationships was provided by the 1972 Democratic Convention, over which Yvonne Braithwaite Burke, a black woman, presided as chairperson. She moderated the convention with great skill and confidence, often quelling boisterous delegates, many of whom were men, some from the South. Although the viewers were not the direct subordinates, they viewed the subordinate role relationships between chairperson and convention delegates. As an impressive keynote speaker for the 1976 convention, Barbara Jordan further exposed mainstream America to a positive image of black women.

The increase of role relationships in which women and minorities are in superordinate positions should have strong effects on traditional relations between the races and the sexes. Although the exact effects of these experiences await further research, it seems highly likely that at least three changes in race and sex relations will occur: 1) changes in the flow of power and influence; 2) a reduction of negative stereotypes about women and minorities and a rise in prestige for these groups; and 3) changes in socialization patterns for future generations of women and minorities.

Recent small-group research provides a vehicle for discussing changes in power and influence, as well as changes in negative stereotypes. Several experimental studies involving black and white students in task-oriented games show that when groups are untreated, or given no new experiences, equal status interaction between white and black is not likely to occur. Even with social class held constant, white persons are consistently more likely to dominate blacks in game situations and to exert a far more lasting influence on group decisions (Katz, *et al.*, 1958; Katz and Benjamin, 1960). The interpretation of these studies is usually that strong racist beliefs are still embedded in our culture. In open situations of interaction, prior racist expectations appear to structure the situation; white persons become more assertive, black persons more passive.

An important study of the kind mentioned (Cohen and Roper, 1972) indicates that equal-status interaction among black and white high school students is possible, but only when the expectations of both whites and blacks are changed through experimental manipulation before the game. In this experiment, black subjects were teachers and white subjects their students; the task was the building of a transistor radio. In addition to direct interaction, a reinforcement of black competence was presented to both white and black participants by the use of video tapes, which recorded and played back the competent behavior of the black teacher. In a subsequent game situation (having nothing to do with building radios) there was found to be a transferral of the treatment in that whites did not dominate the new situation, and the flow of influence was equalitarian.

The small-group research cited above has wide-ranging societal implications. As more women and minority persons move into superordinate role relationships, it is quite possible that the effect of this movement will be to equalize the flow of power and influence between the races and sexes. Males and white subordinates will be experiencing a kind of stereotype-breaking treatment much like the white subjects in the Cohen-Roper small group study. For example, people will no longer assume that women are to take domestic or subordinate roles. When women are seen as highly competent business managers and when black people are visible on a daily basis as highly competent mayors of cities, popular stereotypes are undoubtedly affected. Stereotypic beliefs are directly challenged.

New generations of minority persons and women are likely to be socialized in a very different way. Hitherto, whatever their personal motivation, academic achievement, and IQ, women have been conditioned to take the role of motherhood and homemaker and a limited number of sex-typed occupations (Bem and Bem*, 1972; Berk and Berk, 1976). The socializing forces of the school, family, and mass media have successfully combined to create a potent "nonconsciousness ideology" (Bem and Bem*, 1972). That is, sex-role conditioning has been so complete that women voluntarily seek the limited options provided. With an increased number of women in traditionally male occupations and especially occupations in which women have authority over both male and female subordinates, the aspirations and definitions of what is "normal" women's work are likely to change.

Figure 13–1 summarizes the formulation of ethnic and sex mobility into positions of dominance in conventional role relationships.

Incomplete Mobility

Incomplete mobility refers to instances in which people who have attained high status in occupation, authority over others, or education are denied the full prerogatives of that status because of their race, sex, or age. In this situation, a person fails to move ahead unimpeded on one hierarchy because of his or her position on another. That is, mobility in the class hierarchy is not accompanied by full access to power, privilege, and prestige. The person has "made it" from a class achievement standpoint, but inequities remain because of the person's ascribed status. For example, a female manager, a black professional, or a business executive nearing retirement age each has attained a high class position but may experience limited authority over others or access to information, full respect of co-workers or decision-making opportunities because of their race, sex, or age. (See chapter 8, discussion on "low ascribed/high achieved combinations" for another version of this discussion.) Most people assume that if the class achievement battle is won, a person or a group has arrived. The progress of blacks, Chicanos, and women is viewed in class terms with the unstated assumption that if there were socioeco-

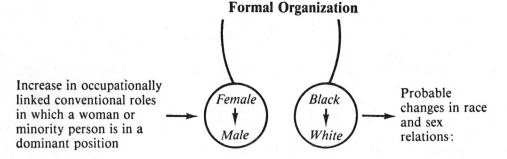

Formal Organization

Increase in occupationally linked conventional roles in which a woman or minority person is in a dominant position → *Female* → *Male*   *Black* → *White* →

Probable changes in race and sex relations:

1. Equalization of power and influence in formal and informal situations.

2. Reduction in stereo-types.

3. Socialization to new role models.

Figure 13-1. *Movement into Positions of Dominance in Conventional Role Relationships*

nomic parity between majority and minority groups, all social problems of these groups would be solved.

Several important articles illustrate the incomplete mobility of high-achieving women. Miller, *et al,** (1975) shows that inequities remain for women in high authority positions of formal organization. Women of all ranks were more likely to be rated low by coworkers in perceived influence and professional respect, and to be more isolated from persons in positions of authority. One would logically expect that women who had reached higher positions in organizations would be more favorably rated. Especially surprising was the finding that women in *higher* positions of authority, education, and occupational rank faced the greatest inequities in respect, influence, and access to information. Although they had reached a higher position in the organizational hierarchy, their access to power and influence was less than that of men in the same position. Women in high positions also expressed a great deal more job strain and job dissatisfaction compared with men in the same rank or with women lower in the hierarchy.

There are similar barriers to women's advancement in the professions such as law, medicine, dentistry, and engineering. The professions involve a high degree of informal interaction. They are "closed worlds" in which colleagues develop many interdependencies, such as exchanging information essential to the performance of the job, or giving opinions and judgments of each other's work. In many professions, a sponsor-protegé system exists. A senior colleague (usually male) in a profession may be eager to pass on his knowledge and skills to younger protegés, but many male sponsors may hesitate to accept a female protegé. The male sponsor may

> . . . prefer a male candiate to a female in the belief that she has less commitment to the profession. When the woman is accepted as a protegé, her other role partners—husband, father, child, etc.—may be jealous and suspicious of her loyalty to the sponsor and her dependence on him. The sponsor's wife may also resent the intimacy of the relationship between the sponsor and his female protegé and object to it (Epstein, 1970:969).

Traditionally, channels of ascent in the professions depend on male inheritance and support. Without this kind of help, women are not as likely as men to reach the highest echelons of their profession. Achievement does not fully override ascription.

Convergence of Two or More Kinds of Mobility

Another form of combinations mobility occurs when people ascend or descend on more than one hierarchy. If a person or group moves in relation to two hierarchies, the possibilities for mobility would be:

- moving up on both
- ascending on one and descending on another
- ascending on one and remaining stationary on another
- moving down on both

The clearest examples of dual mobility deal with the class and age hierarchies. In general, most people simultaneously ascend the class and age hierarchies; increases in age are accompanied by increases in responsibility, in authority over others, and in salary. This dual-track or concomitant mobility often continues until retirement. The process of dual mobility occurs in bureaucracies where persons enter the organization in young adulthood and progress through a series of promotions according to length of time in the organization.

For a great many women and minority persons, however, age mobility is not accompanied by concomitant increases in class privileges. Women are often employed in dead-end clerical jobs that bring no increases in responsibility and power past some initial entry point. Similarly, minority persons are disproportionately employed in unskilled jobs such as janitor or semi-skilled machine operator, that reach ceilings rapidly in pay and responsibility. In short, for women and minority persons there is one common pattern of dual mobility—ascending on one hierarchy and remaining stationary on another. For white males, there is quite a different pattern—moving up on both. The two patterns create differential privilege and prestige. For example, as women begin to age and decline in physical attractiveness, they have few class compensations in authority, status, and career satisfaction. But as men grow older and lose physical attractiveness, they have many class compensations; they gain authority, status, and job statisfaction. The aging woman, who is ascending on one and remaining stationary on another hierarchy, is placed under greater strain and loses more than the aging man who is moving up on both age and class hierarchies (Bell, 1970; Sontag,* 1972).

Status-Attainment Combinations

The status-attainment model deals with variables that explain why some individuals achieve very high positions on the occupational ladder and others do not. Status-attainment models often explore variables such as social class of origin; respondent's IQ; peer-group pressure to achieve; point of entry into the labor force; amount of education of respondent; and, finally, the resulting occupational attainment of respondent. Figure 13–2 illustrates the connections between these variables. Since the person's class of origin comes first in the career sequence it is placed first in the path diagram. Each of the arrows represents a causal connection. For example, a person's class of origin is related to his or her score on IQ tests and the degree of peer pressure to achieve. IQ and peer pressure are, in turn, related to educational attainment and point of entry into the labor force, and these latter two variables are, in turn, related to occupational achievment.

Until very recently, data on status-attainment patterns were based entirely on white males. New research considers variations in status-attainment based on race and sex. Porter (1974) contrasted young white and black males and found marked differences in the career pathways of the two groups. For example,

1. For black males the influence of significant others—for example, the amount of education a boy's friends planned to obtain—had no effect on his ambition. For white males, significant others did have an important influence on ambition.
2. One of the most crucial determinants of ambition and occupational attainment for black males was the extent to which a boy subscribed to the middle-class mores of society—the degree to which a black child projected a self-concept "that is aligned with a stereotype of a solid middle class American youth" (Porter, 1974:308). This conformity to middle-class mores was much less important as a determinant of ambition for white boys.

Variables that were important for understanding the status-attainment of black males were often not important for white males and vice versa. Black males who are successful

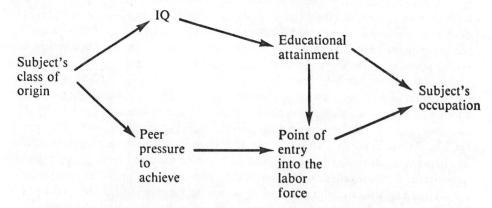

Figure 13–2. *Typical Status Attainment Path*

in their occupations may therefore have to adopt quite different strategies from white males. But what if black females are added to this combinations approach?

Treas* (1978) compared career pathways of black women and black men. On entering the labor force, black women start at much lower-paying, more menial jobs than their qualifications would warrant. Regardless of the education they have attained, black women start at a much lower occupational level than comparably educated white women. Race—not social origins—excludes black women from jobs for which they might otherwise qualify.

The career mobility of black males also is affected by racial discrimination, but discrimination occurs at a different point. Although entry into the labor force may be at a low level, given their background and education credentials, black males usually begin employment that conforms to their skills and training. However, getting off to a fair start does not ensure a lifetime of equal opportunity. For black males, discrimination comes not so much at the point of entry or first job (as it does for black females) but occurs later, in terms of channels for upgrading and promotion. Black men are often "passed over for promotion or excluded from on-the-job training" (Treas,* 1978:397). Given equal starting points and comparable skills, the employment advantages for black males fall behind those for comparable white males during the course of their careers.

Even in the Army—an organization known for its nonracist policies of entrance and promotions and as one employing a proportion of blacks far higher than their percentage of the population—one finds examples of discriminatory career advancement for black males. Butler (1976) analyzed movement of black and white men into noncommissioned ranks, using a data base of all enlisted Army personnel. One of the most important findings of the study was that blacks of high educational attainment and high intelligence took longer—in some cases, much longer—to be promoted than comparably trained whites. Again, a minority person achieves in terms of education but does not receive the privileges of his new status. This time, discrimination surfaces in the form of a longer wait to reach the higher enlisted ranks (E5 to E9). It was especially among bright, educated, high-achieving blacks that the time discrepancy between black and white was the greatest. The discrepancy also depended on the rank. Black soldiers waited the longest (compared to whites) for being promoted to the rank of E5. It is interesting that this is the first military rank that involves authority over others. Greater discrimination may operate when a promotion involves exercising authority over white subordinates (Miller and Ransford, 1978). In sum, the status-attainment process works differently for black males and black females. Both groups eventually are confined to occupations at lower levels than comparably trained white males and females.

SUMMARY: COMBINATIONS MOBILITY

In this section we have presented four instances of combinations mobility: 1) occupational mobility and sex or ethnicity, which describes reversals of authority in conventional role relationships; 2) incomplete mobility, in which people of high-achieved ranks, for example, are denied full access to power and privileges that usually accompany those high ranks; 3) convergence of two or more kinds of mobility, which occurs when people move up on one hierarchy and descend or remain stationary on another;

and 4) status-attainment combinations, which describes patterns of mobility that, for example, vary according to sex and race. In each case, the consideration of the joint effects of two or more hierarchies led to explanations or insights that could not be derived from a single focus on class mobility. To give meaning to such social phenomena as blacks in *super*ordinate positions or the differences between black male and black female career patterns, we need to take into account more than social class. Class ethnicity, sex, and age must be considered together.

REFERENCES

Alvarez, Rodolfo. 1973. "The Psycho-Historical and Socioeconomic Development of the Chicano Community in the United States." *Social Science Quarterly* 53 (March): 920–942.

Bell, Inge Powell. 1970. "The Double Standard: Age." *Trans-Action* (Nov.-Dec.): 75–80.

Bem, Sandra L. & Daryl J. Bem. 1972. "Homogenizing the American Woman: The Power of an Unconscious Ideology." Revised version of a paper originally published in Daryl J. Bem, *Beliefs, Attitudes and Human Affairs*. Belmont, Calif: Brooks/Cole, 1970.

Berk, Sarah Fenstermaker, Richard A. Berk & Catherine White Berheide. 1976. "The Non-Division of Household Labor." Paper presented at the Annual Pacific Sociological Association Meeting, San Diego, California, 1976.

Bureau of the Census. 'The Social and Economic Status of the Black Population in the United States, 1974." Series P-23, no. 54.

_____. "Differences Between Incomes of White and Negro Families by Work Experience of Wife and Region 1970, 1969, and 1959." Series P-23, no. 39.

_____. "Persons of Spanish Origin in the United States: March, 1975." Series P-20, no. 290.

_____. *Current Population Reports*, Series P-20, no. 302.

_____. "A Statistical Portrait of Women in the United States." Series P-23, no. 58.

_____. "Demographic Aspects of Aging and the Older Population in the United States." Series P-23, no. 59.

Butler, John S. 1976. "Inequality in the Military: An Examination of Promotion Time for Black and White Enlisted Men." *American Sociological Review* 14 (October): 807–818.

Chase, Ivan D. 1975. "A Comparison of Men's and Women's Intergenerational Mobility in the United States." *American Sociological Review* 40 (August): 483–505.

Cohen, Elizabeth & Susan S. Roper. 1972. "Modification of Interracial Interaction Disability: An Application of Status Characteristic Theory." *American Sociological Review* 37 (December): 643–657.

Elder, G. H. 1969. "Appearance and Education in Marriage Mobility:" *American Sociological Review* 34:519–33.

Epstein, Cynthia. 1970. "Encountering the Male Establishment: Sex-Status Limits on Women's Careers in the Professions." *American Journal of Sociology* 75 (May): 965–982.

Farley, Reynolds. 1977. "Trends in Racial Inequalities: Have the Gains of the 1960's Disappeared in the 1970's?" *American Sociological Review* 42 (April): 189–208.

Glenn, Norvall D., Adreain A. Ross, & Judy Corder Tully. 1974. "Patterns of Intergenerational Mobility of Females through Marriage." *American Sociological Review* 39 (October): 683–99.

Hill, Robert B. 1978. *The Illusion of Black Progress*. Washington, D.C.: National Urban League.

Katz, I. & L. Benjamin. 1960. "Effects of White Authoritarianism in Biracial Work Groups." *Journal of Abnormal Social Psychology* 61 (November): 643–657.

Katz, I., Judith Goldston & L. Benjamin. 1958. "Behavior and Productivity in Biracial Work Groups." *Human Relations* 11 (May): 123–141.

Kluegel, James R. 1978. "Causes and Costs of Racial Exclusion From Job Authority." *American Sociological Review* 43 (June): 285–301.

Marshall, Harvey & Deborah Meyer. 1975. "Assimilation and the Election of Minority Candidates: The Case of Black Mayors." *Sociology and Social Research* 60 (October): 1–21.

Marx, Gary T. 1967. *Protest and Prejudice*. New York: Harper & Row.

Miller, Jon, Sanford Labovitz & Lincoln Fry. 1975. "Inquiries in the Organizational Experiences of Women and Men." *Social Forces* 54 (December): 365–381.

Miller, Jon & H. Edward Ransford. 1978. "Inequality in the Military: Implications for Organizations, Occupational Mobility, and Social Stratification." *Journal of Political and Military Sociology*. 6 (Spring): 65–74.

Moore, Joan W. 1970. *Mexican Americans*. Englewood Cliffs, N.J.: Prentice-Hall.

Moynihan, Daniel P. 1972. "The Schism in Black America." *The Public Interest* 27 (Spring): 3–24.

New York Law Journal. 1974. January (15): 1–4.

Palmore, Erdman & Frank Whittington. 1971. "Trends in the Relative Status of the Aged." *Social Forces* 50 (September): 84–90.

Penalosa, Fernando. 1971. "The Changing Mexican-American in Southern California." In Norman R. Yetman & C. Hoy Steele (eds.), *Majority and Minority*. Boston: Allyn & Bacon.

Porter, James N. 1974. "Race, Socialization and Mobility in Educational and Early Occupational Attainment" *American Sociological Review* 39 (June): 303–316.

Searles, Ruth & J. Allen Williams, Jr. 1962. "Negro College Students Participation in Sit-Ins." *Social Forces* 40 (March): 215–220.

Sontag, Susan. 1972. "The Double Standard of Aging." *Saturday Review* (Sept. 23, 1972).

Steiner, Stan. 1968. *The New Indians*. New York: Dell Publishing Co.

Szymanski, Albert. 1974. "Race, Sex, and the U.S. Working Class." *Social Problems* 21 (June): 706–725.

Treas, Judith. 1978. "Differential Achievement: Race, Sex, and Jobs." *Sociology and Social Research* 62 (3): 387–400.

Tyree, Andrea & Judith Treas. 1974. "The Occupational and Marital Mobility of Women." *American Sociological Review* 39 (June): 293–302.

U.S. Department of Labor, Wage and Labor Standards Administration, Women's Bureau. November 1968, WB 69–63.

U.S. Department of Labor, Bureau of Statistics. *Employment and Unemployment Trends During 1977*. Special Labor Force Report 211: p. A20.

Waldman, Elizabeth. 1972. "Changes in the Labor Force Activity of Women." In Nona Glazer-Malbin & Helen Youngelson Waehner (eds.), *Women in a Man-Made World*. New York: Rand McNally and Co.

Wattenberg, Ben J. & Richard M. Scammon. 1973. "Black Progress and Liberal Rhetoric." *Commentary* (April): 35–44.

The Psycho-Historical and Socioeconomic Development of the Chicano Community in the United States[1]

Rodolfo Alvarez

THE CLOSEST approximation to objective knowledge can be gained from the confrontation of honestly different perspectives that subsume the same or related sets of facts. What is presented in this paper is a marshalling of historical fact from a perspective not traditionally taken into account in scholarly discourse on Mexican Americans. The objective is to confront the reality of Mexican American society as we have experienced it and from that basis to generate hypotheses for future multidisciplinary research in this area. For this purpose we identify four historical periods and describe the climate of opinion within the generation of Mexican Americans that numerically dominate the period. What I mean by a "generation" is that a critical number of persons, in a broad but delimited age group, had more or less the same socialization experiences because they lived at a particular time under more or less the same constraints imposed by a dominant United States society. Each generation reflects a different state of collective consciousness concerning its relationship to the larger society; psycho-historical

differences related to, if not induced by, the economic system.

We begin our analysis with the assertion that, *as a people,* Mexican Americans are a creation of the imperial conquest of one nation by another through military force. Our people were thrown into a new set of circumstances, and began to evolve new modes of thought and action in order to survive, making Mexican American culture different from the culture of Mexicans in Mexico. Because we live in different circumstances we have evolved different cultural modes; just as we are neither identical to "Anglos" in the United States nor to Mexicans in Mexico, we, nevertheless incorporate into our own ethos much from both societies. This is because we respond to problems of existence that confront us in unique ways, distinct from the way in which Anglos and Mexicans experience them.

How, then, did we pass from being a sovereign people into a state of being compatriots with the newly arrived Anglo settlers, coming mostly from the southern United States, and, finally, into the condition of becoming a conquered people—a charter minority on our own land?

The coming of the Spaniards to Mexico began the development of a mestizo people which has come to be the largest category of Mexican society. The mestizo is the embodiment of biological, cultural and social heterogeneity. This sector of Mexican society was already numerically as-

Reprinted with permission from *Social Science Quarterly,* Vol. 53, (March 1973), pp. 920–942.

1. This paper is an extension of the ideas developed by the author in: Rodolfo Alvarez, "The Unique Psycho-Historical Experience of the Mexican American People," *Social Science Quarterly,* 52 (June, 1971), pp. 15–29. I am indebted to Reynaldo Flores Macias and Victor Velasquez for extensive editorial and research assistance.

cendant by the time Mexico gained its independence from Spain. Sovereign Mexico continued more or less the identical colonization patterns that had been developed by Spain by sending a cadre of soldiers, missionaries, and settlers to establish a mission and presidio where Indians were brought in and "Christianized."[2] Once the Indians were socialized to the peculiar mixture of Indian and Hispanic-Western cultural patterns which constituted the mestizo adaptation to the locale, they were granted tracts of land, which they cultivated to support themselves in trade with the central settlement, and through that, with the larger society with its center in Mexico City.[3] As the settlement grew and prospered, new outposts were developed further and further out into the provinces. Thus, Mexican society, like the Spanish society before it, was after *land* and *souls* in its development of the territories over which it held sovereignty.[4] The Indian quickly was subjugated into the lowest stratum of society to do the heaviest and most undesirable work at the least cost possible—although biologically "pure," but fully acculturated Indians frequently entered the dominant mestizo society. They also tended to marry settlers coming north from central Mexico to seek their fortunes.[5] Light and dark skinned alike were "Mexican."

What is of historic significance here is that in the early 1800's, particularly on the land now called Texas, this imperialistic system came into direct conflict with another;[6] that sponsored by England which resulted in the creation of the United States of America. Both systems set out aggressively to induce the economic development of the area. However, while the Hispanic system sought economic development through the acquisition of *land* and *souls,* the Anglo system that had been established on the northern Atlantic seabord was one of acquiring *land, but not souls.*[7] An Indian could not have been elected president of the United States as Don Benito Juarez was in Mexico. Rather, the Indian was "pushed back" as the European settlement progressed.[8] He had to be either manifestly cooperative in getting out of the way (and later into reservations), or be exterminated. The new society in the United States was, therefore, a great deal more homogeneous than in Mexico since it was fundamentally a European adaptation to the new land and not in any way a mixture of Indian and European elements.

It should be said here, without wanting to overemphasize, that there is some evidence from correspondence between Thomas Jefferson and James Monroe that these and other key figures in the United States had intended to take the Southwest long before U.S. settlers started moving into Texas.[9] Insofar as the stage was not yet set for this final move, the coming of United States citizens into Texas was a case study in peaceful cooperation between peoples with fundamentally different ideological perspectives. The Anglo settlers initially and publicly made the minimal necessary assertions of loyalty to Mexico—despite the fact that they did not live up to the letter of the settlement contracts[10] which called for them to become Mexican citizens and Roman Catholic.[11]

This cooperation experience lasted until approximately 1830–35. During this time Texas was being rapidly settled by Mexicans moving north ("rapidly," considering their form of colonization). Also, some Europeans, a few of them Roman Catholic, arrived in Galveston and settled throughout the territory.[12] Others, in a stream that was ultimately to become the majority, came

2. Wayne Moquin and Charles Van Doren, *A Documentary History of the Mexican American* (New York: Bantam Books, 1972), pp. 2–3.

3. George L. Rives, *The United States and Mexico, 1821–1848* (New York: Scribner's Sons, 1913), Vol. II, p.29.

4. *Ibid.,* pp. 24–25.

5. Herbert L. Priestly, *The Coming of the White Man, 1492–1848* (New York: Macmillan, 1929).

6. Samuel Harmon Lowrie, *Culture Conflict in Texas, 1821–1835* (New York: AMS Press, Inc., 1967).

7. Eugene C. Barker, *Mexico and Texas, 1821–1835* (Dallas: P.L. Turner Co., 1928), p. 72. Also, Edward H. Spicer, *Cycles of Conquest: The Impact of Spain, Mexico, and the United States on the Indians of the Southwest, 1533–1960* (Tucson: University of Arizona Press, 1962), pp. 279–367.

8. Priestly, *Coming of the White Man,* pp. 220–221.

9. Rives, *United States and Mexico,* pp. 23–24.

10. Lowrie, *Culture Conflict,* p. 52.

11. Antonio Lopez de Santa Ana, *et al., The Mexican Side of the Texas Revolution, 1836* (Dallas: P.L. Turner Co., 1928), p. 307.

12. George Conclin, *A New History of Texas; and a History of the Mexican War* (Cincinnati: District Court of Ohio, 1847), p. 150.

from the southern region of the United States.[13] I call this the cooperative experience because there is historical evidence that all of these people, regardless of their point of origin, cooperated relatively well with each other. The frontier was sufficiently rugged that all needed each other's help and ideas in order to survive. Because everyone was given title to generous amounts of land, there was no struggle over land, which was the capital that they all sought. This period may be characterized as one in which every group could, apparently, optimize accomplishment of its objectives. The Mexican government needed to settle the area to secure its claim over the land and to reap the economic gain from its productivity; the settlers, whatever their origin (Indian, mestizo, European, or Anglo) came to develop their own personal economic assets. Because the country was so biologically and culturally heterogeneous, the question of how to develop a stable functioning society was crucial, once the break with Spain had been accomplished. During this period, some Anglo filibustering (insurrectionist activity in a foreign country) did take place. However, there is evidence that other Anglo groups were instrumental in helping to put these activities down. The *general* tone of the times was that of intercultural cooperation. Each group learned from the others as they applied their resources to the economic development of the area.

Somewhere around 1835 began what I call the ''revolutionary experience.'' This was a revolutionary experience, in the usual sense of the term, only toward the end of this phase, as was perhaps inevitable given wide-spread territorial ambitions in the United States (subsequently labeled ''manifest destiny'' by historians of the period). The conflict was exacerbated by an ideological struggle within Mexican society between federalists and centralists. These political philosophies, while based to a considerable degree on economic self-interest of the partisans of either faction, also embodied widely divergent views on the nature of man himself.

The centralists were for administrative control over all Mexican territory by the governing elite in Mexico City. The federalists, on the other hand, were idealists trying to implement in Mex-

ico the noble political principles, of the rights of man as enunciated by the United States Constitution (after which the federalist constitution of 1824 was modeled) and by French political theorists of the Enlightenment. They were for egalitarianism in practice within a culturally and racially heterogeneous society, and not only in principle within a relatively racially and culturally homogeneous society, as in the United States. The centralists were skeptical of the possibility of self-government by a heterogeneous population, the major proportion of whom they considered inferior culturally, especially so because a poor country, such as Mexico, could not invest sufficient resources to educate the masses, who were mostly Indian.[14]

It appeared to the majority of settlers in Texas—Mexicans, as well as others—that federalism would provide the best economic outcome for them. The province of Texas became a stronghold of federalism,[15] and the majority decided to remain loyal to the federalist Mexican constitution of 1824. Santa Ana by this time had switched his ideological stance from federalism to centralism and had taken control of the central government in Mexico City. His reaction to events in Texas was to send troops to discipline the dissident province. However, the poorly professionalized army acted badly in Texas and alienated much of the populace by the unnecessary spilling of blood. The fact that many of these settlers came from the slaveholding South probably did not make relations with Mexicans, whom they considered inferior, easier. Heightened sentiment led to hostile actions and a revolution was started. The upshot was that Santa Ana personally came to command the army that was to put down the revolution and was himself defeated. Once the chief executive and the army of the sovereign country of Mexico were defeated, there was no real pressure for the dissident province to remain a loyal entity within the mother country—even though many of the settlers had set out originally simply to attain a

13.   Barker, *Mexico and Texas.*

14.   Benjamin Keen, *Readings in Latin American Civilization: 1942 to Present* (2nd ed.; Boston: Houghton Mifflin Co., 1967), pp. 165–166.

15.   Joseph M. Nance, *After San Jacinto: The Texas-Mexican Frontier, 1836–42* (Austin: University of Texas Press, 1963), pp. 172, 142–251.

federalist rather than a centralist government in Mexico. Furthermore, when the fighting broke out, adventurers and fortune seekers poured from the United States into Texas to participate in the fight. Evidence that these people, as well as their friends and relatives who remained behind, had a great sense of their "manifest destiny" to acquire more land for the United States,[16] is abundant and is illustrated by the fact that from as far away as Cincinnati, Ohio, came contributions of cannons and supplies as soon as it appeared that separating Texas from Mexico was a possibility.[17] Once hostilities began and these people began to pour in, the federalists loyal to Mexico were outnumbered and full-blown independence from Mexico was declared. When Santa Ana was ultimately defeated, it was still not clear that Mexico would be incapable of reassembling an army and returning to discipline the dissident province. The extreme biological and cultural heterogeneity which characterized Mexico then (as it does today) was one of the bases of Mexico's difficulty in self-government.[18] The depth of Mexico's internal disarray became apparent soon enough. Texas was absorbed into the United States, provoking armed conflict with Mexico. If Mexico had not been able to discipline Texas, it certainly was no match for the well trained and well equipped U.S. Army backed by a *relatively* homogeneous society. By 1848 Mexico had lost approximately 50 percent of its territory. It appears that perhaps Santa Ana may have personally profited by Mexico's disarray.[19] With the signing of the Treaty of Guadalupe Hidalgo,[20] the Mexican American people were created *as a people*: Mexican by birth, language and culture; United States citizens by the might of arms.

16.   Ramon Eduardo Ruiz, *The Mexican War: Was it Manifest Destiny?* (New York: Holt, Rinehart and Winston, 1963).

17.   Seymour V. Connor, *Texas: A History* (New York: Crowell Co., 1971).

18.   Leopoldo Zea, *The Latin American Mind* (Norman: University of Oklahoma Press, 1963). Also, Daniel Cosio Villegas, *American Extremes* (Austin: University of Texas Press, 1964.

19.   Santa Ana, *The Mexican Side.*

20.   Mexico and the United States, *El Tratado de Guadalupe Hidalgo, 1848* (Sacramento: Telefact Foundation, 1968).

THE CREATION GENERATION

Following incorporation of the Southwest into the United States in the mid-1800's there developed the experience of economic subjugation, followed by race and ethnic prejudice.[21]

Mexico . . . simply had to accept the best deal possible under the circumstances of military defeat; that deal meant that Mexico lost any respect it might have had in the eyes of the Mexicans living on the lands annexed by the United States. This rapid change must, certainly, have given them a different social-psychological view of self than they had prior to the break. The break and annexation meant that they were now citizens of the United States, but surely they could not have changed their language and culture overnight merely because their lands were now the sovereign property of the United States; thus they maintained their "Mexicanness." Because their cultural ties were to Mexico, they were, in effect, "Mexicans" in the United States. As the number of "Americans" in the region increased, "Mexicans" became an ever smaller proportion of the population. They were . . . a minority. They thought, spoke, dressed, acted, and had all of the anatomical characteristics of the defeated Mexicans. In fact, were they not still "Mexicans" from the point of view of "Americans" even though they were United States citizens by virtue of the military defeat and treaties that gave sovereignty to the United States? For all of these reasons and more, the "Mexican" minority could be viewed as the deviants onto whom all manner of aggressions could be displaced whenever the Calvinistic desire for material acquisition was in the least frustrated.[22]

It is the psycho-historical experience of a rapid and clear break with the culture of the parent country, and subsequent subjugation against the will of the particular population under analysis—all of this taking place on what the indigenous population considered to be its "own" land—that makes the experience of Mexican

21.   Edward E. Hale, *How to Conquer Texas Before They Conquer Us* (Boston: Redding and Co., March 17, 1845), p. 8.

22.   Alvarez, "Psycho-Historical Experience," pp. 19–20.

Americans different from all other ethnic populations that migrated to this country in the nineteenth and twentieth centuries.

All of the factors necessary for the development of race prejudice against Mexicans, now Mexican Americans, were present after 1836 in Texas. Any bloody war will engender very deeply felt animosity between contending factions. Furthermore, in order to kill, without feelings of remorse, it may be necessary to define the enemy as being sub-human and worthy of being killed. In the case of the fight between centralist and federalist forces in Texas it should be noted that the centralist army was almost exclusively Mexican, having been recruited deep in Mexico and brought north by Santa Ana.[23] The federalist forces in the province of Texas, on the other hand, were a mixture of Mexican, European, and U.S. settlers.[24] However, once the centralist forces were defeated, the hatred toward them, that had now become a hatred of Mexico and Mexicans, could easily be displaced onto settlers who in every respect could be said to be Mexicans, even though they had been federalists and had fought for Texas independence.

Second, since most of the settlers in Texas who came from the United States were from the slave-holding South, the idea of racial inferiority was not unknown to them and could easily be used to explain the hostile emotions they held toward the Mexicans, against whom they had just fought a winning fight.

A third factor making for the development of intense race prejudice against Mexican Americans was economic. Once Texas became independent it left the door open wide for massive migration from the United States. Title to the land had already been parceled out under Mexican sovereignty. Through legal and extra-legal means, the land was taken away from those provincial Mexicans, who as Texans had cooperated to try to give the province a measure of autonomy. These were the betrayed people, betrayed by their fellow Texans, once Texas became fully autonomous. By 1900 even those provincial Mexicans who had

owned large tracts of land and who had held commanding social positions in Texas and throughout southwestern society had been reduced to a landless, subservient wage-earner class—with the advent of a new English language legal system, masses of English speaking, land hungry migrants, and strong anti-Mexican feelings—both by force of arms and through legal transactions backed up by force of arms.[25] Furthermore, it was the importation of race prejudice that created an impenetrable caste boundary between the dominant provincials of northern European background and the provincial Mexicans. Once race prejudice was imported and accepted on a broad scale as an adequate explanation and justification for the lower caste condition of local "Mexicans," these attitudes could spread rapidly into the rest of the Southwest, when the United States acquired a large proportion of northern Mexico. The experience of socioeconomic and political subjugation was repeated throughout the Southwest, with some variations for peculiar circumstances in specific areas, New Mexico in particular. Many of the distinctly Mexican American attitudes throughout the country today stem from the subjugation experience of this period.

THE MIGRANT GENERATION

By 1900 the socioeconomic as well as political subservience of the Mexican American throughout the Southwest was well established. At the same time, the United States population was slowly becoming urbanized and was increasing *very rapidly* in size.[26] Instead of small farms and ranches that provided income for one family, agriculture was increasingly conducted on very large farms in order to grow massive quantities of food profitably. Despite the growing mechanization during this period (after 1900 and before World War II),

23.   George P. Garrison, *Texas: A Contest of Civilization* (Boston and New York: Houghton Mifflin Co., 1903), pp. 104–105.

24.   *Ibid.*, p. 105.

25.   Clark S. Knowlton had documented the procedure by which the lands were taken away from the newly become Mexican Americans in his "Culture Conflict in Natural Resources," in William Burch, *et al.*, *Social Behavior, Natural Resources, and the Environment* (New York: Harper, 1972), pp. 109–145.

26.   Moquin and Van Doren, *A Documentary History*, p. 329.

the large farms and ranches of the Southwest required massive manual labor at certain periods in the growing season. Cheap Mexican labor was inexpensive and required much less care than the machines that were only then coming on the farms.

To provide the massive agricultural labor needed, recruiters were sent deep into Mexico to spread the word of higher wages on the large farms in the United States. Coincidently with this "pull," political upheavals in Mexico created a population "push." The resulting huge waves of migrants[27] coming north to work the fields give the name "Migrant Generation" to this period. Until the 1920's the migrant stream flowed north predominantly through Texas (where racial attitudes were imposed) and then beyond Texas to spread out over the agricultural region of the Great Lakes and western United States. It was not until after World War II that the migrant flow began to come predominantly through California. These people have been called "immigrants" by social scientists and by policy makers because they moved from one sovereign country to another. However true their "immigrant" status might have been *legally,* they were not immigrants either *sociologically* or *culturally* because of the peculiar psycho-historical experience of Mexican Americans in the Southwest prior to 1900. Even those who eventually settled around the Great Lakes and later in the Northwest usually lived for a period of time in the Southwest where they were socialized into the cultural mode of the period.

There are at least four reasons why Mexicans arriving after 1900 but before World War II should be sociologically viewed as "migrants" who simply expanded the number of people who had more or less the same consciousness of lower caste status as those Mexicans who were here prior to 1900. First, the post-1900 waves of Mexican nationals coming into the United States did not come into a fresh social situation where they were meeting the host society for the first time. They did not arrive with the "freedom" to define themselves in the new society in accordance with their own wishes and aspirations. Not only were they denied the social-psychological process of "role taking" among the established higher sta-

tus occupations, but demands and impositions of the dominant society were such that neither could they experiment with the process of "role-making"; i.e., the creation of alternative but equal status occupations.[28] They did not arrive with the "freedom" that comes from having one's self-image and self-esteem determined almost exclusively from one's presentation-of-self to strangers, where these strangers have no prior experience with which to question or invalidate the social claims being made by the performance.[29] Immigrants from other lands arrived in the United States, and their place in the social hierarchy was, in a sense, freshly negotiated according to what the group as a whole could do here.[30] The social situation that the post-1900 waves of Mexicans entering the United States encountered was very different from that of immigrants from other lands. Their experience upon entering the United States was predefined by the well established social position of pre-1900 Mexican Americans as a conquered people (politically, socially, culturally, economically, and in every other respect). They came to occupy the category closest to simple beasts of burden in the expanding regional economy.

The people coming from Mexico, in very large numbers after 1900, viewed themselves and were viewed by the dominant host society as the "same" as those Mexican Americans who had been living on the land long before,[31] during, and after the psycho-historical experience described above as resulting in the "Creation Generation." Before they came they knew they would find, and when they arrived they did find, a large, indigenous population with whom they had language, kinship, customs, and all manner of other genetic, social, cultural, and psychological aspects in common. The very interesting and highly peculiar circumstances in the case of the post-1900 migrant from Mexico is that he left a

28.   Ralph Turner, "Role Taking: Process versus Conformity," in Arnold Rose, ed., *Human Behavior and Social Process* (Boston: Houghton Mifflin, 1962).

29.   Erving Goffman, *Presentation of Self in Everyday Life* (New York: Anchor Books, 1959)

30.   Harold Garfinkel, *Studies in Ethnomethodology* (Englewood Cliffs, N.J.: Prentice Hall, 1967).

31.   Moquin and Van Doren, *A Documentary History,* p. 331.

27.   *Ibid.*

lower *class* status in Mexico to enter a lower *caste* status in the United States without being aware of it. The reasons he was unaware of it are multiple, reflecting the great network of characteristics in common with the people already here. The fact is that the vast majority of Mexican Americans never realized they were in a caste, as opposed to a class, category because they never tried to escape in any substantial numbers. The permeability of normative boundaries need never be an issue, so long as no one attempts to traverse them. Until World War II there existed a state of pluralistic ignorance between these few individuals and groups of Mexican Americans who tried to escape the caste and the majority of relatively unaware members of the Mexican American population. The state of development of mass communications probably prevented widespread knowledge across the Southwest of the many isolated incidents that took place during this period. When a critical proportion of Mexican Americans began to earn enough money to pay for their children's education and began to expect services that they saw non-Mexican American members of the society enjoying, they found out that they were not viewed just simply as members of a less affluent class, but, rather, as members of a despised caste. This was the critical test. If they had achieved skills and affluence in Mexico, race and ethnicity would have been no barrier to personal mobility into a higher socioeconomic class. It was the attempt to permeate the normative boundaries and the subsequent reaction by the larger society that brought out in the open the way they were perceived by the dominant host society. During the period designated as the "Migrant Generation," there were many isolated instances of great conflict between groups of Mexican Americans trying to alter their lower caste status, but they were locally overpowered, and a general state of acquiescence became the state of collective consciousness.

A second factor that characterized post-1900 incoming Mexicans as migrants rather than immigrants is that the land they came to was virtually identical to the land they left.[32] Today there is a sharp contrast between the terrain north and south of the border because of mechanization and irrigation for large scale industrialized farm-

ing on the United States side, and the same old water-starved flatland on the Mexican side. However, in the early period when the great waves of migrants came, the land was sufficiently similar to what they had left behind that it did not require a cognitive reorientation for them.

The fact that the land they came to was very similar, physically, to the land they left behind is very important because it had been part of Mexico. Thus, the post-1900 migrant from Mexico to the United States was not leaving land to which he had a deep identity-giving psychological relationship and going off to another, very different "foreign" land, to which he needed to develop another sort of identity-giving relation. The Irish immigrant, for example, experienced a great discontinuity between the land of origin and the land of destination. Furthermore, the nation-state and the culture identified with the land to which he was going had never been part of the nation-state and culture he was leaving behind. When the Irish immigrant left "Ireland" to go to "America," there surely must have been a very clear psychic understanding that he was leaving behind a land to which he had a very special relationship that made him an "Irishman." The post-1900 migrant from Mexico need not have noticed any change. He was simply moving from one part of his identity-giving land to another. The work that he was to perform on the land of destination was identical to the work he performed on the land of origin.

A third set of factors that distinguished the Migrant Generation from immigrants from other countries involves the physical nature of the border that they had to cross to come into the United States. Over large distances the border between the United States and Mexico was never more than an imaginary line. Even in that part of Texas separated from Mexico by the Rio Grande, the natural obstacles are minimal. During much of the year people could simply walk across, and certainly at other times they could cross the river as any other river might be crossed. The amount of *time* that it takes to cross the border also affects the degree of anticipatory socialization that the person can engage in prior to arrival at his point of destination. The Irish immigrant spent the better part of *two weeks* crossing an enormous physical obstacle, the Atlantic Ocean. The great physi-

32. *Ibid.*

cal boundary separating his land of origin from his land of destination could not escape his notice. The time it took to traverse that boundary afforded the immigrant the opportunity gradually, but profoundly, to engage in serious contemplation that allowed him to significantly "disassociate" his identity from one nation-state and its culture and to engage in more or less effective anticipatory socialization for his new identity and new life in another nation-state and its culture. The point here is that the nature of the physical border (its overpowering size) and the time it took to traverse it made it virtually impossible for the immigrant not to be deeply conscious of the fact that he was entering a new society and therefore, a new place within the structure of that society. This was not the case with the Mexican migrant.

A fourth set of factors distinguishing Mexicans of the Migrant Generation from immigrants from other countries is the nature of their activity in coming to this country. There is undoubtedly a significant psychic impact deriving from the degree to which the individual is a free and autonomous agent in determining the course of his own behavior. The greater the degree to which the individual perceives himself as self-determining, the less his behavior will precipitate a change of his already established identity. Conversely, the more the individual perceives (and his perceptions are validated) that his behavior is significantly determined by others, the greater will be the impact of that realization on his identity. The Irish immigrant, for example, had significant others affecting his behavior in such a way that he could not avoid considering the identity that he was rejecting and the one he was assuming. He had to ask for official permission to leave his country of origin, be physically conveyed across an ocean to enter a country he had to obtain official permission to enter. Those actions forced him to consider his purpose in making the crossing, and whether he was prepared to abandon one identity for the other; whether he was prepared to pay the psychic price. The Mexican migrants, on the other hand, were "active agents," more or less in control of their own movement. They did not, in the early 1900's, have to ask anyone for permission to leave one country to enter the other. If they made their own personal decision to go, they simply went. There was no official transaction that in any

way impinged on their collective self-identity. It took seven minutes to cross a river. The significance of the decision to swim or use the bridge is analogous to the modern-day decision either to walk downtown or to pay for a taxi—hardly an identity-making decision. It was not until the mid-1930's that the border was "closed," that is, when an official transaction was required to cross the border. By this time, however, such an enormous number of people had already crossed, and the Mexican American population, within the lower caste existing in the southwestern United States, was so large that it did not matter in terms of the conceptual argument. The later migrant waves simply inflated the lower caste and took on its psychic orientation (i.e., its collective state of consciousness), despite the fact that by the official transaction they were made conscious that they were now in the sovereign territory of another nation-state. This was so because all other factors still applied, and, in addition, the impact of the large population into which they moved was overwhelming.

The post-1900 migrants came mainly to Texas and California. There they assumed the already established lower caste position we have described, as a consequence of the prior established social structure. Socio-psychologically, the migrants, too, were a conquered people, both because their land of origin had been conquered by the United States and because the Mexican Americans, with whom they were completely commingled, had been treated as a lower caste of conquered people inside the now expanded version of the United States. As such, they were powerless appendages of the regional economy. Their manual labor was essential to the agricultural development of the area. But whenever the business cycle took a turn for the worse, they were easily forced to go back to Mexico;[33] they were forcibly deported. Their United-States-born children were deported right along with the parents. The deportation of Mexican Americans—United States citizens—was not uncommon, since to the U.S. Border Patrol, U.S. Immigration Service ("Migra"), and the Texas Rangers there frequently seemed little or no difference between

33. *Ibid.*

Mexican Americans and Mexicans nationals; they were all simply "Mexicans."[34]

There is for Mexican Americans a very bitter irony in all of this. The irony is that the post-1900 migrants and the pre-1900 lower caste citizens of Mexican descent learned to live more or less comfortably with all of this largely because of their frame of reference. Both constantly compared themselves to Mexican citizens in Mexico. That they should have Mexico as their cultural frame of reference is understandable. The irony is, however, that they never compared themselves to other minority groups in this country, possibly because of geographic isolation. The price the Mexican American had to pay in exchange for higher wages received for stoop labor in the fields and for lower status work in the cities was a pervasive, universal subjugation into a lower caste that came about silently and engulfed him, long before he became aware of it. He became aware of his lower caste, economically powerless position only when he (or his children) tried to break out of the caste and was forced to remain in it. By that time it was too late. He had learned to enjoy a higher wage than he would have had in Mexico and to accept a degrading lower caste position. His lower socioeconomic position in the United States was never salient in his mind.

THE MEXICAN AMERICAN GENERATION

Starting somewhere around the time of the Second World War, and increasing in importance up to the war in Vietnam, there has developed another state of collective consciousness which I call the "Mexican American Generation." This generation increasingly has turned its sense of cultural loyalty to the United States. As members of this generation were achieving maturity, they began to ask their parents:

What did Mexico ever do for you? You were poor and unwanted there. Your exodus reduced the unemployment rate and welfare problems that powerful economic elements in Mexico would have had to contend with, so they were happy to see you leave. You remained culturally loyal to the memory of Mexico, and you had dreams of returning to spend your dollars there. You sent money back to your family relations who remained in Mexico. Both of these acts of cultural loyalty on your part simply improved Mexico's dollar balance of payment. And what did Mexico do for you except help labor contractors and unscrupulous southwestern officials to further exploit you?

I am an "American" who happens to be of Mexican descent. I am going to participate fully in this society because, like descendents of people from so many other lands, I was born here, and my country will guarantee me all the rights and protections of a free and loyal citizen.[35]

What the members of the Mexican American generation did not realize was that, relative to the larger society, they were still just as economically dependent and powerless to affect the course of their own progress as the members of the older Migrant Generation. If the Migrant Generation had Mexicans in Mexico as their socioeconomic reference, the Mexican American Generation, in similar fashion, did not effectively compare its own achievements to those of the larger society, but to the achievements of the Migrant Generation. This comparison was a happy one for the Mexican American Generation. They could see that they were economically better off than their parents had ever been. They could see that they had achieved a few years of schooling while their parents had achieved virtually none.

What the Mexican American Generation did not realize was that their slight improvement in education, income, political efficacy, and social acceptance was an accomplishment only by virtue of comparison to the Migrant Generation which started with nothing. The Mexican American Generation was far behind the black population as the black population was behind the Anglo on every measure of social achievement; i.e., years of education achieved, political efficacy, annual income per family, etc. But these comparisons were rarely made during this period when Mexican

34. Carey McWilliams, *North from Mexico* (New York: Greenwood Press, 1960).

35. Alvarez, "Psycho-Historical Experience," pp. 24–25.

Americans changed from being a predominantly rural population employed in agricultural stoop labor to an urban population employed predominantly in unskilled service occupations. Today, for example, approximately 83 percent of the Mexican American population lives in cities, even though in most instances the mass media still portrays Mexican Americans as rural stoop laborers. This was the period when the first relatively effective community protective organizations began to be formed. The organizing documents are so painfully patriotic as to demonstrate the conceptualized ambitions of the membership rather than their actual living experience.

The change of Mexican Americans from a rural to an urban population was precipitated by the rapid industrialization of agriculture that was brought about initially by the production requirements of World War II (and the simultaneous manpower drain required for the military) and was subsequently sustained and enhanced by the scientific and technological revolution that followed the war. Agriculture had increasingly been organized around big farms since 1900 in order to meet the demands of an expanding population. The massive production required by World War II, in the absence of Mexican American labor—since the Mexican American population participated disproportionately in the war—led to the increasingly rapid conversion of agriculture to resemble the industrialized factory. During the initial phases of the war, much stoop labor was imported from Mexico,[36] but later this became less necessary because machines increasingly were filling the need for all but the most delicate agricultural picking jobs. The entire economic system reached the highest development of the ideals of industrialized society. Perhaps more money and somewhat better working conditions were to be found in cities, but that was not because of any gains on the part of Mexican Americans; it was rather because of the nature of urban living and industrial production of post-World War II era of United States capitalism. Compared to the majority, the Mexican American still had no determinative input into the economic system. Lack of unions and lack of political effectiveness meant

that the Mexican American was earning less than any other group of comparable work. Lack of education meant that the Mexican American did not have sufficient understanding of the nature of the society in which he lived and its economic system to even know that he was being treated unfairly. To the extent that he became conscious of his economically disadvantaged position, he was powerless to do anything about it.

At this point it is fair to ask: If the Mexican American Generation was so poorly educated, how did it ever get the training, skills, and general awareness of things to be able to move in large numbers from the fields to the cities and survive? Here, we have to introduce another statement about socioeconomic dependency. About the time of World War II when industrialization was beginning to be felt out in the fields, a substantial proportion of the Migrant Generation was nearing old age. Older people began to move to the cities to do the lighter work that was available there. At the same time, the young people were being moved into the war effort, young men to the military and young women to work in the war production industries and the skills and technical competency that young Mexican Americans acquired in the military were directly transferable to industrial employment in the cities after the war ended.[37]

Finally, the fact that they fought and saw their military friends and neighbors die in defense of the United States led Mexican Americans generally not to question their relative status in the economy and their lack of control over it. Little did they realize that everyone else was also experiencing both a real and an inflationary increase in economic standing; that other groups were experiencing a faster rate of economic increase because of their more effective direct participation in bringing it about. The Mexican American was only experiencing a kind of upward coasting with the general economy and was not directly influencing his own economic betterment. As a group, Mexican Americans remained at the bottom of the socioeconomic ladder.

36. Carey McWilliams, *Brothers Under the Skin* (Rev. ed.: Boston: Little, Brown and Co., 1964), p. 128.

37. Matt S. Meier and Feliciano Rivera, *The Chicanos: A History of Mexican Americans* (New York: American Century Series, Hill and Wang, 1972), pp. 200–201.

Many Mexican Americans attempted to escape their caste-like status by leaving the Southwest to seek employment in the industrial centers of the mid-western Great Lakes region and in the cities of the Northwest.[38] Others went to California. A high degree of industrialization and a very heterogenerous population (religiously, ethnically, and politically) have always been the factors that attenuated discrimination against Mexican Americans in California. In fact, it is in California (and of course in the Midwest to a smaller extent) that the Mexican American first began to have the characteristics of a lower *class* population on a massive scale, as opposed to the lower *caste* experience. Of course, among the southwestern states on a smaller but widespread scale, the state of New Mexico seems to have come to a condition of class as compared to caste emphasis in a prolonged, gradual manner. This was perhaps due to the fact that the experience of the Migrant Generation never took place as intensely in New Mexico. The post-1900 immigrants came in large numbers to Texas early in the period and to California later (circa W. W. II).[39] However, New Mexico was essentially bypassed by the Migrant Generation. Furthermore, in New Mexico the experience of the Creation Generation was neither as severe nor as complete as it was in Texas and California. In New Mexico the Creation Generation experience did take place, but so-called Hispaños managed to retain some degree of political and economic control since they represented such a large percentage of population—even with, or in spite of, all the extensive land swindles by invading Anglos.[40] Interestingly, the fact that the Mexicans in middle and northern New Mexico were never fully subjugated into a lower caste position is reflected in the linguistic labels they use to identify themselves. It may be argued that in order to differentiate themselves from those who had been subjugated into a lower caste,[41] the so-called His-

paños in New Mexico started calling themselves Spanish Americans some time around the First World War, despite the fact that their anatomical features were those of Mexican mestizaje and did not resemble Spaniards. At that time, their previous geographic isolation began to be ended by large numbers of Anglos from Texas who came to settle in the southeastern part of the state of New Mexico. The Texans brought with them their generalized hatred of Mexicans and their view of them as lower caste untouchables. Thus, out of self-protection, New Mexicans started to call themselves Spanish Americans and to insist that they could trace their racial and ethnic origins to the original Spanish settlements in the area. The linguistic ruse worked so well that Mexican Americans in New Mexico came to believe their own rhetoric. The point to be made here is that this linguistic device was used by a large and isolated population that had not been fully subjugated into a lower caste to maintain in New Mexico the semblance of a class position. It is in New Mexico more than in any of the other southwestern states that Mexican Americans have participated in the society as people who have had the freedom and possibility of social mobility to become members of various social classes. They did this, however, at the price of altering their identity to make themselves acceptable to stronger economic, if not political, interests in the state. Today, however, the younger members of the post-World War II period are developing a new consciousness even in New Mexico. It is the current high school and college age offspring of the so-called Spanish Americans who are using the term Chicano and who are demanding documentation for the presumed historic culture links to Spain.[42] What they are finding—the greater links to Mexican and to Indian culture—is beginning to have an effect on their parents, many of whom are beginning to view themselves as Mexican Americans with some measure of pride.

Some of the tensions within the Mexican American community during this period of time could be explained in terms of the generalized attempt to be more like "Anglo" citizens. Those people who were themselves born in the United States had greater legitimation for their claims of

38. Moquin and Van Doren, *A Documentary History*, p. 402.

39. Leo Grebler, *Mexican Immigration to the United States: The Record and its Implications* (Advance Report # 2, Mexican American Study Project). Also, Manuel Gamio, *Mexican Immigration to the United States, 1883–* (Chicago: University of Chicago Press, 1930).

40. Knowlton, "Culture Conflict."

41. Moquin and Van Doren, p. 394.

42. Meier and Rivera, *The Chicanos*, pp. 270–272.

loyalty to the United States and for their psychic sense of security on the land. They in fact would, in various disingenuous ways, disassociate themselves from those whose claim to belonging could not be as well established; even parents or family elders who were born in Mexico and came over during the period described as the Migrant Generation would be viewed as somehow less legitimate. In the cities a slight distinction was made between the older Mexican Americans who now held stable working class and small entrepreneurial positions as compared to newly arrived migrants from Mexico who entered the urban unskilled labor pool. This, of course, increased the insecurity and decreased the willingness to engage in collective action among the members of the Migrant Generation. They were in a particularly insecure position psychically, economically, and in almost every other regard. They were rejected and mistreated by the dominant Anglo population and rebuffed (as somehow deserving of that mistreatment) by their offspring.

The Mexican American Generation purchased a sense of psychic "security" at a very heavy price. They managed to establish their claims as bona fide citizens of the United States in the eyes of only *one* of the social psychologically relevant populations: *themselves.* The dominant Anglo population never ceased to view them as part of the "inferior" general population of Mexican Americans. The Migrant Generation never fully believed that their offspring would be able to become "Anglos" in any but the most foolhardy dreams of aspiring youth. They had a very apt concept for what they saw in the younger person wanting to become an Anglo facsimile: "Mosca en leche!" The Mexican American who so vehemently proclaimed his United States citizenship and his equality with all citizens never realized that all of the comparisons by which he evaluated progress were faulty. Because of his psychic identification with the superordinate Anglo, he abandoned his own language and culture and considered himself personally superior to the economically subordinate Migrant Generation. The fact that he could see that he was somewhat better off educationally and economically than the Migrant Generation led the Mexican American of this period to believe himself assimilated and accepted into the larger society. He did not fully

realize that his self-perceived affluence and privileges existed only in comparison to the vast majority of Mexican Americans. He did not realize that for the same amount of native ability, education, personal motivation and actual performance, his Anglo counterpart was much more highly rewarded than he. He never made the observation that even when he achieved a higher education, he still remained at the bottom of the ladder in whatever area of economic endeavor he might be employed. Individuals, sometimes with the help of protective organizations, did bring some legal action against personal cases of discrimination. But despite a growing psychic security as citizens of the United States, they did not make effective collective comparisons. The greater security that the Mexican American Generation achieved was a falsely based sense of self-worth. To be sure, because a sizeable proportion of the population managed to exist for several decades with a sense of self-worth, they could give birth to what will be called the Chicano Generation in the next section of this paper. However much the Mexican American Generation may have been discriminated against educationally and especially economically, they did achieve enough leisure and economic surplus so that their offspring did not begin from a hopeless disadvantage at birth. This extra measure of protection was perhaps the greatest indicator that the Mexican American Generation was now part of a class and not a caste system.

THE CHICANO GENERATION

In the late 1960's a new consciousness began to make itself felt among Mexican Americans. By this time the population was solidly urban and well entrenched as an indisputable part of the country's working underclass. Migration from Mexico had slowed and was predominantly to urban centers in the United States. Theories of racial inferiority were dying, not without some sophisticated revivals, to be sure, but in general the country was beginning to accept the capacity of human populations given equal opportunities and resources. Moreover, despite the ups and downs of the market-place, it was becoming clear to all that both technological sophistication and economic potential existed in sufficient abundance to erradicate abject poverty in the United States. These conditions had not existed in the Southwest with regard to the Mexican American population since that historical period immediately preceeding the Creation Generation.

The Chicano Generation is now comparing its fortunes with those of the dominant majority as well as with the fortunes of other minorities within the United States. This represents an awareness of our citizenship in a pluralistic society. It is perhaps early to be writing the history of the Chicano Generation, but already it is clear that we have gone through an initial phase and are now in a second phase. The first phase consisted of the realization that citizenship bestows upon those who can claim it many rights and protections traditionally denied to Mexican Americans. The second phase, only now achieving widespread penetration into the population's consciousness, is that citizenship also entails obligations and duties, which we have traditionally not been in a position to perform. These two perspectives are rapidly colliding with each other. The general mental health of the Chicano community is being severely buffeted by the change in comparative focus and the relative current inability to achieve measurable success according to the new standards.

The parameters of the Mexican American population had been slowly changing, until by the mid-1960's the bulk of the post-World War II baby boom had reached draftable age and now faced the prospect of military service in the war in Vietnam. As a cohort, these young Mexican Americans were the most affluent and socio-politically liberated ever. The bulk were the sons and daughters of urban working class parents. However, a small proportion were the offspring of small businessmen; and an even smaller proportion were the offspring of minor bureaucratic officials, semiprofessionals, and professionals. Especially in these latter types of families, a strong sense of the benefits of educational certification and of the rights of citizenship had been developed. When the bulk of this cohort of young people reached draftable age, which is also the age when young people generally enter college, they made some extremely interesting and shocking

discoveries, on which they were able to act because they had the leisure and resources to permit self-analysis and self-determining action.

Despite the fact that the Mexican American population has the highest school dropout rate of any ethnic population in the country, by the mid-1960's a larger proportion than ever before were finishing high school. These young people then faced three major alternative courses of action, all of them unsatisfactory. One course was to enter an urban-industrial labor force for which they were ill-prepared because a high school education is no longer as useful as in previous generations. And even for those positions for which a high school education is sufficient, they were ill-prepared because the high schools located in their neighborhoods were so inadequate compared to those in Anglo neighborhoods.[43] Moreover, persistent racial discrimination made it difficult to aspire to any but lower working class positions. Another course of action, which a disproportionate number of young men took, was to go into military service as a way to travel, gain salable skills, and assert one's citizenship, as so many Mexican Americans had done in the previous generation. But unlike the Mexican American going into the military of World War II, the young Chicano of the mid-1960's went into a highly professionalized military, the technical skills for which he found difficult to acquire because of his inadequate high school preparation. So instead of acquiring skills for the modern technical society into which he would eventually be released, he disproportionately joined the ranks of the foot soldier and was disproportionately on the war casualty list. A third course of action open to the young Mexican American leaving high school in the mid-1960's was to make application for and enter college. This alternative was unsatisfactory because colleges and universities were not prepared to accept more than the occasional few—and then only those who would be willing to abandon their ethnicity. Refusal to admit was, of course, based on assertions of incapacity or lack of preparation. The former has racist underpinings, while the lat-

43. Herschel T. Manuel, *The Education of Mexican and Spanish Speaking Children in Texas* (Austin: University of Texas, 1930). Also, Thomas P. Clark, *Mexican Americans in School: A History of Educational Neglect* (New York: College Entrance Examination Board, 1970).

ter is class biased since poverty and the inferior schools in which Chicano youth were concentrated did not permit adequate preparation for college and eventual middle class certification.

No matter which course of action the bulk of the young people took they disproportionately faced dismal futures. The larger society in which this ethnic minority exists had become so technical, bureaucratized, and professionalized—in short, so *middle class*—that the strictly lower working class potential of the bulk of the Mexican American population was irrelevant to it. Faced with the prospect of almost total economic marginality, the Chicano Generation was the first generation since the Creation Generation to confront the prospect of large-scale failure—of, in effect, losing ground, of psychically accomplishing less than the Mexican American Generation. The low-skill, labor-intensive society into which the Migrant Generation broke from its caste-like condition and within which the Mexican American Generation had established a firm, but strictly lower working class status, was disappearing. The United States was now predominantly professionalized and middle class, with increasingly fewer labor-intensive requirements. It is in this relatively more limited context that the Chicano Generation came to have relatively higher aspirations.

With higher aspirations than any previous generation, with the prospect of a severe psychic decline compared to its parent generation, and now, because of its greater affluence and exposure, it had to compare itself to its youth counterpart in the dominant society. The broader exposure comes from many sources, including television and greater schooling in schools that, however inferior, were better than those to which prior generations were even minimally exposed. The Chicano Generation very painfully began to ask of what value its United States citizenship was going to be. At this time a significantly large proportion of the black population of this country "revolted." That may well have been the spark that ignited the Chicano movement. The Mexican American Generation had asserted its United States citizenship with great pride, asserting a relationship between economic success and their complete "Angloization" which was now shown to be false. The Chicano Generation came to realize that it was even more acculturated than the

previous generation, yet it did not have any realistic prospects of escaping its virtually complete lower and working class status. Its new consciousness came into being at a time when the Chicano Generation could hardly find any older role models with certified middle class status. Comparatively, for example, out of a population of twenty-four million there are 2,200 black persons who have earned Ph.D. degrees in all disiplines combined.[44] Among the eight million (approximately) Mexican Americans there are only 60 who have earned Ph.D.'s degrees, when a similar level of disadvantage would lead us to expect approximately 730. The number of Ph.D.'s in a population is used here as a sort of barometric indicator of the level and quality of technically trained and certified leadership available to a population within a predominantly middle class society. This is so because one can guess at the ratio of lawyers and doctors as well as master and bachelor degrees for each Ph.D. Thus, the Mexican American population which began to enter colleges and universities in noticeable numbers only as late as the mid-1960's is almost completely lacking in certification for middle class status.

Another indication of the lack of certified leadership that is self-consciously concerned with the welfare of the community is the lack of institutions of higher learning of, for, and by Chicanos. There are over 100 black institutions of higher learning (both privately and publicly supported, including colleges, universities, law schools and medical schools). As recently as five years ago there were no such institutions for Chicanos. Now there are a handful of schools that either have been created *ad hoc* or where a significant number of Chicanos have moved into administrative positions due to pressures from large Chicano student enrollments. The point here is that however inadequate the black schools may have been, compared to "white" schools, they provided the institutional foci within which a broad sector of the black population has been trained and certified for middle class status since prior to 1900. Mexican Americans could neither get into institutions of the dominant society, nor did we have our own alternate institutions. Thus, the difficulty of acquiring broad scale conscious-

44. Author's records, unpublished research.

ness of the condition of our people is apparent, as is the insecure ethnic identification of the early few who entered "white" institutions.

The Chicano Generation has experienced the pain of social rejection in essentially the same fashion (in the abstract) that it was experienced by the Creation Generation. That is, having been ideologically prepared to expect egalitarian co-participation in the society in which it exists, it had instead been confronted with the practical fact of exclusion from the benefits of the society. Because it can no longer compare itself to its immediate predecessors (no matter what the quantity of accomplishments of the Mexican American Generation), it has to compare itself to other groups in the larger society. Relative to them it is more disadvantaged than any other ethnic group, except the American Indian with whom it has much in common both culturally and biologically. Every new demographic analysis gives the Chicano Generation more evidence of relative deprivation,[45] which leads to the rise of a psychic sense of betrayal by the egalitarian ideology of the United States not unlike that experienced by the Creation Generation. Members of the Chicano Generation are therefore saying to the previous generation:

> So you are a loyal "American," willing to die for your country in the last three or four wars; what did your country ever do for you? If you are such an American, how come your country gives you less education even than other disadvantaged minorities, permits you only low status occupations, allows you to become a disproportionately large part of casualties in war, and socially rejects you from the prestige circles? As for me, I am a Chicano, I am rooted in this land, I am the creation of a unique psycho-historical experience. I trace part of my identity to Mexican culture and part to United States culture, but most importantly my identity is tied up with those contested lands called Aztlán! My most valid claim to existential reality is not false pride and unrequited loyalty of either the Migrant Generation or the Mexican American Generation. Rather, I trace my beginnings to the original contest over the lands of

Aztlán, to the more valid psycho-historical experience of the Creation Generation. I have a right to inter-marriage if it suits me, to economic achievement at all societal levels, and to my own measure of political self-determination within this society. I have a unique psycho-historical experience that I have a right to know about and to cultivate as part of my distinctive cultural heritage.[46]

The concerns of the Chicano Generation are those which predominantly plague the middle class: sufficient leisure and affluence to contemplate the individual's origin and potential future, sufficient education and affluence to make it at least possible for the individual to have a noticeable impact on the course of his life's achievements, but not so rich an inheritance that the individual's prominence in society is virtually assured.[47] The Chicano Generation is the first sizable cohort in our history to come to the widespread realization that we can have a considerable measure of self-determination within the confines of this pluralistic society. Yet we are only at the threshold of this era and have hardly begun to legitimate our claims to effective self-determination, i.e., acquisition of professional-technical certification as well as establishment of relatively independent wealth. Our capacity to secure middle class entry for a sizable proportion of our population is threatened on two major fronts.

First, we are threatened by our redundancy or obsolescence at the bottom of the social structure. This has two dimensions: we cannot earn enough money to support a United States standard of living on laborer's wages; even if we were willing to do the few remaining back-breaking jobs, there would not be enough work to go around because these are being automated, and the few that are around will be taken over by cheap Mexican labor from Mexico, unless we organize factory and farmworkers effectively.[48]

45.   Leo Grebler, J. Moore, Ralph Guzman, *The Mexican-American People* (New York: Free Press, 1970).

46.   Alvarez, "Psycho-Historical Experience," p. 25.

47.   George C. Homans, *Social Behavior: Its Elementary Forms* (New York: Harcourt Brace & World, 1961).

48.   Richard B. Craig, *The Bracero Program* (Austin: University of Texas Press, 1971).

Thus, in a sense, the economic bottom of our community is falling away.

Second, we are threatened because just as the middle class sector of the larger society is getting ready to acknowledge our capacities and our right to full participation, we find that the major proportion of our population does not have the necessary credentials for entry—i.e., college, graduate and professional degrees. When large corporate organizations attempt to comply with federal equal employment regulations concerning the Spanish speaking population, they do not care whether the person they hire comes from a family that has been in the United States since 1828 or whether the person arrived yesterday from Mexico or some other Latin American country. The irony is that as discrimination disappears or is minimized, those who have historically suffered the most from it continue to suffer its after affects. This is so because as multi-national corporations have begun their training programs throughout Latin America, and especially in Mexico, a new technically skilled and educated middle class has been greatly expanded in those countries. Many of these persons begin to question why they should perform jobs in their home country at the going depressed salaries when they could come to the United States and receive higher salaries for the same work and participate in a generally higher standard of living. This, in effect, is part of the brain drain experienced by these countries from the point of view of their economy. From the point of view of the Chicano community, however, we experience it as being cut off at the pass. That is, just as the decline of prejudice and the increase in demand for middle class type positions might pull us up into the secure middle class, a new influx of people from another country comes into the United States economy above us. Because it would cost corporations more to develop Chicanos for these positions, and because we do not have a sufficiently aware and sufficiently powerful Chicano middle class to fight for the selection of Chicanos, and because of federal regulations which only call for Spanish surname people to fill jobs, without regard to place of origin, it is conceivable that the bulk of our population might become relegated into relatively unskilled working class positions. Thus, the

plight of the urban Chicano in the 1970's is not technically complicated (how do you acquire middle class expertise with working class resources), but psychically complex (how do you relate to urban middle class immigrants from Spanish speaking countries and to rapidly organizing rural Mexican Americans) at a time when the general economy of the United States appears to be in a state of contraction, making competition for positions severe. Unless we can deal creatively with these trends, we will remain at the bottom of the social structure. This, in spite of outmoded social theories that postulated that each wave of new immigrants would push the previous wave up in the socioeconomic structure.

The introspectiveness of the Chicano generation is leading to new insights. The psycho-historical links of the Chicano Generation with the Creation Generation are primarily those of collective support against a common diffuse and everywhere present danger. The threat of cultural extinction had led the Chicano to deep introspection as to what distinguishes him both from Mexicans in Mexico and from "Anglos" in the United States. This introspection had led to deep appreciation for the positive aspects of each culture and a creative use of our inheritance in facing the future. The fight for self-definition is leading to a reanalysis of culture. For example, Anglo research has defined "machismo" as unidimensional male dominance, whereas, its multi-dimensional original meaning placed heavier emphases on personal dignity and personal sacrifice on behalf of the collectivity—i.e., family or community. This concern for the collectivity comes through again in the emphasis placed on "la familia" in activities within a Chicano movement perspective. The fight for professional and middle class certification is the fight for our collectivity to be heard. The objective is to produce enough certified professionals who can articulate and defend our peculiarly distinct culture in such a manner that educational and other institutions of the dominant society will have to be modified. Until we have our own certified savants, we will continue to be defined out of existence by outsiders insensitive to the internal dynamic of our own collectivity. The willingness to fight may be what will get us there. YA MERO!

Differential Achievement:
Race, Sex, and Jobs*

Judith Treas

ABSTRACT

Both black men and black women get lower status jobs than their white counterparts. Analysis of data from the 1967 NLS and 1962 OCG surveys demonstrates that lower social origins and educational attainments are insufficient explanations of blacks' occupational disadvantage. Although black women get as much schooling as white women with similar social origins, they take humbler first jobs. This status gap narrows over the course of a career, but black women never overcome this inauspicious labor force entry. Black men experience unique barriers to schooling. Although their career beginnings may not be lower than those of white men with limited educations, black men do not enjoy the upward career trajectory which characterizes their white counterparts.

BLACKS ARE known to be occupationally disadvantaged, hailing from lower social origins and arriving at lower occupational destinations than do others in the labor force. This persistent inequity has prompted an impressive body of empirical research. However, the labor market mechanisms which sort blacks into poorer jobs warrant further specification—especially for women whose achievement patterns and processes have only recently attracted scholarly attention.

Reprinted by permission of SOCIOLOGY & SOCIAL RESEARCH, University of Southern California, Los Angeles, CA 90007.

*This research was supported in part by Administration on Aging grant 90-A-1015. This paper benefitted from the careful reading of anonymous reviewers.

Status attainment research on men has demonstrated that lower social origins are insufficient explanation for the occupational deficits of black men, whose family background and educational credentials hold less currency in the job market (Duncan, 1968; Duncan, Featherman, and Duncan, 1972). Despite evidence of converging stratification processes between the races, the occupations of black men are not so easily predicted as those of white men by models positing socioeconomic payoffs to privileged birth or prolonged schooling (Featherman and Hauser, 1976a). It is not known whether the occupational disadvantage of black women reflects the same barriers to achievement since sociological concern has focused on comparisons between men and women in allocative processes, rather than on color cleavages in women's attainments (See, for example, Tyree and Treas, 1974; Featherman and Hauser, 1976a, McClendon, 1976; and Featherman and Hauser, 1976b). It was from this perspective of sex comparisons that Treiman and Terrell (1975a) conducted parallel analyses for white and nonwhite men and women. They find overall similarities in attainment processes in that jobs depend on education and (to a lesser extent) on social origins. However, they note that nonwhite women are more successful at converting education into occupational status than are their brothers and that their occupational achievements are more strongly determined by parental status and educational attainment than are those of other workers.

This study explores the influence of race on women's careers and compares the placement mechanisms relegating black women to poor jobs with those operating to depress the job prospects of black men. This analytic focus on racial inequities existing for each sex recognizes the tenacity of occupational sex differences which persist even as racial differences wane (Treiman and Terrell, 1975b). This analysis is informed by a theoretical perspective characterizing much status attainment research. Our model reduces to the developmental proposition that occupational status is an extension of previous social status, both ascribed and achieved. Ascriptive variables—race, father's education, and father's occupation—are treated as exogenous determinants of respondent's educational attainment. Career beginnings are predicated on these four variables, and current occupation depends on initial job as well as antecedent factors.

DATA AND METHODOLOGICAL CONSIDERATIONS

Our study employs data from the initial wave of the National Longitudinal Survey of Work Experience of Women 30–44 Years of Age (hereafter called NLS). Sponsored by the U.S. Department of Labor, the NLS is the undertaking of Ohio State University and the U.S. Bureau of the Census (Parnes, *et al.,* 1970). The 1967 survey yielded interviews with about 5000 women, including an oversampling of blacks. Our analysis is restricted to employed women, native-born of nonfarm origins. This subsample consists of 274 black women and 655 nonblack women. (For convenience we refer to nonblack women as white since only 1.4 percent of these women are of other races.) We also draw upon data on men from the benchmark 1962 Occupational Changes in a Generation (OCG) Study, a Current Population Survey supplement (Blau and Duncan, 1967). The OCG population of interest here is the experienced civilian labor force of native men, 30–44, whose family heads were not working at farm jobs when the respondent was 16 years old. The OCG subsample consists of 373 blacks and 5646 nonblacks.[1]

For both data sources, educational attainment is expressed as years of schooling completed while occupation is measured by the Duncan (1961) Socioeconomic Index. The Duncan scale

arose as a solution to the limited occupational coverage of the 1947 NORC survey in which a national sample of respondents evaluated the prestige of 78 occupations. Prestige scores were regressed on the age-standardized income and education characteristics of male workers in the 78 occupations, as reported in the 1950 Census of Population. Weights from the resulting regression equation permitted the estimation of status scores for the 270 detailed occupations of the 1950 Census. There are problems attendant in the application of Duncan scores to women. First, the NORC study consciously eliminated "women's occupations" from the survey instrument (Reiss, 1961). Had feminine occupations been included, the regression weight for income might have been reduced since men doing women's work receive lower pay, net of education (Treiman and Terrell, 1975b). Second, Duncan scores are predicated on the objective characteristics of *male* incumbents of occupations. However, scores generated from the characteristics of female workers in 1950 may be shown to correlate .93 over individuals with Duncan scores. This error is the necessary cost of comparability with the OCG data.[2]

Given a focus on the articulation of race and careers, we consider career beginnings as well as current occupation. It should be noted that the wording of first job items differ for NLS and OCG studies. OCG respondents were asked about their first full-time job after leaving school (not counting military service, summer vacations, and part-time employment). The questionable temporal ordering of OCG reports on first job and eventual educational attainment is well documented (B. Duncan, 1965). NLS women answered different questions depending on family status. For example, the overwhelming majority, ever-married women, were asked about "the longest job you had between the time you stopped going to school full-time and your first marriage." (Items are not applicable to a quarter of the sample who married while in school or who did not work before marriage). Since the NLS instrument specified jobs of some duration, women may have reported fewer short-term, stopgap jobs as career beginnings than did OCG men. Nevertheless, these jobs were said by most female respondents to have been their *first full-time* work after schooling.

Racial Effects on Women's Achievement

Black women in the NLS sample are at a disadvantage in the job market. Their mean occupational score in 1967 was 27, almost 15 points below the mean for white women. Is this discrepancy attributable to a real liability of color or does it simply reflect the perpetuation of urban poverty? Although the jobs of white fathers averaged 33 points, the mean for black fathers was only 19. Might not these humbler origins, perhaps mediated by education, suffice to account for the poorer job showings of black working women? Must we postulate labor market mechanisms furthering or checking the job status of women on the basis of race?

In Table 1, we explicitly incorporate race into a model of occupational attainment. We assume for the moment that racial effects are additive.[3] Race is treated as an exogenous dummy variable, coded "0" for blacks and "1" for nonblacks. The correlation coefficients demonstrate the modest positive association of white status with other background variables, particularly occupational origins. While hardly associated with

educational achievement, race proves to be as closely related to first job as is father's education or father's occupation; it is only slightly less associated with current occupation than are other background variables.

Standardized partial regression coefficients in Table 1 permit a causal explanation of correlational evidence on the relation of race and occupation. Even apart from social origins, race is seen to influence the jobs women get, especially when they are new to the labor force. The direct path from race is .230 at career beginnings. Furthermore, the entire influence of color on career beginnings is an unmediated one since race is virtually uncorrelated with the intervening variable, education. The unstandardized partial regression coefficients in Table 2 provide a concrete interpretation of race's impact on career start: a black woman may expect her first job to be 13.5 SEI points lower than that of a white woman with comparable social origins and educational level. Despite the modest direct path (.077) from race to current job, race also registered a small indirect effect (.101) by virtue of its causal impact via first job. Although, the total effect of race on current occupation (.178) is less than that for career be-

Table 1. *Path Coefficients (above diagonal) and Means, Standard Deviations, and Correlation Coefficients (below diagonal) for NLS Native Women, 30–44, of Nonfarm Origin: 1967*

			Variables*			
Variables	H	V	X	U	W	Y
Residual				.881	.771	.727
H				.015	.230	.077
V	.101			.258	.003	.025
X	.206	.576		.257	.005	−.005
U	.094	.407	.408		.556	.336
W	.287	.285	.298	.593		.401
Y	.224	.281	.281	.589	.627	
Mean	.88	8.57	31.06	11.66	39.93	39.13
Standard Deviation	.33	3.86	22.02	2.50	19.41	20.56

*H, race; V, father's (or family head's) educational attainment; X, father's (or family head's) occupational status; U, respondent's educational attainment; W, occupational status of respondent's first job; Y, respondent's occupational status, April, 1967.

Table 2. *Partial Regression Coefficients and Standard Errors (in parentheses) for NLS Native Women, 30–44, of Nonfarm Origin; 1967*

	Variables*				
Variables	H	V	X	U	W
U	.111	.167	.029		
	(.226)	(.023)	(.004)		
W	13.598	.165	.005	4.036	
	(1.524)	(.160)	(.029)	(.221)	
Y	4.790	.134	− .005	2.759	.425
	(1.588)	(.160)	(.029)	(.263)	(.033)

*H, race; V, father's (or family head's) educational attainment; X, father's (or family head's) occupational status; U respondent's educational attainment; W, occupational status of respondent's first job; Y, respondent's occupational status, April, 1967.

ginnings, the net liability of black skin persists; it was 4.8 SEI points in 1967.

Evidently black working women did not attend school quite as long as did other working women, because blacks had lower social origins. Color itself does not work to depress educational attainments. Rather, it is modestly correlated with parental status which does influence schooling. While race no doubt affects the quality of schooling received, it has no direct impact on the years of schooling completed. Any biases in the urban educational system influencing school continuation rates of girls would appear to be biases against those from poor, lower class homes rather than against blacks *per se.* On the other hand, race is a notable determinant of achievement in the occupational sphere. The career beginnings of black women are considerably lower than expected on the basis of their social origins and educations. In fact, race is the only ascribed status directly impinging on occupational success among women workers. Color is most salient at the start of a career. Race influences later achievement in part because black women get off to such a poor start in the labor force.

Those familiar with men's occupational achievement processes may have noted already that parental status characteristics are less salient to the occupational placement of daughters than of sons. The correlation between parental occupation and respondent's current job, for example, is .28 instead of the .4 we have come to expect for men. Paths from social origins to occupation virtually drop out of the model. This is not to say that parental achievement is without influence on daughter's job, but this influence is limited to determining the amount of schooling she gets. Multiplying along paths, we find each socioeconomic background variable exerts an indirect effect via education of .14 on daughter's initial job. It is clear that socioeconomic origin exercises a moderate influence over the amount of education received. Families do not provide comparably unique advantages or disadvantages to their daughters in the work place, for once a woman has completed her education, her socioeconomic background ceases to affect directly her achievement. Rather, educational attainment, with all the tastes, skills, and talents it connotes, is preeminent.

First job is substantially determined by educational qualifications. The experience, skills, and contacts acquired with the entry level job strongly shape subsequent employment, but education continues to be causally important to ultimate achievement, even apart from its role in initial occupational placement. While the intervening variables, education and first job, provide credentials for employers and facilitate satisfactory job performance, these achievement variables also influence occupational outcomes to the extent that they form each woman's definition of personally appropriate, attainable, and acceptable employment. Occupational preferences may be especially pertinent to women's occupational attainments. Having alternative sources of support such as husband's income, alimony, or AFDC, some women can afford to exercise the option of not working if available jobs don't suit them.

Why should fathers directly affect the occupations of sons but not daughters? We can only speculate. Perhaps fathers have more knowledge of and control over employment opportunities for men. Doubtless, it is easier for the machinist to secure a job for his son in the shop than for his daughter in the front office; the banker's resources may be more important to his son's success in business than to his daughter's in elementary school teaching. Alternately, we might hypothesize greater uniformity across socioeconomic strata in the socialization of girls than boys. Since work has been less central to women's lives, they may not receive the socialization inspiring in their brothers the job-related motivations, aspirations, and values which distinguish them from sons of other strata. If there is socioeconomic variation in the occupational drive and involvement of daughters, it may be that the occupational structure less readily recognizes and/or rewards high work commitment, exceptional job performance, and occupational ambition in women.[4]

To sum up, black women find their lower social origins—not their color—an impediment to getting the educational credentials valued in the labor market. However, when they seek work, race—not social origins—excludes them from jobs for which they might otherwise qualify. Since class privilege does not figure directly in the occupational recruitment of women, the intrusion of race is of particular concern.

Labor market discrimination would seem a most likely explanation for the net disadvantage confronting black women new to the labor force. Doubtless, employer bias and institutional racism have relegated many young black women to jobs beneath what might be predicted on the basis of their formal qualifications. If some employers exercise a "taste for discrimination" by refusing to hire blacks, they foster higher unemployment among this group. If they employ black women only in humble capacities, they restrict the employment opportunities of better educated blacks. The high teenage unemployment, the more limited economic resources of black families

at each occupational level, residential segregation, and the strong tradition of black female labor force participation may induce many black girls to accept first jobs for which they are overqualified, rather than wait indefinitely for appropriate work. After an inauspicious beginning, black women may be less able to opt out of the labor force than are white women who fail to find "suitable" employment—that is, jobs on or above the regression line.

Even were employers not to discriminate, race still might depress first job status. Since blacks often receive substandard schooling, they may not possess the same knowledge and skills as comparably educated whites. Color biases within the educational institution may not be manifest in terms of grades completed by working women, but they may still handicap black women for competition in the labor market. For example, Baker and Levenson's (1975) case study of a vocational high school reveals that black and Puerto Rican girls are tracked into lower skill training programs and then referred to lower status jobs by school placement personnel aware of employer's racial preferences.

The influence of color persists in 1967, in part because of racial disadvantages in early career. An additional racial handicap (above and beyond that of career beginnings) is also seen. Even without this direct agency of color, however, occupational tracking in first jobs would act to perpetuate black women's lower status. Because their entry jobs are unexpectedly low in status, black women are less likely to acquire occupational experience requisite to better jobs, to maintain special skills (like stenography) learned in school, to have access to information about higher status employment opportunities, or to retain aspirations for work more befitting their educational credentials.[5]

A Comparison of Racial Disadvantage in Achievement for Men and Women

An alternative analysis supports our conclusions regarding the influence of color on achievement. If we "standardize" for differences between the black and white female populations on independent variables, any remaining gap in achievement may be taken as a measure of the liability of being black. To ascertain the cost of color, the means for black women workers are substituted into regression equations generated for white working women.[6] (See Duncan, 1968 for further description of this approach and an extended comparison on white and black males' achievements). For each dependent variable we derive an expected value which rests on two assumptions: 1) on the average, white women are no different than their black counterparts in terms of antecedent statuses but 2) white women enjoy a distinctive rate of return on those statuses. The results of this exercise are summarized in Table 3.

Consider educational attainment. White women averaged 11.8 years of schooling compared to 11.0 for blacks. If we insert the black educational and occupational origin mean (7.4 and 18.6, respectively) into the equation for white women (U = .160V + .029X + 9.4, where V is father's education and X his job status), we obtain an expected value of 11.1 grades. Thus controlling for social background differences, the color gap in educational attainment is reduced from .8 to .1 years. This confirms that the educational attainment advantage enjoyed by white working women derives almost exclusively from their advantaged social origins, not from educational discrimination against black women.

On the other hand, standardizing for social origins and educational attainment scarcely reduces the racial gap in the first job status. Over 80 percent of this differential (or 15 SEI points) is attributable to what we will call discrimination. (Obviously, others might choose to interpret this

Table 3. *Black (b)—Nonblack (b̄) Differences in Means for Education, First Job, and Current Job and Components of Differences Attributable to Given Control Variables for Native Employed Women, 30–44, with Nonfarm Origins (April, 1967) and Native Men, 30–44, with Nonfarm Origins in the Experienced Civilian Labor Force (March, 1962).*

	Education (U) Means		First job (W) Means		Current job (Y) Means		Controlled Variables*
Women (b̄)	11.8		(b̄) 41.8		(b̄) 40.9		
		.7		2.9		2.2	v,x
	11.1		38.9		38.7		
		.1		.6		1.4	v, x, u
(b)	11.0		38.3		37.3		
				15.0		8.4	v, x, u, w
			(b) 23.3		28.7		
						1.9	
					(b) 27.0		
Total color difference		.8		18.5		13.9	
Men (b̄)	11.8		(b̄) 29.2		(b̄) 42.5		
		1.1		6.5		7.4	v, x
	10.7		22.7		35.1		
		1.6		5.1		7.0	v, x, u
(b)	9.1		17.6		28.1		
				.7		.1	v, x, u, w
			(b) 16.9		28.0		
						8.3	
					(b) 19.7		
Total color difference		2.7		12.3		22.8	

*V, father's education; X, father's occupation; U, respondent's education; W, respondent's first job.

residual as indicative of racial discrepancies in talents, training, or motivation). Much of the white advantage in current jobs may be seen to result from first job inequality. Were whites to have the same background, education, and career beginnings as black women, their current status advantage would be reduced to less than two points. Of course, it is possible that black women encounter more discrimination in current employment than our measure indicates, but that they overcome such economic bias due to extraordinary motivation, greater work experience, or other factors uncontrolled in this analysis. It should be pointed out that black women as a group made modest occupational advancements from first jobs averaging 23.3 to current jobs averaging 27.0 SEI points. While such limited upward mobility may not signify much change for the life style and life chances of black women, it is noteworthy given the career stagnation of white women whose mean occupational status, if anything, declines. What color convergence occurs over the course of careers may well reflect the longer and more continuous work histories of black women (Mincer and Polachek, 1974).

A parallel exercise for OCG men suggests sex differences in the influence of color on achievement. As the lower panel of Table 3 demonstrates, standardizing for social origins leaves half of the racial gap in men's educational attainment unaccounted for. To explain the residual 1.6 grade deficiency of black men, we must posit 1) mechanisms of educational discrimination which are not operative against black school girls or 2) depressed educational aspirations among black males (or some other sex-specific attitudinal or behavioral handicaps to school success).

Given their lower social origins and unimpressive educational attainments, black men are not seen to be greatly disadvantaged in work force entry. Antecedent statuses account for virtually all of the first job differential for men versus only 1/5 for women. In the labor market, black skin is initially a greater liability among women than among men, for white women maintain a 15-point advantage in career beginnings even net of social origins and education. This initial advantage goes a long way toward explaining the 1967 color discrepancy in female occupational achievement: largely because they get off to a poor start

in the labor force, black women are not as occupationally successful as whites although they do manage to narrow the gap between first and current jobs. Although black men don't get off to such a bad start given their background and educational credentials, they fall farther behind their white counterparts over the course of a career; the racial differential widens between first and current jobs, and over a third of the 1962 gap cannot be explained by differences in origins or earlier attainments.

These comparisons suggest different mechanisms may check the achievement of black men than work against black women. After they leave school, black women confront a labor market relegating them immediately to less desirable jobs than attained by white novices with comparable credentials. Young black men begin working at jobs not unlike those of their white counterparts only to find channels for upgrading are closed to them. Many youths may undertake manual jobs, but such work is typically a stepping stone for whites and a dead end for blacks. It would seem that any discrimination against black women occurs largely in initial placement while that against black men takes the form of blocked career mobility.

The locus of black men's career immobility may be labor market barriers to occupational advancement. Black men may be passed over for promotion or excluded from on-the-job training. They may confront more firings and layoffs—involuntary job shifts with limited chance for status gain (Sorensen, 1975). Racial differences in the articulation of labor force participation and schooling might also contribute to differing intragenerational mobility. After labor force entry, black men are less likely to acquire vocational training outside the regular school system or to resume formal education (Kohen and Andrisani, 1974). The latter would imply that black men (like black women) are disadvantaged at career beginnings since ultimate educational attainment would overstate the schooling of white men at labor force entry.

DISCUSSION

Although lower social origins and more modest education attainments contribute to the occupational disadvantage of blacks, labor market mechanisms also check achievement. Color impedes occupational achievement at different career stages for men than for women. Black women suffer no greater impediments to educational attainment than do white schoolmates of similar social origins, but their brothers encounter unique barriers to schooling. On entering the labor force, black women are relegated to humbler jobs than expected on the basis of their qualifications. Although managing to close the color gap in occupational status over the course of the career, they never overcome the handicap of initial job placement. Black men may not fare poorly at labor force entry (given their limited schooling), but since they fail to advance during their careers, they fall behind upwardly mobile white males.

Any policy prescription must take account of the biographical differences in occupational disadvantage for black men and black women. Although black men might benefit from measures designed to raise school retention rates, additional years of schooling hold less socioeconomic promise for their sisters. Rather, educational reforms geared to women might best focus on educational quality, curriculum placement, and career counseling. While intervention at labor force entry might reduce the occupational deficit of women, black men might be better served by employee training programs and career ladders. Clearly, students of socioeconomic stratification would do well to consider both race and sex. Because white men constitute a majority of the labor force, their labor market histories might be regarded as archetypal of American workers. However, our findings make clear that not all groups of workers conform to the notions of intergenerational status transmission or of career mobility predicated on the experience of white males.

NOTES

1. Pairwise deletion procedures were employed to exclude cases with missing data. Subsample size represents the unweighted number of cases for the pair with the least usable data—the correlations between first job and father's education. Although this underestimates the sample base for other correlations, it permits a conservative test of statistical significance. Although nonresponse occurs dispro-

portionately among women of low education and social origin, a comparison of the distributions with other sources found an upward bias in means or reduction in variance to be minimal. Bivariate response rates were also compared with the maximum and minimum possible given the constraints of univariate response. Although some correlated nonresponse was evident, few associations exceeded that expected under statistical independence.

2. To entertain the possibility that women's scores deviate from men's scores due only to random error, NLS correlation coefficients were corrected for attenuation by a factor of .93 (or .93^2 for the correlation of two occupation variables). This exercise did little to reconcile disparities between men's and women's matrices so any differences must arise from sex differences in the attainment processes themselves or from more serious and systematic biases in the measures.

3. Although later findings will call into question this specification of no racial interaction effects, the results of such a model are instructive.

4. Alternately, it may be mothers, not fathers, that transmit socioeconomic traits to daughters.

5. Although this paper does not attempt an analysis of internal labor markets (Blau and Jusenius, 1976), the findings of this article suggest the usefulness of such an institutional approach. It seems likely that sex and race differences in attainment processes reflect the fact that different groups confront different labor markets. Administrative rules and customs allocate some workers to occupations with well-defined career ladders and others to more marginal employment. While this paper does not identify the occupational and industrial constellations available to different groups, it does show careers to be more or less constrained by apparent institutional barriers to entry and roadblocks to advancement.

6. On the other hand, the means for white women might be entered into the equations for black women, yielding different estimates of the status cost of color.

7. That black women, not whites, are upwardly mobile from first job is inconsistent with findings in the previous section where the net YH path implied whites enjoy more career mobility. In fact, the positive YH path is an artifact of interaction effects not incorporated in the model. While not reported here, the model was estimated separately for each racial group, and several racial differences were noted. For example, parental education can further or check the achievement of black daughters to a greater extent than is the case for whites. The puzzling YH path reflects in part the fact that education stands black women in better stead than

whites when it comes to later jobs. In the present standardization, we ask what the socioeconomic outcome might be in the absence of such racial interaction effects.

REFERENCES

Baker, Sally Hillsman and Bernard Levenson. 1975. "Job opportunities of black and white working-class women." *Social Problems* 22:510–33.

Blau, Francine D. and Carol L. Jusenius. 1976. "Economists' approaches to sex segregation in the labor market: An appraisal." In Martha Blaxall and Barbara Regan (eds.), *Women and the Workplace: The Implications of Occupational Segregation.* Chicago: University of Chicago: University of Chicago Press.

Blau, Peter, M. and Otis Dudley Duncan. 1967. *The American Occupational Structure.* New York: John Wiley and Sons, Inc.

Duncan, Beverly. 1965. *Family Factors and School Dropout: 1920–1960,* Final Report, Cooperative Research Project No. 2258. U.S. Office of Education, Ann Arbor, Michigan: University of Michigan.

Duncan, Otis Dudley. 1961. "A socioeconomic index for all occupations." In Albert J. Reiss *et al., Occupations and Social Status.* New York: Free Press.

_____. 1968. "Inheritance of poverty or inheritance of race?" In Daniel P. Moynihan (ed.), *On Understanding Poverty.* New York: Seminar Press.

Duncan, Otis Dudley, David L. Featherman, and Beverly Duncan. 1972. *Socioeconomic Background and Achievement.* New York: Basic Books.

Featherman, David L. and Robert M. Hauser. 1976a.

"Changes in the socioeconomic stratification of the races, 1962–1973." *American Journal of Sociology* 82:621–51.

_____. 1976b. "Sexual inequalities and socioeconomic achievement in the U.S., 1962–73." *American Sociological Review* 41:462–483.

Kohen, Andrew I. and Paul Andrisani. 1974. *Career Thresholds,* Volume 4. Washington, D.C.: U.S. Department of Labor, Manpower Research Monograph No. 16.

McClendon, McKee J. 1976. "The occupational status attainment processes of males and females." *American Sociological Review* 41:52–64.

Mincer, Jacob and Solomon Polachek. 1974. "Family investments in human capital: earnings of women." *Journal of Political Economy,* 82:S-76–S108.

Parnes, Herbert S., John R. Shea, Ruth S. Spitz, and Frederick A. Zeller. 1970. *Dual Careers,* Volume 1. Washington, D.C.: U.S. Department of Labor, Manpower Research Monograph No. 21.

Reiss, Albert J. 1961. *Occupations and Social Status.* Glencoe, Ill.: Free Press.

Sørensen, Aage B. 1975. "The structure of intragenerational mobility." *American Sociological Review* 40:456–71.

Treiman, Donald J. and Kermit Terrell. 1975a. "Sex and the process of status attainment: A comparison of working women and men." *American Sociological Review* 40:2 (April): 174–200.

_____. 1975b. "Women, work and wages: Trends in the female occupational structure." In Kenneth Land and Seymour Spilerman (eds.), *Social Indicator Models.* New York: Russell Sage Foundation.

Tyree, Andrea and Judith Treas. 1974. "The occupational and marital mobility of women." *American Sociological Review* 39:3 (June): 293–302.

Inequities in the Organizational Experiences of Women and Men*

Jon Miller, Sanford Labovitz and Lincoln Fry

ABSTRACT

Women face consistent disadvantages in their experiences in organizations, as evidenced by inequities in interpersonal attractiveness, social isolation, job satisfaction, and work strain. The question raised is whether these disadvantages are due simply to differences in access to key organizational resources (expertise, professional rank, and authority), or to the advantages men have in realizing their vested interests in the face of competition from women. The vested interest interpretation receives strong inferential support, while the interpretation based on differential access to resources receives little confirmation. The concept of compartmentalized rationality *is developed in exploring the implications of the findings.*

DIFFERENCES IN the experiences of women and men in some sorts of social activity have been much studied and, as a result, are generally familiar in the discipline. Yet, in organizational research, direct comparisons between men and women are rare. The reasons for this vary. Some

Reprinted from *Social Forces* 54 (December 1975): 365–381. "Inequities in the Organizational Experiences of Women and Men" by Jon Miller, Sanford Labovitz, and Lincoln Fry. Copyright © the University of North Carolina Press.

*This research was sponsored in part by NIMH grant no. 23274–01A1 and by the Social Sciences Research Institute of the University of Southern California. We are grateful to Steven Bloch for his assistance in the analysis of the data, and to our colleagues, too numerous to list, for their perceptive comments on early versions of the paper.

have speculated that women react to work in organizations in a fundamentally different way than men do (Etzioni), and this has occasionally caused women to be excluded from an analysis altogether (Shepard). Others have studied women at work but have not explored the importance of sex, per se, in determining behavior. (For a comment on this, see Acker and van Houten.) Whatever the reason for the oversight, given our ignorance on the subject there is little doubt that the interaction patterns and exchanges of rewards that develop in organizations would stand out more clearly if sexual differentiation were taken into account.

With this in mind, we have investigated patterns of sexual differentiation in five small, highly professionalized organizations. Information from these organizations was used previously to explore the social-psychological implications of Weber's model of bureaucracy (Miller and Fry), but this is the first time that the possibility of sexual inequities has been directly investigated.

The research proceeded in two stages. First, the differences between men and women in three areas of organizational activity were determined:

1. differences in access to organizational networks of interaction were examined, using sociometric measures of interpersonal *attractiveness* (specifically, friendship, perceived influence, professional respect and organizational knowledge) and *isolation* (amount of contact with persons in authority and with individuals who are popular, respected, or considered to be influential);[1]

2. differences in *job strain* were explored, based on concern over job clarity, autonomy at work, job progress and job tension;
3. differences in *job satisfaction* were investigated, including satisfaction with work and satisfaction with the organization.

In the second stage of the study, the objective was to determine whether the baseline findings on interaction patterns, job strain and job satisfaction could be attributed to differences in official position, occupational rank and education. If so, the differences could be explained by the rationalistic theory that links influence with access to important organizational resources. If not, we would need to entertain a more complex explanation that emphasizes practices that duplicate, in the work setting, the vested interests and inequities that exist in the external system.[2] The assumptions underlying these two approaches will now be outlined in more detail.

THEORETICAL STATEMENT

Resources and Influence

The resource theory of influence, succinctly stated by Bierstedt, has been applied to sex-related differences in the family by Blood and Wolfe and critically reexamined by Heer (a;b) and Liu et al. From this perspective, men generally dominate women because they control resources such as information, income, occupational status, and expertise that are vital to the relationship. This differentiation is largely independent of cultural expectations about what the distribution of power between the sexes should be like. Therefore, whenever control of important resources shifts toward a more equal distribution between men and women, the balance of privilege and decision-making shifts accordingly.

This approach is very similar to rationalistic views of organizational reality, especially the Weberian model. In the ideal type, individuals who are high in professional rank and technical expertise will dominate the decision-making process and many other dimensions of activity because the effectiveness of the organization depends so much on its ability to apply technical intelligence

to its basic goals. Because this principle of organization is predicated on universalistic criteria of technical merit, it assumes that the distribution of rewards is based on objective contributions to the work of the organization and that the system is largely blind to ascribed or inherited differences such as class, race, sex, and the like.

Other things equal, it would follow that any observed imbalances in rewards between men and women must be the product of differences in training and social mobility that persist in the external system. The internal system, left to its own devices, would be essentially nondiscriminatory and, if anything, would have a leveling effect on social and economic differences generated outside the organization (Weber). In this rationalistic model, as in the resource theory of influence, it can be predicted that when differences in position, occupational training and expertise are controlled, the effects of the corresponding differences in organizational influence will be minimized and, as a consequence, access to the networks of interaction and other social rewards will be equalized for men and women.

Vested Interests and Discrimination

A completely rational organization, in reality, is as unlikely as a truly nondiscriminatory set of practices in the larger external system. Nevertheless, in the earlier analysis of the organizations that provided the present data, strong support was found for the rationalistic features of Weber's model (Miller and Fry). By a variety of formal and informal criteria, people in positions of greatest influence and reward were found, organization by organization, to be more qualified and more respected professionally than others. But the possibility of an inequitable structure favoring men in their competition with women was not explored. A competitive structure based on one set of criteria for men and another for women could appear rational, overall, if the only question asked is whether those gaining rewards generally have a greater-than-average contribution to make, in terms of their skills and their prestige in the eyes of others. A structure could evolve that excludes unqualified males and unqualified females from privileged positions but at the same time offers qualified women less return for their skills and contributions than what their qualified male counterparts can expect.

Such a dualistic system can be detected by testing for differences in interaction patterns, job strain and work satisfaction: if the differences observed on these variables do not decrease markedly when official position, occupational rank, and expertise are controlled, this would indicate that more is involved than the possession of vital organizational resources. By inference, it would indicate that the organizational structure, and particularly its mechanism for distributing rewards, functions to preserve men's vested interests by allowing interpersonal barriers to exist that could not be anticipated by the rationalistic view of organizational influence. In fact, in some situations women might find their problems intensified with increasing expertise and status because they represent a greater threat to male dominance than those who occupy statuses traditionally defined as women's positions. In short, in this view the rational principle of expertise functions within *and is limited by* an inequitable system imposed by the surrounding culture.

This *vested interest* argument is more complex than the resource theory (as we have stated it), but it would still be an oversimplification if it overlooked an important complicating factor. It is possible that the work experiences of women, however discriminatory objectively, may be consistent with what they anticipate, because, as Coser and Rokoff (539) state, ". . . women tend to limit their options by 'wanting to do what they have to do'. . . ." If so, subjective variables such as work strain and job satisfaction may not differ greatly between women and men and, in fact, women may be more satisfied with less. Applying controls for occupation, status, and expertise would not substantially alter the picture. This is what Emerson would call a cost-reducing mechanism that enables those who cannot materially alter their circumstances to achieve a more subjectively tolerable balance of rewards to costs. What is important is that a structure that is objectively inequitable would be imperfectly mirrored in personal reactions if such a mechanism were operating.[3] We will be sensitive to this possibility in the analysis that follows.

RESEARCH SETTING AND MEASURES

The data were provided by 178 men and 157 women in five organizations, including a small public school system (24 men, 51 women); two survey research organizations (one with 31 men and 32 women, the other with 28 men and 19 women); a national food processing concern (67 men and 25 women in the research component); and members of four clinics in an alcoholism rehabilitation agency (29 men, 30 women). The 335 respondents represent better than 90 percent of the personnel of each of the five organizations. The totals in the analysis vary because of different rates of completion on some questionnaire items.

Though the organizations differ in their personnel and their basic activities, their internal bureaucratic processes are quite similar. (See Miller and Fry.) All five have established expertise as both the formal and informal criterion for advancement; all five have achieved a close correspondence between authority and control; and the formal and informal status and influence structures are clearly legitimated by most of their members. There is no a priori reason to expect that the basic dynamics of sexual differentiation differ appreciably from one organization to another, or that the process will be atypical compared to what would be found in other types of organizations. For these reasons, the respondents of the five organizations were combined for purposes of the present analysis. Although not randomly selected, these organizations are probably fairly representative of relatively small, highly professionalized organizations. With caution, it is not unreasonable to set such organizations in general as the target universe for inferences from the study.

Background questions provided information on *authority* (whether the individual's position involves direct supervision of other employees); *occupational rank* in the organization (professional, semi-professional, service, clerical); and *education* (number of years of formal education, which is statistically interchangeable in this sample with academic degree). Men have an advantage on each of these. Only 6 percent of the women have authority, compared with 29 percent of the men. Similarly, 37 percent of the women have graduate training compared to 63 percent of the men; and only 15 percent of the women have professional occupations, while 53 percent of the men fall into this category.[4] Given their superordinate status on these variables, it would be surprising if men did not also enjoy advantages on other dimensions of organizational activity.[5]

The dependent variables are operationalized as follows:

Attractiveness and Isolation. Interpersonal attractiveness is measured sociometrically by the number of choices received on questions measuring *friendship* ("Of the people whom you know at work, who are your closest friends?"); perceived *influence* ("Who are the five people . . . who you feel actually have the most to say about how the organization is run?"); and professional *respect* ("Who are the five people whose opinion of your work you respect most highly?"). A communications checklist was used to determine how often an individual was seen as a useful source of information; scores on this variable are used to measure *organizational knowledge.*

Interpersonal isolation is also measured sociometrically, by determining how much *actual working contact* the individual reports with *persons in positions of authority* and with his or her own *nominees on the criteria of friendship, influence and prestige.* Each individual was asked to make five selections on each sociometric criterion. Therefore, scores could range from 0 to 5, depending on how many of the names listed on a given sociometric question reappeared in response to this question measuring contact: "Who are the people with whom you have worked most closely in the last month . . . ?" An "isolate" is a person who reports little or no interaction with a given category of co-worker.

Job Strain. A series of 19 statements relating to four dimensions of job strain (job clarity, autonomy, progress, and tension) was presented to the respondents in all but the school system (which was surveyed using a shorter version of the questionnaire). Individuals recorded their reactions by indicating how often in their work they were troubled by each item; or (in two cases) how favorably they rated the organization on a given item.

Five of the items were summed to form an index of *job clarity*, reflecting how clearly defined the duties and responsibilities of the job are. Included were statements such as "[How often are you] unclear on the scope and responsibilities of your job[?]" and "[How often do you feel that] . . . you can't get the information you need to do your job[?]."

The *autonomy* index (the second dimension of job strain) is based on six items measuring ability to function independently and to influence the actions of those of superior official status. As an illustration, a lack of autonomy is indicated if an individual reported being frequently troubled by the ". . . feeling that you have too little authority to carry out the responsibilities assigned to you," or by the inability to ". . . influence one's immediate superior's decisions. . . ."

Job progress includes three items intended to tap perceptions of the structure of mobility in the organization (". . . not knowing what opportunities for promotion or advancement exist for you"; ". . . feeling that your progress on the job is not what it could or should be"; and ". . . how do you feel about the progress you have [actually] made in this company [organization]?").

Finally, *job tension* (five items) refers to the pressures created by the work load (to illustrate, ". . . thinking that the amount of work you have to do interferes with how well it gets done,") and by the disruptions caused by the job (for example, ". . . feeling that your job interferes with your family life.").

Job Satisfaction. An index of *job satisfaction* was constructed along the same general lines as the job strain indexes. Six items are included that measure satisfaction with the work (for example: "Other things aside, how do you like just the kind of work you do?"), and the organizational setting in which the work takes place ("How do you like working for this company?"). Again, because the same questions were not asked in the school system, the analysis of job satisfaction involves only the members of the other four organizations in the survey.

A brief comment on the statistical procedures is also called for. Somer's d_{yx} is used as the measure of association in Tables 1 and 3 because of its directional and reduction-in-error interpretations. The coefficients in Tables 2 and 4 are partial d_{yx}s, calculated by examining the relationship between sex and the dependent variables within successive categories of education, occupation, authority and a summary index, overall status. The logic involved is the logic of "specification" (Lazarsfeld) which indicates how the strength of a bivariate relationship changes within different values of some third variable. The basic cross-tabulations upon which the measures are based are given in Tables 1 and 3, but this is not possible (for reasons of space) in Tables 2 and 4. To simplify the interpretation, positive coefficients reflect situations favoring men, negative coefficients favor women.

ANALYSIS OF THE FINDINGS

Differences in Interpersonal Attractiveness and Isolation

The data in part A of Table 1 indicate that men enjoy an advantage on each of the measures of interpersonal attractiveness. More men than women (42% versus 29%) receive a large number of friendship choices; and men are more likely to

Table 1. *Differences Between Women and Men in Sociometric Attractiveness and Social Isolation*

A. SOCIOMETRIC ATTRACTIVENESS

	Low	Medium	High	Totals
1. Number of friendship choices received[a]				
Women[b]	29(26%)	69(45%)	44(29%)	152
Men	34(20%)	65(38%)	72(42%)	171
	(d_{yx} = .14; p = .000)			
2. Number of information contacts received[c]				
Women	56(37%)	60(39%)	36(24%)	152
Men	56(33%)	54(32%)	61(36%)	171
	(d_{yx} = ,11; p = .01)			
3. Number of informal control choices[d]				
Women	101(66%)	40(26%)	11(7%)	152
Men	65(38%)	57(33%)	49(29%)	171
	(d_{yx} = .34; p = .000)			
4. Number of professional respect choices[e]				
Women	46(30%)	81(53%)	25(16%)	152
Men	33(19%)	57(33%)	81(47%)	171
	(d_{yx} = .31; p = .000)			
5. Total number of sociometric choices				
Women	48(32%)	77(51%)	27(18%)	152
Men	40(23%)	56(33%)	75(44%)	171
	(d_{yx} = .25; p = .000)			

[a]Time mentioned by others as a close friend.
[b]Female = 1; male = 2. Positive d_{yx} favors men.
[c]Times contacted for information relevant to work.
[d]Times mentioned as influential in organization.
[e]Times mentioned as one whose opinion of others' work is most respected.

Table 1. (*continued*)

B. SOCIAL ISOLATION[f]

	Low Contact	Medium Contact	High Contact	Totals
1. Isolation from friends at work				
Women	64(42%)	44(29%)	44(29%)	152
Men	56(33%)	46(27%)	69(40%)	171
		$(d_{yx} = .12; p = .000)$		
2. Isolation from informal control				
Women	50(33%)	57(37%)	45(30%)	152
Men	55(32%)	58(34%)	58(34%)	171
		$(d_{yx} = .03; p = .21)$		
3. Isolation from respected co-workers				
Women	49(32%)	45(30%)	58(38%)	152
Men	53(31%)	58(34%)	60(35%)	171
		$(d_{yx} = - .01; p = .38)$		
4. Isolation from authority				
Women	56(37%)	60(40%)	36(24%)	152
Men	47(27%)	57(33%)	67(39%)	171
		$(d_{yx} = .17; p = .000)$		

	Low Contact	Intermediate Contact	Contact	High Contact	Totals
5. Total isolation score					
Women	45(30%)	46(30%)	26(17%)	35(23%)	152
Men	32(19%)	44(26%)	36(21%)	59(35%)	171
		$(d_{yx} = .18; p = .000)$			

[f]Number of work contacts with own friends, people considered influential, respected co-workers, or people in positions of authority.

be turned to for work-related information (36% versus 24%). On the remaining two sociometric criteria, the differences are more pronounced: men are four times more likely to be perceived as influential (29% versus 7%) and they are roughly three times as likely to be named frequently as a person whose professional judgment is respected (47% versus 16%). In terms of total number of choices received, the advantage of men is again clear; 44 percent of the men compared to 18 percent of the women received a large number of nominations overall.

On the measures of isolation, the relationships are less pronounced (part B of Table 1). Men have some advantage in being able to interact with their friends and they have greater access to persons in positions of authority. However, when it comes to contact with those who are informally influential, the difference between men and women is not at all large. Finally, there is no evidence that men enjoy greater access to those whose work-related judgment is most respected.

To summarize, the data on attractiveness and isolation reveal the advantages men have, advantages that are most evident when it comes to influence and respect and when the freedom to interact with friends and authority figures is involved.[6] However, it is also clear that men do not enjoy a monopoly of privilege on any of these dimensions.[7]

Statistical Controls for Education, Occupational Rank and Authority

When these relationships are reconsidered with statistical controls, the impression changes, in some instances dramatically (Table 2). In most cases, the disadvantages that women face are more pronounced for those who have advanced education, high occupational rank and superior authority. These resources simply do not pay off for women the way they do for men. The credibility of the vested interest interpretation is consid-

Table 2. *Partial Measures of Association (d_{yx}) Between Sex and the Sociometric Dependent Variables Where Education, Occupation, Authority and Overall Status are Sequentially Controlled (N = 335)*[a]

A. INTERPERSONAL ATTRACTIVENESS

Relationship Between:	Correlations within Successive Categories of Control Variables			
	Low	Intermediate		High
1. Sex and number of friendship choices, controlling for:				
education	.07	.10	.05	.19†
occupation	−.07	.08	−.10	.27†
authority	.02	—	—	.53†
status	.10	−.07	.02	.80†
2. Sex and number of information contacts, controlling for:				
education	.04	−.02	.16	.03
occupation	−.01	−.12	−.19†	.19*
authority	.03	—	—	.34†
status	.15*	−.17*	−.09	.41†
3. Sex and number of informal control choices, controlling for:				
education	−.12	.07	.45†	.40†
occupation	−.02	−.14	.10	.37†
authority	.23	—	—	.18
status	.10	.12	.35†	.28*
4. Sex and number of professional respect choices, controlling for:				
education	.05	.01	.38†	.33†
occupation	−.06	−.15	−.07	.51†
authority	.16†	—	—	.49†
status	.11	−.01	.25	.51†
5. Sex and total number of sociometric choices, controlling for:				
education	−.30	.06	.36	.27†
occupation	−.12	−.23†	−.05†	.30†
authority	.10*	—	—	.35†
status	.02	.04	.14	.47†

[a]Education scores grouped as follows: 12 years or less; 13–15 years; 16 years; more than 16 years. Occupational ranks are: Clerical; Service (e.g., maintenance, repair, technical); Semi-professional (lab technician, teacher, research assistant, social worker); and Managerial and Professional. Authority is a dichotomy determined by whether a person's job involves official supervision of the work of others. Overall status is an additive combination of education, occupational rank and authority, where each of these three variables is dichotomized.

Table 2. (*continued*)

B. SOCIAL ISOLATION

Relationship Between:	Correlations within Successive Categories of Control Variables			
	Low	Intermediate		High
1. *Sex and isolation from friends, controlling for:*				
education	− .03	.24†	− .20*	.19†
occupation	.12	.52†	− .03	.04†
authority	.16†	—	—	.17
status	.33†	− .10	.10	.35†
2. *Sex and isolation from informal control, controlling for:*				
education	.14	.03	− .08	.02
occupation	− .04	− .01	.05	− .05
authority	.03	—	—	.09
status	.09	.06	− .04	.07
3. *Sex and isolation from respected co-workers, controlling for:*				
education	− .40†	− .02	− .24*	.12*
occupation	− .26*	− .08	.01	.06
authority	− .02	—	—	.30†
status	− .08	− .08	.01	.52†
4. *Sex and isolation from authority figures, controlling for:*				
education	− .06	.14	.29†	.08
occupation	− .28†	.32†	.03	.08
authority	.05	—	—	.25†
status	.09	.03	.01	.39†
5. *Sex and total isolation score, controlling for:*				
education	.09	.24	.02	.26†
occupation	.03	.04	.22†	.27†
authority	.17†	—	—	.39†
status	.05	.25†	.21†	.63†

*$p < .05$
†$p < .01$

erably enhanced, although in a small number of cases the resource theory offers a closer fit to the data.

Looking first at interpersonal attractiveness (part A of Table 2), there are only two clear exceptions to the vested interest interpretation. Controlling for education has no stable effect on the relationship between sex and organizational knowledge, and increasing authority reduces (very slightly) men's advantage on perceived control.

But aside from these two exceptions the data on interpersonal attractiveness indicate that education, occupation, and authority may not be assets for women in the networks of social exchange. In fact, there are several instances in which women of the lower status have a small advantage (indicated by negative correlations) that turns to a disadvantage for those with higher status. One example of this is the relationship between sex and informal control, which changes from − .12 to

+ .40 with increasing education. A similar pattern shows up on total number of sociometric choices received.

Some of the information on social isolation (part B of Table 2) confirms this pattern; but overall, the data on isolation are again mixed. The vested interest thesis is moderately supported by the total isolation scores and by the data on isolation from respected co-workers and isolation from authority figures. Note, however, that partialling on education and occupation does not always show men improving their advantage as status increases, but sometimes shows women in higher positions lacking the small advantages of lower-status women. It is only when authority is controlled that a consistent increase in the advantage of men appears.

For the other two dimensions of isolation, the findings are not conclusive for either of the two theoretical approaches. On isolation from perceived control, the advantage of men in the low education group disappears with increasing education, offering some support for the resource hypothesis. However, controlling for occupational rank produces changes that are minor and inconsistent, as does the control for official authority. The findings on isolation from friends are also mixed. Partialling on education, women in the next-to-highest category (four years of college) have some advantage over men, but otherwise they generally rank below men. When occupation is controlled, the data show an unusual advantage for men in the "service" (technical) category that does not appear for the other occupational categories. Finally, the advantage of men is the same for both categories of official authority, favoring the vested interest hypothesis insofar as it fails to show women gaining equality as they achieve supervisory status.

To summarize: the data in Tables 1 and 2 generally show that men have an advantage over women, more so on attractiveness than on isolation. This impression is strengthened when statistical controls are applied, again particularly for interpersonal attractiveness. The patterns of differentiation are less clear for social isolation, although even here there is little to indicate that women profit by increasing their educational level or their occupational rank, or by achieving a position of official responsibility. It is also clear (judging from the inconclusive findings on some dimensions of isolation) that variables not examined here also have an influence on patterns of contact and interaction at work.

Differences in Job Strain

The measures of job strain reflect individuals' subjective reactions to their jobs. It will be clear as we go along that the resource theory receives almost no support from these data. However, the interpretation that does fit the data is less straightforward than in the case of the attractiveness and interaction measures, because the analysis must proceed from different baseline findings. In Table 3, there is nothing to suggest that men experience less job strain than women. In fact, although the differences are very small, the advantages on clarity, autonomy, and progress favor women, while job tension is apparently unrelated to the male–female distinction.[8] But this impression is changed by partialling on education, occupation, and authority (see Table 4, part A). Most of the partials modestly favor women in the lower categories of education, occupation, and authority, but these advantages almost always disappear in the high categories of these variables.

For example, in the low education category fewer women than men indicate that they are troubled by a lack of clarity in their jobs. To add some detail that the partials do not directly show, 5 of 19 women (26%) compared to 4 of 10 men (40%) appear in the "high strain" category on job clarity; conversely, the "low strain" category includes 6 of 19 women (32%) compared to 2 of 10 men (20%). By a similar margin, women in the low education category more frequently express a sense of autonomy in their jobs, and they are substantially less often troubled about their chances for progress (16% of the women in contrast to 40% of the men show high concern; 53% of the women but only 20% of the men show little or no concern). Women are also a little less likely to express tension over their work load and over interference of their work with their activities off the job. On the first three dimensions of job strain (clarity, autonomy, and progress), this pattern in the low education category

Table 3. *Differences Between Women and Men in Expressions of Job Strain and Job Satisfaction*

A. JOB STRAIN

	High Concern	Medium	Low Concern	Totals
1. *Concern over job clarity*[a]				
Women	29(29%)	46(46%)	26(26%)	101
Men	45(31%)	70(48%)	32(22%)	147
	$d_{yx} = -.04$			
2. *Concern over autonomy at work*[b]				
Women	17(17%)	56(55%)	28(28%)	101
Men	36(25%)	75(51%)	36(25%)	147
	$d_{yx} = -.08$			
3. *Concern over job progress*[c]				
Women	33(33%)	26(26%)	42(42%)	101
Men	54(37%)	41(28%)	52(35%)	147
	$d_{yx} = -.07$			
4. *Concern over job tension*[d]				
Women	29(29%)	48(47%)	24(24%)	101
Men	40(27%)	74(50%)	33(22%)	147
	$d_{yx} = .002$			

B. JOB SATISFACTION[e]

	Low Satisfaction	Medium	High Satisfaction	Totals
Women	11(11%)	33(33%)	57(56%)	101
Men	27(18%)	53(36%)	67(46%)	147
	$d_{yx} = -.13$			

[a]Five-item index based on extent to which duties and expectations of the job are clearly specified for the individual. (Item-to-item correlations range from .36 to .70.)

[b]Six-item index based on extent to which individual has autonomy and discretion in the way the duties of the job are performed. (Of 18 item-to-item correlations, 2 are negative, one is +.09, and the others range from .20 to .76. When the item showing a negative relation to other items is dropped, analysis is unaffected.)

[c]Three-item index measuring clarity of criteria for advancement and feelings about own progress on the job. (Item-to-item correlations range from .59 to .72.)

[d]Five-item index based on pressures created by work load, interference of the job with family life and personal feelings of friendship with others at work. Positive correlation would indicate that males are *less troubled* by job tension; negative correlation would favor women. (Item-to-item correlations range from .19 to .78.)

[e]Six-item index computed from answers to questions measuring satisfaction with work and with broader organizational context of work. (Item-to-item correlations range from .20 to .96.)

(N = 29) carries over to some extent into the two intermediate educational categories (Ns of 77 and 35, respectively). The numbers in these comparisons are not large, but the pattern is consistent.

The important point, however, is that on all four dimensions of job strain the situation changes in the highest education category (which includes 21 women and 86 men who have had

Table 4. *Partial Measures of Association (d$_{yx}$) Between Sex and Job Strain and Job Satisfaction, Where Education, Occupational Rank, Authority and Overall Status are Sequentially Controlled (N = 248)*

A. JOB STRAIN

Relationship Between:	Correlations within Successive Categories of Control Variables		
	Lowest Category	Intermediate Categories	Highest Category
1. Sex and job clarity, controlling for:			
education	− .18	.01 − .11	.07
occupation	− .23*	− .19 .10	.16
authority	− .08*	— —	.34†
status	− .21†	.00 .03	.52†
2. Sex and autonomy, controlling for:			
education	− .16	− .25† − .11	.15*
occupation	− .13	− .23† − .10	.05
authority	− .09*	— —	.16
status	− .16†	− .17 .13	.24
3. Sex and job progress, controlling for:			
education	− .39†	− .10 − .24*	.02
occupation	− .02	− .38† − .08	− .14
authority	− .09*	— —	− .04
status	− .23†	− .14 .01	− .02
4. Sex and job tension, controlling for:			
education	− .11	.06 .03	.16*
occupation	.10	.00 .19*	.21*
authority	.01	— —	.33†
status	.01	− .02 .14	.51†

B. JOB SATISFACTION

Relationship between sex and job satisfaction, controlling for:	Lowest Category	Intermediate Categories	Highest Category
education	− .51†	− .10 − .36†	.03
occupation	− .26*	− .41† − .15	.07
authority	− .17†	— —	.14
status	− .32†	− .07 − .13	.31*

*p < .05
†p < .01

graduate work). The modest advantages of women in the lower educational categories disappear on the dimensions of clarity and progress, and where autonomy and tension are concerned, the pattern that favors men begins to reappear. Having graduate training (and not just increasing education) is apparently the key. Among the men who have crossed this important barrier concern is generally lower, but for women with postgraduate training, the level of concern is higher. Once the critical point corresponding to college graduation is surpassed, women begin to pay a price for their advancement that men apparently do not have to pay.

With only two exceptions (both involving progress), the changes that occur when education is controlled also appear when occupational rank and authority are controlled: women express more job strain only in the high categories of these two variables.

In interpreting these findings, it must be kept in mind that the measures of job strain reflect the way the subjects evaluate their work circumstances and the content of their jobs. This is important because the findings indicate that, overall—excluding those in the highest-status categories—women are consistently a little more favorable than men in their reactions to their jobs, even though they rarely compare favorably with men in interpersonal attractiveness or access to the networks of social interaction. In other words, with the exception of the highest-status categories, women's evaluations of their work are more favorable than their objective circumstances would suggest.

This could mean that women adjust to their work because they expect less and have fewer alternatives to turn to, as the literature on inducements-contributions would suggest. (See especially March and Simon.) But even if this is the case, these cost-reducing adjustments operate only up to a point. Among women who have managed some graduate training, who have achieved professional occupational status, or who have moved into positions of official authority, in short, among those who have a great deal invested and more than the average to contribute, the uncritical view of their jobs that characterizes lower-status women begins to disappear on every dimension of job strain except, to a limited degree, the dimension involving progress. In fact, women in higher-status categories are generally more likely to be critical of their job content, and this is especially true for women in positions of authority. In the language of social exchange theory, distributive justice has turned to their disadvantage, and their reactions reflect it.

Job Satisfaction

The analysis of job satisfaction does not change the overall picture. Women generally are a little more satisfied with their work and with their organization than men are (see part B of Table 3),[9] a pattern that is even more characteristic of those in the low categories of education, occupation and authority (see part B of Table 4). Again, the disproportionately favorable responses of women carry over into the intermediate categories of education and occupation. But, just as before, this favorable picture disappears in the high categories of all three control variables.

Clearly, then, the resource theory of influence does not adequately account for differences in either job strain or job satisfaction. But without qualification, neither does the vested interest hypothesis. In a system that is characterized by clearly inequitable differences, many disadvantaged individuals can continue to respond favorably to their work, subjectively. However, the fact that a point is reached where favorable subjective reactions change to unfavorable ones suggests that an inequitable system that affects the work experiences of all women creates much greater pressures for those whose achievements confront the basic pattern of discrimination directly. After all, women who have moved into organizational positions and occupations that allow some access to decision-making and policy formation threaten the very core of male dominance.

CONCLUSIONS AND IMPLICATIONS

The data do not directly test discrimination, and we can only guess about process from data collected at one point in time. But the indication is that, unlike men, women who improve their positions by increasing their expertise, by moving up occupationally, or by moving into positions of authority may also run the risk of losing friendship and respect, influence, and access to information. They can expect that the strains created by the work might increase, and almost none of this will improve with time.[10] It is not surprising, then, that their level of job satisfaction (compared to men) also declines with time. Longitudinal data on career development patterns is called for to test this impression more carefully.

The findings have implications for sociological theory in general and for organizational theory in particular. A strong impression is that the discrimination that prevails in the larger society carries over into particularistic practices in the world of work. Nearly 25 years ago, Hacker pointed to just such a pattern as her justification for calling women a minority group, with all the social deprivation that term conveys. There is also a parallel between these findings and the conclusions reached by Blau and Duncan in their analysis of racial differentiation.

However, the data also have implications for a fundamental change in the way sex is used as a sociological variable. At times the justification for using the dichotomy "male–female" is clear, because distinctions with profound consequences are made using only this item of information. But there are some contexts in which the dichotomy masks important differences within each category. To illustrate, the vested interest thesis postulates that it is to the advantage of men to discriminate against women in order to maintain their favored positions in the social structure (including the work situation). A more detailed conceptualization would now stipulate that only certain kinds of females will be the primary targets of discrimination, namely, those with high status, expertise or authority. The point is that male–female only crudely reflects some important underlying behavioral dimensions of sex. Hence we need to refine our reconceptualization of sex as a sociological variable.

As for the organizational implications of the data, it is clear that, by the abstract standards of the ideal type, the organizations in this survey are engaged in practices of differentiation that are manifestly irrational because they do not have a "leveling effect" on potentially wasteful differences that carry over from the external system. Almost half the personnel (the 47% who are women) are vulnerable in a situation in which rewards are linked with increased contribution to the work of the organization. There is a striking paradox here: otherwise this finding could disappear along with dozens of other observations about the inconsistencies of bureaucratic practice. The paradox is that the organizations that furnished the data were considered earlier to be remarkable because of their conformity to the ideal-typical model, precisely in terms of their ability to establish rational systems of control. This was evidenced by high correlations among the distributions of expertise, influence, and legitimacy, and by a relatively harmonious co-existence between the formal and informal systems of control (Miller and Fry).

Because both the earlier analysis and present findings are accurate, the indication is that organizations can continue to function, and to outward appearances quite well, when their internal structures are decidedly two-faced. It would seem to take a kind of ingenious (if not ingenuous) organizational schizophrenia to maintain a system that appears to be rational and effective from one perspective while at the same time confronting a large number of members with a situation in which inducements are not reliably related to contributions. Having left the data safely behind, we can now ask how such wasteful and seemingly irrational arrangements may be able to persist.

The answer may lie in the notion of compartmentalized rationality. *For the organization* (as distinct from the individuals in it), internal discrimination may not make any appreciable difference and the leveling effect predicted by Weber will not occur so long as: (1) the basic goals of the organization are not directly threatened (as might be the case in an organization created to extend equality of opportunity); (2) the men who move into top positions are in fact qualified to exercise control and are recognized to be qualified (as previous research in the present organizations suggests is the case); and (3) if the resentment and alienation that may accompany discrimination do not increase to the point that they indirectly threaten the effectiveness of the organization. (This is an area where changing attitudes and extra-organizational influences may have their greatest impact.) In short, if we leave moral considerations aside, not all discrimination is prohibitively costly, *organizationally,* so long as the basic rationality of the system (technically qualified people in control) is intact, however compartmentalized that rationality may have become. From the point of view of organizational theory, this is a complexity of no small importance, for it suggests that most of the intraorganizational research that has recently appeared needs to be reconsidered with the possibility of this kind of compartmentalization in mind.

NOTES

1. For reasons of space and complexity, several dimensions of social interaction and isolation will be left for future analyses. One especially critical item concerns whether women interact predominantly with other women, or whether those who are not isolates are integrated into the prevailing patterns of work in such a way that they also interact with men.

2. The logic of this approach is similar to that of Blau and Duncan in their attempt to isolate racial discrimination in the occupational structure. The concept of discrimination, though not directly measured, came into play in their analysis only when alternative models (predicated on differences in education, region, family background and the like) failed to account for economic and occupational differentiation.

3. The vested interest argument also overlooks the possibility that the participants may consider some task-related activities to be more critical than others, and that these are more likely to be points of contention between the sexes. People in privileged positions may strenuously defend their advantages on matters directly involving important rewards and decison-making, for instance. But this may *not* be true of matters that in their view offer no immediate threat, such as the ability to interact informally with friends. Again, a less than monolithic discriminatory system would exist and the data on interpersonal relations would reflect this.

4. The correlations (d_{yx}) between sex and authority, education and occupation are .23, .25 and .46. In each case, $p < .0001$. This pattern of relationships between sex and education, occupational rank and authority holds true in each organization separately, though the relations are, surprisingly, more pronounced in the two survey research organizations. Data available upon request.

    Because only 9 of 157 women occupied positions of authority in these five organizations, the results using this variable as a control should be regarded with caution.

5. Education, professional rank, and authority are clearly not orthogonal to each other (correlations range from .28 to .56, a pattern that appears in each organization), and it is not argued that each makes a separate and unique contribution to the comparative situations of women and men. Recognizing this, a simple additive index combining the three variables (called "overall status") is also reported in the tables to summarize and to simplify the interpretation of the findings.

6. When the data on interpersonal attractiveness and social isolation are analyzed separately by organization, substantially the same patterns appear as have been reported for the aggregate data. Detailed data available upon request.

7. The suggestion that men might preserve their advantages on more vital dimensions of organizational activity while relinquishing their dominance in other areas (see note 3) is only partially confirmed. The data on interpersonal attractiveness offer limited support, since men enjoy a greater edge on professional respect and influence (which are directly tied to formal task-related activities) than on friendship and organizational knowledge (which are more clearly dimensions of the informal system). However, the isolation data are less supportive. The greatest difference appears on access to formal authority figures, which supports the idea of compartmentalization. Beyond this the picture changes, because differences in contact with friends are more, rather than less, pronounced than the differences in contact with influential and respected co-workers.

8. Of 19 job strain items, 11 show slight to moderate negative correlations, 6 show low but positive correlations, and 2 show no relationship to sex. This pattern of relationships between sex and job strain does not vary greatly from one organization to another, except on the variable job clarity. On this variable, women have a clear advantage in the commercial organization and a modest advantage in one of the two survey research organizations, but men have the advantage in the other survey research organization. In the remaining organization (the alcoholism rehabilitation organization) there is little apparent connection between sex and concern over job clarity.

9. Sex and job satisfaction are related in substantially the same way in each organization.

10. In searching for at least one organizational feature that favors women, the effect of tenure on their work experience was examined. This analysis indicated that, to a degree, job tension lessens for women over time, but job clarity and job satisfaction apparently decline, and feelings of autonomy

first improve then ultimately decline with time. Individuals' estimates of their job progress are largely unaffected (not improved) by increasing tenure. On the measures of attractiveness and isolation no improvement at all is apparent for women with long tenure, and in most cases the opposite is true.

A second piece of additional information deals with the channels of mobility in these organizations. Specifically, it was asked whether women's prospects for actually moving into positions of authority improve with education, occupational rank, specialized professional training (in addition to formal education) or tenure. The answer is no. Where edcucation is low (less than four years college), sex is unrelated to authority ($d_{yx} = .01$), but where education is high (college graduate or better), men have the advantage ($d_{yx} = .30; p = .000$). The same pattern applies to professional rank, specialized professional training, and tenure. Apparently, neither the passage of time nor the channels of mobility within these organizations promises much by way of alleviating the disadvantages women face.

REFERENCES

Acker, J., and D. R. Van Houten. 1974. "Differential Recruitment and Control: The Sex Structuring of Organizations."*Administrative Science Quarterly* 19 (June): 152–63.

Bierstedt, R. 1950. "An Analysis of Social Power." *American Sociological Review* 15 (December): 730–38.

Blau, Peter, and Otis D. Duncan. 1967. *The American Occupational Structure.* New York: Wiley.

Blood, Robert O., and Donald M. Wolfe. 1960. *Husbands and Wives: The Dynamics of Married Living.* Glencoe: Free Press.

Coser, R. L., and G. Rokoff. 1971. "Women in the Occupational World: Social Disruption and Conflict." *Social Problems* 18 (Spring): 535–54.

Emerson, R. M. 1962. "Power-dependence Relations." *American Sociological Review* 27 (February): 31–41.

Etzioni, Amitai. 1964. *Modern Organizations.* Englewood Cliffs: Prentice-Hall.

Hacker, H. 1951. "Women as a Minority Group." *Social Forces* 30 (October): 60–90.

Heer, D. a:1962. "Husband and Wife Perceptions of the Family Power Structure." *Marriage and Family Living* 24 (February).

_____. b:1963. "The Measurement and Bases of Family Power: An Overview." *Marriage and Family Living* 25 (May).

Lazarsfeld, P. F. 1958. "Evidence and Inference in Social Research." *Daedalus* 37 (No. 4): 99–130.

Liu, W. T. et al. 1973. "Conjugal Power and Decision Making: A Methodological Note on Cross-Cultural Study of the Family." *American Journal of Sociology* 79 (July): 84–98.

March, James, and Herbert Simon. 1958. *Organizations.* New York: Wiley.

Miller, J., and L. J. Fry. 1973. "Social Relations in Organizations: Further Evidence for the Weberian Model." *Social Forces* 51 (March): 305–19.

Shepard, J. M. 1973. "Technology, Division of Labor, and Alienation." *Pacific Sociological Review* 16 (January): 61–88.

Weber, Max. 1947. *The Theory of Social and Economic Organization.* New York: Free Press.

Name Index

Subject Index